FIELDS OF BLOOD

Karen Armstrong is one of the world's leading commentators on religious affairs. She spent seven years as a Roman Catholic nun in the 1960s and then read English at St Anne's College, Oxford. In 1982, she became a full-time writer and broadcaster. Her books include *A History of God*, *The Bible: A Biography*, *The Case for God* and, most recently, *Twelve Steps to a Compassionate Life*.

Armstrong has addressed members of the United States Congress, has participated in the World Economic Forum and, in 2005, was appointed by Kofi Annan to join the High Level Group of the United Nations initiative 'The Alliance of Civilizations'. In 2008 she was awarded the Franklin D. Roosevelt Four Freedoms Medal and, in the same year, won the TED prize. In 2013 she received the British Academy's inaugral Nayef Al-Rodhan Prize for improving Transcultural Understanding.

KAREN ARMSTRONG

Fields of Blood

Religion and the History of Violence

VINTAGE

1 3 5 7 9 10 8 6 4 2

Vintage
20 Vauxhall Bridge Road,
London SW1V 2SA

Vintage is part of the Penguin Random House group of companies
whose addresses can be found at global.penguinrandomhouse.com

Copyright © Karen Armstrong 2014

Karen Armstrong has asserted her right under the Copyright, Designs
and Patents Act 1988 to be identified as the author of this work

First published in Vintage in 2015
First published in hardback by The Bodley Head in 2014

www.vintage-books.co.uk

A CIP catalogue record for this book is
available from the British Library

ISBN 9780099564980

Typeset by Palimpsest Book Production Limited, Falkirk, Stirlingshire
Printed and bound by CPI Group (UK) Ltd, Croydon CR0 4YY

Penguin Random House is committed to a sustainable future
for our business, our readers and our planet. This book is made
from Forest Stewardship Council® certified paper.

MIX
Paper from
responsible sources
FSC® C018179
www.fsc.org

For Jane Garrett

CONTENTS

Now Hevel became a shepherd of flocks, and Kayin became a worker
   of the soil . . .
But then it was, when they were out in the field
that Kayin rose up against Hevel his brother
and he killed him.
YHWH said to Kayin:
Where is Hevel your brother?
He said:
I do not know. Am I the watcher of my brother?
Now he said:
What have you done!
Hark – your brother's blood cries out to me from the soil!

GENESIS 4: 2, 8–10; translated by Everett Fox

Every year in ancient Israel the high priest brought two goats into the Jerusalem temple on the Day of Atonement. He sacrificed one to expiate the sins of the community and then laid his hands on the other, transferring all the people's misdeeds on to its head, and sent the sin-laden animal out of the city, literally placing the blame elsewhere. In this way, Moses explained, 'the goat will bear all their faults away with it into a desert place'.[1] In his classic study of religion and violence, René Girard argued that the scapegoat ritual defused rivalries among groups within the community.[2] In a similar way, I believe, modern society has made a scapegoat of faith.

In the West the idea that religion is inherently violent is now taken for granted and seems self-evident. As one who speaks on religion, I constantly hear how cruel and aggressive it has been, a view that, eerily, is expressed in the same way almost every time: 'Religion has been the cause of all the major wars in history.' I have heard this sentence recited like a mantra by American commentators and psychiatrists, London taxi drivers and Oxford academics. It is an odd remark. Obviously the two world wars were not fought on account of religion. When they discuss the reasons people go to war, military historians acknowledge that many interrelated social, material and ideological factors are involved, among the chief of them competition for scarce resources. Experts in political violence or terrorism also insist that people commit atrocities for a complex range of reasons.[3] Yet so indelible is the aggressive image of religious faith in our secular consciousness that we routinely load the violent sins of the twentieth century on to the back of 'religion' and drive it out into the political wilderness.

Even those who admit that religion has not been responsible for all the violence and warfare of the human race still take its essential belligerence for granted. They claim that 'monotheism' is especially intolerant and that once people believe that 'God' is on their side, compromise becomes impossible. They cite the Crusades, the Inquisition and the Wars of Religion of the sixteenth and seventeenth centuries. They also point to the recent spate of terrorism committed in the name of religion to prove that Islam is particularly aggressive. If I mention Buddhist nonviolence, they retort that Buddhism is a secular philosophy not a religion. Here we come to the heart of the problem. Buddhism is certainly not a *religion* as this word has been understood in the West since the seventeenth and eighteenth centuries. But our modern Western conception of 'religion' is idiosyncratic and eccentric. No other cultural tradition has anything like it and even pre-modern European Christians would have found it reductive and alien. In fact, it complicates any attempt to pronounce on religion's propensity for violence.

To complicate things still further, for about fifty years now it has been clear in the academy that there is no universal way to define religion.[4] In the West we see 'religion' as a coherent system of obligatory beliefs, institutions and rituals, centring on a supernatural God, whose practice is essentially private and hermetically sealed off from all 'secular' activities. But words in other languages that we translate as 'religion' almost invariably refer to something larger, vaguer and more encompassing. The Arabic *din* signifies a whole way of life. The Sanskrit *dharma* is also 'a "total" concept, untranslatable, which covers law, justice, morals, and social life'.[5] The *Oxford Classical Dictionary* firmly states: 'No word in either Greek or Latin corresponds to the English "religion" or "religious."'[6] The idea of religion as a personal and systematic pursuit was entirely absent from classical Greece, Japan, Egypt, Mesopotamia, Iran, China and India.[7] Nor does the Hebrew Bible have any abstract concept of religion; and the Talmudic rabbis would have found it impossible to express what they meant by faith in a single word or even in a formula, since the Talmud was expressly designed to bring the whole of human life into the ambit of the sacred.[8]

The origins of the Latin *religio* are obscure. It was not 'a great objective something' but had imprecise connotations of obligation and taboo; to say that a cultic observance, a family propriety or keeping an oath was *religio* for you meant that it was incumbent on you to do it.[9] The word acquired an important new meaning among early Christian theologians: an attitude of reverence towards God and the universe as a whole. For St Augustine (*c.* 354–430 BCE), *religio* was neither a system of rituals and doctrines nor a historical institutionalised tradition but a personal encounter with the transcendence that we call God as well as the bond that unites us to the divine and to one another.[10] In medieval Europe, *religio* came to refer to the monastic life and distinguished the monk from the 'secular' priest, someone who lived and worked in the world (*saeculum*).[11]

The only faith tradition that does fit the modern Western notion of religion as something codified and private is Protestant Christianity, which, like 'religion' in this sense of the word is also a product of the early modern period. At this time Europeans and Americans had begun to separate religion and politics, because they assumed, not altogether accurately, that the theological squabbles of the Reformation had been entirely responsible for the Thirty Years War. The conviction that religion must be rigorously excluded from political life has been called the charter-myth of the sovereign nation state.[12] The philosophers and statesmen who pioneered this dogma believed that they were returning to the more satisfactory state of affairs that had existed before ambitious Catholic clerics had confused two utterly distinct realms. But in fact their secular ideology was as radical an innovation as the modern market economy that the West was concurrently devising. To non-Westerners, who had not been through this particular modernising process, both these innovations would seem unnatural and even incomprehensible. The habit of separating religion and politics is now so routine in the West that it is difficult for us to appreciate how thoroughly the two co-inhered in the past. It was never simply a question of the state 'using' religion; the two were indivisible. Dissociating them would have seemed like trying to extract the gin from a cocktail.

In the pre-modern world, religion permeated all aspects of life. We shall see that a host of activities now considered mundane were experienced as deeply sacred: forest-clearing, hunting, football matches, dice games, astronomy, farming, state-building, tugs of war, town planning, commerce, imbibing strong drink, and, most particularly, warfare. Ancient peoples would have found it impossible to see where 'religion' ended and 'politics' began. This was not because they were too stupid to understand the distinction but because they wanted to invest everything they did with ultimate value. We are meaning-seeking creatures and, unlike other animals, fall very easily into despair if we fail to make sense of our lives. We find the prospect of our inevitable extinction hard to bear. We are troubled by natural disasters and human cruelty and acutely aware of our physical and psychological frailty. We find it astonishing that we are here at all and want to know why. We also have a great capacity for wonder. Ancient philosophies were entranced by the order of the cosmos; they marvelled at the mysterious power that kept the heavenly bodies in their orbits, the seas within bounds and ensured that the earth regularly came to life again after the dearth of

winter, and they longed to participate in this richer and more permanent
existence.

They expressed this yearning in terms of what is known as the perennial
philosophy, so-called because it was present, in some form, in most pre-
modern cultures.[13] Every single person, object or experience was seen as
a replica, a pale shadow, of a reality that was stronger and more enduring
than anything in their ordinary experience but which they only glimpsed
in visionary moments or in dreams. By ritually imitating what they understood to be the gestures and actions of their celestial alter egos – whether
gods, ancestors or culture heroes – pre-modern folk felt themselves to be
caught up in their larger dimension of existence. We humans are profoundly
artificial and tend naturally towards archetypes and paradigms.[14] We
constantly strive to improve on nature or approximate to an ideal that
transcends the day-to-day. Even our contemporary cult of celebrity can be
understood as an expression of our reverence for and yearning to emulate
models of 'super-humanity'. Feeling ourselves connected to such extraordinary realities satisfies an essential craving. It touches us within, lifts us
momentarily beyond ourselves, so that we seem to inhabit our humanity
more fully than usual and feel in touch with the deeper currents of life. If
we no longer find this experience in a church or temple, we seek it in art,
a musical concert, sex, drugs – or warfare. What this last may have to do
with these other moments of transport may not be so obvious but it is one
of the oldest triggers of ecstatic experience. To understand why, it will be
helpful to consider the development of our neuro-anatomy.

Each of us has not one but three brains which coexist uneasily. In the
deepest recess of our grey matter we have an 'old brain' that we inherited
from the reptiles that struggled out of the primal slime 500 million years
ago. Intent on their own survival with absolutely no altruistic impulses, these
creatures were solely motivated by mechanisms urging them to feed, fight,
flee (when necessary) and reproduce. Those best equipped to compete mercilessly for food, ward off any threat, dominate territory and seek safety naturally passed along their genes, so these self-centred impulses could only
intensify.[15] But some time after mammals appeared, they evolved what neuroscientists call the limbic system, perhaps about 120 million years ago.[16] Formed
over the core brain inherited from the reptiles, the limbic system motivated
all sorts of new behaviours, including the protection and nurture of young
as well as the formation of alliances with other individuals that were invaluable in the struggle to survive. And so for the first time sentient beings
possessed the capacity to cherish and care for creatures other than themselves.[17]

Although these limbic emotions would never be as strong as the 'me-first' drives still issuing from our reptilian core, we humans have evolved a substantial hard-wiring for empathy with other creatures and special affinity with our fellow humans. Eventually, the Chinese philosopher Mencius (371–288 BCE) would insist that nobody was wholly without such feeling. If a man sees a child teetering on the brink of a well, about to fall in, he would feel her predicament in his own body and would reflexively, without thought for himself, lunge forward to save her. There would be something radically wrong with anyone who could walk past such a scene without a flicker of disquiet. For most these sentiments were essential, though, Mencius thought, somewhat subject to individual will. You could stamp on these shoots of benevolence just as you could cripple or deform yourself physically. On the other hand, if you cultivated them they would acquire a strength and dynamism of their own.[18]

We cannot entirely understand Mencius' argument without considering the third part of our brain. About twenty thousand years ago during the Palaeolithic age, human beings evolved a 'new brain', the neocortex, home of the reasoning powers and self-awareness that enable us to stand back from the instinctive, primitive passions. Humans thus became roughly as they are today, subject to the conflicting impulses of their three distinct brains. Palaeolithic men were proficient killers. Before the invention of agriculture, they were dependent on the slaughter of animals and used their big brains to develop a technology enabling them to kill creatures much larger and more powerful than themselves. But their empathy may have made them uneasy. Or so we might conclude from modern hunting societies. Anthropologists observe that tribesmen feel acute anxiety about having to slay the beasts they consider their friends and patrons and try to assuage this distress by ritual purification. In the Kalahari Desert, where wood is scarce, Bushmen are forced to rely on light weapons that can only graze the skin. So they anoint their arrows with a poison that kills the animal – but very slowly. Out of ineffable solidarity, the hunter stays with his dying victim, crying when it cries, and participating symbolically in its death throes. Other tribes don animal costumes or smear the kill's blood and excrement on cavern walls as a means of returning the creature to the underworld from which it came.[19]

Palaeolithic hunters may have had a similar understanding.[20] The cave paintings in northern Spain and south-west France are among the earliest extant documents of our species. These decorated caves almost certainly had a ceremonial function, so from the very beginning art and ritual were inseparable. Our neocortex makes us intensely aware of the tragedy and perplexity of our existence and in art, as in some forms of religious expression, we find a means of letting go and encouraging the softer, limbic emotions to predominate. The frescoes and engravings in the labyrinth of Lascaux in the Dordogne, the earliest of which are 17,000 years old, still evoke awe in visitors. In their numinous depiction of the animals, the artists have captured the hunters' essential ambivalence. Intent as they were to acquire food, their ferocity was tempered by respectful sympathy for the beasts they were obliged to kill, whose blood and fat they mixed with their paints. Ritual and art helped hunters express their empathy with and reverence (*religio*) for their fellow creatures – just as Mencius would describe some seventeen millennia later – and helped them to live with their need to kill them.

In Lascaux, there are no pictures of the reindeer which featured so largely in the diet of these hunters.[21] But not far away in Montastruc, a small sculpture has been found, carved from a mammoth tusk in about 11,000 BCE, at about the same time as the later Lascaux paintings. Now lodged in the British Museum, it depicts two swimming reindeer.[22] The artist must have watched his prey intently as they swam across lakes and rivers in search of new pastures, making themselves particularly vulnerable to the hunters. He also felt a tenderness towards his victims, conveying the unmistakable poignancy of their facial expressions without a hint of sentimentality. As Neil MacGregor, director of the British Museum, has noted, the anatomical accuracy of this sculpture shows that it 'was clearly made not just with the knowledge of a hunter but also with the insight of a butcher, someone who had not only looked at his animals but had cut them up'.[23] Rowan Williams, the former Archbishop of Canterbury, has also reflected insightfully on the 'huge and imaginative generosity' of these Palaeolithic artists:

> In the art of this period, you see human beings trying to enter fully into the flow of life, so that they become part of the whole process of animal life that's going on all around them . . . and this is actually a very religious impulse.[24]

From the first, then, one of the major preoccupations of both religion and art was to cultivate a sense of community – with nature, the animal world and with our fellow humans.

We would never wholly forget our hunter-gatherer past, which was the longest period in human history. Everything that we think of as most human – our brains, bodies, faces, speech, emotions and thoughts – bears the stamp of this heritage.[25] Some of the rituals and myths devised by our prehistoric ancestors appear to have survived in the religious systems of later, literate cultures. In this way, animal sacrifice, the central rite of nearly every ancient culture, preserved prehistoric hunting ceremonies and the honour accorded the beast that gave its life for the community.[26] Earliest religion was rooted in an acknowledgement of the tragic fact that life depended on the destruction of other creatures; rituals were addressed to helping human beings face up to this insoluble dilemma. Despite their real respect, reverence and even affection for their prey, ancient huntsmen remained dedicated killers, however. Millennia of fighting large aggressive animals meant that these hunting parties became tightly bonded teams that were the seeds of our modern armies, ready to risk everything for the common good and to protect their fellows in moments of danger.[27] And there was one more conflicting emotion to be reconciled: they probably loved the excitement and intensity of the hunt.

Here again the limbic system comes into play. The prospect of killing may stir our empathy, but in the very acts of hunting, raiding and battling this same seat of emotions is awash in serotonin, the neurotransmitter responsible for the sensation of ecstasy that we associate with some forms of religious experience. So it happened that these violent pursuits came to be perceived as natural religious activities, however bizarre that may seem to our understanding of religion. People, especially men, experienced a strong bond with their fellow warriors, a heady feeling of altruism at putting their lives at risk for others, and of being more fully alive. This response to violence persists in our nature. The *New York Times* war correspondent Chris Hedges has aptly described war as 'a force that gives us meaning':

War makes the world understandable, a black and white tableau of them and us. It suspends thought, especially self-critical thought. All bow before the supreme effort. We are one. Most of us willingly accept war as long as we can fold it into a belief system that paints the ensuing suffering as necessary for a higher good, for human beings seek not only happiness but meaning. And tragically war is sometimes the most powerful way in human society to achieve meaning.[28]

It may be, too, that as they give free rein to the aggressive impulses from the deepest region of their brains, warriors feel in tune with the most elemental and inexorable dynamics of existence, those of life and death. Put another way, war is a means of surrender to reptilian ruthlessness, one of the strongest of human drives.

The warrior, therefore, experiences in battle the ecstatic self-affirmation that others find in ritual, sometimes to pathological effect. Psychiatrists who treat war veterans for post-traumatic stress disorder have noted that in the destruction of other people soldiers can experience a self-affirmation that is almost erotic.[29] Yet afterwards, as they struggle to disentangle their emotions of pity and ruthlessness, PTSD sufferers may find themselves unable to function as coherent human beings. One Vietnam veteran described a photograph of himself holding two severed heads by the hair; the war, he said, was 'hell', a place where 'crazy was natural' and everything 'out of control', but, he concluded:

> The worst thing I can say about myself is that while I was there I was so alive. I loved it the way you can like an adrenaline high, the way you can love your friends, your tight buddies. So unreal and the realest thing that ever happened . . . And maybe the worst thing for me now is living in peacetime without a possibility of that high again. I hate what that high was about but I loved that high.[30]

'Only when we are in the midst of conflict does the shallowness and vapidness of much of our lives become apparent,' Chris Hedges explains. 'Trivia dominates our conversation and increasingly our airwaves. And war is an enticing elixir. It gives us a resolve, a cause. It allows us to be noble.'[31] One of the many, intertwined motives driving men to the battlefield has been the tedium and pointlessness of ordinary domestic existence. The same hunger for intensity would compel others to become monks and ascetics.

The warrior in battle may feel connected with the cosmos, but afterwards he cannot always resolve these inner contradictions. It is fairly well established that there is a strong taboo on killing our own kind – an evolutionary stratagem that helped the species to survive.[32] Still, we fight. But to bring ourselves to do so, we envelop the effort in a mythology – often a 'religious' mythology – that puts distance between us and the enemy. We exaggerate his differences – racial, religious, or ideological. We develop narratives to convince ourselves that he is not really human but monstrous, the antithesis of order and goodness. Today we may tell ourselves that we are fighting for God and country or that a particular war is 'just' or 'legal'. But this encouragement doesn't always take hold. During the Second World War, for instance, Brigadier General S. L. A. Marshall of the United States Army and a team of historians interviewed thousands of soldiers from over 400 infantry companies that had seen close combat in Europe and the Pacific. Their findings were startling: only 15–20 per cent of infantrymen were able to fire at the enemy directly; the rest tried to avoid it and had developed complex methods of misfiring or reloading their weapons to escape detection.[33]

It is hard to overcome one's nature. To become efficient soldiers, recruits must go through a gruelling initiation, not unlike what monks or yogins undergo, to subdue their emotions. As the cultural historian Joanna Bourke explains the process:

> Individuals had to be broken down to be rebuilt into efficient fighting men. The basic tenets included depersonalization, uniforms, lack of privacy, forced social relationships, tight schedules, lack of sleep, disorientation followed by rites of reorganization according to military codes, arbitrary rules, and strict punishment. The methods of brutalization were similar to those carried out by regimes where men were taught to torture prisoners.[34]

So, we might say, the soldier has to become as inhuman as the 'enemy' he has created in his mind. Indeed, we shall find that in some cultures, even – or perhaps especially – those that glorify warfare, the warrior is somehow tainted, polluted and an object of fear – both an heroic figure and a necessary evil, to be dreaded, set apart.

Our relationship to warfare is, therefore, complex, possibly because it is a relatively recent human development. Hunter-gatherers could not afford the organised violence that we call war, because warfare requires large armies, sustained leadership and economic resources that were far beyond their reach.[35] Archaeologists have found mass graves from this period that suggest some kind of massacre,[36] yet there is little evidence that early humans regularly fought one another.[37] But human life changed for ever in about 9000 BCE when pioneering farmers in the Levant learned to grow and store wild grain. They produced harvests that were able to support larger populations than ever before and eventually they grew more food than they needed.[38] As a result, the human population increased so dramatically that in some regions a return to hunter-gatherer life became impossible. Between about 8500 BCE and the first century of the Common Era – a remarkably short period given the four million years of our history – all around the world, quite independently, the great majority of humans made

the transition to agrarian life. And with agriculture came civilisation; and
with civilisation warfare.

In our industrialised societies, we often look back to the agrarian age
with nostalgia, imagining that people lived more wholesomely then, close
to the land and in harmony with nature. But initially agriculture was experienced as traumatic. These early settlements were vulnerable to wild
swings in productivity that could wipe out the entire population, and their
mythology describes the first farmers fighting a desperate battle against
sterility, drought and famine.[39] For the first time, back-breaking drudgery
had become a fact of human life. Skeletal remains show that plant-fed humans
were a head shorter than meat-eating hunters, prone to anaemia, infectious
diseases, rotten teeth and bone disorders.[40] The Earth was revered as the
Mother Goddess and her fecundity experienced as an epiphany; she was
called Ishtar in Mesopotamia, Demeter in Greece, Isis in Egypt and Anat in
Syria. Yet she was not a comforting presence but extremely violent. The
Earth Mother regularly dismembered consorts and enemies alike – just as
corn was ground to powder and grapes crushed to unrecognisable pulp.
Farming implements were depicted as weapons that wounded the Earth, so
farming fields became fields of blood. When Anat slew Mot, god of sterility,
she cut him in two with a ritual sickle, winnowed him in a sieve, ground
him in a mill and scattered his scraps of bleeding flesh over the fields. After
she slaughtered the enemies of Baal, god of life-giving rain, she adorned
herself with rouge and henna, made a necklace of the hands and heads of
her victims, and waded knee-deep in blood to attend the triumphal banquet.[41]

These violent myths reflected the political realities of agrarian life. By
the beginning of the ninth millennium BCE, the settlement in the oasis of
Jericho in the Jordan Valley had a population of 3,000 people, which would
have been impossible before the advent of agriculture. But Jericho was a
fortified stronghold protected by a massive wall that must have consumed
tens of thousands of hours of manpower to construct.[42] In this arid region,
Jericho's ample food stores would have been a magnet for hungry nomads.
Intensified agriculture, therefore, created conditions that could endanger
everyone in this wealthy colony and transform its arable land into fields of
blood. Jericho was unusual, however – a portent of the future. Warfare
would not become endemic in the region for another five thousand years,
but it was already a possibility and from the first, it seems, large-scale
organised violence was linked not with religion but with organised theft.[43]

But agriculture had also introduced another type of aggression: an institutional or structural violence in which a society compels people to live in

such wretchedness and subjection that they are unable to better their lot.
This systemic oppression has been described as possibly 'the most subtle
form of violence'[44] and, according to the World Council of Churches, it is
present whenever

> Resources and powers are unequally distributed, concentrated in the hands
> of the few, who do not use them to achieve the possible self-realisation of
> all members, but use parts of them for self-satisfaction or for purposes of
> dominance, oppression and control of other societies or of the underprivi-
> leged in the same society.[45]

Agrarian civilisation made this systemic violence a reality for the first time
in human history.

Palaeolithic communities had probably been egalitarian because hunter-
gatherers could not support a privileged class that did not share the hardship and danger of the hunt.[46] Because these small communities lived at
near-subsistence level and produced no economic surplus, inequity of wealth
was impossible. The tribe could survive only if everybody shared what food
they had. Government by coercion was not feasible because all able-bodied
males had exactly the same weapons and fighting skills. Anthropologists
have noted that modern hunter-gatherer societies are classless, that their
economy is 'a sort of communism',[47] and that people are honoured for
skills and qualities, such as generosity, kindness and even-temperedness,
which benefit the community as a whole.[48] But in societies that produce
more than they need, it is possible for a small group to exploit this surplus
for its own enrichment, gain a monopoly of violence, and dominate the
rest of the population.

As we shall see in Part One, this systemic violence would prevail in all
agrarian civilisations. In the empires of the Middle East, China, India and
Europe, which were economically dependent on agriculture, an elite group,
comprising not more than 2 per cent of the population, with the help of
a small band of retainers, systematically robbed the masses of the produce
they had grown in order to support their aristocratic lifestyle. Yet, social
historians argue, without this iniquitous arrangement human beings would
probably never have advanced beyond subsistence level, because it created
a privileged class with the leisure to develop the civilised arts and sciences
that made progress possible.[49] All pre-modern civilisations adopted this
oppressive system; there seemed to be no alternative. This inevitably had
implications for religion, which permeated all human activities, including

state-building and government. Indeed, we shall see that pre-modern politics was inseparable from religion. And if a ruling elite adopted an ethical
tradition, such as Buddhism, Christianity or Islam, the clergy usually adapted
their ideology so that it could support the structural violence of the state.[50]

In Parts One and Two we shall explore this dilemma. Established by
force and maintained by military aggression, warfare was essential to the
agrarian state. When land and the peasants who farmed it were the chief
sources of wealth, territorial conquest was the only way an agrarian kingdom
could increase its revenues. Warfare was, therefore, indispensable to any
agrarian economy. The ruling class had to maintain its control of the peasant
villages, defend its arable land against aggressors, conquer more land, and
ruthlessly suppress any hint of insubordination. A key figure in this story
will be the Indian emperor Ashoka (c.268–223 BCE). Appalled by the
suffering his army had inflicted on a rebellious city, he tirelessly promoted
an ethic of compassion and tolerance but could not in the end disband his
army. No state can survive without its soldiers. And once states grew and
warfare had become a fact of human life, an even greater force, the military
might of empire, often seemed the only way to keep the peace.

So necessary to the rise of states and ultimately empires is military force
that historians regard militarism as a mark of civilisation. Without disciplined, obedient and law-abiding armies, human society, it is claimed, would
probably have remained at a primitive level or have degenerated into ceaselessly warring hordes.[51] But like our inner conflict between violent and
compassionate impulses, the incoherence between peaceful ends and violent
means would remain unresolved. Ashoka's dilemma is the dilemma of civilisation itself. And into this tug of war religion would enter too. Since all
pre-modern state ideology was imbued with religion, warfare inevitably
acquired a sacral element. Indeed every major faith tradition has tracked
that political entity in which it arose; none has become a 'world religion'
without the patronage of a militarily powerful empire and every tradition
would have to develop an imperial ideology.[52] But to what degree did
religion contribute to the violence of the states with which it was inextricably linked? How much blame for the history of human violence can we
ascribe to religion itself? The answer is not as simple as much of our popular
discourse would suggest.

Our world is dangerously polarised at a time when humanity is more
closely interconnected – politically, economically and electronically – than
ever before. If we are to meet the challenge of our time and create a global
society where all peoples can live together in peace and mutual respect,

we need to assess our situation accurately. We cannot afford oversimplified assumptions about the nature of religion or its role in the world. What the American scholar William T. Cavanaugh calls 'the myth of religious violence'[53] served Western people well at an early stage of their modernisation, but in our global village we need a more nuanced view in order fully to understand our predicament.

This book focuses mainly on the Abrahamic traditions of Judaism, Christianity and Islam because they are the ones most in the spotlight at the moment. But since there is such a widespread conviction that monotheism, the belief in a single God, is especially prone to violence and intolerance, Part One of the book will examine it in comparative perspective. In traditions preceding the Abrahamic faiths we will see not only how military force and religion were both essential to the state, but also how from earliest times there were those who agonised about the dilemma of necessary violence and proposed 'religious' ways to counter aggressive urges and channel them towards more compassionate ends.

Time would fail me to cover all instances of religiously articulated violence, but we will explore some of the most prominent in the long history of the three Abrahamic religions, such as Joshua's holy wars, the call to jihad, the Crusades, the Inquisition, and the European Wars of Religion. It will become clear that when pre-modern people engaged in politics they thought in religious terms and that faith imbued their struggle to make sense of the world in a way that seems strange to us today. But that is not the whole story. To paraphrase a British commercial: 'The weather does lots of different things – and so does religion.' In religious history, the struggle for peace has been just as important as the holy war. Religious people have found all kinds of ingenious methods of dealing with the assertive machismo of the reptilian brain, curbing violence, and building respectful life-enhancing communities. But as with Ashoka, who came up against the systemic militancy of the state, they could not radically change their societies; the most they could do was to propose a different path to demonstrate kinder and more empathic ways for people to live together.

When we come to the modern period, in Part Three, we will, of course, explore the wave of violence claiming religious justification that erupted during the 1980s and culminated in the atrocity of September 11, 2001. But we will also examine the nature of secularism, which, despite its manifold benefits, has not always offered a wholly irenic alternative to a religious state ideology. The early modern philosophies that tried to pacify Europe after the Thirty Years War in fact had a ruthless streak of their own, particularly when dealing with casualties of secular modernity who found it alienating rather than empowering and liberating. This is because secularism did not so much displace religion as create alternative religious enthusiasms. So ingrained is our desire for ultimate meaning that our secular institutions, most especially the nation state, almost immediately acquired a 'religious' aura, though they have been less adept than the ancient religions at helping people face up to the grimmer realities of human existence for which there are no easy answers. But secularism has by no means been the end of the story. In some societies attempting to find their way to modernity, it has succeeded only in damaging religion and wounding psyches of people unprepared to be wrenched from ways of living and understanding that had always supported them. Licking its wounds in the desert, the scapegoat, with its festering resentment, has rebounded on the city that drove it out.

PART ONE

Beginnings

I

FARMERS AND HERDSMEN

Gilgamesh, named in the ancient King-Lists as the fifth ruler of Uruk, was remembered as 'the strongest of men – huge, handsome, radiant, perfect'.[1] He may well have existed but soon acquired a legendary aura. It was said that he had seen everything, travelled to the ends of the earth, visited the underworld, and achieved great wisdom. By the early third millennium BCE, Uruk in what is now southern Iraq was the largest city-state in the federation of Sumer, the world's first civilisation. The poet Sin-leqi, who wrote his version of Gilgamesh's remarkable life in about 1200 BCE, was still bursting with pride in its temples, palaces, gardens and shops. But he begins and ends his epic with an exuberant description of the magnificent city wall, six miles long, that Gilgamesh had restored for his people. 'Walk on the wall of Uruk!' he urges his readers excitedly. 'Follow its course around the city, inspect its mighty foundations, examine its brickwork, how masterfully it is built!'[2] This splendid fortification showed that warfare had become a fact of human life. Yet this had not been an inevitable development. For hundreds of years, Sumer had felt no need to protect its cities from outside attack. Gilgamesh, however, who probably ruled around 2750 BCE, was a new kind of Sumerian king, 'a wild bull of a man, unvanquished leader, hero on the front lines, beloved by his soldiers – *fortress* they called him, *protector of the people, raging flood that destroys all defences*'.[3]

Despite his passion for Uruk, Sin-leqi had to admit that civilisation had its discontents. Poets had begun to tell Gilgamesh's story soon after his death because it is an archetypal tale, one of the first literate accounts of the hero's journey.[4] But it also wrestles with the inescapable structural violence of civilised life. Oppressed, impoverished and miserable, the people of Uruk begged the gods to grant them some relief from Gilgamesh's tyranny:

> The city is his possession, he struts
> Through it, arrogant, his head raised high,
> Trampling its citizens like a wild bull.
> He is king, he does whatever he wants
> The young men of Uruk he harries without a warrant,
> Gilgamesh lets no son go free to his father.[5]

These young men may have been conscripted into the labour-bands that rebuilt the city wall.[6] Urban living would not have been possible without the unscrupulous exploitation of the vast majority of the population. Gilgamesh and the Sumerian aristocracy lived in unprecedented splendour, but for the peasant masses civilisation brought only misery and oppression.

The Sumerians seem to have been the first people to commandeer the agricultural surplus grown by the community and create a privileged ruling class. This could have been achieved only by force. Enterprising settlers had first been drawn to the fertile plain between the Tigris and the Euphrates in about 5000 BCE.[7] It was too dry for farming, so they designed an irrigation system to control and distribute the snowmelt from the mountains that flooded the plain each year. This was an extraordinary achievement. Canals and ditches had to be planned, designed and maintained in a co-operative effort and the water allocated fairly between competing communities. The new system probably began on a small scale, but would soon have led to a dramatic increase in agricultural yield and thus to a population explosion.[8] By 3500, Sumer numbered a hitherto unimaginable half-million souls. Strong leadership would have been essential but what actually transformed these simple farmers into city-dwellers is a topic of endless debate; however, a number of interlocking and mutually reinforcing factors were probably involved: population growth, unprecedented agricultural fecundity, and the intensive labour required by irrigation – not to mention sheer human ambition – all contributed to a new kind of society.[9]

All that we know for certain is that by 3000 BCE there were twelve cities in the Mesopotamian plain, each supported by produce grown by peasants in the surrounding countryside. Theirs was subsistence-level living. Each village had to bring its entire crop to the city it served; officials allocated a portion to feed the local peasants and the rest was stored for the aristocracy in the city temples. In this way, a few great families with the help of a class of retainers – bureaucrats, soldiers, merchants and household servants – appropriated between half and two-thirds of the revenue.[10] They used this surplus to live a different sort of life altogether, freed for various pursuits that depend on leisure and wealth. In return, they maintained the irrigation system and preserved a degree of law and order. All pre-modern states feared anarchy: a single crop-failure caused by drought or social unrest could lead to thousands of deaths so the elite could tell themselves that this system benefited the population as a whole. But robbed of the fruits of their labours, the peasants were little better than slaves: ploughing, harvesting, digging irrigation canals, forced into degradation and penury, their hard labour in the fields draining their lifeblood. If they failed to satisfy their overseers, their oxen were knee-capped and their olive trees chopped down.[11] They left fragmentary records of their distress. 'The poor man is better dead than alive,' one peasant lamented.[12] 'I am a thoroughbred steed,' complained another, 'but I am hitched to a mule and must draw a cart and carry weeds and stubble.'[13]

Sumer had devised the system of structural violence that would prevail in every single agrarian state until the modern period, when agriculture ceased to be the economic basis of civilisation.[14] Its rigid hierarchy was symbolised by the ziggurats, the giant stepped temple-towers that were the hallmark of Mesopotamian civilisation: Sumerian society too was stacked in narrowing layers culminating in an exalted aristocratic pinnacle, each individual locked inexorably into place.[15] Yet, historians argue, without this cruel arrangement that did violence to the vast majority of the population, humans would not have developed the arts and sciences that made progress possible. Civilisation itself required a leisured class to cultivate it, and so our finest achievements were for thousands of years built on the backs of an exploited peasantry. By no coincidence, when the Sumerians invented writing, it was for the purpose of social control.

What role did religion play in this damaging oppression? All political communities develop ideologies that ground their institutions in the natural order as they perceive it.[16] The Sumerians knew how fragile their ground-breaking urban experiment was. Their mud-brick buildings needed constant maintenance; the Tigris and Euphrates frequently broke their banks and ruined the crops; torrential rains turned the soil into a sea of mud, and terrifying storms damaged property and killed livestock. But the aristocrats had begun to study astronomy and discovered regular patterns in the move-ments of the heavenly bodies. They marvelled at the way the different elements of the natural world worked together to create a stable universe, and concluded that the cosmos itself must be a kind of state in which everything had its allotted function. They decided that if they modelled their cities on this celestial order, their experimental society too would be in tune with the way the world worked and would, therefore, thrive and endure.[17]

The cosmic state, they believed, was managed by gods who were inseparable from the natural forces and nothing like the 'God' worshipped by
Jews, Christians and Muslims today. These deities could not control events
but were bound by the same laws as humans, animals and plants. There was
also no vast ontological gap between human and divine; Gilgamesh, for
example, was one third human, two-thirds divine.[18] The Anunnaki, the higher
gods, were the aristocrats' celestial alter egos, their most complete and
effective selves, differing from humans only in that they were immortal. The
Sumerians imagined these gods as preoccupied with town planning, irrigation
and government, just as they were. Anu, the Sky, ruled this archetypal state
from his palace in the heavens but his presence was also felt in all earthly
authority. Enlil, Lord Storm, was revealed not only in the cataclysmic
thunderstorms of Mesopotamia but also in any kind of human force and
violence. He was Anu's chief counsellor in the Divine Council (on which
the Sumerian assembly was modelled), and Enki, who had imparted the arts
of civilisation to human beings, was its Minister of Agriculture.

Every state – even our secular nation state – relies on a mythology that
defines its special character and mission. The word 'myth' has lost its force
in modern times and tends to mean something that is not true, that never
happened. But in the pre-modern world, mythology expressed a timeless
rather than a historical reality and provided a blueprint for action in the
present.[19] At this very early point in history, when the archaeological and
historical record is so scanty, the mythology that they preserved in writing
is the only way we can enter the Sumerians' minds. For these pioneers of
civilisation, the myth of the cosmic state was an exercise in political science.
The Sumerians knew that their stratified society was a shocking departure
from the egalitarian norm that had prevailed from time immemorial, but
were convinced that it was somehow enshrined in the very nature of things
and that even the gods were bound by it. Long before humans existed, it
was said, the gods had lived in the Mesopotamian cities, growing their own
food and managing the irrigation system.[20] After the Great Flood, they had
withdrawn from earth to heaven and appointed the Sumerian aristocracy
to govern the cities in their stead. Answerable to their divine masters, the
ruling class had had no choice in the matter.

Following the logic of the perennial philosophy, the Sumerians' political
arrangements imitated those of their gods; this, they believed, enabled their
fragile cities to participate in the strength of the divine realm. Each city
had its own patronal deity and was run as this god's personal estate.[21]
Represented by a life-sized statue, the ruling god lived in the chief temple

with his family and household of divine retainers and servants, each one of
whom was also depicted in effigy and dwelt in a suite of rooms. The gods
were fed, clothed and entertained in elaborate rituals and each temple
owned huge holdings of farmland and herds of livestock in their name.
Everybody in the city-state, no matter how menial his or her task, was
engaged in divine service – officiating at the gods' rites, working in their
breweries, factories and workshops, sweeping their shrines, pasturing and
butchering their animals, baking their bread and clothing their statues. There
was nothing secular about the Mesopotamian state and nothing personal
about their religion. This was a theocracy in which everybody – from the
highest aristocrat to the lowliest artisan – performed a sacred activity.

Mesopotamian religion was essentially communal; men and women did
not seek to encounter the sacred only in the privacy of their hearts but
primarily in a sacred community. Pre-modern religion had no separate
institutional existence; it was embedded in the political, social and domestic
arrangements of a society, providing it with an overarching system of
meaning. Its goals, language and rituals were conditioned by these mundane
considerations. Providing the template for society, Mesopotamian religious
practice seems to have been the polar opposite of our modern notion of
'religion' as a private spiritual experience: it was essentially a political
pursuit and we have no record of any personal devotions.²²The gods' temples
were not just places of worship but were central to the economy, because
the agricultural surplus was stored there. The Sumerians had no word for
'priest': aristocrats who were also the city's bureaucrats, poets and astron-
omers officiated at the city cult. This was only fitting, since for them, all
activity – and especially politics – was sacred.

This elaborate system was not simply a disingenuous justification of the
structural violence of the state but was primarily an attempt to invest this
audacious and problematic human experiment with meaning. The city was
humanity's greatest artefact: artificial, vulnerable and dependent on institutionalised coercion. Civilisation demands sacrifice, and the Sumerians had
to convince themselves that the price they were exacting from the peasantry
was necessary and ultimately worth it. In claiming that their inequitable
system was in tune with the fundamental laws of the cosmos the Sumerians
were, therefore, expressing an inexorable political reality in mythical terms.

It seemed like an iron law because there was no alternative. By the end
of the fifteenth century CE, agrarian civilisations would be established in
the Middle East, South and East Asia, North Africa and Europe and in every
single one – whether in India, Russia, Turkey, Mongolia, the Levant, China,

Greece or Scandinavia – aristocrats would exploit their peasants as the Sumerians did. Without this aristocratic violence, it would have been impossible to force peasants to produce an economic surplus, because population growth would have kept pace with advances in productivity. Unpalatable as this may seem, by forcing the masses to live at subsistence level, the aristocracy kept population growth in check and made human progress feasible. Had their surplus not been taken from the peasants, there would have been no economic resource to support the technicians, scientists, inventors, artists and philosophers who eventually brought our modern civilisation into being.[23] And, as the American Trappist monk Thomas Merton pointed out, all of us who have benefited from this systemic violence are implicated in the suffering inflicted for over five thousand years on the vast majority of men and women.[24] Or, as the philosopher Walter Benjamin put it: 'There is no document of civilization that is not at the same time a document of barbarism.'[25]

Agrarian rulers saw the state as their private property and felt free to exploit it for their own enrichment. There is nothing in the historical record to suggest that they felt any responsibility for their peasants.[26] As Gilgamesh's people complain in the *Epic*: 'The city is his possession . . . He is king, he does whatever he wants.' Yet Sumerian religion did not entirely endorse this inequity. When the gods heard these anguished complaints, they exclaimed to Anu: 'Gilgamesh, noble as he is, splendid as he is, has exceeded all bounds. The people suffer from his tyranny . . . Is this how you want your king to rule? Should a shepherd savage his own flock?'[27] Anu shakes his head but cannot change the system.

The narrative poem *Atrahasis* (*c.* 1700 BCE) is set in the mythical period when the gods were still living in Mesopotamia and 'gods instead of man did the work' on which civilisation depends.[28] The poet explains that the Anunnaki, the divine aristocracy, have forced the Igigi, the lower gods, to carry too great a load: for three thousand years they have ploughed and harvested the fields and dug the irrigation canals – they even had to excavate the river-beds of the Tigris and Euphrates. 'Night and day, they groaned and blamed each other' but the Anunnaki take no heed.[29] Finally an angry mob gathers outside Enlil's palace: 'Every single one of us gods has declared war. We have put a stop to the digging!' they cry. 'The load is excessive. It is killing us!'[30] Enki, Minister of Agriculture, agrees. The system is cruel and unsustainable and the Anunnaki were wrong to ignore the Igigis' plight: 'Their work was too hard, their trouble too much! Every day the earth resounded. The warning signal was loud enough!'[31] But if nobody does any

productive work civilisation would collapse, so Enki orders the Mother
Goddess to create human beings to take the Igigis' place.[32] For the plight
of their human labourers too the gods feel no responsibility. The toiling
masses are not allowed to impinge on their privileged existence, so when
humans become so numerous that their noise keeps their divine masters
awake, the gods simply decide to cull the population with a plague. The
poet graphically depicts their suffering.

> Their faces covered in scabs, like malt,
> Their faces looked sallow,
> They went out in public hunched,
> Their well-set shoulders slouched,
> Their upstanding bearing slouched.[33]

But yet again aristocratic cruelty does not go uncriticised. Enki, whom the
poet calls 'far sighted', bravely defies his fellow gods, reminding them that
their lives depend on their human slaves.[34] The Anunnaki grudgingly agree
to spare them and withdrew to the peace and quiet of heaven. This was a
mythical expression of a harsh social reality: the gulf separating the nobility
from the peasants had become so great that they effectively occupied different
worlds.

The *Atrahasis* may have been intended for public recitation and the story
seems also to have been preserved orally.[35] Fragments of this text have been
found spanning a thousand years, so it seems that this tale was widely
known.[36] Thus writing, originally invented to serve the structural violence
of Sumer, had begun to record the disquiet of the more thoughtful members
of the ruling class, who could find no solution to civilisation's dilemma but
tried at least to look squarely at the problem. We shall see that others —
prophets, sages and mystics — would also raise their voices in protest, and
try to devise a more equitable way for human beings to live together.

The *Epic of Gilgamesh*, set in the middle of the third millennium when Sumer
had been militarised, presents martial violence as the hallmark of civilisation.[37] When the people beg the gods for help, Anu attempts to alleviate
their suffering by giving Gilgamesh someone of his own size to fight with
and siphon off some of his excessive aggression. So the Mother Goddess
creates Enkidu, primeval man. He is huge, hairy and has prodigious strength
but is a gentle, kindly soul, wandering happily with the herbivores and
protecting them from predators. But to fulfil Anu's plan, Enkidu has to

make the transition from peaceable barbarian to aggressive civilised man. The priestess Shamhat is given the task of educating him and, under her tutelage, Enkidu learns to reason, understand speech and eat human food; his hair is cut, sweet oil is rubbed into his skin and finally 'he turned into a man. He put on a garment, became like a warrior.'[38] Civilised man was essentially a man of war, full of testosterone. When Shamhat mentions Gilgamesh's military prowess, Enkidu becomes pale with anger. 'Take me to Gilgamesh!' he cries, pounding his chest. 'I will shout in his face: I am the mightiest! I am the man who can make the world tremble! I am supreme!'[39] No sooner do these two alpha males set eyes on each other than they begin wrestling, careering through the streets of Uruk, thrashing limbs entwined in a near-erotic embrace, until finally, satiated, they 'kissed each other and formed a friendship'.[40]

By this period, the Mesopotamian aristocracy had begun to supplement its income with warfare, so in the very next episode Gilgamesh announces that he is about to lead a military expedition of fifty men to the Cedar Forest guarded by the fearsome dragon Humbaba to bring this precious wood back to Sumer. It was probably by such acquisition raids that the Mesopotamian cities came to dominate the northern highlands which were rich in the luxury goods favoured by the aristocracy.[41] Merchants had long been dispatched to Afghanistan, the Indus Valley and Turkey to bring back timber, rare and base metals, and precious and semiprecious stones.[42] But for an aristocrat like Gilgamesh the only noble way to acquire these scarce resources was by force. In all future agrarian states, aristocrats would be distinguished from the rest of the population by their ability to live without working.[43] The cultural historian Thorstein Veblen has explained that in such societies, 'labor comes to be associated . . . with weakness and subjection'. Work, even trade, was not only 'disreputable . . . but *morally* impossible to the noble freeborn man'.[44] Because an aristocrat owed his privilege to the forcible expropriation of the peasants' surplus, 'the obtaining of goods by other methods than seizure comes to be accounted unworthy'.[45]

For Gilgamesh, therefore, the organised theft of warfare is not only noble but moral, undertaken not just for his personal enrichment but for the benefit of humanity. 'Now we must travel to the Cedar Forest, where the fierce monster Humbaba lives,' he announces self-importantly: 'We must kill him and drive out evil from the world.'[46] For the warrior, the enemy is always monstrous, the antithesis of everything good. But significantly the poet refused to give this military expedition any religious or ethical sanction. The gods are solidly against it. Enlil has specifically appointed Humbaba to guard the forest against any such predatory attack; Gilgamesh's mother, the goddess Ninsun, is horrified by the plan and at first blames Shamash, the sun god and Gilgamesh's patron, for planting this appalling idea in her son's mind. But when questioned, Shamash seems to know nothing about it.

Even Enkidu initially opposes the war. Humbaba, he argues, is not evil; he is carrying out an ecologically sound task for Enlil, and being frightening is part of his job description. But Gilgamesh is blinded by the aristocratic code of honour.[47] 'Why, dear friend, do you speak like a coward?' he taunts Enkidu: 'If I die in the forest on this great adventure, won't you be ashamed when people say, "Gilgamesh met a hero's death battling the monster Humbaba. And where was Enkidu? He was safe at home!"'[48] It is not the gods nor even simply greed but pride, an obsession with martial glory and the desire for a posthumous reputation for courage and daring that drive Gilgamesh to battle. 'We are mortal men,' he reminds Enkidu:

> Only the gods live forever. *Our* days
> are few in number, and whatever we achieve
> is a puff of wind. Why be afraid then,
> since sooner or later death must come? . . .
> But whether you come along or not,
> I will cut down the tree, I will kill Humbaba,
> I will make a lasting name for myself,
> I will stamp my fame on men's minds forever. [49]

Gilgamesh's mother blames his 'restless heart' for this hare-brained project.[50] A leisured class has a lot of time on its hands; collecting rents and supervising the irrigation system was tame work for a species bred to be intrepid hunters. The poem indicates that already young men were chafing against the triviality of civilian life which, as Chris Hedges explained, would lead so many of them to seek meaning on the battlefield.

The outcome is tragic. There is always a moment in warfare when the horrifying reality breaks through the glamour.[51] Humbaba turns out to be a very reasonable monster, who pleads for his life and offers Gilgamesh and Enkidu all the wood they want, but still they hack him brutally to pieces. Afterwards a gentle rain falls from heaven as though nature itself grieves for this pointless death.[52] The gods show their displeasure with the expedition by striking Enkidu down with a fatal illness and Gilgamesh is forced to come to terms with his own mortality. Unable to assimilate the consequences of warfare, he turns his back on civilisation, roaming unshaven through the wilderness and even descending into the underworld to find an antidote to death. Finally, weary but resigned, he is forced to accept the limitations of his humanity and return to Uruk. On reaching the outskirts of the city, he draws his companion's attention to the great wall surrounding the city: 'Observe the land it encloses, the palm trees, the gardens, the orchards, the glorious palaces and temples, the shops and market-places, the houses, the public squares.'[53] He personally will die, but will achieve an immortality of sorts by cultivating the civilised life and pleasures that are enabling humans to explore new dimensions of existence. But Gilgamesh's famous wall was now essential for the survival of Uruk, since after centuries of peaceful cooperation, the Sumerian city-states had begun to fight one another. What had caused this tragic development?

Not everybody in the Middle East aspired to civilisation: nomadic herdsmen preferred to roam freely in the mountains with their livestock. They had once been part of the agricultural community, living at the edge of the farmland so that their sheep and cattle did not damage the crops. But gradually, they moved further and further away until they finally abandoned the constraints of settled life and took to the open road.[54] The pastoralists of the Middle East had probably become an entirely separate community as early as 6000 BCE, though they continued to trade their hides and milk products with the cities in return for grain.[55] They soon discovered that the easiest way to replace lost animals was to steal the cattle of nearby villages and rival tribes. Fighting, therefore, became essential to the pastoralist economy. Once they had domesticated the horse and acquired wheeled vehicles, these herdsmen spread all over the Inner Asian Plateau, and by the early third millennium some had reached China.[56] By this time, they were formidable warriors, equipped with bronze weaponry, war chariots, and the deadly composite bow, which could shoot with devastating accuracy at long range.[57]

The pastoralists who settled in the Caucasian steppes of southern Russia in about 4500 BCE shared a common culture. They called themselves *Arya* ('noble; honourable'), but we know them as 'Indo-Europeans' because their language became the basis of several Asiatic and European tongues.[58] In about 2500 BCE, some of the Aryans left the steppes and conquered large areas of Asia and Europe, becoming the ancestors of Hittites, Celts, Greeks, Romans, Germans, Scandinavians and Anglo-Saxons. Meanwhile those tribes who had remained in the Caucasus had drifted apart. They continued to live side by side – not always amicably – speaking different dialects of the proto-Indo-European tongue until, in about 1500 BCE, they too migrated from the steppes, the Avestan-speakers settling in what is now Iran and the Sanskrit-speakers colonising the Indian subcontinent.

Aryans saw the warrior's life as infinitely superior to the tedium and steady industry of agrarian existence. The Roman historian Tacitus (c. 55–120 CE) would later note that the German tribes he encountered far preferred 'to challenge the enemy and earn the honour of wounds' to the drudgery of ploughing and the tedium of waiting for the crops to appear: 'Nay, they actually think it tame and stupid to acquire by the sweat of toil what they might win by their blood.'[59] Like urban aristocrats, they too despised labour, saw it as a mark of inferiority, and as incompatible with the 'noble' life.[60] Moreover, they knew that the cosmic order (rita) was possible only because chaos was kept in check by the great gods (devas*) – Mithra, Varuna and Mazda – who compelled the seasons to rotate regularly, kept the heavenly bodies in their proper places, and made the earth habitable. Human beings too could live together in an orderly, productive way only if they were forced to sacrifice their own interests to those of the group.

Violence therefore lay at the heart of social existence and in most ancient cultures this truth was expressed in the ritualised bloodshed of animal sacrifice. Like the prehistoric hunters, Aryans had absorbed the tragic fact that life depends upon the destruction of other beings. They expressed this conviction in the mythical story of a king who nobly allows himself to be slain by his brother, a priest, and thus brings the ordered world into being.[61] A myth was never simply the story of an historical event; rather, it expressed a timeless truth underlying a people's daily existence. A myth is always about *now*. The Aryans re-enacted the tale of the sacrificed king every day by ritually slaying an animal to remind themselves of the sacrifice demanded of every single warrior, who daily put his life at risk for his people.

It has been argued that Aryan society was originally peaceful and did not resort to aggressive raiding until the end of the second millennium.[62] But other scholars note that weapons and warriors figure in the very earliest texts.[63] The mythical stories of the Aryan war gods – Indra in India, Verethragna in Persia, Hercules in Greece and Thor in Scandinavia – follow a similar pattern, so this martial ideal must have developed in

* In Avestan, the Sanskrit *devas* became *daevas*.

the steppes before the tribes went their different ways. It was based on the hero Trito, who conducts the very first cattle raid against the three-headed Serpent, one of the indigenous inhabitants of a land recently conquered by the Aryans. Serpent had the temerity to steal the Aryans' cattle. Not only does Trito kill him and recover the livestock, but this raid becomes a cosmic battle that, like the death of the sacrificed king, restores the cosmic order.[64]

Aryan religion gave supreme sanction to what was essentially organised violence and theft. Every time they set out on a raid, warriors drank a ritual draught of the intoxicating liquor pressed from Soma, a sacred plant which filled them with frenzied rapture, just as Trito had done before pursuing Serpent; they thus felt at one with their hero. The Trito myth implied that all cattle, the measure of wealth in pastoral society, belonged to the Aryans and that other peoples had no right to these resources. The Trito story has been called 'the imperialist's myth par excellence' because it provided a religious justification for the Indo-European military campaigns in Europe and Asia.[65] The figure of Serpent presented those native peoples who dared to resist the Aryan onslaught as inhuman, misshapen monsters. But cattle and wealth were not the only prizes worth fighting for: like Gilgamesh, Aryans would always also seek honour, glory, prestige and posthumous fame in battle.[66] People rarely go to war for one reason only; rather, they are driven by interlocking motivations – material, social and religious. In Homer's *Iliad*, when the Trojan warrior Sarpedon urges his friend Glaukos to make a highly dangerous assault on the Greek camp, he quite unselfconsciously lists all the material perks of a heroic reputation – special seating, the best cuts of meat, booty, and 'a great piece of land' – as an integral part of a warrior's nobility.[67] It is significant that the English words 'value' and 'valour' both have a common Indo-European root, as do 'virtue' and 'virility'.

But while Aryan religion glorified warfare, it also acknowledged that this violence was problematic. Any military campaign involves activities that would be abhorrent and unethical in civilian life.[68] In Aryan mythology, therefore, the war god is often called a 'sinner', because a soldier is forced to act in a way that calls his integrity into question. The warrior always carries a taint.[69] Even Achilles, one of the greatest Aryan warriors, does not escape this stain. Here is Homer's description of the *aristeia* ('triumphal rampage') in which Achilles frenziedly slaughtered one Trojan soldier after another:

As inhuman fire sweeps on in fury through the deep angles
Of drywood mountain and sets ablaze the depth of the timber
And the blustering wind lashes the flame along, so Achilleus
Swept everywhere with his spear, like something more than a mortal.[70]

Achilles has become an inhuman force of purely destructive power. Homer compares him to a thresher crushing barley on the threshing floor, but instead of producing nourishing food, 'trampling alike dead men and shields' as if the two were indistinguishable, his 'invincible hands . . . [were] spattered with bloody filth'.[71] Warriors would never attain the first rank in Indo-European society.[72] They always had to struggle 'to be the best' (Greek: *aristos*); yet they were still relegated to the second class, below the priests. Herdsmen could not survive without raiding; their violence was essential to the pastoralist economy but the hero's aggression often repelled the very people who revered him.[73]

The *Iliad* is certainly not an anti-war poem, but at the same time as it celebrates the feats of its heroes, it reminds us of the tragedy of war. As in the *Epic of Gilgamesh,* the sorrow of mortality sometimes breaks through the excitement and idealism. The third person to be killed in the poem is the Trojan Simoeisios, a beautiful young man who, Homer says, should have known the tenderness of family life but is beaten down by the Greek warrior Ajax:

He dropped then to the ground in the dust, like some black poplar
Which in the land low-lying about a great marsh grows
Smooth trimmed yet with branches growing at the uttermost tree-top:
One whom a man, a maker of chariots, fells with the shining
Iron, to bend it into a wheel for a fine-wrought chariot,
And the tree lies hardening by the banks of a river.[74]

In the *Odyssey,* Homer goes even further, undermining the entire aristocratic ideal. When Odysseus visits the underworld he is horrified by the swarming crowds of gibbering dead, whose humanity has so obscenely degenerated. Coming upon the disconsolate shade of Achilles, he tries to console him: was he not honoured like a god before he died and does he not now rule the dead? But Achilles will have none of it. 'Don't gloss over death to me in order to console me,' he replies: 'I would rather be above the ground still and labouring for some poor peasant man than be the lord over the lifeless dead.'[75]

* * *

We have no firm evidence for this, but it was probably pastoralists living in the mountainous regions surrounding the Fertile Crescent who introduced warfare to Sumer.[76] The herdsmen would have found the cities' wealth irresistible and they had perfected the art of the surprise attack, their speed and mobility terrifying the city-dwellers, who had not yet mastered the art of horsemanship. After a few such lightning raids, the Sumerians would have taken steps to protect their people and storehouses. But these raids probably gave them the idea of using similar techniques to seize loot and arable land from a neighbouring Sumerian city.[77] By the middle of the third millennium BCE, the Sumerian plain was mobilised for warfare: archaeologists have discovered a marked increase in walled fortifications and bronze weaponry in this stratum. This had not been unavoidable; there was no such escalation of armed conflict in Egypt, which had also developed a sophisticated civilisation but was a far more peaceful agrarian state.[78] The Nile flooded the fields with almost unfailing regularity and Egypt was not exposed to the tumultuous climate of Mesopotamia; nor was it encircled by mountains full of predatory herdsmen.[79] The Egyptian kingdoms probably had an ad hoc militia to repel an occasional nomadic attack from the desert, but the weapons unearthed by archaeologists are crude and rudimentary. Most ancient Egyptian art celebrates the joy and elegance of civilian life and there is little glorification of warfare in early Egyptian literature.[80]

We can only piece together the progress of Sumerian militarisation from fragmentary archaeological evidence. Between 2340 and 2284 BCE, the Sumerian king-lists record thirty-four inter-city wars.[81] The first kings of Sumer had been priestly specialists in astronomy and ritual; now increasingly they were warriors like Gilgamesh. They discovered that warfare was an invaluable source of revenue that brought them booty and prisoners who could be put to work in the fields. Instead of waiting for the next breakthrough in productivity, they found that war yielded quicker and more ample returns. The Stele of Vultures (c. 2500 BCE), now in the Louvre, depicts Eannatum, king of Lagash, leading a tightly knit and heavily armed phalanx of troops into battle against the city of Umma; this was clearly a society equipped and trained for warfare. The Stele records that even though they begged for mercy, three thousand Ummaite soldiers were killed that day.[82] Once the plain had become militarised, each king had to be prepared to defend and if possible extend his territory, the source of his wealth. Most of these Sumerian conflicts were tit-for-tat campaigns for booty and territory. None seem to have been decisive and there are signs that some people saw the whole business as futile. 'You go and carry off the enemy's land;' reads one inscription: 'the enemy comes and carries off your land.'[83] Yet still disputes were settled by force rather than diplomacy and no state could afford to be militarily unprepared. 'The state weak in armaments,' commented another inscription, 'the enemy will not be driven from its gates.'[84]

During these inconclusive wars, Sumerian aristocrats and retainers were wounded, killed and enslaved, but the peasants suffered far more. Because they were the basis of any aristocrat's wealth, they and their livestock were regularly slaughtered by an invading army, their barns and homes demolished, and their fields soaked with blood. The countryside and peasant villages would become a wasteland, and the destruction of harvests, herds and agricultural equipment often meant severe famine.[85] The inconclusive nature of these wars meant that everybody suffered and that there would be no permanent gain for anybody, since today's winner was likely to be tomorrow's loser. This would become the besetting problem of civilisation, since equally matched aristocracies would always compete aggressively for scarce resources. Paradoxically, warfare that was supposed to enrich the aristocracy often damaged productivity. Already at this very early date it had become apparent that to prevent this pointless and self-destructive suffering it was essential to hold these competing aristocracies in check. A higher authority had to have the military muscle to impose the peace.

In 2330 BC a new type of ruler emerged in Mesopotamia when Sargon, a common soldier of Semitic origins, staged a successful coup in the city of Kish, marched to Uruk and deposed its king. He repeated this process in one city after another until, for the first time, Sumer was ruled by a single monarch. Sargon had created the world's first agrarian empire.[86] It was said that with his massive standing army of 5,400 men, he conquered territory in present-day Iran, Syria and Lebanon. He built Akkad, an entirely new capital city, which may have stood near modern Baghdad. In his inscriptions, Sargon – his name meaning 'True and Rightful King' – claimed to have ruled 'the totality of lands under heaven' and later generations would revere him as a model hero, not unlike Charlemagne or King Arthur. For millennia, in his memory, Mesopotamian rulers would style themselves 'Lord of Akkad'. Yet we know very little about either the man or his empire. Akkad was remembered as an exotic, cosmopolitan city and an important trade centre, but its site has never been discovered. The empire has left little archaeological trace, and what we know of Sargon's life is largely legendary.

Yet his empire was a watershed. The world's first supra-regional polity, it became the model for all future agrarian imperialism, not simply because of Sargon's prestige but because there was no viable alternative. An empire was achieved by the conquest of foreign territory: subject peoples were reduced to vassals, and kings and tribal chieftains became regional governors, their task to extort taxes in kind from their people – silver, grain, frankincense, metals, timber and animals – and send them to Akkad. Sargon's inscriptions claim that he fought thirty-four wars during his exceptionally long reign of fifty-six years. In all later agrarian empires, warfare would be the norm; it was not simply the 'sport of kings' but an economic and social necessity.[87] Besides gaining plunder and loot, the chief goal of any imperial campaign was to conquer and tax more peasants. As the British historian Perry Anderson explains, 'war was possibly the most *rational* and *rapid* single mode of economic expansion, of surplus extraction, available for any given ruling class'.[88] Fighting and obtaining wealth were inseparable: freed from the need to engage in productive work, the nobility had the leisure to cultivate their martial skills.[89] They certainly fought for honour, glory and the sheer pleasure of battle, but warfare was, 'perhaps above all, a source of profit, the nobleman's chief industry'.[90] It needed no justification: its necessity seemed self-evident.

We know so little about Sargon that it is hard to be precise about the role of religion in his imperial wars. In one of his inscriptions, he claimed that after he defeated the cities of Ur, Lagash and Umma, 'the god Enlil [did] not let him have a rival, gave him the Lower and the Upper Sea and the citizens of Akkad held [posts of] government'.[91] Religion had always been central to Mesopotamian politics. The city was viable because it fed and served its deities; doubtless, the oracles of these gods endorsed Sargon's campaigns. His son and successor Naram-Sin (r. 2260–2223 BCE), who further extended the Akkadian empire, was actually known as the 'god of Akkad'. As a new city, Akkad could not claim to have been founded by one of the Anunnaki, so Naram-Sin declared that he had become the mediator between the divine aristocracy and his subjects. As we shall see, agrarian emperors would often be deified in this way and it gave them a useful propaganda device that justified major administrative and economic reforms.[92] As ever, religion and politics co-inhered, the gods serving as the alter ego of the monarch and sanctifying the structural violence that was essential to the survival of civilisation.

The agrarian empire made no attempt to represent the people or serve their interests. The ruling class regarded the peasant population as virtually a different species. The ruler saw his empire as his personal possession and his army as his own private militia. As long as their subjects produced and relinquished the surplus, the ruling class left them to their own devices so peasants policed and governed their own communities; pre-modern communications did not permit the imperial ruling class to impose its religion or culture on the subject peoples. A successful empire supposedly prevented a repetition of the destructive tit-for-tat warfare that had plagued Sumer but, even so, Sargon died suppressing a revolt and besides constantly subduing would-be usurpers, Naram-Sin also had to defend his borders against pastoralists who had founded their own states in Anatolia, Syria and Palestine.

After the decline of the Akkadian empire, there were other imperial experiments in Mesopotamia. From 2113 to 2029, Ur ruled the whole of Sumer and Akkad from the Persian Gulf to the southern Jezirah (today's al-Jazirai) as well as large parts of western Iran. Then, in the nineteenth century BCE, Sumu-abum, a Semitic-Amorite chieftain, founded a dynasty in the small town of Babylon. King Hammurabi (c. 1792–1750 BCE), the sixth in line, gradually gained control of southern Mesopotamia and the western regions of the middle Euphrates. In a famous stele, he is shown standing before Marduk, the sun god, receiving the laws of his kingdom. In his law code, Hammurabi announced that he had been appointed by the gods 'to cause justice to prevail in the land, to destroy the wicked and the evil, that the strong might not oppress the weak'.[93] Despite the structural violence of the agrarian state, Middle Eastern rulers would regularly make this claim. Promulgating such laws was little more than a political exercise in which the king claimed that he was powerful enough to bypass the lower aristocrats and become a supreme court of appeal for the oppressed masses.[94] His benevolent laws, his code concluded, were the 'laws of righteousness, which Hammurabi, *the strong king* established'.[95] Significantly, he published this code at the end of his career, after he had successfully oppressed whole populations and established a system of taxation throughout his domains that enriched his capital in Babylon.

But no agrarian civilisation could advance beyond a certain limit. An expanding empire always outran its resources, once its requirements exceeded what nature, peasants and animals could produce. And despite the lofty talk about justice for the poor, prosperity had to be confined to an elite. While modernity has institutionalised change, radical innovation was rare in premodern times: civilisation seemed so fragile that it was deemed more important to preserve what had been achieved rather than risk something entirely new. Originality was not encouraged, because any

new idea that required too great an economic outlay would not be implemented and this could cause social unrest. Hence novelty was suspect, not
out of timidity but because it was economically and politically hazardous.
The past remained the supreme authority.[96]

Continuity was politically essential. Thus the Akitu festival, inaugurated
by the Sumerians in the mid-third millennium, was celebrated each year
by every Mesopotamian ruler for over two thousand years. Originally
performed in Ur in honour of Enlil when Sumer had become militarised,
in Babylon the Akitu rituals centred on the city's patron, Marduk.[97] As always
in Mesopotamia, this act of worship had an important political function
and was essential to the regime's legitimacy. We shall see in Chapter 4 that
a king could be deposed for failing to perform these ceremonies, which
marked the start of the New Year when the old year was dying and the
king's power waning.[98] By ritually rehearsing cosmic battles that had ordered
the universe at the beginning of time, the ruling aristocracy hoped to make
this powerful surge a reality in their state for another twelve months.

On the fifth day of the festival, the presiding priest would ceremonially
humiliate the king in Marduk's shrine in the Esagil ziggurat, evoking the
terrifying spectre of social anarchy by confiscating the royal regalia, striking
the king on the cheek and throwing him roughly to the ground.[99] The
bruised and abject king would plead with Marduk that he had not behaved
like an evil ruler:

> I did not destroy Babylon; I did not command its overthrow; I did not destroy
> the temple . . . Esagil. I did not forget its rites; I did not rain blows on the
> cheeks of the protected citizens. I did not humiliate them. I watched out
> for Babylon. I did not smash its walls.[100]

The priest then slapped the king again, so hard that tears rose to his eyes
– a sign of repentance that satisfied Marduk. Thus reinstated, the king now
clasped the hands of Marduk's effigy, the regalia were returned, and his rule
was secure for the coming year. The statues of all the patronal gods and
goddesses of all the cities in Mesopotamia had to be brought to Babylon for
the festival as an expression of cultic and political loyalty. If they were not
all present, the Akitu could not be celebrated and the realm would be
endangered. The liturgy was as crucial for a city's security as its fortifications
and it had reminded the people, only the day before, of the city's fragility.

On the fourth day of the festival, priests and choristers had filed into
Marduk's shrine for the recitation of *Enuma Elish*, the hymn that recounted

Marduk's victory over cosmic and political chaos. The first gods to emerge
from the slimy primal matter (similar to Mesopotamia's alluvial soil) were
'nameless, natureless, futureless'.[101] As in the primeval rural societies, they
were virtually inseparable from the natural world and were the enemies of
progress. But the next gods to emerge from the slime became progressively
more distinct until the divine evolution culminated in Marduk, the most
splendid of the Anunnaki. In the same way, Mesopotamian culture had
developed from rural communities immersed in the natural rhythms of the
countryside which were now regarded as sluggish, static and inert. But the
old times could return: this hymn expressed the fear of civilisation lapsing
back into abysmal nothingness. The most dangerous of the primitive gods
was Tiamat, whose name means 'Void'; she was the salty Sea, which, in the
Middle East, symbolised both primeval chaos and the social anarchy that
could bring starvation, disease and death to the entire population. She
represented an ever-present threat that every civilisation, no matter how
powerful, had to be ready to confront.

The hymn also gave sacred sanction to the structural violence of
Babylonian society. Tiamat creates a horde of monsters to fight the Anunnaki,
a 'growling roaring rout, ready for battle', suggestive of the danger the
lower classes presented to the state. Their monstrous forms represent the
perverse defiance of normal categories and the confusion of identity associated with social and cosmic chaos. Their leader is Tiamat's spouse Kingu,
a 'clumsy labourer', one of the Igigi, whose name means 'Toil'.[102] The
narrative of the hymn is repeatedly punctuated with this pounding refrain:

> She has made the Worm, the Dragon, the Female Monster, the Great Lion,
> the Mad Dog, the Mad Scorpion and the Howling Storm, the Fish-Man, the
> Centaur.[103]

But Marduk defeats them all, casting them into prison and creating an
ordered universe by splitting Tiamat's corpse in two and separating heaven
and earth. He then orders the gods to build the city of *bab-ilani*, 'gate of
the gods', as their earthly home and creates the first man by mixing Kingu's
blood with a handful of dust to perform the labour on which civilisation
depended. 'Sons of toil', the masses are sentenced for life to menial labour
and are held in subjection. Liberated from work, the gods sing a hymn of
praise and thanksgiving. The myth and its accompanying rituals reminded
the Sumerian aristocracy of the reality on which their civilisation and
privilege depended; they must be perpetually primed for war to keep down

rebellious peasants, ambitious aristocrats and foreign enemies who threatened the civilised order. Religion was deeply implicated in this imperial violence and could not be separated from the economic and political realities that sustained any agrarian state.

The fragility of civilisation became clear during the seventeenth century BCE, when Indo-European hordes repeatedly attacked the cities of Mesopotamia. Even Egypt now became militarised, when Bedouin tribesmen, whom the Egyptians called Hyksos ('chieftains from foreign lands'), managed to establish their own dynasty in the delta area in the sixteenth century.[104] The Egyptians expelled them in 1567 BCE, but ever afterwards the ruling pharaoh was depicted as a warrior at the head of a powerful army. Empire seemed the best defence, so Egypt secured its frontier by subjugating Nubia in the south and coastal Palestine in the north. But by the middle of the second millennium the ancient Near East was dominated by foreign conquerors; Kassite tribes from the Caucasus took over the Babylonian empire (c. 1600–1155); an Indo-European aristocracy created the Hittite empire in Anatolia (1420–1200); and the Mitanni, another Aryan tribe, controlled Greater Mesopotamia from about 1500 until they were conquered by the Hittites in the mid-fourteenth century BCE. Ashur-uballik I, ruler of the city of Ashur in the eastern Tigris region, who was able to exploit the turbulence that followed the collapse of the Mitanni, made Assyria a new power in the Middle East.

Assyria was not a traditional agrarian state.[105] Situated in an area that had not been agriculturally productive since the nineteenth century BCE, Ashur had relied more than other cities on commerce, setting up trading colonies in Cappadocia and planting mercantile representatives in several Babylonian cities. For about a century Ashur was a trading hub, importing tin (crucial for the manufacture of bronze) from Afghanistan and exporting it together with Mesopotamian textiles to Anatolia and the Black Sea. The historical record is so slight, however, that we do not know how this affected the farmers of Ashur or whether commerce mitigated the structural violence of the state. Nor do we know much about Ashur's religious practices. Its kings built impressive temples to the gods, but we know nothing about the personality and exploits of Ashur, its patronal deity, whose mythology has not survived.

The Assyrians began to dominate the region when their king Adad-nirari I (1307–1275) conquered the old Mitanni territories from the Hittites as well as land in southern Babylonia. The economic incentive was always prominent in Assyrian warfare. The inscriptions of Shalmaneser I (1274–45) stressed his martial prowess: he was a 'valiant hero, capable of battle with his enemies, whose aggressive battle flashes like a flame and whose weapons attack like a merciless death-trap'.[106] It was he who began the Assyrian practice of forcibly moving people around his empire not simply, as was once thought, to demoralise the conquered peoples but principally to stimulate the agricultural economy by replenishing underpopulated regions.[107]

The reign of his son Tukulti-Ninurta I (1244–08), who made Assyria the most formidable military and economic power of the day, is better documented. He turned Ashur into the ritual capital of his empire and instituted the Akitu festival there, with the god Ashur in the starring role; it appears that the Assyrians introduced a mock battle re-enacting Ashur's war with Tiamat. In his inscriptions, Tukulti-Ninurta was careful to credit his victories to the gods: 'Trusting in Ashur and the great gods, my lord, I struck and brought about their defeat.' But he also makes it clear that warfare was never simply an act of piety:

> I made them swear by the great gods of heaven [and] underworld, I imposed
> upon them the yoke of my lordship, [and then] released them to return to
> their lands . . . Fortified cities I subdued at my feet and imposed corvée.
> Annually I receive with ceremony their valuable tribute in my city Ashur.[108]

Assyrian kings too were plagued by internal dissent, intrigue and rebellion, yet Tigleth-Pileser I (c. 1115–1093) continued to expand the empire, maintaining his domination of the region by continuous campaigning and large-scale deportations, so that his reign was in effect one continuous war.[109] Punctilious as he was in his devotion to the gods and as an energetic builder of temples, his strategy was always dictated by economic imperatives. His chief motive for expanding northward into Iran, for instance, was the acquisition of booty, metal and animals, which he sent home to boost productivity in Syria at a time of chronic crop failure.[110]

Warfare had become a fact of human life, central to the political, social and economic dynamics of the agrarian empire and, like every other human activity, it always had a religious dimension. These states would not have survived without a continuous military effort and the gods, the alter egos of the ruling class, represented a yearning for a strength that could transcend human instability. But the Mesopotamians were not credulous fanatics. Religious mythology may have endorsed their structural and martial violence, but it also regularly called it into question. There was a strong vein of scepticism in Mesopotamian literature. One aristocrat complained that he had always been righteous, joyfully followed the gods' processions, taught all the people on his estate to worship the Mother Goddess, and instructed his soldiers to revere the king as the gods' representative. Yet he had been afflicted with disease, insomnia and terror and 'no god came to my aid or grasped my hand'.¹¹¹ Gilgamesh too gets no help from the gods as he struggles to accept Enkidu's death. When he meets Ishtar, the Mother Goddess, he denounces her savagely for her inability to protect men from the grim realities of life: she is like a waterskin that soaks its carrier, a shoe that pinches its wearer, and a door that fails to keep out the wind. In the end, as we have seen, Gilgamesh found resignation but the *Epic* as a whole suggests that mortals had no choice but to rely on themselves rather than the gods. Urban living was beginning to change the way people thought about the divine, but one of the most momentous religious developments of the period occurred at about the same time as Sin-leqi wrote his version of Gilgamesh's life. It did not happen in a sophisticated city, however, but was a response to the escalation of violence in an Aryan pastoral community.

Early one morning in about 1200 BCE, an Avestan-speaking priest in the Caucasian steppes went to the river to collect water for the morning sacrifice. There he had a vision of Ahura Mazda, 'Lord Wisdom', one of the greatest gods in the Aryan pantheon. Zoroaster had been horrified by the cruelty of the Sanskrit-speaking cattle-raiders, who had vandalised one Avestan community after another. As he meditated on this crisis, the logic of the perennial philosophy led him to conclude that these earthly battles must have a heavenly counterpart. The most important daevas – Varuna, Mithra and Mazda who had the honorary title *ahura* ('Lord') – were guardians of cosmic order and stood for truth, justice, and respect for life and property. But the cattle-raiders' hero was the war god Indra, a second-ranking daeva. Perhaps, Zoroaster reflected, the peace-loving ahuras were being attacked in the heavenly world by the wicked daevas. In his vision, Ahura Mazda told him that he was correct and must mobilise his people in a holy war against terror. Good men and women must no longer sacrifice to Indra and the lower daevas but worship the Wise Lord and his fellow ahuras instead: the daevas and the cattle-raiders, their earthly henchmen, must be destroyed.¹¹²

We shall see again and again that the experience of an unusual level of violence would in the future shock its victims into a dualistic vision that splits the world into two irreconcilable camps. Zoroaster concluded that there must be a malevolent deity, Angra Mainyu, the 'Hostile Spirit', who was equal in power to the Wise Lord but was his polar opposite. Every single man, woman and child, therefore, must choose between absolute Good and absolute Evil.[113] The Wise Lord's followers must live patient, disciplined lives, bravely defending all good creatures from the assault of evildoers, caring for the poor and weak and tending their cattle kindly, instead of driving them from their pastures like the cruel raiders. They must pray five times a day and meditate on the menace of evil in order to weaken its power.[114] Society must not be dominated by these fighters (nar-) but by men (viras) who were kind and dedicated to the supreme virtue of truth.[115] But so traumatised was Zoroaster by the ferocity of the raiders' attacks that this gentle, ethical vision was itself permeated with violence. He was convinced that the whole world was rushing towards a final cataclysm in which the Wise Lord would annihilate the wicked daevas and incinerate the Hostile Spirit in a river of fire. There would be a Great Judgment and the daevas' earthly followers would be exterminated. The earth would then be restored to its original perfection. There would be no more death and disease and the mountains and valleys would be levelled to form a great plain where gods and humans could live together in peace.[116]

Zoroaster's apocalyptic thinking was unique. As we have seen, traditional Aryan ideology had long acknowledged the disturbing ambiguity of the violence that lay at the heart of human society. Indra may have been a 'sinner' but his struggles against the forces of chaos – however tainted by the lies and deceitful practices to which he had to resort – had contributed as much to the cosmic order as the work of the great ahuras. But by projecting all the cruelty of his time on to Indra, Zoroaster had demonised violence and made him a figure of absolute evil.[117] Yet Zoroaster made few converts in his lifetime. No community could survive in the steppes without the fighters that he had rejected. The early history of Zoroastrianism remains obscure, but we do know that when the Avestan Aryans migrated to Iran, they took their faith with them. Suitably adapted to the needs of the aristocracy, Zoroastrianism would become the ideology of the Persian ruling class and Zoroastrian ideals would infiltrate the religion of Jews and Christians living under Persian rule. But that lay in the distant future. In the meantime, the Sanskrit-speaking Aryans began to bring the cult of Indra to the Indian subcontinent.

INDIA: THE NOBLE PATH

For the Aryans who migrated to the Indian subcontinent, springtime was the season of yoga. After a winter of 'settled peace' (*ksema*) in the encampment, it was time to summon Indra to lead them on the warpath into battle once again and the priests performed a ceremony that re-enacted the god's miraculous birth.[1] They also chanted a hymn celebrating his cosmic victory over the chaos-dragon Vritra, who had imprisoned the life-giving waters in the primal mountain so that the world was no longer habitable. During this heroic battle, Indra had been strengthened by hymns sung by the Maruts, the storm gods.[2] Now priests chanted these same hymns to fortify the Aryan warriors, who like Indra before his battles drank a draught of soma. At one now with Indra, exalted by the intoxicating liquor, they harnessed their horses to their war chariots in the formalised *yug* ('yoking') ritual and set off to raid the villages of their neighbours, firm now in their conviction that they too were setting the world to rights. The Aryans regarded themselves as 'noble', and yoga marked the start of the raiding season when they really lived up to their name.

As for the pastoralists of the Near East, Indian Aryan ritual and mythology glorified organised theft and violence. For the Indo-Aryans too, cattle-rustling needed no justification: like any aristocrat, they regarded forcible seizure as the only noble way to obtain goods, so raiding was, per se, a sacred activity. In their battles, they experienced an ecstasy that gave meaning and intensity to their lives, performing thus a 'religious' as well as an economic and political function. But the word 'yoga', which has such different connotations for us today, alerts us to a curious dynamic: in India, Aryan priests, sages and mystics would frequently use the mythology and rhetoric of warfare to subvert the warrior ethos. No myth ever had a single, definitive meaning; it was constantly recast and its meaning changed. The same stories, rituals and set of symbols that could be used to promote an ethic of war could also promote an ethic of peace. By meditating on the violent mythology and rituals that shaped their worldview, the people of India would work as energetically to create a noble path of nonviolence (*ahimsa*) as their ancestors had in promoting the sanctity of the warpath.

But that dramatic reversal would not begin until almost a millennium after the first Aryan settlers arrived in the Punjab during the nineteenth century BCE. There was no dramatic invasion; they arrived in small groups, gradually infiltrating the region over a very long period.[3] During their travels, they would have seen the ruins of a great civilisation in the Indus Valley, which at the height of its power (*c.* 2300–2000 BCE) had been larger than either Egypt or Sumer, but they made no attempt to rebuild these cities, because, like all pastoralists, they despised the security of settled life. A rough, hard-drinking people, Aryans earned their living by stealing the herds of rival Aryan tribes and fighting the indigenous peoples, the *dasas* ('barbarians').[4] Because their agricultural skills were rudimentary, they could support themselves only by cattle-raiding and plunder. They owned no territory but let their animals graze on other people's lands. Driving relentlessly eastward in search of new pastures, they would not wholly abandon this peripatetic life until the sixth century BCE. Continually on the move, living in temporary encampments, they left no archaeological record. For this early period we are entirely dependent on ritual texts that were transmitted orally and that allude, in veiled, riddling fashion, to the mythology that the Aryans used to give shape and significance to their lives.

In *c.* 1200, a group of learned Aryan families began the monumental task of collecting the hymns that had been revealed to the great seers (*rishis*) of old, adding new poems of their own. This anthology of more than a thousand poems, divided into ten books, would become the *Rig Veda,* the most sacred of four Sanskrit texts known collectively as *Veda* ('knowledge'). Some of these hymns were sung during the Aryans' sacrificial rituals to the accompaniment of traditional mimes and gestures. Sound would always have sacred significance in India and as the musical chant and the enigmatic words stole into their minds, Aryans felt in touch with the mysterious potency that held the disparate elements of the universe together in a cosmic coherence. The Rig Veda was rita, divine order, translated into human speech.[5] But to a modern reader these texts do not seem at all 'religious'. Instead of personal devotion, they celebrate the glory of battle, the joy of killing, the exhilaration of strong drink and the nobility of stealing other people's cattle.

Sacrifice was essential to any ancient economy. The wealth of society was thought to depend on gifts bestowed by the gods who were its patrons.

Humans responded to this divine generosity by giving thanks, thus enhancing
the gods' honour and ensuring further benefaction. So Vedic ritual was
based on the principle of reciprocal exchange: *do ut des* – 'I give to make
you give.' The priests would offer the choicest portions of the sacrificial
animal to the gods: this was transferred to the heavenly world by Agni, the
sacred Fire, while the leftover meat was the gods' gift to the community.
After a successful raid, warriors would distribute their spoils in the *vidatha*
ritual, which resembled the 'potlatch' of the north-western Native
Americans.[6] This too was not what we would call a spiritual affair. The
chieftain (*raja*) hosting the sacrifice proudly exhibited the cattle, horses,
soma and crops he had seized to the elders of his own clan and to neighbouring rajas. Some of these goods were sacrificed to the gods, others were
presented to the visiting chieftains, and the rest were consumed in a riotous
banquet. Participants were either drunk or pleasantly mellow; there was
casual sex with slave girls and aggressively competitive chariot races,
shooting matches and tugs of war; there were dice games for high stakes
and mock battles. This was not just a glorified party, however; it was
essential to the Aryan economy: a ritualised way of redistributing newly
acquired resources with reasonable equity and imposing an obligation on
other clans to reciprocate. These sacred contests also trained young men
in military skills and helped rajas identify talent, so that an aristocracy of
the best warriors could emerge.

It was not easy to train a warrior to put himself in harm's way day after
day. Ritual gave meaning to an essentially grim and dangerous struggle. The
soma dulled inhibitions and the hymns reminded warriors that by fighting
indigenous peoples they were continuing Indra's mighty battles for cosmic
order. It was said that Vritra had been 'the worst of the Vratras', the native
warrior tribes who lurked menacingly on the fringes of Vedic society.[7] The
Aryans of India shared Zoroaster's belief that an immense struggle was
raging in heaven between the warlike devas and the peace-loving *asuras*.*
But unlike Zoroaster they rather despised the sedentary asuras and were
staunchly on the side of the noble devas 'who drove their chariots, while
the asuras stayed at home in their halls'.[8] Such was their hatred of the
tedium and triviality of settled life that only in their marauding did they
feel fully alive. They were, so to speak, spiritually programmed: the
constantly repeated ritual gestures imprinted in their bodies and minds an
instinctive knowledge of how an alpha male should comport himself; and

* *Asura* is the Sanskrit version of the Avestan *ahura* ('lord').

the emotive hymns implanted a deep-rooted sense of entitlement, an entrenched belief that Aryans were born to dominate.[9] All this gave them the courage, tenacity and energy to traverse the vast distances of north-west India, eliminating every obstacle in their path.[10]

We know practically nothing about Aryan life during this period, but because mythology is not wholly about the heavenly world but essentially about the here and now, in these Vedic texts we catch glimpses of a community fighting for its life. The mythical battles – between devas and asuras and Indra and his cosmic dragons – reflected the wars between Aryans and dasas.[11] The Aryans experienced the Punjab as confinement and the dasas as perverse adversaries who were preventing them from attaining the wealth and open spaces that were their due.[12] This emotion ran through many of their stories. They imagined Vritra as a huge snake, coiled around the cosmic mountain and squeezing it so tightly that the waters could not escape.[13] Another story spoke of the demon Vala, who had incarcerated the sun together with a herd of cows in a cave so that without light, warmth and food the world would die. But after chanting a hymn beside the sacred Fire, Indra had smashed into the mountain, liberated the cows and set the sun high in the sky.[14] The names Vritra and Vala both derived from the Indo-European root *vr; 'to obstruct, enclose, encircle', and one of Indra's titles was Vrtrahan ('beating the resistance').[15] It was for the Aryans to fight their way through their encircling enemies as Indra had done. Liberation (moksha) would be another of the symbols that later generations would reinterpret; its opposite was amhas ('captivity'), cognate with the English 'anxiety' and the German Angst, evoking a claustrophobic distress.[16] Later sages would conclude that the path to moksha lay in the realisation that less is more.

By the tenth century, the Aryans had reached the Doab region between the Yamuna and the Ganges rivers. There they established two small kingdoms, one founded by the confederation of the Kuru and Panchala clans, the other by the Yadava. But every year when the weather was cooler, the Kuru-Panchala dispatched warriors to establish a new Aryan outpost a little further to the east, where they would subjugate the local populations, raid their farms and seize their cattle.[17] Before they could settle in this region, the dense tropical forests had to be cleared by fire, so the fire god Agni became the colonists' divine alter ego in this incremental drive eastward and the inspiration of the Agnicayana, the ritualised battle that consecrated the new colony. First, the fully armed warriors processed to the riverbank to collect clay to build a brick fire-altar, a provocative assertion of their right to this territory, fighting any locals who stood in their way. The colony became a reality only when Agni leapt forth on the new altar.[18] These blazing altars distinguished Aryan encampments from the darkness of the barbarian villages. The settlers also used Agni to lure away their neighbours' cattle which would follow the flames. 'He should take brightly burning fire to the settlement of his rival,' says a later text. 'He thereby takes his wealth, his property.'[19] Agni symbolised the warrior's courage and dominance, his most fundamental and divine 'self' (*atman*).[20]

Yet like Indra, his other alter ego, the warrior was tainted. It was said that Indra had committed three sins that had fatally weakened him: he had killed a Brahmin priest, broken a pact of friendship with Vritra, and seduced another man's wife by disguising himself as her husband; he had thus, progressively, forfeited his spiritual majesty (*tejas*), his physical strength (*bala*) and his beauty.[21] This mythical disintegration now paralleled a profound change in Aryan society during which Indra and Agni would become inadequate expressions of divinity to some of the rishis. It was the first step in a long process that would undermine the Aryans' addiction to violence.

We do not know exactly how the Aryans established their two kingdoms in the Doab, the 'Land of the Arya', but they can only have done so by force. Events may well have conformed to what social historians call the 'conquest theory' of state-establishment.[22] Peasants have much to lose from warfare, which destroys their crops and kills their livestock. When the economically poorer but militarily superior Aryans attacked them, it is possible that, rather than suffer this devastation, some of the more pragmatic peasants decided to submit to the raiders and offer them part of their surplus instead. For their part, the raiders learned not to kill the goose that lays the golden egg since they could acquire a steady income by returning to the village to demand more goods and, over time, this robbery may have been institutionalised to become regular tribute. Once the Yadavas and Kuru-Panchalas subjugated enough villages in the Doab in this way, they had become in effect aristocratic rulers of agrarian kingdoms, though they still dispatched annual raiding parties to the east.

This transition to agrarian life meant major social change. We can, of course, only speculate, but up to this point, it seems that Aryan society had not been rigidly stratified: the lesser clansmen fought alongside their chieftains, and priests often took part in the raiding.[23] But with agriculture came specialisation. The Aryans found that they now had to integrate the *dasas*, the native farmers with agricultural know-how, into their community, so the Vritra myths demonising the dasas were becoming obsolete, since without their labour and expertise the agrarian economy would fail. The demands of production also meant that Aryans themselves had to toil in the fields, while others became carpenters, metalsmiths, potters, tanners and weavers. They would now stay at home, while the best warriors were dispatched to fight in the east. There were probably power struggles between the rajas, who wielded power, and the priests who gave it legitimacy. Breaking with centuries of tradition, these innovations had to be grafted on to the Vedic mythos.

Their new wealth and leisure gave the priests more time for contemplation and they began to refine their concept of divinity. They had always seen the gods as participating in a loftier, more encompassing reality that was Being itself, which by the tenth century BCE they had started to call *Brahman* ('The All').[24] Brahman was the power that held the cosmos together and enabled it to grow and develop. It was nameless, indefinable and utterly transcendent. Devas were simply different manifestations of Brahman: 'They call him Indra, Mitra, Naruna, Agni, and he is heavenly noble-winged Garatman. To what is One, sages give many a title.'[25] With almost forensic determination, the new breed of rishis were intent on discovering this mysterious unifying principle and the all-too-human devas were not only a distraction but were becoming an embarrassment: they concealed rather than revealed the Brahman. Nobody, one rishi insisted, not even the highest of the gods, knew how our world came into being.[26] The old stories of Indra slaying a monster to order the cosmos now seemed positively infantile.[27] Gradually the gods' personalities began to shrink.[28]

One of these later hymns gave sacred endorsement to the stratification of Aryan society.[29] This rishi meditated on the ancient myth of the king whose sacrificial death had given birth to the cosmos, whom the rishi called 'Purusha', the primordial 'Person'. He described him lying down on the freshly mown grass of the ritual arena and allowing the gods to kill him. His corpse was then dismembered and became the components of the universe: birds, animals, horses, cattle, heaven and earth, sun and moon, and even the great devas Agni and Indra, all emerged from different parts of his body. Yet only 25 per cent of Purusha's being formed the finite world; the other 75 per cent was unaffected by time and mortality, transcendent and illimitable. In Purusha's self-surrender the old cosmic battles and agonistic sacred contests had been replaced by a myth in which there was no fighting: the king gave himself away without a struggle.

The new social classes of the Aryan kingdom also sprouted from Purusha's body:

> When they divided Purusha, how many portions did they make?
>
> What did they call his mouth, his arms?
>
> What do they call his thighs and feet?
>
> The priest (*Brahmin*) was his mouth; of both of his arms was the warrior
> (*rajanya*) made.
>
> His thighs became the commoner (*vaishya*), from his feet the servant
> (*shudra*) was produced.[30]

Thus the newly stratified society, the hymns claimed, was not a dangerous break with the egalitarian past but was as old as the universe itself. Aryan society was now divided into four social classes – the seed of the elaborate caste system that would develop later. Each class (*varna*) had its own sacred 'duty' (*dharma*). Nobody could perform the task allotted to another class, any more than a star could leave its path and encroach on a planet's circuit.

Sacrifice was still fundamental; members of each varna had to give up their own preferences for the sake of the whole. It was the dharma of the Brahmins, who came from Purusha's mouth, to preside over the rituals of society.[31] For the first time in Aryan history, the warriors now formed a distinct class called the *rajanya*, a new term in the Rig Veda; later they would be known as *Kshatriya* ('the empowered ones'). They came from Purusha's arms, chest and heart, the seat of strength, courage and energy, and their dharma was daily to put their lives at risk. This was a significant development, because it limited violence in the Aryan community. Hitherto all able-bodied men had been fighters and aggression the *raison d'être* of the entire tribe. The hymn acknowledged that the rajanya was indispensable, because the kingdom could not survive without force and coercion. But henceforth *only* the rajanya could bear arms. Members of the other three classes – Brahmins, vaishyas and shudras – now had to relinquish violence and were no longer allowed to take part in raids nor fight in their kingdom's wars.

In the two lower classes we see the systemic violence of this new society. They came from Purusha's legs and feet, the lower and largest part of the body; their dharma was to serve, to run errands for the nobility, and bear the weight of the entire social frame, performing the productive labour on which the agrarian kingdom depended.[32] The dharma of the vaishya, the ordinary clansmen, now forbidden to fight, was food production; the Kshatriya aristocracy would now confiscate their surplus. The vaishya were thus associated with fertility and productivity, but also, being taken from a place close to Purusha's genitals, with carnal appetite, which, according to the two upper classes, made them unreliable. But the most significant development was the introduction of the shudra: the dasa at the base of the social body was now defined as a 'slave', one who labours for others, performing the most menial tasks and therefore stigmatised as impure. In Vedic law, the vaishya was to be oppressed but the shudra could be removed or slain at will.[33]

The Purusha Hymn thus acknowledged the structural violence that lay at the heart of the new Aryan civilisation. The new system may have limited fighting and raiding to one of the privileged classes but implied that the forcible subjugation of vaishya and shudra was part of the sacred order of the universe. For the Brahmins and Kshatriyas, the new Aryan aristocracy, productive work was not their dharma, so they had the leisure to explore the arts and sciences. While sacrifice was expected of everybody, the greatest sacrifice was demanded of the lower classes, condemned to a life of servitude and stigmatised as inferior, base and impure.[34]

The Aryan conversion to agriculture continued. By about 900 BCE, there were several rudimentary kingdoms in the land of the Arya. Thanks to the switch from wheat cultivation to wet-rice production, the kingdoms enjoyed a larger surplus. Our knowledge of life in these emerging states is limited, but again, mythology and ritual can throw some light on the developing political organisation. In these embryonic kingdoms, the raja, though still elected by his Kshatriya peers like a tribal chieftain, was well on his way to becoming a powerful agrarian ruler and was now invested with divine attributes during his year-long royal consecration, the *rajasuya*. During this ceremony, another Kshatriya challenged the new king, who had to win his realm back in a ritualised game of dice. If he lost, he was forced into exile but would return with an army to unseat his rival. If he won, he downed a draught of soma and led a raid into the neighbouring territories, and when he returned laden with plunder, the Brahmins acknowledged his kingship: 'Thou, O King, art Brahman.' The raja was now 'The All', the hub of the wheel that pulled his kingdom together and enabled it to prosper and expand.

A king's chief duty was to conquer new arable land, a duty sacralised by the Horse Sacrifice (*Ashvameda*) in which a white stallion was consecrated, set free and allowed to roam unmolested for a year, accompanied by the king's army, which was supposed to protect it. A stabled horse will always make straight for home, however, so the army was in fact driving the horse into territory that the king was intent on conquering.[35] Thus in India, as in any agrarian civilisation, violence was woven into the texture of aristocratic life.[36] Nothing was nobler than death in battle. To die in his bed was a sin against the Kshatriya's dharma and if he felt that he was losing his strength he was expected to seek out death in the field.[37] A commoner had no right to fight, however, so if he died on the battlefield his death was regarded as a monstrous departure from the norm – or even a joke.[38]

Yet during the ninth century BCE, some of the Brahmins in the Kuru kingdom began yet another major reinterpretation of ancient Aryan tradition and embarked on a reform that systematically extracted all violence from religious ritual and even persuaded the Kshatriyas to change their ways. Their ideas were recorded in the scriptures known as the Brahmanas, which date from the ninth to the seventh centuries BCE. There would be no more crowded potlatches or rowdy, drunken contests. In this entirely new ritual, the Patron (who paid for the sacrifice) was now the only layman present and was guided through the elaborate ceremony by four priests. Ritualised raids and mock-battles were replaced by anodyne chants and symbolic gestures, although traces of the old violence remained: a gentle hymn bore the incongruous title 'The Chariot of the Devas', and a stately antiphon was compared to Indra's deadly mace, which the singers were hurling back and forth 'with loud voices'.[39] Finally, in the reformed Agnicayana ritual, instead of fighting for new territory, the Patron simply picked up the fire-pot, took three steps to the east, and put it down again.[40]

We know very little about the motivation that lay behind this reform movement. According to one scholar, it sprang from the insoluble conundrum that the sacrificial ritual, which was designed to give life, actually involved death and destruction. The rishis could not eliminate military violence from society, but they could strip it of religious legitimacy.[41] There was also a new concern about cruelty to animals. In one of the later poems of the Rig Veda, a rishi tenderly soothes the horse about to be slaughtered in the Ashvameda:

> Let not thy dear soul burn thee as thou comest, let not the hatchet linger
>   in thy body
> Let not a greedy, clumsy immolator, missing the joints, mangle thy limbs
>   unduly.
> No, here thou diest not, thou art not injured: by easy paths unto the
>   Gods thou goest.[42]

The Brahmanas described animal sacrifice as cruel, recommending that the beast be spared and given as a gift to an officiating priest.[43] If it had to be killed, the animal should be dispatched as painlessly as possible. In the old days, the victim's decapitation had been the dramatic climax of the sacrifice; now the animal was suffocated in a shed at a distance from the sacrificial ground.[44] Some scholars, however, contend that the reform was driven not by a revulsion from violence per se; rather, violence was now experienced as polluting and, anxious to avoid defilement, priests preferred to delegate the task to assistants, who killed the victim outside the sacred centre.[45] Whatever their motivation, the reformers were beginning to create a climate of opinion that looked askance at violence.

They also directed the Patron's attention towards his inner world. Instead of inflicting death on the hapless animal, he was now instructed to assimilate death, experiencing it internally in a symbolic rite.[46] During the ceremony, his death was enacted ritually so that for a time he entered the world of the immortal gods. A more internal spirituality was beginning to emerge, one closer to what we call 'religion'; and it was rooted in a desire to avoid violence. Instead of mindlessly going through the motions of external rituals, participants were required to become aware of the hidden significance of the rites, making themselves conscious of the connections that, in the logic of the perennial philosophy, linked every single action, liturgical utensil and mantra to a divine reality. Gods were assimilated with humans, humans with animals and plants, the transcendent with the immanent, and the visible with the invisible.[47]

This was not simply self-indulgent make-believe but part of the endless human endeavour to endow the smallest details of life with meaning. Ritual, it has been said, creates a controlled environment in which for a while we lay aside the inescapable flaws of our mundane existence. Yet by so doing we paradoxically become acutely aware of them. After the ceremony, when we return to daily life, we can recall our experience of the way things ought to be. Ritual is, therefore, the creation of fallible human beings who can never fully realise their ideals.[48] So while the day-to-day world of the Aryans was inherently violent, cruel and unjust, in these new rites participants had the chance to inhabit – if only temporarily – a world from which aggression was rigorously excluded. They could not abandon the violence of their dharma, because society depended on it. But, as we will see, some Kshatriyas began to become acutely aware of the taint that the warrior had always carried in Aryan society ever since Indra had been called a 'sinner'. Some would build on the experience of the new rituals to create an alternative spirituality that would undermine the aggressive martial ethos.

But in the new segmented society, very few people took part in the Vedic rites, which now became the preserve of the aristocracy. Most lower-class Aryans made simpler offerings to their favourite devas in their own home and worshipped a variety of gods – some adopted from the indigenous population – which would form the multifarious Hindu pantheon that finally emerged during the Gupta Period (320–540 CE). But the most spectacular rituals, such as the royal consecration, made an impression on the public and people would talk about them for a long time. They also helped to support the class system. The priest who performed the rites was able to assert his superiority over the raja or Kshatriya patron and thus maintain his place at the head of the body politic. In turn, the raja, who paid for the sacrifice, could invoke divine authority to extract more of the surplus from the vaishyas.

If these infant kingdoms were to become mature states, the king's authority could no longer depend on a sacrificial system based on reciprocal exchange. In the Punjab, all the booty and captured cattle had been ritually redistributed and consumed, so the raja had been unable to accumulate wealth independently. But a more developed state required resources of its own to pay for its bureaucracy and institutions. Now, thanks to the massive increase of agricultural productivity in the Doab, the rajas were becoming rich. They controlled the agrarian surplus and were no longer dependent on booty acquired in a raid and ritually distributed among the community. They were becoming both economically and politically independent of the Brahmins, who had once presided over and regulated the distribution of resources.

By the sixth century BCE, the Aryans had reached the eastern Gangetic basin, a region with higher rainfall and even greater agricultural yield. They were now able to grow rice, fruit, cereal, sesame, millet, wheat, grains and barley, and with this enhanced surplus support more elaborate states.[49] As more powerful rajas conquered smaller chiefdoms, sixteen large kingdoms emerged, including Magadha in the north-east of the Gangetic plain and Koshala in the south-west, all competing for scarce resources. The priests still insisted that it was their rituals and sacrifices that preserved the cosmic and social order,[50] but the religious texts acknowledged that in reality the political system depended on coercion:

The whole world is kept in order by punishment . . . If the king did not, without tiring, inflict punishment on those worthy to be punished, the stronger would roast the weaker like fish on a spit. The crow would eat the sacrificial cake and the dog would lick the sacrificial viands, and ownership would not remain with anyone, and the lower ones would usurp the place of the higher ones . . . Punishment alone governs all created beings, punishment alone protects them, punishment watches over them while they sleep . . . Punishment is . . . the king.[51]

We lack the archaeological evidence to know about the organisation of these kingdoms, however; here too we have to rely on religious texts, especially the Buddhist scriptures, which were composed and preserved orally and not committed to writing until the first century CE.

An entirely different polity, however, had also emerged in the foothills of the Himalayas and on the edge of the Ganges plain: the *gana-sanghas* or 'tribal republics' that rejected monarchy and were ruled by assemblies of clan chieftains. They may have been founded by independently minded aristocrats, who were unhappy with the autocracy of the kingdoms and wanted to live in a more egalitarian community. The tribal republics rejected Vedic orthodoxy and had no interest in paying for expensive sacrifices; instead they invested in trade, agriculture and warfare, and power was wielded not by a king but by a small ruling-class.[52] Because they had no priestly caste, there were only two classes: a Kshatriya aristocracy and the *dasa-karmakaru*, 'slaves and labourers', who had no rights or access to resources, although it was possible for enterprising merchants and artisans to achieve higher social status. With their large standing armies, the tribal republics were a significant challenge to the Aryan kingdoms and proved to be remarkably resilient, surviving well into the middle of the first millennium CE.[53] Clearly their independence and at least nominal egalitarianism appealed to something fundamental in the Indian psyche.

The kingdoms and sanghas were both still reliant on agriculture but the Ganges region was also experiencing a commercial revolution, which produced a merchant class and a money economy. Cities linked by new roads and canals – Savatthi, Saketa, Kosambi, Varanasi, Rajagaha and Changa – were becoming centres of industry and business. This challenged the structural violence of the class system, since most of the nouveau riche merchants and bankers were vaishyas and some were even shudras.[54] A new class of 'untouchables' (*chandalas*), who had been thrown off their land by the incoming Aryans, now took the place of these aspiring workers at the bottom of the social hierarchy.[55] City life was exciting. The streets were crowded with brightly painted carriages and huge elephants carrying merchandise from distant lands. People of all classes and ethnicities mingled freely in the marketplace and new ideas began to challenge the traditional Vedic system. The Brahmins, therefore, whose roots were in the countryside, had begun to seem irrelevant.[56]

As often in times of flux, a new spirituality emerged, and it had three interrelated themes: *dukkha, moksha* and *karma*. Surprisingly, despite this prosperity and progress, pessimism was deep and widespread. People were experiencing life as *dukkha,* 'unsatisfactory', 'flawed' and 'awry'. From the trauma of birth to the agony of death, human existence seemed fraught with suffering, and even death brought no relief because everything and everybody was caught up in an inescapable cycle (*samsara*) of rebirth, so the whole distressing scenario had to be endured again and again. The great eastward migration had been fuelled by the Aryans' experience of claustrophobic confinement in the Punjab; now they felt imprisoned in their overcrowded cities. It was not just a feeling: rapid urbanisation typically leads to epidemics, particularly when the population rises above 300,000, a sort of tipping-point for contagion.[57] No wonder the Aryans were obsessed by sickness, suffering and death and longed to find a way out.

Rapid change of circumstance also made people more conscious of cause and effect. They could now see how the actions of one generation affected the next and they began to believe that their deeds (*karma*) would also determine their next existence: if they were guilty of bad karma in this life, they would be reborn as slaves or animals, but with good karma they might become kings or even gods next time. Merit was something that could be earned, accumulated and finally 'realised' in the same way as mercantile wealth.[58] But even if you were reborn as a god, there was no lasting escape from life's dukkha because even gods had to die and would be reborn to lower status. In an attempt, perhaps, to shore up the now vulnerable class system, the Brahmins tried to reconfigure the concepts of karma and samsara: you could endure a good rebirth only if you strictly observed the dharma of your class.[59]

But others would draw upon these new ideas to challenge the social system. In the Punjab, the Aryans had tried to fight their way to 'liberation' (*moksha*); now some, building on the internalised spirituality of the Brahmanas, were looking for a more spiritual freedom and would investigate their inner world as vigorously as the Aryan warriors had once explored the untamed forests. The new wealth gave the nobility the time and leisure that was essential for such introspective contemplation. The new spirituality was, therefore, strictly for the aristocracy; it was one of the civilised arts that relied on the state's structural violence. No shudra or chandala would be permitted to spend hours in the meditations and metaphysical discussions that between the sixth and second centuries BCE produced the texts known as the *Upanishads*.

These new teachings may originally have been formulated by Brahmins who lived in the towns and understood the problems arising from urban living.[60] But significantly, many new practices were attributed to Kshatriya warriors and the discussions reported in the Upanishads often took place in the raja's court. They drew on the more interior spirituality of the Brahmins and took it a step further. The Brhadaranyaka Upanishad, one of the earliest of these texts, was almost certainly composed in the kingdom of Videha, a frontier state on the easternmost point of Aryan expansion.[61] Videha was scorned by the conservative Brahmins in the Doab, but there was a great admixture of peoples in these easterly territories, including Indo-Aryan settlers from earlier waves of migration and tribes from Iran, as well as peoples indigenous to India. Some of these foreigners assimilated to the varna (classes) but brought their own traditions with them – including, perhaps, scepticism about Vedic orthodoxy. These new encounters were intellectually stimulating and the early Upanishads reflect this excitement.

The social and political developments in these new states inspired some of the warrior class to imagine a new world, free of priestly ascendancy. Thus the Upanishads denied the necessity of the Vedic sacrifices and completed the devas' downgrading by simply assimilating the gods into the contemplative's psyche: "'Sacrifice to this god. Sacrifice to that god.' People do say these things, but in reality each of these gods is his own creation, for he himself is all these gods.'[62] The worshipper now turned within. The focus of the Upanishads was the atman, the 'self', which, like the devas, was also a manifestation of the Brahman. If the sage could discover the inner core of his own being, he would automatically enter into the ultimate reality. Only by the ecstatic knowledge of the self, which would free him or her of the desire for ephemeral things here below, would a man or woman be liberated from the ceaseless cycle of rebirth and re-death. This was a discovery of immense importance. The idea that the ultimate reality, 'All' that is, was an immanent presence in every single human being would become a central insight in every major religious tradition. There was, therefore, no need to perform the elaborate rituals that had upheld the structural violence of the varna system, because once they encountered the core of reality within themselves, humans were one with 'the All': 'If a man knows "I am *brahman*" in this way, he becomes this whole world. Not even the gods are able to prevent it, for he becomes their very self (*atman*).'[63] It was a defiant declaration of independence, a political as well as a spiritual revolution. The Kshatriya could now cast aside his dependence on the priest who dominated the ritual arena. At the same time as vaishyas and shudras were climbing the social ladder, the warrior aristocracy was making a bid for the first place in society.

Yet the Upanishads also challenged the Kshatriya martial ethos. The atman had originally been Agni, the deepest, divine 'self' of the warrior which he had attained by fighting and stealing. The heroic Aryan drive eastward had been motivated by desire for earthly things – cows, plunder, land, honour and prestige. Now the Upanishad sages urged their disciples to renounce such desire. Anyone who remained fixated on mundane wealth could never be liberated from the cycle of suffering and rebirth, but 'a man who does not desire – who is without desires, who is freed from desires, whose only desire is his self (*atman*) – his vital functions do not depart. Brahman he is and to *brahman* he goes'.[64] New meditative techniques induced a state of mind that was 'calm, composed, cool, patient and collected': in short, the very opposite of the agitated old Aryan mentality.[65] One of the Upanishads actually described the warrior god Indra, no less, living peacefully as a humble student in the forest with his teacher and relinquishing violence in order to find perfect tranquillity.[66]

Aryans had always considered themselves inherently superior to others; their rituals had bred within them a deep sense of entitlement that had fuelled their raids and conquests. But the Upanishads taught that because the atman, the essence of every single creature, was identical with the Brahman, all beings shared the same sacred core. The Brahman was the subtle kernel of the banyan seed from which a great tree grows.[67] It was the sap that gave life to every part of the tree; it was also the most fundamental reality of every single human being.[68] Brahman was like a chunk of salt left overnight to dissolve in a beaker of water; even though it could not be seen the next morning, it was still present in every sip.[69] Instead of repudiating this basic kinship with all beings, as the warrior did when he demonised his enemy, these sages were deliberately cultivating an awareness of it. Everyone liked to imagine that he was unique, but in reality his special distinguishing features were no more permanent than rivers that all flowed into the same sea. Once they left the river-bed, they became 'just the ocean', no longer proclaiming their individuality, crying 'I am that river', 'I am this river.' Such strident assertion of the ego was a delusion that could only lead to pain and confusion. Release (moksha) from such suffering was dependent on the acknowledgement that at base everybody was Brahman and should, therefore, be treated with absolute reverence. The Upanishads bequeathed to India a sense of the profound unity of all beings, so that your so-called 'enemy' was no longer the heinous other but inseparable from you.[70]

Indian religion had always endorsed and informed the structural and martial violence of society. But as early as the eighth century BCE, the 'renouncers' (samnyasin) mounted a disciplined and devastating critique of this inherent aggression, withdrawing from settled society to adopt an independent life-style. Renunciation was not, as is often thought in the West, simply life-negating. Throughout Indian history, asceticism has nearly always had a political dimension and has often inspired a radical reappraisal of society. That certainly happened in the Gangetic plain.[71] Aryans had always possessed the 'restless heart' that had made Gilgamesh weary of settled life, but instead of leaving home to fight and steal, the renouncers eschewed aggression, owned no property and begged for their food.[72] By about 500 BCE, they had become the chief agents of spiritual change and a direct challenge to the values of the agrarian kingdoms.[73] This movement was in part an offshoot of brahmacharya, the 'holy life' led by the Brahmin student, who would spend years with his guru, studying the Vedas, begging humbly for his bread, and living alone in the tropical forests for a given period. In other parts of the world too, Aryan youths lived in the wild as part of their military training, hunting for food and learning the arts of self-sufficiency and survival. But because the Brahmin's dharma did not include violence, the brahmacharin was forbidden to hunt, to harm animals, or to ride in a war chariot.[74]

Moreover, most of the renouncers were adult Brahmins when they embarked on their solitary existence, their apprenticeship long past.[75] A renouncer made a deliberate choice. He repudiated the ritual sacrifices that symbolised the Aryan political community and rejected the family household, the institutional mainstay of settled life. He had in effect stepped right outside the systemic violence of the varna system and extracted himself from the economic nexus of society in order to become a 'beggar' (bhiksu).[76] Some renouncers returned home, only to become social and religious irritants within the community, while others remained in the forest and challenged the culture from without. They condemned the aristocratic preoccupation with status, honour and glory, yearned for insults 'as if they were nectar'[77] and deliberately courted contempt by behaving like madmen or animals.[78] Like so many Indian reformers, the renouncers drew upon the ancient mythology of warfare to model a different kind of nobility. They evoked the heroic days in the Punjab, when men had proved their valour and virility by braving the untamed forest. Many saw the bhiksu as a new kind of pioneer.[79] When a famous renouncer came to town, people of all classes flocked to listen to him.

Perhaps the most important martial ritual revised by the renouncers was yoga, which became the hallmark of renouncer spirituality. Originally, as we have seen, the term had referred to the tethering of the draught animals to the war chariots before a raid; now it became a contemplative discipline that 'yoked' the yogin's mental powers in a raid on the unconscious impulses (*vrittis*) of passion, egotism, hatred and greed that had fuelled the warrior ethos and were so deeply entrenched in the psyche that they could be extirpated only by sheer mental force. Yoga may have been rooted in the indigenous traditions of India but by the sixth century BCE it had become central to the Aryan spiritual landscape. A systematic assault on the ego, it expunged the 'I' from the yogin's mind, nullifying the warrior's proud self-assertion: 'I am the mightiest! I am supreme!' The ancient warriors of the Punjab had been like the devas, perpetually on the move and constantly engaged in martial activity. Now the new man of yoga sat for hours in one place, holding himself in such unnatural stillness that he seemed more like a statue or a plant than a human being. If he persevered, a skilled yogin had intimations of a final liberation from the confines of egotism that bore no relation to ordinary experience.

But before he was allowed even to sit in the yogic position, an aspirant had to complete an arduous ethical programme, observing five 'prohibitions' (*yamas*).[80] The first of these was ahimsa, nonviolence: not only was he forbidden to kill or injure another creature, but he could not even speak unkindly or make an irritable gesture. Second, he was forbidden to steal: instead of seizing other people's property like the raiders, the yogin had to cultivate an indifference to material possessions. Lying was also prohibited: truth-telling had always been central to the Aryan warrior ethos but the exigencies of war had occasionally forced even Indra into deceit; the aspirant, however, was not permitted to be economical with the truth, even to save his own life. He also abstained from sex and intoxicating substances that could enervate the mental and physical energies that he would need in this spiritual expedition. Finally he must study the teaching (dharma) of his guru and cultivate habitual serenity, behaving kindly and courteously to everybody without exception. This was an initiation into a new way of being human, one that eschewed the greed, self-preoccupation and aggression of the warrior. By dint of practice, these ethical disciplines would become second nature to the yogin and when that happened, the texts explained, he would experience 'indescribable joy'.[81]

Some renouncers broke even more completely with the Vedic system and were denounced as heretics by the Brahmins. Two in particular made a lasting impact and, significantly, both came from the tribal republics. Destined for a military career, Vardhamana Jnatraputra (*c.* 599–527) was the son of a Kshatriya chieftain of the Jnatra clan of Kundagrama, north of modern Patna. At the age of thirty, however, he changed course and became a renouncer. After a long, difficult apprenticeship, he achieved enlightenment and became a *Jina* ('conqueror'), so his followers became known as Jains. Even though he went further than anybody else in his renunciation of violence, it was natural for him, as a former warrior, to express his insights in military imagery. His followers called him *Mahavira* ('Great Champion'), the title of an intrepid warrior in the Rig Veda. Yet his regime, based wholly on non-violence, was one that vanquished every impulse to harm others. For Mahavira, the only way to achieve liberation was to cultivate an attitude of friendliness towards everyone and everything.[82] Here, as in the Upanishads, we encounter the requirement found in many great world traditions that it is not enough to confine our benevolence to our own people or those we find congenial; this partiality must be replaced by a practically expressed empathy for everybody, without exception. If this was practised consistently, violence of any kind – verbal, martial or systemic – becomes impossible.

Mahavira taught his male and female disciples to develop a sympathy that had no bounds, to realise their profound kinship with all beings. Every single creature – even plants, water, fire, air and rocks – had a *jiva,* a living 'soul', and must be treated with the respect that we wish to receive ourselves.[83] Most of his followers were Kshatriyas seeking an alternative to the warfare and structural segmentation of society. As warriors, they would have routinely distanced themselves from the enemy, carefully stifling their innate reluctance to kill their own kind. Jains, like the Upanishadic sages, taught their disciples to recognise their community with all others and relinquish the preoccupation with 'us' and 'them', which made fighting and structural oppression impossible, because a true 'conqueror' did not inflict harm of any kind.

Later, Jains would develop a complex mythology and cosmology, but in the early period nonviolence was their only precept:

All breathing, existing, living, sentient creatures should not be slain, nor
treated with violence, nor abused, nor tormented, nor driven away. This is
the pure, unchangeable law, which the enlightened ones who know have
proclaimed.[84]

Unlike warriors who trained themselves to become impervious to the agony
they inflicted, Jains deliberately attuned themselves to the pain of the world.
They learned to move with consummate caution lest they squash an insect
or trample on a blade of grass; they did not pluck fruit from a tree but
waited till it fell to the ground. Like all renouncers, they had to eat what
they were given, even meat, but must never ask for any creature to be
killed on their behalf.[85] Jain meditation consisted simply of a rigorous
suppression of all antagonistic thoughts and a conscious effort to fill the
mind with affection for all creatures. The result was *samayika* ('equanimity'),
a profound, life-changing realisation that all creatures were equal. Twice a
day, Jains stood before their guru and repented of any distress they might,
even inadvertently, have caused: 'I ask pardon of all living creatures. May
all creatures pardon me. May I have friendship for all creatures and enmity
toward none.'[86]

Towards the end of the fifth century, a Kshatriya from the tribal republic
of Sakka in the foothills of the Himalayas shaved his head and donned the
renouncer's yellow robe.[87] After an arduous spiritual quest during which
he studied with many of the leading gurus of the day, Siddhattha Gotama,
later known as the Buddha ('awakened one'), achieved enlightenment by
a form of yoga based on the suppression of antagonistic feelings and the
careful cultivation of kindly, positive emotions.[88] Like Mahavira, his near-
contemporary, the Buddha's teaching was based on nonviolence. He
achieved a state that he called *nibbana*,* because the greed and aggression
that had limited his humanity had been extinguished like a flame.[89] Later
the Buddha devised a meditation that taught his monks to direct feelings
of friendship and affection to the ends of the earth, desiring that all creatures be free of pain, and finally freeing themselves of any personal attachment and partiality by loving all sentient beings with 'even-mindedness'
(*upeksha*). Not a single creature was to be excluded from this radius of
concern.[90]

* *Nibbana* is the equivalent of the Sanskrit *nirvana* in the Pali dialect which may have been
spoken by the Buddha. Its literal meaning is 'blowing out'.

It was summed up in the early prayer, attributed to the Buddha, recited daily by his monks and lay disciples:

> Let all beings be happy! Weak or strong, of high, middle or low estate
> Small or great, visible or invisible, near or far away,
> Alive or still to be born – may they all be perfectly happy!
> Let nobody lie to anybody or despise any single being anywhere.
> May nobody wish harm to any single creature, out of anger or hatred!
> Let us cherish all creatures as a mother her only child!
> May our loving thoughts fill the whole world, above, below, across, –
> Without limit; a boundless goodwill toward the whole world,
> Unrestricted, free of hatred and enmity![91]

The Buddha's enlightenment had been based on the principle that to live morally was to live for others. Unlike the other renouncers, who retreated from human society, Buddhist monks were commanded to return to the world to help others find release from pain. 'Go now,' he told his first disciples, 'and travel for the welfare and happiness of the people, out of compassion for the world, for the benefit, welfare and happiness of gods and men.'[92] Instead of simply eschewing violence, Buddhism demanded a positive campaign to assuage the suffering and increase the happiness of 'the whole world'.

The Buddha summed up his teaching in four 'Noble Truths': that existence is dukkha; that the cause of our pain is selfishness and greed; that nibbana releases us from this suffering; and that the way to achieve this state is to follow the programme of meditation, morality and resolution he called the 'Noble Path', which was designed to produce an alternative aristocracy. The Buddha was a realist and did not imagine that he could single-handedly abolish the oppression inherent in the varna system, but he insisted that even a vaishya or a shudra would be ennobled if they behaved in a selfless, compassionate manner and 'abstained from the killing of creatures'.[93] By the same token, a man or woman became a 'commoner' (pathujjana) by behaving cruelly, greedily and violently.[94] His Sangha, or order of monks and nuns, modelled a different kind of society, an alternative to the aggression of the royal court. As in the tribal republics, there was no autocratic rule and decisions were made in common. King Pasenedi of Koshala was greatly impressed by the 'smiling and courteous' demeanour of the monks, 'alert, calm and unflustered, living on alms, their minds remaining as gentle as wild deer'. At court, he said wryly, everybody competed acrimoniously for wealth and status, whereas in the Sangha he saw monks 'living together as uncontentiously as milk with water, looking at one another with kind eyes'.[95] The Sangha was not perfect – it could never entirely transcend class distinctions – but it became a powerful influence in India. Instead of melting away into the forests like other renouncers, the Buddhists were highly visible. The Buddha used to travel with an entourage of hundreds of monks, their yellow robes and shaven heads demonstrating their dissent from the mainstream, walking along the trade routes beside the merchants. And behind them, in wagons and chariots laden with provisions, rode their lay-supporters, many of them Kshatriyas.

The Buddhists and Jains made an impact on mainstream society because they were sensitive to the difficulties of social change in the newly urbanised society of northern India. They enabled individuals to declare their independence of the big agrarian kingdoms, as the tribal republics had done. Like the ambitious vaishyas and shudras, Buddhists and Jains were self-made men, reconstructing themselves at a profound psychological level to model a more empathic humanity. Both were also in tune with the new commercial ethos. Because of their absolute rejection of violence, Jains could not engage in agriculture, which involved the killing of creatures, so they turned to trade and became popular in the new merchant communities. Buddhism did not demand complex metaphysics or elaborate, arcane rituals but was based on principles of reason, logic and empirical experience that were congenial to the merchant class. Moreover, Buddhists and Jains were pragmatists and realists: they did not expect everybody to become a monk but encouraged lay disciples to follow their teachings insofar as they could. Thus these spiritualties not only entered the mainstream but even began to influence the ruling class.

Already during the Buddha's lifetime, there were signs of empire-building in the Gangetic plain. In 493 BCE, Ajatashatru became king of Magadha; it was said that, impatient for the throne, he had murdered his father King Bimbisara, the Buddha's friend. Ajatashatru continued his father's policy of military conquest and built a small fort on the Ganges, which the Buddha visited shortly before his death; it later became the famous metropolis of Pataliputra. Ajatashatru also annexed Koshala and Kashi and defeated a confederacy of tribal republics, so that when he died in 461, the Kingdom of Magadha dominated the Gangetic plain. He was succeeded by five unsatisfactory kings, all parricides, until the usurper Mahapadma Nanda, a shudra, founded the first non-Kshatriya dynasty and further extended the borders

of the kingdom. The wealth of the Nandas, based on a highly efficient taxation system, became proverbial and the idea of creating an imperial state
began to take root. When the young adventurer Chandragupta Maurya,
another shudra, usurped the Nanda throne in 321 BCE, the Kingdom of
Magadha became the Mauryan empire.

In the pre-modern period, no empire could create a unified culture; it
existed solely to extract resources from the subject peoples, who would,
inevitably, rise up from time to time in revolt. Thus an emperor was usually
engaged in almost constant warfare against rebellious subjects or against
aristocrats who sought to usurp him. Chandragupta and his successors ruled
from Pataliputra, conquering neighbouring regions that had strategic and
economic potential by force of arms. These areas were incorporated into
the Mauryan state and administered by governors who answered to the
emperor. On the fringes of the empire, peripheral areas rich in timber,
elephants and semiprecious stones served as buffer zones; the imperial state
did not attempt direct rule in these areas, but used local people as agents
to tap their resources; periodically these 'forest peoples' resisted Mauryan
dominance. The main task of the imperial administration was to collect
taxes in kind. In India, the rate of taxation varied from region to region,
ranging from one-sixth to a quarter of agricultural output. Pastoralists were
taxed according to the size and productivity of their herds, and commerce
was subject to taxes, tolls and custom dues. The crown claimed ownership
of all uncultivated land, and, once an area had been cleared, shudras living
in overpopulated regions of the Mauryan empire were forcibly resettled
there.[96]

The empire, therefore, depended entirely on extortion and force. Not
only did military campaigns increase the wealth of the state by acquiring
more arable land, but plunder was an important supplementary revenue
and prisoners of war provided valuable manpower. So it may seem strange
that the first three Mauryan emperors were patrons of nonviolent sects.
Chandragupta abdicated in 297 to become a Jain ascetic; his son Bindusara
courted the strictly ascetical Ajivaka school; and Ashoka, who succeeded
to the throne in 268 BCE after murdering two of his brothers, favoured
the Buddhists. As shudras, they had never been permitted to take part in
the Vedic rituals and probably regarded them as alien and oppressive. The
independent, egalitarian spirit of these unorthodox sects, on the other hand,
would have been highly congenial. But Chandragupta realised that Jainism
was incompatible with royal rule and Ashoka did not become even a lay
Buddhist until the end of his reign. Yet alongside Mahavira and the Buddha,

Ashoka would become one of the most central political and cultural figures of ancient India.[97]

On his accession, he took the title Devanampiya, 'Beloved of the Gods', and continued to expand the empire, which now extended from Bengal to Afghanistan. In the early years of his reign Ashoka had lived a somewhat dissolute life and acquired a reputation for cruelty. But that changed in about 260, when he accompanied the imperial army to put down a rebellion in Kalinga (in modern Odisha) and had an extraordinary conversion experience. During the campaign, 100,000 Kalingan soldiers were killed in battle, many times more perished from wounds and disease afterwards, and 150,000 were deported to the peripheral territories. Ashoka was profoundly shocked by the suffering he witnessed. He had what we might call a 'Gilgamesh moment', when the sensory realities of warfare broke through the carapace of cultivated heartlessness that makes warfare possible. He recorded his remorse in an edict inscribed on a massive rock face. Instead of jubilantly listing the numbers of enemy casualties, like most kings, Ashoka confessed that 'the slaughter, death and deportation is extremely grievous to Devanampiya and weighs heavily on his mind'.[98] He warned other kings that military conquest, the glory of victory and the trappings of royalty were fleeting. If they had to dispatch an army, they should fight as humanely as possible and enforce their victory 'with patience and light punishment'.[99] The only true conquest was personal submission to what Ashoka called *dhamma,* a moral code of compassion, mercy, honesty and consideration for all living creatures.

Ashoka inscribed similar edicts outlining his new policy of military restraint and moral reform on cliff faces and colossal cylindrical pillars throughout the length and breadth of his empire.[100] These edicts were intensely personal messages but could also have been an attempt to give the far-flung empire ideological unity; they may even have been read aloud to the populace on state occasions. Ashoka urged his people to curb their greed and extravagance; promised that, as far as possible, he would refrain from using martial force; preached kindness to animals and vowed to replace the violent sport of hunting, the traditional pastime of kings, with royal pilgrimages to Buddhist shrines. He also announced that he had dug wells, founded hospitals and rest-houses, and planted banyan trees 'which will give shade to beasts and men'.[101] He insisted on the importance of respect for teachers, obedience to parents, consideration for slaves and servants, and reverence for all sects – for the orthodox Brahmins as well as for Buddhists, Jains and other 'heretical' schools: 'Concord is to be commended,' he declared, 'so that men may hear one another's principles.'[102]

It is unlikely that Ashoka's dhamma was Buddhist. This was a broader ethic, an attempt to find a benevolent model of governance based on the recognition of human dignity, a sentiment shared by many contemporary Indian schools. In Ashoka's inscriptions, we hear the perennial voice of those repelled by killing and cruelty who have, throughout history, tried to resist the call to violence. But even though he preached 'abstention from killing living beings',[103] he had tacitly to acknowledge that, as emperor and for the sake of the region's stability, he could not renounce force nor, in these times, could he abolish capital punishment, or legislate against the killing and eating of animals (although he listed species that should be protected). Moreover, despite his distress about the plight of the Kalingans who had been deported after the battle, there was no question of repatriating them since they were essential to the imperial economy. And, as head of state, he could certainly not abjure warfare or disband his army. He realised that even if he abdicated and became a Buddhist monk, others would fight to succeed him and unleash more havoc, and, as always, the peasants and the poor would suffer most.

Ashoka's dilemma is the very dilemma of civilisation itself. As society developed and weaponry became more deadly, the empire, founded and maintained by violence, would paradoxically become the most effective means of keeping the peace. Despite its violence and exploitation, people looked for an absolute imperial monarchy as eagerly as we search for signs of a flourishing democracy today.

Ashoka's dilemma may lie behind the story of the *Mahabharata,* India's great epic. This massive work – eight times the length of Homer's *Iliad* and *Odyssey* combined – is an anthology of many strands of tradition transmitted orally from about 300 BCE but not committed to writing until the early Common Era. The *Mahabharata* is more than a narrative poem, however. It remains the Indian national saga and is the most popular of all India's sacred texts, familiar in every home. It contains the *Bhagavad-gita,* which has been called India's 'national gospel'.[104] In the twentieth century, during the build-up to independence, the *Gita* would play a central role in the discussions about the legitimacy of waging war against Britain.[105] Its influence in forming attitudes to violence and its relation to religion has, therefore, been unparalleled in India. Long after Ashoka had been forgotten, it compelled people of all ranks to grapple with Ashoka's dilemma, which thus became central to the collective memory of India.

Even though the text was finally redacted by Brahmins, at its heart the

epic depicts the pathos of the Kshatriya who could not achieve enlightenment because he was obliged by the dharma of his class to be a man of
war. The story is set in the Kuru-Panchala region before the rise of the
large sixth-century kingdoms. Yudishthira, eldest son of King Pandu, had
lost his kingdom to his cousins, the Kauravas, who had rigged the ritual
game of dice during his consecration, so that he, his four brothers and their
wife had to go into exile. Twelve years later, the Pandavas regain the throne
in a catastrophic war in which nearly everyone on both sides is killed. The
final battle brings the Heroic Age of history to an end and ushers in what
the epic calls the Kali Yuga – our own deeply flawed era. It should have
been a simple war of good versus evil. The Pandava brothers were all
fathered by gods: Yudishthira by Dharma, guardian of cosmic order; Bhīma
by Vayu, god of physical force; Arjuna by Indra; and the twins Nakula and
Sahadeva by the Ashvins, patrons of fertility and productivity. The Kauravas,
however, are incarnations of the asuras so their struggle replicates on earth
the war between devas and asuras in heaven. But even though the Pandavas,
with the help of their cousin Krishna, chieftain of the Yadava clan, finally
defeat the Kauravas, they have to resort to dubious tactics and when they
contemplate the devastated world at the end of the war, their victory seems
tainted. The Kauravas, on the other hand, although they are fighting on the
'wrong' side, often act in an exemplary manner. When their leader
Duryodhana is killed, devas sing his praises and cover his body with a shower
of petals.

The *Mahabharata* is not an anti-war epic: innumerable passages glorify
warfare and describe battles enthusiastically and in gory detail. Even though
it is set in an earlier time, the epic probably reflects the period after Ashoka's
death in about 223 BCE, when the Mauryan empire began its decline and
India entered a dark age of political instability that lasted until the rise of
the Gupta dynasty in 320 CE.[106] There is, therefore, an implicit assumption
that empire – or in the poem's terms, 'world-rule' – is essential to peace.
And although the poem is unsparing about the ferocity of empire, it poign-
antly recognises that nonviolence in a violent world is not only impossible
but can actually cause *himsa* ('harm'). Brahmin law insisted that the king's
chief duty was to prevent the fearful chaos that would ensue if monarchical
authority failed and for this, military coercion (*danda*) was indispensable.[107]
Yet while Yudishthira is divinely destined to be king, he hates war. He
explains to Krishna that even though he knows that it is his duty to regain
the throne, warfare brings only misery. True, the Kauravas usurped his
kingdom, but to kill his cousins and friends – many of them good and noble

men – would be 'a most evil thing'.[108] He knows that every Vedic class has its particular duty: 'The shudra obeys, the vaishya lives by trade . . . The Brahmin prefers the begging bowl', but the Kshatriyas 'live off killing' and 'any other way of life is forbidden to us'. The Kshatriya is therefore doomed to misery. If defeated, he will be reviled, but if he achieves victory by ruthless methods, he incurs the taint of the warrior, is 'deprived of glory and reaps eternal infamy'. 'For heroism is a powerful disease that eats up the heart, and peace is found only by giving it up or by serenity of mind,' Yudishthira tells Krishna. 'On the other hand if final tranquillity were ignited by the total eradication of the enemy that would be even crueller.'[109]

To win the war, the Pandavas have to kill four Kaurava leaders who are inflicting grave casualties on their army. One of them is the general Drona, whom the Pandavas love dearly because he was their teacher and initiated them in the art of warfare. In a council of war, Krishna argues that if the Pandavas want to save the world from total destruction by establishing their rule, they must cast virtue aside. A warrior is obliged to be absolutely truthful and keep his word but Krishna tells Yudishthira that he can only kill Drona by lying to him. In the midst of the battle, he must tell him that his son Ashwatthaman has died so that, overcome with grief, Drona will lay down his weapons.[110] Most reluctantly, Yudishthira agrees, and when he delivers this terrible news Drona never imagines that Yudishthira, the son of Dharma, would lie. So Drona stops fighting and sits down in his chariot in the yogic position, falls into a trance and ascends peacefully to heaven. In terrible counterpoint, the chariot of Yudishthira, which has always floated a few inches above the ground, comes crashing down to earth.

Krishna is no Satan, tempting the Pandavas to sin. This is the end of the Heroic Age and his dark stratagems have become essential because, as he tells the desolate Pandavas, the Kauravas 'could not have been slain by you on the battlefield in a fair fight'. Had not Indra lied and broken his oath to Vritra in order to save the cosmic order? 'Not even the world-guardian gods themselves could have killed by fair means those four noble warriors,' Krishna explains. 'When enemies become too numerous and powerful, they should be slain by deceit and stratagems. This was the path formerly trodden by the devas to slay the asuras; and a path trodden by the virtuous may be trodden by all.'[111] The Pandavas feel reassured and acknowledges that their victory had at least brought peace to the world. But bad karma can only have a bad outcome and Krishna's scheme has appalling consequences that resonate horribly with us today.

Crazed with sorrow, Ashwatthaman, Drona's son, vows to avenge his father and offers himself to Shiva, the ancient god of the indigenous peoples of India, as a self-sacrifice. Entering the Pandava camp by night, he slaughters the sleeping women, children and warriors who are 'exhausted and weaponless', and hacks horses and elephants to pieces. In his divine frenzy, 'his every limb doused in blood, he seemed like Death himself, unloosed by fate . . . inhuman and utterly terrifying'.[112] The Pandavas themselves escape, having been warned by Krishna to sleep outside the camp, but most of their family are killed. When they finally catch up with Ashwatthaman, they find him sitting serenely with a group of renouncers beside the Ganges. He fires off a magical weapon of mass destruction and Arjuna retaliates with a weapon of his own. Had not two of the renouncers, 'desiring the welfare of all creatures', positioned themselves between the contending weapons, the world would have been destroyed. But Ashwatthaman's weapon is diverted into the wombs of the Pandava women, who from then on will bear no more children.[113] So Yudishthira had been right: a destructive cycle of violence, betrayal and lies has rebounded on the perpetrators, resulting in destruction for both sides.

Yudishthira reigns for fifteen years, but he has incurred the ancient stain of the warrior. The light has gone out of his life and after the war he would have become a renouncer had not his brothers and Krishna strongly opposed it. The king's rod of force is essential for the welfare of the world, Arjuna argues. No king has ever attained glory without slaying his enemies; indeed, it is impossible to exist without harming other creatures: 'I don't see anyone living in the world with nonviolence. Even ascetics cannot stay alive without killing.'[114] Like Ashoka, who was also unable to stem the violence of imperial warfare, Yudishthira focuses on kindness to animals, the only form of ahimsa that he is able realistically to practise. At the end of his life, he refuses to enter heaven without his devoted dog and is congratulated for his compassion by his father Dharma.[115] For centuries, the Indian national epic has compelled its audience to appreciate the moral ambiguity and tragedy of warfare; whatever the warrior's heroic code maintained, it was never a wholly glorious activity. Yet it was essential not only to the survival of the state but also for civilisation and progress and, as such, had become an unavoidable fact of human life.

Even Arjuna, who is often irritated by his brother's yearning for nonviolence, has an 'Ashoka moment'. In the Bhagavad-gita, he and Krishna debate these problems before the final battle with the Kauravas. As he stands in his chariot beside Krishna in the front line, Arjuna is suddenly horrified to see his cousins and beloved friends and teachers in the enemy ranks. 'I see no good in killing my kinsmen in battle,' he tells Krishna. 'I do not want to kill them, even if I am killed.'[116] Krishna tries to hearten him by citing all the traditional arguments but Arjuna is not impressed: 'I will not fight!' he cries.[117] So Krishna introduces an entirely novel idea: a warrior must simply dissociate himself from the effects of his actions and perform his duty without any personal animus or agenda of his own. Like a yogin, he must take the 'I' out of his deeds, so that he acts impersonally – indeed, *he* will not be acting at all.[118] Instead, like a sage, even in the frenzy of battle he will remain fearless and without desire.

We do not know whether this would have convinced Arjuna, because he is suddenly blasted by a terrifying epiphany. Krishna reveals that he is really an incarnation of the god Vishnu, who descends to earth whenever the cosmic order is in jeopardy. As Lord of the World, Vishnu is *ipso facto* involved in the violence that is an inescapable part of human life, but he is not damaged by it, 'since I remain detached in all my actions, Arjuna, as if I stood apart from them'.[119] As he gazes at Krishna, Arjuna sees that everything – gods, humans, and the natural order – is somehow present in Krishna's body, and although the battle has not even begun, he sees that the Pandava and Kaurava warriors are already hurtling into the god's blazing mouth. Krishna/Vishnu has already annihilated both armies and it makes no difference whether Arjuna fights or not. 'Even without you,' Krishna told him, 'all these warriors . . . will cease to exist.'[120] Many politicians and generals have similarly argued that they were only instruments of destiny when they committed atrocities – though few have emptied themselves of egotism and become 'Free from attachment, hostile to no creature'.[121]

The *Bhagavad-gita* has probably been more influential than any other Indian scripture. But both the *Gita* and the *Mahabharata* remind us that there are no easy answers to the problems of war and peace. True, Indian mythology and ritual often glorified greed and warfare, but they also helped people to confront its tragedy and even devised ways of extirpating aggression from the psyche, pioneering ways for people to live together without any violence at all. We are flawed creatures with violent hearts that long for peace. At the same time as the *Gita* was being composed, the people of China were coming to a similar conclusion.

3

CHINA:

WARRIORS AND GENTLEMEN

The Chinese believed that at the beginning of time human beings were indistinguishable from animals. Creatures that would eventually become human had 'snake bodies with human faces or the heads of oxen with tiger noses',[1] while future animals could speak and had human skills. These creatures lived together in caves, naked or clad in skins, eating raw meat and wild plants. Humans developed differently not because of their biological make-up but because they were taken in hand by five great kings, who had discerned the order of the universe and taught men and women to live in harmony with it. These Sage Kings drove the other beasts away and forced humans to live separately. They developed the tools and technology essential to organised society and instructed their people in a code of values that aligned them with the cosmic forces. Thus for the Chinese, humanity was neither a given nor did it evolve naturally: it was shaped and crafted by the rulers of states. Those who did not live in civilised Chinese society, therefore, were not really human; and if the Chinese succumbed to social disorder, they too could lapse into bestial savagery.[2]

Some two thousand years after the dawn of their civilisation, however, the Chinese were wrestling with some profound social and political dilemmas. For guidance, they turned to their history – or what they imagined it to be in the absence of the scientific and linguistic techniques we employ today. The myths about the Sage Kings were formed during the turbulent Warring States period (c. 485–221 BCE), when the Chinese were making a traumatic transformation from a multi-state society system to a united empire, but they may have originated from the mythology of the shamans of hunter-gatherer times. Yet these tales also reflected the Chinese view of themselves in the intervening millennia.

This mythology made it clear that civilisation could not survive without violence. The first Sage King, Shen Nung, the 'Divine Farmer', was the inventor of agriculture on which progress and culture depended. He could summon rain at will and conjure grain from the sky; he created the plough, taught his people how to plant and till the soil, and liberated them from the need to hunt and kill their fellow creatures. A man of peace, he refused to punish disobedience and outlawed violence in his kingdom. Instead of creating a ruling class he decreed that everyone should grow his own food, so Shen Nung would become the hero of those who repudiated the exploitation of the agrarian state. But no state could abjure violence. Because the Divine Farmer's successors had had no military training, they were unable to deal adequately with the natural aggression of their subjects which, unchecked, grew to such monstrous proportions that humans seemed about to slide back into animality.[3] Fortunately, however, a second Sage King appeared. He was called Huang Di, the 'Yellow Emperor', because he had recognised the potential of China's ochre-coloured soil.

To farm successfully, people must organise their lives around the seasons; they are dependent on the sun, winds and storms located in Heaven (Tian),* the transcendent realm of the Sky. So the Yellow Emperor established human society in the 'Way' (Dao) of Heaven by processing annually across the world, visiting each of the four compass points in turn – a ritual that maintained the regular cycle of the seasons and would be imitated by all future Chinese kings.[4] Associated with storm and rain, the Yellow Emperor, like other storm gods, was a great warrior. When he came to power, the arable land was desolate, rebels were fighting one another and there was drought and famine. He also had two external enemies: the animal-warrior Chi You, who was harassing his subjects, and the Fiery Emperor, who was scorching the cultivated land. The Yellow Emperor, therefore, drew on his great spiritual 'potency' (de) and trained an army of animals – bears, wolves and tigers – that managed to defeat the Fiery Emperor but could make no headway against the brutality of Chi You and his eighty brothers:

> They had the bodies of beasts, the speech of men, bronze heads and iron brows. They ate sand and stones, and created weapons such as staves, knives, lances, and bows. They terrorised all under Heaven and slaughtered barbarically; they loved nothing and nurtured nothing.[5]

* In this chapter, I have used the Pinyin method of romanising the Chinese script; I have given the Wade-Giles version as an alternative in cases when this form may be more familiar to a Western audience.

The Yellow Emperor tried to help his suffering people, but because 'he practised love and virtuous potency (de)' he could not overpower Chi You with force.[6] So he cast up his eyes to Heaven in silent appeal, and a celestial woman descended bearing a sacred text that revealed the secret art of warfare. The Yellow Emperor could now instruct his animal soldiers in the proper use of weaponry and military conduct and as a result they defeated Chi You and conquered the entire world. While Chi You's savage violence had turned men into beasts, the Yellow Emperor transformed his army of bears, wolves and tigers into human beings by teaching them to fight according to the rhythms of Heaven.[7] A civilisation founded on the twin pillars of agriculture and the organised violence of warfare could now begin.

By the twenty-third century BCE, two other Sage Kings, Yao and Shun, had established a golden age in the Yellow River plain, which was known for ever after as 'the Great Peace'. But during Shun's reign, the land was devastated by floods, so the king commissioned Yu, his chief of public works, to build canals, drain the marshes, and lead the rivers safely to the sea. Because of Yu's heroic labours, the people could grow rice and millet. Shun was so grateful that he arranged for Yu to succeed him, and he became the founder of the Xia dynasty.[8] Chinese history records three successive ruling dynasties before the establishment of the empire in 221 BCE: Xia, Shang and Zhou. It seems, however, that the three coexisted throughout antiquity and although the dominant ruling clan of the kingdom changed, the other lineages remained in charge of their own domains.[9] We have no documentary or archaeological evidence for the Xia period (c. 2200–1600 BCE), but it is likely that there was an agrarian kingdom in the great plain by the end of the third millennium.[10]

The Shang, a nomadic hunting people from northern Iran, seized control of the great plain from the Huai Valley to modern Shantung in about 1600 BCE.[11] The first Shang cities may have been founded by the masters of the guilds that pioneered the manufacture of the bronze weapons, war chariots and the magnificent vessels that the Shang used in their sacrifices. The Shang were men of war. They developed a typical agrarian system but their economy was still heavily subsidised by hunting and plunder and they did not establish a centralised state. Their kingdom consisted of a series of small towns, each governed by a representative of the royal family and surrounded by massive ramparts of packed earth to guard against flooding and attack. Each town was designed as a replica of the cosmos, its four walls oriented to the compass directions. The local lord and his warrior aristocracy lived in the royal palace, served by retainers – craftsmen, chariot-builders, makers of bows and arrows, blacksmiths, metal-workers, potters and scribes – who dwelt in the south of the city. This was a rigorously segmented society. The king was at the apex of the social pyramid; next in rank were the princes who ruled the cities, and the barons who lived on revenues from the rural territories, while the *shi*, the ordinary warriors, were the lowest-ranking members of the nobility.

Religion permeated Shang political life and endorsed its oppressive system. Because they were not part of their culture, the aristocracy regarded their peasants as an inferior species that was scarcely human. The Sage Kings had created civilisation by driving the animals away from human habitations; the peasants therefore never set foot in the Shang towns and lived quite separately from the nobility in subterranean dwelling pits in the countryside. Meriting no more regard than the Yellow Emperor had shown towards Chi You's horde, they led brutally miserable lives. In the spring the men moved out of the village and took up permanent residence in huts in the fields. During this season of work they had no contact with their wives and daughters, except when the women brought out their meals. After the harvest, the men moved back home, sealed up their dwellings and stayed indoors for the whole of the winter. This was their period of rest, but now the women began their season of labour – weaving, spinning and wine-making. The peasants had their own religious rites and festivals, traces of which have been preserved in the Confucian classic, *The Book of Songs*.[12] They could be conscripted in the military campaigns of the aristocracy and are described as lamenting so loudly when they were dragged away from their fields that they were gagged during the march. They did not take part in the actual fighting – that was the privilege of the aristocracy – but acted as valets, servants and carriers and looked after the horses; still, they were strictly segregated from the nobility, marching and camping separately.[13]

The Shang aristocracy appropriated the surplus produce from the peasants, but otherwise took only a ceremonial interest in agriculture. They offered sacrifices to the Earth and to the spirits of the mountains, rivers and winds to obtain a good harvest, and one of the king's tasks was to perform rituals to maintain the agricultural cycle on which the economy depended.[14] But apart from these liturgical rites, the aristocracy left agriculture entirely to the *min*, the 'common people'. At this date, however, very little of the region was given over to cultivation. Most of the Yellow River Valley was still covered by dense woods and marshes. Elephants, rhinoceroses, buffaloes, panthers and leopards roamed through the forests, together with deer, tigers, wild oxen, bears, monkeys and game. Still, the Shang state depended on the surplus produced by the peasants, but like all agrarian aristocracies, the nobility regarded productive work as a mark of inferiority.

Only the Shang king was permitted to approach Di Shang Di, the sky god who was so exalted that he had no dealings with other human beings. This placed the king in a position similar to Di's, a state of exception that consigned the rest of the nobility to a subordinate place.[15] It invested one man with such absolute privilege that he had no rivals and no need to compete with others. In his presence, a nobleman was as vulnerable as a peasant; the king was above all factions or conflicts of interest, so was free to embrace the concerns of the entire social body.[16] He alone could impose peace by offering sacrifice to Di, consulting him about the advisability of a military expedition or the founding of a new settlement. The aristocracy supported him by devoting themselves to three sacred activities that all involved the taking of life: sacrifice, warfare and hunting.[17] The min took no part in any of these pursuits, so violence was the *raison d'être* and distinguishing characteristic of the nobility.

These three duties were intricately interconnected in a way that shows how impossible it is to separate religion from other spheres of life in agrarian society. Sacrifice to the ancestors was deemed essential to the kingdom, because the fate of the dynasty depended on the goodwill of their deceased kings, who could intercede with Di on its behalf. So the Shang held lavish 'hosting' (*bin*) ceremonies at which vast quantities of animals and game were slaughtered – sometimes as many as a hundred beasts in a single ritual – and gods, ancestors and humans shared a feast.[18] Meat-eating was another privilege strictly reserved for the nobility. The sacrificial meat was cooked in exquisite bronze vessels that, like the bronze weapons that had subjugated the min, could be used only by the nobility and symbolised their exalted position.[19] The meat for the bin ceremony was supplied by the hunting expeditions, which were virtually indistinguishable from military campaigns.[20] Wild animals could endanger the crops, and the Shang killed them with reckless abandon. Their hunt was not simply a sport: it was a ritual that imitated the Sage Kings, who by driving the animals away had created the first civilisation.

A considerable part of the year was devoted to military campaigning. The Shang had no great territorial ambitions but made war simply to enforce their authority: extorting tribute from peasants, fighting invaders from the mountains, and punishing rebellious cities by carrying off crops, cattle, slaves and craftsmen. Sometimes they fought the 'barbarians', the peoples who surrounded the Shang settlements and had not yet assimilated to Chinese civilisation.[21] These militant circuits around the kingdom were a ritualised imitation of the Sage Kings' annual processions to maintain cosmic and political order.

The Shang attributed their victories to Di, the war god. But there seems to have been considerable anxiety, because it was impossible to rely on him.[22] As we can see from the surviving oracle bones and turtle shells on which the royal diviners inscribed questions for Di, he often sent drought, flooding and disaster and was an undependable military ally. Indeed, he could 'confer assistance' on the Shang but just as easily support their enemies. 'The Fang are harming or attacking us,' mourned one oracle. 'It is Di who orders them to make disaster for us.'[23] These scattered pieces of evidence suggest a regime constantly poised for attack, surviving only by ceaseless martial vigilance. There are also references to human sacrifice: prisoners of war and rebels were routinely executed and, although the evidence is not conclusive, may have been offered up to the gods.[24] Later generations certainly associated the Shang with ritual murder. The philosopher Mozi was clearly revolted by the elaborate funerals of a Shang aristocrat: 'As for the men who are sacrificed in order to follow him, if he should be a [king], they will be counted in hundreds or tens. If he is a great officer or a baron, they will be counted in tens or units.'[25] Shang rituals were violent because martial aggression was essential to the state. And even though the kings implored Di for help in their wars, in reality they owed their success to their military skills and bronze weapons.

In 1045 BCE the Shang were defeated by the Zhou, a less sophisticated clan from the Wei Valley in the west of the great plain. The Zhou established a feudal system: the king ruled from his western capital but also maintained a presence in a new royal city in the east; the other cities were parcelled out to Zhou princes and allies, who ruled as his vassals and bequeathed these fiefs to their descendants; and the Shang retained a domain in Song. Continuity was always important in pre-modern civilisation, so the Zhou were anxious to continue the Shang ancestral cult to uphold their regime. But how could they plausibly do so when they had executed the last Shang king? The Duke of Zhou, regent for his nephew, the young King Cheng, found a solution that he announced at the consecration of the new eastern capital. Di, whom the Zhou called 'Heaven' (*Tian*), had made the Zhou his instrument to punish the Shang, whose last kings had been cruel and corrupt.

Filled with pity for the suffering people, Heaven had revoked the Shangs' mandate to rule and appointed the Zhou to succeed them, making King Cheng the new Son of Heaven. But this was also a warning for Cheng, who must learn to be 'reverently careful' of 'the little people', because Heaven would take its mandate away from any ruler who oppressed his subjects. Heaven had chosen the Zhou because of their deep commitment to justice, so King Cheng must not inflict harsh punishments on the min.[26] Even though this did little to reduce the systemic violence of the Chinese state in practice, the mandate of Heaven was an important religious and political development, because, if only in theory, it made the ruler morally accountable to his people and instructed him to feel responsible for them. It would remain an important ideal in China.

Heaven was obviously a very different kind of deity from the Di of the Shang, who had had no interest in human behaviour. Heaven would never issue commandments or intervene directly in human affairs, however, for Heaven was not supernatural but inseparable from the forces of nature and active also in the royal potency of the king and princes who ruled as Heaven's sons. Heaven was also not omnipotent, because it could not exist without Earth, its divine counterpart. Unlike the Shang, the Zhou exploited the agricultural potential of the great plain on a grand scale, and because Heaven's influence could be implemented on earth only through the work of human beings, farming, forest clearance and road-building became sacred tasks that completed the creation Heaven had begun. The Chinese were clearly more interested in sanctifying the world they lived in than finding a transcendent holiness beyond.

The Zhou king was supported by a four-tier aristocracy of 'gentlemen' (*junzi*); Western scholars have translated their titles as 'duke', 'marquis', 'earl' and 'baron'. The *shi,* children of younger sons and second-class wives, served as men-at-arms but also as scribes and ritual experts, forming an early 'civil' wing of government. The Zhou confederacy of more than a hundred small principalities survived until 771 when their western capital was overrun by the Qong Rang barbarians. The Zhou fled to the east but never fully recovered. The succeeding period witnessed not merely the decline of a dynasty but saw the decay of the feudal system. The kings remained nominal rulers but were increasingly challenged by the more aggressive 'gentlemen' in the principalities, who were casting aside the deference on which feudalism depended.[27] The boundaries of the Chinese states were also shifting. By this time, the Chinese had absorbed several 'barbarian' populations, all with very different cultural traditions that challenged the old Zhou ethos. Cities located far away from the traditional centres of Chinese civilisation were becoming locally prominent, and by the end of the eighth century, when Chinese history starts to emerge from the mists of legend, they had become capitals of kingdoms: Jin in the north, Qi in the north-west, Qin in the west and Chu in the south. These states ruled thousands of barbarian subjects, whose grasp of Chinese custom was at best superficial. The small principalities in the centre of the great plain had now become extremely vulnerable, since these peripheral states were determined to expand. During the seventh century, they broke with tradition and began to mobilise peasants as fighting foot soldiers; Jin and Chu even brought barbarians into the army, offering them land in return for military service.

Deeply threatened by these aggressive kingdoms, some of the traditional principalities were also riven by internal conflict. With the decline of the Zhou, public order had deteriorated and, increasingly, brute force was becoming the norm. It was not uncommon for princes to kill ministers who dared to challenge their policies; ambassadors could be murdered and rulers assassinated during visits to another principality. To add to the tension, it seems that there was also an environmental crisis.[28] Centuries of aggressive hunting and land clearance that destroyed animal habitats meant that huntsmen were returning empty handed and there was far less meat at the bin banquets, so the old carefree extravagance was no longer possible. In this climate of uncertainty, people wanted clear directives, so the *shi* ritual experts of the principality of Lu re-codified the traditional Chinese custumal law to provide guidance.[29]

The Chinese had an aristocratic code, known as the *li* ('rituals'), which ruled the behaviour of both the individual and the state, and functioned in a way similar to our international law. The *ru* ('ritualists') now based their reform of this code on the conduct of the Sage Kings Yao and Shun whom they presented as models of restraint, altruism, forbearance and kindness.[30] This new ideology was obviously critical of regimes guided by violent, arrogant or selfish policies. Yao, it claimed, had been so 'reverent, intelligent, accomplished, sincere, and mild' that the potency (de) of these qualities had radiated from him to all Chinese families and created the Great Peace.[31] In an extraordinary act of self-abnegation, Yao had bequeathed the empire to the low-born Shun, passing over his own son because he was deceitful and quarrelsome. Shun even behaved with courtesy and respect to his father, who had tried to murder him. The reformed *li* were designed to help the gentlemen cultivate these same qualities. A junzi's demeanour should be 'sweet and calm'.[32] Instead of asserting himself aggressively, he should 'yield' (*rang*) to others and, far from stifling him, this would perfect his humanity (*ren*). The reformed li were expressly designed to curb belligerence and chauvinism.[33] Political life should instead be dominated by restraint and yielding.[34] 'The li teach us that to give free rein to one's feelings and let them follow their bent is the way of barbarians,' explained the ritualists; 'the ceremonial fixes degrees and limits.'[35] In the family, the eldest son should minister to his father's every need, addressing him in a low, humble voice, never expressing anger or resentment; in return, a father must treat all his children fairly, kindly and courteously. The system was so designed that each family member received a measure of reverence.[36] We do not know exactly how this worked out in practice; certainly many Chinese continued to strive aggressively for power, but it seems that by the end of the seventh century a significant number of those living in the traditional principalities were beginning to value moderation and self-control and even the peripheral states of Qi, Jin, Chu and Qin accepted these ritualised imperatives.[37]

The li tried to control the violence of warfare by turning it into a courtly game.[38] Killing large numbers of enemies was considered vulgar — it was the 'way of barbarians'. When an officer boasted that he had slaughtered six of the enemy, his prince had gravely replied: 'You will bring great dishonour on your country.'[39] It was not proper to slay more than three fugitives after a battle and a true junzi would fight with his eyes shut so that he would fail to shoot his enemy. During a battle, if the defeated driver of a war chariot paid a ransom on the spot, his opponents would always let him escape. There should be no unseemly triumphalism. A victorious prince once refused to build a monument to commemorate a victory: 'I was the cause that two countries exposed the bones of their warriors to the sun! It is cruel!' he cried. 'There are no guilty here, only vassals who have been faithful to the end.'[40] Nor should a commander ever take unfair advantage of the enemy's weakness. In 638 the Duke of Song was anxiously waiting for the army of the Chu principality, which greatly outnumbered his own. When they heard that Chu troops were crossing a nearby river, his commander urged him to attack at once: 'They are many: we are few: let us attack them before they get across!' The Duke was horrified and refused to follow this advice. When the Chu had crossed but still not drawn up their battle lines, his commander again urged that they should attack. But again the Duke demurred. Even though Song was soundly defeated in the ensuing battle, the Duke was unrepentant: 'A junzi worthy of the name does not seek to overcome the enemy in misfortune. He does not beat his drum before the ranks are formed.'[41]

Warfare was legitimate only if it restored the Way of Heaven by repelling a barbarian invasion or quashing a revolt. This 'punitive warfare' was a penal exercise to rectify behaviour. A military campaign against a rebellious Chinese city was therefore a highly ritualised affair, which began and ended with sacrifices at the Earth altar. When battle commenced, each side bullied the other with acts of outrageous kindness to prove its superior nobility. Boasting loudly of their prowess, warriors threw pots of wine over the enemy's wall. When a Chu archer used his last arrow to shoot a stag that was blocking his chariot's path, his driver immediately presented it to the enemy team that was bearing down upon them. They at once conceded defeat, exclaiming: 'Here is a worthy archer and well-spoken warrior! These are gentlemen!'[42] But there were no such limitations in a campaign against barbarians, who could be pursued and slaughtered like wild animals.[43] When the Marquis of Jin and his army came by chance upon the local Rong tribe peaceably minding their own business, he ordered his troops to massacre the entire tribe.[44] In a war of civilised 'us' against bestial 'them' any form of treachery or deceit was permitted.[45]

Despite the ritualists' best efforts, towards the end of the seventh century violence escalated on the Chinese plain. Barbarian tribes attacked from the north, and the southern state of Chu increasingly ignored the rules of courtly warfare and posed a real threat to the principalities. The Zhou kings were too weak to provide effective leadership, so Prince Huan of Qi, by now the most powerful Chinese state, formed a league of states that bound themselves by oath not to attack each other. But this attempt would fail, because the nobility, addicted to personal prestige, still wanted to preserve their independence. After Chu destroyed the league in 597 the region became engulfed in an entirely new kind of warfare. Other large peripheral states also began to cast aside traditional constraints, determined to expand and conquer more territory even if this meant the enemy's annihilation. In 593, for example, after a prolonged siege, the people of Song were reduced to eating their children. Small principalities were drawn into the conflict against their will when their territories became battlefields of competing armies. Qi, for example, encroached so frequently on the tiny dukedom of Lu that it was forced to appeal to Chu for help. But by the end of the sixth century, Chu had been defeated and Qi had become so dominant that the Duke of Lu managed to retain a modicum of independence only with the help of the western state of Qin. There was also civil strife: Qin, Jin and Chu were all fatally weakened by chronic infighting and in Lu three baronial families effectively created their own sub-states and reduced the legitimate duke to a mere puppet.

Archaeologists have noted a growing contempt for ritual observance at that time: people were placing profane objects in their relatives' tombs instead of the prescribed vessels. The spirit of moderation was also in decline. Many Chinese had developed a taste for luxury that put an unbearable strain on the economy, as demand outstripped resources, and some of the lower-ranking nobility tried to ape the lifestyle of the great families. As a result many of the shi at the bottom of the aristocratic hierarchy became impoverished and were forced to leave the cities to scrape a living as teachers among the min.

One shi, who held a minor administrative post in Lu, was horrified by the greed, pride and ostentation of the usurping families. Kon Qiu (c. 551–479 BCE) was convinced that the li alone could curb this destructive violence. His disciples would call him Kongfuzi ('our Master Kong') so in the West we call him Confucius. He never achieved the political career he hoped for and died believing that he was a failure, but he would define Chinese culture until the 1911 Revolution. With his little band of followers, most of them from the warrior aristocracy, Confucius travelled from one principality to another, hoping to find a ruler who would implement his ideas. In the West, he is often regarded as a secular rather than a religious philosopher, but he would not have understood this distinction: in ancient China, as the philosopher Herbert Fingarette has reminded us, the secular *was* sacred.[46]

Confucius' teachings were anthologised long after his death, but scholars believe that the *Analects,* a collection of short unconnected maxims, is a reasonably reliable source.[47] His ideology, which sought to revive the virtues of Yao and Shun, was deeply traditional, but his ideal of equality based on a cultivated perception of our shared humanity was a radical challenge to the systemic violence of agrarian China. Like the Buddha, Confucius redefined the concept of nobility.[48] The hero of the *Analects* is the junzi who is no longer a warrior but a profoundly humane scholar and somewhat deficient in the martial arts. For Confucius, a junzi's chief quality was ren, a word that he consistently refused to define because its meaning transcended any of the concepts of his day, but later Confucians would describe it as 'benevolence'.[49] The junzi was required to treat all others at all times with reverence and compassion, a programme of action that Confucius summed up in what is called the Golden Rule: 'Do not impose upon others what you yourself do not desire.'[50] It was, Confucius said, the 'single thread' that ran through all his teaching and should be practised 'all day and every day'.[51] A true junzi had to look into his heart, discover what gave him pain and then refuse under any circumstances to inflict that pain on anybody else.

This was not simply a personal ethic but a political ideal. If they practised ren, rulers would not invade another prince's territory, because they would not like this to happen to their own. They would hate to be exploited, reviled and reduced to poverty, so they must not oppress others. What would you make of a man who could 'extend this benevolence to the common people and bring succour to the multitudes'? asked Confucius' disciple Zigong.[52] Such a man would be a sage! his master exclaimed:

> Yao and Shun would have found such a task daunting! You yourself desire rank and standing; then help others to get rank and standing. You want to turn your merits to account; then help others to turn theirs to account – in fact, the ability to take one's feelings as a guide – that is the sort of thing that lies in the direction of ren.[53]

If a prince ruled solely by force, he might control his subjects' external behaviour but not their inner disposition.[54] No government, Confucius insisted, could truly succeed unless it was based on an adequate conception of what it meant to be a fulfilled human being. Confucianism was never a private pursuit for the individual; it always had a political orientation and sought nothing less than a major reformation of public life. Its goal, quite simply, was to bring peace to the world.[55]

All too often the li had been used to enhance a nobleman's prestige, as had been the case in the aggressive courtesy of ritualised warfare. But properly understood, Confucius believed, the li taught people 'all day and every day' to put themselves in somebody else's shoes and see a situation from another perspective. If such an attitude became habitual, a junzi would transcend the egotism, greed and selfishness that were tearing China apart. How can I achieve ren? asked his disciple Yan Hui. It was quite simple, Confucius replied: 'Curb your ego and surrender to the li.'[56] A junzi must submit every detail of his life to the rituals of consideration and respect for others. 'If for one day, you managed to restrain yourself and return to the rites,' Confucius continued, 'you could lead the entire world back to ren.'[57] But to achieve this, a junzi had to work on his humanity, as a sculptor crafts a rough stone to make it a ritual vessel, a bearer of holiness.[58] He could thus replace the current greed, violence and vulgarity and restore dignity and grace to human intercourse, transforming the whole of China.[59]

The practice of ren was difficult because it required the junzi to dethrone himself from the centre of his world,[60] although the ideal of ren was deeply rooted in our humanity.[61]

Confucius emphasised the importance of 'yielding'. Instead of asserting themselves belligerently and fighting for power, sons should yield to their fathers, warriors to their enemies, noblemen to their rulers, and rulers to their retainers. Instead of seeing family life as an impediment to enlightenment, like the renouncers of India, Confucius saw it as the school of the spiritual quest because it taught every family member to live for others.[62] Later philosophers criticised Confucius for concentrating exclusively upon the family, but Confucius saw each person as the centre of a constantly growing series of concentric circles to which he or she must relate, cultivating a sympathy that went beyond the claims of family, class, state or race.[63] Each of us begins life in the family, so the family li start our education in self-transcendence, but it does not end there. A junzi's horizons would gradually expand. The lessons he had learned by caring for his parents, spouse and siblings would enable him to feel empathy with more and more people: first his immediate community, then the state in which he lived, and finally the entire world.

Confucius was too much of a realist to imagine that human beings could ever abandon warfare; he deplored its waste of life and resources[64] but understood that no state could survive without its armies.[65] When asked to list the priorities of government, he replied: 'Simply make sure there is sufficient food and sufficient armaments,' although he added that if one of these had to go, it should be weaponry.[66] In the past, only the Zhou king had been able to declare war, but now his vassals had usurped this royal prerogative and were fighting one another. If this continued, Confucius feared, violence would proliferate throughout society.[67] 'Punitive expeditions' against barbarians, invaders and rebels were essential, because the government's chief task was to preserve the social order.[68] This, he believed, was why the structural violence of society was necessary. While Confucius always spoke of the min with genuine concern and urged rulers to appeal to their sense of self-respect instead of seeking to control them by force and fear, he knew that if they were not punished when they transgressed, civilisation would collapse.[69]

The fourth-century Confucian philosopher Mencius too could only regard the min as born to be ruled: 'There are those who use their minds and there are those who use their muscles. The former rule; the latter are ruled. Those who rule are supported by those who are ruled.'[70] The min could never join the ruling class because they lacked 'teaching' (*jaio*) which in China always implied a degree of force: the pictograph *jaio* showed a hand wielding a rod to discipline a child.[71] Warfare too was a mode of instruction, essential to civilisation: 'To wage a punitive war,' Mencius wrote, 'is to rectify';[72] indeed, Mencius had even convinced himself that the masses yearned for such correction and that the barbarians vied with one another to be conquered by the Chinese.[73] But it was never permissible to fight equals: 'A punitive expedition is waged by one in authority against his subordinates. It is not for peers to punish one another by war.'[74] The current interstate warfare between rulers of equal status, therefore, was perverse, illegal and a form of tyranny. China desperately needed wise rulers like Yao and Shun, whose moral charisma could restore the Great Peace. 'The appearance of a true King has never been longer overdue than today,' wrote Mencius; 'and the people have never suffered more under tyrannical government than today.' If a militarily powerful state were to govern benevolently, 'the people would rejoice as if they had been released from hanging by the heels'.[75]

Despite their convictions about equality, the Confucians were aristocrats who could not transcend the assumptions of the ruling class. In the writings of Mozi (*c.* 480–390), however, we hear the voice of the commoner. Mozi headed a brotherhood of 180 men, who dressed like peasants and craftsmen and travelled from one state to another, instructing rulers in the new military technology for defending a city when it was besieged by the enemy.[76] Mozi was almost certainly an artisan and he regarded the elaborate rituals of the nobility as a waste of time and money. But he too was convinced that ren was China's only hope, and he emphasised the danger of political sympathy extending no further than one's own kingdom even more strongly than Confucius. 'Others must be regarded like the self,' he insisted. This 'concern' (*ai*) must be 'all-embracing and exclude nobody'.[77] The only way to stop the Chinese destroying one another was to persuade them to practise *jian ai* ('concern for everybody'). Instead of simply worrying about their own kingdom, he urged each prince to 'regard another's state as your own'; for if rulers truly had such concern, they would not go to war. Indeed, the root cause of all the 'world's calamities, dispossessions, resentments and hatreds is lack of *jian ai*'.[78]

Unlike the Confucians, Mozi had nothing positive to say about war. From a poor man's perspective, it made no sense at all. Warfare ruined harvests, killed multitudes of civilians, and wasted weapons and horses. Rulers claimed that the conquest of territory enriched the state and made it more secure, but in fact only a tiny proportion of the population benefited and the capture of a small town could result in such heavy casualties that there was nobody left to farm the land.[79] Mozi believed that a policy could only be called virtuous if it enriched the poor, prevented pointless death, and contributed to public order. But humans were egotists: they would adopt jian ai only if they were convinced by irrefutable arguments that their own well-being depended on the welfare of the entire human race, so that jian ai was essential to their *own* prosperity, peace and security.[80] Hence *The Book of Mozi* included the first Chinese exercises in logic, all dedicated to proving that warfare was not in a ruler's best interests. In words that still ring true today, Mozi insisted that the only way out of the destructive cycle of warfare was for rulers 'not to be concerned for themselves alone'.[81]

In ancient China, Mozi was revered more than Confucius, because he spoke so directly to the problems of this violent time. By the fifth century, the small principalities were surrounded by seven large Warring States – Jin, which had split into the three kingdoms of Han, Wei and Zhao; Qi, Qin and its neighbour Shu in the west; and Chu in the south. Their huge armies, iron weaponry and lethal crossbows were so formidable that any state that could not match them was doomed.[82] Along their frontiers their engineers built defensive walls and fortresses, which were manned by professional garrisons. Supported by strong economies, their armies fought with a deadly efficiency based on unified command, skilful strategy and trained troops. Brutally pragmatic, they had no time for ren or ritual and in battle they spared no one: 'all who have or keep any strength are our enemies, even if they are old men,' one commander maintained.[83] Yet, on purely pragmatic grounds, their new military experts advised against excessive plunder and violence,[84] and in their campaigns they were careful not to endanger agricultural output, the state's primary resource.[85] Warfare was no longer a courtly game governed by li to curb aggression; instead it had become a science, governed by logic, reason and cold calculation.[86]

To Mozi and his contemporaries, it seemed that the Chinese were about to destroy one another, but, with hindsight, we can see that in fact they were moving painfully towards a centralised empire that would impose a measure of peace. The chronic warfare of the Warring States period revealed one of the ubiquitous dilemmas of the agrarian state. Unless they were held in check, aristocrats who were bred to fight and had developed a prickly sense of honour would always compete aggressively for land, wealth, property, prestige and power. In the fifth century, the Warring States began to annihilate the traditional principalities and battle compulsively against each other until in 221 BCE only one of them was left. Its victorious ruler would become the first emperor of China.

We find in this period of Chinese history a fascinating pattern that shows how mistaken it is to imagine that a given set of 'religious' beliefs and practices will lead inexorably to violence. Instead, we find people drawing on the same pool of mythology, contemplative disciplines and ideas but embarking on radically different courses of action. Even though the Warring States were moving towards an ethos that approached modern secularism, their hard-headed strategists regarded themselves as sages and saw their warfare as a species of religion. Their hero was the Yellow Emperor and these commanders were convinced that, like his textbook of military strategy, their own treatises were divinely revealed.

The Sage Kings had discovered an orderly design in the cosmos that showed them how to organise society; similarly the military commander could discern a pattern in the chaos of the battlefield that enabled him to find the most efficient way to achieve victory. 'The one with many strategic factors in his favour wins, the one with few strategic factors in his favour loses,' explained Sunzi, or Sun Tzu, a contemporary of Mencius. 'Observing the matter in this way, I can see who will win and who will lose.'[87] A good commander could even defeat the enemy without any fighting at all. If the odds were stacked against him, the best policy was to wait until the enemy, believing that you were weak, became over-confident and made a fatal mistake. The commander should regard his troops as mere extensions of his will and control them as the mind directs the body. Even though he was of noble birth, an able commander would live among his peasant soldiers, sharing their hardships and becoming the model to which they must conform. He would inflict terrible punishments on his men to make them fear him more than death on the battlefield; indeed, a good strategist would deliberately put his troops into such danger that they had no option but to fight their way out.[88] A soldier could have no mind of his own but should be as subservient and passive in relation to his commander as a woman. Warfare had been 'feminised'. Indeed, feminine weakness could be more effective than masculine belligerence: the best armies might seem to be as weak as water – but water could be extremely destructive.[89]

'The military is a Way (Dao) of Deception,' said Sunzi. The name of the game was to deceive the enemy:

Thus when able, manifest inability. When active, manifest inactivity.

When near, manifest as far. When far, manifest as near.

When he seeks advantage, lure him.

When he is in chaos, take him.

When he is substantial, prepare against him.

When he is strong, avoid him.

Attack where he is unprepared. Emerge where he does not expect.[90]

Sunzi knew that civilians would look askance at this martial ethic, but their state could not survive without its army.[91] The army should therefore be kept apart from mainstream society and be governed by its own laws, because its modus operandi was the 'extraordinary' (*qi*), the counter-intuitive, doing exactly what did *not* come naturally. This would be disastrous in all other affairs of state,[92] but if a commander learned how to exploit the qi, he could achieve a sage-like alignment with the Way of Heaven:

Thus one skilled at giving rise to the extraordinary is as boundless as Heaven and Earth, as inexhaustible as the Yellow River and the ocean.

Ending and beginning again, like the sun and moon. Dying and then being born, like the four seasons.[93]

The dilemma of even the most benign state was that it was obliged to maintain at its heart an institution committed to treachery and violence.

The cult of the 'extraordinary' was not new but was widespread among the population, especially among the lower classes, and might even date back to the Neolithic period. It had strong connections with the mystical school that we call Daoism (or Taoism) in the West, which was far more popular with the masses than the elite.[94] Daoists opposed any form of government and were convinced that when rulers interfered in their subjects' lives they invariably made matters worse – an attitude similar to the strategists' preference for 'doing nothing' and refraining from rushing into action. Forcing people to obey man-made laws and perform unnatural rituals was simply perverse, argued the ebullient hermit Zhuangzi (*c.* 369–286 BCE). It was better to 'do nothing', practising 'action by inaction (*wu wei*)'. It was deep within yourself, at a level far below the reasoning powers, that you would encounter the Way (Dao) things really were.[95]

In the West, we tend to read the mid-third-century treatise known as the *Daodejing* ('Classic of the Way and its Potency')* as a devotional text for a personal spirituality but it was actually a manual of statecraft, written for the prince of one of the vulnerable principalities.[96] Its anonymous author wrote under the pseudonym Laozi, or Lao-Tzu – 'Old Master'. Rulers should imitate Heaven, he taught, which did not interfere with the Ways of men; so if they abandoned their meddlesome policies, royal 'potency' (de) would emerge spontaneously: 'If I cease to desire and remain still, the empire will be at peace of its own accord.'[97] The Daoist king should practise meditative techniques that rid his mind of busy theorising so that it becomes 'empty' and 'still'. Then the Dao of Heaven could act through him and 'To the end of one's days one will meet with no danger.'[98] Laozi offered the beleaguered principalities a stratagem for survival. Statesmen usually preferred to engage in frenzied activity and shows of strength when they should be doing the exact opposite. Instead of posturing aggressively, they should present themselves as weak and small. Like the military strategists, Laozi used the analogy of water, which seemed 'submissive and weak' yet could be far more powerful than 'that which is hard and strong'.[99] The Daoist ruler should abandon masculine self-assertion and embrace the softness of the 'mysterious female'.[100] What goes up must come down, so when you strengthened your enemy by appearing to submit, you were actually hastening his decline. Laozi agreed with the strategists that military action should always be the last resort: weapons were 'ill-omened instruments', he argued, which a sage-king used only 'when he cannot do otherwise'.[101]

> The good leader is not warlike
> The good fighter is not impetuous
> The best conqueror of the enemy is he who never takes the offensive.[102]

The wise leader should not even retaliate after an atrocity because this would simply provoke a counter-attack. By practising wu wei instead, he would acquire the potency of Heaven itself: 'Because he does not contend, there is no one in the world who can contend with him.'[103]

This, alas, proved not to be the case. The victor in the long struggle of the Warring States was not a Daoist sage-king but the ruler of Qin, who was successful simply because he had the most territory, manpower and resources. Instead of depending on ritual, as previous Chinese states had

* *Tao Te Ching* in the Wade-Giles system

done, Qin had developed a materialistic ideology based solely on the economic realities of warfare and agriculture, shaped by a new philosophy known as *Fajia* ('School of the Law') or 'Legalism'.[104] *Fa* did not mean 'law' in the modern sense; rather, it was a 'standard' like the carpenter's square that made raw materials conform to a fixed pattern.[105] It was the Legalist reforms of Lord Shang (c. 390–338 BCE) that put Qin ahead of its rivals.[106] Shang believed that the people must be forced by strict punishments to submit to their subordinate role in a state designed solely to enhance the ruler's power.[107] He eliminated the aristocracy and replaced it with a hand-picked administration wholly dependent on the king. The country was now divided into thirty-one districts, each ruled by a magistrate who answered directly to the capital and conscripted recruits for the army. To boost productivity and free enterprise, peasants were encouraged to buy their land. The nobility of the junzi was irrelevant: honour was achieved only by a brilliant performance on the battlefield. Anyone who commanded a victorious unit was given land, houses and slaves.

Qin had arguably developed the first secular state-ideology but Shang separated religion from politics not because of religion's inherent violence but because religion was impracticably humane. Religious sentiment would make a ruler too benign, which ran counter to the state's best interests. 'A State that uses good people to govern the wicked will be plagued by disorder and be destroyed,' Shang insisted. 'A state that uses the wicked to govern the good always enjoys peace and becomes strong.'[108] Instead of practising the Golden Rule a military commander should inflict on the enemy exactly what he did *not* wish for his own troops.[109] Unsurprisingly, Qin's success was deeply troubling to the Confucians. Xunzi (c. 310–219 BCE), for example, believed that a ruler who governed by ren would be an irresistible force for good and his compassion would transform the world. He would take up arms only

> to put an end to violence, and to do away with harm, not in order to compete with others for spoil. Therefore when the soldiers of the benevolent man encamp they command a godlike respect; and where they pass, they transform the people.[110]

But his pupil Li Si laughed at him: Qin was the most powerful state in China, because it had the strongest army and economy; it did not owe its success to ren but to its opportunism.[111] During Xunzi's visit to Qin, King Zhao told him bluntly: 'The Confucians (ru) are no use in running a state.'[112]

Shortly afterwards, Qin conquered Xunzi's native state of Zhao, and even though the Zhao king surrendered, Qin troops buried 400,000 of his soldiers alive. How could a junzi exert any restraining influence over such a regime? Xunzi's pupil Li Si now emigrated to Qin, became its prime minister and masterminded the lightning campaign that resulted in Qin's final victory and the establishment of the Chinese empire in 221 BCE.

Paradoxically, the Legalists drew on the same pool of ideas and spoke the same language as the Daoists. They also believed that the king should 'do nothing' (wu wei) to interfere with the Dao of the Law, which should run like a well-oiled machine. The people would suffer if the laws kept changing, maintained the Legalist Han Feizi (280–233), so a truly enlightened ruler 'waits in stillness and emptiness' and 'lets the tasks of themselves be fixed'.[113] He did not need morality or knowledge but was simply the Prime Mover, who remained immobile but set his ministers and subjects in motion:

> Having courage, he does not use it to rage
> He draws out all the warlike in his ministers
> Hence by doing without knowledge he possesses clear-sightedness
> By doing without worthiness he gets results
> By doing without courage, he achieves strength[114]

There was, of course, a world of difference between the two: Daoists deplored rulers who forced their subjects to conform to an unnatural fa; their sage-king meditated to achieve selflessness, not to 'get results'.[115] But the same ideas and imagery informed the thinking of political scientists, military strategists and mystics. People could have the same beliefs but act upon them very differently. Military strategists believed that their brutally pragmatic writings came to them by divine revelation, and contemplatives gave strategic advice to kings. Even the Confucians now drew on these notions: Xunzi believed that the Way could be comprehended only by a mind that was 'empty, unified and still'.[116]

Many people must have been relieved when Qin's victory put a stop to the endless fighting and hoped that the empire would keep the peace. But they had a shocking introduction to imperial rule. Acting on the advice of Prime Minister Li Si, the First Emperor became an absolute ruler. The Zhou aristocracy – 120,000 families – were forcibly moved to the capital and their weapons confiscated. The emperor divided his vast territory into thirty-six commanderies, each headed by a civil administrator, a military commander and an overseer; each commandery was in turn divided into counties governed by magistrates, and all officials answered directly to the central government.[117] The old rituals that had presented the Zhou king as head of a family of feudal lords were replaced by a rite that focused on the emperor alone.[118] When the court historian criticised this innovation, Li Si told the emperor that he could no longer tolerate such divisive ideologies: any school that opposed the Legalist programme must be abolished and its writings publicly burned.[119] There was a massive book-burning and 460 teachers were executed. One of the first inquisitions in history had therefore been mandated by a proto-secular state.

Xunzi had been convinced that Qin would never rule China because its draconian methods would alienate the people. He was proved right when they rose up in rebellion after the death of the First Emperor in 210 BCE. After three years of anarchy, Liu Bang, one of the local magistrates, founded the Han dynasty. His chief military strategist Zhang Liang, who had studied Confucian ritual in his youth, embodied Han ideals. It was said that a military text was revealed to him after he had behaved with exemplary respect towards an elderly man and even though he had no military experience, he led Bang to victory. Zhang was not a bellicose man. He was a Daoist warrior: 'not warlike', frequently ill and unable to command on the field. He treated people with humility, practised Daoist meditation and breath control, abstained from grains, and at one point seriously considered retiring from politics for a life of contemplation.[120]

The Han had learned from Qin's mistakes. But Bang wanted to preserve the centralised state and knew that the empire needed Legalist realism because no state could function without coercion and the threat of violence. 'Weapons are the means by which the sage makes obedient the powerful and savage, and brings stability in times of chaos,' wrote the Han historian Sima Qian:

> Instruction and corporal punishment cannot be abandoned in a household, mutilating punishments cannot be halted under Heaven. It is simply that in using them some are skilful and some clumsy, in carrying them out some are in accord [with Heaven] and some against it.[121]

But Bang knew that the state also needed a more inspiring ideology. His solution was a synthesis of Legalism and Daoism.[122] Still reeling from the Qin inquisition, people yearned for 'empty', open-minded governance. Han emperors would maintain absolute control over the commanderies but would refrain from arbitrary interventions; there would be strict penal law but no draconian punishments.

The patron of the new regime was the Yellow Emperor. All empires need theatre and pageantry and the Han rituals gave a new twist to the ancient Shang complex of sacrifice, hunting and warfare.[123] In autumn, the season for military campaigning, the emperor held a ceremonial hunt in the royal parks, which teemed with every kind of animal, to provide meat for the temple sacrifice. A few weeks later, there were military reviews in the capital to show off the skills of elite troops and help maintain the martial competence of the min, who manned the imperial armies. At the end of winter, there were hunting contests in the parks. These rituals, designed to impress visiting dignitaries, all recalled the Yellow Emperor and his animal troops. Men and animals fought as equal combatants, just as they had at the beginning of time before the Sage Kings separated them. There were football matches in which players kicked the ball from one side of the field to the other, to reproduce the alteration of *yin* and *yang* in the seasonal cycle. 'Kickball deals with the power of circumstances in the military. It is a means to train warriors and recognize who have talent,' explained the historian Liu Xiang (77–6 BCE). 'It is said that it was created by the Yellow Emperor.'[124] Like the Yellow Emperor, Han rulers would use religious rituals in an attempt to take the bestial savagery out of warfare so that it became humane.

At the start of his reign, Liu Bang had commissioned the Confucian ritualists (ru) to devise a court ceremonial and when it was performed for the first time, the emperor exclaimed: 'Now I realize the nobility of being a Son of Heaven!'[125] The ru slowly gained ground at court and as the memory of the Qin trauma faded, there was a growing desire for more solid moral guidance.[126] In 136 BCE, the court scholar Dong Zhongshu (179–104) suggested to Emperor Wu (r. 140–87) that there were too many competing schools and recommended that the six classical Confucian texts become the official state teaching. The emperor agreed: Confucianism supported the family; its emphasis on cultural history would forge a national identity; and state education would create an elite class that could counter the enduring appeal of the old aristocracy. But Wu did not make the mistake of the First Emperor. In the Chinese empire there would be no sectarian intolerance: the Chinese would continue to see merit in all schools, which could supplement one another. Thus however diametrically opposed the two schools might be, there would be a Legalist–Confucian coalition: the state still needed Legalist pragmatism, but the ru would temper Fajia despotism.

In 124 BCE, Wu founded the Imperial Academy and for over two thousand years all Chinese state officials would be trained in a predominantly Confucian ideology, which presented the rulers as Sons of Heaven governing by moral charisma. This gave the regime spiritual legitimacy and became the ethos of the civil administration. But like all agrarian rulers the Han controlled their empire by systemic and martial violence, exploiting the peasantry, killing rebels and conquering new territory. The emperors depended on the army (*wu*) and in the newly conquered territories the magistrates summarily expropriated the land, deposed existing landlords, and seized between 50 and 100 per cent of the peasants' surplus. Like any pre-modern ruler, the emperor had to maintain himself in a state of exception as the 'one man' to whom ordinary rules did not apply. At a moment's notice, therefore, he could order an execution and nobody dared object. Such irrational and spontaneous acts of violence were an essential part of the mystique that held his subjects in thrall.[127]

Thus while the ruler and the military lived by the 'extraordinary', the Confucians promoted the predictable, routinised orthodoxy of *wen,* the civil order based on benevolence (ren), culture and rational persuasion. They performed the invaluable task of persuading the public that the emperor really had their interests at heart. They were not mere lackeys – many of the ru were executed for reminding the emperor too forcibly of his moral duty – but their power was limited. When Dong Zhongshu objected that the imperial usurpation of land caused immense misery, Emperor Wu seemed to agree but ultimately Dong had to compromise, settling for a moderate limitation of land tenure.[128] The fact was that while the administrators and bureaucrats championed Confucianism, the rulers themselves preferred the Legalists, who despised the Confucians as impractical idealists; in their view, King Zhao of Qin had said it all: 'The ru are no use in running a state.'

In 81 BCE, in a series of debates about the monopoly of salt and iron, the Legalists argued that the uncontrolled, private 'free enterprise' advocated by the ru was wholly impractical.[129] The Confucians were nothing but a bunch of impoverished losers:

> See them now present us with nothing and consider it substance, with
> 'emptiness' and call it plenty! In their coarse gowns and cheap sandals they

walk gravely along, sunk in meditation as though they had lost something. These are not men who can do great deeds and win fame. They do not even rise above the vulgar masses.[130]

The ru could therefore only bear witness to an alternative society. The word *ru* is related etymologically to *ruo* ('mild') but some modern scholars argue that it meant 'weakling' and was first used in the sixth century to describe the impoverished shi who had scraped a meagre living by teaching.[131] In imperial China, Confucians were political 'softies', economically and institutionally weak.[132] They could keep the benevolent Confucian alternative alive and make it a presence in the heart of government, but would always lack the 'teeth' to push their policies through.

That was the Confucian dilemma — similar to the impasse that Ashoka had encountered on the Indian subcontinent. Empire depended on force and intimidation, because the aristocrats and the masses had to be held in check. Even if he had wanted to, Emperor Wu could not afford to rule entirely by ren. The Chinese empire had been achieved by warfare, wholesale slaughter and the annihilation of one state after another; it retained its power by military expansion and internal oppression and developed religious mythologies and rituals to sacralise these arrangements. Was there a realistic alternative? The Warring States period had shown what happened when ambitious rulers with new weapons and large armies competed pitilessly for dominance, devastating the countryside and terrorising the population in the process. Contemplating this chronic warfare, Mencius had longed for a king who would rule 'all under Heaven' and bring peace to the great plain of China. The ruler who had been powerful enough to achieve this was the First Emperor.

4

THE HEBREW DILEMMA

When Adam and Eve were expelled from the Garden of Eden, they probably did not fall into a state of original sin, as St Augustine believed, but into an agrarian economy.[1] Man (*adam*) had been created from the soil (*adamah*) which in the Garden of Eden was watered by a simple spring. Adam and his wife were free agents, living a life of idyllic liberty, cultivating the garden at their leisure and enjoying the companionship of their god Yahweh. But because of a single act of disobedience, Yahweh condemned them both to a life sentence of hard agricultural labour:

> Accursed be the soil because of you! With suffering shall you get your food from it every day of your life. It shall yield you brambles and thistles, and you shall eat wild plants. With sweat on your brow shall you eat your bread, until you return to the soil as you were taken from it. For dust you are, and to dust you shall return.[2]

Instead of peacefully nurturing the soil as its master, Adam had become its slave. From the very beginning, the Hebrew Bible strikes a different note from most of the texts we have considered so far. Its heroes were not members of an aristocratic elite; Adam and Eve had been relegated to mere field hands, scratching a miserable subsistence from the blighted land.

Adam had two sons: Cain, the farmer, and Abel, the herdsman – the traditional enemy of the agrarian state. Both dutifully brought offerings to Yahweh, who, somewhat perversely, rejected Cain's sacrifice but accepted Abel's. Baffled and furious, Cain lured his brother into the family plot and killed him, his arable land becoming a field of blood that cried out to Yahweh for vengeance. 'Damned be you from the soil, which opened up its mouth to receive your brother's blood!'[3] Yahweh cried. Henceforth Cain would wander in the Land of Nod as an outcast and fugitive. From the start, the Hebrew Bible condemns the violence at the heart of the agrarian state. It is Cain, the first murderer, who builds the world's first city and one of his descendants is Tubal the Smith (*Kayin*), 'ancestor of all metal-workers in bronze and iron', who crafted its weapons.[4] Immediately after the murder, when Yahweh asks Cain: 'Where is your brother, Abel?' he replies: 'Am I my brother's guardian?'[5] Urban civilisation denied that relationship with and responsibility for all other human beings that is embedded in human nature.

The Pentateuch, the first five books of the Bible, did not reach its final form until about the fourth century BCE. For the historians, poets, prophets, priests and lawyers of Israel, it became the organising narrative around which they constructed their worldview. Over the centuries, they would change that story and embroider it, adding or reinterpreting events in order to address the particular challenges of their own time. This story began in about 1750 BCE, when Yahweh commanded Abraham, Israel's ancestor, to turn his back on the agrarian society and culture of Mesopotamia and settle in Canaan, where he, his son Isaac and grandson Jacob would live as simple herdsmen. Yahweh promised that their descendants would one day possess this land and become a nation as numerous as the sands on the seashore.[6] But Jacob and his twelve sons (founders of the tribes of Israel) were forced by famine to leave Canaan and migrate to Egypt. At first they prospered, but eventually the Egyptians enslaved them and they languished in serfdom until about 1250 BCE, when Yahweh brought them out of Egypt under Moses' leadership. For forty years, the Israelites wandered in the Sinai wilderness before reaching the Canaanite border, where Moses died, but his lieutenant Joshua led the Israelites to victory in the Promised Land, destroying all the Canaanite cities and killing their inhabitants.

The archaeological record, however, does not confirm this story. There is no evidence of the mass destruction described in the Book of Joshua and no indication of a powerful foreign invasion.[7] But this narrative was not written to satisfy a modern historian; it is a national epic that helped Israel create a cultural identity distinct from her neighbours. When we first hear of Israel in a non-biblical source, coastal Canaan was still a province of the Egyptian empire. A stele dating from *c.* 1201 mentions 'Israel' as one of the rebellious peoples defeated by Pharaoh Merneptah's army in the Canaanite highlands, where a network of simple villages stretched from lower Galilee in the north to Beersheba in the south. Many scholars believe that their inhabitants were the first Israelites.[8]

During the twelfth century, a crisis that had long been brewing in the Mediterranean accelerated, perhaps occasioned by sudden climate change.

We have no record of what happened to wipe out the region's empires and destroy the local economies. But by 1130 BCE, it was all over: the Hittite capital in Mitanni was in ruins, the Canaanite ports of Ugarit, Megiddo and Hazor had been destroyed; and desperate, dispossessed peoples roamed through the region. It had taken Egypt over a century to relinquish its hold over its foreign provinces. The fact that Pharaoh Merneptah himself had been forced to fight a campaign in the highlands at the turn of the century suggests that even by this early date the Egyptian governors of the Canaanite city-states were no longer able to control the countryside and needed reinforcements from home. During this lengthy, turbulent process, one city-state after another collapsed.[9] There is nothing in the archaeological record to suggest that these cities were destroyed by a single conqueror. After the Egyptians had left, there may have been conflict between the city elites and the villages, or rivalries amongst the urban nobility. But it was during this long period of decline that settlements began to appear in the highlands, pioneered perhaps by refugees fleeing the chaos of the disintegrating cities. One of the very few ways in which peasants could act to better their lot was simply to decamp when circumstances became intolerable, leave their land and become fiscal fugitives.[10] At a time of such political chaos, the Israelite peasants had a rare opportunity to make an exodus from these failing cities and establish an independent society, without fear of aristocratic retaliation. Advances in technology had only recently made it possible to settle in this difficult terrain but by the early twelfth century it seems that the highland villages already housed some 80,000 people.

If these settlers were indeed the first Israelites, some must have been native to Canaan, though they may have been joined by migrants from the south who brought Yahweh, a god of the Sinai region, with them. Others – notably the tribe of Joseph – may even have come from Egypt. But those Canaanites who had lived under Egyptian rule in the coastal city-states of Palestine would also have felt that in a very real sense they had 'come out of Egypt'. The Bible acknowledges that Israel was made up of diverse peoples bound together in a covenant agreement,[11] and its epic story suggests that the early Israelites had made a principled decision to turn their back on the oppressive agrarian state. Their houses in the highland villages were modest and uniform and there were no palaces or public buildings: this seems to have been an egalitarian society that may have reverted to tribal organisation to create a social alternative to the conventionally stratified state.[12]

* * *

The final redaction of the Pentateuch occurred after the Israelites had suffered the destruction of their own state by Nebuchadnezzar in 587 BCE and had been deported to Babylonia. The biblical epic is not simply a religious document but also an essay in political philosophy: how could a small nation retain its freedom and integrity in a world dominated by ruthless imperial powers?[13] When they defected from the Canaanite city-states, Israelites had developed an ideology that directly countered the systemic violence of the agrarian state. Israel must not be 'like the other nations'. Their hostility to 'Canaanites' was, therefore, every bit as much political as it was religious.[14] The settlers seem to have devised laws to ensure that instead of being appropriated by an aristocracy, land remained in the possession of the extended family; that interest-free loans to needy Israelites were obligatory; that wages were paid promptly; that contract servitude was restricted; and that there was special provision for the socially vulnerable – orphans, widows and foreigners.[15]

Later, Jews, Christians and Muslims would all make the biblical god a symbol of absolute transcendence, similar to Brahman or Nirvana.[16] In the Pentateuch, however, Yahweh is a war god, similar to Indra or Marduk but with one important difference. Like Indra, Yahweh had once fought chaos-dragons to order the universe, notably a sea monster called Leviathan,[17] but in the Pentateuch he fights earthly empires to establish a people rather than a cosmos. Moreover, Yahweh is the intransigent enemy of agrarian civilisation. The story of the Tower of Babel is a thinly veiled critique of Babylon.[18] Intoxicated by fantasies of world conquest, its rulers were determined that the whole of humanity should live in a single state with a common language; they believed that their ziggurat could reach heaven itself. Incensed by this imperial hubris, Yahweh reduced the entire political edifice to 'confusion' (*babel*).[19] Immediately after this incident, he ordered Abraham to leave Ur, at this date one of the most important Mesopotamian city-states.[20] Yahweh insisted that the three Patriarchs – Abraham, Isaac and Jacob – exchange the stratified tyranny of urban living for the freedom and equality of the herdsman's life. But the plan was flawed: again and again, the land that Yahweh had selected for the Patriarchs failed to sustain them.[21]

This was the Hebrew dilemma: Yahweh insisted that his people abandon the agrarian state but time and again they found that they could not live without it.[22] To escape starvation Abraham had to take temporary refuge in Egypt.[23] His son Isaac had to abandon pastoral life and take up farming during a famine but became so successful that he was attacked by predatory neighbouring kings.[24] Finally, when 'famine had grown severe throughout the world', Jacob was forced to send ten of his sons to Egypt to buy grain. To their astonishment, they met their long-lost brother Joseph in Pharaoh's court.[25]

As a boy, Joseph – Jacob's favourite son – had dreams of agrarian tyranny that he foolishly described to his brothers: 'We were binding sheaves in the countryside, and my sheaf, it seemed, stood upright; then I saw your sheaves gather round and bow to my sheaf.'[26] The brothers were so incensed that they stuttered in fury: 'Would you be king, yes, king over us?'[27] Such fantasies of monarchy violated everything the family stood for and Jacob took the boy to task: 'Are all of us, then, myself, your mother and your brothers to come and bow to the ground before you?'[28] But he continued to indulge Joseph, until, driven beyond endurance, his brothers had him sold into slavery in Egypt, telling their father he had been killed by a wild beast. Yet after a traumatic beginning, Joseph, a natural agrarian, cheerfully abandoned the pastoral ethos and assimilated to aristocratic life with spec-tacular success. He got a job in Pharaoh's court, took an Egyptian wife and even called his first son Manasseh – 'He Who Makes Me Forget', meaning 'God has made me forget . . . my entire father's house'.[29] As vizier of Egypt, Joseph saved the country from starvation: warned by a dream of impending agricultural blight, he commandeered the harvest for seven years, sending fixed rations to the cities and storing the surplus, so that when the famine struck Egypt had grain to spare.[30] But Joseph had also turned Egypt into a house of bondage because all the hard-pressed Egyptians who had been forced to sell their estates to Pharaoh in return for grain were reduced to serfdom.[31] Joseph saved the lives of his family when hunger forced them to seek refuge in Egypt, but they too would lose their freedom, since Pharaoh would forbid them to leave again.[32]

Readers of the Pentateuch are often confused by the Patriarchs' ethics. None of them are particularly admirable characters: Abraham sold his wife to Pharaoh to save his own skin; Joseph was arrogant and self-centred; and Jacob was shockingly indifferent to the rape of his daughter Dinah. But these are not morality tales. If we read them as political philosophy, things become clearer. Doomed to marginality, Israel would always be vulnerable to more powerful states. Ordered to leave civilisation yet unable to survive without it, the Patriarchs were in an impossible position. Yet despite his flaws, Abraham still compares favourably with the rulers in this story, who appropriate their subjects' wives, steal their wells, and rape their daughters with impunity.[33] While kings routinely confiscated other people's posses-sions, Abraham was always meticulously respectful of property rights. He would not even keep the booty he acquired in a raid he had fought simply to rescue his nephew Lot, who had been kidnapped by four marauding kings.[34] His kindness and hospitality to three passing strangers stands in stark contrast to the violence they experienced in civilised Sodom.[35] When Yahweh told Abraham that he planned to destroy Sodom, Abraham begged him to spare the city, because unlike rulers who had scant respect for human life, he had a horror of shedding innocent blood.[36]

When the biblical authors tell us about Jacob on his deathbed blessing his twelve sons and prophesying their future, they are asking what kind of leader is needed to create a viable egalitarian society in such a ruthless world. Jacob rejected Simeon and Levi, whose reckless violence meant that they should never control territory, populations and armies.[37] He predicted that Judah, who could admit and correct his mistakes, would make an ideal ruler.[38] But no state could survive without Joseph's political savvy so when the Israelites finally escaped from Egypt, they took Joseph's bones with them to the Promised Land. Then there were occasions when a nation might need Levi's radicalism, because without the aggressive determination of the Levite Moses, Israel would never have left Egypt.

The Book of Exodus depicts Egyptian imperialism as an extreme example of systemic oppression. The pharaohs made the Israelites' lives 'unbearable', compelling them to 'work with clay and with brick, all kinds of work in the fields; [forcing] on them every kind of labour'.[39] To stem their rising birth rate, Pharaoh even ordered the midwives to kill all Israelite male babies, but the infant Moses was rescued by Pharaoh's daughter and brought up as an Egyptian aristocrat. One day in instinctive revulsion from state tyranny, Moses, a true son of Levi, killed an Egyptian who was beating a Hebrew slave.[40] He had to flee the country, and Yahweh, who had not revealed himself to Moses the Egyptian aristocrat, first spoke to him when he was working as a shepherd in Midian.[41] During the Exodus, Yahweh could liberate Israel only by using the same brutal tactics as any imperial power, terrorising the population, slaughtering their children and drowning the entire Egyptian army. Peaceful tactics were of no avail against the martial might of the state. Yahweh divided the Sea of Reeds (Red Sea) in two so that the Israelites could cross dry shod as effortlessly as the sun god Marduk had slit Tiamat, the primal Ocean, in half to create heaven and earth, but instead of an ordered universe, he had brought a new nation into being that would provide an alternative to the aggression of imperial rule.

Yahweh sealed his pact with Israel on Mount Sinai. The earliest sources, dating from the eighth century BCE, do not mention the Ten Commandments being given to Moses on this occasion. Instead, they depict Moses and the elders of Israel experiencing a theophany on the summit of Sinai during which they 'gazed upon God' and shared a sacred meal.[42] The stone tablets that Moses received, 'written with the finger of God',[43] were probably inscribed with Yahweh's instructions for the construction and accoutrements of the tent-shrine in which he would dwell with Israel in the wilderness.[44] The Ten Commandments would be inserted into the story later by seventh-century reformers, who, as we shall see, were also responsible for some of the most violent passages in the Hebrew Bible.

After Moses' death, it fell to Joshua to conquer the Promised Land. The biblical Book of Joshua still contains some ancient material but this was radically revised by these same reformers, who interpreted it in the light of their peculiarly xenophobic theology. They give the impression that, acting under Yahweh's orders, Joshua massacred the entire population of Canaan and destroyed their cities. Yet not only is there no archaeological evidence for this wholesale destruction but the biblical text itself admits that for centuries Israelites coexisted with Canaanites, intermarried with them and that large swathes of the country remained in Canaanite hands.[45] On the basis of the reformers' work, it is often claimed that monotheism, the belief in a single god, made Israel especially prone to violence. It is assumed that its denial of other gods reveals a rabid intolerance not found in the generous pluralism of paganism.[46] But the Israelites were not mono-theists at this date and would not begin to be so until the sixth century BCE. Indeed, both the biblical and the archaeological evidence suggest that the beliefs and practices of most early Israelites differed little from those of their Canaanite neighbours.[47] There are in fact very few unequivocally monotheistic statements in the Hebrew Bible.[48] Even the first of the reformers' Ten Commandments takes the existence of rival deities for granted and simply forbids Israel to worship them: 'You are not to have any other gods before my presence.'[49]

In the earliest strand of the conquest narratives, Joshua's violence was associated with an ancient Canaanite custom called the 'ban' (herem).[50] Before a battle, a military leader would strike a deal with his god: if this deity undertook to give him the city, the commander promised to 'devote' (HRM) all valuable loot to his temple and offer the conquered people to him in a human sacrifice.[51] Joshua had made such a pact with Yahweh before attacking Jericho, and Yahweh responded by delivering the town to Israel in a spectacular miracle, causing its famous walls to collapse when the priests blew their rams' horns. Before allowing his troops to storm the city, Joshua explained the terms of the ban and stipulated that no one in the city should be spared, since everybody and everything in the town had been 'devoted' to Yahweh. Accordingly, the Israelites 'enforced the ban on everything in the town, men and women, young and old, even the oxen and sheep and donkeys, massacring them all'.[52] But the ban had been violated when one of the soldiers kept booty for himself and consequently the Israelites failed to take the town of Ai the following day. After the culprit had been found and executed, the Israelites attacked Ai again, this time successfully, setting fire to the city so that it became a sacrificial pyre and slaughtering anybody who tried to escape: 'The number of those who fell that day, men and women together, were twelve thousand, all [the] people of Ai.'[53] Finally Joshua hanged the king from a tree, built a monumental cairn over his body, and reduced the city to 'a ruin for ever more, a desolate place, even today'.[54]

Ninth-century inscriptions discovered in Jordan and southern Arabia record conquests that follow this pattern to the letter. They recount the burning of the town, the massacre of its citizens, the hanging of the ruler, and the erection of a cultic memorial claiming that the enemy had been eliminated and the town never rebuilt.[55] The ban was not, therefore, the invention of 'monotheistic' Israel but was a local pagan practice. One of these inscriptions explains that King Mesha of Moab was commanded by his god Kemosh to take Nebo from King Omri of Israel (r. 885–874 BCE). 'I seized it and killed every one . . . ,' Mesha proclaimed, 'seven thousand foreign men, native women, foreign women, concubines – for I devoted it (HRM) to destruction to Ashtur Kemosh'.[56] Israel had 'utterly perished forever'.[57] This was wishful thinking, however, because the Kingdom of Israel would survive for another 150 years. In the same vein, the biblical authors record Yahweh's decree that Jericho remain a ruin for ever, even though it would become a thriving Israelite city. New nations in the Middle East seem to have cultivated the fiction of a conquest that made the land a *tabula rasa* for them.[58] The narrative of the 'ban', therefore, was a literary trope that could not be read literally. Secular as well as religious conquerors would later develop similar fictions claiming that the territory they occupied was 'unused' and 'empty' until they took possession of it.

True to their mandate to create an alternative society, Israelites were reluctant at first to establish a regular state 'like the other nations' but seem to have lived in independent chiefdoms without a central government. If they were attacked by their neighbours, a leader or 'judge' would rise up and mobilise the entire population against an attack. This is the arrangement we find in the Book of Judges, which was also heavily revised by the seventh-century reformers. But over time, without strong rule, Israelites succumbed to moral depravity. One sentence recurs throughout the book: 'In those days there was no king in Israel, and every man did as he pleased.'[59] We read of a judge who made a human sacrifice of his own daughter;[60] a tribe that exterminated an innocent people instead of the enemy assigned them by Yahweh;[61] a group of Israelites who gang-raped a woman to death;[62] and a civil war in which the tribe of Benjamin was almost exterminated.[63] These tales are not held up for our edification; rather, they explore a political and religious quandary. Can our natural proclivity for violence be controlled in a community without a degree of coercion? It appears that the Israelites had won their freedom but lost their souls and monarchy seemed the only way to restore order. Moreover, the Philistines, who had established a kingdom on the southern coast of Canaan, had become a grave military threat to the tribes. Eventually, the Israelite elders approached their judge Samuel with a shocking request: 'Give us a king to rule over us like the other nations.'[64]

Samuel responded with a remarkable critique of agrarian oppression, which listed the regular exploitation of every pre-modern civilisation:

> These will be the rights of the king who is to reign over you. He will take your sons and assign them to his chariotry and cavalry, and they will run in front of his chariot. He will use them as leaders of a thousand and leaders of fifty; he will make them plough his ploughland and harvest his harvest and make his weapons of war and the gear for his chariots. He will also take your daughters as perfumers, cooks and bakers. He will take the best of your fields, of your vineyards and olive groves and give them to his officials. He will take the best of your manservants and maidservants, of your cattle and your donkeys, and make them work for him. He will tithe your flocks and you yourselves will become his slaves. When that day comes, you will cry out on account of the king you have chosen for yourselves, but on that day Yahweh will not answer you.[65]

Unlike most religious traditions which endorsed this system, albeit reluctantly, Israel had utterly rejected its structural violence but failed to establish a viable alternative. Despite their dreams of freedom and equity, Israelites had discovered, time and again, that they could not survive without a strong state.

Saul, Israel's first king, still ruled as judge and chieftain. But David, who deposed him, would be remembered as Israel's ideal king, even though he was clearly no paragon. The biblical authors did not express themselves as bluntly as the Chinese Legalist Lord Shang, but they probably understood that saints were not likely to be good rulers. David expanded Israelite territory on the east bank of the Jordan, united the separate regions of Israel in the north and Judah in the south, and conquered the Hittite-Jebusite city-state of Jerusalem, which became the capital of his united kingdom. There was no question of putting the Jebusites 'under the ban', however: David adopted the existing Jebusite administration, employed Jebusites in his bureaucracy, and took over the Jebusite standing army – a pragmatism that may have been more typical of Israel than Joshua's alleged zealotry. David probably did not set up a regular tributary system, however, but taxed only the conquered populations and supplemented his income with booty.[66]

In this young, hopeful kingdom we find a heroic ethos that has nothing 'religious' about it.[67] We see it first in the famous account of the young David's duel with the Philistine giant Goliath. Single combat was one of the hallmarks of chivalric war.[68] It gave the warrior a chance to show off his martial skills and both armies enjoyed watching the clash of champions. Moreover, in Israel's chivalric ethos, warriors formed a caste of champions, respected for their valour and expertise even if they were fighting for the enemy.[69] Every morning, Goliath would appear before the Israelite lines, challenging one of them to fight him, and when nobody came forward, he taunted them for their cowardice. One day, the shepherd boy David, armed only with a sling, called Goliath's bluff, knocked him out with a pebble, and decapitated him. But the heroic champion could also be utterly ruthless in battle. When David's army arrived outside the walls of Jerusalem, the Jebusites taunted him: 'You will not get in here. The blind and lame will hold you off.'[70] So in their hearing David ordered his men to kill *only* 'the blind and lame', a ruthlessness designed to terrify the enemy. The biblical text here is fragmentary and obscure, however, and may have been edited by a redactor who was uncomfortable with this story. One later tradition even claimed that David was forbidden by Yahweh to build a temple in Jerusalem, 'since you have shed so much blood on the earth in my presence'. That honour would be reserved for David's son and successor Solomon, whose name was said to derive from the Hebrew *shalom,* 'peace'.[71] But Solomon's mother, Bathsheba, was a Jebusite and his name could also have derived from Shalem, the ancient deity of Jerusalem.[72]

Solomon's temple was built on the regional model and its furniture showed how thoroughly the cult of Yahweh had accommodated itself to the pagan landscape of the Near East. There was clearly no sectarian intolerance in Israelite Jerusalem. At the temple's entrance were two Canaanite standing stones (*matzevoth*) and a massive bronze basin, representing Yam, the sea monster fought by Baal, supported by twelve brazen oxen, common symbols of divinity and fertility.[73] The temple rituals too seem to have been influenced by Baal's cult in neighbouring Ugarit.[74] The temple was supposed to symbolise Yahweh's approval of Solomon's rule.[75] There is no reference to his short-lived empire in other sources, but the biblical authors tell us that it extended from the Euphrates to the Mediterranean and was achieved and maintained by force of arms. Solomon had replaced David's infantry with a chariot-army, engaged in lucrative arms deals with neighbouring kings, and restored the ancient fortresses of Hazor, Megiddo and Arad.[76] In purely material terms, everything seemed perfect: 'Judah and Israel lived in security: each man under his vine and fig tree!'[77] But this kind of state, maintained by war and taxes, was exactly what Yahweh had always abhorred. Unlike David, Solomon even taxed his Israelite subjects and his building projects required massive forced labour.[78] As well as farming their own plots to produce the surplus that supported the state, peasants also had to serve in the army or the corvée for one month in every three.[79]

Some biblical redactors tried to argue that Solomon's empire failed because he had built shrines for the pagan gods of his foreign wives.[80] But it is clear that the real problem was its structural violence, which offended deep-rooted Israelite principles. After Solomon's death a delegation begged his son Rehoboam not to replicate his father's 'harsh tyranny'.[81] When Rehoboam contemptuously refused, a mob attacked the manager of the corvée and ten of the twelve tribes broke away from the empire to form the independent Kingdom of Israel.[82]

Henceforth the two kingdoms went their separate ways. Situated near important trade routes, the northern Kingdom of Israel prospered, with royal shrines in Bethel and Dan and an elegant capital in Samaria. We know very little about its ideology, because the biblical editors favoured the smaller and more isolated Kingdom of Jerusalem. But both probably conformed to local traditions. Like most Middle Eastern kings, the king of Judah was raised to a semi-divine 'state of exception' during the coronation ritual, when he became Yahweh's adopted son and a member of the Divine Assembly of gods.[83] Like Baal, Yahweh was celebrated as a warrior god who defended his people from their enemies: 'When he grows angry he shatters kings, he gives the nations their deserts; smashing their skulls, he heaps the world with corpses.'[84] The chief responsibility of the king was to secure and extend his territory, the source of the kingdom's revenues. He was, therefore, in a perpetual state of conflict with neighbouring monarchs, who had exactly the same goals. Israel and Judah were thus drawn inexorably into the local network of trade, diplomacy and warfare.

The two kingdoms had emerged when the imperial powers of the region were in eclipse, but during the early eighth century Assyria was in the ascendant again, its military might forcing weaker kings into vassal status. Yet some of these conquered kingdoms flourished. King Jeroboam (786–46 BCE) became a trusted Assyrian vassal and the Kingdom of Israel enjoyed an economic boom. But because the rich became richer and the poor even more impoverished, the king was castigated by the prophet Amos.[85] The prophets of Israel kept the old egalitarian ideals of Israel alive. Amos chastised the aristocracy for trampling on the heads of ordinary people, pushing the poor out of their path,[86] and cramming their palaces with the fruits of their extortion.[87] Yahweh, he warned, was no longer unconditionally on Israel's side, but would use Assyria as his instrument of punishment.[88] The Assyrians would invade the kingdom, loot and destroy its palaces and temples.[89] Amos imagined Yahweh roaring in rage from his sanctuary at the war crimes committed by the local kingdoms, Israel included.[90] In Judah too, the prophet Isaiah inveighed against the exploitation of the poor and the expropriation of peasant land: 'Cease to do evil. Learn to do good, search for justice, help the oppressed, be just to the orphan, and plead for the widow.'[91] But the dilemma was that this ruthlessness was essential to the agrarian economy, and had the kings of Israel and Judah fully implemented these compassionate policies, they would have been easy prey for Assyria.[92]

In 745 King Tiglath-Pileser III abolished the system of vassalage and incorporated all the conquered peoples directly into the Assyrian state. At the merest hint of dissent, the entire ruling class would be deported and replaced by people from other parts of his empire. The army left a trail of destruction in its wake and the countryside was deserted as peasants took refuge in the towns. When King Hosea refused to pay tribute in 722, Shalmaneser III simply wiped the Kingdom of Israel off the map and deported its aristocracy. Because of its isolated position, Judah survived until the turn of the century, when Sennacherib's army besieged Jerusalem. The Assyrian army was finally forced to withdraw, possibly because it was smitten by disease, but Lachish, Judah's second city, was razed to the ground and the countryside devastated.[93] King Manasseh (687–42 BCE) was determined to keep on the right side of Assyria, and Judah enjoyed peace and prosperity during his long reign.[94] Manasseh rebuilt rural shrines to Baal and brought an effigy of Asherah, the Canaanite Mother Goddess, into Yahweh's temple; he also set up statues of the divine horses of the sun in the temple, which may have been emblems of Ashur.[95] Few of Manasseh's subjects objected since, as archaeologists have discovered, many of them had similar effigies in their own homes.[96]

During the reign of Manasseh's grandson Josiah (640–609 BCE), however, a group of prophets, priests and scribes attempted a far-reaching reform. By this time, Assyria was in decline: Pharaoh Psammetichus had forced the Assyrian army to withdraw from the Levant and Josiah technically became his vassal. But Egypt was occupied elsewhere and Judah enjoyed a brief period of de facto independence. In 622, Josiah began extensive repairs on Solomon's temple, emblem of Judah's golden age, perhaps as an assertion of national pride. But Judaeans could not forget the fate of the Kingdom of Israel. Surrounded by huge predatory empires, with Babylon now becoming the dominant power in Mesopotamia, how could Judah hope to survive? Fear of annihilation and the experience of state violence often radicalise a religious tradition. Zoroaster had been a victim of excessive aggression, and this had introduced an apocalyptic violence into his initially peaceable alternative to the belligerent cult of Indra. Now in seventh-century Judah, reformers who dreamed of independence but were terrified by the aggression of the great imperial powers brought a wholly new intransigence into the cult of Yahweh.[97]

During the construction work in the temple, the high priest, one of the leading reformers, made a momentous discovery: 'I have found the book of the law (*sefer torah*) in the temple of Yahweh,' he announced.[98] Until this point, there was no tradition of a written text given on Mount Sinai; in fact, until the eighth century reading and writing had little place in the religious life of Israel, so in the early biblical traditions Moses imparted Yahweh's teachings orally.[99] But the reformers claimed that the scroll they had discovered had been dictated to Moses by Yahweh himself.[100] Tragically, this precious document had been lost, but now that they had recovered this 'second law' (Greek: *deuteronomion*) that supplemented Yahweh's verbal teaching on Mount Sinai, the people of Judah could make a new start and, perhaps, save their nation from total destruction. So authoritative was the past in an agrarian state that it was quite customary for people who were promoting an innovative idea to attribute it to an iconic historical figure. The reformers believed that at this time of grave danger they were speaking for Moses and put forward their own teachings in the speech they make Moses deliver, shortly before his death, in the Book of Deuteronomy.

For the very first time, these reformers insisted that Yahweh demanded exclusive devotion. 'Listen, Israel,' Moses tells his people, 'Yahweh is our god, Yahweh alone!'[101] He had not only emphatically forbidden Israelites to worship any other god but had also commanded them to wipe out the indigenous peoples of the Promised Land:

> You must lay them under ban. You must make no covenant with them nor show them any pity. You must not marry with them . . . for this would turn away your son from following me to serving other gods and the anger of Yahweh would blaze out against you and soon destroy you. Instead, deal with them like this: tear down their altars, smash their standing-stones, cut down their sacred poles and set fire to their idols.[102]

Because they had lost this 'second law' recorded by Moses, Israelites had been ignorant of his command; they had condoned the cult of other gods, married Canaanites and made treaties with them. No wonder Yahweh's anger had 'blazed out' against the northern Kingdom of Israel. Moses, the reformers insisted, had warned the Israelites what would happen. 'Yahweh will scatter you among the peoples, from one end of the earth to the other . . . In the morning you will say, "how I wish it were evening!" and in the evening, "how I wish it were morning!" Such terror will grip your heart, such sights your eyes will see.'[103] When the scroll was read aloud to Josiah, its teachings were so startling that the king burst into tears, crying: 'Great indeed must be the anger of Yahweh, blazing out against us.'[104]

It is difficult for us today to realise how strange this insistence on cultic exclusivity would have been in the seventh century BCE. Our reading of the Hebrew Bible has been influenced by 2,500 years of monotheistic teaching. But Josiah, of course, had never heard of the First Commandment – 'Thou shalt not have strange gods before my presence' – which the reformers would place at the top of the Decalogue. It pointedly condemned Manasseh's introduction of the effigies of 'strange gods' into the temple where Yahweh's 'presence' (shechinah) was enthroned in the Holy of Holies. But pagan icons had been perfectly acceptable there since Solomon's time. Despite the campaigns of such prophets as Elijah, who had urged the people to worship Yahweh alone, most of the population of the two kingdoms had never doubted the efficacy of such gods as Baal, Anat or Asherah. The prophet Hosea's oracles showed how popular the cult of Baal had been in the Northern Kingdom during the eighth century and the reformers themselves knew that Israelites 'offered sacrifice to Baal, to the sun, the moon, the constellations and the whole array of heaven'.[105] There would be great resistance to monotheism. Thirty years after Josiah's death, Israelites were still devotees of the Mesopotamian goddess Ishtar and Yahweh's temple was once again full of 'the idols of the house of Israel'.[106] For many it seemed unnatural and perverse to ignore such a divine resource. The reformers knew that they were asking Judaeans to relinquish beloved and familiar sanctities and embark on a lonely, painful severance from the mythical and cultural consciousness of the Middle East.

Josiah was completely convinced by the sefer torah and at once inaugurated a violent orgy of destruction, eradicating the cultic paraphernalia introduced by Manasseh, burning the effigies of Baal and Asherah, abolishing the rural shrines, pulling down the house of sacred male prostitutes and destroying the Assyrian horses. In the old territories of the Kingdom of Israel he was even more ruthless, not only demolishing the ancient temples of Yahweh in Bethel and Samaria, but slaughtering the priests of the rural shrines and contaminating their altars.[107] This fanatical aggression was a new and tragic development, which excoriated sacred symbols that had been central to both the temple cult and the piety of individual Israelites.[108] A religious tradition often develops a violent strain in a symbiotic relationship with excessive state coercion. The reformers now regarded the Canaanite cults that Israelites had long enjoyed as 'detestable' and 'loathsome'; they insisted that any Israelite who participated in them must be hunted down mercilessly.[109] 'You must not give way to him, nor listen to him, you must show him no pity,' Moses had commanded. 'You must not spare him, and you must not conceal his guilt. No, you must kill him.'[110] An Israelite town guilty of this idolatry must be put under the 'ban', burned to the ground and its inhabitants slaughtered.[111]

But this was all so novel that in order to justify these innovations, the reformers had literally to rewrite history. They began a massive editorial revision of the texts in the royal archives that would one day become the Hebrew Bible, changing the wording and import of earlier law codes and introducing new legislation that endorsed their proposals. They recast the history of Israel, adding fresh material to the older narratives of the Pentateuch and giving Moses a prominence that he may not have had in some of the earlier traditions. The climax of the Exodus story was no longer a theophany but the gift of the Ten Commandments and the sefer torah. Drawing on earlier sagas, now lost to us, the reformers put together a history of the two kingdoms of Israel and Judah, which became the books of Joshua, Judges, Samuel and Kings, 'proving' that the idolatrous iniquity of the Northern Kingdom had been the cause of its destruction. When they described Joshua's conquests, they depicted him slaughtering the local population of the Promised Land and devastating their cities like an Assyrian general. They transformed the ancient myth of the ban so that it became an expression of God's justice and a literal rather than a fictional story of attempted genocide. Their history culminated in the reign of Josiah, the new Moses who would liberate Israel from Pharaoh once again, a king who was even greater than David.[112] This strident theology left an indelible trace on the Hebrew Bible; many of the writings so frequently quoted to prove the ineradicable aggression and intolerance of 'monotheism' were either composed or recast by these reformers.

Yet the Deuteronomist reform was never implemented. Josiah's bid for independence ended in 609 when he was killed in a skirmish with Pharaoh Neco. The new Babylonian empire replaced Assyria and competed with Egypt for the control of the Middle East. For a few years, Judah dodged between these great powers but eventually, after an uprising in 597, Nebuchadnezzar, king of Babylon, deported eight thousand Judaean aristocrats, soldiers and skilled artisans.[113] Ten years later, he destroyed the temple, razed Jerusalem to the ground and deported five thousand more Judaeans, leaving only the lower classes in the devastated land. In Babylonia the Judaean exiles were reasonably well treated. Some lived in the capital; others were housed in undeveloped areas near the new canals and could, to an extent, manage their own affairs.[114] But exile is a spiritual as well as a physical dislocation. In Judah, the deportees had been the elite class; now they had no political rights and some even had to work in the corvée.[115] But then, it seemed that Yahweh was about to liberate his people again. This time the exodus would not be led by a prophet but instigated by a new imperial power.

In 559 BCE, Cyrus, a minor member of the Persian Achaemenid family, became king of Anshan in what is now southern Iran.[116] Twenty years later, after a series of spectacular victories in Media, Anatolia and Asia Minor, he invaded the Babylonian empire and, astonishingly, without fighting a single battle, was greeted by the population as a liberator. Cyrus was now the master of the largest empire the world had yet seen. At its fullest extent, it would control the whole of the eastern Mediterranean, from what are now Libya and Turkey in the west to Afghanistan in the east. For centuries to come, any king who aspired to world rule would try to replicate Cyrus' achievement.[117] But he was not only a pivotal figure in the politics of the region: he also modelled a more benign form of empire.

According to Cyrus' victory proclamation, when he arrived in Babylonia, 'All the people . . . of Sumer and Akkad, nobles and governors, bowed down before him and kissed his feet, rejoicing over his kingship, and their faces shone'.[118] Why such enthusiasm for a foreign invader? Ten years earlier, shortly after Cyrus had conquered Media, the Babylonian author of the poem 'The Dream of Nabonidus' had given him a divine role.[119] Media had been a threat to Babylon, and the sun god Marduk, the poet claimed, had appeared in a dream to Nabonidus (r. 556–39), the last Babylonian king, to assure him that he was still controlling events and had chosen Cyrus to solve the Median problem. But ten years later, the Babylonian empire was in decline. Nabonidus, engaged in conquests abroad, had been absent from Babylon for several years and had incurred the wrath of the priesthood by failing to perform the Akitu ritual. During this ceremony all Babylonian kings had to swear not 'to rain blows on the cheeks of the protected citizen', but Nabonidus had imposed forced labour on the freemen of the empire. Disaffected priests announced that the gods had abrogated his rule and abandoned the city. When Cyrus marched on Babylonia, these priests almost certainly helped him to write his victory speech, which explained that when the people of Babylon had cried out in anguish to Marduk, the god had chosen Cyrus as their champion:

> He took the hand of Cyrus, king of the city of Anshan, and called him by name, proclaiming him aloud for the kingship over all of everything . . . He ordered that he should go to Babylon. He had him take the road to [Babylon], and, like a friend and companion, he walked at his side . . . He had him enter without fighting or battle, right into Shuanna; he saved his city Babylon from hardship. He handed over to him Nabonidus, the king who did not fear him.[120]

Ritual and mythology, crucial as they were to kingship, did not always endorse state tyranny. Nabonidus was in effect deposed by the priestly establishment for his excessive violence and oppression.

Cyrus' vast multilingual and multicultural empire needed a different mode of government, one that respected the traditional rights of the conquered peoples and their religious and cultural traditions. Instead of humiliating and deporting his new subjects, tearing down their temples and desecrating the effigies of their gods as the Assyrians and Babylonians had done, Cyrus announced a wholly new policy, preserved in the Cyrus Cylinder, now in the British Museum. Cyrus, it claimed, had arrived in Babylonia as the harbinger of peace rather than war; he had abolished the corvée, repatriated all the peoples who had been deported by Nebuchadnezzar, and promised to rebuild their national temples. An anonymous Judaean exile in Babylonia therefore hailed Cyrus as the *messhiah,* the man 'anointed' by Yahweh to end Israel's exile.[121] But this prophet, of course, was convinced that it was not Marduk but Yahweh who had taken Cyrus by the hand and shattered the bronze gates of Babylon: 'It is for the sake of my servant Jacob, of Israel, my chosen one, that I have called you by your name, conferring a title, though you do not know me,' Yahweh had told Cyrus.[122] A new era was at hand in which the earth would be restored to its primal perfection: 'Let every valley be filled in, every mountain laid low,' cried the prophet, clearly influenced by the Zoroastrian traditions of his Persian messiah, 'let every cliff become a plain, and the ridges a valley.'[123]

Most of the Judaean exiles chose to stay in Babylonia and many acculturated successfully.[124] According to the Bible, more than forty thousand of them chose to return to Judaea with the liturgical utensils confiscated by Nebuchadnezzar, determined to rebuild Yahweh's temple in the devastated city of Jerusalem. The Persians' decision to allow the deportees to return home and rebuild their temples was enlightened and sensible: they believed it would strengthen their empire, since gods ought to be worshipped in their own countries, and it would win the gratitude of the subject peoples. As a result of this benign policy, the Middle East enjoyed a period of relative stability for some two hundred years.

But the Pax Persiana still depended on military force and taxes extorted from the subject races. Cyrus made a point of mentioning the unparalleled might of his army; as he and Marduk marched on Babylon, 'his vast troops whose number, like the water in the river, could not be counted, were marching fully-armed at his side'.[125] His victory proclamation also noted the tributary system that Cyrus had enforced: at Marduk's 'exalted command, all kings who sit on thrones, from every quarter, from the Upper Sea to the Lower Sea, those who inhabit remote districts and the kings of the land of Amurru who live in tents, all of them, brought their weighty tribute into Shuanna and kissed my feet.'[126] Even the most peaceable empire required sustained military aggression and massive expropriation of resources from the populations it conquered. If imperial officials and soldiers felt any moral qualms about this, it would sap the empire's energy; but if they could be persuaded that these policies would ultimately benefit everyone, they would find them more palatable.[127]

In the inscriptions of Darius I, who came to the Persian throne after the death of Cyrus' son Cambyses in 522, we find a combination of three themes that would recur in the ideology of all successful empires: a dualistic worldview that pits the good of empire against evildoers who oppose it; a doctrine of election that sees the ruler as a divine agent; and a mission to save the world.[128] Darius' political philosophy was strongly influenced by Zoroastrianism, which he had skilfully adapted to sacralise the imperial project.[129] A large number of the royal inscriptions that have survived in the Persian heartland of the empire referred to the Zoroastrian creation myth.[130] They describe Ahura Mazda, the Wise Lord who had appeared to Zoroaster, ordering the cosmos in four stages, creating successively earth, sky, humanity and, finally, 'happiness' (*shiyati*), which consisted of peace, security, truth and abundant food.[131] At first there had been only one ruler, one people and one language.[132] But after the assault of the Hostile Spirit ('the Lie'), humanity split into competing groups, governed by people who called themselves kings. There was war, bloodshed and disorder for centuries. Then, on 29 September 522 BCE, Darius ascended the throne and the Wise Lord inaugurated the fifth and final stage of creation: Darius would unite the world and restore the original happiness of mankind by creating a worldwide empire.[133]

Here we see the difficulty of adapting a predominantly peaceful tradition to the realities of imperial rule. Darius shared Zoroaster's horror of lawless violence. After Cambyses' death, he had had to suppress rebellions all over the empire. Like any emperor, he had to quash ambitious aristocrats who sought to unseat him. In his inscriptions, Darius associated these rebels with the illegitimate kings who had brought war and suffering to the world after the Lie's assault. But to restore peace and happiness, the 'fighting men' whom Zoroaster had wanted to exclude from society were indispensable. The apocalyptic restoration of the world that Zoroaster had predicted at the end of time had been transposed to the present and Zoroastrian dualism was employed to divide the political world into warring camps. The empire's structural and martial violence had become the final, absolute good while everything beyond its borders was barbaric, chaotic and immoral.[134] Darius' mission was to subdue the rest of the world and purloin its resources in order to make other people 'good'. Once all lands had been subjugated, there would be universal peace and an era of *frasha*, 'wonder'.[135]

Darius' inscriptions remind us that a religious tradition is never a single, unchanging essence that impels people to act in a uniform way. It is a template that can be modified and altered radically to serve a variety of ends. For Darius, *frasha* was no longer spiritual harmony but material wealth; he described his palace in Susa as *frasha*, a foretaste of the redeemed, reunited world.[136] Inscriptions listed the gold, silver, precious woods, ivory and marble brought in tribute from every region of the empire, explaining that after the Lie's assault, these riches had been scattered all over the world but had now been reassembled in one place, as the Wise Lord had originally intended. The magnificent Apadama relief in Persepolis depicted a procession of the delegates of conquered peoples from far-flung lands duly bringing their tribute to Susa. The ethical vision of Zoroaster, victim of violence and theft on the Caucasian steppes, had been inspired by the shocking aggression of the Sanskrit raiders; now that vision had been used to sacralise organised martial violence and imperial extortion.

The Judaeans who returned from Babylon in 539 found their homeland a desolate place and had to contend with the hostility of the foreigners who had been drafted into the country by the Babylonians. They also faced the resentment of those Judaeans who had not been deported and were now strangers to the returnees who had been born into an entirely different culture. When they finally rebuilt their temple, Persian Judaea became a temple-state governed by a Jewish priestly aristocracy in the name of Persia. The writings of these priestly aristocrats have been preserved in parts of the Pentateuch and the two books of Chronicles, which rewrote the strident history of the Deuteronomists and attempted to adapt ancient Israelite traditions to the new circumstances.[137] These scriptures reflect the exiles' concern that everything stay in its proper place. In Babylon the Judaeans had preserved their national identity by living apart from the local people; now the priests insisted that to be 'holy' (*qaddosh*) was to be 'separate; other'.

Yet unlike the Deuteronomist scriptures, which had demonised the foreigner and yearned to eliminate him, these priestly texts, drawing on exactly the same stories and legends, had developed a remarkably inclusive vision. Again, we see the impossibility of describing any religious tradition as a single, unchanging essence that will always inspire violence. The priests insisted that the 'otherness' of every single creature was sacred and must be respected and honoured. In the priestly Law of Freedom, therefore, nothing could be enslaved or owned, not even the land.[138] Instead of seeking to exterminate the *ger,* the 'resident alien', as the Deuteronomists had insisted, the true Israelite must learn to love him: 'If a stranger lives with you in your land do not molest him. You must treat him as one of your own people and love him as yourselves. For you were strangers in Egypt.'[139] These priests had arrived at the Golden Rule: the experience of living as a minority in Egypt and Babylonia should teach Israelites to appreciate the pain that these uprooted foreigners might be feeling in Judah. The command to 'love' was not about sentiment: *hesed* meant 'loyalty' and was used in Middle Eastern treaties when former enemies agreed to be helpful, trustworthy and give each other practical support.[140] This was not an unrealistically utopian ideal but an ethic within everybody's reach.

To temper the harsh rejectionism of the Deuteronomists, the priestly historians included moving stories of reconciliation. The estranged brothers Jacob and Esau finally see the 'face of God' in each other.[141] The Chroniclers show Moses refraining from retaliation when the king of Edom refused to grant the Israelites safe passage through his territory during their journey to the Promised Land.[142] The most famous of these priestly writings is the creation story that opens the Hebrew Bible. The biblical redactors placed this priestly creation story before the earlier eighth-century tale of Yahweh creating a garden for Adam and Eve and their fall from grace. This priestly version extracted all the violence from the traditional Middle Eastern cosmogony. Instead of fighting a battle and slaying a monster, the God of Israel simply uttered words of command when he ordered the cosmos. On the last day of creation, he 'saw everything that he had made, and indeed it was very good'.[143] This god had no enemies: he blessed every single one of his creatures, even his old enemy Leviathan.

This principled benevolence is all the more remarkable when we consider that the community of exiles was under almost constant attack by hostile groups in Judea. When Nehemiah, dispatched from the Persian court to supervise the rebuilding of Jerusalem, was overseeing the restoration of the city wall, each of the labourers 'did his work with one hand while gripping his weapon with the other'.[144] The priestly writers could not afford to be anti-war but they seem troubled by military violence. They deleted some of the most belligerent episodes in the Deuteronomist history and brushed over Joshua's conquests. They told the stories of David's chivalric warfare but omitted his grim order to kill the blind and lame in Jerusalem, and it was the Chronicler who explained that David was forbidden to build the temple because he had shed too much blood. They also recorded a story about a military campaign against the Midianites, who had enticed the Israelites into idolatry.[145] There was no doubt that it was a just cause and the Israelite armies behaved in perfect accordance with Deuteronomist law: the priests led the troops into battle, the soldiers killed the Midianite kings, set fire to their town, and condemned to death both the married women who had tempted the Israelites and the boys who would grow up to be warriors. But even though they had 'cleansed' Israel, they had been tainted by this righteous bloodshed. 'You must camp for seven days outside the camp,' Moses told the returning warriors: 'Purify yourselves, you and your prisoners.'[146]

In one remarkable story, the Chronicler condemned the savagery of the Kingdom of Israel in a war against an idolatrous Judaean king, even though Yahweh himself had sanctioned the campaign. Israelite troops had killed 120,000 Judaean soldiers and marched 200,000 Judaean prisoners back to Samaria in triumph. But the prophet Oded greeted these conquering heroes with a blistering rebuke:

> You have slaughtered with such fury as reaches to heaven. And now you propose to reduce these children of Judah and Jerusalem to being your serving men and women! And are you not all the while the ones who are guilty before Yahweh your God? Now listen to me – release the prisoners you have taken of your brothers, for the fierce anger of Yahweh hangs over you.[147]

The troops immediately released the captives, relinquished all their booty, and specially appointed officials 'saw to the relief of the prisoners. From the booty, they clothed all those of them who were naked; they gave them clothing and sandals, and provided them with food, drink and shelter. They mounted all those who were infirm on donkeys, and took them back to their kinsmen in Jericho.'[148] These priests were probably monotheists; in Babylonia, paganism had lost its allure for the exiles. The prophet who had hailed Cyrus as the messiah also uttered the first fully monotheistic statement in the Bible: 'Am I not Yahweh?' he makes the God of Israel demand repeatedly: 'There is no other god beside me.'[149] But the monotheism of these priests had not made them intolerant, bloodthirsty or cruel; rather, the reverse is true.

But other post-exilic prophets were more aggressive. Inspired by Darius' ideology, they looked forward to a 'day of wonder' when Yahweh would rule the entire world and there would be no mercy for nations who resisted: 'Their flesh will moulder while they are still standing on their feet; their eyes will rot in their sockets; their tongues will rot in their mouths.'[150] They imagined Israel's former enemies processing meekly each year to Jerusalem, the new Susa, bearing rich gifts and tribute.[151] Others had fantasies of the Israelites who had been deported by Assyria being carried tenderly home,[152] while their former oppressors prostrated themselves before them and kissed their feet.[153] One prophet had a vision of Yahweh's glory shining over Jerusalem, the centre of a redeemed world and a haven of peace – yet a peace achieved only by ruthless repression.

These prophets may have been inspired by the new 'monotheism'. It seems that a strong monarchy often generates the cult of a supreme deity, creator of the political and natural order. A century or more of experiencing the strong rule of such monarchs as Nebuchadnezzar or Darius may have led to the desire to make Yahweh as powerful as they. It is a fine example of the 'embeddedness' of religion and politics, which works two ways: not only does religion affect policy but politics can shape theology. But these prophets were also surely motivated by that all too human desire to see their enemies suffer as they had – an impulse that the Golden Rule had been designed to modify. They would not be the last to adapt the aggressive ideology of the ruling power to their own traditions and in so doing distort them. In this case, Yahweh, originally the fierce opponent of the violence and cruelty of empire, had been transformed into an arch-imperialist.

PART TWO

Keeping the Peace

5

JESUS: NOT OF THIS WORLD?

Jesus of Nazareth was born in the reign of the Roman emperor Caesar Augustus (r. 30 BCE–14 CE) when all the world was at peace.[1] Under Roman rule, a large group of nations, some of them former imperial powers, was able for a significant period to coexist without fighting each other for resources and territory – a remarkable achievement.[2] Romans made the three claims that characterise any successful imperial ideology: they had been specially blessed by the gods; in their dualist vision all other peoples were 'barbarians' with whom it was impossible to deal on equal terms; and their mission was to bring the benefits of civilisation and peace to the rest of the world. But the Pax Romana was enforced pitilessly.[3] Rome's fully professional army became the most efficient killing-machine the world had ever seen.[4] Any resistance at all justified wholesale massacre.[5] When they took a city, said the Greek historian Polybius, their policy was 'to kill everyone they met and spare no one' – not even the animals.[6] After the Roman conquest of Britain, the Scottish leader Calgacus reported that the island had become a wasteland: 'The uttermost parts of Britain are laid bare; there are no other tribes to come; nothing but sea and cliffs and more deadly Romans . . . To plunder, butcher and ravage – these things they falsely name empire.'[7]

Polybius understood that the purpose of this savagery was 'to strike terror' into the subject nations.[8] It usually worked, but it took the Romans nearly two hundred years to tame the Jews of Palestine, who had ousted an imperial power before and believed they could do it again. After Alexander the Great had defeated the Persian empire in 333 BCE, Judaea had been absorbed into the Ptolemid and Seleucid empires of his 'successors' (*diadochoi*). Most of these rulers did not interfere in the personal lives of their subjects. But in 175 BCE the Seleucid emperor Antiochus IV attempted a drastic reform of the temple cult and banned Jewish dietary laws, circumcision and Sabbath observance. The Hasmonean priestly family, led by Judas

Maccabeus, had led a rebellion and managed not only to wrest Judaea and
Jerusalem from Seleucid control, but even to establish a small empire by
conquering Idumaea, Samaria and Galilee.[9]

These events inspired a new apocalyptic spirituality without which it is
impossible to understand the early Christian movement. Crucial to this
mindset was the perennial philosophy: events on earth were an *apokalupsis,*
an 'unveiling' that revealed what was simultaneously happening in the
heavenly world. As they struggled to make sense of current events, the
authors of these new scriptures believed that while the Maccabees were
fighting the Seleucids, Michael and his angels were battling the demonic
powers that supported Antiochus.[10] The Book of Daniel, a historical novella
composed during the Maccabean wars, was set in Babylonia during the
Jewish exile. At its centre was the Judaean prophet Daniel's vision of four
terrifying beasts, representing the empires of Assyria, Babylon, Persia and,
finally, Antiochus' Seleucid empire, the most destructive of all. But then,
'coming on the clouds of heaven', Daniel saw 'one like the son of man'
representing the Maccabees. Unlike the four bestial empires, his rule would
be just and humane and God would give him 'an eternal sovereignty which
shall never pass away'.[11]

But once they had achieved imperial rule, alas, the Hasmoneans' piety
was unable to sustain the brute realities of political dominance and they
became as cruel and tyrannical as the Seleucids. At the end of the second
century BCE, a number of new sects sought a more authentically Jewish
alternative; Christianity would later share some of their enthusiasms. To
initiate their disciples, all these sects set up the systems of instruction that
became the closest thing to an educational establishment in Jewish society.
Both the Qumran sect and the Essenes – two distinct groups that are often
erroneously identified – were attracted to an ethical community life: meals
were eaten together, ritual purity and cleanliness were stressed, and goods
held in common. Both were critical of the Jerusalem temple cult, which,
they believed, the Hasmoneans had corrupted. Indeed, the Qumran
commune beside the Dead Sea regarded itself as an alternative temple: on
the cosmic plane the children of light would soon defeat the sons of darkness, and God would build another temple and inaugurate a new world
order. The Pharisees were also committed to an exact and punctilious
observance of the biblical law. We know very little about them at this date,
however, even though they would become the most influential of these new
groups. Some Pharisees led armed revolts against the Hasmoneans but finally
concluded that the people would be better off under foreign rule. In 64

BCE, therefore, the Hasmonean excesses having become intolerable, the Pharisees sent a delegation to Rome requesting that the empire depose the regime.

The following year, the Roman general Pompey invaded Jerusalem, killing 12,000 Jews and enslaving thousands more. Not surprisingly, most Jews hated Roman rule but no empire can survive unless it is able to co-opt at least some of the local population. The Romans ruled Palestine through the priestly aristocracy in Jerusalem but they also created a puppet king: Herod, a prince of Idumaea and a recent convert to Judaism. Herod built magnificent fortifications, palaces and theatres throughout the country in the Hellenistic style and on the coast constructed Caesarea, an entirely new city, in honour of Augustus. His masterpiece, however, was a magnificent new temple for Yahweh in Jerusalem, flanked significantly by the Antonia fortress, manned by Roman troops. A cruel ruler, with his own army and secret police, Herod was extremely unpopular. The Jews of Palestine were, therefore, ruled by two aristocracies: the Herodians and the Sadducees, the Jewish priestly nobility. Both collected taxes, so Jews bore a double tax burden.[12]

Like all agrarian ruling classes, both aristocracies employed an order of dependent retainers, who in return for extending their masters' influence among the common people enjoyed higher social status and a share in the surplus.[13] They included the publicans or tax-farmers, who in the Roman empire were obliged to pass on a fixed sum to the colonial government but were allowed to retain the difference between that and what they managed to extort from the peasants. As a result, they gained a certain independence, but, as is apparent in the Gospels, they were hated by the common people.[14] The 'scribes and Pharisees' of the Gospels were another group of retainers who interpreted the Torah, Jewish custumal law, in a way that supported the regime.[15] Not all Pharisees assumed this role, however. Most concentrated on the stringent observance of the Torah and the development of what would become rabbinic exegesis, and did not ally themselves too closely with the nobility. Had they done so, they would not have retained their popularity with the people. Indeed, so great was the esteem in which they were held that any Jew who hoped for a political career had to study civil law with the Pharisees. Josephus, the first-century CE Jewish historian, for example, probably became a disciple of the Pharisees to acquire the legal education that qualified him for public life, although he may never have become a full member of the sect.[16]

Once colonised, a people often depends heavily on its religious practices,

over which it still has some control and which recall a time when it had
the dignity of freedom. In the Jewish case, hostility towards their rulers
tended to reach new heights during the important temple festivals which
spoke explosively to the Jews' political subjugation: Passover commemorated
Israel's liberation from Egypt's imperial control; Pentecost celebrated the
revelation of the Torah, a divine law that superseded all imperial edicts; and
the harvest festival of Weeks was a reminder that the land and its produce
belonged to Yahweh, not the Romans. This simmering discontent erupted
in 4 BCE when Herod was on his deathbed. He had recently installed in
the temple a large golden eagle, symbol of imperial Rome, and Judas and
Matthias, two of the most respected Torah teachers, denounced it as an
offensive challenge to Yahweh's kingship.[17] In a well-planned protest, forty
of their students climbed on to the temple roof, hacked the eagle to pieces
and then 'courageously awaited the attack' of Herod's soldiers.[18] Galvanised
by fury, Herod rose from his bed and sentenced the students and their
teachers to death, before dying in agony himself two days later.[19]

It is important to note that most of the protests against imperial rule in
Roman Palestine were nonviolent; far from being fanatically driven to
suicidal aggression by their faith, as Josephus would later suggest, Jews
conducted principled demonstrations that resorted to armed force only
under extreme pressure. When angry crowds protested about the cruel
death of their beloved teachers, Archelaus, Herod's eldest son, asked them
what he could do for them. The response reveals that their hostility to
Rome was not solely inspired by religious intransigence: 'Some clamoured
for a lightening of direct taxation, some for the abolition of purchase-tax,
and others for the release of prisoners.'[20] Even though Jerusalem still rang
with lamentation, there was no violence against the authorities until
Archelaus panicked and sent troops into the temple. Even then the crowds
merely pelted them with stones before returning to their devotions. The
situation could have been contained, had not Archelaus sent in the army,
that killed 3,000 worshippers.[21] Protests then spread to the countryside
where popular leaders, acclaimed as 'kings', waged guerrilla warfare against
Roman and Herodian troops. Again, taxation rather than religion was the
main issue. Mobs attacked the estates of the nobility and raided local
fortresses, storehouses and Roman baggage trains to 'take back the goods
that had been seized from the people'.[22] It took P. Quintilius Varus, governor
of neighbouring Syria, three years to restore the Pax Romana, during which
he burned the Galilean city of Sepphoris to the ground, sacked the
surrounding villages and crucified 2,000 rebels outside Jerusalem.[23]

Rome now decided that Herod's realm should be divided among his three sons: Archelaus was given Idumaea, Judaea and Samaria; Antipas Galilee and Peraea; and Philip the Transjordan. But Archelaus' rule was so cruel that Rome soon deposed him and for the first time Judaea was governed by a Roman prefect, supported by the Jewish priestly aristocracy, from his residence in Caesarea. When Coponius, the first governor, arranged for a census as a prelude to tax assessment, a Galilean named Judas urged the people to resist. His religious commitment was inseparable from his political protest:[24] paying Roman taxes, Judas insisted, 'amounted to slavery, pure and simple' because God was 'the only leader and master' of the Jewish people. If they remained steadfast in their opposition and did not shrink 'from the slaughter that might come upon them', God would intervene and act on their behalf.[25]

Typically, peasants did not resort to violence. Their chief weapon was non-cooperation: working slowly or even refraining from work altogether, making their point economically and often cannily. Most Roman governors were careful to avoid offending Jewish sensibilities, but in 26 CE Pontius Pilate ordered the troops in the Antonia fortress to raise military standards displaying the emperor's portrait right next to the temple. At once a mob of peasants and townsfolk marched to Caesarea, and when Pilate refused to remove the standards, they simply lay motionless outside his residence for five days. When Pilate summoned them to the stadium, they found that they were surrounded by soldiers with drawn swords and fell to the ground again, crying that they would rather die than break their laws. They may have relied on divine intervention but they also knew that Pilate would risk massive reprisals had he slaughtered them all. And they were right: the Roman governor had to admit defeat and take down the standards.[26] The chances of such a bloodless outcome were much slimmer when, twenty-five years later, Emperor Gaius Caligula would order his statue to be erected in the Jerusalem temple. Once again, the peasants took to the road, 'as if at a single signal . . . leaving their houses and villages empty'.[27] When the legate Petronius arrived at the port of Ptolemais with the offending statue, he found 'tens of thousands of Jews' with their wives and children massed on the plain in front of the city. Again, this was not a violent protest. 'On no account would we fight,' they told Petronius, but they were prepared to remain in Ptolemais until after the planting season.[28] This was a politically savvy peasants' strike: Petronius had to explain to the emperor 'that since the land was unsown, there would be a harvest of banditry, because the requirements of the tribute would not be met'.[29] Caligula was rarely moved by rational considerations, however, and the episode could have ended tragically had he not been assassinated the following year.

These peasant communities may have voiced their opposition to Roman rule in terms of their egalitarian Jewish traditions but they were neither crazed by their fervour nor were they violent or suicidal. Later popular movements failed because their leaders were less astute. During the fifties CE, a prophet called Theudas would lead 400 people into the Judaean desert in a new exodus, convinced that if the people took the initiative God would send deliverance.[30] Another rebel leader marched a crowd of 30,000 through the desert to the Mount of Olives, 'ready to force an entry into Jerusalem, overwhelm the Roman garrison, and seize supreme power'.[31] These movements had no political leverage and were ruthlessly put down. Both protests were inspired by the apocalyptic and perennial belief that activity on earth could influence events on the cosmic plane. This was the political context of Jesus' mission in the villages of Galilee.

Jesus was born into a society traumatised by violence. His life was framed by revolts. The uprisings after Herod's death occurred in the year of his birth and he was brought up in the hamlet of Nazareth, only a few miles from Sepphoris which Varus had razed to the ground; the peasants' strike against Caligula would occur just ten years after his death. During his lifetime, Galilee was governed by Herod Antipas, who financed an expensive building programme by imposing heavy taxes on his Galilean subjects. Failure to pay was punished by foreclosure and confiscation of land, and this revenue swelled the huge estates of the Herodian aristocrats.[32] When they lost their land, some peasants were forced into banditry, while others – Jesus' father, the carpenter Joseph, perhaps, among them – turned to menial labour: artisans were often failed peasants.[33] The crowds who thronged around Jesus in Galilee were hungry, distressed and sick. In his parables we see a society split between the very rich and the very poor: people who are desperate for loans; peasants who are heavily indebted, and the dispossessed who have to hire themselves out as day labourers.[34]

Even though the Gospels were written in an urban milieu decades after the events they describe, they still reflect the political aggression and cruelty of Roman Palestine. After Jesus' birth, King Herod slaughtered all the male infants of Bethlehem, recalling Pharaoh, the archetypal evil imperialist.[35] John the Baptist, Jesus' cousin, was executed by Herod Antipas.[36] Jesus predicted that his disciples would be pursued, flogged and killed by the Jewish authorities,[37] and he himself was arrested by the high-priestly aristocracy and tortured and crucified by Pontius Pilate. From the start, the Gospels present Jesus and his teachings as an alternative to the structural violence of imperial rule. Roman coins, inscriptions and temples regularly called Augustus, who had brought peace to the world after a century of brutal warfare, 'Son of God', 'lord' and 'saviour', and announced the 'good news' (*euaggelia*) of his birth. Thus when the angel announced the birth of Jesus to the shepherds, he proclaimed: 'Listen, I bring you *euaggelion* of great joy! Today a Saviour has been born to you.' Yet this 'son of God' was born homeless and would soon become a refugee.[38]

One sign of the acute distress of the population was the large number of people afflicted with neurological and psychological symptoms attributed to demons who came to Jesus for healing. He and his disciples seem to have had the skill to 'exorcise' these disorders.[39] When they cast out demons, Jesus explained, they were replicating God's victory over Satan in the cosmic sphere: 'I watched Satan fall like lightning from Heaven,' he told his disciples when they returned from a successful healing tour.[40] So-called spirit possession seems often linked with economic, sexual or colonial oppression, when people feel taken over by an alien power they cannot control.[41] In one telling incident, when Jesus cast out a host of demons from a possessed man, these satanic forces told him that their name was 'legion', identifying themselves with the Roman troops that were the most blatant symbol of the occupation. Jesus did what many colonised people would like to do: he cast 'legion' into a herd of swine, the most polluted of animals, which rushed headlong into the sea.[42] The ruling class seems to have regarded Jesus' exorcisms as political provocation: they were the reason why Antipas decided to take action against Jesus.[43]

In Jesus' mission, therefore, politics and religion were inextricable. The event that may have led to his death was his provocative entrance into Jerusalem at Passover, when he was hailed by the crowds as 'Son of David' and 'king of Israel'.[44] He then staged a demonstration in the temple itself, turning over the money-changers' tables and declaring that God's house was a 'den of thieves'.[45] This was not, as is sometimes assumed, a plea for a more spiritual style of worship. Judaea had been a temple-state since the Persian period so the temple had long been an instrument of imperial control and the tribute was stored there – although the high priests' collaboration with Rome had recently brought the institution into such disrepute that peasants were refusing to pay the temple tithes.[46] But neither did Jesus' preoccupation with imperial misrule mean that he was 'confusing' religion with politics. As he upturned the tables, he quoted the prophets who had severely castigated those who ignored the plight of the poor but whose religious observance was punctilious. Oppression, injustice and exploitation had always been religiously charged issues in Israel. The idea that faith should not involve itself in such politics would have been as alien to Jesus as it had been to Confucius.

It is not easy to assess Jesus' attitude to violence but there is no evidence that he was planning military insurrection. He forbade his disciples to injure others and to retaliate aggressively.[47] He did not resist his arrest and rebuked the disciple who cut off the ear of the high priest's servant.[48] But he could be verbally abusive: he fulminated against the rich;[49] cruelly lambasted those 'scribes and Pharisees' who served as retainers;[50] and called down God's vengeance on villages that rejected his disciples.[51] As we have seen, the Jewish peasants of Palestine had a tradition of nonviolent opposition to imperial rule and Jesus knew that any confrontation with either the Jewish or the Roman ruling classes – he did not distinguish the two – would be dangerous. Any disciple, he warned, must be ready to 'take up his cross'.[52] It seems that, like Judas of Galilee, Jesus may have relied on God to intervene. While she was pregnant with him, his mother had predicted that God had already begun to create a more just world order:

He has shown the power of his arm

He has routed the proud of heart.

He has pulled down princes from their thrones and exalted the lowly.

The hungry he has filled with good things; the rich sent empty away.

He has come to the help of Israel his servant.[53]

Like Judas the Galilean, Jesus may have believed that if his disciples did not shrink 'from the slaughter that would come upon them' and took the first step, God would overthrow the rich and powerful.

One day the Pharisees and Herodian retainers asked Jesus a trick question: 'Is it permissible to pay taxes to Caesar or not? Should we pay, yes or no?' Taxation was always an inflammable issue in Roman Palestine and if Jesus said 'no' he risked arrest. Pointing to Caesar's name and image on the denarius, the coin of tribute, Jesus replied: 'Give back (*apodote*) to Caesar what belongs to Caesar and to God what belongs to God.'[54] In a purely imperial context, Caesar's claim was legitimate: the Greek verb *apodote* was used of a rendition made when one recognised a rightful claim.[55] But as all Jews knew that God was their king and that everything belonged to him, there was in fact little to 'give back' to Caesar. In Mark's Gospel,

Jesus followed this incident with a warning to the retainers who helped to implement Roman rule and trampled on the poor and vulnerable:

> Beware of the scribes who like to walk about in long robes, to be greeted obsequiously in the market squares, to take the front seats in the synagogues and the places of honour at banquets; these are the men who swallow the property of widows, while making a show of lengthy prayers.[56]

When God finally established his Kingdom, their sentence would be severe.

That Kingdom of God was at the heart of Jesus' teaching.[57] Setting up an alternative to the violence and oppression of imperial rule could hasten the moment when God's power would finally transform the human condition. So his followers must behave *as if* the Kingdom had already arrived.[58] Jesus could not drive the Romans from the country, but the 'kingdom' he proclaimed, based on justice and equity, was open to everybody – especially those whom the current regime had failed. You should not merely invite your friends and rich neighbours to a festivity, he told his host: 'No, when you have a party, invite the poor, the crippled, the lame, and the blind.' Invitations should be issued in 'the streets and alleys of the town' and 'the open roads and hedgerows'.[59] 'How happy are you who are destitute (*ptochos*);' Jesus exclaimed, 'yours is the kingdom of God!'[60] The poor were the only people who could be 'blessed', because anybody who benefited in any way from the systemic violence of imperial rule was implicated in their plight.[61] 'Alas for you who are rich, you are having your consolation now,' Jesus continued. 'Alas for you who have your fill now; you shall go hungry.'[62] In God's Kingdom, the first would be last and the last first.[63] The Lord's Prayer is for people who were terrified of falling into debt and could hope only for bare subsistence, one day at a time: 'Give us today our daily bread. And forgive us our debts, as we forgive those who are in debt to us. And do not put us to the test, but save us from the evil one.'[64] Jesus and his closest companions threw in their lot with the most indigent peasants; they lived rough, itinerant lives, had nowhere to lay their heads, and depended on the support of Jesus' more affluent disciples, such as Lazarus and his sisters Martha and Mary.[65]

Yet the Kingdom was not a utopia that would be established at some distant date. At the very beginning of his mission, Jesus had announced: 'The time has come and the Kingdom of God has already arrived.'[66] The active presence of God was evident in Jesus' miracles of healing. Everywhere he looked he saw people pushed to the limit, abused, crushed and desperate:

'He felt sorry for them because they were harassed (*eskulmenoi*) and dejected (*errimmenoi*), like a sheep without a shepherd.'[67] The Greek verbs all have political connotations, of being 'beaten down' by imperial predation.[68] These people would have been suffering from the hard labour, poor sanitation, overcrowding, indebtedness and anxiety commonly endured by the masses in agrarian society.[69] Jesus' kingdom challenged the cruelty of Roman Judaea and Herodian Galilee by approximating more closely to God's will – 'on earth as it is in heaven'.[70] Those who feared indebtedness must release others from debts; they had to 'love' even their enemies, giving them practical and moral support. Instead of taking violent reprisals, like the Romans, people in God's kingdom would live according to the Golden Rule:

> To the man who slaps you on one cheek, present the other cheek too; to the man who takes your cloak from you, do not refuse your tunic. Give to everyone who asks you, and do not ask for your property back from the man who robs you. Treat others as you would like them to treat you.[71]

Jesus' followers must live as compassionately as God himself, giving generously to all and refraining from judgement and condemnation.[72]

After his crucifixion, Jesus' disciples had visions which convinced them that he had been raised to the right hand of God and would shortly return to inaugurate the Kingdom definitively.[73] Jesus had worked in rural Roman Palestine and had generally avoided the towns and cities.[74] But Paul, a diaspora Jew from Tarsus in Cilicia, who had not known Jesus, believed that he had been commissioned by God to bring the 'good news' of the Gospel to the gentile world, so he preached in the Graeco-Roman cities along the major trade routes in Asia Minor, Greece and Macedonia. This was a very different milieu: Paul's converts could not beg for their bread but had to work for their living, as he did, and a significant number of them were men and women of means. Writing in the fifties CE, Paul is the earliest extant Christian author and his teachings influenced the accounts of Jesus' life in the Gospels of Mark, Matthew and Luke (known as the Synoptics), written in the seventies and eighties. And while the Synoptics also drew upon the earliest Palestinian traditions about Jesus, they were writing in an urban environment permeated by Graeco-Roman religion.

Neither the Greeks nor the Romans had ever separated religion from secular life. They would not have understood our modern conception of 'religion'. They had no authoritative scriptures, no compulsory beliefs, no distinct clergy, and no obligatory ethical rules. There was no ontological gulf separating the gods from men and women; each human being had a *numen* or *genius* that was divine, and gods regularly took human form.[75] Gods were part of the citizen body so the Graeco-Roman city was essentially a religious community. Each city had its own divine patron, and civic pride, financial interest and piety were intertwined in a way that would seem strange in our secularised world. Participation in the religious festivals in honour of the city's gods was essential to city life: there were no public holidays or weekends so the Lupercalia in Rome or the Panathenaea in Athens were rare opportunities for relaxation and celebration. These rituals defined what it meant to be a Roman or an Athenian, put the city on show, invested civic life with transcendent meaning, presented the community at its best, and gave citizens the sense of belonging to a civic family. Participating in these rituals was just as important as any personal devotion to the gods. To belong to a city, therefore, was to worship its gods – though it was perfectly acceptable to worship other deities too.[76]

This was potentially problematic for Paul's Jewish and gentile converts in Antioch, Corinth, Philippi and Ephesus, who, as monotheists, regarded Roman religion as idolatrous. Judaism was respected as a tradition of great antiquity and Jews' avoidance of the public cult was accepted in the Roman empire. At this point, Judaism and Christianity were not yet distinct traditions:[77] Paul's gentile converts saw themselves as part of Israel.[78] But in the crowded Graeco-Roman cities, Christians often came into conflict with the local synagogue and, when they proudly claimed to belong to a 'new Israel', seemed to be behaving with impiety towards the parent faith – an attitude that Romans deplored.[79] Paul's letters show that he was concerned that his converts were becoming conspicuous in a society where difference and novelty could be dangerous. He urged them to observe the customary dress codes,[80] to behave with the decorum and self-control expected of Roman citizens, and to avoid excessively ecstatic demonstrations of piety.[81] Instead of defying the Roman authorities, Paul preached obedience and respect: 'You must all obey the governing authorities. Since all government comes from God, the civil authorities are appointed by God, and so anyone who resists authority is rebelling against God's decisions.'[82] Rome was not an evil empire but the guarantor of order and stability, so Christians must pay their taxes, 'since all government officials are God's officers. They serve God by collecting taxes.'[83] But Paul knew that this was a temporary state of affairs, because

Jesus' Kingdom would be established on earth in his own lifetime: 'The world as we know it is passing away.'[84]

While waiting for Jesus' triumphant return, members of his community (*ekklesia*) should live as Jesus had taught them – kindly, supportively and generously. They would create an alternative to the structural violence of imperial rule and the self-serving policies of the aristocracy. When they celebrated the Lord's Supper, the communal meal in Jesus' memory, rich and poor should sit at the same table and share the same food. Early Christianity was not a private affair between the individual and God: people derived their faith in Jesus from the experience of living together in a close-knit, minority community that challenged the unequal distribution of wealth and power in stratified Roman society. No doubt the author of the Acts of the Apostles gives an idealised picture of the early ekklesia in Jerusalem, but it reflected a Christian ideal:

> The whole group of believers was united, heart and soul; no one claimed
> for his own use anything that he had, as everything they owned was held in
> common . . . None of their members was ever in want, as all those who
> owned land or houses would sell them, and bring the money from them, to
> present it to the apostles; it was then distributed to any members who might
> be in need.[85]

Living in this way gave Christians intimations of new possibilities in humanity epitomised by the man Jesus whose self-abnegation had raised him to God's right hand. All former social divisions, Paul insisted, had become irrelevant: 'In the one Spirit we were all baptised, Jews as well as Greeks, slaves as well as citizens.' This sacred community of people who previously had nothing in common made up the body of the risen Christ.[86] In one memorable story, Luke, the evangelist who is closest to Paul, showed that Christians would come to know the risen Jesus not by a solitary mystical experience but by opening their hearts to the stranger, reading their scriptures together, and eating at the same table.[87]

But despite Paul's best efforts, the early Christians would never fit easily into Graeco-Roman society. They held aloof from the public celebrations and civic sacrifices that bound the city together and revered a man who had been executed by a Roman governor. They called Jesus 'lord' (*kyrios*), but this had nothing in common with the conventional aristocracy which clung to status and regarded the poor with disdain.[88] Paul quoted an early Christian hymn to the Philippi ekklesia, to remind them that God had bestowed the title of kyrios on Jesus because he had 'emptied himself (*heauton ekenosen*) to assume the condition of a slave . . . and was humbler yet, even to accepting death, death on a cross'.[89] The ideal of *kenosis*, 'emptying', would become crucial to Christian spirituality. 'In your minds, you must be the same as Christ Jesus,' Paul told the Philippians:

> There must be no competition among you, no conceit; but everybody is to be self-effacing. Always consider the other person to be better than yourself, so that nobody thinks of his own interests first, but everybody thinks of other people's interests instead.[90]

Like the followers of Confucius and the Buddha, Christians were cultivating the ideals of reverence and selflessness that countered the aggressive self-assertion of the warrior aristocracy.

A tightly knit and isolated community, however, can develop an exclusivity that ostracises others. In Asia Minor, a number of Jewish-Christian assemblies, who traced their origins to the ministry of Jesus' apostle John, had developed a different view of Jesus. Paul and the Synoptics had never regarded Jesus as God; the very idea would have horrified Paul who, before his conversion, had been an exceptionally punctilious Pharisee. They all used the term 'Son of God' in the conventional Jewish sense: Jesus had been an ordinary human being commissioned by God with a special task. Even in his exalted state, there was, for Paul, always a clear distinction between Jesus *kyrios Christos* and God, his Father. The author of the Fourth Gospel, however, depicted Jesus as a cosmic being, God's eternal 'Word' (*logos*) who had existed with God before the beginning of time.[91] This high Christology seems to have separated these congregations from other Jewish-Christian communities. Their writings were composed for an 'in-group' with a private symbolism that was incomprehensible to outsiders. In the Fourth Gospel, Jesus frequently baffles his audience by his enigmatic remarks. For these so-called 'Johannine' Christians, having the correct view of Jesus seemed more important than working for the coming of the Kingdom. They too had an ethic of love, but it was reserved only for loyal members; they turned their back on 'the world',[92] condemning defectors as 'anti-Christs' and 'children of the devil'.[93] Spurned and misunderstood, they had developed a dualistic vision of a world polarised into light and darkness, good and evil, life and death. Their most extreme scripture was the Book of Revelation, probably written while the Jews of Palestine were fighting a desperate war against the Roman empire.[94] The author, John of Patmos, was convinced that the days of the Beast, the Evil Empire, were numbered. Jesus was about to return, ride into battle, slay the Beast, fling him into a pit of fire, and establish his Kingdom for a thousand years. Paul had taught his converts that Jesus, the victim of imperial violence, had achieved a spiritual and cosmic victory over sin and death. John, however, depicted Jesus, who had taught his followers not to retaliate violently, as a ruthless warrior who would defeat Rome with massive slaughter and bloodshed. Revelation was admitted to the Christian canon only with great difficulty but would be scanned eagerly in times of social unrest when people were yearning for a more just and equitable world.

The Jewish revolt had broken out in Jerusalem in 66 CE after the Roman governor had commandeered money from the temple treasury. Not everybody supported it. The Pharisees in particular feared that it would make trouble for diaspora Jews, but the new party of Zealots (*kanaim*) thought that they had a good chance of success because the empire was currently split by internal dissension. They managed to drive out the Roman garrison and set up a provisional government, but the emperor Nero responded by dispatching to Judaea a massive army led by Vespasian, his most gifted general. Hostilities were suspended during the disturbances that followed Nero's death in 68, but after Vespasian became emperor, his son Titus took over the siege of Jerusalem, forced the Zealots to capitulate, and on 28 August 70 burned city and temple to the ground.

In the Middle East, a temple carried such symbolic weight that an ethnic tradition could barely sustain its loss.[95] Judaism owed its survival to a group of scholars led by Yohanan ben Zakkai, leader of the Pharisees, who transformed a faith based on temple worship into a religion of the book.[96] In the coastal town of Yavneh, they began to compile three new scriptures: the Mishnah, completed around 200, and the Jerusalem and Babylonian Talmuds, which reached their final form in the fifth and sixth centuries respectively. At first, most of the rabbis probably assumed that the temple would be rebuilt, but those hopes were quashed when the emperor Hadrian visited Judaea in 130 and announced that he would build a new city on the ruins of Jerusalem called Aelia Capitolina. The following year, as part of his policy of uniting the empire culturally, he outlawed circumcision, the ordination of rabbis, the teaching of the Torah, and public Jewish gatherings. Inevitably, perhaps, there was another revolt and the tough Jewish soldier Simon bar Koseba planned his guerrilla campaign so skilfully that he held Rome at bay for three years. Rabbi Akiva, a leading Yavneh scholar, hailed him as the messiah, calling him Bar Kokhba ('Son of the Star').[97] But Rome finally gained control, systematically destroying almost a thousand Jewish villages, and killing 580,000 Jewish rebels, while countless civilians were either burned to death or died of hunger and disease.[98] After the war, Jews were expelled from Judaea and would not be permitted to return for over five hundred years.

The violence of this imperial assault profoundly affected Rabbinic Judaism. Instead of allowing Jews to bring their more aggressive traditions to the fore, the rabbis deliberately marginalised them, determined to prevent any more catastrophic military adventures.[99] In their new academies in Babylonia and Galilee, the rabbis therefore evolved a method of exegesis that excised any adulation of chauvinism or belligerence. They were not particularly peaceable men – they fought their scholarly battles fiercely – but they were pragmatists.[100] They had learned that Jewish tradition could survive only if Jews learned to rely on spiritual rather than physical strength.[101] They could not afford any more heroic messiahs.[102] They recalled Rabbi Yohanan's advice: 'If there is a seedling in your hand and you are informed "King Messiah has arrived", first plant your seedling and then go forth to greet him.'[103] Other rabbis went further: 'Let him come, but let me not see him!'[104] Rome was a fact of life and Jews must come to terms with it.[105] The rabbis scoured their biblical and oral traditions to show that God had decreed Rome's imperial power.[106] They praised Roman technology and instructed Jews to make a blessing whenever they saw a gentile king.[107] They devised new rules forbidding Jews to bear arms on the Sabbath or to bring weapons into the House of Studies, since violence was incompatible with Torah scholarship.

The rabbis make it clear that instead of being an inflammatory force, religious activity can be used to quell violence. They either ignored the bellicose passages of the Hebrew Bible or gave them a radically new interpretation. They called their exegetical method Midrash – a word derived from *darash*: 'to investigate; go in search of something'. The meaning of scripture was not, therefore, self-evident; it had to be ferreted out by diligent study, and because it was God's Word, it was infinite and could not be confined to a single interpretation. Indeed, every time a Jew confronted the sacred text it should mean something different.[108] The rabbis felt free to argue with God, defy him and even change the words of scripture to introduce a more compassionate reading.[109] Yes, God was often described as a divine warrior in the Bible but Jews must imitate only his compassionate behaviour.[110] The true hero was no longer a warrior but a man of peace: 'Who is the hero of heroes?' asked the rabbis: 'He who turns an enemy into a friend.'[111] A 'mighty' man did not prove his mettle on the battlefield, but was one 'who subdues his passions'.[112] When the prophet Isaiah had seemed to praise a soldier 'who thrusts back his attacker to the gate' he was really speaking of 'those who thrust a parry in the way of Torah'.[113] The rabbis described Joshua and David as pious Torah scholars and even argued that David had had no interest in warfare at all.[114] When the Egyptian army drowned in the Sea of Reeds, some of the angels had wanted to sing Yahweh's praises, but he had rebuked them: 'My children lie drowned in the sea, and you would sing?'[115]

The rabbis acknowledged that there were divinely ordained wars in their scriptures. They concluded that the campaigns against the Canaanites had been 'obligatory' wars, but the Babylonian rabbis ruled that because these peoples no longer existed, warfare could no longer be compulsory.[116] The Palestinian rabbis, however, whose position in Roman Palestine was more precarious, argued that Jews were still obliged to fight sometimes – but only in self-defence.[117] David's territorial wars had been 'discretionary', but the rabbis pointed out that even kings had to ask permission of the Sanhedrin, the Jewish governing body, before taking the field. Yet they concluded that because the monarchy and Sanhedrin were no more, discretionary wars were no longer legitimate. They also interpreted a verse in the Song of Songs in such a way as to discourage mass uprisings that could lead to gentile reprisals: 'I charge you, daughters of Jerusalem, by the gazelles, by the hinds of the field, not to stir my love, nor rouse it, till it please to awake.'[118] Israelites must not take provocative action ('to stir love'); there must be no mass migrations to the Land of Israel and no more rebellions against gentile rule until God issued a directive ('till it please to awake'). If they remained quiet, God would not permit persecution, but if they disobeyed they would, 'like the hinds of the field', be fair game for gentile violence.[119] This abstruse piece of exegesis effectively put a brake on Jewish political action for over a millennium.[120]

By the middle of the third century CE, the Roman empire was in crisis. The new Sassanian dynasty in Persia had conquered Roman territory in Cilicia, Syria and Cappadocia; the Gothic tribes in the Danube basin continuously attacked the frontier; and Germanic warrior bands harried Roman garrisons in the Rhine Valley. In a short span of sixteen years (268–84), eight emperors were assassinated by their own troops. The economy was in ruins and local aristocracies fought for power in the cities.[121] Rome was

eventually saved by a military revolution, led by professional soldiers from
the frontier region, which transformed the Roman army. [122] Aristocrats no
longer filled the top positions, the army doubled in size and legions were
broken up into smaller, more flexible detachments. A mobile cavalry force,
the *comitatus,* supported the garrisons on the borders, and for the first time
Roman citizens were taxed to finance the army. By the end of the third
century, the barbarians in the Balkans and northern Italy had been repulsed,
the Persian advance had been halted, and Rome had recovered its lost territory. The new Roman emperors were no longer of noble birth: Diocletian
(r. 284–305) was the son of a freedman of Dalmatia, Galerius (r. 305–11)
a former cattle-herder in Carpathia, and Constantius Chlorus (r. 305–06)
an undistinguished country gentleman from Nis. They centralised the empire,
taking direct control of taxation instead of leaving it to the local nobility
and, most significantly, Diocletian shared power with three co-emperors
by creating the tetrarchy ('rule of four'): Maximian and Constantius Chlorus
governed the western provinces and Diocletian ruled in the east with
Galerius. [123]

The third-century crisis brought Christianity to the attention of the
imperial authorities. Christians had never been popular; by refusing to take
part in the civic cult they seemed suspect and easily became scapegoats at
times of social tension. According to Tacitus, Nero had blamed Christians
for the great fire of Rome and put many to death – these people may be
the martyrs seated near God's throne in the Book of Revelation. [124] The
North African theologian Tertullian (*c.* 160–220) complained: 'If the Tiber
rises to the walls, if the Nile fails to rise and flood the fields, if the sky
withholds its rain, if there is earthquake or famine or plague, straightway
the cry arises: "The Christians to the lions!"' [125] But it was not customary
for an agrarian ruling class to interfere in the religious lives of their subjects
and the empire had no standard policy of persecution. In 112, when Pliny,
governor of Bithynia, asked the emperor Trajan how he should treat
Christians who were brought before him, Trajan replied that there was no
official procedure. Christians should not be actively hunted out, he advised,
but if they came before the courts for some reason and refused to sacrifice
to the Roman gods, they should be executed for defying the imperial
government. Christians who did die in this way were venerated in their
communities and the Acts of the Martyrs, which recorded the stories of
their deaths in lurid detail, were read aloud in the liturgy.

Yet against all odds, by the third century Christianity had also become
a force to be reckoned with. We still do not really understand how this

came about.[126] It has been suggested that the rise of other new religious movements in the empire had made Christianity appear less bizarre. People were now seeking the divine in a human being who was a 'friend of God' rather than in a holy place, and secret societies, not unlike the Church, were mushrooming throughout the empire. Like Christianity, many of these had originated in the eastern provinces, and they too required a special initiation, offered a new revelation, and demanded a conversion of life.[127] Christianity was also beginning to appeal to merchants and artisans like Paul, who had left their home towns and taken advantage of the Pax Romana to travel and settle elsewhere; many had lost touch with their roots and were open to new ideas. The egalitarian ethic of Christianity made it popular with the lower classes and slaves. Women too found the Church attractive, because the Christian scriptures instructed husbands to treat their wives considerately. Like Stoicism and Epicureanism, Christianity promised inner tranquillity, but its way of life could be followed by the poor and illiterate as well as by members of the aristocracy. The Church had also begun to appeal to some highly intelligent men, such as the Alexandrian Platonist Origen (185–254), who interpreted the faith in a way that interested the educated public. As a result of all this the Church had become a significant organisation. It was not *religio licita,* one of the approved traditions of the empire, so could not own property, but it had ejected some of its wilder elements and, like the empire itself, it claimed to have a single rule of faith, was multiracial, international and administered by efficient bureaucrats.[128]

One of the most cogent reasons for the Church's success was its charitable work, which made it a strong presence in the cities. By 250, the Church in Rome was feeding 1,500 poor people and widows every day, and during a plague or a riot its clergy were often the only group able to organise food supplies or bury the dead. At a time when the emperors were so preoccupied with defending the frontier that they seemed to have forgotten the cities, the Church had become firmly established there.[129] But in this time of social tension, its prominence could be threatening to the authorities, who now began more systematically to seek Christians out for execution.

It is important to explore the ideal of martyrdom, which has surfaced alarmingly in our own time and is now associated with violence and extremism. Christian martyrs, however, were victims of imperial persecution and did not kill anybody else. The memory of this harassment would loom large in the consciousness of the early Church and shape the Christian worldview. However, until the third-century crisis, there had been no official empire-wide persecution but only sporadic local outbreaks of hostility, and even in the third century there were only about ten years when the Roman authorities intensively pursued Christians.[130] In an agrarian empire, the ruling aristocracy expected its religion to be different from that of its subjects, but ever since Augustus, the worship of the gods of Rome was deemed essential to the empire's survival. The Pax Romana was thought to rely on the *Pax deorum,* the peace imposed by the gods, who in return for regular sacrifice would guarantee the empire's security and prosperity.

So when Rome's northern frontier was threatened by the barbarian tribes in 250, the emperor Decius ordered all his subjects to sacrifice to his *genius* to procure the gods' aid on pain of death. This decree was not directed specifically against Christians; moreover, it was difficult to implement and the authorities do not seem to have hunted down anybody who failed to turn up to the official sacrifice.[131] When Decius was killed in action the following year, the edict was rescinded. In 258, however, Valerian was the first emperor to target the Church specifically, ordering that its clergy be executed and the property of high-ranking Christians confiscated. But again, few people seem to have been killed, and two years later Valerian was taken prisoner by the Persians and died in captivity. His successor Galienus revoked the legislation and Christians enjoyed forty years of peace.

Clearly Valerian had been troubled by the Church's organisational strength rather than by its beliefs and rituals. The Church was a new phenomenon. Christians had exploited the empire's improved communications to create an institution with a unity of structure that none of the traditions we have discussed so far had attempted. Each local church was headed by a bishop, the 'overseer' who was said to have derived his authority from Jesus' apostles, and was supported by presbyters and deacons. The network of such near-identical communities seemed almost to have become an empire within the Empire. Irenaeus, the bishop of Lyons (*c.* 130–200), who was anxious to create an orthodoxy that excluded aggressive sectarians, had claimed that the Great Church had a single rule of faith, because the bishops had inherited their teaching directly from the apostles. This was not only a novel idea but a total fantasy. Paul's letters show that there had been considerable tension between him and Jesus' disciples, and his teachings bore little relation to those of Jesus. Each of the Synoptics had his own take on Jesus and the Johannines were different again; there was also a host of other gospels in circulation. When Christians finally established a scriptural canon – between the fourth and sixth centuries – these diverse visions were included side by side.

Unfortunately, however, Christianity would develop a peculiar yearning for intellectual conformity that would not only prove to be unsustainable but set it apart from other faith traditions. The rabbis would never attempt to create a single central authority; not even God, much less another rabbi, could tell another Jew what to think.[132] The Buddha had adamantly rejected the idea of religious authority; the idea of a single rule of faith and a structured hierarchy was entirely alien to the multifarious traditions of India; and the Chinese were encouraged to see merit in all the great teachers, despite their disagreements.

Christian leaders would make the Church even more threatening to the authorities during the forty peaceful years after Valerian's death. When the newly elected emperor Diocletian moved into his palace in Nicomedia in 287, a Christian basilica was clearly visible on the opposite hill, seeming to confront the imperial palace as an equal. He made no move against the Church for sixteen years but as a firm believer in the *Pax deorum* at a time when the fate of the empire hung in the balance, Diocletian would find the Christians' stubborn refusal to honour the gods increasingly intolerable.[133] On 23 February 303, he demanded that the presumptuous basilica be demolished; the next day, he outlawed Christian meetings and ordered the destruction of churches and the confiscation of Christian scriptures. All men, women and children were required on pain of execution to gather in the empire's public squares to sacrifice to the gods of Rome. Yet the legislation was implemented in only a few regions and in the west, where there were few Christian communities, hardly at all. It is difficult to know how many people died as a result. Christians were rarely pursued if they failed to show up for the sacrifice; many apostatised and others found loopholes.[134] Most of those who were put to death had defiantly presented themselves to the authorities as voluntary martyrs, a practice the bishops condemned.[135] When Diocletian abdicated in 305, these edicts expired, though they were renewed for a period of two years (311–13) by Emperor Maximianus Daia.

The cult of the martyrs, however, became central to Christian piety because they proved that Jesus had not been unique: the Church had 'friends of God' with divine powers in its very midst. The martyrs were 'other Christs' and their imitation of Christ even unto death had brought him into the present.[136] The Acts of the Martyrs claimed that these heroic deaths were miracles that manifested God's presence because the martyrs seemed impervious to pain. 'Let not a day pass when we do not dwell on these tales,' Victricius, the fifth-century bishop of Rouen, urged his congregation. 'This martyr did not blench under torturers; this martyr hurried up the slow work of the execution; this one eagerly swallowed the flames; this one was cut about but stood up still.'[137] 'They suffered more than is possible for human beings to bear, and did not endure this by their own strength but by the grace of God,' explained Pope Gelasius (r. 492–96).[138] When the Christian slave-girl Blandina was executed in Lyons in 177, her companions 'looked with their eyes through their sister to the One who was crucified for them'.[139]

When the young wife and mother Vibia Perpetua was imprisoned in Carthage in 203, she had a series of remarkable dreams which proved even to her persecutors that she enjoyed special intimacy with the divine. The prison governor himself perceived 'that there was a rare power in us', her biographer recalled.[140] Through these 'friends of God', Christians could claim respect and even superiority over pagan communities. Yet there would always be more than a hint of aggression in the martyr's 'witness' to Christ. On the night before her execution, Perpetua dreamed that she had been turned into a man and wrestled with an Egyptian in the stadium, a man huge and 'foul' of aspect, but with an infusion of divine strength she was able to throw him to the ground. When she woke, she knew that she would not be fighting wild beasts that day but 'the Fiend' himself and that 'the victory would be mine'.[141]

Martyrdom would always be the protest of a minority, yet the violent deaths of the martyrs became a graphic demonstration of the structural violence and cruelty of the state. Martyrdom was and would always be a political as well as a religious choice. Targeted as enemies of the empire and in a relationship of starkly asymmetrical power with the authorities, these Christians' deaths were a defiant assertion of a different allegiance. They had already achieved an eminence that was intrinsically superior to Rome's and by laying their deaths at the door of the oppressors, the martyrs had effectively demonised them. But these Christians were beginning to develop a history of grievance that gave their faith a newly aggressive edge. They were convinced that, like Jesus in the Book of Revelation, they were engaged in an ongoing eschatological battle; when they fought, like gladiators, with wild beasts in the stadium, they were battling with demonic powers (embodied in the imperial authorities) and would expedite Jesus' triumphant return.[142] Those who voluntarily presented themselves to the authorities were committing what would later be called 'revolutionary suicide'. By forcing the authorities to put them to death, they laid bare for all to see the intrinsic violence of the so-called Pax Romana and their suffering would, they firmly believed, hasten its end.

But other Christians did not regard the empire as satanic; rather they experienced a remarkable conversion to Rome.[143] Again, this shows that it is impossible to point to an 'essential' Christianity that promoted identical courses of action. Origen, for instance, believed that Christianity was the culmination of the classical culture of antiquity; like the Hebrew scriptures, Greek philosophy had also been an expression of the Logos, the Word of God. The Pax Romana had been providentially ordained: 'It would have hindered Jesus' teaching from being spread through the whole world,' Origen believed, 'if there had been many kingdoms.'[144] The statesmanship and wise decision-making of the bishops of the Mediterranean cities gained them a reputation for being the 'friends of God'.[145] Cyprian, bishop of Carthage (200–258), claimed that he presided over a privileged society that was invested with a majesty every bit as powerful as Rome.[146]

In 306, Valerius Aurelius Constantinus, who had distinguished himself as a soldier under Diocletian, succeeded his father Constantius Chlorus as one of the two rulers of the empire's western provinces. Determined to achieve sole supremacy, he campaigned against his co-emperor Maxentius. On the night before their final battle at the Milvian Bridge near Rome in 312, Constantine had a vision of a flaming cross in the sky embellished with the motto: 'In this conquer!' A dreamer and visionary, Constantine also saw himself as a 'friend of God' and would always attribute his subsequent victory to this miraculous omen. That year he declared Christianity to be *religio licita*.

Constantine employed the philosopher Lucius Caelius Lactantius (c. 260–325) as a tutor for his son Crispus. Lactantius had been converted to Christianity by the courage of the martyrs who had suffered under Maximianus Daia. The state was, he believed, inherently aggressive and predatory. Romans might talk loftily about virtue and respect for humanity but did not practise what they preached. The goals of any political power, Rome included, were always 'to extend the boundaries which are violently taken from others, to increase the power of the state, to improve the revenues' and this could only be achieved by *latrocinium*, violence and robbery.[147] There was no such thing as a 'just' war, because it was never permissible to take human life.[148] If Romans really wanted to be virtuous, Lactantius concluded, they should 'restore the possessions of others' and abandon their wealth and power.[149] That might have been what Jesus would have done but it was not likely to happen in Christian Rome.

6

BYZANTIUM:
THE TRAGEDY OF EMPIRE

In 323 Constantine defeated Licinius, emperor of the eastern provinces, and became sole ruler of the Roman empire. His ultimate ambition, however, was to command the civilised world from the shores of the Mediterranean to the Iranian Plateau as Cyrus had done.[1] As a first step, he moved his capital from Rome to the city of Byzantium at the Bosporus, the juncture of Europe and Asia, which he renamed Constantinople. Here he was greeted by Eusebius (c. 264–340), the bishop of Caesarea:

> Let the friend of the All-Ruling God be proclaimed our sole sovereign . . .
> who has modelled himself after the archetypal form of the Supreme Sovereign,
> whose thoughts mirror the virtuous rays by which he has been made perfectly
> wise, good, just, pious, courageous and God-loving.[2]

This was a far cry from Jesus' criticism of such worldly authority, but in antiquity the rhetoric of kingship had always been virtually interchangeable with the language of divinity.[3] Eusebius regarded monarchy, the rule of 'one' (monos), as a natural consequence of monotheism.[4] There was now one God, one empire and one emperor.[5] By his military victories, Constantine had finally established Jesus' Kingdom, which would soon spread to the entire world. Eusebius understood Constantine's Iranian ambitions perfectly and argued that the emperor was not only the Caesar of Roman Christians but also the rightful sovereign of the Christians of Persia.[6] By crafting and articulating an imperial Christianity and baptising the latrocinium of Rome – its 'robbery and violence' – Eusebius had entirely subverted the original message of Jesus.

Constantine's conversion was clearly a coup. Christianity was not yet the official religion of the Roman Empire but had at last been recognised in Roman law. The Church could now own property, build basilicas and churches, and make a distinctive contribution to public life. But those Christians who had accepted imperial patronage so joyfully failed to notice some glaring incongruities. Jesus had told his followers to give all they had to the poor, but the Christian emperor enjoyed immense wealth. In the Kingdom of God, rich and poor were supposed to sit at the same table, but Constantine lived in an exalted state of exception and Christianity would inevitably be tainted by its connection with the oppressive agrarian state. Eusebius believed that Constantine's conquests were the culmination of sacred history:[7] Jesus had given his disciples all power in heaven and earth and the Christian emperor had made this a political reality.[8] Eusebius chose to ignore the fact that he had achieved this with the Roman legions that Jesus had condemned as demonic. The close union of church and empire that began in 312 meant that warfare inevitably acquired a sacral character – though Byzantines would always be reluctant to call war 'holy'.[9] Neither Jesus nor the first Christians could have imagined so great an oxymoron as the notion of a Christian emperor.

Yet again, we see that a tradition that had once challenged state aggression was unable to sustain this ethical stance when it became identified with aristocratic rule. The Christian empire would inevitably be tainted by the 'robbery and violence' that, Lactantius believed, characterised all imperialism. As in Darius' imperial Zoroastrianism, eschatological fulfilment had been projected on to a political system that was inevitably flawed. Eusebius maintained that Constantine had established the Kingdom that Christ was supposed to inaugurate at his Second Coming. He taught the Christians of Byzantium to believe that the ruthless militarism and systemic injustice of the Roman empire would be transformed by the Christian ideal. But Constantine was a soldier, with very little knowledge of his new faith. It was more likely that Christianity would be converted to imperial violence.

Constantine may have felt the ambiguity of his position, because he delayed his baptism until he was on his deathbed.[10] In the very last year of his life, he was planning an expedition against Persia, but when he fell sick, Eusebius reported, 'he perceived that this was the time to purify himself from the offences which he had at any time committed, trusting that whatever sins it had been his lot as a mortal to commit, he could wash them from his soul'.[11] He told the bishops: 'I shall now set for myself rules of life which befit God', tacitly admitting, perhaps, that for the last twenty-five years he had been unable to do so.[12]

The emperor had experienced these contradictions before he arrived in the east when he had to deal with a case of Christian heresy in North

Africa.[13] Constantine felt quite entitled to intervene in such matters because, as he famously said: 'I have been established by God as the supervisor of the external affairs of the church.'[14] Heresy (*airesis*) was not simply a dogmatic issue but also a political one; the word meant 'to choose another path'. Because religion and politics were inseparable in Rome, lack of consensus in the Church threatened the Pax Romana. In matters of state, no Roman emperor could permit his subjects to 'go their own way'. Once he had become sole emperor of the western provinces, Constantine had been bombarded with appeals from the Donatist separatists and was concerned that 'such disputes and altercations . . . might perhaps arouse the highest deity not only against the human race, but also against myself, to whose care he has . . . committed the regulation of all things earthly'.[15] A significant number of North African Christians had refused to accept the episcopal consecration of Caecilian, the new bishop of Carthage, and had set up their own church with Donatus as their bishop.[16] Because Caecilian's orders were accepted as valid by all the other African churches, the Donatists were destroying the consensus of the Church and Constantine decided that he had to act.

Like any Roman emperor, his first instinct was to crush dissent militarily but he settled instead for the confiscation of Donatist property.[17] Tragically, however, when the imperial troops marched into a Donatist basilica to carry out the edict, the unarmed congregation resisted and a massacre followed. At once the Donatists loudly complained that the Christian emperor was persecuting his fellow Christians and that despite Constantine's conversion nothing had changed since the days of Diocletian.[18] Constantine was forced to revoke the edict, left the Donatists in peace and instructed orthodox bishops to turn the other cheek.[19] He would have been uneasily aware that the Donatists had got away with it. Henceforth he and his successors would be wary of any theological or ecclesiastical discourse that threatened the Pax Christiana on which the security of the empire, they believed, now depended.[20]

Constantine was reluctant to promote his Christianity in the sparsely Christianised west, but his arrival in the east marked his political conversion to the faith.[21] There could as yet be no question of making Christianity the official religion of the empire and pagans still held public office, but Constantine closed down some pagan temples and expressed his disapproval of sacrificial worship.[22] Christianity's universal claims seemed ideally suited to Constantine's ambition to achieve world rule and he believed that its ethos of peace and reconciliation were in perfect alignment with the Pax Romana. But to Constantine's horror, the eastern churches, far from being united in brotherly love, were bitterly divided by an obscure – and, to Constantine, incomprehensible – theological dispute.

In 318, Arius, presbyter of Alexandria, had put forward the idea that Jesus, the Word of God, had not been divine by nature. Quoting an impressive array of biblical texts, he contended that God had simply conferred divinity upon the man Jesus as a reward for his perfect obedience and humility. At this point there was no orthodox position on the nature of Christ and many of the bishops felt quite at home with Arius' theology. Like their pagan neighbours, they did not experience the divine as an impossibly distant reality; in the Graeco-Roman world, it was taken for granted that men and women regularly became fully-fledged gods.[23] Eusebius, the leading Christian intellectual of his day, taught his congregations that God had revealed himself in human form before: firstly to Abraham, who had entertained three strangers at Mamre and discovered that Yahweh was participating in the conversation; later Moses and Joshua had had similar theophanies.[24] For Eusebius, God's Word or Logos – the divine element in a human being[25] – had simply returned to earth once more, this time in the person of Jesus of Nazareth.[26]

But Arius was vehemently opposed by Athanasius, his bishop's young, combative assistant, who argued that God's descent to earth was not a repetition of previous epiphanies but a unique, unprecedented and unrepeatable act of love. This resonated in some quarters, where there had been a major shift in the perception of the divine; many Christians no longer felt that they could ascend to God by their own efforts, as, Arius claimed, Jesus had done. There seemed an unbridgeable gulf between the God that was life itself and the material world, which now appeared chronically fragile and moribund. Dependent on God for their every breath, humans were powerless to save themselves. But paradoxically, Christians still found that when they contemplated the man Jesus they saw a new divine potential in humanity, which moved them to look upon themselves and their neighbours differently. There was also a new appreciation of the human body. Christian spirituality had been strongly influenced by Platonism, which sought to liberate the soul from the body, but in some circles in the early fourth century, people were beginning to hope that their hitherto despised bodies could bring men and women to the divine – or at least that it was not a reality separate from the physical, as the Platonists held.[27]

Athanasius' doctrine of incarnation spoke directly to this changed mood. In the person of Jesus, he claimed, God had leaned across the dividing chasm and in an astounding act of kenosis ('self-emptying') had taken mortal flesh, shared our weakness, and had utterly transformed fragile, perishable human nature. 'The Logos became human that we might become divine,' Athanasius insisted. 'He revealed himself through a body that we might receive an idea of the invisible Father.'[28] The good news of the Gospel was the coming of new life, human because it was divine.[29] Nobody was compelled to 'believe' this doctrine; people embraced it because it reflected their personal experience. Athanasius' doctrine of the 'deification' (*theosis*) of humanity made perfect sense to those Christians who had become convinced that in some mysterious way they had already been transformed and that their humanity had acquired a new, divine dimension. But theosis seemed nonsensical to those who had not experienced this.

Two new 'Christianities' had therefore emerged in response to a shift in the intellectual environment, both of which could claim support from past scriptures and luminaries. With quiet and sustained reflection, this dispute could easily have been settled peaceably. But instead it became entangled with imperial politics. Constantine, of course, had no understanding of theological issues but was determined nevertheless to repair this breach of ecclesiastical consensus. In May 325 he summoned the bishops to a council in Nicaea to settle the matter once and for all. Here Athanasius managed to get the emperor's ear and forced his position through. Most of the bishops, anxious not to incur Constantine's displeasure, signed Athanasius' creed but continued to preach as they had before. Nicaea solved nothing and the Arian controversy dragged on for another sixty years. Constantine, out of his depth theologically, would eventually veer to the other side and take the Arian position that was promoted by the more cultured, aristocratic bishops.[30] Athanasius, no aristocrat himself, was reviled by his enemies as an upstart 'from the lowest depths of society' who was 'no different from a common artisan'. But for all his talk of kenosis, Athanasius never lost his pointy elbows or his theological certainty, which was inspired in no small part by the new monastic movement that had emerged in the deserts around Alexandria.

In 270, the year of Constantine's birth, a young Egyptian peasant had walked to church lost in thought. Antony had just inherited a sizeable piece of land from his parents but found this good fortune an intolerable burden. He was only eighteen years old yet now he had to provide for his sister, take a wife, have children, and toil on the farm for the rest of his life to support them all. In Egypt, where famine loomed whenever the Nile failed to flood, starvation was always a real threat, and most people accepted this relentless struggle as inevitable.[31] But Jesus had said: 'I am telling you not to worry about your life and what you are to eat and about your body and how to clothe it.'[32] Antony also remembered that the first Christians had sold all their possessions and given the proceeds to the poor.[33] Still musing on these texts, he entered the church, only to hear the priest reading Jesus' words to a rich young man: 'If you wish to be perfect, go and sell what you own and give the money to the poor, and you will have treasure in heaven.'[34] Immediately Antony sold his property and embarked on a quest for freedom and holiness that would become a counter-cultural challenge to both the Christianised Roman state and the new worldly, imperial Christianity. Like other monastic communities we have considered, Antony's followers would try to model a more egalitarian and compassionate way for people to live together.

For the first fifteen years, like other 'renouncers' (*apotaktikoi*), Antony lived at the very edge of his village; then he moved to the tombs on the periphery of the desert, and finally ventured further into the wilderness than any other monk, living for years in an abandoned fortress beside the Red Sea until, in 301, he began to attract disciples.[35] In the immensity of the desert, Antony discovered a tranquillity (*hesychia*) that put worldly care into perspective.[36] St Paul had insisted that Christians must support themselves,[37] so Egyptian monks either worked as day labourers or sold their produce in the market. Antony grew vegetables so that he could offer hospitality to passing travellers, because learning to live kindly with others and sharing your wealth was essential to his monastic programme.[38]

For some time, Egyptian peasants had engaged in this type of disengagement (*anchoresis*) to escape economic or social tension. During the third century, there had been a crisis of human relations in the villages. These farmers were prosperous but acerbic and quick with their fists, yet the village's tax burden and the need for cooperation to control the flood waters of the Nile obliged them to live in unwelcome proximity with uncongenial neighbours.[39] Success was often resented: 'Although I possess a good deal of land and am occupied with its cultivation,' one farmer explained, 'I am not involved with any person in the village but keep to myself.'[40] When neighbourly relationships became unendurable, therefore, people would sometimes retire to the very edge of the settlement.[41] But once Christianity reached the Egyptian countryside in the late third century, anchoresis was no longer a disgruntled withdrawal but had become a positive choice to live according to the Gospel in a way that offered a welcome and challenging alternative to the acrimony and tedium of settled life. The monk (*monachos*) lived alone (*monos*) seeking the 'freedom from care' (*amerimmia*) that Jesus had prescribed.[42]

Like the renouncers of previous times, the monks set up a counter-culture, casting off their functional role in the agrarian economy and rejecting its inherent violence. A monk's struggle began as soon as he left his village.[43] At first, explained one of the greatest of these anchorites, he was plagued by terrifying thoughts 'of lengthy old age, inability to perform manual labour, fear of the starvation that will ensue, of the sickness that follows undernourishment, and the deep shame of having to accept the necessities of life from the hands of others'.[44] Their greatest task, however, was to still the violent impulses that lurk in the depths of the human psyche. The monks often described their struggle as a battle with demons, which we moderns usually understand as sexual temptations. But they were less preoccupied by sex than we are: Egyptian monks usually avoided women because they symbolised the economic burden they wanted to escape.[45] Far more threatening than sex to these sharp-tongued Egyptian peasants was the 'demon' of anger.[46] However provocative the circumstances, monks must never respond aggressively to any attack. One abbot ruled that there was no excuse for violent speech, even if your brother 'plucks out your right eye and cuts off your right hand'.[47] A monk must not even look angry or make an impatient gesture.[48] These monks meditated constantly on Jesus' command to 'love your enemies' because most of them *did* have enemies in the community.[49] Evagrius of Pontus (d. 399), one of the most influential monastic teachers, drew on Paul's doctrine of kenosis and instructed monks to empty their minds of the rage, avarice, pride and vainglory that tore the soul apart and made them close their hearts to others. By following these precepts, some learned to transcend their innate belligerence and achieved an interior peace that they experienced as a return to the Garden of Eden when human beings had lived in harmony with each other and with God.

The monastic movement spread more rapidly, demonstrating a widespread hunger for an alternative to a Christianity that was increasingly tainted by imperial associations. By the end of the fifth century, tens of thousands of monks were living beside the Nile and in the deserts of Syria, Egypt, Mesopotamia and Armenia.[50] They had, wrote Athanasius, created a spiritual city in the wilderness that was the antithesis of the worldly city, which was supported by taxation, oppression and military aggression.[51] Instead of establishing an aristocracy that lived off the labour of others, monks were self-sufficient, existed at subsistence level, and gave whatever surplus they produced to the poor. Instead of the Pax Romana enforced by martial violence, they cultivated hesychia and systematically rid their minds of anger, violence and hatred. Like Constantine, Antony was venerated by many as *epigeios theos,* a 'god on earth', but he ruled with kindness rather than coercion.[52] The monks were the new 'friends of God' whose power had been achieved by a self-effacing lifestyle that had no earthly profit.[53]

After the Council of Nicaea, some Christians began to fall out of love with their emperors. They had expected Christian Rome to become a utopia that would somehow eliminate the cruelty and violence of the imperial state, but found instead that Roman belligerence had infiltrated the Church. Constantine, his son Constantius II (r. 337–61) and their successors continued the struggle for consensus, using force when necessary, and their victims called them 'persecutors'. First, it was Athanasius' 'Nicenes' who suffered, but after the Council of Constantinople (381), which made Athanasius' creed the official faith of the empire, it was the Arians' turn. There were no formal executions but people were massacred when soldiers invaded a church to break up a heretical gathering and increasingly both sides complained far more about their opponents' violence than about their theology. In the early years, while Athanasius still enjoyed Constantine's favour, Arians complained of his 'greed, aggression and boundless ambition'[54] and accused him of 'force', 'murder' and the 'killing of bishops'.[55] For their part, the Nicenes vividly described the rattling weapons and flashing swords of the imperial troops, who thrashed their deacons and trampled worshippers underfoot.[56] Both sides dwelt obsessively on their enemies' vicious treatment of the consecrated virgins,[57] and both revered their dead as 'martyrs'. Christians were developing a history of grievance that intensified during the brief but dramatic reign of the emperor Julian (361–63), known as 'the Apostate'.

Despite his Christian upbringing, Julian had come to detest the new faith, convinced it would ruin the empire. Many of his subjects felt the same. Those who still loved the old rites feared that this violation of the *Pax deorum* would result in political catastrophe. Throughout the imperial domains, Julian appointed pagan priests to sacrifice to the One God worshipped under many names – as Zeus, Jupiter, Helios or, in the Hebrew Bible, 'God Most High'.[58] He removed Christians from public office, gave special privileges to towns that had never adopted Christianity, and announced that he would rebuild the Jewish temple in Jerusalem. Julian was careful to avoid outright persecution, but merely boosted pagan sacrifice, refurbished pagan shrines, and covertly encouraged anti-Christian violence.[59] Over the years a great deal of pent-up resentment had accumulated against the Church, and when Julian's edicts were published, in some towns pagans rioted against Christians, who now discovered how vulnerable they really were.

Once again, some Christians responded to the state that had suddenly turned against them with the defiant gesture of martyrdom. Most of the martyrs who died in these two years were either killed by pagan mobs or put to death by local officials for their provocative attacks on pagan religion.[60] As Jews began work on their new temple and pagans gleefully refurbished their shrines, throughout the empire conflict centred on iconic buildings. Ever since Constantine, Christians had become accustomed to seeing the decline of Judaism as the essential concomitant to the triumph of the Church. Now as they watched the purposeful activity of the Jewish workmen on the temple site in Jerusalem, they felt as if the fabric of their own faith had been undermined. At Merum in Phrygia, there was a more ominous development. While the local pagan temple was being repaired and the statues of the gods polished, three Christians, 'unable to endure the indignity put upon their religion and impelled by a fervent zeal for virtue, rushed by night into the temple and broke the images in pieces'. This amounted to a suicide attack on a building that seemed to epitomise their new humiliation. Even though the governor urged them to repent, they refused, 'declaring their readiness to undergo any sufferings, rather than pollute themselves by sacrificing'. Consequently, they were tortured and roasted to death on a gridiron.[61] A new spate of martyr stories appeared, even more sensational than the original Acts of the Martyrs.

In this aggressive form of martyrdom, the martyrs were no longer the innocent victims of imperial violence: their battles now took the form of a symbolic assault upon the enemies of the faith. Like some modern religious extremists, Christians felt that they had suffered a sudden loss of power and prestige – all the more acute in their case because the memory of their days as a despised minority were so recent.[62] Christians courted martyrdom by smashing the pagan gods' effigies, disrupting rituals and destroying the temples that symbolised their degradation, and by loudly praising those who had defied Julian's 'tyranny'. When Julian was killed in a military expedition against Persia, and Jovian, a Christian, was proclaimed emperor in his place, it seemed like a divine deliverance. But Julian's reign, which had so rudely shattered the Christians' new-found security and entitlement, had created a polarised religious climate and, at least among the lower classes, had exacerbated hostility between Christians and pagans. 'Never again!' would be the Christian watchword as they contemplated renewed attacks on the pagan establishment in the coming years.[63] State repression leaves a history of injury that often radicalises a religious tradition and can even push an originally irenic vision into a campaign of violence.

Christian and pagan aristocrats, however, still shared a common culture that did much to mitigate this aggression among the upper classes. Throughout the empire, young noblemen and talented individuals of humble birth were inducted into a 'formation' (*paedeia*) dating from ancient times.[64] It was not a purely academic programme, though it was intellectually rigorous, but was primarily an initiation that shaped the behaviour of the ruling class and profoundly moulded their attitudes. As a result, wherever they travelled in the empire, they found that they could relate to their peers. Paedeia was an important antidote to the violence of late Roman society, where slaves were regularly beaten to death, where the flogging of social inferiors was perfectly acceptable, and where councillors were publicly thrashed for tax arrears. A truly cultivated Roman was unfailingly courteous and self-controlled, since anger, vituperative speech and aggressive gestures were unbecoming to a gentleman, who was expected to yield graciously to others and behave at all times with restraint, calm and gravitas.

Because of paedeia, the old religion remained an integral part of late Roman culture and its ethos was also absorbed into the life of the Church, where young men brought these attitudes with them to the baptismal font; some even saw paedeia as an indispensable preparation for Christianity.[65] 'With measured words, I learn to bridle rage,' the Cappadocian bishop Gregory of Nazianzus (329–90) told his congregation.[66] His friends, Basil, bishop of Caesarea (c. 330–79) and Gregory, bishop of Nyssa (331–95), Basil's younger brother, were not baptised until after they had completed this traditional training.[67] The restraint of paedeia also informed the doctrine of the Trinity, which these three men, often known as the Cappadocian Fathers, developed towards the end of the Arian crisis. They had been uneasy about these disputes, both sides of which had been strident and had cultivated an inappropriate certainty about these ineffable matters. The Cappadocians practised the silent, reticent prayer designed by Evagrius of Pontus in part to strip the mind of such angry dogmatism. They knew that it was impossible to speak about God as we speak about ordinary matters and the Trinity was designed firstly to help Christians realise that what we call God lies beyond the reach of words and concepts. But they would also introduce Christians to a meditation on the Trinity that would help them to develop attitudes of restraint in their own lives that would counter aggressive and bellicose intolerance.

Many Christians had been confused by the creed of Nicaea. If there was only one God, how could Jesus be divine? Did that mean that there were two gods? And was there a third: what was the 'holy spirit', which had been dealt with so perfunctorily in Athanasius' creed? In the New Testament, this Jewish term had referred to the human experience of the power and presence of God, which could never measure up to the divine reality itself. The Trinity was an attempt to translate this Jewish insight into a Hellenistic idiom. God, the Cappadocians explained, had one inaccessible essence (*ousia*) that was totally beyond the reach of the human mind, but it had been made known to us by three manifestations (*hypostases*): the Father (source of being), the Logos (in the man Jesus) and the Spirit that we encounter within ourselves. Each 'person' (from the Latin *persona*, meaning 'mask') of the Trinity was merely a partial glimpse of the divine *ousia* that we could never comprehend. The Cappadocians introduced converts to the Trinity in a meditation, which reminded them that the divine could never be encapsulated in a dogmatic formula. Constantly repeated, this meditation taught Christians that there was a kenosis at the heart of the Trinity, since the Father ceaselessly emptied himself, transmitting everything to the Logos. Once that Word had been spoken, the Father no longer had an 'I' but remained eternally silent and unknowable. The Logos likewise had no self of its own but was simply the 'Thou' of the Father, while the Spirit was the 'We' of Father and Son.[68] The Trinity expressed the paedeia's values of restraint, deference and self-abnegation, with which the more aristocratic bishops countered the new Christian stridency. Other bishops, alas, were all too ready to embrace it.

Constantine had given the bishops new authority for the exercise of imperial power, and some, especially those of humble birth, strove for the episcopate as aggressively as politicians compete for parliamentary seats today.[69] Some even staged coups, taking over a church by night and barricading the doors during their illegal consecration.[70] 'At present we have men who claim to be bishops – a lowly breed who are bogged down in acquiring money and military operations and striving for honourable positions,' complained the historian Palladius.[71] They became known as 'tyrant bishops'. In ancient Greece, a *tyrannos* was a strong man who seized power by unlawful violence; in the later Roman empire, the word had general connotations of misrule, cruelty and unrestrained anger.[72] When Athanasius became a bishop, his opponents regularly called him a tyrant because, they claimed, he was motivated not by the desire to defend the faith but by personal ambition. He was described as 'raging like a tyrant' when he sentenced Arians to prison, flogging and torture, and, it was noted, his entourage included 'the military and officials of the imperial government'.[73] It was clearly easier to imperialise the faith than to Christianise the empire.

In the late fourth century, rioting became a regular feature of city life. Barbarian tribes were ceaselessly attacking the frontiers, brigandage was rife in the countryside and refugees poured into the towns.[74] Overcrowding, disease, unemployment and increased taxes created a tension that often exploded violently but because the army was needed to defend the borders, governors had no military forces to quell these uprisings and passed the responsibility for crowd control to the bishops.[75] 'It is the duty of a bishop like you to cut short and restrain any unregulated movements of the mob,' wrote the Patriarch of Antioch to a colleague.[76] The bishops of Syria already relied on local monks to man their soup kitchens and serve as stretcher-bearers, hospital porters and gravediggers. These monks were greatly loved by the people, especially the urban poor, who enjoyed their aggressive denunciations of the rich. Now they began to police the riots and in the process acquired martial skills.

Unlike Antony's Egyptian monks, the monks of Syria had no interest in fighting the demon of anger. Known as *boskoi*, 'grazers', they had no fixed abode but roamed through the mountains at will, feeding on wild plants.[77] One of the most famous boskoi was Alexander the Sleepless, who had left a regular community of monks because he disapproved of its property ownership. He had wholly imbibed the post-Julian ethos of 'Never Again' and his first act, on emerging from seven solitary years in the desert, was to burn down the largest temple in a pagan village. There could be zero tolerance for the icons of the old religion, which were a standing threat to the security of the Church. Alexander lost out on the palm of martyrdom, however, because he preached so eloquently to the mob that came to kill him that it converted to Christianity on the spot. He founded an order dedicated to 'freedom from care', so instead of working for their living, like Antony, his monks lived on alms, refusing to engage in productive labour. And instead of trying to control their anger, they gave it free rein.[78] During the 380s, four hundred of them formed a massive prayer gang and began a twenty-year trek along the Persian border, singing in shifts all around the clock in obedience to Paul's instructions to 'pray without ceasing'.[79] The hapless inhabitants of the villages on either side of the frontier were terrorised as the monks chanted the psalmists' blood-curdling denunciations of idolatry. Their aggressive begging made them an intolerable burden to these rural communities that could barely support themselves. When they arrived in a city, they squatted in a public space in the centre, attracting huge crowds of urban poor who flocked to hear their fiery condemnation of the rich.

But those who did not feel badgered by them respected the monks for expressing the values of Christianity in an absolute way. For them, Alexander's virulent intolerance of paganism showed that he really believed that Christianity was the one true faith. After Julian, Christians increasingly defined themselves as a beleaguered community. They gathered around the tombs of local martyrs, listened avidly to the stories of their suffering, and piously preserved the memory of Julian's persecution, keeping alive their sense of grievance. Many had no time for the courteous tolerance of the more aristocratic bishops.[80] The pagan temples, which had symbolised the brief pagan revival, seemed a standing threat that became increasingly intolerable. To add fuel to these flames, the emperors were now ready to exploit the monks' popularity and let these zealots loose on the pagan world. They would enforce the Pax Christiana as aggressively as they had previously imposed the Pax Romana.

Theodosius I (r. 346–95) was a recent convert and a man of humble Spanish origins. A brilliant soldier, he had pacified the Danube region and arrived in Constantinople in 380 determined to implement his aggressive form of Christianity in the east. It was he who summoned the Council of Constantinople that made Nicene orthodoxy the official religion of the empire in 381. He patronised the Roman aristocracy when it suited him, but his sympathies really lay with the man in the street and he decided to create a power base by wooing the disaffected townsfolk through their beloved monks. He could see the point of destroying the pagan temples; his empress Aelia Flacilla had already distinguished herself in Rome by leading a crowd of noble women to attack pagan shrines. In 388, Theodosius gave the monks the go-ahead and they fell on the village shrines of Syria like a plague; with the connivance of the local bishop, they also destroyed a synagogue at Callinicum on the Euphrates. The pagan orator Libanius urged the emperor to prosecute this 'black-robed tribe' who were guilty of latrocinium, describing the 'utter desolation' that followed their vicious attacks on the temples 'with sticks and stones and bars of iron, and in some cases, disdaining these, with hands and feet'. The pagan priests had no option but to 'keep quiet or die'.[81] The monks became the symbolic vanguard of violent Christianisation. The mere sound of their chanting was enough to make the governor of Antioch adjourn his court and flee the city. Even though there were no boskoi on Minorca, the leader of the Jewish community there dreamed in 418 that his synagogue was in ruins and its site occupied by psalm-singing monks. A few weeks later the synagogue was in fact destroyed – though not by monks but by fanatic local Christians.[82]

Some bishops opposed this vandalism, but not consistently. Because Roman law protected Jewish property, Theodosius ordered the bishop who had instigated the burning of the Callinicum synagogue to pay for its repair. But Ambrose (339–97), bishop of Milan, forced him to rescind this decree, since rebuilding the synagogue would be as humiliating to the true faith as Julian's attempt to restore the Jewish temple.[83] The Christianisation of the empire was now, increasingly, equated with the destruction of these iconic buildings. In 391, after Theodosius had permitted Theophilus, bishop of Alexandria, to occupy the temple of Dionysus, the bishop pillaged all the temples in the city and paraded the looted treasure in an insulting display.[84] In response, the pagans of Alexandria barricaded themselves into the magnificent temple of Serapis with some Christian hostages, whom they forced to re-enact the trauma of Diocletian's persecution:

> These they forced to offer sacrifice on the altars where fire was kindled; those who refused they put to death with new and refined tortures, fastening some to gibbets and breaking the legs of others and pitching them into the caverns which a careworn antiquity had built to receive the blood of sacrifices and the other impurities of the temple.[85]

When the pagan leader thought he heard monks singing in some distant part of the shrine he knew he was doomed. In fact, the Serapaeum was destroyed by imperial soldiers acting under the bishop's orders, but the monks who turned up afterwards carrying relics of John the Baptist and squatted in the ruins became the symbols of this Christian triumph.[86] It was reported that many pagans were so shocked by these events that they converted on the spot.

The success of these attacks convinced Theodosius that the best way of achieving ideological consensus in the empire was to ban sacrificial worship and close down all the old shrines and temples. His son and successor Arcadius (r. 395–408) expressed this policy succinctly: 'When [the temples] are overthrown and obliterated, the material foundations for all superstition will have been done away with.'[87] He urged local aristocracies throughout the empire to let their zealots loose on the temples to prove that the pagan gods could not even defend their own homes. As one modern historian notes: 'Silencing, burning and destruction were all forms of theological demonstration; and when the lesson was over, monks and bishops, generals and emperors had driven the enemy from the field.'[88]

It was Aurelius Augustine, bishop of Hippo in North Africa, who gave the most authoritative blessing to this Christian state violence. He had found by experience that militancy brought in new converts.[89] Writing twenty-five years after agents of the Western emperor Honorius had torn down the temples and idolatrous shrines of Carthage in 399, he asked: 'Who does not see how much the worship of the name of Christ has increased!'[90] When Donatist monks had raged through the African countryside in the 390s, destroying the temples and attacking the estates of the nobility, Augustine had at first forbidden the use of force against them, but he soon noticed that it was the stern imperial edicts that terrified the Donatists and made them return to the Church. It is no coincidence, therefore, that it was Augustine who would develop the 'just war' theory, the foundation of all future Christian thinking on the subject.[91] When Jesus had told his disciples to turn the other cheek when attacked, Augustine argued, he had not asked them to be passive in the face of wrongdoing.[92] What made violence evil was not the act of killing but the passions of greed, hatred and ambition that had prompted it.[93] Violence was legitimate, however, if inspired by charity – by a sincere concern for the enemy's welfare – and should be administered in the same way as a schoolmaster beat his pupils for their own good.[94] But force must always be authorised by the proper authority.[95] An individual, even if acting in self-defence, would inevitably feel an inordinate desire (libido) to inflict pain on his assailant, whereas a professional soldier, who was simply obeying orders, could act dispassionately. In putting violence beyond the reach of the individual, Augustine had given the state almost unlimited powers.

When Augustine died in 430, the Vandals were besieging Hippo. During the last years of his life, one western province after another had fallen to the barbarian tribes, who had set up their own kingdoms in Germany and Gaul, and in 410 Alaric and his Gothic horsemen had sacked the city of Rome itself. In response, Theodosius II (r. 408–50) built a massive fortifying wall around Constantinople, but the Byzantines had long been oriented to the east, still dreaming of replicating Cyrus' empire, and were able to survive the loss of old Rome without undue repining.[96] Lacking imperial supervision, western Europe became a primitive backwater, its civilisation lost, and for a while it looked as though Christianity itself would perish there. But the western bishops stepped into the shoes of the departing Roman officials, maintaining a semblance of order in some regions, and the Pope, the bishop of Rome, inherited the imperial aura. The popes sent missionaries out to the new barbarian kingdoms who converted the Anglo-Saxons in Britain and the Franks in the old province of Gaul. Over the coming centuries, the Byzantines would look with increasing disdain on these 'barbarian' Christians. They would never accept the popes' claim that, as the successors of St Peter, they were the true leaders of the Christian world.

In Byzantium, the debates on the nature of Christ were resumed even more aggressively than before. It might seem that this conflict, which had always expressed itself violently, was caused wholly by religious zeal for correct dogma. The bishops were still searching for a way to express their vision of humanity, vulnerable and moribund as it was, as somehow sacred and divine. But the discussions were fuelled in equal measure by the internal politics of the empire. The leading protagonists were 'tyrant bishops', men with worldly ambitions and huge egos, and the emperors continued to muddy the waters. Theodosius II patronised the lawless monks even more assiduously than his grandfather. One of his protégés was Nestorius, Patriarch of Constantinople, who argued that Christ had two natures, one human and one divine.[97] Where the Nicene Creed saw humanity and divinity as entirely compatible, however, Nestorius insisted that they could not coexist. His argument was thoughtful and nuanced and if the debate had been conducted in a peaceable, open-hearted manner, the issue could have been resolved. But anxious to curb Nestorius' rising star, Cyril, Patriarch of Alexandria, vehemently accused him of outright heresy, arguing that when God stooped to save us, he did not go halfway, as Nestorius seemed to suggest, but embraced our humanity in all its physicality and mortality. At the Council of Ephesus (431), which met to decide the issue, both sides accused each other of 'tyranny'. Nestorius claimed that Cyril had sent a horde of 'fanatical monks' to attack him and that he had been compelled to surround his house with an armed guard.[98] Contemporary historians had no respect for either side, dismissing Nestorius as a 'firebrand' and Cyril as 'power-hungry'.[99] There was no serious doctrinal conflict, argued Palladius; these men 'tore the church asunder' simply 'to satisfy their desire for the episcopal office or even the primacy of the episcopate'.[100]

In 449, Eutyches, a revered monastic leader in Constantinople, maintained that Jesus had only one nature (mono physis), since his humanity had been so thoroughly deified that it was no longer like our own. He accused his opponents – quite inaccurately – of 'Nestorianism'. Flavian, his bishop, tried to settle the matter quietly but Eutyches was a favourite of the emperor and insisted on making a legal case of it.[101] The result was a virtual civil war over doctrine, in which emperor and monks formed an unholy alliance against the more moderate bishops. A second council was convened at Ephesus in 449 to settle the 'Monophysite' problem, headed by the 'tyrant bishop' Dioscorus, Patriarch of Alexandria, who was determined to use the council to establish himself as primate of the Eastern Church. To make matters worse, Theodosius brought the monk Barsauma and his crew to Ephesus, ostensibly to represent 'all the monks and pious people of the east' but actually to be his stormtroopers.[102] Twenty years earlier, Barsauma and his monastic thugs had ritually re-enacted Joshua's campaign in Palestine and Transjordan, systematically destroying synagogues and temples at all the holy places along the route, and in 438 they had killed Jewish pilgrims on the Temple Mount in Jerusalem. 'He has sent thousands of monks against us,' his victims complained later, 'he has devastated all of Syria; he is a murderer and a slayer of bishops.'[103]

When the delegates arrived at Ephesus, they were met by hordes of monks wielding clubs and attacking Eutyches' opponents:

> They were carrying off men, some of them from the ships and others of them from the streets and others from the houses and others from the churches where they were praying and were pursuing others of them that fled; and with all zeal they were searching out and digging [out] even those who were hiding in caves and in holes of the earth.[104]

Hilary of Poitiers, the Pope's envoy, thought he was lucky to get out alive and Bishop Flavian was beaten so badly that he died shortly afterwards. Dioscorus refused to allow any dissenting voice to be heard, doctored the minutes, and called in the imperial troops when it came to the vote.

The following year, however, Theodosius died and the monks lost their imperial support. A new council met at Chalcedon in 451 to reverse Second Ephesus and create a neutral theological middle ground.[105] The 'Tome' of Pope Leo, which declared diplomatically that Jesus was fully God and fully man, now became the touchstone of orthodoxy.[106] Dioscorus was deposed; and the roaming Syrian boskoi reined in. Henceforth all monks were required to live and remain in their monastery, forbidden to participate in both worldly and ecclesiastical affairs, and were to be financially dependent on and controlled by the local bishop. But Chalcedon, hailed as the triumph of law and order, was actually an imperial coup. At the beginning of the fourth century, Christians had denounced the presence of imperial troops in their churches as sacrilegious; but after the horror of Second Ephesus, the moderate bishops begged the emperor to take control. Consequently a committee of nineteen of the highest military and civil officials of the empire presided over Chalcedon, set the agenda, silenced dissenting voices, and enforced correct procedure. Henceforth in the Syrian-speaking world, the Chalcedonian Church was known as 'Melkite' – 'the emperor's Church'. In every previous empire, the religion of the ruling class had been distinct from the faith of the subjugated masses, so the Christian emperors' attempt to impose their theology on their subjects was a shocking break with precedent and was experienced as an outrage. Opponents of this imperialised Christianity espoused Eutyches' 'Monophysitism' in protest. In fact, the theological difference between 'Monophysites' and 'Nicenes' was minimal, but the Monophysites could point to other Christian traditions – not least Jesus' stance against Rome – to claim that the Melkites had made an unholy alliance with earthly power.

The debates about the nature of Christ had been an attempt to build a holistic view of reality, one with no division between the physical and the spiritual realms or the divine and the human. In human society too, the emperor Justinian (r. 527–65) believed, there should be a *symphonia* of church and state, a harmony and concord based on the Incarnation of the Logos in the man Jesus.[107] Just as the two natures – human and divine – were found in a single person, there could be no separation of church and empire; together they formed the Kingdom of God, which would soon spread to the entire world. But there was, of course, a massive difference between Jesus' Kingdom and the Byzantine state.

As the barbarians crept ever closer to the walls of Constantinople, Justinian became even more zealous in restoring the divine unity by vigorously enforcing the supremacy of 'the emperor's church'. His attempts to suppress the Monophysite party permanently alienated the people of Palestine, Syria and Egypt. He declared that Judaism was no longer *religio licita:* Jews were now debarred from public office and the use of Hebrew was prohibited in the synagogue. In 528, Justinian gave all pagans three months to be baptised, and the following year, he closed the Academy in Athens that had been founded by Plato. In every province, from Morocco to the Euphrates, he commissioned churches, built after the style of Constantinople, to symbolise the unity of the empire. Instead of providing a challenging alternative to imperial violence, the tradition that had begun in part as a protest against the systemic oppression of empire had become the tool of Rome's aggressive coercion.

In 540 Khusrow I of Persia began to transform his ailing kingdom into the economic giant of the region in a reform based on a classic definition of the agrarian state:[108]

> The monarchy depends on the army, the army on money; money comes from the land tax; the land tax comes from agriculture. Agriculture depends on justice; justice on the integrity of officials, and integrity and reliability on the ever-watchfulness of the king.[109]

Khusrow devised a more efficient method of tax collection and invested heavily in the irrigation of Mesopotamia, which previous Persian kings had neglected. With the proceeds, he was able to create a professional army to replace the traditional aristocratic levies. War with Christian Rome was now inevitable, since both powers aspired to dominate the region. Khusrow employed Arab tribesmen to police his southern border, and the Byzantines reciprocated by hiring the Banu Ghassan, even though they had converted to Monophysite Christianity, to patrol the frontier from their winter camp near Damascus.

In Khusrow's Persia, there was zero tolerance for rebellion but no religious discrimination: on the eve of a revolt, the king warned that he would 'kill every man who persists in insubordination against me – be he a good Zoroastrian, a Jew or a Christian'.[110] Like most traditional agrarian rulers, the Persian kings had no interest in imposing their faith on their subjects; even Darius' imperial version of Zoroastrianism had been strictly confined to the aristocracy. Their subjects worshipped as they chose, living in communities of Christians, Jews and pagans, governed by their own laws and customs, and ruled by religious officials who were agents of the state – an arrangement that determined the social organisation of Middle Eastern society for over a millennium. After Khusrow's death, there was a civil war in Persia and the Byzantine emperor Maurice intervened to put the young Khusrow II (591–628) on the throne. Alienated from the Persian nobility, Khusrow II surrounded himself with Christians, but the splendours of his court set the tone for Middle Eastern monarchy for centuries to come. He continued his father's reforms, making Mesopotamia a vibrant, rich and creative region. The Jewish community at Ctesiphon (near modern

Baghdad) became the intellectual and spiritual capital of world Jewry, and
Nisibis, dedicated to the study of Christian scripture, another great intellectual centre.[111] While Byzantine horizons were shrinking, Persians were
broadening their outlook.

When his ally Maurice was assassinated in a coup in 610, Khusrow
seized the opportunity to conduct massive raids for slaves and booty in
Byzantium. And when Heraclius, governor of Roman North Africa, gained
the imperial throne in another coup, Khusrow embarked on a huge
offensive, conquering Antioch (613), large areas of Syria and Palestine
(614), Egypt (619), and in 626 the Persian army even besieged
Constantinople. But in an extraordinary riposte, Heraclius and his small
disciplined army defeated the Persian forces in Asia Minor and invaded
the Iranian Plateau, attacking the unprotected estates of the Zoroastrian
nobility and destroying their shrines before he was forced to withdraw.
Utterly discredited, Khusrow was assassinated by his ministers in 628.
Heraclius' campaign had been more overtly religious than any previous
war of Christian Rome. Indeed, so intertwined were church and empire
by now that Christianity itself had seemed under attack during the siege
of Constantinople. When the city was saved, the victory was attributed
to Mary, mother of God, whose icon had been paraded to deter the
enemy from the city walls.

During the Persian wars a monk finally brought the Christological
disputes to an end. Maximus (580–662) insisted that these issues could not
be settled simply by a theological formulation: 'deification' was rooted in
the experience of the Eucharist, in contemplation, and in the practice of
charity. It was these communal rites and disciplines that taught Christians
to see that it was impossible to think 'God' without thinking 'man'. If
human beings emptied their minds of the jealousy and animosity that ruin
their relations with one another, they could, even in this life, become divine:
'The whole human being could become God, deified by the grace of God
become man – whole man, soul and body, by nature and becoming whole
God, soul and body by grace.'[112] Every single person, therefore, had sacred
value. Our love of God was inseparable from our love of one another.[113]
Indeed, Jesus had taught that the iron test of our love of God was that we
love our enemies:

> Why did he command this? To free you from hatred, anger and resentment,
> and to make you worthy of the supreme gift of perfect love. And you cannot
> attain such love if you do not imitate God and love all men equally. For God

loves all men equally and wishes them 'to be saved and to come to the knowledge of the truth.'[114]

Unlike the 'tyrant bishops' who vied for the emperor's backing, Maximus became a victim not a perpetrator of imperial violence. Having fled to North Africa during the Persian wars, in 661 he was forcibly brought to Constantinople, where he was imprisoned, condemned as a heretic and mutilated; he died shortly afterwards in exile. But he was vindicated at the third Council of Constantinople in 680 and would become known as the Father of Byzantine theology.

The doctrine of deification celebrates the transfiguration of the entire human being in the here and now, not merely in a future state, and this has indeed been the living experience of individual Christians. But this spiritual triumph hardly resembles the 'realised eschatology' promoted by emperors and 'tyrant bishops'. After Constantine's conversion, they had convinced themselves that the empire was the Kingdom of God and a second manifestation of Christ. Not even the catastrophe of the second Council of Ephesus or the military vulnerability of their empire could shake their belief that Rome would become intrinsically Christian and win the world for Christ. In other traditions, people had tried to create a challenging alternative to the systemic violence of the state, but right up to the fall of Constantinople to the Turks in 1453 Byzantines continued to believe that the Pax Romana was compatible with the Pax Christiana. The enthusiasm with which they had greeted imperial patronage was never accompanied by a sustained critique of the role and nature of the state, or its ineluctable violence and oppression.[115]

By the early seventh century, both Persia and Byzantium had been ruined by their wars for imperial dominance. Syria, already weakened by a devastating plague, had become an impoverished region and Persia had succumbed to anarchy, its frontier fatally compromised. Yet while Persians and Byzantines eyed one another nervously, the real danger emerged elsewhere. Both empires had forgotten their Arab clients and failed to notice that the Arabian Peninsula had experienced a commercial revolution. Arabs had been watching the wars between the great powers very closely and knew that both empires were fatally weakened; they were about to undergo an astonishing spiritual and political awakening.

7

THE MUSLIM DILEMMA

In 610, the year that saw the outbreak of the Persian–Byzantine war, a merchant from Mecca in the Arabian Hejaz experienced a dramatic revelation during the sacred month of Ramadan. For some years, Muhammad ibn Abdullah had made an annual retreat on Mount Hira, just outside the city.[1] There he fasted, performed spiritual exercises, and gave alms to the poor while he meditated deeply on the problems of his people, the tribe of Quraysh. Only a few generations earlier, their ancestors had been living a desperate life in the intractable deserts of northern Arabia. Now they were rich beyond their wildest dreams and, since farming was virtually impossible in this arid land, their wealth had been entirely created by commerce. For centuries the local nomads (*badawin*) had scratched out a meagre living by herding sheep and breeding horses and camels, but in the sixth century they had invented a saddle that enabled camels to carry heavier loads than before. As a result, merchants from India, East Africa, Yemen and Bahrain began to take their caravans through the Arabian steppes to Byzantium and Syria, using the Bedouin to guide them from one watering-hole to another. Mecca had become a station for these caravans, and the Quraysh started their own trade missions to Syria and Yemen, while the Bedouin exchanged goods in an annual circuit of regular *suqs* ('markets') around Arabia.[2]

Mecca's prosperity also depended on its status as a pilgrimage centre. At the end of the suq season, Arabs came from all over Mecca during the month of Hajj to perform the ancient rituals around the Kabah, the ancient cube-shaped shrine in the heart of the city. Cult and commerce were inseparable: the climax of the *hajj* (pilgrimage) was the *tawaf*, the seven circumambulations of the Kabah that mirrored the suq circuit, giving the Arabs' mercantile activities a spiritual dimension. Yet despite its extraordinary success, Mecca was in the grip of a social and moral crisis. The old tribal spirit had succumbed to the ethos of an infant market economy and families now vied with one another for wealth and prestige. Instead of sharing their goods, as had been essential for the tribe's survival in the desert, families were building private fortunes, and this emerging commercial aristocracy ignored the plight of the poorer Quraysh and seized the inheritances of orphans and widows. The rich were delighted with their new security but those who fell behind felt lost and disoriented.

Poets exalted Bedouin life, but in reality it was a grim, relentless struggle in which too many people competed for too few resources. Perpetually on the brink of starvation, tribes fought endless battles for pastureland, water and grazing. The *ghazu*, or 'acquisition raid', was essential to the Bedouin economy. In times of scarcity, tribesmen would invade their neighbours' territory and carry off camels, cattle, food or slaves, taking care to avoid killing anybody since this would lead to a vendetta. Like most pastoralists, they saw nothing reprehensible in raiding. The ghazu was a kind of national sport, conducted with skill and panache according to clearly defined rules, which the Bedouin would have thoroughly enjoyed. It was a brutal yet simple way of redistributing wealth in a region where there was simply not enough to go round.

The tribesmen had little interest in the supernatural but they gave meaning to their lives by formulating a code of virtue and honour. They called it *muruwah,* a term that is difficult to translate: it encompasses courage, patience and endurance. Muruwah had a violent core. Tribesmen had to avenge any wrong done to the group, protect its weaker members, and defy its enemies. Each member had to be ready to leap to the defence of his kinsmen if the tribe's honour was impugned. But above all, he had to share his resources. Tribal life on the steppes would be impossible if individuals hoarded their wealth while others went hungry; nobody would help you in a lean period if you had been miserly in your good days. But by the sixth century the limitations of muruwah were becoming tragically apparent, as the Bedouin got caught up in an escalating cycle of inter-tribal warfare. They began to regard those outside their kin group as worthless and expendable, and felt no moral anguish when killing in defence of the tribe, right or wrong.[3] Even their ideal of courage was now essentially combative, since it lay not in self-defence but in the pre-emptive strike.[4] Muslims traditionally call the pre-Islamic period *jahiliyyah,* which is usually translated as 'the time of ignorance'. But the primary meaning of the root *JHL* is 'irascibility' – an acute sensitivity to honour and prestige, excessive arrogance and, above all, a chronic tendency to violence and retaliation.[5]

Muhammad had become intensely aware of both the oppression and the injustice of Mecca and the martial danger of jahiliyyah. Mecca had to be a place where merchants from any tribe could gather freely to do business without fear of attack, so in the interests of commerce, the Quraysh had abjured warfare, maintaining a position of aloof neutrality. With consummate skill and diplomacy, they had established the 'sanctuary' (haram), a twenty-mile zone around the Kabah where all violence was forbidden.[6] But it would take more than that to subdue the jahili spirit. Meccan grandees were still chauvinistic, touchy, and liable to explosions of ungovernable fury. When Muhammad, the pious merchant, began to preach to his fellow Meccans in 612, he was well aware of the precariousness of this volatile society. Gathering a small community of followers, many from the weaker, disadvantaged clans, his message was based on the Quran ('Recitation'), a new revelation for the people of Arabia. The ideas of the civilised peoples of the ancient world had travelled down the trade routes and had been avidly discussed by the Arabs. Their own local lore had it that they themselves were descended from Ishmael, Abraham's eldest son,[7] and many believed that their high god Allah, whose name simply meant 'God', was identical with the God of the Jews and Christians. But the Arabs had no concept of an exclusive revelation or of their own special election. The Quran was to them simply the latest in the unfolding revelation of Allah to the descendants of Abraham, a 'reminder' of what everybody knew already.[8] Indeed, in one remarkable passage of what would become the written Quran, Allah makes it clear that he made no distinction between the revelations of any of the prophets.[9]

The bedrock message of the Quran was not a new abstruse doctrine, such as had riven Byzantium, but simply a 'reminder' of what constituted a just society that challenged the structural violence emerging in Mecca: that it was wrong to build a private fortune but good to share your wealth with the poor and vulnerable, who must be treated with equity and respect. The Muslims formed an ummah, a 'community' that provided an alternative to the greed and systemic injustice of Meccan capitalism. Eventually the religion of Muhammad's followers would be called islam, because it demanded that individuals 'surrender' their whole being to Allah; a muslim was simply a man or woman who had made that surrender. But at first the new faith was called tazakka, which can be roughly translated as 'refinement'.[10] Instead of hoarding their wealth and ignoring the plight of the poor, Muslims were exhorted to take responsibility for one another and feed the destitute, even when they were hungry themselves.[11] They traded the irascibility of jahiliyyah for the traditional Arab virtue of hilm – forbearance, patience and mercy.[12] By caring for the vulnerable, freeing slaves, and performing small acts of kindness on a daily, even hourly basis, they believed that they would gradually acquire a responsible, compassionate spirit and purge themselves of selfishness. Unlike the tribesmen, who retaliated violently at the slightest provocation, Muslims must not strike back but leave revenge to Allah,[13] consistently treating all others with gentleness and courtesy.[14] Socially, the surrender of *islam* would be realised by learning to live in a community: believers would discover their deep bond with other human beings, whom they would strive to treat as they would wish to be treated themselves. 'Not one of you can be a believer,' Muhammad is reported to have said, 'unless he desires for his neighbour what he desires for himself.'

At first, the Meccan establishment took little notice of the ummah, but when Muhammad began to emphasise the monotheism of his message they became alarmed, for commercial rather than theological reasons. Outright rejection of the local deities would be bad for business and alienate the tribes who kept their totems round the Kabah and came specifically to visit them during the hajj. A serious rift now developed: Muslims were attacked; the ummah, still only a small segment of the Quraysh, was economically and socially ostracised; and Muhammad's life was in jeopardy. When Arabs from Yathrib, an agrarian colony some 250 miles to the north, invited the ummah to settle with them, it seemed the only solution. In 622, therefore, some seventy Muslim families left their homes for the oasis that would become known as *al-Madinat*, or Medina, the City of the Prophet.

This *hijrah* ('migration') from Mecca was an extraordinary step. In Arabia, where the tribe was the most sacred value, to abandon one's kinsfolk and accept the permanent protection of strangers was tantamount to blasphemy. The very word hijrah suggests painful severance: *HJR* has been translated as 'he cut himself off from friendly or loving communication . . . he ceased . . . to associate with them'.[15] Henceforth, Meccan Muslims would be called the *Muhajirun* ('Emigrants'), this traumatic dislocation becoming central to their identity. In taking in these foreigners, with whom they had no blood relationship, the Arabs of Medina who had converted to Islam, the *Ansar* ('Helpers'), had also embarked on an audacious experiment. Medina was not a unified city but a series of fortified hamlets, each occupied by a different tribal group. There were two large Arab tribes – the Aws and the Khasraj – and twenty Jewish tribes and they all fought each other constantly.[16] Muhammad, as a neutral outsider, became an arbitrator and crafted an agreement that united Helpers and Emigrants in a super-tribe – 'one community to the exclusion of all men' – that would fight all enemies as one.[17] This is how Medina became a primitive 'state' and how it found, almost immediately, that despite the ideology of hilm it had no option but to engage in warfare.

The Emigrants were a drain on the community's resources. They were merchants and bankers but there was little opportunity for trade in Medina; they had no experience of farming and in any case there was no available land. It was essential to find an independent source of income, and the *ghazu* (raid), the accepted way of making ends meet in times of scarcity, was the obvious solution. In 624, therefore, Muhammad began to dispatch raiding parties to attack the Meccan caravans, a step that was controversial only in that the Muslims attacked their own tribe. But because the Quraysh had abjured warfare long ago, the Emigrants were inexperienced *ghazis* and their first raids failed. When they finally got the hang of it, the raiders broke two Arabian cardinal rules by accidentally killing a Meccan merchant and fighting during one of the Sacred Months when violence was prohibited throughout the peninsula.[18] Muslims could now expect reprisals from Mecca. Three months later, Muhammad himself led a ghazu to attack the most important Meccan caravan of the year. When they heard about it, the Quraysh immediately sent their army to defend it, but in a pitched battle at the well of Badr, the Muslims achieved a stunning victory. The Quraysh responded the following year by attacking Medina and defeating the Muslims at the Battle of Uhud, but in 627, when they attacked Medina again, the Muslims trounced the Quraysh at the Battle of the Trench, so-called because Muhammad dug a defensive ditch around the settlement.

The ummah also had internal troubles. Three of Medina's Jewish tribes – the Qaynuqa, Nadir and Qurayzah – were determined to destroy Muhammad, because he had undermined their political ascendancy in the oasis. They had sizable armies and pre-existing alliances with Mecca so they were a security risk. When the Qaynuqa and Nadir staged revolts and threatened to assassinate him, Muhammad expelled them from Medina. But the Nadir had joined the nearby Jewish settlement of Khaybar and drummed up support for Mecca among the local Bedouin. So after the Battle of the Trench, when the Qurayzah had put the entire settlement at risk by plotting with Mecca during the siege, Muhammad showed no mercy. In accordance with Arab custom, the 700 men of the tribe were slaughtered and the women and children sold as slaves. The other seventeen Jewish tribes remained in Medina and the Quran continued to instruct Muslims to behave respectfully to the 'People of the Book' (*ahl al-kitab*) and stress what they all held in common.[19] Even though the Muslims sentenced the tribesmen of Qurayzah for political not religious reasons, this atrocity marked the lowest point in the Prophet's career. From then on, he intensified his diplomatic efforts to build relationships with the Bedouin, who had been impressed by his military success, and established a powerful confederacy. Bedouin allies did not have to convert to Islam but swore merely to fight the ummah's enemies: Muhammad must be one of the few leaders in history to build an empire largely by negotiation.[20]

In March 628, during the month of the hajj and to everybody's astonishment, Muhammad announced that he intended to make the pilgrimage to Mecca, which, since pilgrims were forbidden to carry weapons, meant riding unarmed into enemy territory.[21] About a thousand Muslims volunteered to accompany him. The Quraysh dispatched their cavalry to attack the pilgrims, but their Bedouin allies guided them by a back route into the sanctuary of Mecca where all violence was forbidden. Muhammad then ordered the pilgrims to sit beside the Well of Hudaybiyyah and wait for the Quraysh to negotiate. He knew that he had put them in an extremely difficult position: if the guardians of the Kabah killed pilgrims on sacred ground they would lose all credibility in the region. Yet when the Qurayshi envoy arrived, Muhammad agreed to conditions that seemed to throw away every advantage the ummah had gained during the war. His fellow pilgrims were so horrified that they almost mutinied, yet the Quran would praise the truce of Hudaybiyyah as a 'manifest victory'. While the Meccans had behaved with typical jahili belligerence when they tried to slaughter the unarmed pilgrims, God had sent down the 'spirit of peace' (sakina) upon the Muslims.[22] Muhammad's first biographer declared that this nonviolent victory was the turning-point for the young movement: during the next two years 'double or more than double as many entered Islam as ever before,'[23] and in 630 Mecca voluntarily opened its gates to the Muslim army.

Our main source for Muhammad's life is the Quran, the collection of revelations that came to the Prophet during the twenty-three years of his mission. The official text was standardised under Uthman, the third caliph, some twenty years after Muhammad's death. But it had originally been transmitted orally, recited aloud and learned by heart; as a result, during and after the Prophet's life, the text remained fluid and people would have remembered and dwelt on different parts they had heard. The Quran is not a coherent revelation: it came to Muhammad piecemeal in response to particular events, so as in any scripture there were inconsistencies – not least about warfare. *Jihad* is not one of the Quran's main themes: in fact the word and its derivatives occur only forty-one times and just ten of these refer unambiguously to warfare. The 'surrender' of islam requires a constant *jihad* ('struggle') against our inherent selfishness; this sometimes involves fighting (*qital*) but bearing trials courageously and giving to the poor in times of personal hardship was also described as jihad.[24]

There is no univocal or systematic Quranic teaching about military violence.[25] Sometimes God demands patience and restraint rather than fighting;[26] sometimes he gives permission for defensive warfare and condemns aggression; but at other times he calls for offensive warfare within certain limits;[27] and occasionally these restrictions are lifted.[28] In some passages, Muslims are told to live at peace with the People of the Book;[29] in others they are required to subdue them.[30] These contradictory instructions occur throughout the Quran and Muslims developed two exegetical strategies to rationalise them. The first linked each verse of the Quran with a historical event in Muhammad's life and used this context to establish a general principle. But because the extant text does not place the revelations in chronological order, the early scholars found it difficult to determine these *asbab al-nuzal* ('occasions of revelations'). The second strategy was to abrogate verses: scholars argued that while the ummah was still struggling for survival, God could give Muslims only temporary solutions to their difficulties, but once Islam was victorious he could issue permanent commands. Thus the later revelations – some of which call for unrestrained warfare – were God's definitive words and rescinded the earlier more lenient directives.[31]

Scholars who favoured abrogation argued that when Muslims were still a vulnerable minority in Mecca, God told them to avoid fighting and confrontation.[32] But after the hijrah, when they had achieved a degree of power, God gave them permission to fight – but only in self-defence.[33] As they grew stronger, some of these restrictions were lifted[34] and finally, when the Prophet returned in triumph to Mecca, Muslims were told to wage war against non-Muslims wherever and whenever they could.[35] God had, therefore, been preparing Muslims gradually for their global conquests, tempering his instructions to their circumstances. But modern researchers have noted that the early exegetes did not always agree about which revelation should be attached to which particular 'occasion', or which verse abrogated which. The American scholar Reuven Firestone has suggested that the conflicting verses instead expressed the views of different groups within the ummah during the Prophet's life and after.[36]

It would not be surprising if there were disagreements and factions in the early ummah. Like the Christians, Muslims would interpret their reve- lation in radically divergent ways and, like any other faith, Islam developed in response to changing circumstances. The Quran seems aware that some Muslims would not be happy to hear that God had encouraged fighting: 'Fighting has been ordained for you, though it is hateful to you.'[37] Once the ummah had started to engage in warfare, it seems that one group, which was strong enough to warrant extensive rebuttal, consistently refused to take part:

> Believers, why, when it is said to you, 'Go and fight in God's cause' do you
> feel weighed down to the ground? Do you prefer this world to the world
> to come? How small is the enjoyment of this world compared with the life
> to come! If you do not go out and fight, God will punish you severely and
> put others in your place.[38]

The Quran calls these people 'laggers' and 'liars', and Muhammad was reproved for allowing them to 'stay at home' during campaigns.[39] They are accused of apathy, cowardice and equated with the *kufar,* the enemies of Islam.[40] But this group could point to the many verses in the Quran that instruct Muslims not to retaliate but to 'forgive and forbear', responding to aggression with mercy, patience and courtesy.[41] At other times, the Quran looks forward confidently to a final reconciliation: 'Let there be no argu- ment between us and you – God will gather us together and to Him we shall return.'[42] The impressive consistency of this irenic theme throughout the Quran, Firestone believes, must reflect a strong tendency that survived in the ummah for some time – perhaps until the ninth century.[43]

Ultimately, however, the more militant groups prevailed, possibly because by the ninth century, long after the Prophet's death, the more aggressive verses reflected reality since by this time Muslims had established an empire that could be maintained only by military force. Their favourite text was the 'Sword Verse', which they regarded as God's last word on the subject – though even here the endorsement of total warfare segues immediately into a demand for peace and leniency:

> When the forbidden months are over wherever you encounter the idolaters,
> kill them, seize them, besiege them, wait for them at every look-out post;
> but if they repent, maintain the prayer, and pay the prescribed alms, let them
> go on their way, for God is most merciful and forgiving.[44]

There is thus a constant juxtaposition of ruthlessness and mercy in the Quran: believers are repeatedly commanded to fight 'until there is no more sedition and religion becomes God's'[45] but are at once told that the moment the enemy sues for peace there must be no further hostilities.[46]

Muhammad's Confederacy broke up after his death in 632 and his 'successor' (*khalifa*), Abu Bakr, fought the defecting tribes to prevent Arabia from sliding back into chronic warfare. As we have seen elsewhere, the only way to stop this chronic infighting was to re-establish a strong hegemonic power that could enforce the peace. Within two years, Abu Bakr succeeded in restoring the Pax Islamica and after his death in 634, Umar ibn al-Khattab (r. 634–44), the second caliph, believed that peace could only be preserved by an outwardly directed offensive. These campaigns were not religiously inspired: there is nothing in the Quran to suggest that Muslims must fight to conquer the world. Umar's campaigns were driven almost entirely by the precarious economy of Arabia. There could be no question of establishing a conventional agrarian empire in Arabia, because there was so little land suitable for cultivation. The Quraysh's modest market economy clearly could not sustain the entire peninsula and the Quran forbade members of the Islamic Confederacy to fight each other. How, therefore, could a tribe feed itself in times of scarcity? The ghazu, the acquisition raid against neighbouring tribes, had been the only way to redistribute the meagre resources of Arabia but this was now off limits. Umar's solution was to raid the rich settled lands beyond the Arab peninsula, which, as the Arabs knew well, were in disarray after the Persian–Byzantine wars.

Under Umar's leadership, the Arabs burst out of the peninsula, initially in small local raids but later in larger expeditions. As they expected, they met with little opposition. The armies of both the great powers had been decimated and the subject peoples were disaffected. Jews and Monophysite Christians were sick of harassment from Constantinople and the Persians were still reeling from the political upheaval that had followed Khusrow II's assassination. Within a remarkably short period, the Arabs forced the Roman army to retreat from Syria (636) and crushed the depleted Persian army (637). In 641, they conquered Egypt and though they had to fight some fifteen years to pacify the whole of Iran, they were eventually victorious in 652. Only Byzantium, now a rump state shorn of its southern provinces, held out. Thus, twenty years after the Battle of Badr, the Muslims found themselves masters of Mesopotamia, Syria, Palestine and Egypt. When they finally subdued Iran, they had fulfilled the dream that

had eluded both the Persians and Byzantines and recreated Cyrus'
empire.[47]

It is hard to explain their success. The Arabs were accomplished raiders
but had little experience of protracted warfare and had no superior weapons
or technology.[48] In fact, like the Prophet, in the early years of the conquest
period they gained more territory by diplomacy than by fighting: Damascus
and Alexandria both surrendered because they were offered generous
terms.[49] The Arabs had no experience of state-building and simply adopted
Persian and Byzantine systems of land tenure, taxation and government.
There was no attempt to impose Islam on the subject peoples. The People
of the Book – Jews, Christians and Zoroastrians – became *dhimmis*
('protected subjects'). Critics of Islam often denounce this arrangement as
evidence of Islamic intolerance, but Umar had simply adapted Khusrow I's
Persian system: Islam would be the religion of the Arab conquerors – just
as Zoroastrianism had been the exclusive faith of the Persian aristocracy
– and the dhimmis would manage their own affairs as they had in Iran and
pay the *jizya*, a poll tax, in return for military protection. After centuries
of forcible attempts by the Christian Roman empire to impose religious
consensus, the traditional agrarian system had reasserted itself and many
of the dhimmis found this Muslim polity a relief.

When Umar took Jerusalem from the Byzantines in 632, he immediately
signed a charter to ensure that the Christian shrines were undisturbed and
cleared the site of the Jewish temple which had been left in ruins since its
destruction in CE 70 and was used as the city's garbage dump. Henceforth
this holy site would be called the Haram al-Sharif, the 'Most Noble
Sanctuary', and become the third-holiest place in the Muslim world, after
Mecca and Medina. Umar also invited Jews, who had been forbidden
permanent residence in Judaea since the Bar Kokhba revolt, to return to
the City of the Prophet Da'ud (David).[50] In the eleventh century, a Jerusalem
rabbi still recalled with gratitude the mercy God had shown his people
when he allowed the 'Kingdom of Ishmael' to conquer Palestine.[51] 'They
did not inquire about the profession of faith,' wrote the twelfth-century
historian Michael the Syrian, 'nor did they persecute anybody because of
his profession, as did the Greeks, a heretical and wicked nation.'[52]

The Muslim conquerors tried at first to resist the systemic oppression
and violence of empire. Umar did not allow his officers to displace the local
peoples or establish estates in the rich land of Mesopotamia. Instead, Muslim
soldiers lived in new 'garrison towns' (*amsar*; singular: *misr*) built in strategic
locations: Kufah in Iraq, Basra in Syria, Qum in Iran, and Fustat in Egypt;

Damascus was the only old city to become a misr. Umar believed that the
ummah, still in its infancy, could retain its integrity only by living apart from
the more sophisticated cultures. The Muslims' ability to establish and maintain a stable, centralised empire was even more surprising than their military
success. Both the Persians and the Byzantines imagined that, after their initial
victories, the Arabs would simply ask to settle in the empires they had
conquered. This, after all, was what the barbarians had done in the western
provinces and they now ruled according to Roman law and spoke Latin
dialects.[53] Yet when their wars of expansion finally ceased in 750, the Muslims
ruled an empire extending from the Himalayas to the Pyrenees, the largest
the world had yet seen, and most of the conquered peoples would convert
to Islam and speak Arabic.[54] This extraordinary achievement seemed to
endorse the message of the Quran, which taught that a society founded on
the Quranic principles of justice would always prosper.

Later generations would idealise the Conquest Era but it was a difficult
time. The failure to defeat Constantinople was a bitter blow. By the time
Uthman, the Prophet's son-in-law, became the third caliph (r. 644–56),
Muslim troops had become mutinous and discontented. The distances were
now so vast that campaigning was exhausting and they were taking less
plunder. Far from home, living perpetually in strange surroundings, soldiers
had no stable family life.[55] This disquiet is reflected in the *hadith* (plural:
ahadith) literature, in which the classical doctrine of jihad began to take
shape.[56] The *ahadith* ('reports') recorded sayings and stories of the Prophet
not included in the Quran. Now that he was no longer with them, people
wanted to know how Muhammad had behaved and what he had thought
about such subjects as warfare. These traditions were collected and anthologised during the eighth and ninth centuries and became so numerous that
criteria were needed to distinguish authentic reports from the obviously
spurious. Few of the ahadith date back to the Prophet himself but even the
more dubious ones throw light on attitudes in the early ummah as Muslims
reflected on their astounding success.

Many ahadith saw the wars as God's way of spreading the faith: 'I have
been sent to the human race in its entirety,'[57] the Prophet says; 'I have been
commanded to fight the people until they bear witness: "There is no god
but Allah"'.[58] Empire-building works best when soldiers believe that they
are benefiting humanity, so the conviction that they had a divine mission
would cheer flagging spirits. There is also contempt for the 'laggers' who
'stayed at home'; the soldiers probably resented those Muslims who benefited from the conquests but did not share their hardships. Thus in some

ahadith, Muhammad is made to condemn settled life: 'I was sent as a mercy and a fighter, not as a merchant and a farmer; the worst people of this ummah are the merchants and the farmers, [who are] not among those who take religion (din) seriously.'[59] Other reports emphasise the privations of the warrior who lives daily with death and 'has built a house and not lived in it, who has married a woman and not had intercourse with her'.[60] These warriors were beginning to dismiss other forms of jihad, such as caring for the poor, and saw themselves as the only true jihadis. Some ahadith claim that fighting was the Sixth Pillar or 'essential practice' of Islam, alongside the profession of faith (shehadah), almsgiving, prayer, the Ramadan fast and the hajj. Some said that fighting was far more precious than praying all night beside the Kabah or fasting for many days.[61] The ahadith give fighting a spiritual dimension it had never had in the Quran. There is much emphasis on the soldier's intentions: was he fighting for God or simply for fame and glory?[62] According to the Prophet, 'The monasticism of Islam is the jihad.'[63] The vocation of military life segregated soldiers from civilians, and as Christian monks lived separately from the laity, the garrison towns where Muslim fighters lived apart from their wives and observed the fasts and prayers assiduously were their monasteries.

Because soldiers constantly faced the possibility of an untimely death, there was much speculation about the afterlife. There had been no detailed End-Time scenario in the Quran, and Paradise had been described only in vaguely poetic terms. But now some ahadith claimed that the wars of conquest heralded the Last Days[64] and imagined Muhammad speaking as a doomsday prophet: 'Behold! God has sent me with a sword, just before the Hour.'[65] Muslim warriors are depicted as an elite vanguard fighting the battles of the End Time.[66] When the end came, all Muslims would have to abandon the ease of settled life and join the army, which would not only defeat Byzantium but complete the conquest of Central Asia, India and Ethiopia. Some soldiers were dreaming of martyrdom and the ahadith supplemented with Christian imagery the Quran's brief remarks about the fate of those who die in battle.[67] Like the Greek martus, the Arabic shahid meant 'one who bears witness' to Islam by making the ultimate surrender. Ahadith list his heavenly rewards: he will not have to wait in the grave for the Last Judgment like everybody else, but will ascend immediately to a special place in Paradise.

In the sight of God, the martyr has six [unique] qualities: God forgives him at the first opportunity, and shows him his place in Paradise; he is saved from the torment of the grave, he is safe from the great fright [of the Last Judgment], a crown of honour is placed on his head – one ruby of which is greater than the world and all that is in it – he is married to seventeen of the *houris* [women of Paradise] and he gains the rights to intercede [with God] for his relatives.[68]

As a reward for his hard life in the army, the martyr will drink wine, wear silk clothes and bask in the sexual delights he had forsaken for the jihad. But other Muslims, who were not so wedded to the new military ideal, would insist that any untimely death was a martyrdom: drowning, plague, fire or accident also 'bore witness' to human finitude, showing that there was no security in the human institutions in which people put their trust but only in the illimitable God.[69]

It was probably inevitable that, as they made their astonishing transition from a life of penury to world rule, there would be disagreements about leadership, the allocation of resources, and the morality of empire.[70] In 656, Uthman was killed during a mutiny of soldiers backed by the Quran-reciters, the guardians of Islamic tradition who were opposed to the growing centralisation of power in the ummah. With the support of these malcontents, Ali, the Prophet's cousin and son-in-law, became the fourth caliph; a devout man, he struggled with the logic of practical politics and his rule was not accepted in Syria, where the opposition was led by Uthman's kinsman Muawiyyah, governor of Damascus. The son of one of the Prophet's most obdurate enemies, Muawiyyah was supported by the wealthy Meccan families and by the people of Syria, who appreciated his wise and able rule. The spectacle of the Prophet's relatives and companions poised to attack one another was profoundly disturbing, and to prevent armed conflict, the two sides called for arbitration by neutral Muslims, who decided in favour of Muawiyyah. But an extremist group refused to accept this and were shocked by Ali's initial submission. They believed that the ummah should be led by the most committed Muslim (in this case, Ali) rather than a power-seeker, like Muawiyyah. They now regarded both rulers as apostates, so these dissidents withdrew from the ummah, setting up their own camp with an independent commander. They would be known as *kharaji*, 'those who go out'. After the failure of a second arbitration, Ali was murdered by a Kharajite in 661.

The trauma of this civil war marked Islamic life for ever. Henceforth rival parties would draw upon these tragic events as they struggled to make sense of their Islamic vocation. From time to time, Muslims who protested against the behaviour of the reigning ruler would retreat from the ummah, as the Kharajites had done, and summon all 'true Muslims' to join them in a struggle (jihad) for higher Islamic standards.[71] The fate of Ali became for some a symbol of the structural injustice of mainstream political life and these Muslims, who called themselves the *shiah-i Ali* ('Ali's Partisans'), developed a piety of principled protest, revering Ali's male descendants as the true leaders of the ummah. But, appalled by the murderous divisions that had torn the ummah apart, most Muslims decided that the unity of the ummah must be the first priority, even if that meant accommodating a degree of oppression and injustice. Instead of revering Ali's descendants, they would follow the *sunnah* ('customary practice') of the Prophet. As in Christianity and Judaism, radically different interpretations of the original revelation would make it impossible to speak of a pure essentialist 'Islam'.

The Quran had given Muslims an historical mission: to create a just community in which all members, even the weakest and most vulnerable, would be treated with absolute respect. Politics was, therefore, not a distraction from spirituality but what Christians would call a sacrament, the arena in which Muslims experienced God and which enabled the divine to function effectively in our world. Hence if state institutions did not measure up to the Quranic ideal, if their political leaders were cruel or exploitative and their community humiliated by foreign enemies, a Muslim could feel that his or her faith in life's ultimate purpose was imperilled. For Muslims, the suffering, oppression and exploitation that arose from the systemic violence of the state were moral issues of sacred import and could not be relegated to the profane realm.

After Ali's death, Muawiyyah moved his capital from Medina to Damascus and founded a hereditary dynasty. The Umayyads would create a conventional agrarian empire, with a privileged aristocracy and an unequal distribution of wealth. Herein lay the Muslim dilemma. There was now general agreement that an absolute monarchy was far more satisfactory than a military oligarchy where commanders inevitably competed aggressively for power – as Ali and Muawiyyah had done. The Umayyads' Jewish, Christian and Zoroastrian subjects agreed. They were weary of the chaos inflicted by the Roman–Persian wars and longed for the peace that only an autocratic empire seemed able to provide. Umayyads permitted some of the old Arab informality, but they understood the importance of the monarch's state of exception. They modelled their court ceremonial on Persian practice, shrouded the caliph from public view in the mosque, and achieved a monopoly of state violence by ruling that only the caliph could summon Muslims to war.[72]

But this adoption of the systemic violence condemned by the Quran was very disturbing to the more devout Muslims, and nearly all the institutions now regarded as critical to Islam emerged from anguished discussions that took place after the civil war. One was the Sunni/Shii divide. Another was the discipline of jurisprudence (*fiqh*): jurists wanted to establish precise legal norms that would make the Quranic command to build a just society a real possibility rather than a pious dream. These debates also produced Islamic historiography: in order to find solutions in the present, Muslims looked back to the time of the Prophet and the first four caliphs (*rashidun*). Moreover, Muslim asceticism developed as a reaction against the growing luxury and worldliness of the aristocracy. Ascetics often wore the coarse woollen garments (*tasawwuf*) standard among the poor, as the Prophet had done, so would become known as Sufis. While the caliph and his administration struggled with the problems that beset any agrarian empire and tried to develop a powerful monarchy, these pious Muslims were adamantly opposed to any compromise with systemic injustice and oppression.

One event above all others symbolised the tragic conflict between the inherent violence of the state and Muslim ideals. After Ali's death, the Shii had pinned their hopes on Ali's descendants. Hasan, Ali's elder son, came to an agreement with Muawiyyah and retired from political life. But in 680 when Muawiyyah died, he passed the caliphate to his son Yazid. For the first time, a Muslim ruler had not been elected by his peers and there were Shii demonstrations in Kufa in favour of Husain, Ali's younger son. This uprising was ruthlessly quashed, but Husain had already set out from Medina to Kufa, accompanied by a small band of his followers and their wives and children, convinced that the spectacle of the Prophet's family marching to end imperial injustice would remind the ummah of its Islamic priorities. But Yazid sent out the army and they were massacred on the plain of Karbala, outside Kufa; Husain was the last to die, holding his infant son in his arms. All Muslims lament the murder of the Prophet's grandson but, for the Shiah, Karbala epitomised the Muslim dilemma. How could Islamic justice be realistically implemented in a belligerent imperial state?

Under the Umayyad Caliph Abd al-Malik (685–705), the wars of expansion gained new momentum and the Middle East began to assume an Islamic face. The Dome of the Rock, built by Abd al-Malik in Jerusalem in 693, was as magnificent as any of Justinian's buildings. But the Umayyad economy was in trouble: it was too reliant on plunder and its investment in public buildings was not sustainable. Umar II (r. 717–20) tried to rectify this by cutting down on state expenditure, demobilising surplus military units, and reducing the commanders' allowances. He knew that the dhimmis resented the jizya tax, which they alone had to pay, and that many Muslims believed this arrangement violated Quranic egalitarianism. So even though it meant a drastic loss of income, Umar II became the first caliph to encourage the conversion of the dhimmis to Islam. He did not live long enough to see his reform through, however. Hisham I (724–43), his successor, launched new military offensives in Central Asia and North Africa but when he tried to revive the economy by reimposing the jizya there was a massive revolt of Berber converts in North Africa.

Backed by disaffected Persian converts, a new dynasty, claiming descent from Muhammad's uncle Abbas, challenged Umayyad rule, drawing heavily on Shii rhetoric. In August 749 they occupied Kufa, and defeated the Umayyad caliph the following year. But as soon as they were in power, the Abbasids cast aside their Shii piety and set up an absolute monarchy on the Persian model, which was welcomed by the subject peoples but strayed wholly from Islamic egalitarianism by embracing imperial structural violence. Their first act was to massacre all the Umayyads and a few years later Caliph Abu Jafar al-Mansur (754–75) murdered Shii leaders and moved his capital to the new city of Baghdad, just thirty-five miles south of Ctesiphon. The Abbasids were wholly oriented towards the East.[73] In the West, the victory of the Frankish king Charles Martel over a Muslim raiding party at Poitiers in 732 is often seen as the decisive event that saved Europe from Islamic domination; in fact, Christendom was saved by the Abbasids' total indifference to the West. Realising that the empire could expand no further, they conducted foreign affairs with elaborate Persian diplomacy and the soldier soon became an anomaly at court.

By the reign of Harun al-Rashid (786–809), the transformation of the Islamic empire from an Arab to a Persian monarchy was complete. The caliph was hailed as the 'Shadow of God' on earth and his Muslim subjects – who had once bowed only to God – prostrated themselves before him. The executioner stood constantly beside the ruler to show that he had the power of life and death. He left the routine tasks of government to his vizier; the caliph's role was to be a judge of ultimate appeal beyond the reach of factions and politicking. He had two significant tasks: to lead the Friday prayers and to lead the army into battle. The latter was a new departure since the Umayyads had never personally taken the field with the army so Harun was the first autocratic ghazi-caliph.[74]

The Abbasids had given up trying to conquer Constantinople, but every year Harun conducted a raid into Byzantine territory to demonstrate his commitment to the defence of Islam: the Byzantine emperor reciprocated with a token invasion of Islamdom. Court poets praised Harun for his zeal in 'exerting himself beyond the exertion (*jihad*) of one who fears God'. They pointed out that Haran was a volunteer who put himself at risk in a task not required of him: 'You could, if you liked, resort to some pleasant place, while others endured hardship instead of you.'[75] Harun was deliberately evoking the golden age when every able-bodied man had been expected to ride into battle beside the Prophet. Despite its glorious façade, however, the empire was already in trouble, economically and militarily.[76] The Abbasids' professional army was expensive and manpower always a problem. Yet it was imperative to defend the border against the Byzantines, so Harun reached out to committed civilians who, like himself, were ready to volunteer their services.

Increasingly, Muslims who lived near the empire's frontiers began to see 'the border' as a symbol of Islamic integrity that had to be defended against a hostile world. Some of the *ulema* ('learned scholars') had objected to the Umayyads' monopoly of the jihad because it clashed with Quranic verses and hadith traditions that made jihad a duty for everybody.[77] Hence, when the Umayyads had besieged Constantinople (717–18), ulema, hadith-collectors, ascetics and Quran-reciters had assembled on the frontier to support the army with their prayers. Their motivation was pious but perhaps they were also attracted by the intensity and excitement of the battlefield. Now following Harun's lead, they gathered again in even greater numbers not only on the Syrian/Byzantine border but also on the frontiers of Central Asia, North Africa and Spain. Some of these scholars and ascetics took part in the fighting and in garrison duties but most supplied spiritual support in the form of prayer, fasting and study. 'Volunteering' (*tatawwa*) would put down deep roots in Islam and resurface powerfully in our own day.

During the eighth century, some of these 'fighting scholars' started to develop a distinctively jihadi spirituality. Abu Ishaq al-Fazari (d. *c.* 802) believed he was imitating the Prophet in his life of study and warfare; Ibraham ibn Adham (d. 778), who engaged in extreme fasts and heroic night vigils on the frontier, maintained that there could be no more perfect form of Islam; and Abdullah ibn Mubarak (d. 797) agreed, arguing that the dedication of the early Muslim warriors had been the glue that bonded the early ummah. Jihadis did not need the state's permission but could volunteer whether the authorities and professional soldiers liked it or not. But these pious volunteers could not solve the empire's manpower problem, so eventually Caliph al-Mutasim (833–42) would create a personal army of Turkish slaves from the steppes, who placed the formidable fighting skills of the herdsmen at the service of Islam. Each *mamluk* ('slave') was converted to Islam but because the Quran forbade the enslaving of Muslims their sons were born free. This policy was fraught with contradictions, but the Mamluks became a privileged caste and in the not too distant future, these Turks would rule the empire.

The volunteers had created another variant of Islam, and could claim that their way of life came closest to that of the Prophet, who had spent years defending the ummah against its enemies. But their militant jihad never appealed to the wider ummah. In Mecca and Medina, where the frontier was a distant reality, almsgiving and solicitude for the poor were still seen as the most important form of jihad. Some ulema vigorously opposed the beliefs of the 'fighting scholars', arguing that a man who devoted his life to scholarship and prayed every day in the mosque was just as good a Muslim as a warrior.[78] A new hadith reported that on his way home from the Battle of Badr, Muhammad had said to his Companions: 'We are returning from the Lesser Jihad [the battle] and returning to the Greater Jihad' – the more exacting and important effort to fight the baser passions and reform one's own society.[79]

During the Conquest era, the ulema had begun to develop a distinctive body of Muslim law in the garrison towns. But at that time the ummah had been a tiny minority; by the tenth century, 50 per cent of the empire's population was Muslim and the code of the garrisons was no longer appropriate.[80] The Abbasid aristocracy had its own Persian code known as the *adab* ('culture'), which was based on the literate artistry and courtly manners expected of the nobility and was obviously unsuitable for the masses.[81] The caliphs, therefore, asked the ulema to develop the standardised system of Islamic law that would become the Shariah. Four schools of law (*maddhab*) emerged, all regarded as equally valid. Each school had its distinctive outlook but was based on the practice (*sunnah*) of the Prophet and the early ummah. Like the Talmud, which was a strong influence on these developments, the new jurisprudence (fiqh) aimed to bring the whole of life under the canopy of the sacred. There was, therefore, no attempt to impose a single 'rule of faith'. Individuals were free to select their own maddhab and, as in Judaism, follow the rulings of the scholar of their choice.

Shariah law provided a principled alternative to the aristocratic rule of agrarian society, since it refused to accept a hereditary class system. It had, therefore, revolutionary potential; indeed, two of the maddhab founders – Malik ibn Anas (d. 795) and Muhammad Idris al-Shafii (d. 820) – had taken part in Shii uprisings against the early Abbasids. The Shariah insisted that every single Muslim was directly responsible to God; a Muslim needed no caliph or priest to mediate divine law and everybody – not just the ruling class – was responsible for the ummah's well-being. Where the aristocratic adab took a pragmatic view of what was politically feasible, the Shariah was an idealistic counter-cultural challenge, which tacitly condemned the structural violence of the imperial state and boldly insisted that no institution – not even the caliphate – had the right to interfere with an individual's personal decisions. There was no way that an agrarian state could be run on these lines, however, and although the caliphs always acknowledged the Shariah as the law of God, they could not rule by it. Consequently, Shariah law never governed the whole of society and the caliph's court, where justice was summary, absolute and arbitrary, remained the supreme court of appeal; in theory, any Muslim, however lowly, could appeal to the caliph for justice against members of the lower aristocracy.[82] Nevertheless, the Shariah was a constant witness to the Islamic ideal of equality that is so deeply embedded in our humanity that despite the apparent impossibility of incorporating it in political life we remain stubbornly convinced that it is the natural way for human beings to live together.

Al-Shafii formulated what would become the classical doctrine of jihad which, despite Shariah aversion to autocracy, drew on standard imperial ideology: it had a dualistic worldview, claimed that the ummah had a divine mission, and that Islamic rule would benefit humanity. God had decreed warfare because it was essential for the ummah's survival, al-Shafii argued. The human race was divided into the *dar al-Islam* ('The Abode of Islam') and the non-Muslim world, the *dar al-harb* ('The Abode of War'). There could be no final peace between the two, though a temporary truce was permissible. But since all ethical faiths came from God, the ummah was only one of many divinely guided communities and the goal of jihad was not to convert the subject population. What distinguished Islam from other revelations, however, was that it had a God-given mandate to extend its rule to the rest of humanity. Its mission was to establish the social justice and equity prescribed by God in the Quran, so that all men and women could be liberated from the tyranny of a state run on worldly principles.[83] The reality, however, was that the Abbasid caliphate was an autocracy that depended on the forcible subjugation of the majority of the population;

like any agrarian state, it was constitutionally unable to implement Quranic norms fully. Yet without such idealism, which reminds us of the imperfection of our institutions, their inherent violence and injustice would go without critique. Perhaps the role of religious vision is to fill us with a divine discomfort that will not allow us wholly to accept the unacceptable.

Al-Shafii also ruled against the conviction of the 'fighting scholars' that militant jihad was incumbent upon every Muslim. In Shariah law, the daily prayer was binding on all Muslims without exception, so it was *fard ayn*, an obligation for each individual. But even though all Muslims were responsible for the well-being of the ummah, some tasks, such as cleaning the mosque, could be left to the appointed official and was *fard kifaya*, a duty delegated to an individual by the community. Should this job be neglected, however, others were obliged to take the initiative and step in.[84] Al-Shafii decreed that jihad against the non-Muslim world was *fard kifaya* and the ultimate responsibility of the caliph. So as long as there were enough soldiers to defend the frontier, civilians were exempt from military service. But in the event of an enemy invasion, Muslims in the border regions might be obliged to help. Al-Shafii was writing at a time when the Abbasids had renounced territorial expansion, so he was not legislating for offensive jihad but for defensive warfare. Muslims still debate the legitimacy of jihad in these terms today.

Sunni Muslims had accepted the imperfections of the agrarian system in order to keep the peace.[85] The Shii still condemned its systemic violence but found a practical way of dealing with the Abbasid regime. Jafar al-Sadiq (d. 765), the sixth in the line of imams ('leaders') descended from Ali, formally abandoned armed struggle, because rebellions were always savagely put down and resulted only in unacceptable loss of life. Henceforth the Shia would hold aloof from the mainstream, its disengagement a silent rebuke to Abbasid tyranny and a witness to true Islamic values. As the Prophet's descendant, Jafar enshrined his charisma and remained the rightful leader of the ummah but henceforth he would function only as a spiritual guide. Jafar had, in effect, separated religion and politics. This sacred secularism would remain the dominant ideal of Shiism until the late twentieth century.

Yet the imams remained an unbearable irritant to the caliphs. The imam, a living link with the Prophet, revered by the faithful, quietly dedicated to the contemplation of scripture and charitable works, offered a striking contrast to the caliph whose ever-present executioner was a grim reminder of the violence of empire. Which was the truly Muslim leader? The imams embodied a sacred presence that could not exist safely or openly in a world dominated by violence and injustice, since they were nearly all murdered by the caliphs. When towards the end of the ninth century, the Twelfth Imam mysteriously vanished from prison, it was said that God had miraculously concealed him and that he would one day return to inaugurate an era of justice. In this concealment, he remained the true leader of the ummah and in his absence all government was illegitimate. Paradoxically, liberated from the confines of time and space, the Hidden Imam became a more vivid presence in the lives of Shiis. The myth reflected the tragic impossibility of implementing a truly equitable policy in a flawed and violent world. On the anniversary of Imam Husain's death on the tenth (*ashura*) of the month of Muharram, Shiis would publicly mourn his murder, processing through the streets, weeping and beating their breasts to demonstrate their undying opposition to the corruption of mainstream Muslim life. But not all Shiis subscribed to Jafar's sacred secularism. The Ismailis, who believed that Ali's line had ended with Ismail, the Seventh Imam, remained convinced that piety must be backed up by military jihad for a just society. In the tenth century, when the Abbasid regime was in serious decline, an Ismaili leader established a rival caliphate in North Africa and this Fatimid dynasty later spread to Egypt, Syria and Palestine.[86]

In the tenth century, the Muslim empire was beginning to fragment. Taking advantage of Fatimid weakness, the Byzantines conquered Antioch and important areas of Cilicia, while within the Dar al-Islam Turkish generals established virtually independent states, although they continued to acknowledge the caliph as the supreme leader. In 945, the Turkish Buyid dynasty actually occupied Baghdad and even though the caliph retained his court, the region became a province of the Buyid kingdom. Yet Islam was by no means a spent force. There had always been tension between the Quran and autocratic monarchy and the new arrangement of independent rulers symbolically linked by their loyalty to the caliph was religiously more congenial, if not politically effective. Muslim religious thought subsequently became less driven by current events and would become politically oriented again only in the modern period when the ummah faced a new imperial threat.

The Seljuk Turks from Central Asia gave fullest expression to the new order. They acknowledged the sovereignty of the caliph, but under their brilliant Persian vizier Nizamulmulk (r. 1063–92) they created an empire extending to Yemen in the south, the Oxus River in the east and Syria in the west. The Seljuks were not universally popular. Some of the more radical Ismailis withdrew to mountain strongholds in what is now Lebanon, where they prepared for a jihad to replace the Seljuks with a Shii regime, occasionally undertaking suicidal missions to murder prominent members of the Seljuk establishment. Their enemies called them *hashashin* because they were said to use marijuana to induce mystical ecstasy and this gave us our English word 'assassin'.[87] But most Muslims accommodated easily to Seljuk rule. Theirs was not a centralised empire; the emirs who commanded the districts were virtually autonomous and worked closely with the ulema, who gave these disparate military regimes ideological unity. To raise educational standards, they created the first madrasas and Nizamulmulk established these schools throughout the empire, giving the ulema a power base and drawing the scattered provinces together. Emirs came and went but the Shariah courts were a stable authority in each region. Moreover, Sufi mystics and the more charismatic ulema travelled the length and breadth of the Seljuk empire giving ordinary Muslims a strong sense of belonging to an international community.

By the end of the eleventh century, however, the Seljuk empire had also started to decline. It had succumbed to the usual problem of a military oligarchy, since the emirs began to fight one another for territory. They were so intent on these internal feuds that they neglected the frontier and were incapable of stopping the influx of pastoralists from the steppes who had begun to bring their herds into the fertile settled lands now ruled by their own people. Large groups of Turkish herdsmen moved steadily westward, taking over the choicest pasturage and driving out the local population. Eventually they arrived at the Byzantine frontier in the Armenian highlands. In 1071, the Seljuk chieftain Alp Arslan defeated the Byzantine army at Manzikert in Armenia, and as the Byzantines retreated, the nomadic Turks broke through the unguarded frontier and began to infiltrate Byzantine Anatolia. The beleaguered Byzantine emperor now appealed to the Christians of the West for help.

8

CRUSADE AND JIHAD

Pope Gregory VII (r. 1073–85) was deeply disturbed to hear that hordes of Turkish tribesmen had invaded Byzantine territory and in 1074 he dispatched a series of letters summoning the faithful to join him in 'liberating' their brothers in Anatolia. He proposed personally to lead an army to the east, which would rid Greek Christians of the Turkish menace and then liberate the holy city of Jerusalem from the infidel.[1] *Libertas* and *liberatio* were the buzz-words of eleventh-century Europe; its knights had recently 'liberated' land from the Muslim occupiers of Calabria, Sardinia, Tunisia, Sicily and Apulia and had begun the Reconquista of Spain.[2] In the future, Western imperial aggression would often be couched in the rhetoric of liberty. But *libertas* had different connotations in medieval Europe. When Roman power had collapsed in the western provinces, the bishops had taken the place of the Roman senatorial aristocracy, stepping into the political vacuum left by the departing imperial officials.[3] The Roman clergy thus adopted the old aristocracy's ideal of *libertas*, which had little to do with freedom; it referred to the privileged position of the ruling class, which had to be maintained if society was not to lapse into barbarism.[4] As the successor of St Peter, Gregory believed that he had a divine mandate to rule the Christian world. His 'crusade' was designed in part to reassert papal libertas in the eastern empire, which did not accept the supremacy of the bishop of Rome.

Throughout his pontificate, Gregory struggled but ultimately failed to assert the libertas of the Church against the rising power of the lay rulers. Hence his proposed crusade came to nothing, and in his determined effort to free the clergy from lay control he was ignominiously defeated by Henry IV, Holy Roman Emperor of the West. For eight years the pontiff and the emperor had been locked in a power struggle, each trying to depose the other. In 1084, when Gregory threatened him with excommunication once again, Henry simply invaded Italy and installed an antipope in the Lateran Palace. But the popes had only themselves to blame, for the western empire was their creation. For centuries, the Byzantines had maintained an outpost in Ravenna in Italy, to protect the Church of Rome against the barbarians. By the eighth century, however, the Lombards had become so aggressive in northern Italy that the Pope needed a stronger lay protector, so in 753 Pope Stephen II made an heroic journey over the Alps in the middle of winter to the old Roman province of Gaul to seek an alliance with Pippin, son of the Frankish king Charles Martel, thus giving papal legitimacy to the Carolingian dynasty. Pippin at once began preparations for a military expedition to Italy, while his ten-year-old son Charles – later known as Charlemagne – escorted the exhausted and bedraggled pope to his lodgings.

The Germanic tribes who established kingdoms in the old Roman provinces had embraced Christianity and revered the warrior kings of the Hebrew Bible but their military ethos was still permeated with ancient Aryan ideals of heroism and desire for fame, glory and loot. All these elements blended inextricably in their conduct of war. The Carolingians' wars were presented as holy wars, sanctioned by God, and they called their dynasty the New Israel.[5] Their military campaigns certainly had a religious dimension but material profit was every bit as important. In 732, Charles Martel (d. 741) had defeated a Muslim army on its way to pillage Tours, but after his victory Charles immediately proceeded to loot the Christian communities in southern Francia as thoroughly as the Muslims would have done.[6] During his Italian wars to defend the Pope, his son Pippin forced the Lombards to relinquish a third of their treasure; this massive wealth enabled his clergy to build a truly catholic and Roman enclave north of the Alps.

Charlemagne (r. 772–814) showed what a king could do when supported by such substantial resources.[7] By 785, he had conquered northern Italy and the whole of Gaul; in 792, he moved into Central Europe and attacked the Avars of western Hungary, bringing home wagonloads of plunder. These campaigns were billed as holy wars against 'pagans' but the Franks remembered them for more mundane reasons. 'All the Avar nobility died in the war, all their glory departed. All their wealth and their treasure assembled over so many years were dispersed,' Einhard, Charlemagne's biographer recorded complacently. 'The memory of men cannot remember any war of the Franks by which they were so enriched and their material possessions so increased.'[8] Far from being inspired solely by religious zeal, these wars of expansion were informed by the economic imperative of acquiring more arable land. The episcopal sees in the occupied territories became instruments of colonial control[9] and the mass baptisms of the conquered peoples were statements of political rather than spiritual realignment.[10]

But the religious element was prominent. On Christmas Day, 800, Pope Leo III crowned Charlemagne 'Holy Roman Emperor' in the Basilica of St Peter. The congregation acclaimed him as 'Augustus' and Leo prostrated himself at Charlemagne's feet. The popes and bishops of Italy had long believed that the *raison d'être* of the Roman Empire was to protect the libertas of the Catholic Church.[11] After the empire's fall they knew that the Church could not survive without the king and his warriors. Between 750 and 1050, therefore, the king was a sacred figure who stood at the apex of the social pyramid. 'Our Lord Jesus Christ has set you up as the ruler of the Christian people, in power more excellent than the pope or the emperor of Constantinople,' wrote Alcuin, a British monk and court adviser, to Charlemagne. 'On you alone depends the whole safety of the churches of Christ.'[12] In a letter to Leo, Charlemagne declared that as emperor it was his mission 'everywhere to defend the church of Christ'.[13]

The instability and chaotic flux of life in Europe after the collapse of the Roman empire had created a hunger for tangible contact with the eternal stability of heaven. Hence the popularity of the saints' relics, which provided a physical link with martyrs who were now with God. Even the mighty Charlemagne felt vulnerable in this violent and unstable world: his throne in Aachen had cavities stuffed with relics and the great monasteries of Fulda, Saint Gall and Reichenau, positioned on the borders of his empire as powerhouses of prayer and sanctity, took great pride in their relic collection.[14] The monks of Europe were very different from their counterparts in Egypt and Syria. They were not peasants but members of the nobility; they lived not in desert caves but on estates farmed by serfs who were the monastery's property.[15] Most followed the Rule of St Benedict, written in the sixth century at a time when the bonds of civil society seemed on the point of collapse. Benedict's aim had been to create communities of obedience, stability and *religio* ('reverence' and 'bonding') in a world of violence and uncertainty. The Rule provided *disciplina,* similar to the military *disciplina* of the Roman soldier: it prescribed a series of physical rituals carefully designed to restructure emotion and desire and create an attitude of humility very different from the aggressive self-assertion of the knight.[16] Monastic disciplina set out to defeat not a physical enemy but the unruly psyche and the unseen powers of evil. The Carolingians knew that they owed their success in battle to highly disciplined troops. Hence they appreciated the Benedictine communities and during the ninth and tenth centuries support for the Rule became a central feature of government in Europe.[17]

Monks formed a social order (*ordo*), separate from the disordered world outside the monastery. So abjuring sex, money, fighting and mutability, the most corrupting aspects of secular life, they embraced chastity, poverty, nonviolence and stability. Unlike the restless boskoi, Benedictine monks vowed to remain in the same community for life.[18] A monastery, however, was designed not so much to cater for the individual spiritual quest as to serve a social function by providing occupation for the younger sons of the nobility, who could never hope to own land and might become a destabilising influence in society. At this point, Western Christendom did not distinguish public and private, natural and supernatural. Thus by combating the demonic powers with their prayers, monks were essential to the security of the realm. There were two ways for an aristocrat to serve God: fighting or praying.[19] Monks were the spiritual counterparts of secular soldiers, their battles just as real and far more significant:

> The abbot is armed with spiritual weapons and supported by a troop of monks anointed with the dew of heavenly graces. They fight together in the strength of Christ with the sword of the spirit against the aery wiles of the devils. They defend the king and clergy of the realm from the onslaughts of their invisible enemies.[20]

The Carolingian aristocracy was convinced that the success of their earthly battles depended on their monks' disciplined warfare, even though they fought only with 'vigils, hymns, prayers, psalms, alms and daily offering of masses'.[21]

Originally there had been three social orders in Western Christendom: monks, clerics and the laity. But during the Carolingian period, two distinct aristocratic orders emerged: the warrior nobility (*bellatores*) and the men of religion (*oratores*). Clerics and bishops, who worked in the world (*saeculum*) and had once formed a separate ordo, were now merged with monks and would increasingly be pressured to live like them by abjuring marriage and fighting. In Frankish and Anglo-Saxon society, still influenced by ancient Aryan values, those who shed blood on the battlefield carried a taint that disqualified them from handling sacred things or saying Mass. But military violence was about to receive a Christian baptism.

During the ninth and tenth centuries, Norse and Magyar invaders devastated Europe and brought down the Carolingian empire. Although they would be remembered as wicked and monstrous, in truth a Viking leader was no different from Charles Martel or Pippin: he was simply a 'king on the warpath (*vik*)', fighting for tribute, plunder and prestige.[22] In 962 the

Saxon king Otto managed to repel the Magyars and recreate the Holy Roman Empire in much of Germany. But in Francia, the kings' power had so declined that they could no longer control the lesser aristocrats, who not only fought one another but had begun to loot church property and to terrorise the peasant villages, killing livestock and burning homes if the agricultural yield was poor.[23] A member of the lower aristocracy – called *cniht* ('soldier') or *chevaller* ('horseman') – felt no qualms about such raiding, which was essential to his way of life. For decades French knights had been engaged in almost ceaseless warfare and were now economically dependent on plunder and looting. As the French historian Marc Bloch has explained, besides bringing a knight glory and heroism, warfare was 'perhaps above all, a source of profit, the nobleman's chief industry', so for the less affluent, the return of peace could be 'an economic crisis as well as a disastrous loss of prestige'.[24] Without war, a knight could not afford weapons and horses, tools of his trade, and would be forced into menial labour. The violent seizure of property was, as we have seen, regarded as the only honourable way for an aristocrat to acquire resources, so much so that there was 'no line of demarcation' in early medieval Europe between 'warlike activity' and 'pillaging'.[25] In the tenth century, therefore, many impoverished knights were simply doing what came naturally to them when they robbed and harassed the peasantry.

This surge of violence coincided with the development of the manors, the great landed estates, and a fully-fledged agrarian system in Europe which depended on the forcible extraction of the agricultural surplus.[26] The arrival of the structural violence that maintained it was heralded at the end of the tenth century by the appearance of a new ordo: the *imbelle vulgus*, or 'unarmed commoner', whose calling was *laborare*, 'to work'.[27] The manorial system had abolished the ancient distinction between the free peasant, who could bear arms, and the slave, who could not. Both were now lumped together, forbidden to fight yet unable to defend themselves from the knights' assault, and forced to live at subsistence level. A two-tier stratification had emerged in Western society: the 'men of power' (*potentes*) and the 'poor' (*pauperes*). The aristocracy needed the help of ordinary soldiers to subjugate the poor, so knights became retainers, exempt from servitude and taxation, and members of the nobility.

The aristocratic priests naturally supported this oppressive system and indeed were largely responsible for crafting it, enraging many of the poor by their flagrant abandonment of the egalitarianism of the Gospel. The Church denounced the more vocal of these malcontents as 'heretics' but their dissent took the form of a religiously articulated protest against the new social and political system and was not concerned with theological issues. In the early eleventh century, for example, Robert of Arbrissel wandered barefoot through Brittany and Anjou at the head of a tattered retinue of *pauperes Christi*, his demand for a return to Gospel values attracting widespread support.[28] In southern France, Henry of Lausanne also drew huge crowds when he attacked the greed and immorality of the clergy, and in Flanders, Tanchelm of Antwerp preached so effectively that people stopped attending Mass and refused to pay their tithes. Robert eventually submitted to the Church, founded a Benedictine monastery and became a saint, but Henry remained active in his 'heresy' for thirty years and Tanchelm set up his own church.

The monks of the Benedictine abbey of Cluny in Burgundy responded to the twofold crisis of internal violence and social protest by initiating a reform that attempted to limit the lawless aggression of the knights. They tried to introduce lay men and women to the values of monastic *religio,* in their view the only authentic form of Christianity, by promoting the practice of pilgrimage to sacred sites. Like a monk, the pilgrim made a decision to turn her back on the world and head for the centres of holiness; like a monk, she made a vow in the local church before setting out and donned a special uniform. All pilgrims had to be chaste for the duration of their pilgrimage and knights, forbidden to carry arms, were forced to contain their instinctive aggression for a significant period of time. During the long, difficult and frequently dangerous journey, lay pilgrims formed a community, the rich sharing the privations and vulnerability of the poor, the poor learning that their poverty had sacred value, and both experiencing the inevitable hardship of life on the road as a form of asceticism.

At the same time, the reformers tried to give fighting spiritual value and make knightly warfare a Christian vocation. They decided that a warrior could serve God by protecting the unarmed poor from the depredations of the lower aristocracy and by pursuing the enemies of the Church. The saintly hero of the *Life of St Gerald of Aurillac,* written *c.* 930 by Odo, abbot of Cluny, was neither a king nor a monk nor a bishop but an ordinary knight who achieved sanctity by becoming a soldier of Christ and defending the poor. To further their cult of this 'holy warfare', the reformers devised rituals for the blessing of military banners and swords and encouraged devotion to such military saints as Michael, George and Mercury (who was believed to have murdered Julian the Apostate).[29]

In a related movement, the bishops inaugurated the Peace of God to

limit the knights' violence and protect church property.[30] In central and
southern France, where the monarchy was no longer functioning and society
was degenerating into violent chaos, they began to convene large assemblies
of churchmen, knights and feudal lords in the fields outside the cities.
During these rallies, knights were forced to swear, on pain of excommunication, that they would stop tormenting the poor:

> I will not carry off either ox or cow or any other beast of burden; I will
> seize neither peasant nor merchant; I will not take from them their pence,
> nor oblige them to ransom themselves; and I will not beat them to obtain
> their subsistence. I will seize neither horse, mare nor colt from their pasture;
> I will not destroy or burn their houses.[31]

At these Peace Councils the bishops insisted that anyone who kills his fellow
Christians 'spills the blood of Christ'.[32] They now also introduced the Truce
of God, forbidding fighting from Wednesday evening to Monday morning
each week in memory of Christ's days of passion, death and resurrection.
Although peace became a reality for a specific period of time, it could not
be maintained without violence. The bishops were able to enforce the Peace
and the Truce only by forming 'peace militias'. Anyone who broke the
Truce, explained the chronicler Raoul Glaber (c. 985–1047), 'was to pay
for it with his life or be driven from his own country and the company of
his fellow-Christians'.[33] These peace-keeping forces helped to make knightly
violence a genuine 'service' (*militia*) of God, equal to the priestly and
monastic vocation.[34] The Peace movement spread throughout France and
by the end of the eleventh century, there is evidence that a significant
number of knights had indeed been converted to a more 'religious' lifestyle
and regarded their military duties as a form of lay monasticism.[35]

But for Pope Gregory VII, one of the leading reformers of the day,
knighthood could be a holy vocation only if it fought to preserve the libertas
of the Church. He therefore tried to recruit kings and aristocrats into his
own Militia of St Peter to fight the Church's enemies – and it was with
this militia that he intended to fight his 'crusade'. In his letters, he linked
the ideals of brotherly love for the beleaguered eastern Christians and
liberatio of the Church with military aggression. But very few laymen joined
his Militia.[36] Why indeed would they, since it was clearly designed to enhance
the power of the Church at the expense of the *bellatores*, the lay warrior
nobility? The popes had blessed the predatory violence of the Carolingians
because it had enabled the Church to survive. But as Gregory had learned

in his struggle with Henry IV, fighting men were no longer willing simply to protect the Church's libertas. This political struggle for power between popes and emperors would inform the religiously inspired violence of the Crusading period; both sides were competing for political supremacy in Europe and that meant gaining the monopoly of violence.

In 1074, Gregory's crusade had no takers; twenty years later, the response from the laity would be very different.

On 27 November 1095, Pope Urban II, another Cluniac monk, addressed a Peace Council at Clermont in southern France and summoned the First Crusade, appealing directly to the Franks, the heirs of Charlemagne. We have no contemporary record of this speech and can only infer what Urban might have said from his letters.[37] In keeping with the recent reforms, Urban urged the knights of France to stop attacking their fellow Christians and instead fight God's enemies. Like Gregory VII, Urban urged the Franks to 'liberate' their brothers, the eastern Christians, from 'the tyranny and oppression of Muslims'.[38] They should then proceed to the Holy Land to liberate Jerusalem. In this way, the Peace of God would be enforced in Christendom and God's war fought in the East. The crusade, Urban was convinced, would be an act of love in which the crusaders nobly laid down their lives for their eastern brothers and in leaving their homes they would secure the same heavenly rewards as monks who abjured the world for the cloister.[39] But for all this pious talk, the crusade was also essential to Urban's political manoeuvres to secure the libertas of the Church. The previous year he had ousted Henry IV's antipope from the Lateran Palace and at Clermont he excommunicated King Philip I of France for making an adulterous marriage. Now by dispatching a massive military expedition to the East without consulting either monarch, Urban had usurped the royal prerogative of controlling the military defence of Christendom.[40]

But while a pope might say one thing, less educated listeners could hear something entirely different. Drawing on Cluniac ideas, Urban would always call the expedition a pilgrimage – except that these pilgrims would be heavily armed knights and this 'act of love' would result in the deaths of thousands of innocent people. Urban almost certainly quoted Jesus' words, telling his disciples to take up their cross, and he probably told the crusaders to sew crosses on the back of their clothes and and travel to the land where Jesus had lived and died. The vogue for pilgrimage had already raised the profile of Jerusalem in Europe. In 1033, the millennium of Jesus' death, Raoul Graber reported that, convinced that the End Time was nigh, an 'innumerable multitude' had marched to Jerusalem to fight the 'miserable Antichrist'.[41] Thirty years later, 7,000 pilgrims had left Europe for the Holy Land to force the Antichrist to declare himself so that God could establish a better world. In 1095 many of the knights would have seen the crusade in this populist apocalyptic light. They would also have viewed Urban's call to help the Eastern Christians as a vendetta for their kinsmen and feel as bound to fight for Christ's patrimony in the Holy Land as they would to recover the fief of their feudal lord. One early medieval historian of the Crusades makes a priest ask his listeners: 'If an outsider were to strike any of your kin down would you not avenge your blood relative? How much more ought you to avenge your God, your father, your brother, whom you see reproached, banished from his estates, crucified, whom you hear calling for aid.'[42] Pious ideas would certainly have been fused with more earthly objectives. Many would take up their cross to acquire wealth overseas or fiefs for their descendants, as well as fame and prestige.

Events quickly spiralled out of Urban's control – a reminder of the limitations of religious authority. Urban had imagined an orderly military expedition and had urged the crusaders to wait until after the harvest. But five large armies ignored this sensible advice and began their trek across Europe in the spring. Thousands either died of hunger or were repulsed by the Hungarians, who were terrified by this sudden invasion. It had never occurred to Urban that the crusaders would attack the Jewish communities in Europe, but in 1096 an army of German crusaders slaughtered 4–8,000 Jews in Speyer, Worms and Mainz. Their leader Emicho of Leningen had presented himself as the emperor of popular legend who would appear in the West during the Last Days and fight the Antichrist in Jerusalem. Jesus could not return, Emicho believed, until the Jews had converted to Christianity, so as his troops approached the Rhineland cities with large Jewish communities, Emicho ordered that Jews be forcibly baptised on pain of death. Some crusaders seemed genuinely confused. Why were they going to fight Muslims thousands of miles away when the people who had actually killed Jesus – or so the crusaders mistakenly believed – were alive and well on their very doorstep? 'Look now,' a Jewish chronicler overheard the crusaders saying to one another, 'we are going to take vengeance on the Ishmaelites for our Messiah, when here are the Jews who murdered and crucified him. Let us first avenge ourselves on them.'[43] Later some of the French crusaders would also be puzzled: 'Do we need to travel to distant lands in the East to attack the enemies of God, when there are Jews right before our eyes, a race that is the greatest enemy of God? We've got it all backward!'[44]

The Crusades made anti-Semitic violence a chronic disease in Europe: every time a crusade was summoned, Christians would first attack Jews at home. This persecution was certainly inspired by religious conviction but social, political and economic elements were also involved. The Rhineland cities were developing the market economy that would eventually replace agrarian civilisation; they were therefore in the very early stages of modernisation, a transition that always strains social relations. After the demise of the Roman empire, town life had declined; there was virtually no commerce and no merchant class.[45] Towards the end of the eleventh century, however, increased productivity had given aristocrats a taste for luxury. To meet their demands, a class of specialists – masons, craftsmen and merchants – had emerged from the peasantry and the consequent exchanges of money and goods led to the rebirth of the towns.[46] The nobility's resentment of the *vilain* ('upstart') from the lower classes who was acquiring wealth that they regarded as theirs by right may also have fuelled the violence of the German crusaders, since Jews were particularly associated with this disturbing social change.[47] In the episcopally administered Rhineland cities, the townsfolk had been trying for decades to shake off feudal obligations that impeded commerce but their bishop-rulers had extremely conservative views on trade.[48] There was also tension between rich merchants and poorer artisans, and when the bishops tried to protect the Jews, it appears that these less affluent townsfolk joined the crusaders in the killing.

Crusaders would always be motivated by social and economic factors as well as religious zeal. Crusading was especially appealing to the *juventus*, the knightly 'youth', who completed their military training by roaming freely around the countryside in search of adventure.[49] Primed for violent action, these knights errant were free of the restraints of settled existence and their lawlessness might account for some of the crusading atrocities.[50] Many of the first crusaders came from regions in north-eastern France and western Germany that had been devastated by years of flooding, plague and famine, so they may simply have wanted to leave an intolerable life.[51] There were also inevitably adventurers, robbers, renegade monks and brigands in the crusading hordes, many doubtless drawn by dreams of wealth and fortune, as well as a 'restless heart'.[52]

The leaders of the First Crusade, which left Europe in the autumn of 1096, had mixed motives for joining the expedition. Bohemund, Count of

Taranto in southern Italy, had a very small fief, and made no secret of his worldly ambitions: he left the crusade at the first opportunity to become Prince of Antioch. His nephew Tancred, however, found in the crusade the answer to a spiritual dilemma. He had 'burned with anxiety' because he could not reconcile his profession of fighting with the Gospel and had even considered the monastic life. But as soon as he heard Pope Urban's summons, 'his eyes opened, his courage was born'.[53] Godfrey of Bouillon meanwhile was inspired by the Cluniac ideal that saw fighting the Church's enemies as a spiritual vocation, but his brother Baldwin merely wanted fame, fortune and an estate in the East.

The terrifying experience of crusading soon changed their views and expectations.[54] Many of the crusaders had never left their villages; now they were thousands of miles from home, shut off from everything they had known, and surrounded by fearful enemies in alarming terrain. When they arrived at the Ante-Taurus range, many were paralysed by terror, gazing at these precipitous mountains 'in a great state of gloom, wringing their hands because they were so frightened and miserable'.[55] The Turks operated a scorched-earth policy, so there was no food and the poorer non-combatants and soldiers died like flies. Chroniclers report that during the siege of Antioch:

> The starving people devoured the stalks of beans still growing in the fields, many kinds of herbs unseasoned with salt, and even thistles which because of the lack of firewood were not well cooked and therefore irritated the tongues of those eating them. They also ate horses, camels, dogs, and even rats. The poorer people even ate the hides of animals and the seeds of grain found in manure.[56]

The crusaders soon realised that they were badly led and inadequately provisioned. They also knew they were massively outnumbered: 'Where we have a count, the enemy has forty kings; where we have a regiment, the enemy has a legion,' wrote the bishops who accompanied the expedition in their joint letter home; 'where we have a castle, they have a kingdom.'[57]

Even so, they could not have arrived at a more opportune moment. Not only was the Seljuk empire disintegrating but the sultan had recently died and the emirs were fighting one another for the succession. Had the Turks preserved a united front, the crusade could not have succeeded. But the crusaders knew nothing about local politics and their understanding was derived almost entirely from their religious views and prejudices.[58] Onlookers described the crusading armies as a monastery on the march. At every crisis, there were processions, prayers, and a special liturgy. Even though they were famished, they fasted before an engagement and listened as attentively to sermons as to battle instructions. Starving men had visions of Jesus, the saints, and of deceased crusaders who were now glorious martyrs in heaven. They saw angels fighting alongside them and at one of the lowest moments of the siege of Antioch, they discovered a holy relic – the lance that had pierced Christ's side – which so elated the despairing men that they surged out of the city and put the besieging Turks to flight. When they finally succeeded in conquering Jerusalem on 15 July 1099, they could only conclude that God had been with them. 'Who could not marvel at the way we, a small people among such kingdoms of our enemies, were able not just to resist them but survive?' wrote the chaplain, Fulcher of Chartres.[59]

War has been aptly described as 'a psychosis caused by an inability to see relationships'.[60] The First Crusade was especially psychotic. By all accounts, the crusaders seemed half-crazed. For three years, they had had no normal dealings with the world around them, and prolonged terror and malnutrition made them susceptible to abnormal states of mind. They were fighting an enemy that was both culturally and ethnically different – a factor that, as we have found in our own day, tends to nullify normal inhibitions – and when they fell on the inhabitants of Jerusalem they slaughtered some thirty thousand people in three days.[61] 'They killed all the Saracens and Turks they found,' the author of the *Deeds of the Franks* reported approvingly. 'They killed everyone, male or female.'[62] The streets ran with blood. Jews were rounded up into their synagogue and put to the sword, and 10,000 Muslims who had sought sanctuary in the Haram al-Sharif were brutally massacred. 'Piles of heads, hands and feet were to be seen,' wrote the Provençale chronicler Raymond of Aguilers: 'Men rode in blood up to their knees and bridle reins. Indeed, it was a just and splendid judgment of God that this place should be filled with the blood of unbelievers.'[63] There were so many dead that the crusaders were unable to dispose of the bodies. When Fulcher of Chartres came to celebrate Christmas in Jerusalem five months later, he was appalled by the stench from the rotting corpses that still lay unburied in the fields and ditches around the city.[64]

When they could kill no more, the crusaders processed to the Church of the Resurrection, singing hymns with tears of joy rolling down their cheeks. Beside the Tomb of Christ, they sang the Easter liturgy. 'This day,

I say, will be famous in all future ages, for it turned our labours and sorrows into joy and exultation,' Raymond exulted. 'This day, I say, marks the justification of all Christianity, the humiliation of paganism, the renewal of faith.'[65] Here we have evidence of another psychotic disconnect: the crusaders were standing beside the tomb of a man who had been a victim of human cruelty, yet they were unable to question their own violent behaviour. The ecstasy of battle, heightened in this case by years of terror, starvation and isolation, merged with their religious mythology to create an illusion of utter righteousness. But victors are never blamed for their crimes and chroniclers soon described the conquest in Jerusalem as a turning point in history. Robert the Monk made the astonishing claim that its importance had been exceeded only by the creation of the world and Jesus' crucifixion.[66] As a consequence, Muslims were now regarded in the West as a 'vile and abominable race', 'despicable, degenerate and enslaved by demons', 'absolutely alien to God', and 'fit only for extermination'.[67]

This holy war and the ideology that inspired it represented a complete denial of the pacifist strain in Christianity. It was also the first imperial venture of the Christian West as, after centuries of stagnation, it fought its way back on to the international scene. Five crusader states were established: in Jerusalem, Antioch, Galilee, Edessa and Tripoli. These states needed a standing army and the Church completed its canonisation of warfare by giving monks a sword: the Knights Hospitaller of St John, founded originally to care for poor and sick pilgrims, and the Knights Templar, housed in the Aqsa Mosque on the Haram, who policed the roads. They took vows of poverty, chastity, and obedience to their military commander, and because they were far more disciplined than ordinary knights, they became the first professional fighting force in the West since the Roman legions.[68] St Bernard, abbot of the new Cistercian abbey of Clairvaux, had no time for regular knights, who with their fine clothes, jewelled bridles and delicate hands were motivated only by 'irrational anger, hunger for empty glory, or hankering after some earthly possessions'.[69] The Templars, however, combined the meekness of monks with military power, and their sole motivation was to kill the enemies of Christ. A Christian, Bernard said, should exult when he saw these 'pagans' 'scattered', 'cut away' and 'dispersed'.[70] The ideology of these first Western colonies was permeated through and through with religion, and although later Western imperialism was inspired by a more secular ideology, it would often share the ruthlessness and aggressive righteousness of crusading.

*   *   *

The Muslims were stunned by the crusaders' violence. By the time they reached Jerusalem, the Franj ('Franks') had already acquired a fearsome reputation; it was said that they had killed more than a hundred thousand people at Antioch, and that during the siege they had roamed the countryside, wild with hunger, openly vowing to eat the flesh of any Saracen who crossed their path.[71] But Muslims had never experienced anything like the Jerusalem massacre. For over three hundred years they had fought all the great regional powers, but these wars had always been conducted within mutually agreed limits.[72] Muslim sources reported in horror that the Franks did not spare the elderly, the women or the sick, and even slaughtered devout ulema, 'who had left their homelands to live lives of pious seclusion in the holy place'.[73]

Yet despite this appalling beginning, not only was there no major Muslim offensive against the Franks for nearly fifty years but the crusaders were accepted as part of the political make-up of the region. The Crusader states fitted neatly into the Seljuk pattern of small independent tributary states and when emirs fought one another, they often made alliances with Frankish rulers.[74] For the Turkish commanders, the ideals of classical jihad were dead and when the crusaders had arrived, no 'volunteers' had rushed to defend the frontiers. No longer poised to resist foreign invasion, the emirs had been lax in their defence of the borders; they were unconcerned about the 'infidel' presence, since they were too intent on their campaigns against one another. Even though the crusading ideal resonated with hadith that saw jihad as a form of monasticism, the first Muslim chroniclers to record the crusade completely failed to recognise the Franks' religious passion and assumed that they were driven solely by material greed. They all realised that the Franks owed their success to the emirs' failure to form a united front but after the crusade, there was still no serious attempt to band together. For their part, the Franks who stayed in the Holy Land realised that their survival depended on their ability to coexist with their Muslim neighbours and soon lost their rabid prejudice. They assimilated into the local culture and learned to take baths, dress in the Turkish style and speak the local languages; they even married Muslim women.

But if the emirs had forgotten the jihad, a handful of 'fighting ulema' had not. Immediately after the conquest of Jerusalem, Abu Said al-Harawi, *qadi* (judge) of Damascus, led a deputation of Muslim refugees from Jerusalem to the caliph's mosque in Baghdad, and begged the caliph to call for a jihad against the invaders. Their terrible stories reduced the congregation to tears, but the caliph was now too weak to undertake any military action.[75] In 1105, the Syrian jurist al-Sulami wrote a treatise arguing that jihad against the Franks was fard ayn, an 'individual obligation' incumbent on the local emirs, who must step into the vacuum created by the caliph's incapacity and drive the invaders out of the dar al-Islam. But, he insisted, no military action would be successful unless it was preceded by the 'Greater Jihad', a reform of hearts and minds in which Muslims battled with their fear and apathy. [76]

But still there was little response. Far from being maniacally programmed for holy war by their religion, the Muslims had little appetite for jihad but were preoccupied with new forms of spirituality. In particular, some of the Sufi mystics would develop an outstanding appreciation of other faith traditions. The learned and highly influential Muid ad-Din ibn al-Arabi (1165–1240) would claim that a man of God was at home equally in a synagogue, mosque, temple or church, since all provided a valid apprehension of God:

> My heart is capable of every form.
> A cloister for the monk, a fane for idols,
> A pasture for gazelles, the votary's Kabah,
> The tables of the Torah, the Quran.
> Love is the faith I hold. Wherever I turn
> His camels, still the one true faith is mine.[77]

During the twelfth and thirteenth centuries, the period of the Crusades, Sufism ceased to be a fringe movement and in many parts of the Muslim world became the dominant Islamic mood. Few were capable of achieving the higher mystical states, but Sufi disciplines of concentration, which included music and dancing, helped people to abandon simplistic and narrow notions of God and chauvinist attitudes towards other traditions.

But a few ulema and ascetics found the presence of the Franks intolerable. In 1111, Ibn al-Khashab, qadi of Aleppo, led a delegation of Sufis, imams and merchants to Baghdad, where they broke into the caliph's mosque and smashed his pulpit in an unsuccessful attempt to rouse him from his inertia.[78] In 1119, the troops of Mardin and Damascus were so inspired by the qadi's preaching that they 'wept with emotion and admiration' and achieved their first Muslim victory over the Franks by defeating Count Roger of Antioch.[79] But no sustained action was taken against the crusaders until 1144, when, almost by accident, Zangi, emir of Mosul, conquered the Christian principality of Edessa during his campaign in Syria. To his surprise, Zangi, who had little interest in the Franks, became an overnight hero. The caliph hailed him as 'the pillar of religion' and 'the cornerstone of Islam', though it was hard to see Zangi as a devout Muslim.[80] The Turkish chroniclers condemned his 'roughness, aggression, and insolence that brought death to enemies and civilians' and in 1146 he was murdered by a slave while in a drunken stupor.[81]

It was the spectacle of the huge armies arriving from Europe to recover Edessa in the Second Crusade (1148) that finally galvanised some of the emirs. Even though this crusade was an embarrassing fiasco for the Christians, the local people were beginning to see the Franks as a real danger. The Muslim riposte was led by Nur ad-Din, Zangi's son (r. 1146–74), who took the advice of the 'fighting scholars' and first dedicated himself to the Greater Jihad. He returned to the spirit of the Prophet's ummah, living a frugal life, often passing the whole night in prayer, and setting up 'houses of justice' where anybody, whatever his faith or status, could find redress. He fortified the cities of the region, built madrasas and Sufi convents, and cultivated the ulema.[82] So moribund was the jihad spirit among the populace that reviving it was hard work. Nur ad-Din circulated anthologies of ahadith in praise of Jerusalem and commissioned a beautiful pulpit to be installed in the Aqsa Mosque when the Muslims recovered their holy city. Yet never once in his twenty-eight-year reign did he attack the Franks directly.

His greatest military achievement was the conquest of Fatimid Egypt and it was his Kurdish governor there, Yusuf ibn Ayyub, usually known by his title Salah ad-Din ('Honour of the Faith'), who would reconquer Jerusalem. But Saladin had to spend the first ten years of his reign fighting other emirs in order to hold Nur ad-Din's empire together and during this struggle he made many treaties with the Franks. Saladin too first concentrated on the Greater Jihad and endeared himself to the people by his compassion, humility and charisma, but as his biographer explained, he was passionate about military jihad:

> The Jihad and the suffering involved in it weighed heavily on his heart and his whole being in every limb; he spoke of nothing else, thought only about equipment for the fight, was interested only in those who had taken up arms . . . For the love of Jihad in God's Path, he left his family and his sons, his homeland, his house and all his estates, and chose out of all the world to live in the shade of his tent.[83]

Like Nur ad-Din, Saladin always travelled with an entourage of ulema, Sufis, qadis and imams, who recited Quran and ahadith to the troops as they marched. Jihad, which had been all but dead, was becoming a live force in the region; it had been resurrected not by the inherently violent nature of Islam but by a sustained assault from the West. In the future, any Western intervention in the Middle East, however secular its motivation, would evoke the memory of the fanatical violence of the First Crusade.

Like the Crusaders, Saladin discovered that his enemy could be its own greatest foe. Ultimately, he owed his military success to the chronic infighting of the Franks and the hawkish policies of newcomers from the West who did not understand regional politics. As a result, in July 1187 he was able to destroy the Christian army at the Horns of Hattin in Galilee. After the battle, he released the king of Jerusalem but had the surviving Templars and Hospitallers killed in his presence, judging correctly that they posed the greatest danger to the Muslim Reconquista. When he took possession of Jerusalem, his first impulse was to avenge the crusaders' massacre of 1099, but he was persuaded by a Frankish envoy to take the city without violence.[84] Not a single Christian was killed, the Frankish inhabitants of Jerusalem were ransomed for a very moderate sum, and many were escorted to Tyre, where the Christians maintained a stronghold. Christians in the West were uneasily aware that Saladin had behaved more humanely than their own crusaders and developed legends that made him an honorary Christian. Some Muslims, however, were more critical: Ibn al-Athir argued that this clemency was a serious military and political error, because the Franks managed to retain a narrow coastal state stretching from Tyre to Beirut, which continued to threaten Muslim Jerusalem until the late thirteenth century.[85]

Ironically, as military jihad became embedded in the spirituality of the Greater Jihad, crusading was increasingly driven by material and political interests which sidelined the spiritual.[86] When Pope Urban had summoned the First Crusade, he had usurped the kings' prerogative in his bid for papal supremacy. The Third Crusade (1189–92), led and convened by Holy Roman Emperor Frederick Barbarossa, Philip II of France, and Richard I of England, reasserted the temporal rulers' monopoly of violence. While Saladin inspired his soldiers with hadith readings, Richard offered his men money for every stone of Acre's city wall torn down. A few years later, the Fourth Crusade was hijacked purely for commercial gain by the merchants of Venice, the new men of Europe, who persuaded the crusaders to attack their fellow Christians in the port of Zara and plunder Constantinople in 1204. Western emperors governed Byzantium until 1261, when the Greeks finally managed to expel them, but their incompetence in the intervening period may have fatally weakened this sophisticated state whose polity was far more complex than that of any Western kingdom at this date.[87] Pope Innocent III reclaimed papal libertas in 1213 by summoning the Fifth Crusade, which attempted to establish a Western base in Egypt, but the crusaders' fleet was incapacitated by an epidemic and the land army cut off by the rising flood waters of the Nile during the march to Cairo.

The Sixth Crusade (1228–29) entirely subverted the original crusading ideal since it was led by the Holy Roman Emperor Frederick II who had recently been excommunicated by Pope Gregory IX. Brought up in cosmopolitan Sicily, Frederick did not share the Islamophobia of the rest of Europe and negotiated a truce with his friend Sultan al-Kamil, who had no interest in jihad. Frederick thus recovered Jerusalem, Bethlehem and Nazareth without fighting a single battle.[88] But both rulers had misjudged the popular mood: Muslims were now convinced that the West was their implacable enemy and Christians seemed to think it more important to fight Muslims than to get Jerusalem back. Because no priest would perform the ceremony for an excommunicate, in March 1229 Frederick defiantly crowned himself king of Jerusalem in the Holy Sepulchre Church. The Teutonic Knights of the Holy Roman Empire proudly declared that this ceremony had made him God's vicar on earth, and that it was the emperor not the Pope who stood 'between God and mankind and was chosen to rule the entire world'.[89] By now a crusade's political impact at home seemed more important than what was happening in the Middle East.

Christians lost Jerusalem again in 1244, when the marauding Khwarazmian Turks in flight from the Mongol armies rampaged through the holy city, portent of a terrifying threat to both Christendom and Islamdom. Between 1190 and 1258, Genghis Khan's Mongol hordes had overrun northern China, Korea, Tibet, Central Asia, Anatolia, Russia and Eastern Europe. Any ruler who failed to submit immediately saw his cities laid waste and his subjects massacred. In 1257, Hulugu, Genghis Khan's son, crossed the Tigris, seized Baghdad and strangled the last Abbasid caliph; then he destroyed Aleppo and occupied Damascus, which surrendered and was spared destruction. At first King Louis IX of France and Pope Innocent IV hoped to convert the Mongols to Christianity and let them destroy Islam. Instead the Muslims would save the crusaders' coastal state and, possibly, Western Christendom from the Mongols. Finally, the Mongol rulers who established states in the Middle East would convert to Islam.

In 1250, a group of disaffected Mamluks took over Saladin's Ayyubid empire in a military coup. Ten years later, the brilliant Mamluk commander Baibars defeated the Mongol army at the Battle of Ain Jalut in Galilee. But the Mongols had conquered vast swathes of Muslim territory in Mesopotamia, the Iranian mountains, the Syr-Oxus basin, and the Volga region, where they established four large states. Mongol violence was not caused by religious intolerance: they acknowledged the validity of all faiths and usually built on local traditions once a region had been subjugated, so by the early fourteenth century the Mongol rulers of all four states had converted to Islam. The Mongol aristocracy, however, still followed the Yasa, Genghis Khan's military code. Many of their Muslim subjects were dazzled by their brilliant courts and were fascinated by their new rulers. But so much Muslim scholarship and culture had been lost in the devastation that some jurists decreed that the 'gates of *ijtihad* [independent reasoning] had closed'. This was an extreme version of the conservative tendency of agrarian civilisation, which lacked the economic resources to implement innovation on a large scale, valued social order over originality, and felt that culture was so hard won that it was more important to conserve what had already been achieved. This narrowing of horizons was not inspired by an inherent dynamic of Islam but was a reaction to the shocking Mongol assault. Other Muslims would respond to the Mongol conquests very differently.

Muslims were always ready to learn from other cultures and in the late fifteenth century they did so from the heirs of Genghis Khan. The Ottoman empire in Asia Minor, the Middle East and North Africa, the Safavid empire in Iran, and the Moghul empire in India would be created on the basis of the Mongol army state and become the most advanced states in the world at the time. But the Mongols also unwittingly inspired a spiritual revival. Jalal ad-Din Rumi (1207–73) had fled the Mongol armies with his family, migrating from Iran to Anatolia, where he founded a new mystical Sufi order. One of the most widely read Muslims in the West today, his philosophy is redolent of the refugee's homelessness and sense of separation, but Rumi was also enthralled by the vast extent of the Mongol empire and encouraged Sufis to explore boundless horizons on the spiritual plane and to open their hearts and minds to other faiths.

But no two people will respond to the same trauma identically. Another thinker of the period who has also achieved great influence in our own time is the 'fighting scholar' Ahmed ibn Taymiyyah (1263–1382), also a refugee who, unlike Rumi, hated the Mongols. He saw the Mongol converts, now fellow Muslims, as *kufar* ('infidels').[90] He also disapproved of the suspension of ijtihad: in these fearful times jurists needed to think creatively and adapt Shariah to the fact that the ummah had been weakened by two ruthless enemies: the crusaders and the Mongols. True, the crusaders seemed a spent force, but the Mongols might still attempt the conquest of the Levant. In preparation for a military jihad to defend their lands, Ibn Taymiyyah urged Muslims to engage in the Greater Jihad and return to the pure Islam of the Prophet's time, ridding themselves of such inauthentic practices as philosophy (*falsafah*), Sufi mysticism, Shiism, and the veneration of saints and tombs. Muslims who persisted in these false devotions were no better than infidels. When Ghazan Khan, the first of the Mongol chieftains to convert to Islam, invaded Syria in 1299, Ibn Taymiyyah issued a *fatwa* ('legal ruling') declaring that despite their conversion to Islam the Mongols were infidels, because they observed their own military code, the Yasa, instead of the Shariah, and their Muslim subjects were not bound to obey them. Muslims had traditionally been wary of condemning fellow Muslims as apostates, because they believed that only God could read a person's heart. The practice of *takfir*, declaring that a fellow Muslim has apostatised, would take on new life in our own times when Muslims have once again felt threatened by foreign powers.

During the Crusading period, Europe had also adopted a narrower perspective and become what one historian has called a 'persecuting society'.[91] Until the early eleventh century, Jews had been fully integrated in Europe.[92] Under Charlemagne they had enjoyed imperial protection and held important public posts. They became landowners, craftsmen in all trades, and Jewish physicians were much in demand. Jews spoke the same languages as Christians – Yiddish did not develop until the thirteenth century – and gave their children Latin names. There were no 'ghettos': Jews and Christians lived side by side and bought houses from one another in London until the mid-twelfth century.[93] But during the eleventh century, there had been rumours that Jews had persuaded the Fatimid caliph al-Hakim to destroy the Church of the Resurrection in Jerusalem in 1006, even though the caliph, who seems to have been certifiably insane, had also persecuted Jews and his fellow Muslims as well as Christians.[94] In consequence, Jews were attacked in Limoges, Orleans, Rouen and Mainz. Linked with Islam in the Christian imagination, their position grew more precarious with each crusade. After Richard I took the Cross in London in 1198 there were persecutions in East Anglia and Lincoln, and in 1193 in York Jews who refused baptism committed suicide en masse. The so-called 'blood libel', whereby the deaths of children were blamed on the local Jewish community, first surfaced when a child was killed in Norwich in the 1140s; there were similar cases in Gloucester (1168), Bury St Edmunds and Winchester (1192).[95]

This wave of persecution was certainly inspired by a distorted Christian mythology, but it was also the product of social factors. During its slow transition from a purely agrarian to a commercialised economy, towns were beginning to dominate Western Christendom and by the end of the twelfth century were becoming important centres of prosperity, power and creativity. There were great disparities of wealth. Low-born bankers and financiers were becoming rich at the expense of the aristocracy, while some townsfolk had not only been reduced to abject poverty but had also lost the traditional support structures of peasant life.[96] Money, in common use by the late eleventh century, came to symbolise the disturbing changes caused by this rapid economic growth that undermined the traditional social structure; it was seen as 'the root of all evil' and in popular iconography the deadly sin of avarice inspired visceral loathing and dread.[97] Originally Christians had been the most successful moneylenders, but during the twelfth century Jews had their lands confiscated and many were forced to become bailiffs, financial agents of the aristocracy or moneylenders, and were thereafter tainted by their association with money.[98] The Jew in Peter Abelard's *Dialogue* (1125) explained that because Jews' land tenure was so insecure, 'the principal gain that is left for us is that we sustain our miserable lives here by lending money at interest to strangers. But that just makes us more hated by those who think that they are oppressed by it.'[99] Jews, of course, were not the only scapegoats of Christian anxiety. Since the Crusades, Muslims, once regarded with vague indifference in Europe, now came to be regarded as fit only for extermination. In the mid-twelfth century, Peter the Venerable, abbot of Cluny, depicted Islam as a bloodthirsty religion that had been propagated entirely by the sword – a fantasy that may have reflected hidden guilt about Christian behaviour during the First Crusade.[100]

Disquiet about nascent capitalism and the growing violence of Western society, both of which were so obviously at odds with the radical teachings of Jesus, also surfaced in the 'heresies' that the Church had begun to persecute actively in the late twelfth century. Again, the challenge was political rather than doctrinal. The conditions of peasants had reached their lowest level and poverty had become a major problem.[101] Some had become rich in the towns, but population growth had fragmented inheritances and multiplied the numbers of landless villagers roaming the countryside desperately seeking employment. The structural violence of the 'three estate'

system was the cause of much anxious soul-searching among Christians. In
orthodox as well as heretical circles, the well-to-do were coming to the
conclusion that the only way to save their souls was to give away their
wealth, which they now regarded as sinful. After a serious illness, Francis
of Assisi (1181–1226), son of a wealthy merchant, renounced his patrimony,
lived as a hermit, and founded a new order of friars dedicated to serving
the poor and sharing their poverty; it increased rapidly in membership.
Francis' rule was approved by Pope Innocent III, who hoped thereby to
retain some control of the poverty movement that threatened the entire
social order.

Other groups were not such loyal adherents of the Church. Even after
they had been excommunicated in 1181, the followers of Valdes, a rich
businessman of Lyons who had given all his wealth to the poor, continued
to attract much support as they travelled through the towns of Europe in
pairs like the apostles, barefoot, clad in simple garments and holding all
things in common. Still more worrying were the Cathari, the 'Pure Ones',
who also roamed the countryside, begging for their bread, and were
dedicated to poverty, chastity and nonviolence. They founded churches in
all the major cities of northern and central Italy, enjoyed the protection of
influential laymen, and were especially powerful in Languedoc, Provence,
Tuscany and Lombardy. They embodied the Gospel values far more clearly
and authentically than did the worldly Catholic establishment who, perhaps
because they felt at some level guilty about their reliance on a system that
so clearly contradicted Jesus' teachings, responded viciously. In 1207, Pope
Innocent III (r. 1198–1216) commissioned Philip II of France to lead a
crusade against the Cathars in Languedoc, who, he wrote, were worse than
the Muslims. The Cathar Church 'gives birth continually to a monstrous
brood by which its corruption is vigorously renewed after that offspring
has passed on to others the canker of its own madness and a detestable
succession of criminals emerges'.[102]

Philip was happy to oblige since this would enhance his hold over southern
France, but Counts Raymond VI of Toulouse and Raymond-Roger of Béziers
and Carcassonne refused to join his crusade. When one of Raymond's barons
stabbed the papal legate, Innocent was convinced that the Cathars were
determined 'to annihilate us ourselves' and eliminate orthodox Catholicism
in Languedoc.[103] In 1209, Armand-Amalric, abbot of Cîteaux, led a large
army there, laying siege to the city of Béziers. It is said that when his troops
asked the abbot how they could distinguish orthodox Catholics from the
heretics in the town, he had replied: 'Kill them all; God will know his own.'

There followed indiscriminate slaughter. In fact, it seems that when the Catholics of Béziers were ordered to leave the town, they refused to abandon their Cathar neighbours and chose to die with them.[104] This crusade was as much about regional solidarity against outside intrusion as about religious affiliation.

The extremity of the rhetoric and the military ruthlessness of the Catharist Crusade is symptomatic of a profound denial. Popes and abbots were dedicated to the imitation of Christ but, like Ashoka, they had come up against the dilemma of civilisation, which cannot exist without the structural and military violence against which the Cathars had been protesting. Innocent III was the most powerful pope in history: he had secured the libertas of the Church and, unlike his predecessors, could command kings and emperors as their monarch. But he headed a society that had almost succumbed to barbarism after the collapse of the Roman empire and was now in the process of creating the world's first predominantly commercial economy. All three Abrahamic faiths began with a defiant rejection of inequity and systemic violence, which reflects the persistent conviction of human beings, dating back perhaps to the hunter-gatherer period, that there should be an equitable distribution of resources. But this militated against the way that Western society was heading. Cathars and Franciscans alike felt compromised by this impasse, realising, perhaps, that, as Jesus had pointed out, all who benefit from the structural violence of the state are implicated in its cruelty.

It seems unlikely that Innocent agonised unduly about this dilemma, though his neurotically exaggerated anti-Cathar rhetoric may express some unease with his position. Far more poignant was the stance of Dominic Guzman (c. 1170–1221), founder of the Order of Preachers; like the Franciscans, his friars had adopted a poverty so extreme that they could own no property and so begged for a living. The mendicant Dominicans travelled throughout Languedoc in pairs trying to bring the 'heretics' back to orthodoxy peacefully, reminding them of St Paul's insistence that Christians obey the political authorities. But they were inevitably tainted by their association with the anti-Cathar Crusade, especially after Dominic attended the Lateran Council of 1215 to seek Innocent's approval of his order.

Those Christians who remained loyal to the Church but could see how the systemic violence of Christendom violated the Gospel teaching were inevitably conflicted. Unable to admit that the 'heretics' had a point, yet furious with them for drawing attention to their dilemma, they projected these sentiments outward, in forms monstrous and inhuman. There were paranoid fantasies of a highly organised, clandestine Catharist Church determined to destroy the human race and restore Satan's kingdom.[105] We shall see that similar conspiracy fears would later erupt in other societies that were going through a traumatic modernisation process and would also result in violence. The Council of Rheims (1157) described the Cathars 'hiding among the poor and under the veil of religion . . . moving from place to place and undermining the faith of simple people'.[106] Soon Jews would be said to belong to a similar international conspiracy.[107] Even a fair-minded man like Peter the Venerable, abbot of Cluny, who claimed to be reaching out to the Muslim world with love rather than force, described Islam as a 'heresy and diabolical sect' addicted to 'bestial cruelty'.[108] At the outset of the Second Crusade he wrote to King Louis VII of France that he hoped he would kill as many Muslims as Moses and Joshua had killed Amorites and Canaanites.[109] During this period, Satan, often pictured as a monstrous human being with horns and a tail, became a far more menacing figure in Western Christianity than in either Judaism or Islam. As they made their stressful transition from political backwater to major world power, Europeans were terrified of an unseen 'common enemy', representing what they could not accept in themselves and associated with absolute evil.[110]

Innocent III had achieved a virtual papal monarchy in Europe but no other pope would match his power. Secular rulers, such as Louis VII of France (1137–80), Henry II of England (r. 1154–89) and Frederick II all challenged this papal supremacy. They had built powerful kingdoms with government institutions that could intrude more than ever before into the lives of ordinary people, so they were all zealous persecutors of 'heretics' who threatened the social order.[111] They were not 'secularists' in our sense; they still regarded royal power as sacred and war as holy, but they had developed a Christian theology of war that was quite different from that of the official Church. Again, we find it impossible to pinpoint a single, essentialist Christian attitude to war, fighting and violence. The Christian template could be used to very different effect by different groups.

Bishops and popes had used both the Peace of God and the Crusades to control the warrior aristocracy but during the thirteenth century, the knights responded by developing a chivalric code that declared independence of the papal monarchy. They rejected the Cluniac reform, had no intention of converting to the monastic ideal, and were indifferent to Bernard's scathing critique of knighthood. Their Christianity was laced with the Indo-European warrior code of the Germanic tribes, with its ethos of honour, loyalty and prowess. Where the reforming popes had forbidden knights to kill their fellow Christians, urging them to slaughter Muslims instead, these rebellious knights were happy to fight any Christian who threatened their lord and his people.

In the *chansons de geste,* the 'Songs of Deeds', composed in the early twelfth century, warfare is a natural, violent and sacred activity. These knights clearly loved the excitement and intensity of the battlefield and experienced it with religious fervour. 'Now war is upon us again, all praise to Christ!' cries one of King Arthur's knights.[112] *The Song of Roland*, composed in the late eleventh century, describes an incident that occurred at the end of Charlemagne's campaign in Muslim Spain: Archbishop Turpin kills Muslims with joyous abandon and Roland has no doubt that the souls of his dead companions have gone straight to heaven.[113] His sword Durendal, which has relics embedded in its hilt, is a sacred object and his loyalty to Charlemagne inseparable from his devotion to God.[114] Far from having monastic inspirations, these knights regard monks with disdain. As Archbishop Turpin says robustly, a knight who is not 'forward and fierce in battle' might as well 'turn monk in monastery meek and for his sins pray daily on his knees'.[115]

The Quest of the Holy Grail (c. 1225), a prose fable, takes us into the heart of knightly spirituality.[116] It shows clear influences of the Cistercian ideal, which had introduced a more introspective spirituality into monasticism, but replaced this internal quest with heroism on the battlefield and set the knight's religious world apart from the ecclesiastical establishment. Indeed, knights alone can participate in the quest for the Grail, said to be the cup that Jesus used at the Last Supper. Their liturgy takes place in a feudal castle rather than a church or monastery and their clergy are not abbots or bishops but hermits, many of them former knights. Galahad, not the Pope, is Christ's representative on earth. The knight's loyalty to his earthly lord is a sacred duty and no other commitment can supersede it:

> For the heart of the knight must be so hard and unrelenting to his sovereign's foe that nothing in the world can soften it. And if he gives way to fear, he is not of the company of knights, a veritable companion, who would sooner meet death in battle than fail to uphold the quarrel of their lord.[117]

Killing the enemies of his king, even if they are Christians, is just as holy as killing the Muslim enemies of Christ.

The ecclesiastical establishment found it impossible to control the knights' dissident Christianity. Aware that they were in an unassailable position, these knights simply refused to comply with the Church's demands.[118] 'Everybody should honour them,' wrote an early thirteenth-century cleric, 'for they defend the Holy Church and they uphold justice for us against those who would do us harm . . . Our chalices would be stolen from before us at the table of God and nothing would ever stop it . . . The good would never be able to endure if the wicked did not fear knights.'[119] Why should knights obey the Church? Their victories alone proved that they had a special relationship with the Lord of Hosts.[120] Indeed, one poet argued, the physical effort, skill, tenacity and courage that warfare required made it 'a much nobler work' than any other occupation and put the knight in a superior class of his own. Chivalry, claimed another knight, was 'such a difficult, tough and very costly thing to learn that no coward ventures to take it on'.[121] Knights regarded fighting as an ascetic practice that was far more challenging than a monk's fasts or vigils. A knight really knew what suffering was: every day he took up his cross and followed Jesus on the battlefield.[122]

Henry of Lancaster (c. 1310–61), hero of the first phase of the Hundred Years War between England and France, prayed that the wounds, pain, fatigue and danger of the battlefield would enable him to suffer for Christ 'such afflictions, labours, pains, as you chose, and not merely to win a prize nor to offset my sins, but purely for love of you, as you Lord have done for love of me'.[123] For Geoffroi de Charny, fighting on the other side, the physical struggle of warfare gave his life meaning. Prowess was the highest human achievement because it required such extreme 'pain, travail, fear, and sorrow'. Yet it also brought 'great joy'.[124] Monks had it easy; their so-called sufferings were 'nothing in comparison' to what a soldier endured every day of his life, 'beset by great terrors' and knowing that at any moment he could be 'defeated, or killed, or captured, or wounded'.[125] Fighting for worldly honour alone was useless, but if knights struggled in the path of God, their 'noble souls will be set in paradise for all eternity and their persons will be forever honoured'.[126]

The kings, who also abided by this chivalric code, believed that they too had a direct link to God that was independent of the Church and by the late thirteenth century some of them felt strong enough to challenge papal supremacy.[127] This began in 1296 with a dispute about taxation. The Fourth Lateran Council (1215) had 'liberated' the clergy from the direct jurisdiction of secular princes but now Philip IV of France and Edward I of England asserted their right to tax the clergy in their realms. Even though Pope Boniface VIII objected, they got their way – Edward by outlawing the English clergy and Philip by withholding essential resources from the papacy. In 1301, Philip again went on the offensive, when he ordered a French bishop to stand trial for treason and heresy. When Boniface issued the bull *Unam Sanctam*, insisting that all temporal power was subject to the Pope, Philip simply dispatched Guillaume de Nogaret with a band of mercenaries to bring Boniface to Paris to face charges of usurpation of royal power. Nogaret arrested the Pope at Anagni and held him prisoner for several days before he was able to escape. The shock proved too much for Boniface and he died shortly afterwards.

At this date no king could survive without papal support. But the outrage of Anagni convinced Clement V (1305–14), Boniface's successor, to make the papacy more accommodating and he was the first in a line of French popes to reside in Avignon. Clement meekly restored Philip's legitimacy by repealing all the bulls Boniface had issued against him and, on Philip's orders, disbanded the Templars and confiscated their vast wealth. Subject to the Pope and owing no obedience to the king, the Templars were an enemy to royal ascendancy; they epitomised the crusading ideals of the papal monarchy and had to go. The monks were tortured until they admitted to sodomy, cannibalism and devil worship; many repudiated these confessions at the stake.[128] Philip's ruthlessness did not suggest that royal power would be more irenic than Innocent III's papal monarchy.

It is wrong to claim, as some scholars have done, that Philip created the first modern secular kingdom; these were not yet sovereign states.[129] Philip was re-sacralising kingship; these ambitious kings knew that the king had once been the chief representative of the divine in Europe and argued that the pope had usurped his royal prerogative.[130] Philip was a theocratic ruler whose subjects called him 'semi-divine' (*quasi semi-deus*) and 'king and priest' (*rex et sacerdos*). His land was 'holy' and the French were the new Chosen People.[131] In England too, holiness had 'migrated from the crusade to the nation and its wars'.[132] England, claimed the Chancellor when he opened the parliament of 1376–77, was the new Israel; her military victories proved her divine election.[133] Under this sacral kingship, defence of the realm would acquire a sacral dimension.[134] Soldiers who died fighting for a territorial kingdom would, like the crusaders, be revered as martyrs.[135] People still dreamed of going on crusade and liberating Jerusalem, but in an important development holy warfare was beginning to merge with the patriotism of national war.

PART THREE

Modernity

9

THE ARRIVAL OF 'RELIGION'

On 2 January 1492, the Catholic monarchs Ferdinand of Aragon and Isabella of Castile celebrated their victory over the Muslim kingdom of Granada in southern Spain. Crowds watched the Christian banners unfurling on the city walls with deep emotion and bells pealed triumphantly throughout Europe. Yet despite the triumph of that day, Europeans still felt threatened by Islam. In 1453 the Ottoman Turks had obliterated the Byzantine empire, which for centuries had protected Europe from Muslim encroachment. In 1480, the year after the monarchs' accession, the Ottomans had begun a naval offensive in the Mediterranean and Abu al-Hassan, Sultan of Granada, had made a surprise attack on the port of Zahara in Castile. Spain, therefore, was on the front line of the war with the Muslim world and many believed that Ferdinand was the mythical emperor who was expected to unite Christendom, defeat the Ottomans and usher in the Age of the Holy Spirit in which Christianity would spread to the ends of the earth.[1] Western Europe was indeed about to achieve global dominance, yet in 1492 it still lagged far behind Islam.

The Ottoman empire was the strongest and most powerful state in the world, ruling Anatolia, the Middle East, North Africa and Arabia. But the Safavids in Iran and the Moghuls in India had also established absolute monarchies in which almost every facet of public life was run with systematic and bureaucratic precision. Each had a strong Islamic ideology that pervaded every aspect of their rule: the Ottomans were staunchly Sunni; the Safavids Shii; and the Moghuls leaned towards Falsafah and Sufism. Far more efficient and powerful than any European kingdom at this time, they marked the culmination of the agrarian state,[2] and were the last magnificent expression of the 'conservative spirit' that was the hallmark of pre-modern society.[3] As we have seen, all agrarian societies eventually outran their intrinsically limited resources, which put a brake on innovation. Only fully industrialised societies could afford the constant replication of the infrastructure that unlimited progress required. Pre-modern education could not encourage originality, because it lacked the resources to implement many new ideas. If people were encouraged to think innovatively, but nothing ever came of it, the ensuing frustration could lead to social unrest. In a conservative society, stability and order were far more important than freedom of expression.

In any traditional empire, the purpose of government was not to guide or provide services for the population but to tax them. It did not usually attempt to interfere with the social customs or religious beliefs of its subjects. Rather, a government was set up to take whatever it could from its peasants and prevent other aristocrats from getting their surplus, so warfare – to conquer, expand or maintain the tax base – was essential to these states. Indeed, between 1450 and 1700 there were only eight years when the Ottomans were not involved in warfare.[4] An Ottoman treatise expressed succinctly the agrarian state's dependence on organised violence:

> The world is before all else a verdant garden whose enclosure is the State; the State is a government whose head is the prince; the prince is a shepherd who is assisted by the army; the army is a body of guards which is maintained by money, and money is the indispensable resource which is provided by subjects.[5]

But for centuries now, Europeans had been devising a commercial economy that would result in the creation of a very different kind of state. The modern world is often said to have begun in 1492; in fact, it would take Europeans some four hundred years to create the modern state. Its economy would no longer be based on the agrarian surplus, it would interfere far more in the personal lives of its subjects, it would be run on the expectation of constant innovation, and it would separate religion from its politics.

Present at the ceremony in Granada was Christopher Columbus, the monarchs' protégé; later that year he sailed from the port of Palos in Spain to find a new trade route to the Indies, only to discover the Americas instead. In sponsoring this voyage, Ferdinand and Isabella had unwittingly taken an important step towards the creation of our globalised, Western-dominated world.[6] For some, Western modernity would be empowering, liberating and enthralling; others would experience it as coercive, invasive and destructive. The Spaniards and Portuguese, who pioneered the discovery of the New World, imagined that it was simply waiting to be carved up, plundered and exploited for their benefit. So did Pope Alexander VI, who, as if he were undisputed monarch of the globe, divided it between Spain and Portugal from pole to pole and gave Ferdinand and Isabella a mandate to wage a 'just war' against any native peoples who resisted the European colonialists.[7]

But Alexander was no Innocent III. Papal power had plummeted during the fourteenth century and the balance of power had passed to the kings. Seven successive popes had resided in Avignon (1309–77), firmly under the thumb of the French kings. In 1378, a disputed papal election divided the Church between the supporters of Urban VI in Rome and Clement VII in Avignon and the kings of Europe had taken sides according to their own rivalries. The schism ended only with the election of Martin V at the Council of Constance in 1417 but the popes, now safely back in Rome, never recovered their former prestige. There were reports of corruption and immorality and in 1492 Rodrigo Borgia, father of Cesare and Lucrezia Borgia and two other illegitimate children, had won the papacy by flagrant bribery, taking the name of Alexander VI. His chief goal as pontiff was to break the power of the Italian princes and secure their wealth for his own family. His mandate to Ferdinand and Isabella was, therefore, of dubious spiritual value.

The early colonialists stormed violently into the New World as if they were conducting a giant acquisition raid, greed melding seamlessly with pious intent. The Portuguese set up sugar plantations in the Cape Verde Islands and between three and five million Africans were torn from their homes and enslaved there.[8] No other American colony would be so gravely implicated in slavery. When the Portuguese finally rounded the Cape and exploded aggressively into the Indian Ocean, their bronze cannons made short work of the slender dhows and junks of their rivals. By 1524 they had seized the best ports in East Africa, western India, the Persian Gulf and the Malacca Strait and by 1560 they had an ocean-wide chain of settlements based on Goa.[9] This was purely a trading empire: the Portuguese made no attempt to conquer territory inland. Meanwhile, the Spanish had invaded the Americas, slaughtering the indigenous peoples and seizing land, booty and slaves. They may have claimed to fight in the name of Christianity, but Hernando Cortés was brutally frank about his real motivation: he simply wanted 'to get rich, not to work like a peasant'.[10] In Montezuma's Aztec empire in central Mexico, he would invite local chieftains in each city to the central square and, when they arrived with their retainers, his small Spanish army would gun them down, loot the city and go on to the next.[11] When Cortés arrived in the Aztec capital in 1525, Montezuma was already dead and his now shattered empire passed into Spanish hands. Survivors were decimated by European diseases to which they had no immunity. Some ten years later, Francisco Pizarro, using similar military tactics, brought smallpox to the Inca empire in Peru. For Europeans, colonialism brought unimaginable wealth; for the native peoples it brought death on an unprecedented scale. According to one estimate, between 1519 and 1595 the population of central Mexico fell from 16.9 million to 1 million and between 1572 and 1620 the Inca population had been halved.[12]

Cortés and Pizarro were the heroes of the *conquistadores* ('conquerors'), men of low social status who went to the New World to become Spanish grandees.[13] Their conquests were achieved with martial savagery and maintained by systematic exploitation. When they arrived in a new region, they would read out a formal statement in Spanish, informing the uncomprehending inhabitants that the Pope had given their land to Spain so they must now submit to the Church and the Catholic monarchs: 'We shall take you and your wives and your children, and make slaves of them and we shall take away your goods and do you all the mischief and damage that we can.'[14] The Spanish did not need to import African slaves; they simply enslaved the local peoples to grow cash crops, work in the mines and provide domestic labour. By the end of the sixteenth century, they were shipping on average 300 million grams of silver and 1.9 million grams of gold every year. With these unique resources, Spain established the first global empire, stretching from the Americas to the Philippines and dominating large portions of Europe.[15]

The Spanish colonialists felt no compunction about their treatment of the indigenous peoples – they regarded the 'savage' as scarcely human and had been horrified to discover that the Aztecs practised human sacrifice and cannibalism.[16] But at home the Dominicans adhered more faithfully to Christian principles and spoke up for the conquered peoples. The Church had no jurisdiction over these American 'kings', argued Durandus of San Poinciana in 1506; they should not be attacked unless they were actually harming Europeans. The popes should send missionaries to these new lands, Cardinal Thomas Cajetan argued, but not 'for the purpose of seizing their lands or reducing them to temporal subjection'.[17] Francisco de Vitoria maintained that the conquistadores had no right to 'eject the enemy from their dominions and despoil them of their property'.[18]

The Renaissance humanists, however, were far more sympathetic to the colonial project. In Thomas More's *Utopia* (1516), a fictional account of an ideal society, the Utopians went to war only 'to drive invading armies from the territories of their friends, or to liberate oppressed people in the name of humanity from tyranny and servitude'.[19] All very admirable, but there were limits to this benevolent policy: if the population became too great for their island to support, Utopians felt entitled to send settlers to plant a colony on the mainland, 'wherever the natives have plenty of unoccupied or uncultivated land'. They would farm this neglected soil, which 'previously had seemed too barren and paltry even to support the natives', and make it yield an abundance.[20] Friendly natives could be absorbed into the colony, but the Utopians felt no qualms about fighting those who resisted them: 'The Utopians say that it is perfectly justifiable to make war on people who leave their land idle or waste yet forbid the use and possession of it to others who, by the law of nature, ought to be supported from it.'[21]

There was a strain of ruthlessness and cruelty in early modern thought.[22] The so-called humanists were pioneering a rather convenient idea of natural rights to counter the brutality and intolerance they associated with conventional religion. From the outset, however, the philosophy of human rights, still crucial to modern political discourse, did not apply to all human beings. Because Europe was frequently afflicted by famine and seemed unable to support its growing population, humanists like Thomas More were scandalised by the idea of arable land going to waste. They looked back to Tacitus, an apologist for Roman imperialism, who had been convinced that exiles had every right to secure a place to live, since 'what is possessed by none belongs to everyone'. Commenting on this passage, Alberico Gentili (1552–1608), professor of civil law at Oxford, concluded that because 'God did not create the world to be empty', the 'seizure of vacant places' should be 'regarded as a law of nature':

And even though such lands belong to the sovereign of that territory . . . yet because of that law of nature which abhors a vacuum, they will fall to the lot of those who take them, though the sovereign will retain jurisdiction over them.[23]

Gentili also quoted Aristotle's opinion that some men were natural slaves and that waging war against primitive peoples 'who, though intended by nature to be governed, will not submit', was as necessary as hunting wild animals.[24] Gentili argued that the Mesoamericans clearly fell into this category because of their abominable lewdness and cannibalism. Where churchmen frequently condemned the violent subjugation of the New World, the Renaissance humanists who were trying to create an alternative to the cruelties committed by people of faith endorsed it.

Spain had, however, embarked on a policy that would come to epitomise the fanatical violence inherent in religion. In 1480, with the Ottoman threat at its height, Ferdinand and Isabella had established the Spanish Inquisition. It is significant that, even though the Catholic Monarchs remained the Pope's obedient servants, they insisted that it remain separate from the papal inquisition. Ferdinand may have hoped thereby to mitigate the cruelty of his own inquisition and almost certainly never intended it to be a permanent institution.[25] The Spanish Inquisition did not target Christian heretics but focused on Jews who had converted to Christianity and were believed to have lapsed. In Muslim Spain, Jews had never been subjected to the persecution that was now habitual in the rest of Europe,[26] but as the crusading armies of the Reconquista had advanced down the peninsula in the late fourteenth century, Jews in Aragon and Castile had been dragged to the baptismal font; others had tried to save themselves by voluntary conversion, and some of these *conversos* (converts) became extremely successful in Christian society and inspired considerable resentment. There were riots and converso property was seized, the violence caused by financial and social jealousy as much as religious allegiance.[27] The monarchs were not personally anti-Semitic but simply wanted to pacify their kingdom, which had been shaken by civil war and now faced the Ottoman threat. Yet the Inquisition was a deeply flawed attempt to achieve stability. As often happens when a nation is menaced by an external power, there were paranoid fears of enemies within, in this case of a 'fifth column' of lapsed conversos working secretly to undermine the kingdom's security. The Spanish Inquisition has become a byword for fanatical 'religious' intolerance but its violence was caused less by theological than political considerations.

Such interference with the religious practice of their subjects was entirely new in Spain, where confessional uniformity had never been a possibility. After centuries of Christians, Jews and Muslims 'living together' (*convivencia*), the monarchs' initiative met with strong opposition.[28] Yet while there was no public appetite for targeting observant Jews, there was considerable anxiety about the so-called lapsed 'secret Jews', known as New Christians. When the Inquisitors arrived in a district, 'apostates' were promised a pardon if they confessed voluntarily and 'Old Christians' were ordered to report neighbours who refused to eat pork or work on Saturday, the emphasis always on practice and social custom rather than 'belief'. Many conversos who were loyal Catholics felt it wise to seize the opportunity for amnesty while the going was good, and this flood of 'confessions' convinced both the Inquisitors and the public that the society of clandestine 'Judaisers' really existed.[29] Seeking out dissidents in this way would not infrequently become a feature of modern states, secular as well as religious, in times of national crisis.

After the conquest of 1492, the monarchs had inherited Granada's large Jewish community. The fervid patriotism unleashed by the Christian triumph led to more hysterical conspiracy fears.[30] Some, remembering old tales of Jews helping the Muslim armies when they had arrived in Spain eight hundred years earlier, pressured the monarchs to deport all practising Jews from Spain. After initial hesitation, on 31 March 1492 the monarchs signed the edict of expulsion, which gave Jews the choice of baptism or deportation. Most chose baptism and, as conversos, were now harassed by the Inquisition, but about eighty thousand crossed the border into Portugal and fifty thousand took refuge in the Ottoman empire.[31] Under papal pressure, Ferdinand and Isabella now turned their attention to Spain's Muslims. In 1499 Granada was split into Christian and Muslim zones. Muslims were required to convert, and by 1501 Granada was officially a kingdom of 'New Christians'. But the Muslim converts (*Moriscos*) were given no instruction in their new faith and everybody knew that they continued to live, pray and fast according to the laws of Islam. Indeed, a mufti in Oran in North Africa issued a fatwa permitting Spanish Muslims to conform outwardly to Christianity and most Spaniards turned a blind eye to Muslim observance. A practical convivencia had been restored.

The first twenty years of the Spanish Inquisition were undoubtedly the most violent in its long history. There is no reliable documentation of the numbers of people killed. Historians once believed that about thirteen thousand conversos were burned during this early period.[32] But more recent estimates suggest that most of those who came forward were never brought to trial, that in most cases of conversos who had fled the death penalty was pronounced *in absentia* and they were symbolically burned in effigy, and that between 1480 and 1530 only 1,500 to 2,000 people were actually executed.[33] Nevertheless, this was a tragic and shocking development, which broke with centuries of peaceful coexistence. The experience was devastating for the conversos and proved lamentably counter-productive. Many conversos who had been faithful Catholics when they were detained were so disgusted by their treatment that they reverted to Judaism and became the 'secret Jews' that the Inquisition had set out to eliminate.[34]

Spain was not a modern centralised state but in the late fifteenth century it was the most powerful kingdom in the world. Besides its colonial possessions in the Americas, Spain had holdings in the Netherlands and the monarchs had married their children to the heirs of Portugal, England and the Austrian Habsburg dynasty. To counter the ambitions of its arch-rival France, Ferdinand had campaigned in Italy against France and Venice and seized control of Upper Navarre and Naples. Spain was, therefore, feared and resented, and exaggerated tales of the Inquisition spread through the rest of Europe, which was itself in the violent throes of a major transformation.

By the sixteenth century, a new kind of civilisation was slowly emerging in Europe, based on new technologies and the constant reinvestment of capital. This would ultimately free the continent from many of the restrictions of agrarian society. Instead of focusing on the preservation of past achievements, Western people were acquiring the confidence to look to the future. Where older cultures had required people to remain within carefully defined limits, pioneers like Columbus encouraged them to venture beyond the known world, where they discovered that they not only survived but prospered. Inventions were occurring simultaneously in many different fields; none of them seemed particularly momentous at the time, but their cumulative effect was decisive.[35] Specialists in one discipline found that they benefited from discoveries made in others. By 1600, innovations were made on such a scale and in so many areas at once that progress had become irreversible and religion would either have to adapt to these developments or become irrelevant.

By the early seventeenth century, the Dutch had created the building blocks of western capitalism.[36] In the joint-stock company, members pooled their capital contributions and placed them on a permanent basis under common management, which gave a colonial or trading venture abroad resources and security far greater than one person could provide. The first municipal bank in Amsterdam offered efficient, inexpensive and safe access to deposits, money transfers and payment services both at home and in the growing international market. Finally, the Stock Exchange gave merchants a centre where they could trade in all kinds of commodities. These institutions, over which the Church had no control, would acquire a dynamic of their own and, as the market economy developed, would increasingly undermine old agrarian structures and enable the commercial classes to develop their own power base. Successful merchants, artisans and manufacturers became powerful enough to participate in the politics that had formerly been the preserve of the aristocracy, even to the point of playing off one noble faction against another. They tended to ally themselves with those kings who were trying to build strong centralised monarchies, since this would facilitate trade. With the emergence of the absolute monarchy and the sovereign state in England and France, the commercial classes, or bourgeoisie, became increasingly influential as market forces gradually made the state independent of the restrictions imposed upon it by a wholly agrarian economy.[37] But would it be less structurally or militarily violent than the agrarian state?

In Germany there were no strong, centralising monarchies, just a welter of forty-one small principalities that the Holy Roman Emperor was unable to control. But in 1506, Charles V, the grandson of Ferdinand and Isabella and of the emperor Maximilian, inherited the Habsburg lands in Austria, and in 1516 became king of Aragon and Castile on the death of Ferdinand; in 1519 he was elected Holy Roman Emperor. By an adroit series of marriage alliances, skilful diplomacy and warfare, the Habsburgs had brought more territories under their rule than any previous European rulers. Charles' ambition was to create a pan-European empire similar to the Ottoman empire, but he found that he could not control the German princes who wanted to make their principalities strong monarchies on the model of France and England. Moreover, the towns of central and southern Germany had become the most vital commercial centres in Northern Europe.[38] Economic changes there led to class conflict, and, as usual, discontent focused on Jewish 'usurers' and venal Catholic priests who were said to leech off the poor.

In 1517, Martin Luther (1483–1546), an Augustinian friar, nailed his famous 95 Theses on the castle church door in Wittenberg and set in motion the process known as the Reformation. His attack on the Church's sale of indulgences resonated with discontented townsfolk, who were sick of clerics extorting money from gullible people on dubious pretexts.[39] The ecclesiastical establishment treated Luther's protest with lofty disdain, but young clerics took his ideas to the people in the towns, who initiated local reforms that effectively liberated their congregations from the control of Rome. The more intellectually vigorous clergy spread Luther's ideas in their own books, which, thanks to the new technology of printing, circulated with unprecedented speed, launching one of the first modern mass movements. Like other heretics in the past, Luther had created an anti-church.

Luther and the other great reformers – Ulrich Zwingli (1484–1531) and John Calvin (1509–64) – were addressing a society undergoing fundamental and far-reaching change. Modernisation would always be frightening:

living *in medias res*, people are unable to see where their society is going and find its slow but radical alteration distressing. No longer feeling at home in a changing world, they found that their faith changed too. Luther himself was prey to agonising depressions and wrote eloquently of his inability to respond to the old rituals, which had been designed for another way of life.[40] Zwingli and Calvin both felt a sense of crippling helplessness before experiencing a profound conviction of the absolute power of God, which, they were convinced, alone could save them. In leaving the Roman Church, the reformers were making one of the earliest declarations of independence of Western modernity and, because of their aggressive stance towards the Catholic establishment, they were known as 'Protestants'. They demanded the freedom to read and interpret the Bible as they chose – even though each of the three could be intolerant of views opposed to his *own* teaching. The reformed Christian stood alone with his Bible before his God: Protestants thus canonised the growing individualism of the modern spirit.

Luther was also the first European Christian to advocate the separation of church and state, though his 'secularist' vision was hardly irenic. God, he believed, had so retreated from the material world that it no longer had any spiritual significance. Like other rigorists before him, Luther yearned for spiritual purity and concluded that church and state should operate independently, each respecting the other's proper sphere.[41] In Luther's political writings, we see the arrival of 'religion' as a discrete activity, separate from the world as a whole, which it had previously permeated. True Christians, justified by a personal act of faith in God's saving power, belonged to the Kingdom of God and, because the Holy Spirit made them incapable of injustice and hatred, they were essentially free from state coercion.[42] But Luther knew that such Christians were few in number. Most were still in thrall to sin and, together with non-Christians, belonged to the Kingdom of the World; it was essential, therefore, that these sinners be restrained by the state 'in the same way as a savage wild beast is bound with chains and ropes so that it cannot bite and tear as it would normally do'.[43] Luther understood that, without a strong state, 'the world would be reduced to chaos', and that no government could realistically rule according to the Gospel principles of love, forgiveness and tolerance.[44] To attempt this would be like 'loosing the ropes and chains of the savage wild beasts and letting them bite and mangle everywhere'.[45] The only way the Kingdom of the World, a realm of selfishness and violence ruled by the devil, could impose the peace, continuity and order that made human society feasible was by the sword.

But the state had no jurisdiction over the conscience of the individual and no right, therefore, to fight heresy or lead a holy war. While it could have nothing to do with the spiritual realm, the state *must* have unqualified and absolute authority in temporal affairs. Even if the state were cruel, tyrannical and forbade the teaching of God's Word, Christians must not resist its power.[46] For its part, the true Church, the Kingdom of God, must hold aloof from the inherently corrupt and depraved policies of the Kingdom of the World, dealing only with spiritual affairs. Protestants believed that the Roman Church had failed in its true mission because it had dallied with the sinful Kingdom of the World.

Where pre-modern faith had emphasised the sacredness of community – the Sangha, the ummah, and the Body of Christ – for Luther 'religion' was a wholly personal and private matter. Where previous sages, prophets and reformers had felt impelled to take a stand against the systemic violence of the state, Luther's Christian was supposed to retreat into his own interior world of righteousness and let society, quite literally, go to hell. And in his emphasis on the limited and inferior nature of earthly politics, Luther had given a potentially dangerous endorsement of unqualified state power.[47] Luther's response to the Peasants' War in Germany showed that a secularised political theory would not necessarily lead to a reduction in state violence. Between March and May 1525, peasant communities in southern and central Germany had resisted the centralising policies of the princes that deprived them of traditional rights, and by hard-headed bargaining many villages had managed to wrest concessions from them without resorting to violence. But in Thuringia, in central Germany, lawless peasant bands roamed the countryside, looting and burning convents, churches and monasteries.[48]

In his first pamphlet on the Peasants' War, Luther had tried to be even-handed and had castigated the 'cheating' and 'robbing' of the aristocracy.[49] But in his view the peasants had committed the unpardonable sin of mixing religion and politics. Suffering, he maintained, was their lot; they must obey the Gospel, turn the other cheek and accept the loss of their lives and property.[50] They had had the temerity to argue that Christ had made all men free – an opinion that clearly chimed with New Testament teachings but cut no ice with Luther. He insisted that 'A worldly kingdom cannot exist without an inequality of persons, some being free, some imprisoned, some lords, some subjects.'[51] Luther encouraged the princes to use every possible means to suppress the peasant agitators:

Let everyone who can, smite, slay and stab, secretly or openly, remembering that nothing can be more poisoned, hurtful or devilish than a rebel. It is just as when one must kill a mad dog: if you do not strike him, he will strike you and a whole land with you.[52]

The rebels, he concluded, were in thrall to the devil and killing them was an act of mercy, for it would rescue them from this satanic bondage.

Because this rebellion threatened the entire social structure, the state suppressed it savagely: as many as 100,000 peasants may have died. The crisis was an ominous sign of the instability of early modern states at a time when traditional ideas were being widely questioned. The reformers had called for a reliance on scripture alone but would find that the Bible could be a dangerous weapon if it got into the wrong hands. Once people began reading the Bible for themselves, they soon saw glaring discrepancies between Jesus' teachings and current ecclesiastical and political practice. The Anabaptists ('Re-baptisers') were especially disruptive because their literal reading of the Gospel led them to condemn such institutions as the Holy Roman Empire, the city council and the trade guild.[53] When some Dutch Anabaptists managed to seize control of Münster in north-west Germany in 1534, instituting polygamy and banning private property, Catholics and Protestants – for once in firm agreement – saw this as a political threat that could easily be emulated by other towns.[54] The following year, the Anabaptists of Münster were massacred by joint Catholic and Protestant forces.[55]

The Münster catastrophe and the Peasants' War both affected the way other rulers dealt with religious dissidents. In Western Europe, 'heresy' had always been a political rather than a purely theological matter and had been suppressed violently because it threatened public order. Very few of the elite, therefore, considered it wrong to prosecute and execute 'heretics', who were killed not so much for what they believed as for what they did or failed to do. The Reformation, however, had introduced an entirely new emphasis on 'belief'. Hitherto the Middle English *beleven* (like the Greek *pistis* and the Latin *credo*) had been a practically expressed 'commitment' or 'loyalty'; now it would increasingly come to mean an intellectual accept-ance of a set of doctrinal opinions.[56] As the Reformation progressed, it became important to explain the differences between the new and the old religion, as well as between the different Protestant sects – hence the lists of obligatory 'beliefs' in the Thirty-Nine Articles, the Lambeth Articles and the Westminster Confession.[57] Catholics would do likewise in their own reformation, formulated by the Council of Trent (1545–63), which created a catechism of propositional, standardised opinions.

The doctrinal divisions created by the Reformation became especially significant in states aspiring to strong centralised rule. Hitherto the traditional agrarian state had neither the means nor, usually, the inclination to supervise the religious lives of the lower classes. But those monarchs striving for absolute rule had developed a state machinery that enabled them to supervise their subjects' lives more closely, and increasingly confessional allegiance would become the criterion of political loyalty. Henry VIII (r. 1509–47) and Elizabeth I (r. 1558–1603) of England both persecuted Catholics not as religious apostates but as traitors to the state. When he was Henry VIII's Chancellor, Thomas More had passed harsh sentences on politically dangerous heretics, only to be himself executed for refusing to take the Oath of Supremacy that made Henry head of the Church in England.[58] In France, the Edict of Paris (1543) described Protestant 'heretics' as 'the seditious disturbers of the peace and tranquillity of our subjects and secret conspirators against the prosperity of our state, which depends chiefly on the preservation of the Catholic faith in our kingdom'.[59]

Although the Reformation produced fruitful forms of Christianity, it was in many ways a tragedy. It has been estimated that as many as 8,000 men and women were judicially executed as heretics in Europe during the sixteenth and seventeenth centuries.[60] Policies differed from region to region. In France, judicial proceedings had given way to open warfare, massacre and popular violence by the 1550s. The German Catholic Inquisitors were never overly zealous in pursuing Protestants but Holy Roman Emperor Charles V and his son Philip II of Spain (1556–98) regarded Protestantism in the Netherlands as a political as well as a religious threat so they were unwavering in their attempts to suppress it. In England, policy changed with the faith-allegiance of the monarch. Henry VIII, who upheld his Catholicism, was unswervingly hostile to Lutherans but regarded fidelity to the Pope as a capital offence because it threatened his political supremacy. Under his son Edward VI (r. 1547–53), the pendulum swung in favour of Calvinism and then veered back under the Catholic Mary Tudor (r. 1553–58) who burned some three hundred Protestants. Under Elizabeth I, England became officially Protestant again and the main victims were Catholic missionary priests, trained in seminaries abroad and living in England clandestinely, saying Mass and administering the sacraments to recusant Catholics.

We cannot expect these early modern states to have shared the outlook

of the Enlightenment. Civilisation had always depended upon coercion, so
state violence was regarded as essential to public order. Petty theft, murder,
forgery, arson and the abduction of women were all capital offences, so the
death penalty for heresy was neither unusual nor extreme.[61] Executions
were usually carried out in public as a ritualised deterrent that expressed
and enforced state and local authority.[62] Without a professional police force
and modern methods of surveillance, public order was dependent on such
spectacles. Utterly repugnant as it is to us today, killing dissenters was seen
as essential to the exercise of power, especially when the state was still
fragile.[63] But the suppression of heterodoxy was not wholly pragmatic; an
ideology that was central to an individual's integrity also played a role.
Thomas More, once a ruthless persecutor, would have taken the Oath had
he been motivated solely by political concerns; and Mary Tudor could have
strengthened her regime had she been less zealous against Protestants. But
heresy was different from other capital crimes, because if the accused
recanted, she was pardoned and her life spared. Modern scholars have
shown that officials often genuinely wanted to bring the wayward back into
the fold and that the death of an unrepentant heretic was seen as a defeat.[64]
During the 1550s, the zealous inquisitor Pieter Titlemaus presided over at
least 1,120 heresy trials in Flanders, but only 127 ended in execution.
Twelve attempts were made by Inquisitors, civic authorities and priests to
save the Anabaptist Soetken van den Houte and her three women companions in 1560. Under Mary Tudor, Edmund Bonner, Catholic bishop of
London, tried fifteen times to rescue the Protestant John Philpot, six times
to save Richard Woodman and nine times to redeem Elizabeth Young.[65]

   Catholics, Lutherans and Calvinists could all find biblical texts to justify
the execution of heretics.[66] Some quoted scriptural teachings that preached
mercy and tolerance, but these kinder counsels were rejected by the
majority.[67] Yet even though thousands were indeed beheaded, burned or
hanged, drawn and quartered, there was no fanatical headlong rush to
martyrdom. The vast majority were content to keep their convictions to
themselves and conform outwardly to state decrees.[68] Calvin inveighed
against such cowardice, comparing closet Calvinists to Nicodemus, the
Pharisee who kept his faith in Jesus secret. But 'Nicodemites' in France and
Italy retorted that it was easy for him to take this heroic line while living
safely in Geneva.[69] Under Elizabeth I, there was a strong cult of martyrdom
only among the Jesuits and seminarians training for the English mission
who believed that their sacrifice would save their country.[70] But recruits
were also warned against excessive enthusiasm. A manual of the English

College in Rome in the 1580s pointed out that not everybody was called to martyrdom and that no one should put himself at risk unnecessarily.[71]

The one thing on which Catholics and Protestants could agree was their hatred of the Spanish Inquisition. But despite its gruesome reputation, the crimes of the Inquisition were exaggerated. Even the *auto-da-fé* ('declaration of faith') with its solemn processions, sinister costumes and burning of heretics, which to foreigners seemed the epitome of Spanish fanaticism, was not all it was cracked up to be. The auto-da-fé had no deep roots in Spanish culture.[72] Originally a simple service of reconciliation, it took on this spectacular form only in the mid-sixteenth century and after its brief heyday (1559–70) was held very rarely. Moreover, the burning of the recalcitrant was not the centrepiece of the ritual: the accused were usually put to death unceremoniously outside the city and scores of autos were held without a single execution. After the Inquisition's first twenty years, less than 2 per cent of those who were accused were convicted, and of these most were burned in effigy *in absentia*.[73] Between 1559 and 1566, when the auto was at the peak of its popularity, about a hundred people died, whereas 300 Protestants were put to death under Mary Tudor; twice that number were executed under Henry II of France (r. 1547–59), and ten times as many were killed in the Netherlands.[74]

Very few Protestants were killed by the Spanish Inquisition; most of its victims were the 'New Christians'. By the 1580s, when Spain was at war with other European states, the crown once again turned on the 'enemy within', this time the Moriscos, who, like the Jews before them, were resented less for their beliefs than for their cultural difference and financial success.[75] 'They marry among themselves and do not mix with Old Christians,' a Toledo tribunal complained to Philip II in 1589; 'none of them enters religion, nor joins the army, none enters domestic service . . . they take part in trade and are rich'.[76] Yet again, persecution proved counter-productive because it transformed the beleaguered Moriscos from imaginary to real enemies, courted by the Huguenots and Henry IV of France or turning to the Sultan of Morocco for help. As a result, in 1609, the Moriscos were expelled from Spain, eliminating the last substantial Muslim community from Europe.

Spain was heavily involved in the Wars of Religion that culminated in the horror of the Thirty Years War (1618–48). These conflicts gave rise to what has been called the 'creation myth' of the modern West, because it explains how our distinctively secular mode of governance came into being.[77] The theological quarrels of the Reformation, it is said, so inflamed Catholics and Protestants that they slaughtered one another in senseless wars, until the violence was finally contained by the creation of the liberal state that separated religion from politics. Europe had learned the hard way that once a conflict becomes 'holy', violence will know no bounds and compromise becomes impossible because all combatants are convinced that God is on their side. Consequently, religion should never again be allowed to influence political life.

But nothing is ever quite that simple. After the Reformation, north-eastern Germany and Scandinavia were, roughly speaking, Lutheran; England, Scotland, the northern Netherlands, the Rhineland, and southern France were predominantly Calvinist; and the rest of the continent remained mostly Catholic. This naturally affected international relations but European rulers had other concerns. Many, especially those trying to create absolutist states, were alarmed by the extraordinary success of the Habsburgs, who now ruled the German territories, Spain and the southern Netherlands. Charles V's aspiration to achieve trans-European hegemony on the Ottoman model was opposed by the more pluralistic dynamics in Europe that inclined towards the sovereign nation state.[78] The German princes naturally struggled to resist Charles' ambitions and retain their local power and traditional privileges.

In the minds of the participants, however, these wars were certainly experienced as a life-and-death struggle between Protestants and Catholics. Religious sentiments helped soldiers and generals to distance themselves from the enemy, blot out all sense of a shared humanity, and infuse the cruel struggle with a moral fervour that made it not only palatable but noble; they gave participants an uplifting sense of righteousness. But secular ideologies can do all this too. These wars were not quintessentially 'religious' in the modern sense. If they had been, we would not expect to find Protestants and Catholics fighting on the same side, for example. But, in fact, they often did so and consequently fought their co-religionists.[79] Just two years after Charles became Holy Roman Emperor, the Catholic Church had condemned Luther at the Diet of Worms (1521). But for the first ten years of his reign, Charles, a Catholic, paid little attention to the Lutherans in Germany; instead he concentrated on fighting the Pope and the Catholic kings of France in Italy. Catholic rulers were particularly hostile to decrees of the Council of Trent that sought to limit their powers; this was yet another episode in the long struggle of European monarchs to control the Church in their own realms.[80] As late as 1556, Pope Paul IV went to war

against Charles' son Philip II, the devout Catholic ruler of Spain.[81] The
Catholic kings of France were so alarmed by the Habsburgs that they were
even prepared to make alliances with the Ottoman Turks against them.[82]
For over thirty years (1521–52), they engaged in five military campaigns
against the Catholic emperor, who was supported in these conflicts by many
of the Protestant German princes; Charles rewarded them by granting them
extensive powers over the churches in their domains.[83]

The German princes, Catholic and Lutheran alike, were also alarmed
by Charles' centralising ambitions. In 1531, some Protestant princes and
townsfolk united to form the League Schmalkaldic against him. But during
the first Schmalkaldic War, other prominent Lutheran princes fought on
Charles' side, while the Catholic king Henry II of France joined the Lutheran
League in an attack on the emperor's forces, and the Catholic German
princes remained neutral.[84] Moreover, many of Charles' soldiers in the
imperial army were mercenaries fighting for money rather than faith, and
some were Protestants.[85] Clearly these wars were not simply driven by
sectarian fervour. Eventually, Charles had to admit defeat and signed the
Peace of Augsburg in 1555. The Protestant princes were allowed to keep
the Catholic ecclesiastical properties they had seized and henceforth in
Europe the religious allegiance of the local ruler determined the faith of
his subjects – a principle later enshrined in the maxim *cuius regio, eius
religio*.[86] Charles abdicated and retired to a monastery, and the empire was
divided between his brother Ferdinand, who ruled the German territories,
and his son Philip II, who governed Spain and the Netherlands.

This was a political victory of one set of state-builders over another.[87]
The Catholic and Lutheran princes of Germany had ganged up on Charles,
realising quite correctly that his aim had not been simply to crush heresy
but also to increase his own power at their expense.[88] The peasantry and
the lower classes showed little theological conviction but switched from
Catholicism to Lutheranism and back again as their lords and masters
required.[89] At the end of the struggle, the Peace of Augsburg greatly enhanced
the political power of the princes, Catholic and Protestant alike. They could
now use the Reformation to their own advantage, taxing their clergy,
appropriating Church estates, controlling education and potentially
extending their authority, through the parishes, to every single one of their
subjects.[90]

A similar complexity can be observed in the French Wars of Religion
(1562–98). These too were more than a fight between the Calvinist
Huguenots and the Catholic majority; they were also a political contest

between competing aristocratic factions.[91] The Guises were Catholic and the southern Bourbons Huguenot; the Montmorencies were split, the older generation inclining to Catholicism, the younger to the Huguenots. These aristocrats were defending their traditional rights against the king's ambition to create a centralised state with *un roi, une foi, une loi*. The social and political elements of these struggles were so evident that until the 1970s most scholars believed that faith was merely a front for the purely secular ambitions of kings and nobles.[92] But in a landmark article, Natalie Zemon Davis examined the popular rituals in which both Catholics and Protestants drew on the Bible, the liturgy and folk traditions to dehumanise their enemies, and concluded that the French civil wars were 'essentially religious'.[93] Since then, scholars have re-emphasised the role of religion, pointing out, however, that it is still anachronistic to separate the 'political' from the 'religious' at this date.[94]

On 25 October 1534, Calvinists had pasted vitriolic and satirical placards attacking the Catholic Mass on public landmarks all over Paris, Blois, Orléans and Tours. One even appeared on the door of Francis I's bedchamber. As Catholics made their way to morning Mass, they were confronted by a headline printed in capital letters: 'TRUE ARTICLES ON THE HORRIBLE, GROSS AND INSUFFERABLE ABUSE OF THE PAPAL MASS.' French pamphleteer Antoine Marcourt listed four arguments against the Eucharist, 'by which the whole world . . . will be completely ruined, cast down, lost and desolated': it was blasphemous for the Mass to claim that it repeated Christ's perfect sacrifice on Calvary; Jesus' body was with God in heaven so could not be present in the bread and wine; transubstantiation had no scriptural warrant; and communion was simply an act of remembrance. He concluded with a vicious attack on the clergy:

> By this [mass] they have seized, destroyed and swallowed up everything imaginable, dead or alive. Because of it they live without any duties or responsibility to anyone or anything even to the need to study . . . They kill, burn, destroy and murder as brigands all those who contradict them, for now all they have left is force.[95]

The polemic was so extreme that even Theodore Beza, Calvin's future deputy in Geneva, condemned it in his history of the French Protestant Church. Yet it was this disreputable attack that sparked the French Wars of Religion.

As soon as the king saw the placards he initiated a nationwide persecution of the Huguenots that forced many, including Calvin himself, to flee the country. King Francis was not a theological bigot; he was open to new ideas and had entertained Erasmus and other humanists at his court. But he rightly saw the placards as both a theological diatribe and an attack on the entire political system. The Eucharist was the supreme expression of social bonding, experienced not principally as a private communion with Christ but as a rite that bound the community together,[96] a ritual of 'greeting, sharing, giving, receiving and making peace'.[97] Before receiving the sacrament, Catholics had to beg their neighbours' pardon for outstanding grievances; king, priests, aristocrats and the common folk all ate the same consecrated bread, and in so doing were integrated as one in the Body of Christ. The placards were also understood by both Catholics and Protestants as an implicit assault on the monarchy. The kings of France had always been revered as semi-divine; the Calvinists' denial of the Real Presence of Christ now tacitly denied the fusion of the physical and the sacred that had been crucial to medieval Christianity and which the king embodied in his person.[98] Pasting the scurrilous placard on Francis' door was both a religious and political act; and for Francis, the two were inseparable.

Yet in the ensuing wars it was impossible to divide the French population into neat communities of Protestants and Catholics.[99] Here too people crossed the confessional lines and even changed their religious allegiance.[100] In 1574, Henry of Montmorency, Catholic governor of Languedoc, joined his Huguenot neighbours in supporting a constitution attacking the monarchy.[101] In 1579, a significant number of Huguenots were prepared to fight the king under the banner of the ultra-Catholic Duke of Guise, a pretender to the throne.[102] Even the Catholic kings made alliances with Protestants in their struggle against the Habsburgs, whom the Peace of Augsburg had set back but hardly neutralised. Charles IX (r. 1560–74) fought with the Huguenots against the Spanish Habsburgs in the Netherlands and in 1580 Henry III (r. 1574–89) was prepared to support Dutch Calvinists against Catholic Spain.

In their struggle against the aristocracy, the lower classes also transcended sectarian allegiance. In 1562, hundreds of Catholic peasants joined a revolt against a Catholic nobleman who had forbidden his Huguenot peasants to hold Protestant services.[103] Catholic and Protestant peasants joined forces again to oppose Henry III's excessive tax levy in 1578, rampaging through the countryside for almost a year until they were slaughtered by the royal troops.[104] In another tax protest during the 1590s, twenty-four Protestant and Catholic villages in the Haut-Biterrois set up an alternative system of self-government,[105] and in the south-west Protestants and Catholics engaged in dozens of joint uprisings against the nobility, some of which involved as many as forty thousand people. In Croquants, the most famous of these associations, ignoring religious difference was a condition of membership.[106]

After the murder of Henry III in 1589, the Huguenot leader Henry of Navarre succeeded to the throne as Henry IV and brought the French Wars of Religion to an end by converting to Catholicism and adopting a policy of strict neutrality. In the Edict of Nantes (1598), he granted religious and civil liberties to the Huguenots and when the *parlement* expelled the Jesuits from France, he had them reinstated. This did not mark the birth of the tolerant secular state, however, since Henry had not abandoned the ideal of *une foi;* the Edict of Nantes was simply a temporary settlement, an attempt to buy time by winning the Huguenots over. The French crown was still too weak to achieve the religious uniformity that, the kings believed, would help to centralise the state and bind the nation together.[107]

But despite Henry's policy of toleration, Europe drifted inexorably towards the horror of the Thirty Years War that would kill about 35 per cent of the population of Central Europe. Here again, though religious solidarities were certainly a factor in this series of conflicts, it was never their sole motivation.[108] This was already clear in 1609, nine years before it began, when the Calvinist Frederick V, Elector Palatine, tried to create a pan-European Union of Protestant principalities against the Habsburgs. Very few of the Protestant princes joined but the Union did gain Catholic support from Henry IV and Carlo Emanuele of Savoy. The war started in earnest with an uprising in Catholic Bohemia against the Catholic Habsburg Emperor Ferdinand II: in 1618 the rebels defiantly offered the crown of Bohemia to the Calvinist Frederick V but the other members of the Protestant Union refused to support him and two years later the Union disbanded.[109] It took two years for the Habsburgs to quash the revolt and re-Catholicise Bohemia, and meanwhile the Dutch had opened a new round of hostilities against Habsburg rule.

The princes of Europe resisted Habsburg imperialism, but there was never a wholly solid 'Catholic' or 'Protestant' response. Catholic France nearly always supported the Protestant princes of Germany against the empire. The war was fought by mercenaries available to the highest bidder, so Protestants from Scotland and England, for example, served in the armies of Catholic France.[110] The Catholic general Ernst von Mansfeld led the imperial army against the Catholic Bohemian rebels at the start of the war, but in 1621 switched sides and commanded the troops of the Calvinist Frederick V in Bohemia.[111] Albrecht von Wallenstein, the Bohemian mercenary leader who became supreme commander of the Catholic imperial army, was a Lutheran, and many of his foot soldiers were Protestants who had fled Catholic persecution in their own countries. Wallenstein seemed more interested in military entrepreneurism than religion.[112] He transformed his huge estates into a vast arsenal for his private army of half a million men. Indifferent to the social standing or religious convictions of his associates, he demanded only obedience and efficiency from his troops, who were allowed to live off the countryside and terrorise the rural population.

By 1629, Emperor Ferdinand seemed to have regained control of the empire. But a year later the tide turned, when Cardinal Richelieu, chief minister of France, persuaded the Protestant warrior king Gustavus Adolphus of Sweden to invade the Habsburg empire. Adolphus is often presented as the hero of the Protestant cause, but he did not mention religion in his declaration of intent in June 1630 and found it difficult at first to attract allies.[113] The most powerful German Protestant princes saw the Swedish invasion as a threat and formed a third party, holding aloof from both the Swedes and the Habsburgs. When Lutheran German peasants tried to drive the Lutheran Swedes out of their country in November 1632, they were simply massacred.[114] Eventually, however, after Adolphus' first victory over the Catholic League of German princes at Magdeburg in 1631, many territories that had tried to remain neutral joined the Swedish offensive. Inadequate methods of financing, supplying and controlling the troops meant that Swedish soldiers resorted to looting the countryside, killing huge numbers of civilians.[115] The mass casualties of the Thirty Years War can partly be attributed to the use of mercenary armies which had to provision themselves and could do so only by brutally sacking civilian populations, abusing women and children, and slaughtering their prisoners.

Catholic France had come to the rescue of the Protestant Swedes in January 1631, promising to supply their campaign, and later dispatched troops to fight the imperial forces in the winter of 1634–35. They received the backing of Pope Urban VIII, who wanted to weaken Habsburg control of the Papal States in Italy. But to counter the combined Swedish, French and papal alliance, the Protestant principalities of Brandenburg and Saxony were reconciled with the Catholic emperor at the Peace of Prague (1635) and within a few months most of the Lutheran states also made peace with Ferdinand. The Protestant armies were absorbed into the imperial forces and German Catholics and Protestants fought together against the Swedes. The rest of the Thirty Years War now became largely a struggle between Catholic France and the Catholic Habsburgs.[116] Neither could achieve a decisive victory and after a long, enervating struggle treaties were signed, known collectively as the Peace of Westphalia (1648), which left the Austrian Habsburgs in control of their hereditary lands and the Swedes in possession of Pomerania, Bremen, and the Baltic region. Prussia emerged as the leading German Protestant state and France gained much of the Alsace. Finally, Calvinism became a licit religion in the Holy Roman Empire.[117] By the end of the Thirty Years War, Europeans had fought off the danger of imperial rule. There would never be a large unified empire on the Persian, Roman or Ottoman models; instead Europe would be divided into smaller states, each claiming sovereign power in its own territory, each supported by a standing, professional army and governed by a prince who aspired to absolute rule – a recipe, perhaps, for chronic interstate warfare.

'Religious' sentiments were certainly present in the minds of those who fought these wars; but to imagine that 'religion' was yet distinguishable from the social, economic and political issues is essentially anachronistic. The historian John Bossy has reminded us that before 1700 there was no concept of 'religion' as separate from society or politics. As we shall see later in this chapter, that distinction would not be made until the formal separation of church and state by early modern philosophers and statesmen, and even then the liberal state was slow to arrive. Before that time, 'there simply was no coherent way yet to divide religious causes from social causes; the divide is a modern invention.'[118] People were fighting for different visions of society, but they had as yet no way to separate religious from temporal factors.

This was also true of the English Civil War (1642–48), which resulted in the execution of Charles I and the creation in England of a short-lived Puritan republic under Oliver Cromwell (1599–1658). It is more difficult to list examples of participants in this who crossed denominational lines, since Cromwell's Puritan army and the Royalist troops were all members of the Church of England. They held different views of their faith, however. The 'Puritans' were dissatisfied with the slow and limited progress of the Reformation in their country and wanted to 'purge' the Anglican establishment of 'popish' practices. Instead of worshipping in elaborate church buildings with authoritarian bishops, they formed small, exclusive congregations of those who had experienced a 'born again' conversion. Certainly the heavy-handed attempts of William Laud, Archbishop of Canterbury (1573–1645), to root out Calvinism in the English and Scottish churches, his suspension of Puritan ministers and support of royal absolutism were crucial irritants. Cromwell was convinced that God controlled events on earth and had singled out the English to be his new Chosen People.[119] The success of his New Model Army in defeating the Royalists at the Battle of Naseby in 1645 seemed to prove the 'remarkable providences and appearances of the Lord,'[120] and he justified his brutal subjugation of Ireland as a 'righteous judgment of God'.[121]

But the Civil War is no longer regarded as a last eruption of religious fanaticism laid to rest by Charles II's constitutional monarchy in 1660.[122] It too was part of the larger European struggle against state centralisation. Charles I had been trying to achieve an absolute monarchy similar to those established on the continent after the Thirty Years War,[123] and the Civil War was an attempt to resist this centralisation and protect local interests, freedoms and privileges.[124] Again, transcending sectarian divisions, Scottish Presbyterians and Irish Catholics had for a time fought alongside the Puritans to weaken the monarchy. Even though Charles had tried to impose episcopal rule on the Scots, they made it clear in their Covenant of 1639 that they were fighting not only for religion but also 'to shake off all monarchical government'.[125] In the Grand Remonstrance, presented to Charles in 1641, the Puritans took it for granted that religion and politics were inseparable: 'The root of all this mischief we find to be a malignant and pernicious design of subverting the fundamental laws and principles of government upon which the religion and justice of this kingdom are firmly established.'[126]

As William Cavanaugh explains in *The Myth of Religious Violence,* these wars were neither 'all about religion' nor 'all about politics'. But it is true that they helped create the idea of 'religion' as a private and personal activity, separate from mundane affairs.[127] Chancellor Axel Oxenstierna, who masterminded Sweden's participation in the Thirty Years War, told the Swedish Council that the conflict was 'not so much a matter of religion, but rather of serving the status publicus, wherein religion is also comprehended'.[128] He could speak in this way because the Lutheran Church had already been absorbed or 'comprehended' by the Swedish state. New configurations of political power were beginning to force the Church into a subordinate realm, a process that involved a fundamental reallocation of authority and resources. When the new word 'secularisation' was coined in France during the late sixteenth century, it originally referred to 'the transfer of goods from the possession of the Church into that of the "world" (saeculum)'.[129] Legislative and judicial powers that had been in the Church's remit were gradually transferred to the new sovereign state.

Like most states, these early modern kingdoms were achieved by force: all struggled to annex as much land as possible and had internal battles with the cities, clergy, local associations and aristocracies who jealously guarded traditional privileges and immunities that sovereign states could not permit.[130] The modern state had come into being by militarily defeating rival political institutions: the empire, the city-state, and the feudal lordship.[131] The Church, which had been so integral to medieval government, also had to be subdued. Thus the sixteenth- and seventeenth-century wars were 'the crucible in which some of the competing forces from an earlier age were consumed in the fire and others blended and transmuted into new compounds . . . the matrix of all that came after'.[132]

These political and social developments required a new understanding of the word 'religion'.[133] One of the characteristics of early modern thought was a tendency to assume binary contrasts. In an attempt to define phenomena more exactly, categories of experience that had once co-inhered were now set off against each other: faith and reason, intellect and emotion, and church and state. Hitherto, the 'internal' and 'external' worlds had been complementary, but now 'religion' was becoming a private, internalised commitment separate from such 'external' activities as politics. Protestants, whose reinterpretation of Christianity was itself a product of early modernity, would define 'religion' and set an agenda to which other faith traditions would be expected to conform. This new definition mirrored the programmes of the new sovereign states, which were relegating 'religion' to the private sphere.

A crucial figure in this development was Edward, Lord Herbert of Cherbury (1583–1648), who was not only a philosopher but also a statesman committed to the state control of ecclesiastical affairs. His most important work, *De Veritate*, which influenced such important philosophers as Hugo Grotius (1583–1645), René Descartes (1596–1650) and John Locke (1632–1704), argued that Christianity was neither an institution nor a way of life but a set of five truths that were innate in the human mind: (1) a supreme deity existed, (2) which should be worshipped (3) and served by ethical living and natural piety; (4) human beings were thus required to reject sin and (5) would be rewarded or punished by God after death.[134] Because these notions were instinctive, self-evident and accessible to the meanest intelligence, the rituals and guidance of a church were unnecessary.[135] These 'truths' would, however, seem strange indeed to Buddhists, Hindus, Confucians or Daoists, and many Jews, Christians and Muslims would also find them odd. Herbert was convinced that 'all men will be unanimously eager for this austere worship of God', and since everybody would agree on 'these natural tokens of faith' it was the key to peace; 'insolent spirits' who refused to accept them must be punished by the secular magistracy.[136] Emphasis on the 'natural', 'normal' and 'innate' character of these core ideas implied that those who did not discover them in their minds were in some way unnatural and abnormal: a dark current was emerging in early modern thought. This extreme privatisation of faith, therefore, had the potential to become as divisive, coercive and intolerant as the so-called 'religious' passions it was trying to abolish.

Thomas Hobbes (1588–1679) also saw state control of the Church as essential to peace and wanted a strong monarch to take over the Church and enforce religious unity. A committed Royalist, he wrote his classic *Leviathan* (1651) in exile in Paris after the English Civil War. The disruptive forces of religion, Hobbes argued, must be curbed as effectively as God had subdued Leviathan, the biblical chaos-monster, to create an ordered universe. Hobbes was adamant that pointless squabbling about irrational dogmas had been entirely responsible for the Wars of Religion. Not everybody shared this view. In *Commonwealth of Oceana* (1656), the English political theorist James Harrington discussed the economic and legal issues that had contributed to these conflicts, but Hobbes would have none of it. The preachers alone, he insisted, had been 'the cause of all our late mischief' by leading the people astray with 'disreputable doctrines'.[137] The Presbyterian divines, he believed, had been particularly culpable in stirring up unruly passions before the English Civil War and were 'therefore guilty of all that fell'.[138] Hobbes' solution was to create an absolute state that would crush the tendency of human beings to cling obstinately to their own beliefs, which doomed them to perpetual warfare. Instead, they must learn to recognise the frailty of humanity's grasp on truth, enter into a contractual relationship with one another, elect an absolute monarch and accept his ideas as their own.[139] This ruler would control the clergy in such a way as to prevent even the possibility of sectarian conflict.[140] Alas, history would show that Hobbes' solution was too simplistic; the states of Europe would continue to fight one another savagely, with or without sectarian strife.

John Locke's solution was religious freedom, since, in his view, the Wars of Religion had been caused by a fatal inability to entertain other points of view. 'Religion', he argued, was a 'private search' and as such could not be policed by the government; in this personal quest everyone must rely on 'his own endeavours' rather than an external authority.[141] To mingle 'religion' and politics was a grievous, dangerous and existential error:

> The church itself is a thing absolutely separate and distinct from the common-
> wealth. The boundaries on both sides are fixed and immoveable. He jumbles
> heaven and earth together, the things most remote and opposite, who mixes
> these two societies, which are in their original end, business, and in every-
> thing perfectly and infinitely different from each other.[142]

Locke assumed that the separation of politics and religion was written into
the very nature of things. But, of course, this was a radical innovation that
most of his contemporaries would find extraordinary and unacceptable. It
would make modern 'religion' entirely different from anything that had
gone before. But because of the violent passions it supposedly unleashed,
Locke insisted that the segregation of 'religion' from government was 'above
all things necessary' for the creation of a peaceful society.[143] In Locke we
see the birth of the 'myth of religious violence' that would become ingrained
in the Western ethos.

It is true that Western Christianity had become more internalised during
the early modern period. This is evident in Luther's conception of faith as
an interior appropriation of Christ's saving power, in the mysticism of Teresa
of Avila (1515–82) and in the *Spiritual Exercises* of Ignatius of Loyola (1491–
1556). But in the past, the exploration of the inner world had compelled
Buddhist monks to work 'for the welfare and happiness of the people' and
Confucians to engage in a political effort to reform society. After his solitary struggle with Satan in the wilderness, Jesus had embarked on a ministry
of healing in the troubled villages of Galilee that led to his execution by
the political authorities. Muhammad had left his cave on Mount Hira for a
political struggle against the structural violence of Mecca. In the early
modern period too, the *Spiritual Exercises* had propelled Ignatius' Jesuits all
over the world – to Japan, India, China and the Americas. But modern
'religion' would try to subvert this natural dynamic by turning the seeker
in upon himself and, inevitably, many would rebel against this unnatural
privatisation of their faith.

Unable to extend the natural human rights they were establishing to the
indigenous peoples of the New World, the Renaissance humanists had already
revealed the insidious underside of early modern ideas that still inform our
political life. Locke, who was among the first to formulate the liberal ethos
of modern politics, also revealed the darker aspect of the secularism he
proposed. A pioneer of tolerance, he was adamant that the sovereign state
could not accommodate either Catholicism or Islam;[144] he endorsed a
master's 'Absolute, Arbitrary, Despotical Power' over a slave that included

'the power to kill him at any time'.[145] Himself directly involved in the colonisation of the Carolinas, Locke argued that the native 'kings' of America had no legal jurisdiction or right of ownership of their land.[146] Like the urbane Thomas More, he found it intolerable that the 'wild woods and uncultivated waste of America be left to nature, without any improvement, tillage and husbandry' when it could be used to support the 'needy and wretched' of Europe.[147] A new system of violent oppression was emerging that would privilege the liberal, secular West at the expense of the indigenous peoples of its colonies.

On the issue of colonisation, most early modern thinkers agreed with Locke. Grotius contended that any military action against the natives was just because they had no legal claim to their territory.[148] Hobbes believed that because they had not developed an agrarian economy, the Native Americans – 'few, savage, short-lived, poor and mean' – must relinquish their land.[149] And in a sermon delivered in London in 1622 to the Virginia Company, which had received a royal charter to settle all the terrain between what is now New York and South Carolina, John Donne, Dean of St Paul's Cathedral, argued that: 'In the Law of Nature and Nations, a Land never inhabited by any or utterly derelicted and immemorially abandoned by the former Inhabitants, becomes theirs that will possess it.'[150] The colonists would take this belief with them to North America – but unlike these early modern thinkers, they had absolutely no intention of separating church and state.

THE TRIUMPH OF
THE SECULAR

When the Pilgrim Fathers arrived in Massachusetts Bay in 1620, they would have been horrified to hear that they were about to lay the foundations of the world's first secular republic. They had left England because Archbishop Laud, they believed, had corrupted their Church with popish practices; and they regarded their migration as a new Exodus and America, the 'English Canaan', as their 'land of Promise'.[1] Before landing, John Winthrop, first governor of the Bay Colony, reminded them that they had come to the American wilderness to build a truly Protestant community that would be a light to other nations and inspire Old England to revive the Reformation:[2] 'We must consider that we shall be as a city upon a hill. The eyes of all people are upon us, so that if we shall deal falsely with our God in this work we have undertaken, and so cause him to withdraw his present help from us, we shall be made a story and a by-word throughout the world.'[3] One of their most important missions was to save the Native Americans from the wiles of the French Catholic settlers in North America, making New England a 'bulwark against the kingdom of Antichrist, which the Jesuits labour to rear up in these parts'.[4] Winthrop would have found the notion of a secular state inconceivable and, like most of the colonists, he had no time for democracy. Before they set foot on American soil, he reminded the migrants firmly that God had 'so disposed the condition of mankind, as in all times some must be rich, some poor, some high and eminent in power and dignity, others mean and in subjection'.[5]

The Puritans were convinced that God had given the land to them by a special dispensation, and this covenantal faith blended seamlessly with the humanists' more secular doctrine of natural human rights. On the eve of their departure from Southampton in 1620, their minister John Cotton had listed all the biblical precedents for their migration. So after showing that God had given the children of Adam and Noah, who had both colonised

an 'empty' world, the 'liberty' to inhabit a 'vacant place' without either
buying it from the original inhabitants or asking their leave, he segued quite
naturally into the argument that: 'It is a principle in nature, that in a vacant
soil he that taketh possession of it, and bestoweth culture and husbandry
upon it, his right it is.'[6] England was overcrowded, contended Robert
Cushman, business manager of the Bay Company, and America was 'a vast
and empty chaos' because the Indians were 'not industrious, neither having
art, science, skill or faculty to use either the land or the commodities but
all spoils, rots and is marred for want of manuring, gathering, ordering
etc.' It was therefore 'lawful' for the settlers 'to take a land which none
useth'.[7] This liberal doctrine would inform their dealings with the Native
Americans quite as much as the biblical teachings.

The centrality of Original Sin in their theology predisposed these
staunchly Protestant colonists to an absolutist remedy for man's fallen nature
in their polity. If Adam had not sinned, government would have been
unnecessary; but unredeemed men and women were naturally prone to lie,
steal and murder and these evil impulses could be forcibly held in check
only by a strong, authoritative government. Those who had been 'born
again' enjoyed the freedom of the Sons of God but were at liberty only to
do what God commanded. At their conversion, they had surrendered the
right to follow their own inclinations and must submit to the authorities
God had placed over them.[8]

The Massachusetts Bay Colony was, of course, not the first English
settlement in North America. The founders of Jamestown in Virginia had
arrived in 1607. They were not ardent Puritan Dissenters but mercantilists,
intent on making their colony a profitable commercial enterprise. Yet on
disembarking, the first thing they did was build a makeshift church, with
a sail for a roof and logs for pews.[9] Their colony was almost as strict as
Massachusetts. Church services were obligatory and there were fines for
drunkenness, gambling, adultery, idleness and ostentatious dress. If an
offender failed to change his ways, he was excommunicated and his property confiscated.[10] This was a Christian as well as a commercial enterprise,
hailed in London as a pivotal moment in salvation history.[11] According to
their royal charter, the Virginia Company's chief objective was the conversion of the native peoples rather than financial success.[12] As good early
modern Protestants, Virginians adhered to the principles of the Treaty of
Augsburg: *cuius regio, eius religio*. Where most agrarian rulers had rarely
attempted to control the spiritual lives of their subjects, the commercially
minded Virginians took it for granted that in a properly regulated society

all citizens should have the same faith and that it was the duty of any government to enforce religious observance.

John Locke was not yet born, so in the American colonies, religion, politics and economics were still inseparable. Indeed, the Virginians were incapable of thinking of commerce as a purely secular activity.[13] Samuel Purchas, the company's propagandist, gave fullest expression to their ideology.[14] If Adam had not fallen, the whole world would have retained its original perfection and exploration would have been easy. But with the arrival of sin, men became so depraved that they would have slaughtered one another, so God had scattered them over the earth after the destruction of the Tower of Babel and kept them in ignorance of one another. Yet he had also decreed that commerce would bring them together again. In Eden, Adam had enjoyed all essential commodities but these too had been dispersed after the Fall. Now, thanks to modern maritime technology, a country in one region could supply what was lacking in other places, and God could use the global market to redeem the non-Christian world. In America, the Virginians would supply staples for famine-prone England and at the same time bring the Gospel to the Indians. A company broadsheet explained that God no longer worked through prophets and miracles; the only way to evangelise the world these days was 'mixtly, by discoverie, and trade of marchants'. Living on the Indians' land and trading with them, the colonists would 'sell to them the pearles of heaven' by 'dailie conversation'.[15] So the quest for commodities, Purchas insisted, was not an end in itself, and the Company would fail if it sought only profit.

Purchas initially believed that the land must not be forcibly taken from the Indians because it had been assigned to them by God.[16] His Protestant ideology may have been paternalistic yet there was also a measure of respect for the indigenous peoples. But during the first two terrible winters, when the colonists were starving to death, some of their conscripted labourers had fled to the local Powhatans and when the English governor asked their chief to return the fugitives, he disdainfully refused. Whereupon the English militia descended on the settlement, killed fifteen Native Americans, burned their houses, cut down their corn and abducted the queen, killing her children.[17] So much for peaceful 'dailie conversation'. The Indians were bewildered: 'Why will you destroy us who supply you with food?' asked Chief Powhatan: 'Why are you jealous of us? We are unarmed and willing to give you what you ask, if you come in a friendly manner.'[18]

But by 1622 the Indians had become seriously alarmed by the rapid growth of the colony; the English had taken over a significant acreage of their hunting grounds, depriving them of essential resources.[19] In a sudden attack on Jamestown, the Powhatans killed about a third of the English population. The Virginians retaliated in a ruthless war of attrition: they would allow local tribes to settle and plant their corn and then, just before the harvest, attack them, killing as many natives as possible. Within three years, they had avenged the Jamestown massacre many times over. Instead of founding their colony on the compassionate principles of the Gospel, they had inaugurated a policy of elimination imposed by ruthless military force. Even Purchas was forced to abandon the Bible and rely on the humanists' aggressive doctrine of human rights when he finally agreed that the Indians deserved their fate because, by resisting English settlement, they had broken the law of nature.[20] More pragmatic considerations were beginning to replace the old piety. The company had not been able to produce the staples England needed and investors had not seen an adequate return. The only way their colony could function was to cultivate tobacco and sell it at five shillings a pound. Begun as a holy enterprise, Virginia would gradually be secularised not by Locke's liberal ideology but by pressure of events.[21]

The Puritans of Massachusetts had no qualms about killing Indians.[22] They had left England during the Thirty Years War, had absorbed the militancy of that fearsome time, and justified their violence by a highly selective reading of the Bible. Ignoring Jesus' pacifist teachings, they drew on the bellicosity of some of the Hebrew scriptures. 'God is an excellent Man of War,' preached Alexander Leighton, and the Bible 'the best handbook on war'.[23] Their revered minister John Cotton had instructed them that they could attack the natives 'without provocation' – a procedure normally unlawful – because they had not only a natural right to their territory, but 'a special Commission from God' to take their land.[24] Already there were signs of the exceptionalist thinking that would in future often characterise American politics. In 1636 William Bradford, describing a raid on the Pequot village of Fort Mystic on the Connecticut shore to avenge the murder of an English trader, contemplated the fearsome carnage with lofty complacency:

Those that escaped the fire were slain with the sword; some hewed to pieces, others run through with rapiers, so as they were quickly dispatched, and very few escaped. It was conceived they thus destroyed about 400 at this time. It was a fearful sight to see them thus frying in the fire, and the streams of blood quenching the same, and horrible was the stink and scent thereof,

but the victory seemed a sweet sacrifice, and they gave the prayers thereof
to God, who had wrought so wonderfully for them.[25]

When the Puritans negotiated the Treaty of Hartford (1638) with the few
Pequot survivors, they insisted on the destruction of all Pequot villages and
sold the women and children into slavery. Should Christians have behaved
more compassionately? asked Captain John Underhill, a veteran of the Thirty
Years War. He answered his rhetorical question with a decided negative:
God supported the English, 'so we had sufficient light for our proceedings'.[26]

But thirty years later, some Puritans had begun to question the validity
of these Indian campaigns.[27] After the murder of an Indian convert to
Christianity in 1675, the Plymouth authorities, on very shaky evidence,
pinned the blame on Metacom, chief of the Wampanoag, whom the English
called 'King Philip'. When they executed three of his aides, Metacom with
his Indian allies promptly devastated fifty of the ninety English towns in
Plymouth and Rhode Island; by the spring of 1676 the Indian armies were
within ten miles of Boston. In the autumn, the war turned in the colonists'
favour. Yet they were facing a hard winter and the Narragansetts on Rhode
Island had food and supplies. Accusing them – again on dubious grounds – of
aiding Metacom, the English militia attacked and looted the village, massacred
its inhabitants – most of them non-combatant refugees – and burned the
settlement to the ground. The war continued with atrocities on both sides
– Indian warriors scalped their prisoners alive; the English disembowelled
and quartered theirs – but in the summer of 1676, both sides abandoned
the struggle. Almost half the pre-war Indian population had been eliminated:
1,250 were killed in battle, 625 died of wounds, and 3,000 died of disease
in captivity. The colonies, however, suffered only about eight hundred casualties, a mere 1.6 per cent of the total English population of 50,000.

The Puritan establishment believed that God had used the Indians to
punish the colonists for their backsliding from godly ways and for the decline
in church attendance and were, therefore, unconcerned about the Indian
casualties. But many of the colonists were now less convinced of the morality
of all-out warfare. This time a vocal minority spoke out against the war.
The Quakers, who had first arrived in Boston in 1656 and had themselves
been the victims of Puritan intolerance, vigorously condemned the atrocities. John Easton, governor of Rhode Island, accused the Puritans of
Plymouth of arrogance and over-confidence in provocatively expanding their
settlements and mischievously playing the tribes off against one another.
John Eliot, a missionary to the Indians, argued that this had not been a war

of self-defence; the real aggressors were the Plymouth authorities who had fudged evidence and treated the Indians with rough justice. As in Virginia, flagging piety meant that more rational and naturalistic arguments would gradually replace theological ones in their politics.[28]

As is often the case, a general decline in religious fervour tends to inspire a revival from some dissatisfied element of society. By the early eighteenth century, worship had become more formal in the colonies and elegant churches transformed the skylines of New York and Boston. But to the horror of these polite congregations, a frenzied piety had erupted in the rural areas. The Great Awakening broke out first in Northampton, Connecticut, in 1734, when the deaths of two young people and the powerful preaching of its minister Jonathan Edwards (1703–58) whipped the town into a devotional fever that spread to Massachusetts and Long Island. During Edwards' sermons, the congregation screamed, yelled, writhed in the aisles and crowded around the pulpit, begging him to stop. But Edwards continued inexorably, never looking at the hysterical masses, offering them no comfort, but staring rigidly at the bell-rope. Three hundred people experienced a wrenching conversion, could not tear themselves away from their bibles and forgot to eat. But they also experienced, Edwards recalled, a joyous perception of beauty that was quite different from any natural sensation 'so that they could not forbear crying out with a loud voice, expressing their great admiration'.[29] Others, broken by the fear of God, would sink into an abyss of despair only to soar to an equally extreme elation in the sudden conviction that they were free of sin.

The Great Awakening showed that religion, instead of being an obstacle to progress and democracy, could be a positive force for modernisation. Strangely enough, this seemingly primitive hysteria helped these Puritans to embrace an egalitarianism that would have shocked Winthrop but was far closer to our present norms. The Awakening appalled the Harvard faculty and Yale, Edwards' own university, disowned him, but Edwards believed that a different order – nothing less than the Kingdom of God – was coming painfully to birth in the New World. Edwards was, in fact, presiding over a revolution. The Awakening flourished in the poorer colonies, where people had little hope of earthly fulfilment. While the educated classes were turning to the rational consolations of the European Enlightenment, Edwards brought the Enlightenment ideal of the pursuit of happiness to his unlettered congregation in a form that they could understand and prepared them for the revolutionary upheavals of 1775.[30]

At this date, most colonists still believed that democracy was the worst form of government and that some form of social stratification was God's will. Their Christian horizons were bounded by the systemic violence that had been essential to the agrarian state. In the congregations of New England, only the 'saints' who had experienced a born-again conversion were allowed to participate in the Lord's Supper. Even though they comprised just a fifth of the English population, they alone had a share in God's Covenant with the New Israel. Yet even the saints were not allowed to speak in church but had to wait in silent attendance on the minister, and the unregenerate majority had equality before the law but no voice in government.[31] Edwards' grandfather, Solomon Stoddard of Northampton, had brusquely dismissed the masses as incapable of serious thought: 'Let the government be put into their hands and things will be carried by a tumultuous cry . . . things would quickly be turned upside down.'[32] Yet Stoddard had urged his entire congregation, including the unconverted, to partake of the Lord's Supper and ordered them, in highly emotional gatherings, to stand up and publicly claim the Covenant for themselves.

Jonathan Edwards understood that, despite his autocratic views, his grandfather had in fact given the masses a voice. He now demanded that his congregants speak out in church or be lost for ever. Edwards belonged to the New England aristocracy; he had no interest in political revolution but he had realised that a preacher could no longer expect his audience to listen submissively to eternal verities that did not speak convincingly to their condition. That might have worked in seventeenth-century England, but a different kind of society was coming into being in America, one that was not in thrall to an established aristocracy. In 1748, at the funeral of his uncle Colonel John Stoddard, Edwards delivered a remarkable eulogy, which listed the qualities of a great leader. In this New World, a leader must come down to the people's level.[33] He must have a 'great knowledge of human nature' and acquaint himself with 'the state and circumstances' of the nation, adapting his ideas to the realities of human and social experience. A leader must get to know his people, be attentive to current events and foresee crises. Not until the very end did Edwards say that a leader should belong to a 'good family' but only because education was 'useful' and would make him more effective. A great man could have nothing to do with self-interested people of a 'narrow, private spirit'. Standing before the merchants, businessmen and land speculators of Northampton, Edwards uttered a blistering condemnation of men who 'shamefully defile their hands to gain a few pounds, and . . . grind the faces of the poor and screw upon their neighbours, and will take advantage of their authority to line their own pockets'.[34] This revolutionary assault on the structural violence of colonial society spread to other towns and, two years later, Edwards was driven from his pulpit and forced to take refuge for a time on the frontier with other misfits, acting as chaplain to the Indians of Stockbridge. Edwards was well versed in contemporary thought and had read Locke and Newton but it was his Christianity that enabled him to bring the modern egalitarian ideal to the common people.

The Great Awakening of the 1730s and 40s was America's first mass movement; it gave many ordinary folk their first experience of participating in a nationwide event that could change the course of history.[35] Their ecstatic awakening left many Americans, who would not easily relate to the secular leanings of the revolutionary leaders, with the memory of a blissful state that they called 'liberty'. The revival had also encouraged them to see their emotional faith as superior to the cerebral piety of the respectable classes. Those who remembered the aristocratic clerics' disdain of their enthusiasm retained a distrust of institutional authority that prepared them later to take the drastic step of rejecting the king of England.

In 1775, when the British government tried to tax the colonists to pay for its colonial wars against France, anger flared into outright rebellion. The leaders experienced the American Revolution as a secular event, a sober, pragmatic struggle against an imperial power. They were men of the Enlightenment, inspired by Locke and Newton, and were also deists, who differed from orthodox Christians by rejecting the doctrines of Revelation and the Divinity of Christ. The Declaration of Independence, drafted by Thomas Jefferson, John Adams and Benjamin Franklin, and ratified by the Colonial Congress on 4 July 1776, was an Enlightenment document, based on Locke's theory of self-evident human rights – life, liberty and property[36] – and the Enlightenment ideals of freedom and equality. But these men had no utopian ideas about redistributing wealth or abolishing the class system. For them this was simply a practical, far-reaching but sustainable war of independence.

The Founding Fathers, however, belonged to the gentry and their ideas were far from typical; most Americans were Calvinists who could not relate to this rationalist ethos. Reluctant initially to break with Britain, not all the colonists joined the struggle but those that did were motivated as much by the millennial myths of Christianity as by the Founders' ideals. During the revolution, secularist ideology blended creatively with the religious aspirations of the majority in a way that enabled Americans with very divergent beliefs to join forces against the might of England. When ministers spoke of the importance of virtue and responsibility in government, they helped people make sense of the Founder Samuel Adams' fiery denunciations of British tyranny.[37] When the Founding Fathers spoke of 'liberty' they used a word charged with religious meaning.[38] Timothy Dwight, Jonathan Edwards' grandson and president of Yale University, predicted that the revolution would usher in 'Immanuel's land':[39] the Connecticut preacher Ebenezer Baldwin argued that liberty, religion and learning had been driven out of Europe and moved to America, where Jesus would establish his Kingdom; and Provost William Smith of Philadelphia maintained that the colonies were God's 'chosen seat of Freedom, Arts and Heavenly Knowledge'.[40] John Adams saw the English settlement of America as part of God's plan for the world's enlightenment[41] and Thomas Paine was convinced that 'we have it in our power to begin the world over again. A situation such as the present hath not happened since the days of Noah.'[42]

But this exaltation was laced with hatred for the enemies of God's kingdom. After the passing of the Stamp Act (1765), patriotic songs portrayed its perpetrators – Lords Bute, Grenville and North – as the minions of Satan and during political demonstrations their pictures were carried alongside effigies of the devil.[43] When George III granted religious freedom to the French Catholics in the Canadian territory, he was denounced by the American colonists as the ally of Antichrist;[44] and even the presidents of Harvard and Yale saw the War of Independence as part of God's design for the overthrow of Catholicism.[45] This virulent sectarian hostility enabled the colonists to separate themselves definitively from the Old World, for which many still felt a strong residual affection; hatred of Catholic 'tyranny' would long remain a crucial element in American national identity. The Founders may have been followers of Locke, but 'religion' had not yet been banished from the colonies; had it been so, the revolution might not have succeeded.

As soon as independence was declared in July 1776, the colonies began to compose their new constitutions. In Virginia, Thomas Jefferson (1743– 1826) proposed a formula that would not survive the ratification process: 'All persons shall have full and free liberty of religious opinion; nor shall any be compelled to frequent or maintain any religious institution.'[46] This guaranteed freedom *for* religion and freedom *from* it. But we must bear in mind that Jefferson's conception of 'religion' was based on two early modern innovations to which most of his countrymen did not subscribe. First was the reduction of religion to 'belief' and 'opinion'. As an apostle of Enlightenment empiricism, Jefferson rejected the idea that religious knowledge was acquired by revelation, ritual or communal experience; it was merely a set of beliefs shared by some. Like all Enlightenment *philosophes*, Jefferson and James Madison (1751–1836), the pioneers of religious liberty in America, believed that no idea should be immune from investigation or even outright rejection. Nevertheless, they also insisted on the right of conscience: a man's personal convictions were his own, not subject to the coercion of government. Obligatory belief, therefore, violated a fundamental human right. 'Religious bondage shackles and debilitates the mind and unfits it for every noble enterprise, every expected prospect,' Madison objected.[47] The last fifteen hundred years, he claimed sweepingly, had resulted in 'more or less all places' in 'pride and indolence in the clergy, ignorance and servility in the laity; in both, superstition, bigotry and persecution'.[48] The 'myth of religious violence' had clearly taken root in the minds of the Founders. In the new enlightened age, Jefferson declared in his *Statute for Establishing Religious Freedom in Virginia*, 'Our civil rights have no dependence upon our religious opinions, any more than our opinions in physics or geometry.'[49]

The critique of Jefferson and Madison was a healthy corrective to the idolatrous tendency to give man-made ideas divine status. Freedom of thought would become a sacred value in the modern secular West, an inviolable and unnegotiable human right. It would advance scientific and technological progress and enable the arts to flourish. But the intellectual freedom proclaimed by the Enlightenment *philosophes* was a luxury of modernisation. In the pre-modern agrarian state it had never been possible to permit the entire population to cast tradition aside and freely criticise the established order. Most of the aristocratic Founders, moreover, had no intention of extending this privilege to the common people. They still took it for granted that it was their task, as enlightened statesmen, to lead from above.[50] Like most of the elite, John Adams, second president of the United States (1797–1801), was suspicious of any policy that might lead to 'mob-rule' or the impoverishment of the gentry,[51] though Jefferson's more radical followers protested against this 'tyranny' and, like Edwards, demanded that the people's voices be heard.[52] Still, it was not until the Industrial Revolution shook up the social order that the ideals enshrined by the Founding Fathers could apply broadly to social reality.

The second assumption of Jefferson and Madison was that 'religion' was an autonomous, private human activity essentially separate from politics and that mixing the two had been a great aberration. This may have been self-evident to Locke, but it would still have been a very strange notion to most Americans. The Founders knew their countrymen: a federal constitution would never gain the support of all the states unless it refrained from making any single Protestant denomination official, as many of the state constitutions had done. Precisely because most Americans still approved of religion in their governments, therefore, uniting the several states would require religious neutrality at the federal level.[53] Hence the first lapidary clause of the First Amendment to the Constitution in the Bill of Rights (1791) decreed that 'Congress shall make no law respecting the establishment of religion, or prohibiting the free exercise thereof.' The state would neither promote nor obstruct religion: it would simply leave it alone.[54] But there were political consequences even of that. During the bitterly contested presidential election of 1800, Jefferson the deist was accused of being an atheist and even a Muslim. He replied that although he was not hostile to faith he was adamantly opposed to government meddling in religious affairs. When a group of his Baptist supporters in Danbury, Connecticut asked him to appoint a day of fasting to bring the nation together, Jefferson replied that this lay beyond the president's competence:

> Believing with you that religion is a matter which lies solely between man and his God, that he owes to none other for his faith and worship, that the legislative powers of government reach actions only, and not opinions, I contemplate with solemn reverence that act of the whole American people which declared that their legislature should 'make no law respecting an establishment of religion or prohibiting the free exercise thereof,' thus building a wall of separation of Church and State.

But while such separation could be beneficial to both church and state, it was not, as Jefferson assumed, written into the very nature of things but was a modern innovation. The United States was attempting something entirely new.

Jefferson had borrowed the image of the 'wall of separation' from Roger Williams (1604–83), founder of Providence, Rhode Island, who had been expelled from New England because of his opposition to the intolerant policies of the Puritan government.[55] But Williams was less concerned about the welfare of the state than about his faith, which he believed would be contaminated by any involvement with government.[56] He intended Rhode Island to be an alternative Christian community that came closer to the spirit of the Gospels. Jefferson, by contrast, was more concerned to protect the state from the 'loathsome combination of church and state' that had reduced human beings to 'dupes and drudges'.[57] But he seemed to assume – quite wrongly – that there had been states in the past that had *not* been guilty of this 'loathsome combination'. It remained to be seen whether the secularised United States would be less violent and coercive than its more religious predecessors.

Whatever the Founders wanted, most Americans still took it for granted that the United States would be based on Christian principles. By 1790, some 40 per cent of the new nation lived on the frontiers and were becoming increasingly resentful of the republican government that did not share their hardships but taxed them as harshly as the British had done. A new wave of revivals, known as the Second Great Awakening, represented a grassroots campaign for a more democratic and Bible-based America.[58] The new revivalists were not intellectuals like Edwards but men of the people, who used wild gestures, earthy humour and slang, and relied on dreams, visions and celestial signs. During their mass rallies, they pitched huge tents outside the towns and their Gospel songs transported the crowds to ecstasy. But these prophets were not pre-Enlightenment throwbacks. Lorenzo Dow may have looked like John the Baptist but he quoted Jefferson and Paine and, like any Enlightenment *philosophe*, urged the people to think for themselves. In the Christian commonwealth the first should be last and the last first. God had sent his insights to the poor and unlettered, and Jesus and his disciples had not had college degrees.

James Kelly and Barton Stone railed against the aristocratic clergy who tried to force the erudite faith of Harvard on the people. Enlightenment philosophers had insisted that people must have the courage to throw off their dependence on authority and use their natural reason to discover the truth. Now the revivalists insisted that American Christians could read the Bible without direction from upper-class scholars. When Stone founded his own denomination, he called it a 'declaration of independence': the revivalists were bringing the modern ideals of democracy, equality, freedom of speech and independence to the folk in an idiom that uneducated people could make their own. This Second Awakening may have seemed retrograde to the elite but it was actually a Protestant version of the Enlightenment. Demanding a degree of equality that the American ruling class was not yet ready to give them, the revivalists represented a populist discontent that it could not safely ignore.

At first, this rough, democratic Christianity was confined to the poorer Americans but during the 1840s, Charles Finney (1792–1875) brought it to the middle classes, creating an 'evangelical' Christianity based on a literal reading of the Gospels. Evangelicals were determined to convert the secular republic to Christ and by the mid-nineteenth century, evangelicalism had become the dominant faith of the United States.[59] Without waiting for guidance from the government, from about 1810 these Protestants began to work in churches and schools and established reform associations, which mushroomed in the northern states. Some campaigned against slavery, others against liquor; some worked to end the oppression of women and other disadvantaged groups, others for penal and educational reform. Like the Second Great Awakening, these modernising movements helped ordinary Americans to embrace the ideal of inalienable human rights in a Protestant package. Their members learned to plan, organise and pursue a clearly defined objective in a rational way that empowered them to confront the establishment. We in the West tend to evaluate other cultural traditions by measuring them against the Enlightenment: the Great Awakenings in America show that people can reach these ideals by another, specifically religious route.

In fact, American evangelicals had appropriated some Enlightenment ideals so thoroughly that they created a curious hybrid that some historians have called 'Enlightenment Protestantism'.[60] This paradox had been noted by Alexis de Tocqueville when he visited the United States in the 1830s, remarking that the character of the country combined 'two perfectly distinct elements that elsewhere have often made war with each other, but which, in America, . . . they have succeeded in incorporating somehow one into another and combining marvellously: I mean to speak of the *spirit of religion* and the *spirit of freedom*'.[61] The Founding Fathers had been inspired by the so-called 'moderate' Enlightenment of Isaac Newton and John Locke. The evangelicals, however, repudiated the 'sceptical' Enlightenment of Voltaire and David Hume as well as the 'revolutionary' Enlightenment of Rousseau but embraced the 'common sense' philosophy of the Scottish thinkers Francis Hutcheson (1694–1746), Thomas Reid (1710–96), Adam Smith (1723–90) and Dugald Stewart (1753–1828).[62] This taught them that human beings had an innate and infallible ability to see clear connections between moral causes and their effects in public life. Understanding things was simple, a matter of common sense. Even a child could grasp the essence of the Gospel and figure out for herself what was right. American evangelicals were confident that if they put their minds to it they could create a society in the New World that fully implemented Christian values.[63] The Constitution had established a secular state but had done nothing to encourage the development of a national culture; the Founders had assumed that this would evolve naturally in response to government action.[64] But thanks to the evangelical welfare and reform associations, 'Enlightenment Protestantism', somewhat ironically, became the national ethos of the secular state.[65] You can take religion out of the state but you can't take religion out of the nation. By dint of their energetic missionary work, reform organisations and publications, the evangelicals created a Bible-based culture that pulled the new nation together.

The Americans had shown that it was possible to organise society on a more just and rational basis. In France, the leaders of the bourgeoisie, the rising middle classes, had watched these events very carefully because they too had developed ideologies that emphasised the freedom of the individual.[66] But they had a more difficult task, because they had to depose a long-established ruling class with a professional army, a centralised bureaucracy and an absolute monarchy.[67] But by the end of the eighteenth century, traditional agrarian society was coming under increasing strain in Europe: more people were moving to the towns and working in non-agricultural trades and professions; literacy was more widespread and there was unprecedented social mobility.

In the spring of 1789, Louis XVI's absolutist monarchy was in trouble. Profligate stewardship had plunged the French economy into crisis and now the clergy and nobility (the First and Second Estates) were refusing a new regime of taxation by the crown. To break the deadlock, the king called the Estates General to meet at Versailles on 2 May.[68] The king wanted the three estates – clergy, nobility and commoners – to deliberate and vote separately, but the Third Estate refused to allow the aristocracy to dominate the proceedings and invited the clergy and nobility to join them in a new National Assembly. The first to defect to the Third Estate were 150 of the lower clergy, who came from the same background as the commoners, were weary of the bishops' hauteur and wanted a more collegial church.[69] There were also defections from the Second Estate: the rural gentry disdained by the Parisian aristocracy and the wealthy bourgeois who were impatient with the nobility's conservatism. On 17 June members of the new National Assembly swore that they would not disperse until they had a new Constitution.

The Assembly had intended to conduct a reasoned, enlightened debate on the American model, but it had reckoned without the people. After a bad harvest, food supplies were dangerously low, the price of bread had rocketed in the towns, and there was widespread unemployment. In April, 5,000 artisans had rioted in Paris and revolutionary committees and citizen

militias had formed across the country to contain the unrest. During the
Assembly's discussions, delegates were booed and heckled from the public
galleries and the distraught crowds took to the street, attacking any representative of the *Ancien Régime* that crossed their path. In a crucial development, some of the soldiers dispatched to quell these riots joined the rebels
instead. On 14 July, the mob stormed the Bastille in eastern Paris, released
the prisoners, and hacked the gaol's governor to pieces. Other senior officials met the same fate. In the countryside, the famished peasantry were
gripped by the 'Great Fear', convinced that the grain shortages had been
engineered by the regime to starve them into submission. This suspicion
was compounded by the arrival of impoverished labourers seeking work
who were thought to be the nobility's advance troops.[70] Villagers raided
the chateaux, attacked Jewish moneylenders, and refused to pay their tithes
and taxes.

As the country span out of control, the Assembly became more radical.
It produced the Declaration of the Rights of Man and the Citizen, which
vested sovereignty in the people rather than the monarch and proclaimed
that all men had natural rights of liberty of conscience, property and free
speech and must enjoy equality before the law, personal security and equal
opportunity. Then the Assembly set about dismantling the Catholic Church
in France. As we have seen, the 'myth of religious violence' was founded
on the belief that the separation of church and state would liberate society
from the inherent belligerence of 'religion'. But almost every secularising
reform in Europe and in other parts of the world would begin with an
aggressive assault on religious institutions, which would inspire resentment,
anomie, distress and, in some cases, a violent riposte. On 2 November
1789 the Assembly voted by 568 to 346 to pay off the national debt by
confiscating the wealth of the Church. The Bishop of Autun, Charles Maurice
de Talleyrand, pointed out that the Church did not own property in the
ordinary way; its lands and estates had been given to it so that it could do
good works.[71] The state could now pay the clergy a salary and finance these
charitable activities itself. This decision was followed on 3 February 1790
by the abolition of all religious orders except those engaged in teaching or
hospital work. Many clerics protested vigorously against these measures
and they gravely disturbed many of the common people, but some priests
saw them as an opportunity for reform that could return the Church to
its pristine purity and even inaugurate a new 'national religion'.

The secular regime thus began with a policy of coercion, disempower-
ment and dispossession. On 29 May 1790, the Assembly issued the Civil

Constitution of the Clergy that relegated the Church to a state department. Fifty sees were abolished and in Brittany, many parishioners found themselves without a bishop. Four thousand parishes were eliminated, bishops' salaries were reduced, and in future bishops were to be elected by the people. On 26 November, the clergy were given eight days to take an Oath of Loyalty to the nation, the law and the king. Forty-four clerics in the Assembly refused to take the oath and there were riots in protest against this humiliation of the priestly order in Alsace, Anjou, Artois, Brittany, Flanders, Languedoc and Normandy.[72] Catholicism was so deeply entwined with almost every detail of daily life that, aghast, many of the Third Estate turned against the regime. In western France, parishioners pressured their ministers to refuse the Oath and would have nothing to do with the Constitutional clergy sent in to replace them.

The aggression of the secular state soon segued into outright violence. Neighbouring monarchies began to mobilise against the revolution. As so often happens, an external threat led to widespread fears of the 'enemy within'. When French troops were routed by the Austrians in the summer of 1792, wild rumours circulated of a 'fifth column' of counter-revolutionary priests aiding the enemy. When the Prussian army broke through the frontier and threatened Verdun, the last line of defence before Paris, recalcitrant clerics were imprisoned. In September, amid fears of royalist clergy planning simultaneous uprisings, violent mobs descended on the prisons and murdered 2–3,000 prisoners, many of them priests. Two weeks later, France was declared a republic.

The French and the Americans had adopted diametrically opposed policies on religion: all the American states eventually disestablished their churches, but because their clergy were not implicated in an aristocratic government, there was no virulent hostility to the traditional denominations. But in France, the Church, which had been so deeply involved in aristocratic rule, could be dismantled only by an outright assault.[73] By now it was clear that a secular regime had just as much potential for violence as a religiously constituted one. After the September Massacres, there were more atrocities. On 12 March 1793, an uprising began in the Vendée in western France in protest against conscription to the army, unfair taxation and, above all, the anti-Catholic policies of the revolution.[74] The rebels were especially incensed by the arrival in the Vendée of Constitutional clergy, who had no roots in the region, to replace priests who were known and loved. They formed the Catholic and Royal Army, carried banners of the Virgin and sang hymns as they marched. This was not an aristocratic uprising but an army of the people, who were determined to retain their Catholicism: over 60 per cent were farmers and the others artisans and shopkeepers. Three armies dispatched from Paris to quell the uprising were diverted to deal with the Federalist Revolt in which moderate provincial bourgeois and republicans joined forces with royalists in Bordeaux, Lyons, Marseilles, Toulouse and Toulon in protest against measures taken in Paris.

Once the Federalists were put down with horrible reprisals, four revolutionary armies arrived in the Vendée early in 1794 with instructions from the Committee of Public Safety that recalled the rhetoric of the Catharist Crusade: 'Spear with your bayonets all the inhabitants you encounter along the way. I know there may be a few patriots in this region – it matters not, we must sacrifice all.'[75] 'All brigands found with weapons or suspected of having carried them will be speared by the bayonet,' General Turreau instructed his soldiers. 'We will act equally with women, girls and children . . . Even people only suspected will not be spared.'[76] 'The Vendée no longer exists,' François-Joseph Westermann reported to his superiors at the end of the campaign. 'Following the orders I have received, I have crushed children beneath the hooves of our horses, and massacred women . . . the roads are littered with corpses.'[77] The revolution that had promised liberty and fraternity may have slaughtered a quarter of a million people in one of the worst atrocities of the early modern period.

Human beings have always sought intensity and moments of ecstasy that give their lives meaning and purpose. If a symbol, icon, myth, ritual or doctrine no longer yields a sense of transcendent value, they tend to replace it with something else. Historians of religion tell us that absolutely anything can become a symbol of the divine and that such epiphanies occur 'in every area of psychological, economic, spiritual and social life'.[78] This was soon evident in France. No sooner had the revolutionaries rid themselves of one religion than they invented another, making the nation an embodiment of the sacred. It was the audacious genius of the revolutionary leadership to recognise that the potent emotions traditionally connected with the Church could be just as powerfully felt if directed towards a new symbol. On 10 August 1793, while the nation was tearing itself apart in war and bloodshed, a festival choreographed by the artist Jacques-Louis David celebrated the Unity and Indivisibility of the Republic in Paris. It began at sunrise on the site of the Bastille, where an imposing statue of Nature decanted water from her breasts into a cup held by the president of the National Convention; he then passed it to eighty-six elderly men representing the French *départements* in a holy communion. In the Place de la Révolution the president torched a great bonfire of heraldic symbols, sceptres and thrones before a statue of Liberty, and at the Invalides the public gazed at a giant effigy of the French people as Hercules.[79] These festivals became so frequent that people wrote of 'festomania'.[80] As the nineteenth-century historian Jules Michelet explained, the state rituals celebrated the arrival of 'a strange *vita nuova,* one eminently spiritual'.[81]

The Catholic Mass had been a central feature of the early pageants but by 1793 the priests had been eliminated from these national rites. This was the year that Jacques Hébert enthroned the Goddess of Reason on the high altar of Notre-Dame Cathedral, transforming it into a temple of philosophy. Revolutionary politics was itself becoming an object of worship. Leaders made great use of such terms as 'credo', 'zealot', 'sacrament' and 'sermon' when describing political events.[82] Honoré Mirabeau wrote that 'the Declaration of the Rights of Man has become a political Gospel and the French Constitution a religion for which the people is prepared to die'.[83] The poet Marie-Joseph Chénier told the National Convention: 'You will know how to found on the ruins of dethroned superstition, the single universal religion of which our lawmakers are the preachers, the magistrates the pontiffs, and in which the human family burns its incense only at the altar of the Patrie, common mother and divinity.'[84] Because the revolution 'seemed to be striving for the regeneration of the human race even more than for the reform of France', de Tocqueville observed:

> a new kind of religion, an incomplete religion, it is true, without God, without ritual, and without life after death, but one which nevertheless, like Islam, flooded the earth with its soldiers, apostles and martyrs.[85]

It is interesting that he equated this defiantly secular religiosity with the fanatical violence that Europeans had long attributed to Islam.

The 'civil religion' described first by Jean-Jacques Rousseau (1712–78) was based on belief in God and the afterlife, the social contract and the prohibition of intolerance. Its festivals, Rousseau wrote, would create a sacred bond between participants: 'Let the spectators become an entertainment to themselves; make them actors themselves; do it so that each sees and loves himself in the others so that all will be better united.'[86] But Rousseau's loving tolerance did not extend to those who refused to obey the precepts of civil religion and a similar rigour entered the revolution.[87] A month after the festival celebrating the Unity and Indivisibility of the Republic, the Reign of Terror began when Maximilien de Robespierre

(1758–94) appointed a tribunal to seek out traitors and pursued dissidents with all the zeal of a militant pope. Not only were the king and queen, members of the royal family and the aristocracy executed but one group of apparently loyal patriots after another went to the guillotine. The distinguished chemist Antoine Lavoisier, who had worked all his professional life to improve conditions in French prisons and hospitals, and Gilbert Romme, who had designed the revolutionary calendar, were both beheaded. When the purge ended in July 1794, some seventeen thousand men, women and children had been guillotined and twice as many had either died in the disease-ridden prisons or had been slaughtered by local vigilantes.[88]

Meanwhile, the revolutionary leaders were waging a holy war against the non-revolutionary regimes of Europe.[89] Since the Peace of Westphalia (1648) the continent had known nearly 150 years of relative peace. A balance of power kept the sovereign states in harmony. Brutality on the battlefield was no longer acceptable; moderation and restraint were the new watchwords.[90] Armies were now adequately provisioned so soldiers no longer had to terrorise the peasant population by foraging for themselves.[91] There was greater emphasis on drill, discipline and correct methods of procedure, and between 1700 and 1850 there were no significant developments in military technology.[92] But this peace was shattered when first the revolutionary armies and then Napoleon threw these restraints to the wind.

The French state had certainly not become more irenic after abolishing the Church. On 16 August 1793, the National Convention issued the *levée en masse*: for the first time in history, an entire society was mobilised for war.

> All Frenchmen are permanently requisitioned for service into the armies. Young men will go forth into battle; married men will forge weapons and transport munitions; women will make tents and clothing and serve in the hospitals; children will make lint from old linen; and old men will be brought into the public squares to arouse the courage of the soldiers, while preaching the unity of the Republic and hatred against Kings.[93]

Some 300,000 volunteers, aged between eighteen and twenty-five, brought the French army up to a record-breaking million strong. Hitherto peasants and artisans had been tricked or press-ganged into the military but in this 'Free Army' soldiers were well paid and for the first year officers were elected from the ranks on merit. In 1789, over 90 per cent of French officers had been aristocrats; by 1794 a mere 3 per cent were of noble birth.[94] Even though over a million young men died in the Revolutionary and Napoleonic Wars, more were willing to volunteer. These soldiers fought not with professional decorum but with the raw violence they had learned in the revolution's street battles, and they probably relished the ecstasy of warfare.[95] And because they had to feed themselves, they committed the same kind of atrocities as the mercenaries in the Thirty Years War.[96] For nearly twenty years, the French armies seemed unstoppable, overrunning Belgium, the Netherlands and Germany and effortlessly brushing aside the Austrian and Prussian armies that tried to halt this triumphant progress.

Revolutionary France did not bring liberty to the peoples of Europe, however; instead, Napoleon, the revolution's heir, created a traditional tributary empire that threatened the imperial ambitions of Britain. In 1798, to establish a base in Suez that would cut off the British sea routes to India, Napoleon invaded Egypt and at the Battle of the Pyramids inflicted a devastating defeat on the Mamluk army: only ten French soldiers were killed but the Mamluks lost more than two thousand men.[97] With consummate cynicism, Napoleon then presented himself as the liberator of the Egyptian people. Carefully briefed by the French Institut d'Égypte, he addressed the sheikhs of the Azhar madrasa in Arabic, expressing his deep respect for the Prophet, and promising to free Egypt from the oppression of the Ottomans and their Mamluk agents. Accompanying the French army was a corps of scholars, a library of modern European literature, a laboratory, and a printing press with Arabic type. The ulema were not impressed: 'All this is nothing but deceit and trickery,' they said, 'to entice us.'[98] They were right. Napoleon's invasion, exploiting Enlightenment scholarship and science to subjugate the region, marked the beginning of Western domination of the Middle East.

To many it seemed that the French Revolution had failed. The systemic violence of Napoleon's empire betrayed revolutionary principles and Napoleon also reinstated the Catholic Church. For decades the hopes of 1789 were dashed by one disillusioning event after another. The glory days of the fall of the Bastille were followed by the September Massacres, the Reign of Terror, the Vendée genocide and a military dictatorship. After Napoleon's fall from power in 1814, Louis XVIII (the brother of Louis XVI) was returned to the throne. But the revolutionary dream refused to die. The republic was revived for two brief periods, during the Hundred Days before Napoleon's final defeat at Waterloo in 1815 and for a brief period between 1848 and 1852. In 1870 it was restored yet again, this time lasting until it was destroyed by the Nazis in 1940. Instead of seeing the French Revolution as a failure, therefore, we should perhaps see it as the explosive start of a lengthy process. Such massive social and political change over-turning millennia of autocracy cannot be achieved overnight. Revolutions take a long time. But unlike several other European countries, where aristocratic regimes were so deeply entrenched that they managed to hang on, albeit in limited form, France eventually achieved its secular republic. We should bear this long-drawn-out and painful process in mind before dismissing as failures revolutions that have taken place in our own time: in Iran, Egypt and Tunisia, for example.

The French Revolution may have changed the politics of Europe but it did not affect the agrarian economy. Modernity came of age in Britain's Industrial Revolution, which began in the later eighteenth century, though its social effects would not be truly felt until the early nineteenth.[99] It started with the invention of the steam engine, which provided more energy than the country's entire workforce put together, so the economy grew at an unprece-dented rate. It was not long before Germany, France, Japan and the United States followed Britain's lead and all these industrialised countries were permanently transformed. To man the new machines, the population had to be mobilised for industry instead of agriculture; economic self-sufficiency now became a thing of the past. The government also began to control the lives of ordinary folk in ways that had been impossible in agrarian society.[100] In *Hard Times* (1854), Charles Dickens portrayed the industrial city as an inferno: workers – referred to contemptuously as 'the Hands' – live in abject poverty and have no more than instrumental value. The oppression of the agrarian state had been replaced by the structural violence of indus-trialisation. More benign state ideologies would develop and more people than ever before would enjoy the comfort previously available only to the nobility but, despite the best efforts of some politicians, an unbridgeable gap would always separate rich and poor.

The Enlightenment ideals of toleration, independence, democracy and intellectual freedom were no longer simply noble aspirations but had become practical necessities. Mass production required a mass market, so the common people could no longer be kept at subsistence level: they had to be able to afford manufactured goods. More and more people were drawn into the productive process – as factory workers, printers or office clerks – and needed at least a modicum of education. Inevitably they would begin to demand representation in government, and modern communications would make it easier for workers to organise politically. Because no single group could dominate or even effectively oppose the government, different parties had to compete for power.[101] Intellectual liberty was now essential to the economy, as people could only achieve the innovation that was essential to progress by thinking freely, unconstrained by their class, guild or church. Governments had to exploit all their human resources, so outsiders, such as the Jews in Europe and Catholics in England and America, were brought into the mainstream.

Industrialised countries were soon compelled to seek new markets and resources abroad and would, therefore, as the German philosopher Georg Wilhelm Hegel (1770–1831) had predicted, be pushed towards colonialism.[102] In these new empires, the economic relationship between the imperial power and the subject peoples became just as one-sided as it had been in the agrarian empires. The new colonial power did not help its colonies to industrialise but simply appropriated an 'undeveloped' country to extract raw materials that could feed the European industrial process.[103] In return, the colony received cheap manufactured goods from the West that ruined local businesses. Not surprisingly, colonialism was experienced as intrusive and coercive. The colonialists built modern transport and communications but chiefly for their own convenience.[104] In India, British traders ransacked the assets of Bengal so ruthlessly during the late eighteenth century that this period is regularly described as 'the plundering of Bengal'. The region was pushed into a chronically dependent role and instead of growing their own food villagers were forced to cultivate jute and indigo for the world market. The British did help keep disease and famine at bay, but the consequent population growth led to poverty and overcrowding.[105]

This combination of industrialised technology and empire was creating a global form of systemic violence, driven not by religion but by the wholly secular values of the market. The West was so far ahead, that it was virtually impossible for the subject peoples to catch up. Increasingly the world would be divided between the West and the Rest, and this systemic political and economic inequality was sustained by military force. By the mid-nineteenth century, Britain controlled most of the Indian subcontinent and after the Indian Mutiny (1857), in which 70,000 Indians were killed in a final desperate protest against foreign rule, the British formally deposed the last Moghul Emperor.[106] Because the colony had to fit into the global market, a degree of modernisation was essential: policing, the army and the local economy had to be completely reorganised and some of the 'natives' introduced to modern ideas. Only very rarely had agrarian empires attempted to change the religious traditions of the common people, but in India British innovations had a drastic effect on the religious and political life of the subcontinent.

The ease with which they had been so thoroughly subjugated was profoundly disturbing to the people of India since it implied that something was radically amiss with their social systems.[107] Traditional Indian aristocracies now had to cope not only with a foreign ruling class but with a wholly different socioeconomic order and with the new cadres of clerks and bureaucrats created by the British who often earned more than the old elites. These Westernised Indians had become in effect a new caste, separated by a gulf of incomprehension from the unmodernised majority. The increasing democratisation imposed by their British rulers was alien to the social arrangements of India, which had always been strongly hierarchical and had encouraged synergy among disparate groups rather than organised unity. Moreover, confronted with the bewildering social variety of the subcontinent, the British latched on to the groups they mistakenly thought they understood and divided the population into 'Hindu', 'Muslim', 'Sikh' and 'Christian' communities.

The 'Hindu' majority, however, consisted of multifarious castes, cults and groups that did not see themselves as forming an organised religion, as Western people now understood this term. They had no unifying hierarchy and no standard set of rituals, practices and beliefs. They worshipped numerous unrelated gods and engaged in devotions that had no logical connection with one another. But now they all found themselves lumped together into something the British called 'Hinduism'.[108] The term *hindu* had been used first by the Muslim conquerors to describe the indigenous people; it had no specifically religious connotation but simply meant 'native' or 'local' and the indigenous peoples, including Buddhists, Jains and Sikhs, came to use it of themselves. Under the British, however, 'Hindus' had to become a close-knit group and cultivate a broad, caste-less communal identity that was alien to their age-old traditions.

It was ironic that the British, who had banished 'religion' from the public sphere at home, should classify the subcontinent in such tightly religious terms. They based the Indian electoral system on religious affiliation and in 1871 conducted a census that made these religious communities acutely aware of their numbers and areas of strength in relation to one another. By bringing religion to the fore in this way, the British inadvertently bequeathed a history of communal conflict to South Asia. In the Moghul empire, there had certainly been tension between the Muslim ruling class and their Hindu subjects but this had rarely had a religious coloration. While Western Christians had become more sectarian during their Reformation, India had been moving in the opposite direction. In the thirteenth century, Vedic orthodoxy had begun to be transformed by *bhakti*, a 'devotion' to a personal deity which refused to acknowledge differences of caste or creed. Bhakti drew much inspiration from Sufism, which had become the dominant mode of Islam in the subcontinent and had long insisted that because the omniscient and omnipresent God could not be confined to a single creed, belligerent assertion of orthodoxy was a form of idolatry (*shirk*).

Sikhism had been born in this climate of open-hearted tolerance. The word *sikh* derived from the Sanskrit *shishya* ('disciple'), for Sikhs followed the teachings of Guru Nanak (1469–1539), founder of their tradition, and his nine inspired successors. Born in a village near Lahore in the Punjab, Nanak had insisted that interior apprehension of God was far more important than a strict adherence to doctrines and customs that could divide people from one another – though he scrupulously avoided deriding anybody's faith. Like the Sufis, he believed that human beings must be weaned from the fanaticism that made them attack the beliefs of others: 'Religion lives not in empty words,' he once said. 'He who regards all men as equals is religious.'[109] One of his earliest maxims stated categorically: 'There is no Hindu; there is no Muslim; who shall I follow? I shall follow the way of God.'[110]

Another leading proponent of this openness to other faiths was Akbar, the third Moghul emperor (1542–1605). Out of respect for Hindu sensitivity, he gave up hunting, forbade the sacrifice of animals on his birthday, and became a vegetarian. In 1575 he founded a House of Worship, where scholars from all religious traditions met freely to discuss spiritual matters, and a Sufi order, dedicated to 'divine monotheism' (*tawhid-e-ilahi*) based on the conviction that the one God could reveal himself in any rightly guided religion. But not all Muslims shared this vision and this policy could be sustained only while the Moghuls were in a position of strength. When their power began to decline and various groups began to revolt against imperial rule, religious conflict escalated. Akbar's son Jahangir (r. 1605–27) had to put down one rebellion after another and Aurangzeb (r. 1658–1707) seems to have believed that political unity could only be restored by greater discipline within the Muslim ruling class. He therefore outlawed laxities such as wine-drinking, made Muslim cooperation with their Hindu subjects impossible, and engaged in widespread destruction of Hindu temples. These violent policies, the result of political insecurity as much as religious zeal, were reversed immediately after Aurangzeb's death but were never forgotten.

Sikhs had suffered from the imperial violence. By this time, Sikhs, who had once eschewed all external symbols, had developed some of their own. The fifth guru, Arjan Dev, had made the Golden Temple at Amritsar in the Punjab a place of pilgrimage and had enshrined the Sikh scriptures there in 1604. Sikhism had always abstained from violence. Guru Nanak had said: 'Take up arms that hurt no one; let your coat of mail be understanding; convert your enemies to friends.'¹¹¹ The first four gurus had had no need to bear arms. But Jahangir had tortured the fifth guru to death in 1606, and in 1675 Aurangzeb beheaded Tegh Bahadur, the ninth guru. His successor, Gobind Singh, therefore faced an entirely different world. Henceforth, the tenth guru declared, there would be no more human leaders: in future the Sikhs' only guru would be their scripture. In 1699, he instituted the Sikh Order of Khalsa (the 'purified' or 'chosen'). Like Kshatriya warriors, its members would call themselves *Singh* ('Lion'), carry swords and distinguish themselves from the rest of the population by wearing soldiers' garb and keeping their hair unshorn. Yet again, imperial violence had radicalised an originally irenic tradition and had also introduced a particularism that was entirely alien to the original Sikh vision. Gobind is believed to have written to Aurangzeb that when all else failed, it was only right to lift the sword and fight. Militancy might be necessary to defend the community – but only as a last resort.¹¹²

The Hindu, Sikh and Muslim communities were now in competition for British favour, resources and political influence. Their leaders discovered that the British were more receptive to their ideas if they believed that they represented a larger group, and realised that in order to prosper under colonial rule they would have to adapt to the Western understanding of religion. So new reform movements tended to adopt contemporaneous Protestant norms in a way that distorted these traditions. Luther had tried to return to the practice of the early Church, so the Arya Samaj ('Society of Aryans'), which was founded in the Punjab in 1875 by Swami Dayananda, attempted a return to Vedic orthodoxy. He also tried to create an author-itative scriptural canon, which had no precedent in India. The Arya was, therefore, an extremely reductive form of 'Hinduism', since the Vedic tradition had long been the faith of a small elite and very few people were able to understand ancient Sanskrit. It thus tended to appeal only to the educated classes. But by 1947, when British rule ended, the Arya had

1.5 million members. In other parts of the world too, wherever secular modernity was imposed, there would be similar attempts to return to 'fundamentals'. The Arya illustrated the aggression inherent in such fundamentalism. In his book *Satyarth Prakash* ('The Light of Truth'), Dayananda dismissed Buddhists and Jains as mere offshoots of 'Hinduism', derided Christian theology, claimed that Sikhism was merely a Hindu sect, dismissing Guru Nanak as a well-meaning ignoramus who had no understanding of the Vedic traditions, and was vitriolic in his abuse of the Prophet Muhammad. In 1943, the book inspired violent protests among Muslims in Sind and became a rallying point for those Hindus who were campaigning for an India free of both the British and Islam.[113]

After Devananda's death, the Arya became even more insulting and disrespectful in their denunciation of the Sikh gurus and, perhaps inevitably, inspired an aggressive assertion of Sikh identity. When Arya pamphlets argued that *Sikh Hindu hain* ('The Sikhs are Hindus'), the prominent Sikh scholar Kahim Singh retaliated with his highly influential tract *Ham Hindu nahim* ('We are not Hindus').[114] The irony was, of course, that until the British had arrived nobody had thought of themselves as 'Hindu' in this way. The British tendency to see the different faith communities in stereotypical ways also helped to radicalise the Sikh tradition; they promoted the idea that Sikhs were an essentially warlike and heroic people.[115] In recognition of Sikh support during the 1857 mutiny, the British had overcome their initial reluctance to admit members of the Khalsa into the army; moreover, once they were recruited, they were allowed to wear their traditional uniforms. This special treatment meant that gradually the idea that Sikhs were a separate and distinctive race gained ground.

Hitherto Sikhs and Hindus had lived together peacefully in the Punjab, sharing the same cultural traditions. There had been no central Sikh authority, so variant forms of Sikhism flourished. This had always been the norm in India, where religious identities had been multiple and defined regionally.[116] But in the 1870s Sikhs began to develop their own reform movement in an attempt to adapt to these new realities. By the end of the nineteenth century there were about a hundred Sikh Sabha groups all over the Punjab, dedicated to an assertion of Sikh distinctiveness, building Sikh schools and colleges and producing a flood of polemical literature.[117] On the surface, these groups seemed in tune with Sikh tradition but this separatism entirely subverted Nanak's original vision. Sikhs were now expected to adopt a single identity. Over the years a Sikh fundamentalism would emerge that interpreted the tradition selectively, claiming to return to the martial teachings of the tenth guru but ignoring the peaceful ethos of the early gurus. This new Sikhism was passionately opposed to secularism: Sikhs must have political power in order to enforce this conformity. A tradition that once had been open to all had been invaded by fear of the 'Other', represented by a host of enemies – Hindus, heretics, modernisers, secularists and any form of political dominance.[118]

There was a similar distortion of the Muslim tradition. The British abolition of the Moghul empire had been a traumatic watershed, summarily demoting a people who hitherto had been virtual masters of the globe. For the first time, they were being ruled by hostile infidels in one of the core cultures of the civilised world. Given the symbolic importance of the ummah's well-being, this was not simply a political anxiety but one that touched the spiritual recesses of their being. Some Muslims would therefore cultivate a history of grievance. We have previously seen that the experience of humiliation can damage a tradition and become a catalyst for violence. Segments of the Hindu population, who had been subjected to Muslim rule for seven hundred years, had their own smouldering resentment of imperial rule, so Muslims suddenly felt extremely vulnerable, especially since the British blamed them for the mutiny of 1857.[119]

Many were afraid that Islam would disappear from the subcontinent and that Muslims would lose their identity. Their first impulse was to withdraw from the mainstream and cling to the glories of the distant past. In 1867 in Deoband, near Delhi, a cadre of ulema began to issue detailed fatwas that governed every single aspect of life to help Muslims live authentically under foreign rule. Over time, the Deobandis established a network of madrasas throughout the subcontinent that promoted a form of Islam which was as reductive in its own way as the Arya Samaj. They too attempted a return to 'fundamentals' – the pristine Islam of the Prophet and the first four caliphs – and vehemently decried such later developments as the Shiah. Islam had for centuries displayed a remarkable ability to assimilate other cultural traditions, but their colonial humiliation caused the Deobandis to retreat from the West in rather the same way as Ibn Taymiyyah had recoiled from Moghul civilisation. Deobandi Islam refused to countenance itjihad ('independent reasoning') and argued for an overly strict and literal interpretation of the Shariah. The Deobandis were socially progressive in their rejection of the caste system and their determination to educate the poorest Muslims, but they were radically opposed to any innovation – adamant, for instance, in their condemnation of the compulsory education of women. In the early days, Deobandis were not violent but they would later become more militant. They would have a drastic effect on subcontinental Islam, which had traditionally leaned towards the more inclusive disciplines of Sufism and Falsafah, both of which the Deobandis now virulently condemned. During the twentieth century they would gain considerable influence in the Muslim world and would rank in importance with the prestigious al-Azar Madrasa in Cairo. The British subjugation of India had driven some Hindus, Sikhs and Muslims into a defensive posture that could easily segue into violence.

With the transformation of manufacturing came a portentous technological development: the creation of modern weaponry. The new guns and shells developed by William Armstrong, Claude Minié and Henry Shrapnel made it easy for Europeans to keep their colonial subjects in line. They were initially unwilling to use these new machine guns against their fellow Europeans but by 1851 Minié ball-firing rifles had been issued to British troops overseas.[120] When they were used the following year against Bantu tribesmen, marksmen found that they could pick off the Bantu at a distance of 1,300 yards without having to see the devastating consequences of their action.[121] This distance caused a dulling of the innate reluctance to kill at close quarters. In the early 1890s, during an encounter between the German East Africa Company and the Hehe tribesmen, an officer and a soldier killed around a thousand natives with two machine guns.[122] In 1898 at the Battle of Omdurman in the Sudan, a mere six Maxim guns firing at 600 shots a minute mowed down thousands of the Mahdi's followers. 'It was not a battle, but an execution,' an onlooker reported. 'The bodies were not in heaps . . . but . . . spread evenly over acres and acres.'[123]

The new secular ethos was quickly able to adapt to this horrific violence. It certainly did not share the universalist outlook promoted by some religious traditions that had helped people cultivate a reverence for the sanctity of all human beings. At a conference in The Hague that debated the legality of these weapons the following year, Sir John Ardagh explained that 'Civilised man is much more susceptible to injury than savages . . . The savage, like the tiger, is not so impressionable, and will go on fighting even when desperately wounded.'[124] As late as 1927, US Army Captain Elbridge Colby could argue that 'The real essence of the matter is that devastation and annihilation is the principal method of warfare that savage tribes know.' It was a mistake to allow 'excessive humanitarian ideas' to inhibit the use of superior firepower. A commander who gives in to this misplaced compassion 'is simply being unkind to his own people'. If a few 'non-combatants' were killed, 'the loss of life is probably far less than might have been sustained in prolonged operations of a more polite character. The *inhuman* act thus becomes *actually humane*.'[125] The pervasive view that ethnic difference rendered other groups not quite human had resulted in a casual acceptance of the mass slaughter that mechanised arms had made possible. An age of unimagined violence was dawning.

Industrialisation also gave birth to the nation state.[126] Agrarian empires had lacked the technology to impose a uniform culture; the borders and territorial reach of pre-modern kingdoms could only be loosely defined and the monarch's authority enforced in a series of overlapping loyalties.[127] But during the nineteenth century, Europe was reconfigured into clearly defined states ruled by a central government.[128] Industrialised society required standardised literacy, a shared language, and the unified control of human resources. Even if they spoke a different language from the ruler, subjects now belonged to an integrated 'nation', an 'imaginary community' of people who were encouraged to feel a deep connection with persons they knew nothing about.[129]

Religiously organised agrarian societies had often persecuted 'heretics'; in the secularised nation state, it was 'minorities' who had either to assimilate or disappear. In 1807 Jefferson had instructed his Secretary of War that the Native Americans were 'backward peoples' who must either be 'exterminated' or driven 'beyond our reach' to the other side of the Mississippi 'with the beasts of the forest'.[130] In 1806, Napoleon made Jews full citizens of France, yet two years later he issued the 'Infamous Decrees' ordering them to take French names, privatise their faith and ensure that at least one in every three marriages per family was with a gentile.[131] This forcible integration was regarded as progress. Surely, argued the British philosopher John Stuart Mill (1806–73), it was better for a Breton to accept French citizenship 'than to sulk on his own rocks, the half-savage remnant of past times, revolving in his own little mental orbit, without participation or interest in the general movement of the world'.[132] But the English historian Lord Acton (1834–1902) deplored the notion of nationality, fearing that the 'fictitious' general will of the people that it promoted would crush 'all natural rights and all established liberties for the purpose of vindicating itself'.[133] He could see that the desire to preserve the nation might become an absolute used to justify the most inhumane policies. Even worse:

> By making the State and the nation commensurate with each other in theory,
> [nationality] reduces practically to a subject condition all other nationalities
> that may be within the boundary . . . According, therefore, to the degree
> of humanity and civilization in that dominant body which claims all the rights
> of the community, the inferior races are exterminated or reduced to servi-
> tude, or put in a condition of dependence.[134]

His reservations about nationalism would prove to be all too well grounded.

The new nation state laboured under a fundamental contradiction: the *state* (the governmental apparatus) was supposed to be secular, but the *nation* ('the people') aroused quasi-religious emotions.[135] In 1807–08, while Napoleon was conquering Prussia, the German philosopher Johann Gottlieb Fichte had delivered a series of lectures in Berlin, looking forward to the time when the forty-one separate German principalities would become a unified nation state. The Fatherland, he claimed, was a manifestation of the divine, the repository of the spiritual essence of the *Volk* and, therefore, eternal. Germans must be ready to die for the nation, which alone gave human beings the immortality they craved because it had existed since the dawn of time and would continue after their death.[136] Early modern philos- ophers, such as Hobbes, had called for a strong state to restrain the violence of Europe, which, they believed, had been solely inspired by 'religion'. Yet in France, the nation had been evoked to mobilise all citizens for war and Fichte now encouraged Germans to fight French imperialism for the sake of the Fatherland. The *state* had been devised to contain violence but the *nation* was now being used to release it.

If we can define the sacred as something for which one is prepared to die, the nation had certainly become an embodiment of the divine, a supreme value. Hence national mythology would encourage cohesion, solidarity and loyalty within the confines of the nation. But it had yet to develop the 'concern for everybody' that had been such an important ideal in many of the spiritual traditions associated with religion. The national mythos would not encourage citizens to extend their sympathy to the ends of the earth, to love the stranger in their midst, be loyal even to their enemies, to wish happiness for all beings, and to become aware of the world's pain. True, this universal empathy had rarely affected the violence of the warrior aris- tocracy, but it had at least offered an alternative and a continuing challenge. Now that religion was being privatised, there was no 'international' ethos to counter the growing structural and military violence to which weaker nations were increasingly subjected. Secular nationalism seemed to regard

the foreigner as fair game for exploitation and mass slaughter, especially if
he or she belonged to a different ethnic group.

In America, the colonies and, later, the states had lacked the manpower to
maintain productivity so by 1800, between ten and fifteen million African
slaves had been forcibly transported to North America.[137] They were subdued
brutally: slaves were repeatedly reminded of their racial inferiority, their
families were broken up and they were subjected to hard labour, flogging
and mutilation. None of this seemed to bother the Founders, who had so
proudly asserted that 'all men are created equal' and 'endowed by their
Creator with certain inalienable rights'. Those who would object did so by
invoking not Enlightenment principles but Christian morals. In the Northern
states, Christian abolitionists condemned slavery as a blot on the nation and
in 1860, president-elect Abraham Lincoln (1809–65) announced that he
would prohibit it in any newly conquered territory. Almost at once South
Carolina seceded from the Union and it was clear that other Southern states
would follow.

The political issue – the preservation or dissolution of the Union – was
not in doubt, but to their dismay, both Northerners and Southerners found
that the clergy on whom they relied for ideological guidance could find no
common ground. Supporters of slavery had a host of biblical texts at their
command,[138] but in the absence of any explicit biblical condemnation of
slave-ownership, abolitionists could only appeal to the spirit of scripture.
The Southern preacher James Henry Thornhill argued that slavery was a
'good and merciful' way of organising labour,[139] while in New York Henry
Ward Beecher maintained that it was 'the most alarming and most fertile
cause of national sin'.[140] But the theological split did not coincide neatly
with the North/South divide. In Brooklyn, Henry van Dyke argued that
abolition was evil because it amounted to an 'utter rejection of the
Scriptures',[141] but Taylor Lewis, a professor of Greek and Oriental Studies
at New York University, retorted that van Dyke was not taking 'the vastly
changed condition of the world' sufficiently into account: it was a 'malignant
falsehood' to suggest that ancient institutions could be transplanted wholesale to the modern world.[142]

Lewis' nuanced approach to scripture was based on a scholarly understanding of ancient slavery that was anathema to evangelicals in the North,
who had led the abolitionist movement since its founding in the 1830s.[143]
They still approached scripture with the Enlightenment conviction that
human beings could discover the truth for themselves without authoritative

or expert guidance but now, to their dismay, they found that the Bible that had united the nation after the War of Independence was tearing it apart.[144] The evangelicals had failed to guide the nation at this moment of grave crisis. When, however, the political unity of the states foundered with the election of Abraham Lincoln and the secession of the Confederacy, the problem of slavery was settled by the battles of the Civil War (1861–65), not by the Bible.

This is not to say that wartime saw an eclipse of religious sentiment. On the contrary: though the American state would regard its effort as a principled defence of the Constitution, for the American nation, it was a conflict charged with religious conviction. The Civil War armies have been described as the most religiously motivated in American history.[145] Northerners and Southerners both believed that God was on their side and that they knew exactly what he was doing.[146] And when it was all over, Southerners would see their defeat as divine retribution, while Northern preachers would celebrate their victory as God's endorsement of their political arrangements. 'Republican institutions have been vindicated in this experience as they never were before,' Beecher exulted; 'God, I think, has said, by the voice of this event to all the nations of the earth: "Republican liberty, based upon true Christianity, is firm as the foundation of the globe."'[147] 'The Union will no more be thought of as a mere human compact,' exclaimed Howard Bushnell at the Yale Commencement of 1865: 'the sense of nationality becomes even a kind of religion.'[148]

But in fact the outcome had not been decided by God but by modern weaponry. Both sides were armed with Minié rifles, which made it impossible for either to charge – the traditional mode of engagement – without being vulnerable to the gun's substantial range and suffering horrific casualties.[149] But despite the appalling loss of life – 2,000 men could be lost in a single charge – generals continued to order their men to take the offensive.[150] As a result, in eight of the first twelve battles of the war, the Southern Confederacy lost 97,000 men, and in 1864 the Northern general Ulysses Grant lost 64,000 men in the first six months of his campaign against Robert E. Lee in the Wilderness.[151] The infantrymen caught on to this problem before the political or military leaders. Because one had to fire the Minié standing up, foot soldiers on both sides started to dig the trenches that would become the hallmark of early industrialised warfare and its protracted stalemates.[152] With both sides 'dug in', unable to advance decisively, modern wars would drag on for battle after battle.

After the war, the more reflective leaders, such as Oliver Wendell Holmes

Jr, Andrew Dixon White and John Dewey, retreated from the certainties of Enlightenment Protestantism.[153] In Europe too Enlightenment confidence had been undermined. In Germany during the late eighteenth and early nineteenth centuries, scholars had applied to scripture the modern historical-critical methodology used to study classical texts. This 'Higher Criticism' revealed that there was no univocal message in scripture; that Moses had not written the Pentateuch, which was composed of at least four different sources; that the miracle stories were little more than a literary trope; and that King David was not the author of the Psalms. A little later, Charles Lyell (1797–1875) argued that the earth's crust had not been shaped by God but by the incremental effects of wind and water; Charles Darwin (1809–82) put forward the hypothesis that *Homo sapiens* had evolved from the same proto-ape as the chimpanzee; and studies revealed that the revered philosopher Immanuel Kant had actually undercut the entire Enlightenment project by maintaining that our ways of thinking bear no relation to objective reality.

In Europe the rising tide of unbelief was born not merely from scepticism but from a hunger for radical social and political change. The Germans had been enthralled by the French Revolution but the social and political situation in their country ruled out anything similar; it seemed better to try to change the way people thought rather than to resort to violence. By the 1830s, a radical cadre of intellectuals had emerged who were theologically literate, were particularly incensed by the social privileges of the clergy, and saw the Lutheran Church as a bastion of conservatism. As part of the corrupt Old Regime, they argued, the churches had to go, together with the God who had supported the system. Ludwig Feuerbach's atheistic statement *The Essence of Christianity* (1841) was avidly read as a revolutionary as well as a theological tract.[154]

In the United States, however, the urban elite had been appalled by the violence of the French Revolution and used Christianity to promote the social reform that would hold such turbulence at bay. Lyell's revelations had caused a brief panic but most Americans remained convinced by Newton's vision of a design in the universe that proved the existence of an intelligent, benign Creator. These more liberal Christians were open to the Higher Criticism and willing to 'christen' Darwinism, largely because they had not yet fully absorbed its implications. Evolution was not yet the bogey in America that it would become during the 1920s. At this point, the liberal elite believed that God had been at work in the process of natural selection and that humanity was gradually evolving towards spiritual perfection.[155]

But after the Civil War, demoralised by their failure to resolve the slavery question, many of the evangelicals withdrew from public life, realising that they had marginalised themselves politically.[156] Their religion thus became separate from their politics, a private affair – just as the Founders had hoped. Instead of bringing a Christian voice to the great questions of the day, they turned inwards and, perhaps because the Bible had seemed to fail them in the nation's darkest hour, they became preoccupied with the minutiae of biblical orthodoxy. That retreat was in some ways a positive development. Evangelicals were still staunchly anti-Catholic and their withdrawal made it easier for Catholic immigrants to be accepted into the American nation, but it also deprived that nation of salutary criticism. Before the war, preachers had concentrated on the legitimacy of slavery as an institution but had neglected the issue of race. Tragically they would remain unable to bring the Gospel to bear on this major American problem. For a hundred years after the abolition of slavery, African Americans in the South would continue to suffer segregation, discrimination and routine terrorism at the hands of white supremacist mobs, which the local authorities did little to suppress.[157]

Shaken by the catastrophe of the Civil War, Americans dismantled their military. Europeans meanwhile came to believe that they had discovered a more civilised and sustainable mode of warfare.[158] Their model for this supposedly efficient warfare was the Prussian chancellor Otto von Bismarck (1815–98) who had invested heavily in railways and telegraph systems and issued his army with the new needle-guns and steel cannon. In three relatively short, bloodless but spectacularly successful wars against states that did not have this advanced technology – the Danish War (1864), the Austro-Prussian War (1866), and the Franco-Prussian War (1870) – Bismarck created a united Germany. Fired by their national myths, the nation states of Europe now embarked on an arms race, each convinced that they too could fight their way to a unique and glorious destiny. The British writer I. F. Clarke has shown that between 1871 and 1914 not a single year passed in which a novel or short story about a future catastrophic conflict did not appear in a European country.[159] The 'Next Great War' was invariably imagined as a terrible but inevitable ordeal, after which the nation would rise to enhanced life. But this would not be as easy as they imagined. What each power failed to reckon was that when all nations had the same new weapons, none would have an advantage and that Bismarck's victories were, therefore, not replicable.

As Lord Acton had predicted, this aggressive nationalism made life even more problematic for minorities. In the nation state, Jews increasingly appeared chronically rootless and cosmopolitan. There were pogroms in Russia, condoned and even orchestrated by the government;[160] in Germany anti-Semitic parties began to emerge in the 1880s; and in 1893 Captain Alfred Dreyfus, the only Jewish officer on the French General Staff, was convicted on false evidence of transmitting secrets to Germany. Many were convinced that Dreyfus was part of an international Jewish conspiracy that was plotting to weaken France. The new anti-Semitism drew on centuries of Christian prejudice but gave it a scientific rationale.[161] Anti-Semites claimed that Jews did not fit the biological and genetic profile of the *Volk* and some argued that they should be eliminated, in the same way as modern medicine cut out a cancer.

It was, perhaps, inevitable that, correctly anticipating an anti-Semitic catastrophe, some Jews would develop their own national mythology. Loosely based on the Bible, Zionism campaigned for a safe haven for Jews in their ancestral land, but Zionists also drew on varied currents of modern thought – Marxism, secularism, capitalism and colonialism. Some wanted to build a socialist utopia in the Land of Israel. The earliest and most vociferous Zionists were atheists who were convinced that religious Judaism had made Jews passive in the face of persecution: they horrified Orthodox Jews, who insisted that only the Messiah could lead Jews back to the Promised Land. But like most forms of nationalism Zionism had a religiosity of its own. Zionists who settled in agricultural colonies in Palestine were called *chalutzim,* a term with biblical connotations of salvation, liberation and rescue; they described their agricultural work as *avodah,* which in the Bible had referred to temple worship; and their migration to Palestine was *aliyah,* a spiritual 'ascent'.[162] Their slogan, however, was 'A land without a people for a people without a land'.[163] Like other European colonists, they believed that an endangered people had a natural right to settle in 'empty' land. But the land was not empty. Palestinians had their own dreams of national independence and when the Zionists finally persuaded the international community to create the State of Israel in 1948, the Palestinians became a rootless, endangered people without a land of their own in a world that now defined itself by nationality.

The First World War (1914–18) destroyed a generation of young men, yet many Europeans initially embraced it with an enthusiasm that shows how difficult it is to resist those emotions long activated by religion and now by nationalism, the new faith of the secular age. In August 1914, the cities of Europe were swept up in a festival atmosphere, which, like the rituals of the French Revolution, made the 'imaginary community' of the nation an incarnate reality. Total strangers gazed enraptured into each other's eyes; estranged friends embraced, feeling a luminous cohesion that defied rational explanation. The euphoria has been dismissed as an outbreak of communal madness, but those who experienced it said that it was the 'most deeply-lived' event of their lives. It has also been called an 'escape from modernity' since it sprang from a profound discontent with industrialised society, in which people were defined and classified by their function and everything was subordinated to a purely material end.[164] The declaration of war seemed a summons to the nobility of altruism and self-sacrifice that gave life meaning.

'All differences of class, rank and language were flooded over at that moment by the rushing feeling of fraternity,' the Austrian writer Stefan Zweig recalled. Everyone 'had been incorporated into the mass, he was a part of the people, and his person, his hitherto unnoticed person, had been given meaning . . . Each one was called upon to cast his infinitesimal self into the glowing mass and there to be purified of all selfishness.'[165] There was a yearning to cast aside an identity that felt too lonely, narrow and confining and to extricate onself from the privacy imposed by modernity.[166] An individual 'was no longer the isolated person of former times', said Zweig.[167] 'No more are we what we had been so long: alone,' declared Marianne Weber.[168] A new era seemed to have begun. 'People realised that they *were* equal,' remembered Rudolf Binding. 'No one wished to count for more than anyone else . . . It was like a rebirth.'[169] It 'transported the body as well as the soul into a trance-like, enormously enhanced love of life and existence,' recalled Carl Zuckmayer, 'a joy of participation, of living-along-with, a feeling, even, of grace'.[170] The triviality of the 'petty, aimless lounging life of peacetime is done with', Franz Schauwecker exulted.[171] For the first time, said Conrad Haenisch, a lifelong critic of German capitalism, he could join 'with a full heart, a clean conscience, and without a sense of treason in the sweeping, stormy song: Deutschland, Deutschland über alles'.[172]

In the trenches, however, volunteers discovered that far from escaping industrialisation, they were entirely dominated by it. Like a sinister religious revelation, the war laid bare the material, technological and mechanical reality that twentieth-century civilisation concealed.[173] 'Everything becomes machinelike,' one soldier wrote; 'one might almost term the war an industry of professionalised human slaughter.'[174] It is a telling indictment of the loneliness and segmentation of modern society that many of these soldiers never forgot the profound sense of community they experienced in the trenches. 'There enwrapped us, never to be lost, the sudden comradeship of the ranks,' T. E. Lawrence recalled.[175] One of Simone de Beauvoir's professors 'discovered the joys of comradeship which overcame all social barriers' and determined never again to submit to 'the segregation which in civil life separates young middle-class men from working chaps . . . something he felt like a personal mutilation'.[176] Many found that they could not even hate the invisible enemy and were shocked when they finally saw the people they had been shelling for months. 'They were showing themselves to us as they really were, men and soldiers like us, in uniform like us,' an Italian soldier explained.[177]

This secular war for the nation had given some of the participants experiences associated with the religious traditions: an *ekstasis*, a sense of liberation, freedom, equanimity, community and a profound relationship with other human beings, even the enemy. Yet the First World War heralded a century of unprecedented slaughter and genocide that was not inspired by religion as people had come to know it, but by an equally commanding notion of the sacred: men fought for power, glory, scarce resources and, above all, for their nation.

RELIGION FIGHTS BACK

During the twentieth century, there would be many attempts to resist the modern state's banishment of religion to the private sphere. To committed secularists, these religious efforts seemed like so many attempts to turn the clock back, but in fact all were modern movements that could have flourished only in our own time. Indeed, some commentators have seen them as postmodern, since they represented a widespread dissatisfaction with many of the canons of modernity. Whatever the philosophers, pundits or politicians claimed, people all over the world expressed a wish to see religion playing a more central role in public life. This type of religiosity is often called 'fundamentalism' – an unsatisfactory term because it does not translate easily into other languages and suggests a monolithic phenomenon. In fact, though these movements share certain family resemblances, each has its own focus and trigger. In almost every region where a secular government has been established, a religious counter-cultural protest has developed as well, similar to the Muslim and Hindu reform movements that had emerged in British-controlled India. The attempt to confine religion to the individual conscience had originated in the West as part of Western modernisation but to others it made no sense. Indeed, many would find the expectation unnatural, reductive and even damaging.

As I have written elsewhere in detail, fundamentalism, be it Jewish, Christian or Muslim, is not in itself a violent phenomenon.[1] Only a tiny proportion of fundamentalists commit acts of terror; most are simply trying to live a devout life in a world that seems increasingly hostile to faith, and nearly all begin with what is perceived as an assault on them by the secular, liberal establishment. These movements tend to follow a basic pattern: first they retreat from mainstream society to create an enclave of authentic faith, rather as the Deobandis did in the subcontinent; at a later stage, some – but by no means all – engage in a counter-offensive to 'convert' the broader society. Every single one of the movements I have studied is rooted in fear – in the conviction that modern society is out to destroy their faith. This is not simply, or even mainly, paranoid. Fundamentalism first became a force in Jewish life, for example, after the Holocaust, Hitler's attempt to exterminate European Jewry. Moreover, we have seen that in the past when people fear annihilation, their horizons tend to shrink and they may lash out violently – though most 'fundamentalists' have confined their antagonism to rhetoric or nonviolent political activity. But it will be our concern to consider the reasons why those exceptional cases turn out as they do.

We can learn a great deal about fundamentalism generally from a crisis in one of the first of these movements, which developed in the United States during and immediately after the First World War. The term itself was coined in the 1920s by American Protestants who resolved to return to the 'fundamentals' of Christianity. Their retreat from public life after the Civil War had narrowed and, perhaps, distorted their vision. Instead of engaging as before with such issues as racial or economic inequality, they focused on biblical literalism, convinced that every single assertion of scripture was literally true. And so their enemy was no longer social injustice but the German Higher Criticism of the Bible, which had been embraced by the more liberal American Christians who were still attempting to bring the Gospel to bear on social problems. For all the claims that fundamentalisms make of a return to basics, however, these movements are highly innovative. Before the sixteenth century, for instance, Christians had always been encouraged to read scripture allegorically; even Calvin did not believe that the first chapter of Genesis was a factual account of the origins of life and he took severely to task those 'frantic persons' who believed that it was.[2] The new fundamentalist outlook required the wholesale denial of glaring discrepancies in scripture itself. Closed to any alternative and coherent only in its own terms, biblical inerrancy created a shuttered mindset born of great anxiety. 'Religion has to fight for its life against a large class of scientific men,' explained Charles Hodge, who formulated this dogma in 1874.[3] This embattled preoccupation with the status of the biblical text reflected a wider Christian concern about the nature of religious authority. Just four years earlier, the First Vatican Council (1870) had promulgated the new – and highly controversial – doctrine of papal infallibility. At a time when modernity was demolishing old truths and leaving crucial questions unanswered, there was a yearning for absolute certainty.

All types of fundamentalisms are often preoccupied by the horror of modern warfare and violence. The shocking slaughter in Europe during the First World War could only be the beginning of the end, the evangelicals concluded; these times of unprecedented carnage must be the battles fore-told in the Book of Revelation. There was a deep concern about the central-isation of modern society and anything approaching world rule. In the new League of Nations, the evangelicals saw the revival of the Roman empire predicted in Revelation, the abode of Antichrist.[4] Fundamentalists now saw themselves grappling with satanic forces that would shortly destroy the world. Their spirituality was defensive and filled with a paranoid terror of the sinister influence of the Catholic minority; they even described American democracy as the 'most devilish rule this world has ever seen'.[5] The American fundamentalists' chilling scenario of the End Time, with its wars, bloodshed and slaughter, is symptomatic of a deep-rooted distress that cannot be assuaged by cool, rational analysis. In less stable countries, it would be all too easy for a similar malaise, despair and fear to erupt in physical violence.

Their horrified recoil from the violence of the First World War also led American fundamentalists to veto modern science. They became obsessed with evolutionary theory. There was a widespread belief that German wartime atrocities were the result of the nation's devotion to Darwinian social theory, according to which existence was a brutal godless struggle in which only the strongest should survive. This was, of course, a vulgar distortion of Darwin's hypothesis but at a time when people were trying to make sense of the bloodiest war in human history, evolution seemed to symbolise every-thing that was most ruthless in modern life. These ideas were particularly disturbing to small-town Americans who felt that their culture was being taken over by the secularist elite – almost as though they were being colo-nised by a foreign power. This anxiety came to a head in the famous Scopes Trial of 1925 in Dayton, Tennessee, when the fundamentalists, represented by the Democratic politician William Jennings Bryan, tried to defend the state legislature's prohibition of the teaching of evolution in the public schools. They were opposed by the rationalist campaigner Clarence Darrow, supported by the newly founded American Civil Liberties Union.[6] Even though the state law was upheld, Bryan's bumbling performance under Darrow's sharp interrogation thoroughly discredited the fundamentalists' cause.

Their response to this humiliation is instructive. The press mounted a virulent campaign exposing Bryan and his fundamentalist supporters as hopeless anachronisms. Fundamentalists had no place in modern society, argued the journalist H. L. Mencken: 'They are everywhere where learning is too heavy a burden for human minds to carry, even the vague, pathetic learning on tap in the little red schoolhouses.' He mocked Dayton as a 'one-horse, Tennessee village' and its citizens as the 'gaping primates of the upland valleys'.[7] Yet whenever a fundamentalist movement is attacked, either with violence or in a media campaign, it almost invariably becomes more extreme. It shows malcontents that their fear is well grounded: the secular world is *really* out to destroy them. Before the Scopes Trial, not even Hodge had believed that Genesis was scientifically sound in every detail but afterwards, 'creation science' became the rallying cry of the fundamentalist movement. Before Dayton, some leading fundamentalists still engaged in social work with people on the left; afterwards, they swung to the far right, retreating altogether from the mainstream and creating their own churches, colleges, broadcasting stations and publishing houses. They grew and grew below the mainstream cultural radar. Once they became aware of their considerable public support, in the late 1970s they would re-emerge from the margins with Jerry Falwell's Moral Majority.

American fundamentalism would ever after vie to be heard as a decisive voice in American politics – with notable success. It would not resort to violence, largely because American Protestants did not suffer as greatly as did, for example, the Muslims of the Middle East. Unlike the secular rulers of Egypt or Iran, the United States government did not confiscate their property, torture and assassinate their clergy, or violently dismantle their institutions. In America, secular modernity was a home-grown product, which was not imposed militarily from outside but had evolved organically over time, and when they arrived on the public scene in the late 1970s, American fundamentalists could use well-established democratic channels to make their point. Although American Protestant fundamentalism was not usually an agent of violence, it was, to a degree, a response to violence: the trauma of modern warfare and the psychological violence of the aggressive disdain of the secularist establishment. Both can distort a religious tradition in ways that reverberate far beyond the community of the faithful. Nevertheless, fundamentalism in America shares with other disaffected groups the sensibility of the colonised in its defiant self-assertion and determination to recover one's own identity and culture against a powerful 'other'.

Muslim fundamentalism, by contrast, has often – though again, not always – segued into physical aggression. This is not because Islam is constitutionally more prone to violence than Protestant Christianity but rather because Muslims had a much harsher introduction to modernity. Before the birth of the modern state in the crucible of colonialism, Islam had continued in many Muslim lands to operate as the organising principle of society. In 1920, after the First World War and the defeat of the Ottoman empire, Britain and France divided Ottoman territories into Western-style nation states and established mandates and protectorates there before granting these new countries independence. But the inherent contradictions of the nation state would be especially wrenching in the Muslim world, where there was no tradition of nationalism. The frontiers drawn up by the Europeans were so arbitrary that it was extremely difficult to create a national 'imaginary community'. In Iraq, for example, where Sunnis were a minority, the British appointed a Sunni ruler to govern both the Shiite majority and the Kurds in the north. In Lebanon, 50 per cent of the population was Muslim and naturally wanted close economic and political relations with their Arab neighbours, but the Christian government selected by the French preferred stronger ties with Europe. The partition of Palestine and the creation of the Jewish State of Israel by the United Nations in 1948 proved no less mischievous. It resulted in the forcible displacement of 750,000 Arab Palestinians, and those who remained found themselves living in a state that was hostile to them. There was the added complication that Israel was a secular state founded for adherents of one of the world's ancient religions. Yet for the first twenty years of its existence the Israeli leadership was aggressively secular, and the violence inflicted on the Palestinians, Israel's wars with its neighbours, and the Palestinian riposte were motivated not by religion but by secular nationalism.

The British partition of the Indian subcontinent into Hindu India and Muslim Pakistan in 1947 was similarly problematic, since both were established as secular states in the name of religion. The brutal process of partition caused the displacement of over seven million people and the deaths of a million others who were attempting to flee from one state to join their co-religionists in the other. In both India and Pakistan, vast numbers found themselves unable to speak the so-called national language. A particularly volatile situation was created in Kashmir, which despite its Muslim majority was given to India because it was ruled by a Hindu maharaja. That British decision is still contested and a similar arbitrariness was felt in the separation of eastern and western Pakistan by a thousand miles of Indian territory.

As they struggled for independence before partition, Hindus had engaged in an intense discussion about the legitimacy of fighting the British, shaped in large part by the *Bhagavad-gita,* a text that has deeply shaped the collective memory of India. Ahimsa was an important spiritual value in India, yet the *Gita* seemed to sanction violence. Mohandas (Mahatma) Gandhi (1869–1948), however, disagreed with this interpretation. He had been born into a vaishya family and had many Jain friends, who influenced his later attitudes. In 1914, after working for years as a lawyer in South Africa to oppose

discriminatory legislation against Indians, he had returned to India and
become interested in the issue of home rule, founding the Natal Indian
Congress party and developing his unique method of resisting colonial
oppression by non-resistance. Besides the Hindu religious tradition, he had
been influenced by Jesus' Sermon on the Mount, Tolstoy's *The Kingdom of
God is Within You*, Ruskin's 'Unto This Last' and Thoreau's *Civil Disobedience*.

Central to Gandhi's worldview was the insight, first developed in the
Upanishads, that all beings were manifestations of the Brahman. Since
everybody shared the same sacred core, violence went against the metaphysical bias of the entire universe. This deeply spiritual vision of the unity
of existence directly countered the aggressive separatism and chauvinism
of the nation state. Gandhi's peaceable refusal to obey the self-serving
obduracy of the British regime was based on three principles: ahimsa,
satyagraha (the 'soul force' that comes with the realisation of truth) and
swaraj ('self-rule'). In the *Gita*, Gandhi maintained, Arjuna's initial refusal
to fight had not been true ahimsa, because he still regarded himself as
different from his enemies and had not realised that they were all, friend
and foe alike, embodiments of the Brahman. Had Arjuna truly understood
that he and Duryodhana, the adversary he was about to fight, were ultimately
one, he would have acquired the 'soul force' that had the power to transform
an enemy's hatred into love.

But, as we have seen, the same texts and spiritual practices can lead to
entirely different courses of action. Others opposed this interpretation of
the *Gita*. The Hindu scholar Aurobindo Ghose (1872–1950) argued that
Krishna's validation of violence in the *Gita* was simply an acknowledgement
of life's grim reality. Yes, it would be nice to remain peacefully above the
fray, but until Gandhi's 'soul force' actually became an effective reality in
the world, the natural aggression inherent in both men and nations 'tram-
ples down, breaks, slaughters, burns, pollutes as we see it doing today'.
Gandhi might discover that he had caused as much destruction of life by
abjuring violence as those who had resorted to fighting.[8] Aurobindo was
voicing the view of Gandhi's critics, who thought that he closed his eyes
to the fact that the British response to his nonviolent campaigns actually
resulted in hideous bloodshed. But Aurobindo was also articulating the
eternal dilemma of Ashoka: is nonviolence feasible in the inescapably violent
world of politics?

Nevertheless, Gandhi saw his theory through to its ultimate conclusion.
Nonviolence meant not only loving your enemies, he maintained, but realising that they were not your enemies at all. He might hate the systemic

and military violence of colonial rule, but he could not allow himself to
hate the people who implemented it:

> Mine is not an exclusive love. I cannot love Moslems or Hindus and hate
> Englishmen. For if I love merely Hindus and Moslems because their ways
> are on the whole pleasing to me, I shall soon begin to hate them when their
> ways displease me, which they may well do [at] any moment. A love that is
> based on the goodness of those whom you love is a mercenary affair.[9]

Without reverence for the sanctity of every single human being and the
'equanimity' long seen in India as the pinnacle of the spiritual quest, 'politics bereft of religion', Gandhi believed, were a 'death-trap because they
kill the soul'.[10] Secular nationalism seems unable to cultivate a similarly
universal ideology, even though all parts of our globalised world are deeply
interconnected. Gandhi could not countenance Western secularism: 'To see
the universal and all-pervading Spirit of Truth face to face one must be able
to love the meanest creature as oneself,' he concluded in his autobiography.
Devotion to this Truth required one to be involved in every field of life; it
had brought him into politics, for 'those who say that religion has nothing
to do with politics do not know what religion means'.[11] Gandhi's last years
were darkened by the communal violence that had erupted during and after
partition. He was assassinated in 1948 by a radical nationalist who believed
that Gandhi had given too many concessions to the Muslims and had made
a large monetary donation to Pakistan.

As they forged their national identities in the peculiarly tense conditions
of India, Muslims and Hindus would both fall prey to the besetting sin of
secular nationalism: its inability to tolerate minorities. And because their
outlook was still infused with spirituality, this nationalist bias distorted their
traditional religious vision. As violence between Muslims and Hindus escalated in the 1920s, Dayananda's Arya Samaj became more militant.[12] At a
conference in 1927, it formed a military cadre, the Arya Vir Dal ('Troop of
Aryan Horses'). They declared that the new Aryan hero must develop the
virtues of the Kshatriya – courage, physical strength and, especially, profi-
ciency in the use of weapons. His principal duty was to defend the rights
of the Aryan nation against the Muslims and the British.[13] The Arya was
anxious not to be outdone by the Rashtriya Svayamsevak Sangh ('National
Volunteer Association'), usually referred to as RSS, founded in central India
three years earlier by Keshav B. Hedgewar. Where the Arya had applied the
British notion of 'religion' to 'Hinduism', RSS had fused traditional religious

ideals with Western nationalism. It was primarily a character-building organisation designed to develop an ethos of service, based on loyalty, discipline and a respect for the Hindu heritage, and appealed particularly to the urban middle classes. Its hero was the seventeenth-century warrior Shivaji who, empowered by his fidelity to traditional Hindu ritual as well as his organisational skills, had led a successful revolt against the Moghuls. He had managed to weld recruits from disparate peasant castes into a unified army and RSS vowed to do the same in British India.[14]

Thus a new religiosity was coming to birth in India, one that cultivated Hindu strength not by evoking ahimsa but by developing the traditional warrior ethos. But the fusion of the Kshatriya ideal with secular nationalism could be toxic. For RSS, Mother India was not a territorial entity but a living goddess. She had always been revered as a holy land and her seas, rivers and mountains regarded as sacred, but for centuries she had been desecrated by foreigners and would shortly be raped by partition. Traditionally, the Mother Goddess had embraced everyone, but with its new Western intolerance of minorities, RSS insisted that she could no longer admit Muslims or East Asian Buddhists.

Hedgewar was an activist rather than an intellectual, his thinking deeply influenced by V. D. Savarkar, a brilliant radical imprisoned by the British whose classic *Hindutva* ('Hinduness') had been smuggled out of prison and published in 1923. It defined the Hindu as a person who acknowledged the integrity of Greater India (which stretched from the Himalayas to Iran and Singapore) and revered the country not only as Fatherland, as other nationalists did, but also as Holy Land.[15] This fusion of religion and secular nationalism was potentially toxic. In Savarkar's books, the emerging Hindu national identity depended upon the exclusion of Islam: the whole complex history of India was reductively presented as a struggle to the death with Muslim imperialism. Even though Hindus had always been the majority population, they had been conditioned by centuries of imperial domination to see themselves as an embattled, endangered minority.[16] Like so many subject peoples, they had developed a history of grievance and humiliation, which can corrode a religious tradition and incline it towards violence. Some experienced their long oppression as a national disgrace. During the 1930s, M. S. Golwalkar, the second leader of the RSS, felt an affinity with the ideals of National Socialism, in part the product of Germany's humiliation by the Allies after the First World War. Foreigners in India had only two options, Golwalkar argued: 'The foreign races must lose their separate existence . . . or [they] may stay in the country, wholly subordinated to the Hindu Nation, claiming nothing, deserving no privileges, far less any preferential treatment – not even citizen's rights.'[17] Golwalkar praised the Germans for 'purging the country of the Semitic Races'; India, he believed, had much to learn from this Aryan 'Race pride'.[18]

The horror of partition could only inflame the history of grievance that was so dangerously poisoning relations between Muslims and Hindus. As the psychologist Sudhir Kakar has explained, for decades hundreds of thousands of Hindu and Muslim children have listened to tales of the violence of that time, which 'dwell on the fierceness of the implacable enemy. This is a primary channel through which historical enmity is transmitted from one generation or the next.'[19] It also created a rift between secularist and religious Hindus.[20] Secularists convinced themselves that such violence could never happen again. Many blamed the British for the tragedy; others regarded it merely as a terrifying aberration. Jawaharlal Nehru, India's first prime minister, believed that the industrialisation of the country and the spread of scientific rationalism and democracy would counter these communal passions.

But there was a disturbing portent of future trouble. In 1949 an image of Ram, incarnation of Vishnu and chief exemplar of Hindu virtue, was discovered in a building at the site of his mythological birthplace in Ayodhya on the eastern Gangetic plain. But this was also the site of a mosque said to have been established in 1528 by Babur, the first Moghul emperor.[21] Devout Hindus claimed that this representation of Ram had been placed there by God; Muslims, naturally, denied this. There were violent clashes and the district magistrate, a member of RSS, refused to remove the icon. Because the gods' effigies require regular worship, Hindus were henceforth permitted to enter the building for devotional chanting on the anniversary of the miraculous arrival of Ram's statue. Forty years later, this sacred geography would trump the scientific rationalism so confidently predicted by the secularists.

The founder of Pakistan, Muhammad Ali Jinnah (1876–1948), was an unabashed secularist who had simply wanted to create a state in which Muslims would not be defined or limited by their religious affiliation. But in fact the nation had been defined by Islam before it had even begun. This inevitably raised certain expectations, and from the beginning, while the government was still resolutely secularist, there was pressure to re-sacralise political life. The Deobandis became particularly powerful in Pakistan. They endorsed the modern system of territorial nationalism and secular democracy and offered free education to the poor in their madrasas at a time when the state school system was collapsing due to lack of funding. Their students would be isolated from mainstream secular life and schooled in the Deobandis' peculiarly rigid and intolerant form of Islam. To protect their Islamic lifestyle, the Deobandis also founded a political party, the JUI (Association of Ulema of Islam). By the late 1960s, having accumulated tens of thousands of students and alumni, they were in an excellent position to pressure the government to Islamise civil law and the banking system, thereby creating jobs for their ultra-religious graduates.

Quite different was the Jamaat-i-Islami, which had been established in India in 1941 to oppose the creation of a separate secular state. Jamaat had no madrasa base and did not cling to the past, as the Deobandis did, but developed an Islamic ideology influenced by the modern ideals of liberty and independence. Abul Ala Maududi (1903–79), its founder, argued that because God alone ruled human affairs, nothing else – 'be it a human being, a family, a class, or a group of people, or even the human race as a whole' – could claim sovereignty.[22] Therefore nobody was obliged to obey any mortal authority. Each generation had to fight the jahiliyyah of its day, as the Prophet had done, since jahili violence, greed and godlessness were an ever-present danger. Western secularism epitomised the modern jahiliyyah because it amounted to a rebellion against God's rule.[23] Islam, Maududi insisted, was not a Western-style 'religion', separate from politics; here he was in full agreement with Gandhi. Rather, Islam was a *din,* a whole way of life which had to include economic, social and political as well as ritualised activities:[24]

> The use of the word [din] categorically refutes the views of those who believe a prophet's message is principally aimed at ensuring worship of the one God, adherence to a set of beliefs, and observance of a few rituals. This also refutes the views of those who think that din has nothing to do with cultural, political, economic, legal, judicial, and other matters pertaining to this world.[25]

Muslims had been charged to reject the structural violence of the jahili state and implement economic justice, social harmony and political equality in public as well as private life, all based on a profound awareness of God (*taqwah*).

Before partition, Jamaat had concentrated on training its members to reform their own lives in the Greater Jihad; only by living an authentically Quranic life could they hope to inspire the people with a longing for Islamic government. But after partition, the movement split. Of its 625 members, 240 remained in India. Since only 11 per cent of the population of India was Muslim, Indian Jamaat could not hope to create an Islamic state; instead its members adopted a qualified appreciation of the moderate (as opposed to atheistic) secularism of the new state of India that forbade discrimination on the basis of religious belief. This, they declared, was a 'blessing' and a 'guarantee for a safe future for Islam in India'.[26] But in Pakistan, where there was the possibility of an Islamic state, Maududi and his 385 Jamaat disciples felt no such constraints. They became the most organised Pakistani political party, gained the support of the educated urban classes, and campaigned vigorously against the dictatorship of Ayub Khan (1958–69), who confiscated all clerical property, and the socialist regime of Zulfikar Ali Bhutto (1971–77), who used Islamic symbols and slogans to win popular support but in reality had nothing but contempt for religion.

Maududi, therefore, was still committed to the struggle (jihad) against jahili secularism, but he always interpreted jihad broadly in the traditional manner so that it did not simply mean 'holy war'; one could 'strive' to achieve God's sovereignty by peaceful political activities, such as writing books or working in education.[27] It is a mistake, therefore, to brand Pakistani Jamaat as fanatically intent on violence; the fact that the party went in two such different directions after partition shows that it had the flexibility to adapt to circumstances. Maududi would have nothing to do with revolutionary coups, assassinations or policies that stirred up hatred and conflict, and insisted that an Islamic state could put down firm roots only if ends and means were 'clean and commendable'.[28] The transition from a secular nation state to a truly Islamic society must, he would always maintain, be 'natural, evolutionary and peaceful'.[29]

But in Pakistan violence had become one of the chief ways of doing politics.[30] Leaders regularly came to power in military coups and in their ruthless suppression of any political opposition neither Khan nor Bhutto could be seen as an example of benign, peaceable secularism. So prevalent was violence becoming in Pakistani society that a group that abjured it had little hope of success. In an effort to gain popular support for Jamaat, Maududi agreed to lead a campaign against the so-called heretical Ahmadi sect in 1953 and wrote an inflammatory pamphlet, which sparked riots and put him in prison.[31] This, however, was an aberration. Maududi continued to denounce the violence of Pakistani politics and condemned the aggressive activities of Jamaat's affiliate IJT (Islami Jamiat-i-Taliban), the Society of Islamic Students, which organised strikes and demonstrations against Bhutto, paralysed the communication systems, disrupted urban commerce and educational establishments, and led violent confrontations with the police.

While other members of Jamaat succumbed to Pakistan's endemic violence, Maududi remained committed to achieving an Islamic state democratically. He repeatedly insisted that an Islamic state could not be a theocracy, because no group or individual had the right to rule in God's name. An Islamic government must be elected by the people for a fixed term; there must be universal adult franchise, regular elections, a multi-party system, an independent judiciary, and guaranteed human rights and civil liberties – a system not very different from the parliamentary democracy of Westminster.[32]

When Zia ul-Haq seized power in a coup in 1977, established a dictatorship, and announced that Pakistan would follow Shariah law, he drew heavily on Maududi's writings in his speeches. He also brought several senior Jamaat officials into his cabinet and employed thousands of Jamaat activists in the civil service, education and the army. Shariah courts were established and traditional Islamic penalties for theft, prostitution, adultery and the use of alcohol introduced. By this time, Maududi was in failing health and the current Jamaat leaders supported Zia's military regime, regarding it as a promising beginning. But Maududi had profound misgivings. How could a dictatorship, which usurped God's sovereignty and ruled with martial and structural violence, be truly Islamic? Shortly before his death, he penned a brief note to this effect:

> The implementation of Islamic laws alone cannot yield the positive result Islam really aims at . . . For, merely by dint of this announcement [of Islamic laws] you cannot kindle the hearts of the people with the light of faith, enlighten their minds with the teachings of Islam, and mould their habits and manners corresponding to the virtues of Islam.[33]

Future generations of Muslim activists would have done well to heed this lesson.

Western modernity had conferred two blessings in the places it was first conceived: political independence and technical innovation. But in the Middle East, modernity arrived as colonial subjugation and there was little potential for innovation, with the West so far ahead that Muslims could only imitate.[34] And the unwelcome changes, imposed as foreign imports from without, were uncongenially abrupt. A process that had taken centuries in Europe had to be effected in a matter of decades, superficially and often violently. The almost insuperable problems faced by modernisers had already become clear in the career of Muhammad Ali (1769–1849). He had become governor of Egypt after Napoleon's invasion and managed the monumental feat of dragging this backward Ottoman province into the modern world within a mere forty years. Yet he could do so only by ruthless coercion. Twenty-three thousand peasants died in the forced labour bands that improved Egypt's irrigation and communications. Thousands more were conscripted into the army; some cut off their fingers and even blinded themselves to avoid military service.[35] There could never be technological self-sufficiency since Muhammad Ali had to buy all his machinery, weapons and manufactured goods from Europe.[36] And there could be no independence: despite his achieving a degree of autonomy from the Ottomans, modernisation eventually led to Egypt's becoming a virtual British colony. Ismail Pasha (1803–95), Muhammad Ali's grandson, made the country too desirable to the Europeans: he had commissioned French engineers to construct the Suez Canal, built 900 miles of railways, irrigated over a million acres of hitherto uncultivable land, set up modern schools for both boys and girls, and transformed Cairo into an elegant modern city. In the process, he bankrupted the country, ultimately giving the British the pretext they needed in 1882 to establish a military occupation to protect the interests of shareholders.

Even when a degree of modernisation was achieved, the European colonial powers managed to snuff it out. Perhaps Muhammad Ali's greatest achievement had been the creation of the cotton industry, which promised to give Egypt a reliable economic base, until Lord Cromer, the first Consul-General of Egypt, put a brake on production, since Egyptian cotton damaged British interests. No friend to the emancipation of women – he was a founding member of the Anti-Women's Suffrage League in London – Cromer also scaled back Ismail's programmes to educate women and blocked them from entering the professions. Every benefaction was less than it seemed. In 1922 the British allowed Egypt a modicum of independence, with a new king, a parliamentary body and a liberal Western-style Constitution, but retained control of military and foreign policy. Between 1923 and 1930 there were three general elections, each won by the Wafd party which campaigned for reduced British presence in Egypt, but each time the British forced the elected government to resign.[37] In the same way, Europeans obstructed the development of democracy in Iran, where modernising clergy and intellectuals had led a successful revolution against the Qajar shah in 1906, demanding constitutional rule and representative government. But almost immediately the Russians helped the shah to close the new parliament (*majlis*) and during the 1920s, the British routinely rigged elections to prevent the majlis from nationalising the Iranian oil that fuelled their navy.[38]

The Muslims of the Middle East had, therefore, experienced the secular rule of the colonial powers as militarily and systemically violent. But things did not improve after they achieved independence in the twentieth century. As the Europeans dismantled their empires and left the region, they ceded power to the pre-colonial ruling classes which were so embedded in the old aristocratic ethos that they were incapable of modernisation. They were usually deposed in coups organised by reform-minded army officers, who were virtually the only commoners to receive a western-style education: Reza Khan in Iran (1921), Colonel Adib Shissak in Syria (1949) and Jamal Abd al-Nasser in Egypt (1952). Like Muhammad Ali, these reformers modernised rapidly, superficially, and even more violently than the Europeans. Used to barracks life and the following of orders without question, they cut down opposition ruthlessly and underestimated the complexities of modernisation.[39] Secularism did not come to their subjects as liberating and irenic. Instead, these secularising rulers effectually terrorised their subjects by tearing down familiar institutions, so that their world became unrecognisable.

Again, you could take religion out of the state but not out of the nation. The army officers wanted to secularise but found themselves ruling devout nations for whom a secularised Islam was a contradiction in terms.[40] Undeterred, these rulers declared war on the religious establishment. Following the aggressive methods of the French revolutionaries, Muhammad Ali had starved the clergy financially, taking away their tax exemption, confiscating the religiously endowed properties (*awqaf*) that were their principal source of income, and systematically robbing them of any shred of power.[41] For the Egyptian ulema, modernity was forever tainted by this ruthless assault and they became cowed and reactionary. Nasser changed tack and turned them into state officials. For centuries, the ulema's learned expertise had guided the people through the intricacies of Islamic law but they had also stood as a protective bulwark between the people and the systemic violence of the state. Now the people came to despise them as government lackeys. This deprived them of a responsible and expert religious authority that was aware of the complexity of the Islamic tradition. Self-appointed religious leaders and more simple-minded radicals would step into the breach, often with disastrous effect.[42]

Throughout the Muslim world, Mustafa Kemal Atatürk (1881–1938), founder of the modern republic of Turkey, seemed to personify the violence of secularism. After the First World War, he had managed to keep the British and French out of Anatolia, the Ottoman heartland, so Turkey had the great advantage of avoiding colonisation. Determined to deprive Islam of all legal, political and economic influence, Atatürk is often admired in the West as an enlightened Muslim leader.[43] But in fact he was a dictator who hated Islam, which he described as a 'putrefied corpse'.[44] He proceeded in the usual belligerent manner to outlaw the Sufi orders, seize their properties, shut down the madrasas, and appropriate the awqaf. Most importantly, he abolished Shariah law, replacing it with a legal code essentially adopted from Switzerland that was meaningless to most of the population.[45] Finally, in 1925, Atatürk declared the caliphate null and void. It had long been a dead letter politically but had symbolised the unity of the ummah and its link with the Prophet; at this bleak moment in their history, Sunni Muslims everywhere experienced its loss as a spiritual and cultural trauma. Western approval of Atatürk led many to believe that the West sought to destroy Islam itself.

In order to control the rising merchant class, the last Ottoman sultans had systematically deported or killed their Greek and Armenian subjects, who constituted about 90 per cent of the bourgeoisie. In 1908, the Young Turks, a party of modernisers, deposed Sultan Abdul Hamid II in a coup. They had absorbed the anti-religious positivism of such Western thinkers as August Comte (1798–1857) as well as the new 'scientific' racism, an outgrowth of the Age of Reason that came into good use in the Age of Empire. During the First World War, in order to create a purely Turkic state, the Young Turks ordered the deportation and 'resettlement' of Armenian Christians from the empire on the pretext that they were conniving with the enemy. This led to the first genocide of the twentieth century, committed not by religious fanatics but by avowed secularists. Over a million Armenians were slaughtered: men and youths were killed where they stood while women, children and the elderly were driven into the desert where they were raped, shot, starved, poisoned, suffocated or burned to death.[46] 'I came into this world a Turk,' declared the physician Mehmet Resid, the 'Executioner Governor'. 'Armenian traitors had found a niche for themselves in the bosom of the fatherland; they were dangerous microbes. Isn't it a duty of a doctor to destroy these microbes?'[47]

When Atatürk came to power, he completed this racial purge. For centuries Greeks and Turks had dwelt together on both sides of the Aegean. Atatürk now partitioned the region and organised a massive exchange of populations. Greek-speaking Christians living in what is now Turkey were deported to what would become Greece, while Turkish-speaking Muslims living in Greece were sent the other way. For many in the Muslim world, therefore, Western secularism and nationalism would be forever associated with ethnic cleansing, virulent intolerance, and the violent destruction of precious Islamic institutions.

In Iran, Reza Khan courted the Westernised upper and middle classes but took no interest in the peasant masses, who therefore relied more than ever on the ulema. Two nations were developing in the country, one modernised, the other excluded from the benefits of modernity and cruelly deprived of the religious traditions that gave their life meaning. Determined to base the state's identity on ancient Persian culture rather than Islam, Reza summarily outlawed the Ashura mourning rituals for Husain, forbade Iranians to make the hajj, and drastically curtailed the scope of the Shariah courts. When Ayatollah Modarris objected, he was imprisoned and executed.[48] In 1928, Reza issued the Laws on the Uniformity of Dress, and with their bayonets his soldiers tore off the women's veils and ripped them to pieces in the street.[49] On Ashura 1929, the police surrounded the prestigious Fayziyah Madrasa in Qum and when the students spilled out after their classes, they were stripped of their traditional clothes and forced into Western garb. In 1935, the police were ordered to open fire on a crowd who had staged a peaceful demonstration against the Dress Laws in the holy shrine of the Eighth Imam in Mashhad and killed hundreds of unarmed Iranians.[50] In the West, the secular nation state had been set up to curb the violence of religion; for many thousands of people in the Middle East, secular nationalism seemed a bloodthirsty, destructive force that deprived them of the spiritual support that had been their mainstay.

The Middle East had thus been brutally initiated into the new system of oppression and violence that had come into being during the colonial period. These former provinces of the mighty Ottoman empire had been aggressively reduced by the colonialists almost overnight to a dependent bloc, their laws replaced by foreign codes, their age-old rituals abolished, and their clergy executed, impoverished and publicly humiliated. Surrounded by modern buildings, institutions and Western-style street layouts, people no longer felt at home in their own countries. The effect of their transformation has been compared to watching a beloved friend slowly disfigured before one's eyes by mortal sickness. Egypt, always a leader in the Arab world, had had a particularly difficult transition to modernity with a much longer period of direct Western rule than many other Middle Eastern countries. This persistent foreign presence and the lack of spiritual and moral leadership had created a dangerous malaise in the country and a corrosive sense of humiliation, which neither the British nor the new Egyptian government seemed willing to address. Some reformers belonging to the traditional Egyptian elite tried to counter this growing alienation. Muhammad Abduh (1849–1905), Sheikh of Al-Azhar, suggested that modern legal and constitutional arrangements should be linked to traditional Islamic norms that would make them comprehensible. As it was, the people were so bewildered by the secular legal system that Egypt was effectively becoming a country without law.[51] Lord Cromer, however, who regarded the social system of Islam as 'politically and socially moribund', would have none of it.[52] In the same vein, Rashid Rida (1865–1935), Abdu's biographer, wanted to establish a college where students would be introduced to modern jurisprudence, sociology and science at the same time as they studied Islamic law, so that it might be possible one day to modernise the Shariah without diluting it and to formulate laws based on authentic Muslim tradition instead of a foreign ideology.[53]

But these reformers failed to inspire disciples who could carry their ideas forward. Far more successful was Hassan al-Banna (1906–49), founder of the Muslim Brotherhood and one of the more positive 'freelances' who would step into the spiritual leadership vacuum created by the modernisers.[54] A schoolteacher, who had studied modern science, Banna knew that modernisation was essential but believed that, because Egyptians were deeply religious, it could succeed only if accompanied by a spiritual refor- mation. Their own cultural traditions would serve them better than alien ideologies that they could never make fully their own. Banna and his friends had been shocked and saddened by the political and social confusion in Egypt and the stark contrast between the luxurious homes of the British and the hovels of the Egyptian workers in the Canal Zone. One night in March 1928, six of his students begged Banna to take action, eloquently articulating the inchoate distress experienced by so many:

> We know not the practical way to reach the glory of Islam and to serve the welfare of the Muslims. We are weary of this life of humiliation and restric- tion. So we see that the Arabs and the Muslims have no status and no dignity. They are no more than mere hirelings belonging to foreigners . . . We are unable to perceive the road to action as you perceive it, or to know the path to the service of the fatherland, the religion and the *ummah*.[55]

That very night Banna created the Society of Muslim Brothers, which inaugurated a grassroots reformation of Muslim society.

The Society clearly answered an urgent need, because it would become one of the most powerful players in Egyptian politics. By the time of Banna's assassination in 1949, there were 2,000 branches throughout Egypt, and the Brotherhood was the only Egyptian organisation that represented every social group – civil servants, students, urban workers and peasants.[56] The Society was not a militant organisation but sought simply to bring modern institutions to the Egyptian public in a familiar Islamic setting. The Brothers built schools for girls and boys beside the mosque and founded the Rovers, a scout movement that became the most popular youth group in the country; they set up night schools for workers and tutorial colleges to prepare students for the civil service examinations; they built clinics and hospitals in the rural areas; and they involved the Rovers in improving sanitation and health education in the poorer districts. The Society also set up trades unions that acquainted workers with their rights; in the factories where the Brotherhood was a presence, they earned a just wage, had health insurance and paid holidays, and could pray in the company's mosque. Banna's counter-culture thus proved that, far from being some obsolete vestige of another era, Islam could become an effective modernising force as well as promoting spiritual vitality. But the Brotherhood's success would prove double-edged, for it called attention to the government's neglect of education and labour conditions. Banna's Society thus came to be perceived as not a help but a grave threat to the regime.

The Society was not perfect: it tended to be anti-intellectual, its pronouncements often defensive and self-righteous, its view of the West distorted by the colonial experience, and its leaders intolerant of dissent. Most seriously, it had developed a terrorist wing. After the creation of the State of Israel, the plight of the Palestinian refugees became a disturbing symbol of Muslims' impotence in the modern world. For some, violence seemed the only way forward. Anwar Sadat, future president of Egypt, founded a 'murder society' to attack the British in the Canal Zone.[57] Other paramilitary groups were attached to the palace and the Wafd, and so it was perhaps inevitable that some Brothers should form the 'Secret Apparatus' (al-jihaz al-sirri). Numbering only about a thousand, the Apparatus was so clandestine that even most of the Brothers had never heard of it.[58] Banna denounced the Apparatus but could not control it and eventually it would both taint and endanger the Society.[59] When the Apparatus assassinated Prime Minister Muhammad al-Nuqraishi on 28 December 1948, the Society condemned the atrocity in the strongest terms. But the government seized this opportunity to suppress it. On 12 February 1949, almost certainly at the behest of the new prime minister, Banna was gunned down in the street.

When Nasser seized power in 1952, the Society had regrouped but was deeply divided. In the early days while he was still unpopular, Nasser courted the Brotherhood, even though he was a committed secularist and an ally of the Soviet Union. When it became clear that Nasser had no intention of creating an Islamic state, however, a member of the Apparatus shot him during a rally. Nasser survived and his courage under attack did wonders for his popularity. He now felt able to move against the Society and by the end of 1954 over a thousand Brothers had been brought to trial and uncounted others, many of whom had committed no greater offence than distributing leaflets, would never have even a day in court but languished in prison without charge for fifteen years. After Nasser became a hero in the larger Arab world by defying the West during the Suez Crisis of 1956, he intensified his efforts to secularise the country. But this state violence simply spawned a more extreme form of Islam that called for armed opposition to the regime.

Religious extremism often develops in a symbiotic relationship with a virulently aggressive secularism. One of the Brothers detained in 1954 was Sayyid Qutb (1906–66), the Society's chief propagandist.[60] As a young man, Qutb had felt no conflict between his faith and secular politics, but he had been alienated by the ruthless policies of the British and shocked by the racial prejudice he experienced during a visit to the United States. Still, his views had remained moderate and tentative; what radicalised him was the violence of Nasser's prison. Qutb was himself tortured, and was devastated to see twenty prisoners slaughtered in a single incident. Dozens more were tortured and executed – not by foreigners but by their own people. Secularism no longer seemed benign but cruel, aggressive and immoral. In prison, Qutb took Maududi's ideas a step further. When he heard Nasser vowing to privatise Islam on the Western model and observed the unfolding horror of his prison life, Qutb came to believe that even a so-called Muslim ruler could be as violently jahili as any Western power. Like others terrorised by violence and injustice, Qutb had developed a dualistic ideology that divided the world starkly into two camps: one accepted God's sovereignty and the other did not. In the career of Muhammad, God had revealed a practical programme for the creation of a properly ordered society. Firstly, acting under God's orders, he had created a *jamaat,* a 'party' committed to justice and equity that held aloof from the pagan establishment. Secondly, at the hijrah, he had effected a complete severance of the Godly from the Godless. Thirdly, Muhammad had established an Islamic state in Medina; and fourthly, he began his jihad against jahili Mecca, which eventually bowed to God's sovereignty.

Qutb formulated these ideas in his book *Milestones*, which was smuggled out of prison and read avidly. He was a learned man but *Milestones* is not the work of an official Islamic authority; it is the outcry of a man who has been pushed too far. Qutb's programme distorted Islamic history, since it made no mention of Muhammad's nonviolent policy at Hudaybiyyah, the turning-point of the conflict with Mecca. Humiliation, foreign occupation and secularising aggression had created an Islamic history of grievance. Qutb now had a paranoid vision of the past, seeing only a relentless succession of jahili enemies – pagans, Jews, Christians, Crusaders, Mongols, Communists, capitalists, colonialists and Zionists – intent on the destruction of Islam.[61] Executed in 1966, he did not live long enough to work out the practical implications of his programme. But unlike some of his later followers, he seems to have realised that Muslims would have to undergo a long spiritual, social and political preparation before they were ready for armed struggle. After his death, however, the political situation in the Middle East deteriorated and the increasing violence and consequent alienation meant that Qutb's work would resonate with disaffected youth, especially those Brothers who had been likewise hardened in Egyptian gaols and felt that there was no time for such a ripening process. When they were released in the early 1970s, they would bring Qutb's ideas into mainstream society, and try to implement them practically.

After the Six Day War between Israel and its Arab neighbours in June 1967, the region experienced a religious revival not only in the Muslim countries but also in Israel. Zionism, we have seen, had begun as a defiantly secular movement and the military campaigns of the Jewish state had had no religious content; their violent suppression of the Palestinian people had been the result of their secular nationalism rather than a religious imperative. Before the war, as they listened to Nasser vowing to throw them all into the sea, many Israelis had been convinced that yet another attempt would be made to exterminate them. They responded with lightning speed, achieving a spectacular victory in which they took the Golan Heights from Syria, the Sinai Peninsula from Egypt, and the West Bank and the Old City of Jerusalem from Jordan.

Although religion had not figured in the action, many Israelis would experience this dramatic reversal of fortune as a miracle similar to the crossing of the Red Sea.[62] Above all, the conquest of the Old City of Jerusalem, closed to Israelis since 1948, was a numinous experience. When in 1898 the Zionist ideologue Theodor Herzl had visited the Western Wall, the last relic of Herod's temple, he had been repelled by the sight of the

Jewish worshippers clinging cravenly to its stones.[63] But in June 1967, tough paratroopers with blackened faces and their atheistic officers leant against the Wall and wept, their secular ethos momentarily transformed by sacred geography. Nationalism, as we have seen, easily segues into a quasi-religious fervour, especially in moments of heightened tension and emotion. Devotion to Jerusalem had been central to Jewish identity for millennia. Long before people began to map their landscape scientifically, they had defined their place in the world emotionally and spiritually, drawn irresistibly to localities that they experienced as radically different from all others. The Israeli experience in 1967 shows that we have still not entirely desacralised the world.[64] The soldiers' 'beliefs' had not changed, but the Wall evoked in them something akin to the way others experienced the sacred – 'something big and terrible and from another world,'[65] yet also 'an old friend, impossible to mistake'.[66] Just as they had narrowly escaped destruction, they recognised the Wall as a survivor like themselves. 'There will be no more destruction,' one soldier said as he kissed the stones, 'and the Wall will never again be deserted.'[67]

'Never again' had been a Jewish watchword since the Holocaust and now generals and soldiers were using it once more. For the first time too, the term 'holy city' entered Zionist rhetoric. But according to the ancient sacred geography of the Middle East, the whole point of a 'holy city' was that nobody could own it because it belonged to the god – to Marduk, Baal or Yahweh. The 'City of David' had been ruled by Yahweh from his throne in the temple, the king merely acting as his anointed representative. Instead of becoming the personal property of the ruler, Jerusalem was 'holy' (qaddosh) precisely because it was 'set apart' for Yahweh. But once the emotions of sacred geography were fused with the Israelis' secular nationalism, in which territorial integrity was all-important, politicians had no doubt that Jerusalem belonged absolutely to the Israeli state. 'We have returned to our most holy places,' said the avowed secularist commander Moshe Dayan; 'we have returned and we shall never leave them.'[68] Jerusalem had become a non-negotiable absolute that transcended all other claims. Even though international law forbade the permanent occupation of territory conquered during a conflict, Abba Eban, Israel's delegate to the United Nations, argued that Jerusalem 'lies beyond and above, before and after, all political and secular considerations'.[69]

The sacred geography of Israel also had a strong moral and political dimension. While Israelis lauded Jerusalem as the city of shalom ('peace', 'wholeness'), the Psalms had insisted that there would be no shalom in

Jerusalem without justice (*tzeddek*). The king was charged by Yahweh to 'defend the poorest, save the children of those in need and crush their oppressors'.[70] In Yahweh's Zion, there could be no oppression and violence; it must be a haven for the poor (*evionim*). But once the 'holiness' of Jerusalem had been fused with the secular nation state, its Palestinian inhabitants became a vulnerable minority and their presence a contamination. On the night of 10 June 1967, after the signing of the armistice, the 619 Palestinian inhabitants of the Maghribi Quarter beside the Wall were given three hours to evacuate their homes. Then, in contravention of international law, the bulldozers came in and reduced this historic district – one of the earliest Jerusalem awqaf – to rubble. On 28 June, the Israeli Knesset formally annexed the Old City and East Jerusalem, declaring them part of the State of Israel.

Secular nationalism had exploited and distorted a religious ideal; but a religious embrace of the modern nation state could be equally dangerous. Well before 1967, Orthodox Jews had sacralised the secular state of Israel and made it a supreme value. A somewhat despised religious version of Zionism had always existed alongside the secular nationalism of most Israelis.[71] It became slightly more prominent during the 1950s, when a group of young Orthodox, including Moshe Levinger, Shlomo Aviner, Yaakov Ariel and Eliezar Waldman, had fallen under the spell of the ageing Rabbi Zvi Yehuda Kook, who regarded the secular State of Israel as a 'divine entity' and the Kingdom of God on earth.[72] In exile it had been impossible to observe the commandments tied to the Land; now there was a yearning for wholeness. Instead of excluding the sacred from political life, Kookists, as the rabbi's followers became known, intended it to pervade the whole of existence once again – 'all the time and in every area'.[73] Political engagement, therefore, had become an 'ascent to the pinnacles of holiness'.[74] The Kookists transformed the Land into an idol, an earthly object that had absolute status and required the unquestioning veneration and commitment that traditionally applied only to the transcendence we call God. 'Zionism is a heavenly matter,' Kook insisted. 'The State of Israel is a divine entity, our holy and exalted state.'[75] For Kook, every clod of Israel's soil was holy; its institutions were divine; and the weapons of Israeli soldiers were as sacred as prayer-shawls. But Israel, like any state, was far from ideal and was guilty of both structural and martial violence. In the past, prophets had challenged the systemic injustice of the state and priests had been critical even of its holy wars. But for the Kookists secular Israel was beyond criticism and essential to the world's salvation. With the establishment of

Israel, Messianic redemption had already begun: 'Every Jew who comes to Eretz Yisrael, every tree that is planted in the soil of Israel, every soldier added to the army of Israel constitutes another spiritual stage; literally, another stage in the process of redemption.'[76]

As we have seen, ancient Israel from the very first had looked askance at state violence; now the Kookists gave it supreme sanction. Once the nation state becomes the supreme value, however, as Lord Acton had predicted, there is no limit to what it can do – literally, anything goes. By elevating the state to the divine level, Kookists had also given sacred sanction to nationalism's shadow side: its intolerance of minorities. Unless Jews occupied the entire Land, Israel, they insisted, would remain tragically incomplete, so annexing Arab territory was a supreme religious duty.[77] A few days after the Six Day War, the Labour government proposed to return some of the occupied territories – including some of the most important biblical sites on the West Bank – to the Arabs in exchange for peace and recognition. The Kookists vehemently opposed the plan and, to their surprise, found that for the first time they had secular allies. A group of Israeli poets, philosophers and army officers, fired by the victory, had come together to prevent any such handover and offered the Kookists moral and financial support. Secular nationalists had now made common cause with the hitherto despised religious Zionists, realising that they had exactly the same objectives.

Enthused by this backing, in April 1968 Moshe Levinger led a small group of families to celebrate Passover in Hebron on the West Bank. They checked into the Park Hotel and, to the embarrassment of the Labour government, refused to leave. But their chutzpah tugged at Labourite heartstrings because it recalled the audacity of the chalutzim, who in the days before the state had defied the British by squatting aggressively in Arab land.[78] Yet again, secular and religious enthusiasms merged dangerously. For the Kookists, Hebron – the burial place of Abraham, Isaac and Jacob – was contaminated by the presence of the Palestinians, who also revered these prophets. They now refused to leave the Cave of the Patriarchs in time for Muslim communal prayer, noisily blocking the entrances and flying the Israeli flag at the shrine on Independence Day.[79] When a Palestinian finally threw a hand grenade, the Israeli government reluctantly established an enclave guarded by the Israeli Defence Force for the settlers outside Hebron; by 1972 Kiryat Arba had 5,000 inhabitants. For Kookists it was an outpost pushing against the frontiers of the demonic world of the 'Other Side'.

Yet still Labour refused to annex the territories. After the October War of 1973, when Egypt and Syria invaded Sinai and the Golan Heights and were repelled only with great difficulty, a group of Kookists, rabbis and hawkish secularists formed Gush Emunim, the 'Bloc of the Faithful'. A pressure group rather than a political party, its objective was nothing less than 'the full redemption of Israel and the entire world'.[80] As a 'holy people', Israel was not bound by United Nations resolutions or international law. Gush's ultimate plan was to colonise the entire West Bank and transplant hundreds of thousands of Jews into the occupied territories. To make their point, they organised hikes and rallies in the West Bank and on Independence Day 1975 nearly twenty thousand armed Jews attended a West Bank 'picnic', marching militantly from one location to another.[81]

The Gush experienced their marches, battles with the army and illegal squats as rituals that brought them a sense of ecstasy and release.[82] But the fact that they attracted so much secularist support showed that they were tapping into nationalistic passions that were felt just as strongly by Israelis who had no time at all for religion. They could also draw on the Western tradition of natural human rights which had long declared that an endangered people – and after the October War, who, they asked, could deny that Israelis *were* endangered? – were entitled to settle in 'vacant' land. Their sacred task was to ensure that it was truly 'empty'. When the Likud party led by Menachem Begin defeated Labour in the 1977 elections and declared its commitment to Israeli settlement on both sides of the Jordan, Kookists believed that God was at work. But the honeymoon was short-lived. On 20 November 1977, President Anwar Sadat of Egypt made his historic journey to Jerusalem to initiate a peace process, and the following year, Begin and Sadat, two former terrorists, signed the Camp David Accords: Israel would return the Sinai Peninsula to Egypt in exchange for Egypt's formal recognition of the State of Israel. Observing this unexpected development, many Western people concluded that secular pragmatism would prevail after all.

But the Iranian revolution shattered that hope. Western politicians had regarded Shah Muhammad Reza Pahlavi as a progressive leader and had put their muscle behind his regime, regardless of the fact that he had no legitimacy among his own people. Iranians were in fact experiencing the structural violence of 'The West and the Rest' in an acute form. Independence, democracy, human rights and national self-determination were for 'the West'; but for Iranians, violence, domination, exploitation and tyranny were to be the order of the day. In 1953 a coup organised by the CIA and British

Intelligence had unseated the secular nationalist premier Muhammad Musaddiq (who had tried to nationalise the Iranian oil industry) and re-instated the shah. This event showed Iranians how little they could command their own destiny. After 1953, like the British before them, the United States controlled the monarch and Iran's oil reserves, demanding diplomatic privileges and trade concessions. American businessmen and consultants poured into the country, and though a few Iranians benefited from the boom, most did not. In 1962, the shah began his White Revolution by closing the Majlis legislature and pushed his unpopular reforms through with the support of SAVAK, the dreaded secret police trained by the CIA and Israeli Mossad. These reforms were applauded in the West, since they established capitalism, undermined feudal land ownership and promoted literacy and women's rights, but in fact they favoured the rich, concentrated on city-dwellers, and ignored the peasantry.[83] There were the usual symptoms of an economy modernising too rapidly: agriculture declined and rural migrants poured into the cities, living in desolate shanty towns and eking out a precarious existence as porters and street-vendors.[84] SAVAK made Iranians feel like prisoners in their own country and clandestine Marxist and Islamist guerrilla groups formed in opposition to a secular regime that violently suppressed all opposition.

But one little-known cleric had the courage to speak out publicly against this oppressive regime. In 1963, Ayatollah Ruhollah Khomeini (1902–89), Professor of Ethics at the Fayziyah Madrasa in Qum, began a sustained attack on the shah, condemning his use of torture, his closing the Majlis, his spineless subservience to the United States and his support for Israel, which denied Palestinians fundamental human rights. On one occasion, he stood with the Quran in one hand and the 1906 Constitution in the other and accused the shah of betraying both.[85] On 22 March 1963, the anniversary of the martyrdom of the Sixth Imam, SAVAK attacked the madrasa, arrested Khomeini, and killed some of the students. After his release, Khomeini resumed the offensive. During the Ashura rituals, in his eulogy for Husain, he compared the shah to Caliph Yazid, the villain of the Karbala tragedy in 680.[86] When Khomeini was arrested for a second time thousands of Iranians poured on to the streets, laymen and mullahs protesting side by side. SAVAK was given shoot-to-kill orders and clerics braved the guns wearing the white shroud of the martyr, demonstrating their willingness to die like Husain in the war against tyranny. By the time peace was finally restored, hundreds of civilians had been killed.[87]

The regime, Khomeini protested, was assaulting its own people. Always he championed the poor, the chief victims of its systemic injustice, ordering the shah to leave his palace and look at the deplorable conditions in the shanty towns. Iran, he claimed on 27 October 1964, was virtually an American colony. It was a rich country and it was a disgrace that people were sleeping in the streets. For decades foreigners had been plundering their oil, so that it was of no benefit to the Iranian people. 'I am deeply concerned about the conditions of the poor next winter, as I expect many to die, God forbid, from cold and starvation,' he concluded. 'The ulema should think of the poor and take action now to prevent the atrocities of last winter.'[88] After this speech Khomeini was deported and went into exile in Iraq. Overnight, he had become a hero in Iran, a symbol of resolute Shii opposition to oppression. Marxist or liberal ideology could have appealed to only a few Iranians, but everybody, especially the urban poor, understood the imagery of Karbala. In the West we are accustomed to extrovert and crowd-pleasing politicians, so it was hard for us to understand Khomeini's appeal, but Iranians recognised his withdrawn demeanour, inward-seeming gaze and monotonous delivery as the sign of a 'sober' mystic, who had achieved full control of the senses.[89] In exile in Najaf too, near the tomb of Imam Ali, Khomeini became closely associated with the Twelve Imams in the minds of the people and, thanks to modern communications, he would continue to direct events from afar – not unlike the Hidden Imam.

In the West, Khomeini would be widely regarded as a fanatic and his success seen as a triumph of superstition over rationality. But his principled opposition to systemic violence and demand for global justice was deeply in tune with contemporaneous religious developments in the West. His message was not dissimilar to that of Pope John XXIII (r. 1958–63), whose encyclical letter *Mater et Magistra* (1961) insisted that unfettered capitalism was immoral and unsustainable; instead, 'all forms of economic enterprise must be governed by the principles of social justice and charity'. The pope also called for global equity. National prosperity was not enough: 'Man's aim must be to achieve social justice in a national and international juridical order . . . in which all economic activity can be conducted not merely for private gain but also in the interests of the common good.'[90] In *Pacem in Terris* (1963), the Pope insisted that human rights rather than economic profit must be the basis of international relations – a plea clearly critical of exploitative Western policies in undeveloped countries.

At about the same time as Khomeini was inveighing against the injustice of the shah, the Catholic Church in Latin America was evolving its Liberation Theology. Priests and nuns encouraged small communities of the poor to study the Bible in order to redress the systemic violence of Brazilian society. In 1968, Latin American bishops met in Medellín, Colombia, to support the emerging themes of this new movement, which argued that Jesus was on the side of the poor and oppressed and that Christians must struggle for justice and equality. In Latin America, as in Iran, this kind of theology was deeply threatening to the political and economic elites. Liberation priests were dubbed 'communists', and, like Iranian clerics, were imprisoned, tortured and executed because they made it clear that the economic order imposed on the 'Third World' by the colonial West was inherently violent:

> For centuries, Latin America has been a region of violence. We are talking of the violence that a privileged minority has been using, since the colonial period, to exploit the vast majority of the people. We are talking of the violence of hunger, of helplessness, of underdevelopment . . . of illegal but existing slavery, of social, intellectual, and economic discrimination.[91]

They insisted that because the world was now so economically interdependent, a North American individual was able to live a comfortable life only because other people, living perhaps in a Brazilian slum, were impoverished; they could purchase goods cheaply because others had been exploited in their production.[92]

In the United States too, religion acquired a revolutionary edge and for the first time in the twentieth century opposed the policies of the American government.[93] While presidents John F. Kennedy and Lyndon B. Johnson were careful to keep religion out of politics, liberal Catholics, Protestants and Jews campaigned in the name of their faith against the structural and military violence of the United States. Like Iranian Shii Muslims, they took to the streets to protest against the Vietnam War and joined Martin Luther King's civil rights movement against racial discrimination at home. In 1962, the National Council of Churches asked Kennedy to commit the nation to 'an all-out effort to abolish [poverty], both at home and abroad'.[94]

Khomeini, often thought in the West to be a rabble-rouser, was not advocating violence. The crowds who protested on the streets were unarmed and their deaths laid bare the ruthless ferocity of the shah's secular regime. The assassination of Martin Luther King, who had insisted that a nonviolent response to injury was 'an absolute necessity for our survival . . . the key to the solution of the problems of our world',[95] also revealed the latent violence of American society. King would have agreed with Khomeini's demand for global justice. He had lamented Kennedy's disastrous colonial misadventure in the Bay of Pigs (1961) and even though Johnson had given African Americans more than any previous president, King refused to support his war in Vietnam. But in the late 1970s, when the Iranian revolution broke out, the mood in the West had changed. In 1978, the conservative bishop of Kraców Karol Wojtyla, a fierce opponent of Liberation Theology, was elected to the papacy, taking the name of John Paul II. The fundamentalist Moral Majority had surged to the forefront of American religious life, and the Democratic president Jimmy Carter, a 'born again' Christian who campaigned vigorously for human rights, was a loyal supporter of the shah's dictatorship.

Viewed from the West, Iran seemed to be booming in the 1970s, but the state had become rich at the expense of the nation; a million people were unemployed, local merchants had been ruined by the influx of foreign goods, and there was widespread resentment of the flourishing American expatriates.[96] After Khomeini's departure, the shah had become even more autocratic and started to secularise more aggressively, confiscating the awqaf and bringing the madrasas under strict bureaucratic control.[97] When Ayatollah Riza Saidi denounced the regime he was tortured to death, and thousands of demonstrators poured on to the streets of Qum.[98] The charismatic lay philosopher Ali Shariati (1933–77), who had studied at the Sorbonne, kept the revolutionary flame alive among the young Westernised Iranians.[99] He told them that if they tried to conform too closely to the Western ideal and abandoned the Shiah, they would lose themselves; the example of Ali and Husain compelled Muslims to stand up and say 'No' to injustice, coercion and tyranny. He too was tortured, imprisoned and died in exile, almost certainly the victim of SAVAK agents. In Najaf in 1971, Khomeini published *Islamic Government,* arguing that the ulema should rule the state. His doctrine of *velayat-e faqih*, 'the government of a [Muslim] jurist', seemed to fly in the face of Western modernity and was shocking to most Shiis, since for centuries the clergy had refused official posts because, in the absence of the Hidden Imam, any government was corrupt. But Khomeini's thought was clearly in line with those Third World intellectuals who defied global structural violence. Islam, he would always claim, was 'the religion of militant individuals who are committed to faith and justice. It is the religion of those who desire freedom and independence. It is the school of those who struggle against imperialism.'[100]

Even though nobody at this date, Khomeini included, believed that it was possible to topple the shah, events were moving faster than he had anticipated. In November 1977, his son Mustafa was assassinated in Iraq, again almost certainly by SAVAK agents,[101] and the shah forbade mourning ceremonies to be held. This only identified Khomeini even more closely with the Shii Imams – since, like Husain, his son had been murdered by an unjust ruler – and cast the shah yet again as Yazid. And at this critical juncture, US President Jimmy Carter cast himself as the 'Great Satan'. In November 1977, while Iran was mourning Mustafa Khomeini, the shah visited Washington and Carter spoke with great emotion of the United States' 'special relationship' with Iran, 'an island of stability in a turbulent corner of the world'.[102] He thus entered the unfolding Karbala drama as the *shaytan*, the 'tempter' who had lured the shah to follow the United States to the detriment of his own people.

The revolution began on 8 January 1978 when the semi-official newspaper *Ettelaat* published a preposterous attack on Khomeini.[103] The next day 4,000 unarmed students in Qum demanded a revival of the 1906 Constitution, freedom of speech, the release of political prisoners and the return of Khomeini. Throughout, Iranians showed that they had fully absorbed the modern ethos, demanding the independence, liberty and constitutional rule that they had been consistently denied by the shah's secular government and the international community. Seventy of these students were killed. With this massacre, the regime had crossed a line. A pattern now emerged. Forty days after the Qum massacre, crowds gathered for the traditional mourning ceremonies for the dead and more people were shot down. Forty days later, there were more ritualised rallies in honour of the new martyrs. Marxists, secularists, and liberals who opposed the shah but knew that they had no grassroots appeal, joined forces with the religiously minded revolutionaries. This was not a violent uprising, however. Cinemas, banks and liquor stores – symbols of the 'great shaytan' – were attacked, but not people.[104] By now, the gaols were full of political prisoners and the mounting death toll showed the world that the shah's secular regime, lauded in the West as progressive and peaceful, was slaughtering its own people.

The revolution was experienced as a religious as well as a political event. Demonstrators carried placards reading 'Everywhere is Karbala, and every day is Ashura', convinced that they were following Husain in their struggle against oppression.[105] They spoke of the revolution as a transforming and purifying experience, as if they were purging themselves of a debilitating poison and regaining authenticity.[106] Many felt as though Husain himself were leading them and that Khomeini, like the Hidden Imam, was directing them from afar.[107] On the last night of Ramadan, 4 September, vast crowds prostrated themselves in prayer in the streets, but – an important turning-point – this time the army did not open fire. Even more significantly, the middle classes began to join in the protests, marching with placards reading: 'Independence, Freedom and Islamic Government!'[108] At six a.m. on 8 September, martial law was declared but the 20,000 demonstrators who were already gathering in Jaleh Square did not know this; when they refused to disperse, the soldiers opened fire. As many as 900 people may have died that day.[109]

That evening, Carter called the shah from Camp David to assure him of his support and the White House, while regretting the loss of life, reaffirmed its special relationship with Iran. The liberty and independence for which the American revolutionaries had fought were clearly not for every-body. On the first three nights of Muharram, men donned the white shroud of the martyr and ran through the streets defying the curfew, while others shouted anti-shah slogans from the rooftops. In these few days alone, the BBC estimated that 700 people had been killed by the Iranian army and police.[110] Yet still there was no mob violence. On 9 December, for six hours a vast procession – at different times numbering between 300,000 and 1.5 million people – wound through the streets of Tehran, walking quietly four abreast. Two million more marched on the day of Ashura itself, carrying green, red and black flags, representing Islam, Martyrdom and the Shiah.[111]

A month later, it was all over. The shah and the royal family flew to Egypt and on 1 February 1979 Khomeini returned to Tehran. His arrival was one of those events, like the storming of the Bastille, that seemed to change the world for ever. For committed liberal secularists, it was a dark moment, the triumph of the forces of unreason over rationality. But for many Muslims, Sunni as well as Shii, it seemed a luminous reversal. As he drove through the streets of Tehran, the crowds greeted him as if he were the returned Hidden Imam, confident that a new age had dawned. Taha Hejazi published a poem of celebration, a tremulous hope for the justice that the shah and the international community had denied them:

> When the Imam returns,
> Iran – this broken, wounded mother –
> Will be forever liberated
> From the shackles of tyranny and ignorance
> And the chains of plunder, torture and prison.[112]

Khomeini liked to quote the hadith in which the Prophet announced after a battle that he was returning from the lesser to the 'Greater Jihad', the implementation of truly Islamic values in society, a struggle far more exacting than the 'lesser', political one. As he looked at the ecstatic crowds that day he must surely have felt apprehension at the more onerous jihad about to begin.

It was indeed a struggle: almost at once, perhaps predictably, the fragile coalition of Marxists, liberals and the devout seemed to unravel. There was opposition to the new Constitution, in 1980 four separate plots against the regime were uncovered, and there were constant street battles between secularist guerrillas and Khomeini's Revolutionary Guards. A reign of terror ensued, not unlike those that followed the French and Russian revolutions, when so-called revolutionary councils, which the government could not control, executed hundreds of people for 'un-Islamic behaviour'. As a crowning blow, on 20 September 1980, the south-west of the country was invaded by Saddam Hussein's Iraqi forces. During this turbulent period, the American hostage crisis proved a godsend to Khomeini. On 4 November 1979, 3,000 Iranian students had stormed the United States embassy in Tehran and taken ninety prisoners. It is not clear whether Khomeini knew of their plan beforehand, and everyone expected him to release the hostages immediately. But although the women hostages and the embassy's Marine guards were allowed to return to America, the remaining fifty-two diplomats were held for 444 days. In the West, this disreputable affair seemed to epitomise Islamic radicalism.

Yet Khomeini's decision to retain the hostages was inspired not by an Islamic imperative but simply by politics. He could see that this focus on the Great Satan would unite Iranians behind him at a difficult juncture. As he explained to his prime minister Bani Sadr:

> This action has many benefits. The Americans do not want to see the Islamic Republic taking root. We keep the hostages, finish our internal work, and then release them. This has united our people. Our opponents do not dare act against us. We can put the constitution to the people's vote without difficulty, and carry out presidential and parliamentary elections. When we have finished all these jobs, we can let the hostages go.[113]

As soon as they were no longer useful, the hostages were released, on 20 January 1981, the inauguration day of the new US president Ronald Reagan and the departure of his 'satanic' predecessor Jimmy Carter. Inevitably the hostage crisis tainted the image and idealism of the Islamic revolution. Many Iranians were unhappy about it, even while appreciating its symbolism. A nation's embassy is regarded as its sovereign territory on foreign soil and some thought it apt that American citizens should be held there, just as for decades Iranians had felt imprisoned in their own country with the conniv- ance of the United States. But this was simply revenge politics and the cruel treatment meted out to the hostages violated cardinal principles of all faith traditions, not least those of Islam. Whatever the regime gained by stopping the clock while it achieved a degree of stability, it would pay for over many years in the ledger of the privileged free world.

The great genius of the Shiah was its tragic perception that it is impos- sible fully to implement the ideals of religion in the inescapably violent realm of politics. Ashoka had discovered this even earlier than the Shii Imams when he promoted his compassionate dharma but could not disband his army. At best, people of faith can either bear witness to these values, as Khomeini did when he castigated the injustice of the Pahlavi regime in the 1960s, or provide an alternative that either challenges or seeks to mitigate state violence. But as we have seen throughout this story, even the most humanitarian tradi- tions are unable to implement their ideals if they identify with a state ideology that inevitably depends upon force. Khomeini believed that the revolution had been a rebellion against the rational pragmatism of the modern world. The goal of his theory of velayat-e faqih was to institutionalise Shii values: the Supreme Jurist (*faqih*) and the ulema on the Council of Guardians would have the power to veto any legislation that violated the principles of Islamic justice.[114] But in practice, Khomeini would often have to reprove the Guardians for playing selfish power games, just as he himself had felt compelled to pursue a cynical realpolitik during the hostage crisis.

We have seen that revolutions can take a long time, and, like the French Revolution, the Iranian revolution has passed through many stages and is still in progress. As in France, Iranians feared that powerful external enemies would destroy their regime. In the summer of 1983 the Iraqis attacked Iranian troops with mustard gas, and with nerve gas the following year.[115] Khomeini was convinced that America would organise a coup similar to the one that had deposed Musaddiq in 1953. Because Iran had antagonised the West, she had forfeited essential equipment, spare parts and technical advice; inflation was high and by 1982 unemployment had risen to 30 per cent of the general population and 50 per cent in the cities.[116] The poor, whose plight Khomeini had championed, were not doing much better under the revolution. Yet Western observers had to acknowledge that, despite the growing opposition of Westernised Iranians, Khomeini never lost the love of the masses, especially the *bazaaris,* the madrasa students, the less-eminent ulema, and the poor.[117] These people, whom the shah's modernisation programme had overlooked, still thought and spoke in a traditionally religious, pre-modern way that many Westerners could not even comprehend.

After the Iranian revolution, one exasperated United States official was heard to exclaim: 'Whoever took religion seriously?'[118] Since the Enlightenment, revolutions were understood to occur at a time when the saeculum had reached maturity and was strong enough to declare its independence of faith.[119] The idea of a popular uprising ushering in a religiously oriented state was almost embarrassing in its upending of accepted wisdom; many Westerners deplored it as atavistic and perverse. But they seemed unable to see that by pursuing their own political and economic agendas that did violence to the Iranian people, Western governments had bred a new species of religion. They had been blind to the particular problems of the post-colonial state and the pitfalls of a modernisation imposed from without rather than effected organically from within.[120] And in deploring the new theocracy, they failed to appreciate a central irony. The Western ideals of liberty had fired the Iranian imagination and inspired Iranians to demand basic freedoms, but the Western secular ideal had been irredeemably tainted for Iranians by the self-interest and cruelty with which it had been pursued. The United States declared that it had a God-given mission to spread liberty throughout the world, but this had evidently not included the people of Iran. 'We did not expect Carter to defend the shah, for he is a religious man who has raised the slogan of defending human rights,' an ayatollah explained to an interviewer after the revolution. 'How can Carter, the devout Christian, defend the shah?'[121] Such perplexity reveals how strange a pre-modern sensibility must find the idea of religion as a private matter.

The Iranian revolution had dramatically changed the status quo in the Persian Gulf. The shah had been one of the key pillars of US policy in the region, permitting the West to access its vast oil reserves at an affordable price. In December 1979, the Soviet Union sought to capitalise on America's loss of influence in the region by invading Iran's neighbour Afghanistan. This Cold War struggle between the superpowers helped to inspire a global jihad that would eventually target the United States and its allies. But it would be some time before the West recognised this danger, because during the 1980s and 90s, it was more concerned with terrorist atrocities and violence in the Middle East and the Indian subcontinent that seemed wholly inspired by 'religion'.

HOLY TERROR

On 18 November 1978, nine hundred and thirteen American citizens died of self-administered cyanide poisoning in the agricultural colony of Jonestown, Guyana.[1] It was, at the time, the largest loss of civilian life in a single incident in United States history. The deceased men, women and children were members of the People's Temple founded during the 1950s in Indianapolis, Indiana, by the charismatic preacher James Warren Jones (1931–78). Its commitment to racial and social equality had attracted chiefly poor, working-class white Americans and African Americans. Members lived a strictly communal life based on what Jones called the 'apostolic socialism' of the Acts of the Apostles. In 1965, after having a vision of a nuclear bomb destroying Chicago, Jones had persuaded his followers to move with him and his family to safety in California. The Temple opened facilities in San Francisco and Los Angeles and gained a reputation for being politically progressive, offering legal services, childcare, housing, and drug and alcohol rehabilitation. Membership increased to about a thousand and in 1976, to escape the systemic violence and injustice that it believed to be inherent in the United States, the Temple moved to Guyana.

Jonestown is often cited by those who claim that religion has been responsible for more death and suffering than any other human activity. Yet even though Jones was an ordained Methodist pastor, who often quoted the Gospels and used religion in recruitment, he was a self-confessed atheist and communist who ridiculed conventional Christianity. Stories about the Temple's violence had begun to circulate in 1972: defectors spoke of beatings, verbal abuse and emotional cruelty. Members were viciously castigated for making racist or sexist remarks, complaining about the communal living arrangements or wasting food. Culprits were subjected to brutal physical punishment and humiliation in public and the community was kept in a state of constant terror. Jones filled their minds with graphic descriptions of CIA torture methods, the Nazi concentration camps, and Ku Klux Klan lynchings. In 1972, while still in California, he announced that the United States government was

> gonna put people in this country in concentration camps. They're gonna put them in gas ovens, just like they did the Jews ... They're gonna put you in the concentration camps that're already in Tule Lake, California, Allentown, Pennsylvania, near Birmingham, outside El Reno, Oklahoma. They've got them all ready ... they still have the concentration camps, they did it to the Japanese, and they'll do it to us.[2]

'I tell you, we're in danger from a corporate dictatorship,' Jones insisted, 'a great fascist state, a great communist state.'[3]

The ultimate terror began in 1978, when members started to rehearse their mass suicide. On 'White Nights' they would be roused suddenly from sleep, informed that they were about to be killed by US agents, and that suicide was the only viable option. They were then given a drink that they believed to be poisoned, and waited to die. On 18 November 1978 the community had been visited by US Congressmen Leo Ryan who had come to investigate reports of human rights abuses. After Ryan left, Jones dispatched Temple members to shoot him at the airstrip and then summoned the entire community to the Jonestown pavilion. There medical staff administered potassium cyanide in a batch of the soft drink Flavor-Aid, which parents fed to their children before taking it themselves. Most seem to have died willingly, though the 200 children were certainly murdered and about a hundred of the elderly may have been injected involuntarily.

They recorded their last messages on audiotape. Jones had taken the concept of 'revolutionary suicide' from Black Panther leader Huey Newton.[4] 'I made the decision to commit revolutionary suicide. My decision has been well thought out,' said one Jonestown resident. 'And in my death, I hope that it would be used as an instrument to further liberation.'[5] 'It's been my pleasure walking with all of you in this revolutionary struggle,' one woman stated. 'No other way I would rather go [than] to give my life for socialism, communism.'[6] People who were convinced that they had no voice in their own society had come to believe they could be heard only in the shocking spectacle of their dying. Jones was the last to take the poison: 'We said – one thousand people who said, we don't like the way the world is. We didn't commit suicide. We committed an act of revolutionary suicide, protesting the conditions of an inhumane world.'[7]

The community dynamics of Jonestown were, of course, complex and imponderable but although religion was clearly not the cause of this tragedy, it has much in common with instances of 'revolutionary suicide' that have been articulated in religious terms. The Temple was a protest against the structural violence of American society; it had a highly developed history of grievance and suffering which, its members claimed, mainstream society chose to ignore. Jonestown was an assault as well as a protest: Temple members were laying their deaths at the door of the United States, a demonstration that its systemic injustice had made their lives so intolerable that death was preferable. Jones obviously believed, however psychotically, that he was engaged in an asymmetrical struggle with a superpower that held all the cards. All these elements would also surface in the wave of religiously inspired terrorism that broke out in the 1980s.

One of the many reasons why the drama of Jonestown is so disturbing is the germ of nihilism it reveals in modern culture. The Temple was haunted by two of the dark icons of modernity: the concentration camp and the mushroom cloud. According to Sigmund Freud (1856–1939), human beings were as strongly motivated by a death wish as by a desire for procreation. The French existentialist Jean-Paul Sartre (1905–80) spoke of a God-shaped hole in human consciousness, a void at the heart of modern culture. By the mid-twentieth century that psychic void had been filled with a terrible reality. Between 1914 and 1945, seventy million people in Europe and the Soviet Union had died violent deaths.[8] Some of the worst atrocities had been perpetrated by Germans, who lived in one of the most cultivated societies in Europe. The Holocaust shook the Enlightenment optimism that education would eliminate barbarism, since it showed that a concentration camp could exist in the same vicinity as a great university. The sheer scale of the Nazi genocide reveals its debt to modernity; no previous society could have implemented such a grandiose scheme of extermination. The Nazis used many of the tools and achievements of the industrial age – the factory, the railways, and the advanced chemical industry – to deadly effect, relying on modern scientific and rational planning in which everything is subordinated to a single, limited and defined objective.[9] Born of modern scientific racism, the Holocaust was the ultimate step in social engineering and the most extreme demonstration of the inability of the nation to tolerate minorities. It showed what can happen once the sense of the sacredness of every single human being – a conviction at the heart of traditional religions that quasi-religious systems seem unable or disinclined to recreate – is lost.

On 6 August 1945, a 3,600-kilogram atomic bomb was dropped on Hiroshima, killing approximately 140,000 people instantaneously. Three days later, a plutonium-type bomb was dropped on Nagasaki, killing some 24,000 people.[10] For centuries, people had dreamed of a final apocalypse wrought by God; now, with weapons of mass destruction, it appeared, human beings no longer needed God to achieve apocalyptic effects. The nation had become a supreme value and the international community acknowledged the legitimacy of a nuclear strike to protect it, despite the prospect of total annihilation that such means suggested. There could be no more potent evidence of the death-wish Freud had described. But it also, perhaps, suggests a flaw in the purely secular ideal that eliminates 'holiness' from its politics – the conviction that some things or people must be 'set apart' from our personal interests. The cultivation of that transcendence – be it God, Dao, Brahman or Nirvana – had, at its best, helped people to appreciate human finitude. But if the nation becomes the absolute value (in religious terms, an 'idol'), there is no reason why we should not liquidate those who appear to threaten it.

This death-wish was, however, not only present in the godless violence of secular nationalism but is also evident in the religiously articulated violence of the late twentieth century. Westerners were quite rightly horrified by the Iranian child-martyrs who died on the battlefields of the Iraq–Iran war. As soon as war was declared, adolescents from the slums and shanty towns had crowded into the mosques, begging to be sent to the front. Radicalised by the excitement of the revolution, they hoped to escape the tedium of their grim lives. And so, as in traditional societies of times past, the potential for achieving ecstasy and intensity through warfare beckoned. The government issued an edict allowing male children as young as twelve to enlist at the front without their parents' permission. They became wards of the Imam and were promised a place in Paradise. Tens of thousands of adolescents poured into the war zone, wearing the martyrs' insignia of crimson headbands. Some, trying to clear minefields, ran ahead of the troops and were blown to pieces. Others attacked as suicide bombers, deploying a tactic that has been used in various contexts of asymmetrical warfare since the eleventh century. Scribes were sent to the front to write the martyrs' wills, many of which took the form of letters to the Imam and spoke of their joy in fighting 'alongside friends on the road to Paradise'.[11] The child-martyrs restored Khomeini's faith in the revolution; like Imam Husain, he claimed, they were dying to bear witness to the primacy of the Unseen. But they had also been exploited to serve the interests of the nation.

But religiously articulated militarism is not restricted to cultures with a pre-modern religious outlook. In the secularised West it has surfaced in response to the terrors of modernity, especially those of modern industrialised warfare. During the early 1980s, disaffected American Protestant groups fearing a Soviet nuclear attack during a particularly tense period of the Cold War established fortified strongholds in remote areas of the northwest. But these survivalists, who trained militarily and stockpiled ammunition and other supplies, felt threatened not only by the godless Soviet bloc, but by the US government as well. Loosely affiliated as Christian Identity, these groups had very little in common with orthodox Christian churches.[12] Claiming direct descent from the Twelve Tribes of Israel (through a preposterous ethnography known as 'British Israelism'), they espoused a brand of white supremacy that saw the federal government and its toxic pluralism as a mortal threat. It is difficult to estimate its numbers, because Identity was and remains merely a network of organisations, but it probably had no more than 100,000 members.[13] And not all shared the same concerns: some were strictly secular survivalists who were simply fleeing the threat of nuclear catastrophe.[14] But there is a religious patina to some of these extremist groups, who use the language of faith to express fears, anxieties and enthusiasms that are widespread, though not openly expressed, in the mainstream.

The reach of the message can be dramatic. Christian Identity's brand of ideology would inspire Timothy McVeigh's bombing of the Alfred P. Murrah federal building in Oklahoma City on 19 April 1995. McVeigh was a self-professed agnostic, however. Like several Identity leaders, he had served in the US army and had a pathological attraction to violence. In the 1991 Gulf War he had helped massacre a group of trapped Iraqi soldiers and taken photographs of their corpses for his personal collection. He was not officially a member of Christian Identity but read its newsletter, had telephone conversations with its officers, and had visited its compound on the Oklahoma–Arkansas border.[15]

How, then, can we try to understand terrorism as a particular species of violence?

Like religion, 'terrorism' is notoriously difficult to define. There are so many competing and contradictory formulations that, according to one scholar, the word is now 'shrouded in terminological confusion'.[16] Part of the problem is that it is such an emotive word, one of the most powerful terms of abuse in the English language, and the most censorious way of characterising any violent act.[17] As such, it is never used of anything we do ourselves, except perhaps in some abjectly penitential confession. Connoting more than it denotes, the word stubbornly refuses to reveal much, especially when both sides of a conflict hurl the same charge at each other with equal passion. Its effect is to accuse an opponent much more than to clarify the nature of the underlying conflict.[18]

One attempt at definition describes the phenomenon as 'the deliberate use of violence, or threat of its use, against innocent people, with the aim of intimidating them specifically or others into a course of action they would not otherwise take'. But this could also be said of some forms of conventional warfare.[19] Indeed, there is a general scholarly agreement that some of the largest-scale acts of terrorist violence against civilians have been carried out by states rather than independent groups or individuals.[20] In the national wars of the twentieth century, hundreds of thousands of civilians were firebombed, napalmed or vaporised. During the Second World War, Allied scientists carefully calculated the mix of explosives and wind patterns to create devastating firestorms in densely populated residential areas in German and Japanese cities precisely to create terror in the population.[21]

There is, however, at least one point on which everybody is in agreement: terrorism is fundamentally and inherently political, even when other motives – religious, economic or social – are involved.[22] Terrorism is *always* about 'power – acquiring it or keeping it'.[23] And so, according to one of the pioneering experts in the field, 'All terrorist organizations, whether their long-term political aim is revolution, national self-determination, preservation or restoration of the status quo, or reform, are engaged in a struggle for political power with a government they wish to influence and replace.'[24] The claim that the primary motivation of a terrorist action is political may seem obvious – but not to those who seem determined to regard such atrocious acts of violence as merely 'senseless'. Many of that view, not surprisingly, find religion, which they regard as a byword for irrationality, to be the ultimate cause. One of the most prominent is Richard Dawkins, who has argued that 'only religious faith is a strong enough force to motivate such utter madness in otherwise sane and decent people'.[25] But this dangerous oversimplification springs from a misunderstanding of both religion and terrorism. It is, of course, a familiar enough expression of the secularist bias of modernity, which has cast 'religion' as a violent, unreasonable force that must be excluded from the politics of civilised nations.[26] Somehow, it fails to consider that all the world's great religious traditions share as one of their most essential tenets the imperative of treating others as one would wish to be treated oneself. This, of course, is not to deny that religion has often been implicated in terrorist atrocities but it is far too easy to make it a scapegoat rather than trying to see what is really going on in the world.

The first act of Islamic terrorism to grab the world's attention was the murder of President Anwar Sadat, winner of the Nobel Peace Prize, hero of the Camp David Accords, and widely regarded in the West as a progressive Muslim leader. Western peoples were aghast at the ferocity of the attack. On 6 October 1981, during a parade celebrating Egypt's victories in the October War of 1973, First-Lieutenant Khaled Islambouli jumped out of his truck, ran towards the presidential stand and opened fire with a machine gun, shooting round after round into Sadat, killing seven people besides the president and injuring twenty-eight others. His political motivation was clearly regime change, but revolutionary fervour was fused with Islamic sentiment. At his trial, Islambouli gave three reasons for murdering Sadat: the suffering of Egyptian Muslims under his tyrannical rule; the Camp David Accords; and Sadat's imprisonment of Islamists a month earlier.

A bevy of Western princes, politicians and celebrities attended Sadat's funeral, but no Arab leaders were present and the streets of Cairo were eerily silent – a very different scene from the tumultuous lamentations at Nasser's funeral. Western politicians had admired Sadat's peace initiative, but many people in Egypt regarded it as opportunistic and self-serving, especially since, three years after Camp David, the plight of the Palestinians had not improved. Sadat had also won Western approval by switching to the 'right' side of the Cold War, dismissing the 1,500 Soviet advisers installed by Nasser in 1972 and announcing an 'Open Door' policy designed to bring Egypt into the capitalist free market.[27] But, as in Iran, although a few entrepreneurs flourished, local businessmen were ruined when foreign imports flooded the markets. Only 4 per cent of the young could find a decent job and housing was so expensive that couples often had to wait years before they could marry. No longer able to afford living in their own country, thousands of Egyptians went to work in Saudi Arabia or the Gulf states, sending money home to their families.[28] The social dislocation of the abrupt Westernisation of Sadat's Egypt was also disturbing. As one observer tried to explain, it was impossible for an Egyptian peasant to maintain his dignity as 'a culture bearer in his own culture', when, after a day's toiling in the hot sun, he had to stand in line for a frozen American chicken and spend the evening in front of the television set purchased with money sent by his son from Saudi Arabia, watching the antics of J. R. Ewing and Sue Ellen on *Dallas*.[29]

The devout element of Egyptian society felt especially betrayed by Sadat. At first, anxious to create an identity for his regime that was distinct from Nasser's he had courted them, releasing the Muslim Brothers from prison, encouraging Muslim student associations to wrest the campuses away from the socialists and Nasserites, and styling himself the Pious President. There was much mosque-building and plenty of airtime devoted to religion. But there was nothing Islamic about Open Door. This was blatant structural violence, which revealed the hollowness of Sadat's devout stance, since he had created conditions of inequity explicitly condemned by the Quran. The president discovered that his economic and political assault on the Egyptian people had inadvertently spawned political Islamist movements dangerously hostile to his regime.

One of these was the Society of Muslims, founded in 1971 by Shukri Mustafa, a member of the Muslim Brotherhood, after his release from prison.[30] He would be one of the most misguided 'free lances' that stepped into the vacuum created by the ulema's marginalisation. By 1976, the Society had about two thousand members, men and women convinced that they were divinely commissioned to build a pure ummah on the ruins of Sadat's jahiliyyah. Taking Qutb's programme in *Milestones* to the limit, Shukri declared not only the government but the entire Egyptian population to be apostate and he and his followers withdrew from the mainstream, living in caves in the desert outside Cairo or in the city's most deprived neighbourhoods. Their experiment ended in violence and lethal immorality when members killed defectors from the group and Shukri murdered a respected judge who had condemned the Society. Yet deeply misguided as it was, Shukri's Society held up a dark mirror image that revealed the darker side of Sadat's regime. Shukri's excommunication of Egypt was extreme, but in Quranic terms Sadat's systemic violence was indeed jahili. The hijrah to the most desperate quarters of Cairo reflected the plight of many young Egyptians who felt there was no place for them in their country; the Society's communes were supported by young men who, like so many others, were sent to work in the Gulf states. The Society condemned all secular learning as a waste of time, and there was a grain of truth in this since a lady's maid in a foreign household could earn more than a junior lecturer.

Far more constructive than the Society of Muslims, however, were the *jamaat al-islamiyyah*, the student organisations that dominated the university campuses during Sadat's presidency, who tried to help themselves in a society that ignored the needs of the young.[31] By 1973 they had organised summer camps at nearly all the major universities, where students could immerse themselves in an Islamic milieu, studying the Quran, keeping night vigils, listening to sermons about the Prophet, and attending classes in sport and self-defence – creating an Islamic alternative to the inadequacies of the secular state.[32] On the lamentably ill-equipped campuses, in order to protect women from harassment they segregated the sexes during lectures, where several students often had to share a single seat, and arranged study hours in the mosque, which was quieter than the overcrowded halls of residence. Those who came from rural backgrounds and were experiencing life in a modern city for the first time were now able to make their way to modernity in a familiar Islamic setting.

Student protests became more aggressive as Sadat drew closer to the West and became more autocratic. In 1978, he issued the Law of Shame: any deviation in thought, word or deed from the establishment was to be punished by loss of civil rights and confiscation of passports and property. Citizens were forbidden to join any group, take part in any broadcast, or publish anything that would threaten 'national unity or social peace'. Even a casual remark, made in the privacy of one's own home, would not go unpunished.[33] In response to government oppression, at the University of Mina students started vandalising Christian churches – associated with Western imperialism – and attacking those who wore Western dress.[34] Sadat closed the jamaat down but suppression nearly always makes such movements more extreme and some students joined a clandestine movement dedicated to armed jihad. Khaled Islambouli had studied at the University of Mina and joined one of these cells. In September 1981, shortly before his assassination, Sadat had rounded up over 1,500 opposition figures, including cabinet ministers, politicians, intellectuals, journalists and ulema, as well as Islamists; one of the latter was Khaled's brother Muhammad.[35]

The ideology of Sadat's murderers had been shaped by Abd al-Salam Faraj, spiritual guide of the Jihad Network, who was executed with Khaled in 1982. His treatise, *The Neglected Duty,* had been circulated privately among members of the organisation and was published after the assassination. This plodding, graceless and ill-informed document shows how misguided the secularising reformers had been to deprive the people of adequate religious guidance. Faraj was another freelancer: he had graduated in electrical engineering and had no expertise in Islamic law. But it seems that by the 1980s the maverick ideas that he was expressing had spread, unchecked by the sidelined ulema, until they were widely accepted in society.[36] The 'neglected duty' of the title was aggressive jihad. Muslims, Faraj argued, had been convinced by feeble-minded apologists that fighting was permissible only in self-defence. Hence Muslims were living in subjection and humiliation and could recover their dignity only by resorting to arms. Sadat was no better than an infidel because he ruled by the 'laws of unbelief' imposed on the ummah by the colonialists.[37] Despite their apparent orthodoxy, Sadat and his government were a pack of apostates who deserved to die. Faraj cited Ibn Taymiyyah's fatwa against the Mongol rulers, who, just like Sadat, had been Muslims only in name. In the time of al-Shafii, Muslims had feared an external attack; but now infidels were actually ruling the ummah. To create a truly Islamic state, therefore, jihad was fard ayn, the duty of every able-bodied Muslim.

Faraj reveals the 'idolatry' that is every bit as present in some forms of political Islamism as in secularist discourse, for he made the ummah a supreme value. 'It is obligatory for every Muslim to seriously strive for the return of the Caliphate,' Faraj argued; anyone who fails to do so 'does not die as a Muslim'.[38] In the past, Islam had been a religion validated by its success. Until the modern period, the powerful position of the ummah had seemed to confirm the message of the Quran: that a rightly guided community would prosper because it was in tune with the way things ought to be. The ummah's sudden demotion has been as theologically shattering for some Muslims as Darwin's evolutionary theory has been for some Christians. The acute sense of shame and humiliation is exacerbated by the sense of past greatness. Much modern Islamism represents a desperate struggle to put history back on track. But this dream of a gloriously restored ummah has become an absolute, an end in itself and, as such, justifies the means of an aggressive jihad – in this case a criminal assassination. In Islamic terms, this constitutes the prime sin of shirk, an idolatry that places a political ideal on the same level as Allah. As one commentator observed, far from condoning lawless violence, the ideal of jihad originally expressed the important insight that 'the final truth for man lies not in some remote and untarnished utopia but in the tension and struggle of applying its ideals to the recalcitrant and obstructive stuff of worldly sorrow'.[39]

Faraj's primitive theology is apparent when he explains why it was more important to fight Sadat than the Israelis: if a truly Islamic state were established in Egypt, he believed, Jerusalem would automatically revert to Muslim rule. In the Quran, God had promised Muslims that he would bring disgrace on their enemies and come to the Muslims' aid. In a nihilistic abandonment both of his modern scientific training and of the Quranic insistence that Muslims use their natural intelligence, Faraj reverted to an extremely naive form of the perennial philosophy that amounted to little more than magical thinking: if Muslims took the initiative, God would 'intervene [and change] the laws of nature'. Could the militants expect a miracle? Faraj answered 'yes'.[40] Observers were puzzled that there was no planned uprising after the assassination. Faraj believed that God would step in and do the rest.[41] He did not. Hosni Mubarak became president with the minimum of fuss and his secular dictatorship remained in power for thirty years.

Terrorism has often cropped up in the Muslim world when the nation's boundaries do not accord with those set up by the colonial powers for the state.[42] Lebanon had been put together particularly ineptly by the colonialists. It had also inherited a pattern of economic disparity, and had its own unique and tragic problems. Its Shii population inhabited the infertile country between Tyre and Sidon which until 1920 had been part of Greater Syria, so they had no historic ties with the Sunni Muslims and Maronite Christians of the north; they had not participated in their modernisation process. A prosperous bourgeoisie had made Beirut the intellectual capital of the Middle East. But southern Lebanon remained undeveloped, because the Constitution made each confessional community responsible for its own welfare and social institutions. Shii poverty meant that most of their 300 villages had neither hospitals nor irrigation and because Shiites tended to be uneducated, they were inadequately represented in the national government. During the 1950s, unable to make a living on the land, thousands migrated to Beirut where they lived in the shanty towns of Maslakh and Karantina, known locally as the 'misery belt'. They never assimilated and were regarded with disdain by the more sophisticated population.

In 1959, however, Musa al-Sadr, a brilliant, cosmopolitan Iranian cleric arrived from Najaf, where a circle of ulema had created a revisionist form of Shiism. Using Shii ideas to help the people reflect on their political and social position, Sadr began to transform this backward community into one of the leading factions in Lebanon. Part of the problem, Sadr believed, was that the traditional quietism of the Shiah had contributed to Shii marginalisation. The Sixth Imam had adopted this policy of sacred secularism in order to protect Shiis from Abbasid violence. But the conditions of the modern world required Shiis to go back to the spirit of Imam Husain and take their destiny into their own hands. In Husain, they could find a model of courage and political choice.[43] Sadr criticised the ulema and feudal landlords for failing to provide for their community. Together with Ayatollah Muhammad Fadl Allah, another member of the Najaf circle, he provided the community with badly needed social services and began to build a culture of Shii self-reliance and resistance to the systemic injustice of Lebanon.[44]

All the elements of the structural violence that typically contributes to the development of an Islamist movement were, therefore, present in Lebanon. A gulf separated a Westernised, privileged elite from the unmodernised masses; urbanisation had been too rapid; there was an inequitable social system, and physical and social dislocation. But the situation of Lebanon was further complicated by the intractable Arab–Israeli conflict. After the Cairo Agreement of 1969, the Palestinian Liberation Organisation was allowed to establish bases in southern Lebanon from which to attack Israel and once they had been expelled from Jordan in 1970, Lebanon became the main base of the PLO. In southern Lebanon, therefore, the Shii suffered heavy casualties in Israel's retaliatory bombardment. The demography of the country had also changed. The Shii birth rate had increased dramatically, the population rising from 100,000 in 1921 to 750,000 in 1975. Because the Sunni and Maronite birth rates had declined, by the mid-1970s the Shii formed 30 per cent of the population and had become the largest confessional community in Lebanon.[45] When both Sunni and Shii Muslims requested a restructuring of political institutions to reflect this change, a catastrophic civil war broke out (1975–78). Lebanon became a dangerously violent place, where fighting was no longer a choice but essential to personal survival.

Shii Islam became militant as a result of ubiquitous warfare and the systemic oppression of Lebanese society. Sadr had already established training camps to teach Shii youth self-defence and after the outbreak of the civil war founded AMAL ('Battalions for Lebanese Resistance'), which brought the poorer classes together with the 'new men' – Shii businessmen and professionals who had managed to climb the economic ladder. They fought Maronite supremacy alongside the Druze, a small, esoteric Shii sect. The Shii probably suffered more than any other group during the civil war. Their shanty towns were destroyed by the Christian militias, thousands were left homeless and thousands more had to flee the south of the country during the ongoing struggle between Israel and the PLO. When Israel invaded southern Lebanon in 1978 to oust the PLO, Shii homes were destroyed and hundreds of thousands were forced to seek refuge in Beirut.

At this crucial moment, Musa al-Sadr made a visit to Libya and disappeared, perhaps murdered by Qaddafi, thus becoming the Lebanese 'Hidden

Imam'. This loss split AMAL: some followed the secularist, American-educated Nabih Berri, who advocated peaceful action, but the more literate 'new men' followed Fadl Allah, a scholar whose views would come to be very controversial in the community of learned authorities. Written in a society torn apart by violent conflict, his *Islam and the Use of Force* (1976) had argued that Muslims must be ready to fight and, if necessary, die like Husain in the struggle for justice and equity. Martyrdom was not just a pious deed but a revolutionary political act, a refusal to submit to oppression and cruelty. Rightly used, force enabled a person to take charge of his life and was the only way to survive with dignity in a violent world:

> Force means that the world gives you resources and wealth; conversely in conditions of weakness, a man's life degenerates, his energies are wasted, he becomes subject to something that resembles suffocation and paralysis. History, the history of war and peace, of science and wealth, is the history of the strong.[46]

Muslims should not shy away from economic success and modern technology but use them to resist injustice and marginalisation. They would not be aping the West, because instead of making the nation state an instrument of the market economy, Shii would build a humane state based on the values of community and self-respect. The ends were Islamic but the means were new.

In 1979, inspired by the Iranian Revolution and with funding and training from Tehran, Fadl Allah founded Hizbollah, the 'Party of God'. Western people were puzzled that the revolution had failed to spread to Shii communities closer to Iran in the Gulf and Saudi Arabia, but had taken root immediately in faraway Lebanon.[47] In fact, Iran and Lebanon had a long relationship. In the sixteenth century, when the Safavids had founded their Shii empire in Iran, then a largely Sunni country, they had asked the Shii scholars of Lebanon to instruct and guide them; so it was natural for Lebanese Shii to join the Iranian revolutionary network. Hizbollah first came to the world's attention during the Israeli invasion (1982) and the subsequent US military intervention (1983–84) when on 25 October 1983 Hizbollah suicide bombers killed 241 American and 58 French peacekeeping troops in their military compound near Beirut airport; this martyrdom operation was followed by further attacks on the US embassy and the US barracks.

To explain its violent actions, Hizbollah communiqués cited the United

States' opposition to Khomeini, and its support for Saddam Hussein, Israel and the Christian Maronites. Fadl Allah spoke of the 'arrogant silence' of Western powers in the face of Third World suffering.[48] These operations were not simply inspired by religious zeal but had a clear political objective: to compel foreign occupiers to leave Lebanon. This was 'revolutionary suicide'. As to methods, Fadl Allah pointed out that the Shii were engaged in an asymmetrical struggle:

> The oppressed nations do not have the technology and destructive weapons that America and Europe have. They must fight with special means of their own . . . We . . . do not regard what oppressed Muslims of the world do with primitive and unconventional means to confront aggressive powers as terrorism. We view this as lawful warfare against the world's imperial powers.[49]

These were not random, bigoted and irrational acts but 'legal obligations governed by rules' which Muslims must not transgress.[50] One of these rules forbade the deliberate targeting of civilians, which is prohibited under Islamic law – though Hizbollah did take American, British, French and German civilians as hostages to secure the release of Shii prisoners held elsewhere. In the West, the suicide attack immediately recalled the Assassins, who symbolised the fanaticism that Westerners had long attributed to Islam. But while Hizbollah had indeed pioneered this controversial method in the modern Middle East, most suicide bombing in Lebanon during the 1980s would be carried out by secularists. According to one survey, Hizbollah was responsible for seven suicide operations; the secular Syrian Nationalist Party for twenty-two, and the socialist Baath party for ten.[51]

By 1986, however, most clerics condemned suicide bombing and hostage-taking as un-Islamic. Hizbollah, it was generally agreed, must change direction, since its operations were too often irresponsible and counter-productive, as it was causing heavy casualties and dividing the Shii community. There was tension between Hizbollah and AMAL and the villages resisted Hizbollah's attempts to impose Islamic rules.[52] By this time Fadl Allah had concluded that violence, after all, did not bring results: what had the PLO achieved with the terrorism that had shocked the world? Lebanese Shii must take a new path, he argued, working 'from within the objective and actual circumstances' in which they found themselves.[53] Fadl Allah knew that it was impossible to establish an Islamic state in Lebanon and in 1989 even suggested that it was time for the Iranians to begin 'the normalisation of relations with the rest of the world', since like any political movement, revolutions go through many stages and change with a changing world:

> Like all revolutions, including the French Revolution, the Islamic Revolution didn't have a realistic line at first. At that time it served to create a state, it proclaimed a mobilisation, a new religious way of thinking and living, with the aim of winning Muslim autonomy and independence from the super-powers.[54]

Hizbollah, therefore, renounced terrorism and became a political party answerable to the electorate and focusing on social activism and a grassroots transformation.

It had already begun to disentangle itself from the melee of Shii militias by developing an underground cell structure and devised a spiritual process designed to replace what Khomeini had called the 'colonised brain' with one that could think outside the parameters imposed by the West.[55] All Hizbollah leaders still attend philosophy classes to develop their capacity to think critically and independently. Like the American civil rights activists, they work with small groups in the villages to discover how each individual can best contribute to the community: they may set someone up in business or train him for an elite militia. Their goal, reminiscent of the Confucian ideal, is to develop a Shii community in which everybody receives and gives a measure of respect and feels valued and needed. Since the 2006 war with Israel, Hizbollah has concentrated especially on anger management: 'We want to turn this anger from a destructive course into something politically useful – building resistance, perhaps – or into some socially constructive activity.'[56]

During that war, Hizbollah modelled an alternative solution to the problem of asymmetrical warfare.[57] In preparation for such a contingency, they had constructed deep underground tunnels and bunkers, some forty feet below the surface, where their militias could sit out Israeli air strikes, before emerging to mount a prolonged rocket and missile attack. They knew that these could not seriously damage the powerful Israeli war machine, but the long duration and unremitting nature of the missile barrages did affect Israeli morale. Hizbollah's goal was to force Israel to launch a ground invasion, whereupon the well-trained Hizbollah guerrilla forces, with inti-mate knowledge of the terrain, could effectively assault Israel's armoured tanks with their shoulder-launched missiles. They had also achieved such a mastery of intelligence and public relations that many Israeli journalists frankly admitted that they preferred Hizbollah's dispatches to the IDF's. Their victory in compelling the Israelis to withdraw demonstrated that terrorism need not be the only way to repel a militarily superior enemy.

As an inspiration for terrorism, however, nationalism has been far more productive than religion. The examples of Egypt and Lebanon both show that the denial of a people's right to national self-determination and the occupation of its homeland by foreign forces has historically been the most powerful recruiting agent of terrorist organisations, whether they have a religious or a secular cast.[58] In Israel we have seen a different dynamic of secular nationalism pushing a religious tradition into a more militant direction: its tendency to make the nation state a supreme value so that its preservation and integrity permits any form of action, however extreme. In May 1980, after the murder of six yeshiva students in Hebron, Gush settlers Menachem Livni and Yehuda Etzion planted bombs in the cars of five Arab mayors, intending not to kill but to mutilate them so that they became living reminders of the consequences of any opposition to Israel.[59] But this operation was a sideline. In April 1984, the Israeli government revealed the existence of a Jewish underground movement that had plotted to blow up the Dome of the Rock in order to bring the Camp David talks to an end.

To curb Jewish aggression that could endanger the nation's survival, the Talmudic rabbis had insisted that the temple could be rebuilt only by the Messiah and, over the centuries, this had acquired the force of a taboo. But Jewish extremists were intensely disturbed by the Dome of the Rock, the third-holiest place in the Muslim world, which was said to stand on the site of Solomon's temple. The magnificent dome, which dominates the skyline of East Jerusalem and is perfectly attuned to the natural environment, was a permanent reminder of the centuries of Islamic domination of the Holy Land. For the Gush, this symbol of the Muslim minority had become demonic. Livni and Etzion described it as an 'abomination' and the 'root cause of all the spiritual errors of our generation'. For Yeshua ben Shoshan, the underground's spiritual adviser, the Dome was the haunt of the evil forces that inspired the Camp David negotiations.[60] All three were convinced that, according to Kabbalistic perennial philosophy, their actions here on earth would activate events in heaven, forcing God, as it were, to effect the Messianic redemption.[61] As an explosives expert in the IDF, Livni manufactured twenty-eight precision bombs that would have destroyed the Dome but not its surroundings.[62] Their only reason for not going ahead was that they could not find a rabbi to bless their operation. The plot was another demonstration of the modern death-wish. The Dome's destruction would almost certainly have caused a war in which, for the first time, the entire Muslim world would have united to fight Israel. Strategists in Washington believed that during the Cold War, when the Soviets supported the Arabs and the United States supported Israel, this might even have sparked a third world war.[63] So crucial was the survival and territorial integrity of the State of Israel to the militants that it justified the destruction of the human race.

Yet far from being inspired by their religious tradition, the militants' conviction violated core teachings of Rabbinic Judaism. The rabbis had repeatedly insisted that violence towards other human beings was tantamount to the denial of God, who had made men and women in his image; murder, therefore, was a sacrilege. God had created *adam*, a single human being, to teach us that whoever destroyed a single life would be punished as though he had destroyed the whole world.[64]

The Dome as a perceived symbol of Jewish humiliation, domination and obliteration fed dangerously into the Jewish history of grievance and suffering, which can become literally explosive. Jews had fought back and achieved a superpower status in the Middle East that would once have seemed inconceivable. For the Gush, the peace process seemed to threaten this hard-won status and, like the monks who obliterated the pagan temples after Julian's attempt to suppress Christianity, their instinctive response was 'Never again'. Hence Jewish radicals, with or without rabbinic approval, continue to flirt with Livni's dangerous idea, convinced that their political designs had some basis in eternal truth. The Temple Mount Faithful have drawn up plans for the Jewish temple that will one day replace the Dome, which they display in a museum provocatively close to the Haram al-Sharif with the ritual utensils and ceremonial robes that they have prepared for the cult. For many, Jewish Jerusalem rising phoenix-like from the ashes of Auschwitz has acquired a symbolic value that is non-negotiable.

The history of Jerusalem shows that a holy place always becomes more precious to a people after they have lost it or feel that their tenure is endangered. Livni's plot therefore helped to make the Haram al-Sharif even more sacred to the Palestinians. When Islam was a great world power, Muslims had the confidence to be inclusive in their devotion to this sacred space. Calling Jerusalem al-Quds ('the Holy'), they understood that a holy place belongs to God and can never be the exclusive preserve of a state. When Umar conquered the city, he left the Christian shrines intact and invited

Jews to return to the City from which they had been excluded for centuries. But now, as they feel that they are losing their city, Palestinian Muslims have become more possessive. Hence the tension between Muslims and Jews frequently erupts into violence at this holy place: in 2000 the provocative visit of the hawkish Israeli politician Ariel Sharon with his right-wing entourage sparked the Palestinian uprising known as the Second Intifada.

Rabbi Meir Kahane also plotted to destroy what he called 'the gentiles' abomination on the Temple Mount'.[65] Most Israelis were horrified when he was elected to a seat in the 1984 Knesset with 1.2 per cent of the vote.[66] For Kahane, to attack any gentile who posed the slightest threat to the Jewish nation was a sacred duty. In New York, he had founded the Jewish Defence League to avenge attacks on Jews by black youths, but when he arrived in Israel and settled in Kiryat Arba he changed its name to Kach ('Thus it is!'), its goal to force the Palestinians to leave the land. Kahane's ideology symbolises the 'miniaturisation' of identity that is one of the catalysts of violence.[67] His fundamentalism was so extreme that it reduced Judaism to a single precept. 'There are not several messages in Judaism,' he insisted. 'There is only one': God simply wanted Jews to 'come to this country to create a Jewish state'.[68] Israel was commanded to be a 'holy' nation, set apart from all others, so 'God wants us to live in a country on our own, isolated, so that we have the least possible contact with what is foreign.'[69] In the Bible, the cult of holiness had prompted the priestly writers to honour the essential 'otherness' of every single human being; it had urged Jews to love the foreigner who lived in their land, using their memories of past suffering not to justify persecution but to sympathise with the distress that these uprooted gentiles were enduring. Kahane, however, embodied an extreme version of the secular nationalism whose inability to tolerate minorities had caused such suffering to his own people. In his view, 'holiness' meant the isolation of Jews, who must be 'set apart' in their own land and the Palestinians expelled.

Some Jews argue that the Holocaust 'summons us all to preserve democracy, to fight racism, and to defend human rights',[70] but many Israelis have concluded that the world's failure to save the Jewish people requires the existence of a militarily strong Israel and they are, therefore, reluctant to engage in peace negotiations. Messianic redemption, Kahane argued, began after the Six Day War. Had Israel annexed the territories, expelled the Arabs and torn down the Dome, redemption would have come painlessly. But because the Israeli government had wanted to appease the international community and had refrained from this violence, redemption would come

in a terrible anti-Semitic calamity, far worse than the Holocaust, which
would force all Jews to leave the diaspora.[71] The Holocaust overshadowed
Kahane's ideology. The State of Israel, he believed, was not a blessing for
Jews but God's revenge on the gentiles: 'He could no longer take the
desecration of his Name and the laughter, the disgrace, and the persecution
of the people that were named after Him.'[72] Every attack on a Jew, therefore, amounted to blasphemy and every act of Jewish retaliation was *Kiddush
ha-Shem*, a sanctification of God's name: 'a Jewish fist in the face of the
astonished gentile world that has not seen it for two millenniums [*sic*]'.[73]
This was the ideology that inspired Kiryat Arba settler Baruch Goldstein
to shoot twenty-nine Palestinian worshippers in the Cave of the Patriarchs
in Hebron on the festival of Purim, 25 February 1994. The massacre was
revenge for the murder of fifty-nine Jews in Hebron on 24 August 1929.
Goldstein died in the attack and is revered by the Israeli Far Right as a
martyr. His action would inspire the first wave of Muslim suicide bombing
in Israel and Palestine.

A collective memory of humiliation and imperial domination has also inspired
a desire for a national character of strength in India.[74] When they look back
in history, Hindus are divided. Some see a paradise of coexistence and a culture
in which Hindu and Muslim traditions combine. But Hindu nationalists see
the period of Muslim rule as a clash of civilisations, in which a militant Islam
forced its culture on the oppressed Hindu majority.[75] The structural violence
of empire is always resented by subject peoples and can persist long after the
imperialists have left. Founded in the early 1980s, the Bharatiya Janata Party
(BJP), the 'Indian National Party', an affiliate of RSS, feeds on this bitterness
and enhances it. It campaigned for a militarily strong India, a nuclear arsenal
(whose warheads are named after Hindu gods), and national distinctiveness.
At first, however, it made no headway in the polls but its fortunes changed
dramatically in 1989, when the issue of the Babri mosque once again hit the
headlines.[76] In India as in Israel, sacred geography has become emblematic of
the nation's disgrace. Here too, the spectacle of a Muslim shrine atop a ruined
temple aroused huge passions, because it so graphically symbolised the Hindu
collective memory of Islamic imperial dominance. In February 1989, activists
resolved to build a new temple to Ram on the site of the mosque and collected
donations from the poorer castes throughout India; in the smallest villages
bricks for the new shrine were cast and consecrated. Not surprisingly, tensions
flared between Muslims and Hindus in the north and Rajiv Gandhi, who had
tried to mediate, lost the election.

The BJP, however, had made large gains at the polls and the following year its president, L. K. Advani, began a *rath yatra* ('chariot pilgrimage'), a thirty-day journey from the west coast to Ayodhya which was to culminate in the rebuilding of the Ram temple. His Toyota van was decorated to resemble Arjuna's chariot in the last battle of the *Mahabharata* and was cheered by fervent crowds lining the route.[77] The pilgrimage began, significantly, at Somnath, where, legend has it, Sultan Mahmud of the Central Asian kingdom of Ghazni had slaughtered thousands of Hindus way back in the eleventh century, razing Shiva's ancient temple to the ground and plundering its treasure. Advani never made it to Ayodhya, because he was arrested on 23 October 1990, but thousands of Hindu nationalists from every region of India had already assembled at the site to begin the mosque's demolition. Scores of them were shot down by the police and hailed as martyrs and Hindu–Muslim riots exploded throughout the country. The Babri mosque was finally dismantled in December 1992, while the press and army stood by and watched. For Muslims, its brutal destruction evoked the horrifying spectre of Islam's annihilation in the subcontinent. There were more riots, the most notorious being a Muslim attack on a train conveying Hindu pilgrims to Ayodhya, which was avenged by a massacre of Muslims in Gujarat.

Like the Islamists, Hindu nationalists are lured by the prospect of rebuilding a glorious civilisation, one that will revive the splendours of India before the Muslims' arrival. They have convinced themselves that their path to this utopian future is blocked by the relics of Moghul civilisation, which have wounded the body of Mother India. Countless Hindus experienced the demolition of the Babri mosque as a liberation from 'slavery'; but others argue that the process is far from complete and dream of erasing the great mosques at Mathura and Varanasi.[78] Many other Hindus, however, were religiously appalled by the Ayodhya tragedy, so this iconoclasm cannot be traced to a violence inherent in 'Hinduism', which has, of course, no single essence, either for or against violence. Rather, Hindu mythology and devotion had blended with the passions of secular nationalism – especially its inability to countenance minorities.

All this meant that for Hindu nationalists the new Ram temple had become a symbol of a liberated India. The emotions involved were memorably expressed by the revered renouncer Rithambra at Hyderabad in April 1991, in a speech which she delivered in the mesmerising rhymed couplets of Indian epic poetry.[79] The temple would not be a mere building, nor was Ayodhya important simply because it was Ram's birthplace: 'The Ram temple

is our honour. It is our self-esteem. It is the image of Hindu unity. We shall
build the temple!'[80] Ram was 'the representation of mass-consciousness';
he was the god of the lowest castes – the fishermen, cobblers and wash-
ermen.[81] Hindus were in mourning for the dignity, self-esteem and spiritual
essence that they had lost. But this new Hindu self could be reconstructed
only by the destruction of the antithetical 'other'. The Muslim was the
obverse of the tolerant, benign Hindu: fanatically intolerant, a destroyer of
shrines, and an arch-tyrant. Throughout, Rithambra laced her speech with
vivid images of mutilated corpses, amputated arms, chests cut open like
those of dissected frogs, and bodies slashed, burned, raped and violated, all
evoking Mother India, desecrated and ravaged by Islam. The 800 million
Hindus of India can hardly claim to be economically or socially oppressed,
so Hindu nationalists feed on such images of persecution and insist that a
strong Hindu identity can be restored only by decisive, violent action.

Until the 1980s, the Palestinians had held aloof from the religious revival
in the rest of the Middle East. Yasser Arafat's PLO was a secular nationalist
organisation. Most Palestinians admired him but the PLO's secularism
appealed mainly to the Westernised Palestinian elite, and observant Muslims
played virtually no part in its terrorist actions.[82] When the PLO was
suppressed in the Gaza Strip in 1971, Sheikh Ahmed Yassin founded Mujama
('Congress'), an offshoot of the Muslim Brotherhood, which focused on
social welfare work. By 1987 Mujama had established clinics, drug-
rehabilitation centres, youth clubs, sporting facilities and Quran classes
throughout Gaza, supported not only by Muslim alms but also by the Israeli
government in an attempt to undermine the PLO. At this point Yassin had
no interest in armed struggle. When the PLO accused him of being Israel's
puppet, he replied that, on the contrary, it was their secular ethos that was
destroying Palestinian identity.[83] Mujama was far more popular than Islamic
Jihad (IJ), formed in the 1980s, which attempted to apply Qutb's ideas to
the Palestinian tragedy and regarded itself as the vanguard of a larger global
struggle 'against the forces of arrogance (jahiliyyah), the colonial enemy,
all over the world'.[84] IJ engaged in terrorist attacks on the Israeli military
but rarely quoted the Quran; its rhetoric was frankly secular. Ironically, the
only thing that was religious about this organisation was its name – and
this may explain its lack of mass support.[85]

The outbreak of the First Intifada (1987–93), led by young secularist
Palestinians, changed everything. Impatient with the corruption and inef-
fectiveness of Fatah, the leading PLO party, they urged the entire population

to rise up and refuse to submit to the Israeli occupation. Women and children threw stones at Israeli soldiers and those shot by the IDF were hailed as martyrs. The intifada made a strong impression on the international community: Israel had long presented itself as plucky David fighting the Arab Goliath but now the world watched heavily armoured Israeli soldiers pursuing unarmed children. As a military man, Yitzhak Rabin realised that harassing women and children would ruin IDF morale and when he became prime minister in 1992, he was prepared to negotiate with Arafat. The following year Israel and the PLO signed the Oslo Accords. The PLO recognised Israel's existence within its 1948 borders and promised to end the insurrection; in return, Palestinians were offered limited autonomy in the West Bank and Gaza for a five-year period, after which final-status negotiations would begin on the issues of Israeli settlements, compensation for Palestinian refugees and the future of Jerusalem.

The Kookists, of course, regarded this as a criminal act. In July 1995, fifteen Gush rabbis ordered soldiers to defy their commanding officers when the IDF began to evacuate the territories – an act that was tantamount to civil war. Other Gush rabbis ruled that Rabin was a *rodef* ('pursuer'), worthy of death under Jewish law for endangering Jewish life.[86] On 4 November 1995, Yigal Amir, an army veteran and student at Bar Ilan University, took this ruling to heart, shooting the prime minister during a peace rally in Tel Aviv.[87]

The success of the intifada made younger Mujama members aware that its welfare programmes were not truly addressing the Palestinian problem, so they broke away to form *HAMAS,* an acronym of *Haqamat al-Muqamah al-Islamiyya* ('Islamic Resistance Movement'), meaning 'Fervour'. They would fight both the PLO and the Israeli occupation. Young men flocked to join up, finding the egalitarian ethos of the Quran more congenial than the secularism of the Palestinian elite. Many recruits came from the lower middle-class intelligentsia, educated now in Palestinian universities, which was no longer prepared to kowtow to the traditional authorities.[88] Sheikh Yassin lent his support and some of his closest associates staffed Hamas' political wing. Instead of drawing on Western ideology, Hamas found inspiration in the history of secular Palestinian resistance as well as Islamic history; religion and politics were inseparable and intertwined.[89] In its communiqués, Hamas celebrated the Prophet's victory over the Jewish tribes at the Battle of Khaybar,[90] Saladin's victory over the Crusaders, and the spiritual status of Jerusalem in Islam.[91] The Charter of Hamas evoked the venerable tradition of 'volunteering' when it urged Palestinians to become *murabitun* ('guardians of the frontiers'),[92] presenting the Palestinian struggle as a classical defensive jihad: 'When our enemies usurp some lands, jihad becomes a duty on all Muslims (*fard ayn*).'[93]

But in the early days fighting was a secondary concern; the Charter quoted none of the Quranic jihad verses.[94] The first priority was the Greater Jihad, the struggle to become a better Muslim. Palestinians, Hamas believed, had been weakened by the inauthentic adoption of Western secularism by the PLO, when, the Charter explained, 'Islam disappeared from life. Thus, rules were broken, concepts were vilified, values changed . . . homelands were invaded, people were subdued'.[95] Hamas did not resort to violence until 1993, the year of the Oslo Accords, when seventeen Palestinians were killed on the Haram al-Sharif and Hamas activists retaliated in a series of operations against Israeli military targets and Palestinian collaborators. After Oslo, support for the militant Islamist groups dropped to 13 per cent of the Palestinian population but it rose to a third when Palestinians found that they were subjected to harsh and exceptional regulations and that Israel would retain indefinite sovereignty over Gaza and the West Bank.[96]

The Hebron massacre was a watershed. After the forty-day mourning period, a Hamas suicide bomber killed seven Israeli citizens in Afula in Israel proper, and this was followed by four operations in Jerusalem and Tel Aviv, the most deadly of which was a bus bombing in Tel Aviv on 19 October 1994, which killed twenty-three people and injured nearly fifty. The murder of innocent civilians and the exploitation of adolescents for these actions was morally repugnant, damaged the Palestinian cause abroad and split the movement. Some Hamas leaders argued that by losing the moral high ground, Hamas had strengthened the Israeli position.[97] Others retorted that Hamas was merely responding in kind to Israel's aggression against Palestinian civilians, which, indeed, had increased after the outbreak of the Second Intifada when there were more bombings, missile attacks and assassinations of Palestinian leaders. Ulema abroad were equally divided. Sheikh Tantawi, Grand Mufti of Egypt, defended suicide bombing as the only way for Palestinians to counter the military might of Israel, and Sheikh al-Qaradawi in Yemen argued that it was legitimate self-defence.[98] But Sheikh al-Sheikh, Grand Mufti of Saudi Arabia, protested that the Quran strictly forbade suicide and that Islamic law prohibited the killing of civilians. In 2005, Hamas abandoned the suicide attack and focused instead on creating a conventional military apparatus in Gaza.

Some Western analysts have argued that suicide killing is deeply embedded in the Islamic tradition.[99] But if that were so, why was 'revolutionary suicide' unknown in Sunni Islam before the late twentieth century; why have not more militant Islamist movements adopted this tactic; and why have both Hamas and Hizbollah abandoned it?'[100] It is certainly true that Hamas drew upon the Quran and hadith to motivate the bombers with fantasies of Paradise. But the suicide attack was in fact invented by the Tamil Tigers of Sri Lanka, a nationalist separatist group with no time for religion, who have claimed responsibility for over 260 suicide operations in two decades.[101] Robert Pape of the University of Chicago has investigated every single suicide attack worldwide between 1980 and 2004 and concluded that 'there is little connection between suicide terrorism and Islamic fundamentalism, or any religion for that matter'. For instance, of thirty-eight suicide attacks in Lebanon during the 1980s, eight were committed by Muslims, three by Christians, and twenty-seven by secularists and socialists.[102] What all suicide operations do have in common, however, is a strategic goal: 'to compel liberal democracies to withdraw military forces from territory that the terrorists consider to be their homeland'. Suicide bombing is, therefore, essentially a political response to military occupation.[103] IDF statistics show that of all Hamas' suicide attacks, only 4 per cent targeted civilians in Israel proper, the rest being directed against West Bank settlers and the Israeli army.[104]

This is not to deny that Hamas is as much a religious as a national move- ment, only that the fusion of the two is a modern innovation. The exalted love of the Fatherland, which has no roots in Islamic culture, is now suffused with Muslim fervour.[105] Islamic and nationalist themes alternate seamlessly in the final videotaped messages of Hamas martyrs. Twenty-year-old Abu Surah, for example, began with a traditional Muslim invocation: 'It is the day of meeting the Lord of the Worlds and bearing witness to the Messenger.' He then called upon 'all the saints and all the mujahidin of Palestine and of every part of the world', moving unselfconsciously from holy men to Palestinian nationalists before finally shifting to a global perspective. Martyrs shed their blood

> for the sake of Allah and out of love for this homeland and for the same and honor of this people in order that Palestine remain Islamic, and Hamas remain a torch lighting the road of all the perplexed and all the tormented and oppressed and that Palestine be liberated.[106]

Like the Iranians, Palestinians regarded their jihad against Israeli occupation as part of a Third World struggle against imperialism. Moreover, they may

be fighting the secular Palestinian Authority, but both share the same nationalist passions: both regard death for Palestine as a great privilege and hate
the enemy with the virulence of any ultra-nationalist whose country is at
war.[107]

Highly stylised videos notwithstanding, one can never know what goes
through the mind of suicide bombers at the moment when they drive trucks
into a building or detonate bombs in a crowded marketplace. To imagine
they do this entirely for God or that they are impelled solely by Islamic
teaching is to ignore the natural complexity of all human motivation.
Forensic psychiatrists who have interviewed survivors find that the desire
to become a hero and achieve posthumous immortality was a strong factor.
Other would-be martyrs cited the ekstasis of battle that gives life meaning
and purpose, a feeling close to religious exaltation, as we have seen, but
not religious per se. In fact, it is said, the Hamas rank-and-file lived not
for 'politics, nor ideology, nor religion . . . but rather an ecstatic camara-
derie in the face of death "on the path of Allah"'.[108] Life under occupation
held little attraction for many of the volunteers; their bleak existence in
Gaza's refugee camps made the possibility of a blissful hereafter and a
glorious reputation here on earth powerfully alluring. But then all communities throughout history have praised the warrior who gives his life for his
people.[109] Palestinians also honour those who are killed involuntarily in the
conflict with Israel; they too are shahid as the hadith made clear: any
untimely death was a 'witness' to both human finitude and the nation's
plight.[110]

It further complicates the question of faith and terrorism that the suicide
killer has been revered as a hero in other religious traditions as well. In
the story of Samson, the judge who died pulling the Temple of Dagon down
upon the Philistine chieftains, the biblical author does not agonise over his
motives but simply celebrates his courage.[111] Samson 'heroically hath finished
a life heroic', the devout Puritan John Milton likewise concluded in *Samson
Agonistes*:[112]

> Nothing is here for tears, nothing to wail
> Or knock the breast; no weakness, no contempt,
> Dispraise or blame; nothing but well and fair,
> And what may quiet us in a death so noble.[113]

Far from inspiring horror, Samson's end left those who witnessed it with
a sense of 'peace and consolation . . . and calm of mind, all passion spent'.[114]

Not coincidentally, Israel calls its nuclear capacity 'The Samson Option', regarding a strike that would inevitably result in the destruction of the nation as an honourable duty and a possibility that the Jewish state has freely chosen.[115] Talal Asad has suggested that the suicide bomber is simply acting out this same appalling scenario on a smaller scale and can, therefore, 'be seen to belong to the modern Western tradition of armed conflict for the defence of the free political community. To save the tradition (or to found its state) in confronting a dangerous enemy, it may be necessary to act without being bound by ordinary moral constraints.'[116]

We are absolutely right to condemn the suicide bomber's targeting of innocent civilians and mourn his victims. But as we have seen, in war the state also targets such victims; during the twentieth century, the rate of civilian deaths rose sharply and now stands at 90 per cent of all deaths.[117] In the West, we solemnise the deaths of our regular troops carefully, and recurrently honour the memory of the soldier who dies for his country. But the civilian deaths we cause are rarely mentioned and there has been no sustained outcry in the West against them. Suicide bombing shocks us to the core; but should it be more shocking than the death of thousands of children in their homelands every year because of landmines? Or collateral damage in a drone strike? 'Dropping cluster bombs from the air is not only less repugnant: it is somehow deemed, by Western people at least, to be morally superior,' says British psychologist Jacqueline Rose. 'Why dying with your victim should be seen as a greater sin than saving yourself is unclear.'[118] The colonial West had created a two-tier hierarchy that privileged itself at the expense of 'the Rest'. The Enlightenment had preached the equality of all human beings, yet Western policy in the developing world often adopted a double standard so that we failed to treat others as we would wish to be treated. Our focus on the nation seems to have made it hard for us to cultivate the global outlook that we need in our increasingly interrelated world. We must deplore any action that spills innocent blood or sows terror for its own sake. But we must also acknowledge and sincerely mourn the blood that we have shed in the pursuit of our national interests. Otherwise we can hardly defend ourselves against the accusation of maintaining an 'arrogant silence' in the face of others' pain and of creating a world order in which some people's lives are deemed more valuable than others.

GLOBAL JIHAD

In the early 1980s, a steady stream of young men from the Arab world made their way to north-west Pakistan, near the Afghan border, to join the jihad against the Soviet Union. The charismatic Jordanian-Palestinian scholar Abdullah Azzam had summoned Muslims to fight alongside their Afghan brothers.[1] Like the 'fighting scholars' who had flocked to the frontiers during the classical period, Azzam was convinced that repelling the Soviet occupation was a duty for every able-bodied Muslim: 'I believe that the Muslim ummah is responsible for the honour of every Muslim woman that is being violated in Afghanistan and is responsible for every drop of Muslim blood that is being shed unjustly,' he declared.[2] Azzam's sermons and lectures electrified a generation distressed by the suffering of their fellow Muslims, frustrated by an inability to help, and youthfully eager to do something about it. By 1984 recruits were arriving in ever-larger numbers from Saudi Arabia, the Gulf States, Yemen, Egypt, Algeria, Sudan, Indonesia, the Philippines, Malaysia and Iraq.[3] One of these volunteers was the scion of a great family fortune, Osama bin Laden, who became the main sponsor for the Services Bureau established in Peshawar to support his comrades, organise recruitment and funding, and provide healthcare, food and shelter for Afghan orphans and refugees.

President Ronald Reagan also spoke of the Afghan campaign as a holy war. In 1983, addressing the National Association of Evangelicals, he branded the Soviet Union an 'evil empire'. 'There is sin and evil in the world,' he told his highly receptive audience, 'and we're enjoined by Scripture and the Lord Jesus to oppose it with all our might.'[4] It seemed entirely proper to Reagan and CIA director William Casey, a devout Catholic, to support Muslim *mujahidin* against the atheistic communists. The massive aid package of US $600 million (annually renewed and matched each year by Saudi Arabia and the Gulf States) transformed the Afghan guerrilla forces into a military juggernaut that battled with the Russians as fiercely as their ancestors had fought the British in the nineteenth century. Some of the Afghan fighters had studied in Egypt and been influenced by Qutb and Maududi but most were from rural societies and their Sufi devotion to saints and shrines was wholly untouched by any hint of modern Islamic thought.

The Americans also gave the 'Arab-Afghans' (as the foreign volunteers were called) every possible encouragement. Supported by funds from Arab entrepreneurs like bin Laden, they were armed by the Americans and trained by Pakistani troops.[5] In training camps around Peshawar they fought alongside the Afghan guerrillas, but their contribution should not be exaggerated. Few actually took part in the fighting; many would engage solely in humanitarian work, never leaving Peshawar, and some would stay only a few weeks. There were rarely more than three thousand Arab fighters in the region at any one time. Some merely spent part of their summer vacation on 'jihad tours', which included a trip over the Khyber Pass where they could be photographed on location. Known as 'The Brigade of the Strangers', the Arab-Afghans tended to keep to themselves; the Pakistanis and Afghans regarded them as somewhat bizarre.

Leading Muslim ulema looked somewhat askance at Azzam but his integrity was very appealing to the young Arab-Afghans, who were disillusioned by the corruption and hypocrisy of their leaders at home. They knew that Azzam had always practised what he preached, thoughout his life combining scholarship with political activism. He had joined the Muslim Brotherhood at the age of eighteen while studying Shariah in Syria, had fought in the Six Day War, and as a student at the Azhar had supervised Brotherhood Youth. While he was a lecturer at Abd al-Aziz University in Jeddah, Saudi Arabia, one of his pupils was the young bin Laden. 'The life of the Muslim ummah,' Azzam declared, 'is solely dependent on the ink of its scholars and the blood of its martyrs.'[6] Scholarship was essential to deepen the ummah's spirituality, but so was the self-sacrifice of its warriors, since no nation had ever achieved distinction without a strong military. 'History does not write its lines, except in blood,' Azzam insisted. 'Honour and respect cannot be established except on a foundation of cripples and corpses.'

Empires, distinguished peoples, states, and societies cannot be established except with examples. Indeed, those who think that they can change reality or change societies without blood, sacrifices and invalids – without pure innocent souls – do not understand the essence of this *din* [Islam] and they do not know the method of the best of Messengers.[7]

Other Muslim leaders had praised the glory of martyrdom but none had dwelt so graphically on its violent reality. A community that cannot defend itself, Azzam insisted, will inevitably be dominated by military power. His goal was to create a cadre of scholar-warriors, whose sacrifice would inspire the rest of the ummah.[8] Jihad, he believed, was the Sixth Pillar, on a par with the shahadah, prayer, almsgiving, the Ramadan fast and hajj. A Muslim who neglected jihad would have to answer to God on the Day of Judgment.[9]

Azzam did not make this theory out of whole cloth. He followed the classical theory of al-Shafii, the eighth-century scholar who had ruled that when the Dar al-Islam was invaded by a foreign power, jihad became fard ayn, the responsibility of every fit Muslim who lived near the frontier. Modern transport now made it possible for *all* Muslims to reach the border of Afghanistan, so jihad, Azzam reasoned, was 'compulsory for each and every Muslim on earth'. Once they had liberated Afghanistan, the Arab-Afghans should go on to recover all the other lands wrested from the ummah by non-Muslim states – Palestine, Lebanon, Bokhara, Chad, Eritrea, Somalia, the Philippines, Burma, South Yemen, Tashkent and Spain.[10]

In his lectures and writings, Azzam depicted the Afghans somewhat idealistically as untouched by the brutal mechanisation of modern jahiliyyah; they represented pristine humanity. Fighting the Soviet Goliath, they reminded him of David when he was but a shepherd boy.[11] His tales of the Afghans and Arabs who died as martyrs in this war inspired Muslim audiences worldwide. But Azzam's martyrs were not suicide bombers or terrorists of any kind. They did not cause their own deaths and did not kill civilians: they were regular soldiers killed in battle by Soviet troops. Azzam was in fact adamantly opposed to terrorism and on this point he would eventually part company with bin Laden and the Egyptian radical Ayman al-Zawahiri. Azzam insistently maintained the orthodox view that killing non-combatants or fellow Muslims like Sadat violated fundamental Islamic teaching. In fact, he believed that a martyr could bear 'witness' to divine truth even if he died peacefully in bed.[12] Azzam's classical jihadism was condemned by some scholars, but it had strong appeal for young Sunnis who were embarrassed by the success of the Shii revolution in Iran. But not all the volunteers were devout; some were not even observant, although in Peshawar many would be influenced by such hard-line Islamists as Zawahiri, who had suffered arrest, torture and imprisonment in Egypt for alleged involvement in the Sadat assassination. And so Afghanistan became a new Islamist hub. Young militants from East Asia and North Africa were sent to the front to increase their commitment and the government of Saudi Arabia actually encouraged its own young to volunteer. [13]

To understand the Saudi influence, one must reckon with what may seem a contradiction. On the one hand, after the Iranian Revolution in 1979, the Kingdom of Saudi Arabia had become one of America's chief regional allies. On the other hand, it subscribed to an extremely reductive form of Islam, which had been developed in the eighteenth century by the Arabian reformer Muhammad ibn Abd al-Wahhab (1703–92). Ibn Abd al-Wahhab had preached a return to the pristine Islam of the Prophet and repudiated such later developments as Shiism, Sufism, Falsafah and the jurisprudence (fiqh) on which all other Muslim ulema depended. He was particularly distressed by the popular veneration of holy men and their tombs, which he condemned as idolatry. Even so, Wahhabism was not inherently violent; indeed, Ibn Abd al-Wahhab had refused to sanction the wars of his patron, Ibn Saud of Najd, because he was simply fighting for wealth and glory. [14] It was only after his retirement that Wahhabis became more aggressive, even to the point of destroying Imam Husain's shrine in Karbala in 1802 as well as monuments in Arabia connected with Muhammad and his Companions. At this time too, the sect insisted that Muslims who did not accept their doctrines were infidels (kufar). [15] During the early nineteenth century, Wahhabis incorporated the writings of Ibn Taymiyyah into their canon and takfir, the practice of declaring another Muslim an unbeliever, which Ibn Abd al-Wahhab himself had rejected, became central to their practice. [16]

The oil embargo imposed by the Gulf States during the 1973 October War had sent the price soaring and the Kingdom now had all the petro-dollars it needed to find practical ways of imposing Wahhabism on the entire ummah. [17] Deeply disconcerted by the success of the Shii revolution in Iran, which threatened their leadership of the Muslim world, the Saudis intensi-fied their efforts to counter Iranian influence and replaced Iran as the chief ally of the United States in the region. The Saudi-based Muslim World League opened offices in every region inhabited by Muslims and the Saudi Ministry of Religion printed and distributed translations of the Quran, Wahhabi doctrinal tracts, and the works of Ibn Taymiyyah, Qutb and Maududi to Muslim communities in the Middle East, Africa, Indonesia, the United States and Europe. In all these places, they funded the building of Saudi-style mosques, creating an international aesthetic that broke with local architectural traditions, and established madrasas that provided free educa-tion for the poor, with, of course, a Wahhabi curriculum. At the same time, the young men from the more disadvantaged Muslim countries, such as Egypt and Pakistan, who came to work in the Gulf, associated their new affluence with Wahhabism.[18] When they returned home they chose to live in new neighbourhoods with Saudi mosques and shopping malls that segregated the sexes. In return for their munificence, Saudis demanded religious conformity. The Wahhabi rejection of all other forms of Islam as well as other faith traditions would reach as deeply into Bradford, England, and Buffalo, New York, as into Pakistan, Jordan or Syria, everywhere gravely undermining Islam's traditional pluralism. The West played an unwitting role in this surge of intolerance, since the United States welcomed the Saudis' opposition to Iran and the Kingdom depended on the US military for its very survival.[19]

The Saudis' experience of modernity had been very different from that of the Egyptians, Pakistanis or Palestinians. The Arabian Peninsula had not been colonised; it was rich, and had never been forced to secularise. Instead of fighting tyranny and corruption at home, therefore, Saudi Islamists focused on the suffering of Muslims worldwide, their Pan-Islamism close in spirit to Azzam's global jihad. The Quran told Muslims that they must take responsibility for one another; King Faisal had always framed his support for the Palestinians in these terms, and the Saudi-based Muslim World League and the Organisation of Islamic Conferences had regularly expressed solidarity with member-states in conflict with non-Muslim regimes. Now television brought images of Muslim suffering in Palestine or Lebanon into Saudis' comfortable homes. They saw pictures of Israelis bulldozing Palestinian houses and in September 1982 witnessed the Christian Maronites' massacre, with the tacit approval of the IDF, of 2,000 Palestinians in the refugee camps of Sabra and Shatila. With so much suffering of this kind in the Muslim world, Pan-Islamist sentiment increased during the 1980s and the government exploited it as a way of distracting their subjects from the Kingdom's internal problems.[20] It was for this reason, too, that the Saudis encouraged the young to join the Afghan jihad, offering airfare discounts, while the state press celebrated their feats on the frontier. The Wahhabi clerical establishment, however, disapproved of the Afghans' Sufi practices and insisted that jihad was not an individual duty for civilians but was still the ruler's responsibility. Yet the Saudi king's civil government supported Azzam's teaching for its own temporal reasons.

A study of Saudis who volunteered for Afghanistan, and later fought in Bosnia and Chechnya, shows that most were chiefly motivated by the desire to help their Muslim brothers and sisters.[21] Nasir al-Bahri, who would become bin Laden's bodyguard, gave the fullest and most perceptive explanation of this concern:

> We were greatly affected by the tragedies we were witnessing and the events we were seeing: children crying, women widowed, and the high number of incidents of rape. When we went forward for jihad, we experienced a bitter reality. We saw things that were more awful than anything we had expected or had heard or seen in the media. It was as though we were like 'a cat with closed eyes' that opened its eyes at these woes. [22]

This was, he said, a political awakening and the volunteers began to acquire a global sense of the ummah that transcended national boundaries: 'The idea of the umma began to evolve in our minds. We realised we were a nation (*ummah*) that had a distinguished place among nations . . . The issue of nationalism was put out of our minds, and we acquired a wider view than that, namely the issue of the umma.' [23] The welfare of the ummah had always been a deeply spiritual as well as a political concern in Islam so the plight of their fellow Muslims cut to the core of their Islamic identity. Many were ashamed that Muslim leaders had responded so inadequately to these disasters. 'After all those years of humiliation, they could finally do something to help their Muslim brothers,' one respondent explained. [24] Another said that 'he would follow the news of his brothers with the deepest empathy and he wanted to do something, anything, to help them'. One volunteer's friend remembered that 'we would often sit and talk about the slaughtering to which Muslims are subjected, and his eyes would fill with tears'. [25]

The survey also found that, in nearly every case, there was more sympathy for the victims than hatred for their oppressors. And despite the United States' support for Israel, there was as yet little anti-Americanism. 'We did not go because of the Americans,' insisted Nasir al-Bahri. [26] Some recruits longed for the glamour of a glorious martyrdom but many were also lured by the sheer excitement of warfare, the possibility of heroism and the comradeship of brothers-in-arms. As ever, the warrior's transcendence of mundane circumstance seemed very much akin to the believer's spiritual transcendence. Nasir al-Bahri remembered how they idolised the volunteers: 'When we used to look at the Afghan suits that the mujahidin who returned from Afghanistan wore as they walked the streets of Jidda, Mecca or Medina, we used to feel that we were living with the generation of the triumphant companions of the Prophet, and hence looked up to them as an example.' [27]

When finally the Soviets were forced to withdraw from Afghanistan in February 1989 and the Soviet Union itself collapsed in 1991, the Arab-Afghans relished a heady, if inaccurate, sense of having defeated a great world power. They now planned to fulfil Azzam's dream of reconquering all the lost Muslim lands. Throughout the world at this time, political Islam seemed in the ascendant. Hamas had become a serious challenge to Fatah. In Algeria, the Islamic Salvation Front (FIS) had won a decisive victory over the secular National Liberation Front (FLN) in the municipal polls of 1990, and the Islamist ideologue Hassan al-Turabi had come to power in the Sudan. After the Soviet withdrawal, bin Laden founded al-Qaeda, which began humbly as an alumni organisation for those Arab-Afghans who wanted to take the jihad forward. At this point, the entity, whose name simply means 'The Base', had no coherent ideology or clear goal. And so some of its affiliates returned home as freelances with the aim of deposing corrupt secularist regimes and replacing them with an Islamic government. Others, still committed to Azzam's classical jihadism, joined local Muslims in their struggle against the Russians in Chechnya and Tajikistan and the Serbs in Bosnia. But to their dismay, they found that they were unable to transform these national conflicts into what they considered a true jihad. Indeed, in Bosnia they were not only de trop but a positive liability.

The Bosnian War (1992–95) saw one of the last genocides of the twentieth century. Unlike the two preceding it, the Turkish genocide and the Holocaust, this mass killing was conducted on the basis of religious rather than ethnic identity. But despite the widespread assumption in the West that the divisions in the Balkans were ancient and ingrained and that the violence was ineradicable because of its strong 'religious' element, such communal intolerance was relatively new. Jews, Christians and Muslims had lived together peacefully under Ottoman rule for five hundred years and continued doing so after the fall of the Ottoman empire in 1918, when Serbs, Slovenians, Slavic Muslims and Croats had formed the multi-religious federation of Yugoslavia ('Land of the South Slavs'). Yugoslavia was dismantled by Nazi Germany in 1941 but was revived after the Second World War by the communist leader Josip Broz Tito (r. 1945–80) under the slogan 'Brotherhood and Unity'. After his death, however, the radical Serbian nationalism of Slobodan Milošević and the equally assertive Croatian nationalism of Franjo Tudjman pulled the country apart, with Bosnia caught in the middle. Slavic nationalism had a strongly Christian flavour – Serbs were Orthodox and Croatians Roman Catholic – but Bosnia, with a Muslim majority and Serbian, Croatian, Jewish and gypsy communities, opted for a secular state that respected all religions. Lacking the military capacity to defend themselves, Bosnian Muslims knew they would be persecuted if they remained part of Serbia and so in April 1992 they declared independence. The United States and the European Union recognised Bosnia-Herzegovina as a sovereign state.

Milošević depicted Serbia as 'a fortress, defending European culture and religion' from the Islamic world, and Serbian clerics and academics similarly described their nation as a bulwark against the Asiatic hordes.[28] Another radical Serbian nationalist, Radovan Karadžić, had warned the Bosnian Assembly that if they declared independence they would lead their nation 'into hell' and 'make the Muslim people disappear'.[29] But this latent hatred of Islam dated only from the nineteenth century, when Serbian nationalists had created a myth that blended Christianity with a national sentiment based on ethnicity: it cast Prince Lazlo, defeated by the Ottomans in 1389, as a Christ figure, the Turkish Sultan as a Christ-slayer, and the Slavs who converted to Islam as 'Turkified' (isturciti). By adopting a non-Christian religion they had renounced their Slavic ethnicity and become Orientals; the Serbian nation would not rise again until these aliens were exterminated.[30] But so deep-rooted were the habits of coexistence that it took Milošević three years of relentless propaganda to persuade the Serbs to revive this lethal blend of secular nationalism, religion and racism. Significantly, the war began with a frantic attempt to expunge the documentary evidence that for centuries Jews, Christians and Muslims had enjoyed a rich coexistence. A month after the Bosnian declaration of independence, Serbian militias destroyed the Oriental Institute in Sarajevo, which housed the largest collection of Islamic and Jewish manuscripts in the Balkans, burned down the National Library and National Museum, and targeted all such manuscript collections for destruction. Between them, Serbian and Croat nationalists also destroyed some fourteen hundred mosques, turning the sites into parks and parking-lots to erase all memory of the inconvenient past.[31]

While they were burning the museums, Serbian militias and the heavily armed Yugoslav National Army overran Bosnia and in the autumn of 1992 the process that Karadžić called 'ethnic cleansing' began.[32] Milošević had opened the prisons and recruited petty gangsters into the militias, letting them pillage, rape, burn and kill with impunity.[33] No Muslim was to be spared and any Bosnian Serb who refused to cooperate must also die. Muslims were herded into concentration camps, and without toilets or other sanitation, filthy, emaciated and traumatised, they seemed scarcely human either to themselves or their tormentors. Militia leaders dulled the inhibitions of their troops with alcohol, forcing them to gang-rape, murder and torture. When Srebrenica, a United Nations 'safe area', was turned over to the Serb army in the summer of 1995 at least eight thousand men and boys were massacred, and by the autumn the last Muslims were either killed or expelled from the Banja Luka region.[34]

The international community was horrified, but made no urgent demand for the killing to be stopped; rather, the prevailing feeling was that all parties were equally guilty.[35] 'I don't care two cents about Bosnia. Not two cents,' said *New York Times* columnist Thomas Friedman. 'The people there have brought on their own troubles. Let them keep on killing one another and the problem will be solved.'[36] To their credit, the Arab-Afghans were the only people to provide military help but the Bosnian Muslims found them intolerant, were baffled by their global jihadism and adamantly rejected all their plans for an Islamic state. Unfortunately, the Arab-Afghans' presence gave the impression abroad that the Bosnian Muslims were also fundamentalists, though in fact many wore their Islam very lightly. Stereotypical views about Islam and fears of an Islamic state on the threshold of Europe may well have contributed to the Western reluctance to intervene; Serbian rhetoric of defensive walls may not have seemed such a bad idea to some Europeans and Americans. Nevertheless in August 1995, NATO did intervene with a series of air strikes against Bosnian Serb positions, which finally brought this tragic conflict to an end. A peace agreement was signed in Dayton, Ohio, on 21 November 1995. But the world was left with a troubling memory. Yet again, there had been concentration camps in Europe, this time with Muslims in them. After the Holocaust, the cry had been 'Never Again' but this did not seem to apply to Europe's Muslim population.

Other Arab-Afghan veterans found, when they returned home, that they were too radical for the local Muslims who had not shared their experience in Afghanistan. The vast majority vehemently rejected their ruthless militancy. In Algeria, Afghan veterans had high hopes of creating an Islamic state, since the Islamic Salvation Front (FIS) seemed certain to gain a majority in the national elections in 1992. But at the last moment, the military staged a coup and the liberal secularist FLN President Benjedid, who had promised democratic reforms, suppressed FIS and imprisoned its leaders. Had a democratic process been thwarted in such an unconstitutional manner in Iran or Pakistan, there would have been worldwide outrage. But because it was an Islamic government that had been blocked by the coup there was jubilation in some sectors of the Western press, which seemed to suggest that in some mysterious way this undemocratic action had made Algeria safe for democracy. The French government threw its support behind the new hard-line FLN President Liamine Zéroual and strengthened his resolve to hold no further dialogue with the FIS.

As we have seen elsewhere, when suppressed, these movements tend almost invariably to become more extreme. The more radical members of the FIS broke away to form a guerrilla organisation, the Armed Islamic Group (GIA) and were joined by the returning Arab-Afghans. At first, the veterans' military training was welcome, but their ruthless methods soon shocked the Algerians. They began a terror campaign in the mountains south of Algiers, assassinating monks, journalists, and secular and religious intellectuals as well as the inhabitants of entire villages. There are indications, however, that the military not only acquiesced but may even have participated in this violence in order to eliminate populations sympathetic to the FIS and discredit the GIA. There was also a chilling preview of future events, when the GIA hijacked a plane flying to France, intending to crash it over Paris to prevent the French government from supporting the Algerian regime. Fortunately, the plane was captured by commandos at Marseilles.[37]

The returning Egyptian Arab-Afghans also found that they had become too extreme for their fellow countrymen. Zawahiri founded Islamic Jihad with the intention of assassinating the entire Mubarak government and establishing an Islamic state. In June 1995, they attempted but failed to murder the president. In April 1996, they killed a busload of thirty Greek tourists – the intended targets had been Israelis, who had switched buses at the last moment – and finally, to weaken the economy by damaging the crucially important tourist industry, Islamic Jihad massacred sixty people, most of them foreign visitors, at Luxor in November 1997. They discovered, however, that they had wholly misjudged the mood of the country. Egyptians saw this violent obsession with an Islamic state as blatant idolatry that violated core Muslim values; they were so appalled by the Luxor atrocity that Zawahiri had no option but to rejoin bin Laden in Afghanistan and merge his Islamic Jihad with al-Qaeda.

Bin Laden fared no better than the other veterans when he returned to Saudi Arabia.[38] When Saddam Hussein invaded Kuwait in 1990, he offered the royal family the services of his Arab-Afghan fighters to protect the Kingdom's oilfields, but to his fury they turned him down in favour of the

United States army. Thus began his estrangement from the Saudi regime. When in 1994 the Saudi government suppressed Sahwa ('Awakening'), a nonviolent reformist party that shared bin Laden's disapproval of American troop deployment in Arabia, his alienation was complete. Convinced now that peaceful resistance was futile, bin Laden spent four years in Sudan, organising financial backing for Arab-Afghan projects. But in 1996, when the United States and the Saudis pressured the Turabi government to expel him, he returned to Afghanistan, where the Taliban had just seized power.

After the Soviet withdrawal, the West lost interest in the region, but both Afghanistan and Pakistan had been gravely derailed by the long conflict. A flood of money and weapons had flowed into Pakistan from the United States as well as from the Persian Gulf, giving extremist groups access to advanced armaments, which were simply stolen as they were being unloaded. These heavily armed extremists had therefore broken the state's monopoly on violence and henceforth could operate outside the law. To defend themselves, nearly all groups in the country, religious and secular, developed paramilitary wings. Moreover, after the Iranian Revolution, Saudi Arabia, aware of the significant Shii community in Pakistan, had stepped up its funding of Deobandi madrasas to counter Shii influence. This enabled the Deobandis to educate even more students from poorer backgrounds and they sheltered the children of impoverished peasants, who were tenants of Shii landlords. Those entered the madrasas, therefore, with an anti-Shiah bias that was greatly enhanced by their education there.

Isolated from the rest of Pakistani society, these 'students' (taliban) bonded tightly with the three million Afghan children who had been orphaned during the war and were brought to Pakistan as refugees. They had all arrived traumatised by war and poverty, and were introduced to a rule-bound, restricted and highly intolerant form of Islam. They had no training in critical thought, were shielded from outside influence, and became rabidly anti-Shii.[39] In 1985, the Deobandis founded the Soldiers of the Companions of the Prophet in Pakistan (SCPP) specifically to harass the Shii, and in the mid-1990s two even more violent Deobandi movements emerged: the Army of Jhangvi, which specialised in assassinating Shiis, and the Partisan Movement, which fought for the liberation of Kashmir. As a result of this onslaught, the Shii formed the Soldiers of the Prophet in Pakistan (SPP), which killed a number of Sunnis. For centuries, Shiis and Sunnis had coexisted amicably in the region. Thanks to the United States' Cold War struggle in Afghanistan and Saudi-Iranian rivalry, they were now tearing the country apart in what amounted to a civil war.

The Afghan Taliban combined their Pashtun tribal chauvinism with Deobandi rigorism, an unholy hybrid and maverick form of Islam that expressed itself in violent opposition to any rival ideology. After the Soviet withdrawal, Afghanistan had descended into chaos, and when the Taliban managed to take control, they seemed to both the Pakistanis and the Americans to be an acceptable alternative to anarchy. Their leader Mullah Omar believed that human beings were naturally virtuous and, if placed on the right path, needed no government coercion, social services or public healthcare. There was, therefore, no centralised government and the population was ruled by local Taliban *komitehs,* whose punishments for the smallest infringement of Islamic law were so draconian that a degree of order was indeed restored. Fiercely opposed to modernity, which had, after all, come to them in the form of Soviet guns and air strikes, the Taliban ruled by their traditional tribal norms, which they identified with the rule of God. Their focus was purely local and they had no sympathy with bin Laden's global vision. But Mullah Omar was grateful to the Arab-Afghans for their support during the war, and when bin Laden was expelled from Sudan, he admitted him to Afghanistan, in return for which bin Laden improved the country's infrastructure.[40]

Other uprooted radicals gathered around bin Laden in Afghanistan, Zawahiri and his Egyptian radicals most especially.[41] But al-Qaeda was still a minor player in Islamist politics. A former militant told ABC Television that even though he had spent ten months in training camps run by bin Laden's aides, he had never heard of the organisation.[42] It seems that, even though he expressed his approval of both operations, bin Laden played no part in the 1993 bombing of the World Trade Center in New York by Arab-Afghan veteran Ramzi Youssef or the 1995 truck bombing in Riyadh that killed five Americans.[43] But al-Qaeda may have provided an ideological focus for militants in Afghanistan, who were feeling increasingly dispirited.[44] Not only had they failed to advance on their three main fronts of Bosnia, Algeria and Egypt, but by the end of the 1990s political Islam itself seemed in terminal decline.[45] In a dramatic turnabout, Hojjat al-Islam Seyyed Muhammad Khatami, running on a democratic ticket, won a landslide victory in the 1997 elections in Iran. He immediately signalled that he wanted a more positive relationship with the West, and dissociated his government from Khomeini's fatwa against Salman Rushdie. In Algeria, the government of President Abdul-Abdelaziz Bouteflika included militant secularists as well as moderate Islamists, and in Pakistan, the secularist colonel Pervez Musharraf toppled Nawaz Sharif, patron of the Islamist parties. In Turkey, the Islamist Prime Minister Necmettin Erbakan had to resign after a single year in office, and Turabi was deposed in a military coup in Sudan. It seemed increasingly urgent to bin Laden to reignite the jihad in a spectacular operation that would catch the attention of the whole world.

In August 1996, he issued his 'Declaration of War' on the United States and Israel, the 'Crusader–Zionist Alliance' which he accused of 'aggression, iniquity and injustice' against Muslims.[46] He condemned the American military presence in the Arabian Peninsula, equating it with the Israeli occupation of Palestine, and denounced American support of corrupt governments in the Muslim world and the sanctions led by Israel and the United States against Iraq, which, he claimed, had caused a million Iraqi deaths. In February 1998 he announced the World Islamic Front against Zionists and Crusaders, stating that all Muslims had a religious obligation to attack the United States and its allies 'in any country in which it is possible to do it' and to drive American troops from Arabia.[47] Three entirely new themes were emerging in bin Laden's ideology.[48] The first was his identification of the United States as the prime enemy rather than Russians, Serbs or 'apostate' Muslim rulers. Secondly, there was his call to attack the United States and its allies anywhere in the world, even in America itself – an unusual step since terrorists usually avoided operations outside their own country, which cost them international support. Thirdly, even though bin Laden never wholly abandoned Qutb's terminology, he drew chiefly on Pan-Islamic themes, focusing particularly on the suffering that Muslims were enduring worldwide.

This last was the core of bin Laden's message and enabled him to claim that his jihad was defensive.[49] In his 'Declaration of War', he exploited the culture of grievance that had been developing in the Muslim world, insisting that for centuries 'the people of Islam have suffered from aggression, iniquity and injustice imposed upon them by the Crusader-Zionist alliance'.[50] In al-Qaeda's propaganda videos, this verbal message is relayed against a collage of pain. They show Palestinian children harassed by Israeli soldiers; piles of corpses in Lebanon, Bosnia or Chechnya; the shooting of a Palestinian child in Gaza; houses bombed and bulldozed; and blind, limbless patients lying inertly in hospital beds. A survey of men recruited by al-Qaeda after 1999 revealed that most of them were still primarily motivated by the desire to assuage such suffering.[51] 'I did not know exactly in what way I would help,' said a Saudi prisoner in Guantanamo, 'but I went to help the people, not to fight.'[52] Feisal al-Dukhayyil, who was not an observant Muslim, was so distressed by a television programme on the plight of Chechen women and children that he enlisted immediately.[53] Despite bin Laden's anti-American rhetoric, hatred of the United States was not a major preoccupation among his recruits; this seems to have developed only during their indoctrination in the al-Qaeda camps in Pakistan, to which all, even those intending to fight in Chechnya, were sent. Muslims from Buffalo, New York, known as the 'Lackawanna Six', later explained that they left their training camp in 2001 because they were shocked by its anti-Americanism.[54]

Bin Laden's 'Crusader–Zionist Alliance' model exploited the conspiracy fears that are widespread in Muslim countries where lack of government transparency makes accurate information hard to come by.[55] It provides an explanation for an otherwise inexplicable concatenation of disasters. Islamists often quote a hadith that was rarely cited in the classical period but became very popular during the Crusades and the Mongol invasions.[56] 'The nations are about to flock against you from every horizon,' the Prophet had told his companions, and Muslims would be helpless because 'weakness (*wahn*) will be placed in your hearts'. What did *wahn* mean? 'Love of this world and fear of death,' Muhammad replied.[57] Muslims had become soft and had abandoned jihad because they were afraid of dying. Their only hope was to summon again the courage at the heart of Islam. Hence the importance of the huge martyrdom operation that would show the world that Muslims were no longer afraid. Their plight was so desperate that they must either fight or be killed. Radicals also love the Quranic story of David and Goliath which concludes: 'How often a small force has defeated a large army!'[58] The more powerful the enemy, therefore, the more heroic the struggle. Killing civilians is regrettable but, fighters argue, the Crusader-Zionists have also shed innocent blood and the Quran commands retaliation.[59] So the martyr must soldier on bravely, stoically repressing pity or moral revulsion for the terrible acts that he is tragically obliged to commit.[60]

The al-Qaeda leadership had been planning the 'spectacular' attack of September 11, 2001 for some time but could not proceed until they found the right recruits. They needed men who were technologically competent, at home in Western society, and had the ability to work independently.[61] In November 1999, Muhammad Atta, Ramzi bin al-Shibh, Marwan al-Shehhi and Ziad Jarrah, on their way (or so they thought) to Chechnya, were diverted to an al-Qaeda safe house in Qandahar. They came from privileged backgrounds, had studied engineering and technology in Europe – Jarrah and al-Shehhi were engineers and Atta was an architect – and would blend easily into American society while they trained as pilots. They were members of a group now known as the Hamburg Cell. Of the four, only bin al-Shibh had a deep knowledge of the Quran. None of them had the madrasa training that is often blamed for Muslim terrorism; instead they had attended secular schools – and until he met the group Jarrah was not even observant.[62] Unused to allegoric and symbolic thought, their scientific education inclined them not to scepticism but to a literalist reading of the Quran that diverged radically from traditional Muslim exegesis. They had no training in the traditional jurisprudence so their knowledge of mainstream Muslim law was at best superficial.

In his study of the 9/11 terrorists and those who worked closely with them – 500 people in all – the forensic psychiatrist Marc Sageman found that only 25 per cent had a traditional Islamic upbringing; that two-thirds were secularly minded until they encountered al-Qaeda; and the rest were recent converts.[63] Their knowledge of Islam was, therefore, limited. Many were self-taught and some did not study the Quran thoroughly until they were in prison. Perhaps, Sageman concludes, the problem was not Islam but ignorance of Islam.[64] The Saudis who took part in the 9/11 operation had had a Wahhabi education, but they were chiefly influenced not by Wahhabism but by the Pan-Islamist ideals, which the Wahhabi ulema had often opposed. The martyr-videos of Ahmed al-Haznawi, who died in the plane that crashed in Pennsylvania, and Abdulaziz al-Omari, who was in the first plane to hit the World Trade Center, dwell intensely on Muslim suffering worldwide. But while the Quran certainly orders Muslims to come to the aid of their brothers, Shariah law forbids violence against civilians, the use of fire in warfare, and prohibits any attack on a country where Muslims are allowed to practise their religion freely.

Muhammad Atta, leader of the Hamburg Cell, was motivated by Azzam's global vision, convinced that every able-bodied Muslim was obliged to defend his brothers and sisters in Chechnya or Tajikistan.[65] But Azzam would have deplored the terrorist activity that this group was to embrace. As moderate members fell away from the cell, they were replaced by others who shared Atta's views. In such closed groups, isolated from divergent opinion, Sageman believes, 'the cause' becomes the milieu in which they live and breathe.[66] Members became deeply attached to one another, shared apartments, ate and prayed together, and watched endless battlefield videos from Chechnya.[67] Most importantly, they identified closely with these distant struggles. Modern media enable people in one part of the world to be influenced by events that happen far away – something that would have been impossible in pre-modern times – and to apply these foreign narratives to their own problems.[68] It is a highly artificial state of consciousness.

The story of the 9/11 terrorists is now well known. Years after the tragedy, the events of that day are still horrifying. Our task in this book is to assess the role of religion in this atrocity. In the West, there was a widespread conviction that Islam, an inherently violent religion, was the chief culprit. A few weeks after September 11, in an article entitled 'This *Is* a Religious War', the American journalist Andrew Sullivan quoted from bin Laden's *Declaration of War*:

> The call to wage war against America was made because America spearheaded the Crusade against the Islamic nation, sending thousands of troops to the Land of the Two Holy Mosques, over and above its meddling in Saudi affairs and its politics, and its support of the oppressive, corrupt and tyrannical regime that is in control.[69]

Sullivan alerted his readers to the use of the word 'Crusade', 'an explicitly religious term', and pointed out that 'bin Laden's beef is with American troops defiling the land of Saudi Arabia, "the Land of the Two Holy Mosques" in Mecca and Medina'.[70] The words 'crusade' and 'mosques' were enough to persuade Sullivan that this really *was* a religious war, whereupon he felt free to embark on a paean to the Western liberal tradition. Way back in the seventeenth century, the West had understood how dangerous it was to mix religion and politics, Sullivan reasoned, but the Muslim world, alas, had yet to learn this important lesson. Yet Sullivan failed to discuss or dwell upon the two highly specific and clearly political aspects of American foreign policy mentioned by bin Laden in the quoted extract: its interference in the internal affairs of Saudi Arabia and its support for the despotic Saudi regime.[71]

Even the 'explicitly religious' terms – 'crusade' and 'holy mosques' – in fact had political and economic connotations. Since the early twentieth century, the Arabic *al-salibiyyah* ('crusade') has become an explicitly *political* term, applied routinely to colonialism and Western imperialism.[72] The deployment of American troops in Saudi Arabia was not only a violation of sacred space but also a humiliating demonstration of the Kingdom's dependence on the United States and America's domination of the region. The American troops involved the Kingdom in expensive arms deals, and its

Saudi base gave the United States easy access to Saudi oil, enabling the US military to launch air strikes against Sunni Muslims during the Gulf War.[73]

The hijackers themselves certainly regarded the 9/11 atrocities as a religious act, but one that bore very little resemblance to normative Islam. A document found in Atta's suitcase outlined a programme of prayer and reflection to help them through the ordeal.[74] If psychosis is 'an inability to see relationships', this is a deeply psychotic document. The principal imperative of Islamic spirituality is *tawhid* ('making one'): Muslims truly understand the unity of God only if they integrate all their activities and thoughts. But this document atomises the mission, dividing it into segments – the 'last night', the journey to the airport, boarding the planes, etc. – so that the unbearable whole is never considered. The terrorists were told to look forward to Paradise and back to the time of the Prophet – in fact, to contemplate anything but the atrocity they were committing in the present.[75] Living from one moment to another, their minds were to be diverted from the appalling finale. The prayers themselves are jarring. Like all Muslim discourse, the document begins with the *bismallah* – 'In the Name of God, the most Merciful and most Compassionate' – but it initiates an action devoid of either mercy or compassion. It then segues to a remark that most Muslims, I suspect, would find idolatrous: 'In the name of God, of myself, and my family'.[76] The hijacker is told to cut off any feelings of pity for his fellow passengers or fear for his own life and exert an immense effort to put himself into this abnormal mindset. He must 'resist' these impulses, 'tame', 'purify' and 'convince' his soul, 'incite' it and 'make it understand'.[77]

The imitation of Muhammad is central to Islamic piety; by imitating his external behaviour, Muslims hope to acquire his interior attitude of total surrender to God. But Atta's document determinedly steers the terrorists away from their inner world by an almost perverse emphasis on the external. As a result, the devotions seem primitive and superstitious. While packing they were to whisper Quranic verses into their hands and rub this holiness on to their luggage, box-cutters, knives, ID and passports.[78] Their clothes must fit snugly, like the garments of the Prophet and his Companions.[79] When they begin to fight the passengers and crew, as a sign of resolution, each one must 'clench his teeth just as the pious forefathers did prior to entering into battle'[80] and 'strike in the manner of champions who are not desirous of returning to this world, and shout *Allahu akbar!* For this shout causes fear in the hearts of the unbelievers.'[81] They must not 'become gloomy' but must recite Quranic verses while they are fighting, 'just as the pious ancestors would compose poetry in the midst of battles to calm their brothers and to cause tranquillity and joy to enter their souls'.[82] To imagine that serenity and joy would be possible in such circumstances indicates a truly psychotic inability to relate their faith to the reality of what they were about to do.

We find here the kind of magical thinking that we noted in Faraj's *The Neglected Duty*. As they went through the security gates of the airport, the hijackers were instructed, they must recite a verse that was almost 'a creedal statement' for radicals.[83] It is found in a Quranic passage about the Battle of Uhud when the 'laggers' urged the more intrepid Muslims to 'stay at home'. But they had simply replied: 'God is enough for us: He is the best protector,' and because of their faith they had 'returned with grace and bounty from God; no harm befell them'.[84] If they repeat these words, the document assured the hijackers, 'You will find matters straightened; and [God's] protection will surround you; no power can penetrate that.' The recitation of this verse would not only keep their fear at bay but overcome all physical obstacles: 'All of their devices, their [security] gates and their technology will not save [the Americans].'[85] The mere repetition of the first part of the shehadah, 'There is no god but God' would itself be enough to secure their entry into Paradise. The hijackers are told to 'consider the awesomeness of this statement' while they were fighting the Americans, remembering that in the Arabic script this verse had 'no pointed letters – this is a sign of perfection and completeness, as the pointed words or letters lessen its power'.[86]

Just over a year after 9/11, Louis Atiyat Allah would write an essay for a jihad website after watching al-Omari's martyr-video. There is absurdity in Allah's extravagant eulogy, which imagines the hijackers – 'mountains of courage, stars of masculinity, and galaxies of merit' – weeping for joy as the planes hit the target.[87] But it was obviously written to rebut widespread criticism of the 9/11 perpetrators. It was not only 'moderates' who deplored the atrocity; even in radical circles Muslims were apparently objecting that the Quran forbids suicide; they believed that the hijackers had acted irresponsibly. Their action had been counter-productive, too: the atrocity had inspired worldwide sympathy for America, and it had weakened the Palestinian cause by strengthening Israel's bond with the United States. In his article rebutting these complaints, Allah retorted that the hijackers had not 'committed suicide' nor were they simply 'crazy people who found planes to hijack'. No, they had a clearly defined political objective: 'To smash the foundations of the tyrant and to demolish the idol of the age, America'.[88] They had also struck a blow against the structural violence of the American-dominated Middle East, rejecting the 'silly [rulers] of Ibn Saud, and Husni [Mubarak], and all the other retards who falsely call themselves "those in authority"' (Quran 4: 59), but who were actually 'nothing but tentacles of the octopus upon you, with the head of the [octopus] being in New York and Washington DC'.[89] The purpose of this operation was to take a 'terrifying historical leap which will . . . extricate the Muslims in one fell swoop from humiliation, dependency and servility'.[90]

These political objectives were certainly uppermost in bin Laden's mind in the immediate aftermath of 9/11, although he would also invoke the divine will. In the videotape released on 7 October 2001, he crowed: 'Here is America struck by God in one of its vital organs, so that its greatest buildings are destroyed',[91] buildings that had been carefully selected as 'America's icons of military and economic power'.[92] Five times bin Laden applied the word *kafir* ('infidel') to the United States, though each time it referred not to the religious beliefs of America but to its violation of Muslim sovereignty in Arabia and Palestine.[93] On the same day, President George W. Bush announced Operation Enduring Freedom, a US-led war against the Taliban in Afghanistan. Like the First Crusade against Islam, this military offensive was couched in the language of liberty: 'We defend not only our precious freedoms, but also the freedom of people everywhere.'[94] He assured the people of Afghanistan that the United States had no quarrel with them, would strike only at military targets, and promised airdrops of food, medicine and supplies. And just a week following the attacks, Bush had made clear that America's quarrel was not with Islam: 'The face of terror is not the true faith of Islam. That's not what Islam is all about. Islam is peace. These terrorists don't represent peace. They represent evil and war.'[95] Like bin Laden, Bush, in this carefully secular presentation, saw the world starkly divided into two camps, one good, the other evil: 'In this conflict there is no neutral ground. If any government sponsors the outlaws and killers of innocents, they have become outlaws and murderers themselves.'[96]

Bush's Manichaean worldview reflected the thinking of the neoconservatives prominent in his administration, who had a semi-mystical belief that nothing must impede America's unique historical mission in the twenty-first century. The 'War on Terror' would be waged against any forces that threatened America's global leadership. Indeed, neoconservatism has been described as 'a faith-based system', because it required absolute fidelity to its doctrine, permitting no deviation from its beliefs.[97] And so the politics of the secular nation was imbued with a quasi-religious fervour and conviction. The United States had a mission to promote the global free market, the One True Economy, everywhere. It was not a religious message but one that nevertheless resonated strongly as such with Bush's base of 100 million American evangelical Christians, who still subscribed to the vision of America as a 'City on a Hill'.

The first three months of the war against Afghanistan, where Taliban gave sanctuary to al-Qaeda, seemed remarkably successful. The Taliban were defeated, al-Qaeda personnel scattered, and the United States established two large military bases at Bagram and Kandahar. But there were two ominous developments. Even though Bush had given instructions that prisoners be treated humanely in accordance with the Geneva Conventions, it seems that in practice troops were told that they could 'deviate slightly from the rules' since terrorists were not covered by the laws relating to prisoners of war. Bush had been careful to insist that this was not a war against Islam, but that was not how it appeared on the ground, where there was little punctiliousness about religious sensibilities. On 26 September 2002, a convoy of mujahidin were captured in Takhar. According to one Muslim account, US troops 'hung one mujahid by his arms for six days, questioning him about Usama bin Laden'. Eventually they gave up and asked him about his faith: He replied that

He trusted in Allah, the Prophet Muhammad and the holy Qur'an. Upon receiving this answer, the US troops replied that 'Your Allah and Muhammad are not here, but the Qur'an is, so let's see what it will do to us.' After this, one US soldier brought a Holy Qur'an and began urinating over it, only to be joined by other US and Northern Alliance troops who did the same.[98]

Despite their manifest contempt for Islam, this does not mean that US troops saw themselves as fighting a war that was specifically directed against Islam. Rather, the unconventional nature of the campaign, defined as a 'War on Terror', a 'different kind of war', had changed the rules of engagement. With this terminology the United States had liberated itself from the rules of conventional conflict.[99] Ground troops seem to have absorbed the view that terrorists were not entitled to the same protection as regular combatants.

Since 9/11, the United States, which still regards itself as a uniquely benign hegemon, has, with the support of its allies, indefinitely retained people who deny involvement in any conflict, conducted violent and humiliating interrogations, or else sent prisoners to countries known to practise torture. As early as December 2001, hundreds of prisoners – by means of 'extraordinary rendition' – were being detained in Guantanamo Bay and Diego Garcia without due process and were subjected to 'stress and duress' (i.e. torture).[100] The frequent – almost routine – reports of abuse in United States prisons suggest that military and political authorities may have condoned a policy of systematic brutality.[101] The second disturbing development in the War on Terror was the large number of civilian casualties. About three thousand civilians were killed in the first three months – roughly the same number as had died in New York, Pennsylvania and Washington on September 11. Thousands more displaced Afghans would die later in refugee camps.[102] As the war dragged on, the casualties became catastrophic: between 2006 and 2012, it has been estimated that 16,179 Afghan civilians had perished.[103]

There was a second wave of terrorist incidents, directed by the 'second generation' of al-Qaeda, which included the failed plot of British 'shoe-bomber' Richard Reid (December 2001), the Djerba bombing in Tunisia (April 2002), and the Bali nightclub attack (October 2002), which killed over two hundred people. After Iyman Faris' foiled plot to destroy the Brooklyn Bridge, however, most of the al-Qaeda central command had either been killed or captured and there were no more major incidents.[104] But just as the situation seemed to be improving, in March 2003 the United States, Britain and their allies invaded Iraq, despite considerable opposition from the international community and strong protests throughout the Muslim world. The reasons for this invasion were allegations that Saddam Hussein possessed weapons of mass destruction and had furnished support for al-Qaeda, both of which eventually proved to be groundless.

Again, the United States presented itself as the bearer of freedom: 'If we must use force,' Bush had promised the American people, 'the United States and our coalition stand ready to help the citizens of a liberated Iraq.'[105] 'We don't seek an empire,' he insisted on another occasion. 'Our nation is committed to freedom for ourselves and for others.'[106] Cheered on by such neo-imperialist intellectuals as Niall Ferguson, the Bush regime believed that it could use the colonial methods of invasion and occupation for purposes of liberation.[107] America would force Iraq into the free global economy and change the politics of the Middle East by creating a liberal, democratic and pro-Western Arab state, one that would also support Israel, embrace market capitalism, and at the same time provide the United States with a military base and access to vast oil reserves.

On 1 May 2003, Bush's Viking jet swooped on to the deck of USS *Abraham Lincoln*, where the president announced a victorious end to the Iraq War.[108]

'We have fought for the cause of liberty and for the peace of the world,' he told the assembled troops. 'Because of you, the tyrant is fallen and Iraq is free.' In this political message, too, were the overtones of a holy war. This war of the American nation was directed by God himself: 'All of you – all in this generation of our military – have taken up the highest calling of history,' he proclaimed, quoting the Prophet Isaiah: 'And wherever you go, you carry a message of hope – a message that is ancient and ever new. To the captives, "come out" – and to those in darkness "be free".'[109] Use of this biblical verse, which Jesus had quoted to describe his own mission,[110] revealed the messianic streak of the Bush administration.

It was ironic that Bush announced the liberation of captives. In October 2003, the media published photographs of US military police abusing Iraqi prisoners in Abu Ghraib, Saddam's notorious prison; later almost identical cruelty was shown to have taken place in British-run prisons. These photographs were a cruder vision of the official US media presentation of the Iraq War. Hooded, naked, writhing on the ground, the Iraqis were depicted as dehumanised, craven, bestial and utterly dominated by America's superior power.[111] The cocky stance of the low-ranking GIs implied: 'We are high, they are low; we are clean, they are dirty; we are strong and brave, they are weak and cowardly; we are lordly, they are virtually animals; we are God's chosen, they are estranged from everything divine.'[112] 'The photos are us,' the late Susan Sontag declared. Nazis were not the only people to commit atrocities; Americans do so too 'when they are led to believe that the people they are torturing belong to an inferior, despicable race or religion'.[113] Clearly the GIs saw nothing untoward in their behaviour and had no fear of punishment. 'It was just for fun,' said Private Lynndie England, who had appeared in the photographs walking a prisoner on a leash like a dog. They behaved in this way, the official investigation concluded, 'Simply because they could'.[114]

Within a month of Bush's aircraft carrier speech, Iraq had descended into chaos. Most Iraqis gave no credence to Bush's exalted rhetoric but were convinced that the United States simply wanted their oil and intended to use their country as a military base from which to defend Israel. They may have been glad to get rid of Saddam but they did not regard the American and British troops as liberators. 'They're walking over my heart,' said one Baghdad resident. 'Liberate us from what?' demanded another. 'We have [our own] traditions, morals, customs.'[115] The Iraqi cleric Sheikh Muhammad Bashir complained that if the Americans had brought freedom to the country it was not for the Iraqis:

It is the freedom of occupying soldiers in doing what they like . . . No one can ask them what they are doing, because they are protected by their freedom . . . No one can punish them, whether in our country or in their country. They expressed the freedom of rape, the freedom of nudity and the freedom of humiliation.[116]

In 2004, the overwhelming US assault on Fallujah, the iconic 'city of mosques', has been called the Arab 9/11: hundreds of civilians were killed and 200,000 made homeless. By the following year, 24,000 civilians had been killed in Iraq and 70,000 injured.[117] Instead of bringing peace to the region, the occupation inspired an insurgency of Iraqis and mujahidin from Saudi Arabia, Syria and Jordan, who like other fighters we have discussed responded to this foreign invasion with the terrorist technique of suicide bombing, eventually breaking the long-standing record of the Tamil Tigers.[118]

As to global terrorism, the situation has become even more dangerous than before the Iraq War.[119] Following the assassination of bin Laden in 2011, al-Qaeda still thrives. Its strength was always more conceptual than organisational – global revolutionary fervour combining an intense political militancy with dubious claims to divine sanction. Its branch affiliates, including the one founded in Iraq (as of this writing increasingly active there and also in the Syrian civil war) as well as those in Somalia and Yemen, continue to promote a restoration of the caliphate as the ultimate objective of their interventions in local politics. Elsewhere, in the absence of any tightly organised cadre, there are thousands of freelance aspirants to terrorism world-wide – radicalised in internet chat rooms, self-trained, poorly educated, and lacking any clear practical objective. Such was the case with Michael Adebolajo and Michael Adebowale, two British-born converts to Islam, who murdered the British soldier Lee Rigby in 2013 in south-east London, claiming that they were avenging the deaths of Muslim innocents at the hands of British troops. Like Mohammed Bouyeri who assassinated the Dutch film-maker Theo van Gogh in 2004 and the Madrid train bombers, who killed 191 people in the same year, they were not directly linked to al-Qaeda.[120] Some self-starters do seek out the al-Qaeda leadership for credentialling and in the hope of being sent to some important operational theatre, but it seems that trainers in Pakistan prefer to send them home to destabilise Western countries instead – as happened with the 7/7 London bombings (July 2005), the Australian bombing plan (November 2005), the Toronto plot (June 2006), and the foiled British project of blowing up several planes over the Atlantic (August 2006).

All these freelance terrorists have very little knowledge of the Quran, and so it is pointless to attempt a debate about their interpretation of scripture or to blame 'Islam' for their crimes.[121] Indeed, Marc Sageman, who has talked with several of them, believes that a normal religious education might have deterred them from their crimes.[122] They are, he has found, chiefly motivated by the desire to escape a stifling sense of insignificance and pointlessness in secular nation states that struggle to absorb foreign minorities. They seek the age-old dream of military glory and believe that by dying a heroic death they will give their lives meaning as local heroes.[123] In these cases, suffice it to say, what we call 'Islamic terrorism' has been transformed from a political cause – inflamed with pious exhortations contrary to Islamic teachings – into a violent acting out of youthful rage. They may claim to be acting in the name of Islam, but when an untalented beginner claims to be playing a Beethoven sonata, we hear only cacophony.

One of bin Laden's objectives had been to draw Muslims all over the world to his vision of jihad. Though he did become a charismatic folk hero to some – a kind of Saudi Che – in this central mission he ultimately failed. Between 2001 and 2007, a Gallup Poll was conducted in thirty-five predominantly Muslim countries. It found that only 7 per cent of respondents thought the 9/11 attacks were 'completely justified'; for these people, the reasons were entirely political. As for the 93 per cent who condemned the attacks, they quoted Quranic verses to show that the killing of innocent people could have no place in Islam.[124] One might well wonder how much more unanimously opposed to terror the Muslim world might have become but for the course the US took in the wake of 9/11. At a time when even in Tehran there were demonstrations of solidarity with America, the Bush and Blair coalition lashed out with its own violent rejoinder, a drive that would culminate in the tragically misbegotten Iraq invasion of 2003. Its most decisive result was to present the world with a new set of images of Muslim suffering in which the West was not only implicated but for which it was, this time, directly responsible. When considering the tenacity of al-Qaeda, it is well to remember that such images of Muslim suffering more than any expansive theory of jihad were what had drawn so many young Muslims to the camps of Peshawar in the first instance.

We routinely and rightly condemn the terrorism that kills civilians in the name of God but we cannot claim the high moral ground if we dismiss the suffering and death of the many thousands of civilians who die in our wars as 'collateral damage'. Ancient religious mythologies helped people to face up to the dilemma of state violence, but our current nationalist ideologies seem by contrast to promote a retreat into denial or hardening of our hearts. Nothing shows this more clearly than a remark of Madeleine Albright when she was still Bill Clinton's ambassador to the United Nations. Later she retracted it, but among people all around the world it has never been forgotten. In 1996, on CBS's *60 Minutes*, Lesley Stahl asked her whether the cost of international sanctions against Iraq was justified: 'We have heard that half a million children have died. I mean, that's more children than died in Hiroshima . . . Is the price worth it?' 'I think this is a very hard choice,' Albright replied, 'but the price, we think the price is worth it.'[125]

On 24 October 2012, Mamana Bibi, a sixty-eight-year-old woman picking vegetables in her family's large, open land in northern Waziristan, Pakistan, was killed by a United States drone aircraft. She was not a terrorist but a midwife married to a retired schoolteacher, yet she was blown to pieces in front of her nine young grandchildren. Some of the children have had multiple surgeries that the family could ill afford because they lost all their livestock; the smaller children still scream in terror all night long. We do not know who the real targets were. But even though the US government claims to carry out thorough post-strike assessments, it has never apologised, never offered compensation to the family, nor even admitted to the American people what happened. CIA director John O. Brennan had previously claimed that drone strikes caused absolutely no civilian casualties; more recently he has admitted otherwise, while maintaining that such deaths are extremely rare. Since then Amnesty International has reviewed some forty-five strikes in the region, finding evidence of unlawful civilian deaths, and has reported several strikes that appear to have killed civilians outside the bounds of law.[126] 'Bombs create only hatred in the hearts of people. And that hatred and anger breed more terrorism,' said Bibi's son. 'No one ever asked *us* who was killed or injured that day. Not the United States or my own government. Nobody has come to investigate nor has anyone been held accountable. Quite simply, nobody seems to care.'[127]

'Am I my brother's guardian?' Cain asked after he had killed his brother Abel. We are now living in such an interconnected world that we are all implicated in one another's history and one another's tragedies. As we – quite rightly – condemn those terrorists who kill innocent people, we also have to find a way to acknowledge our relationship with and responsibility for Mamana Bibi, her family, and the hundreds of thousands of civilians who have died or been mutilated in our modern wars simply because they were in the wrong place at the wrong time.

AFTERWORD

We have seen that, like the weather, religion 'does lots of different things'. To claim that it has a single, unchanging and inherently violent essence is not accurate. Identical religious beliefs and practices have inspired diametrically opposed courses of action. In the Hebrew Bible, the Deuteronomists and the priestly authors all meditated on the same stories but the Deuteronomists turned virulently against foreign peoples, while the priestly authors sought reconciliation. Chinese Daoists, Legalists and military strategists shared the same set of ideas and meditative disciplines, but put them to entirely different uses. St Luke and the Johannine authors all reflected on Jesus' message of love, but Luke reached out to marginalised members of society, while the Johannines confined their love to their own group. Antony and the Syrian boskoi both set out to practise 'freedom from care' but Antony spent his life trying to empty his mind of anger and hatred while the Syrian monks surrendered to the aggressive drives of the reptilian brain. Ibn Taymiyyah and Rumi were both victims of the Mongol invasions, but used the teachings of Islam to come to entirely different conclusions. For centuries, the story of Imam Husain's tragic death inspired Shiis to withdraw from political life in principled protest against systemic injustice; more recently it has inspired them to take political action and say 'no' to tyranny.

Until the modern period, religion permeated all aspects of life, including politics and warfare, not because ambitious churchmen had 'mixed up' two essentially distinct activities, but because people wanted to endow everything they did with significance. Every state ideology was religious. The kings of Europe who struggled to liberate themselves from papal control were not 'secularists' but were revered as semi-divine. Every successful empire has claimed that it has a divine mission; that its enemies are evil, misguided or tyrannical; and that it will benefit humanity. And because these states and empires were all created and maintained by force, religion has been implicated in their violence. It was not until the seventeenth and eighteenth centuries that religion was ejected from political life in the West. When, therefore, people claim that religion has been responsible for *more* war, oppression, and suffering than any other human institution, one has to ask 'more than *what*?' Until the American and French revolutions, there were no 'secular' societies. And, so ingrained is our impulse to 'sanctify' our political activities that no sooner had the French revolutionaries successfully marginalised the Catholic Church than they created a new national religion. In the United States, the first secular republic, the state has always had a religious aura, a manifest destiny and divinely sanctioned mission.

John Locke believed that the separation of church and state was the key to peace, but the nation state has been far from averse to war. The problem lies not in the multifaceted activity that we call 'religion' but in the violence embedded in our human nature and the nature of the state, which from the start required the forcible subjugation of at least 90 per cent of the population. As Ashoka discovered, even if a ruler shrank from state aggression, it was impossible to disband the army. The *Mahabharata* lamented the dilemma of the warrior king doomed to a life of warfare. The Chinese realised very early that a degree of force was essential to civilised life. Ancient Israel tried initially to escape the agrarian state yet Israelites soon discovered that much as they hated the exploitation and cruelty of urban civilisation, they could not live without it; they too had to become 'like all the nations'. Jesus preached an inclusive and compassionate Kingdom that defied the imperial ethos, and was crucified for his pains. The Muslim ummah began as an alternative to the jahili injustice of commercial Mecca, but eventually it had to become an empire, because at that time an absolute monarchy was the best and perhaps the only way to keep the peace. Modern military historians agree that without professional and responsible armies, human society would either have remained in a primitive state or have degenerated into ceaselessly warring hordes.

Before the creation of the nation state, people thought about politics in a religious way. Constantine's empire showed what could happen when an originally peaceful tradition became too closely associated with the government; the Christian emperors enforced the Pax Christiana as belligerently as their pagan predecessors had imposed the Pax Romana. The Crusades were certainly inspired by religious passion but were also deeply political: Pope Urban II let the knights of Christendom loose on the Muslim world to extend the power of the Church eastwards and create a papal monarchy that would control Christian Europe. The Inquisition was a deeply flawed attempt to secure the internal order of Spain after a divisive civil war. The Wars of Religion and the Thirty Years War were certainly exacerbated by the sectarian quarrels of the Reformation but were also the birth pangs of the modern nation state.

When we fight, we need to distance ourselves from the adversary and because religion was so central to the state, its rites and myths depicted its enemies as monsters of evil that threatened cosmic and political order. During the Middle Ages, Christians denounced Jews as child-killers, Muslims as 'an evil and despicable race', and Cathars as a cancerous growth in the body of Christendom. Again, this hatred was certainly religiously motivated, but it was also a response to the social distress that accompanies early modernisation. Christians made Jews the scapegoat for their excessive anxiety about the money-economy and popes blamed Cathars for their own inability to live up to the Gospel. In the process they created imaginary enemies who were distorted mirror images of themselves. But casting off the mantle of religion did not bring an end to prejudice. A 'scientific racism' developed in the modern period that drew on the old religious patterns of hatred and inspired the Armenian genocide and Hitler's death camps. Secular nationalism, imposed so unceremoniously by the colonialists, would regularly merge with local religious traditions, where people had not yet abstracted 'religion' from politics; as a result these religious traditions were often distorted and developed an aggressive strain.

The sectarian hatreds that develop within a faith tradition are often cited to prove that 'religion' is chronically intolerant. These internal feuds have indeed been bitter and virulent, but they too have nearly always had a political dimension. Christian 'heretics' were persecuted for using the Gospel to articulate their rejection of the systemic injustice and violence of the agrarian state. Even the abstruse debates about the nature of Christ in the Eastern Church were fuelled by the political ambitions of the 'tyrant-bishops'. Heretics were often persecuted when the nation feared external attack. The xenophobic theology of the Deuteronomists developed when the Kingdom of Judah faced political annihilation. Ibn Taymiyyah introduced the practice of takfir when Muslims in the Near East were menaced by the Crusaders from the west and the Mongols from the east. The Inquisition took place against the backdrop of the Ottoman threat and the Wars of Religion, just as the September Massacres and the Reign of Terror in revolutionary France were motivated by fears of foreign invasion.

Lord Acton accurately predicted that the liberal nation state would persecute ethnic and cultural 'minorities', who have indeed taken the place of 'heretics'. In Iraq, Pakistan and Lebanon, the traditional Sunni/Shii division has been aggravated by nationalism and the problems of the post-colonial state. In the past, Sunni Muslims were always loath to call their co-religionists 'apostates', because they believed that God alone knew what was in a person's heart. But the practice of *takfir* has become common in our own day when Muslims once again fear foreign enemies. When Muslims attack churches and synagogues today, they are not driven to do so by Islam. The Quran commands Muslims to respect the faith of 'the people of the book'.[1] One of the most frequently quoted jihad verses justifies warfare by stating: 'If God did not repel some people by means of others, many monasteries, churches, synagogues, and mosques, where God's name is much invoked, would have been destroyed.'[2] This new aggression towards religious minorities in the nation state is largely the result of political tensions arising from Western imperialism (associated with Christianity) and the Palestinian problem.[3]

It is simply not true that 'religion' is always aggressive. Sometimes it has actually put a brake on violence. In the ninth century BCE, Indian ritualists extracted all violence from the liturgy and created the ideal of ahimsa, 'nonviolence'. The medieval Peace and Truce of God forced knights to stop terrorising the poor and outlawed violence from Wednesday to Sunday each week. Most dramatically, after the Bar Kokhba war the Rabbis reinterpreted the scriptures so effectively that Jews refrained from political aggression for a millennium. But these successes have been rare. Because of the inherent violence of the states in which we live, the best that prophets and sages have been able to do is provide an alternative. The Buddhist Sangha had no political power, but it became a vibrant presence in ancient India and even influenced emperors. Ashoka included the ideals of ahimsa, tolerance, kindness and respect in the extraordinary inscriptions he promoted throughout the empire. Confucians kept the ideal of humanity (*ren*) alive in the government of imperial China until the revolution. For centuries, the egalitarian code of the Shariah was a counter-cultural challenge to the Abbasid aristocracy; the caliphs acknowledged that it was God's law, even though they could not rule by it.

Other sages and mystics developed spiritual practices to help people to control their aggression and develop a reverence for all human beings. In India, renouncers practised the disciplines of yoga and ahimsa to eradicate egotistic machismo. Others cultivated the ideals of *anatta* ('no self') or *kenosis* ('self-emptying') to control the 'me-first' impulses that so often lead to violence; they sought an 'equanimity' that would make it impossible to see oneself as superior to anybody else, taught that every single person had sacred potential and that people should even love their enemies. Prophets and psalmists insisted that a city could not be 'holy' if the ruling class did not care for the poor and dispossessed. Priests urged their compatriots to draw on the memory of their own past suffering to assuage the pain of others, instead of using it to justify harassment and persecution. They all insisted in one way or another that if people did not treat all others as they would wish to be treated themselves and developed a 'concern for everybody', society was doomed. If the colonial powers had observed the Golden Rule in their colonies we would not be having so many political problems today.

One of the most ubiquitous religious practices was the cult of community. In the pre-modern world, religion was a communal pursuit. People achieved enlightenment and salvation by learning to live harmoniously together. Instead of distancing themselves from their fellow humans as the warrior did, sages, prophets and mystics helped people cultivate a relationship with and responsibility for those they would not ordinarily find congenial. They devised meditations that deliberately extended their benevolence to the ends of the earth; wished all beings happiness; taught their compatriots to revere the holiness of every single person; and resolved to find practical ways of assuaging the world's suffering. Neuroscientists have discovered that Buddhist monks who have practised this compassionate meditation assiduously have physically enhanced those centres of the brain that spark our empathy. Jains cultivated an outstanding vision of the community of all creatures. Muslims achieved the surrender of *islam* by taking responsibility for one another and sharing what they had with those in need. In Paul's churches, rich and poor were instructed to sit at the same table and eat the same food. Cluniac monks made lay Christians live together like monks during a pilgrimage, rich and poor sharing the same hardships. The Eucharist was not a solitary communion with Christ but a rite that bonded the political community.

From a very early date, prophets and poets helped people to contemplate the tragedy of life and face up to the damage they did to others. In ancient Sumeria, the *Atrahasis* could not find a solution to the social injustice on which their civilisation depended but this popular tale made people aware of it. Gilgamesh had to come face to face with the horror of death, which drained warfare of spurious glamour and nobility. The Prophets of Israel compelled rulers to take responsibility for the suffering they inflicted on the poor and lambasted them for their war crimes. The priestly authors of the Hebrew Bible lived in a violent society and could not abjure warfare, but believed that warriors were contaminated by their violence, even if the campaign had been endorsed by God. That was why David was not allowed to build Yahweh's temple. The Aryans loved warfare and revered their warriors; fighting and raiding were essential to the pastoral economy but the warrior always carried a taint. Chinese strategists admitted that the military way of life was a 'way of deception' and must be segregated from civilian life. They drew attention to the uncomfortable fact that even an idealistic state nurtured at its heart an institution dedicated to killing, lying and treachery.

In the West secularism is now a part of our identity. It has been beneficial – not least because an intimate association with government can badly compromise a faith tradition. But it has had its own violence. Revolutionary France was secularised by coercion, extortion and bloodshed; for the first time it mobilised the whole of society for war; and its secularism seemed propelled by an aggression towards religion that is still shared by many Europeans today. The United States did not stigmatise faith in the same way and religion has flourished there. There was an aggression in early modern thought, which failed to apply the concept of human rights to the indigenous peoples of the Americas or to African slaves. In the developing world secularisation has been experienced as lethal, hostile and invasive. There have been massacres in sacred shrines, clerics have been tortured, imprisoned and assassinated, madrasa students shot down and humiliated, and the clerical establishment systematically deprived of resources, dignity and status.

Hence secularisation has sometimes damaged religion. Even in the relatively benign atmosphere of the United States, Protestant fundamentalists became xenophobic and fearful of modernity. The horrors of Nasser's prison polarised the vision of Sayed Qutb; his former liberalism was transformed into a paranoid vision that saw enemies everywhere. Khomeini too frequently spoke of conspiracies of Jews, Christians and imperialists. The Deobandis, bruised by the British abolition of the Moghul empire, created a rigid rule-bound form of Islam and gave us the Taliban travesty, a noxious combination of Deobandi rigidity, tribal chauvinism, and the aggression of the traumatised war orphan. In the Indian subcontinent and the Middle East, the alien ideology of nationalism transformed traditional religious symbols and myths and gave them a violent dimension. But the relationship between modernity and religion has not been wholly antagonistic. Some movements, such as the two Great Awakenings or the Muslim Brotherhood, have actually helped people to embrace modern ideals in a more familiar idiom.

Modern religious violence is not an alien growth: it is part of the modern scene. We have created an interconnected world. It is true that we are dangerously polarised, but we are also linked together more closely than ever before. When shares fall in one region, markets plummet all around the world. What happens in Palestine or Iraq today can have repercussions tomorrow in New York, London or Madrid. We are connected electronically so that images of suffering and devastation in a remote Syrian village or an Iraqi prison are instantly beamed around the world. We all face the possibility of environmental or nuclear catastrophe. But our perceptions have not caught up with the realities of our situation so that in the First World, we still tend to put ourselves in a special privileged category. Yet our policies have helped to create widespread rage and frustration and in the West we bear some responsibility for the suffering in the Muslim world that bin Laden was able to exploit. 'Am I my brother's guardian?' The answer must, surely, be 'Yes.'

War, it has been said, is caused 'by our inability to see relationships. Our relationship with our economic and historical situation. Our relationship with our fellow-men. And above all our relationship to nothingness. To death.'[4] We need ideologies today, religious or secular, that help people to face up to the intractable dilemmas of our current 'economic and historical situation' as the prophets did in the past. Even though we no longer have to contend with the oppressive injustice of the agrarian empire, there is still massive inequality and an unfair imbalance of power. But the dispossessed are not helpless peasants any more; they have found ways of fighting back. If we want a viable world, we have to take responsibility for the world's pain and learn to listen to narratives that challenge our sense of ourselves. All this requires the 'surrender', selflessness and compassion that have been just as important in the history of religion as the Crusades and jihads.

We all wrestle – in secular or religious ways – with 'nothingness', the void at the heart of modern culture. Ever since Zoroaster, religious movements that tried to address the violence of their time have absorbed some of its aggression. Protestant fundamentalism came into being in the United States when evangelical Christians pondered the unprecedented slaughter of the First World War. Their apocalyptic vision was simply a religious version of the 'future war' genre that had developed in Europe. Religious fundamentalists and extremists have used the language of faith to express fears that also afflict secularists. We have seen that some of the cruelest and most self-destructive of these movements have been in part a response to the Holocaust or the nuclear threat. Groups such as Shukri Mustafa's Society in Sadat's Egypt can hold up a distorted mirror image of the structural violence of contemporary culture. Secularists as well as religious people have resorted to the suicide attack, which in some ways reflects the death-wish in modern culture. Religious and secularists have shared the same enthusiasms. Kookism was clearly a religious form of secular nationalism and was able to work closely with the Israeli secular Right. The Muslims who flocked to join the jihad against the Soviet Union were certainly reviving the classical Islamic practice of 'volunteering' but they also experienced the impulse that prompted hundreds of Europeans to leave the safety of home and fight in the Spanish Civil War (1936–39) and Jews to hasten from the diaspora to support Israel on the eve of the Six Day War.

When we confront the violence of our time, it is natural to harden our hearts to the global pain and deprivation that make us feel uncomfortable, depressed and frustrated. But we must find ways of contemplating these distressing facts of modern life or we will lose the best part of our humanity. Somehow we have to find ways of doing what religion – at its best – has done for centuries: build a sense of global community, cultivate a sense of reverence and 'equanimity' for all, and take responsibility for the suffering we see in the world. No state in history, however great its achievements, has not incurred the taint of the warrior. We are all, religious and secularist alike, responsible for the current state of the world. It is a stain on the international community that Mamana Bibi's son can say: 'Quite simply, nobody seems to care.' The scapegoat ritual was an attempt to sever the community's relationship with its misdeeds; it cannot be a solution for us today.

In the fall of 2013, I submitted the manuscript of this book to my publishers. Since then, there have been fresh atrocities which, at first glance, seem to have taken religiously articulated violence to a new level. Yet in fact they follow a familiar trajectory.

Thus, the group that now calls itself 'Islamic State' (IS) has rampaged through Iraq and Syria, capturing large swathes of territory and butchering thousands of civilians. The obscene savagery of IS fighters, with their swords, covered faces and cut-throat executions, seems to belong to a bygone age, but, of course, mass killing has been a tragic part of the modern experience: we need only recall the public beheading of 17,000 men, women and children during the French Revolution (which created the first secular state in Europe); the Armenian massacres; and the Nazi Holocaust. In fact IS is a thoroughly modern movement, with highly professionally managed assets of $2 billion; there is nothing irrational about its hideous execution videos, which are strategically planned to inspire terror and recall the tactics of the Khmer Rouge and Red Guard, who also tried to purge humanity of corruption.

Yet many Western people believe that IS is decisive proof that Islam is chronically addicted to violence. After all, its fighters lard their discourse with Quranic quotations; their leader, Abu Bakr al-Baghdadi, has taken the name of the deeply revered first caliph; and IS imposes a medieval form of Shariah law in its territories. Hence hostility to Islam has increased in the West. In September 2014, a Zogby poll found that only 27 per cent of Americans had a favourable view of Islam – a fall from 35 per cent in 2010, and the Obama administration has been viciously castigated for refusing to identify IS terror with Islam. [1]

Yet IS is no more authentically Islamic than the British National Party is typically British or the Ku Klux Klan genuinely Christian. Leading Muslim institutions and authorities, such as Al-Azhar University, the Islamic Society of North America and the Grand Mufti of Saudi Arabia, have deplored its conduct and ideology in the strongest terms. Sunni and Shii, Salafi and liberal Muslims are united in their denunciation of IS, tirelessly pointing out that its spokesmen simply cherry-pick random Quranic texts that seem to support their views and ignore anything that contradicts them.

We have seen that many of the Muslims convicted for terrorist activities since 2001 have a woefully inadequate knowledge of Islam and this seems true of IS: two wannabe jihadis who left the UK for Syria in May 2014 ordered *Islam for Dummies* from Amazon.[2] Indeed, emerging reports suggest that IS culture is markedly secular. Didier Francois, the French journalist held hostage by IS for ten months, has said that the Quran did not feature in his captors' discourse, which was entirely political. David Kenner of *Foreign Policy* magazine, who held discussions with fifteen IS supporters in Jordan, also noted that they never raised the topic of religion, nor did they answer the muezzin's call to prayer.[3]

So the widespread Western insistence that IS represents the true face of Islam looks like another instance of scapegoating – an attempt to place the blame elsewhere, since IS is the remnant of the insurgency inspired by the American/British-led war in Iraq. New images of Muslim suffering under the occupation impelled yet another wave of 'volunteers' from Saudi Arabia, Syria and Jordan to become suicide bombers in Iraq. The insurgency flared into new life in April 2013 when the Iraqi security forces of the Shii-led Maliki government opened fire on a peaceful demonstration of Sunni Muslims, who were demanding a more equitable reallocation of the oil revenues. Note that this 'sectarian' conflict was not caused by 'religious' zeal but by economic factors.

In IS we see an unholy alliance of debased 'religion' with the worst kind of 'secularism'. In the West we hear little about its crucial alliance with members of Saddam's deposed Baathist regime. In 2010, Haji Bakr, a colonel in Saddam's disbanded army, having spotted the organisational skills of his fellow-Baathist Abu Bakr al-Baghdadi (hitherto disdained in the movement because of his lax religious observance), engineered his appointment to the leadership of what would become IS. Abu Muslim al-Afari al-Turkmani, a Special Forces officer in Saddam's army, became Baghdadi's deputy in Iraq, and former Major General Abu Ali al-Abari, his second in command in Syria. The presence of these highly professional soldiers explains IS' remarkable military success.

Once IS had begun to dismantle the unstable nation states created by European colonialists, yet another wave of 'volunteers' left home to join the fray, some inspired less by 'religion' than by the perennial lure of the battlefield: jihadis told the BBC that life in IS was like living in the computer game 'Call of Duty'.[4] But others, yet again, were chiefly motivated by the misery of Syrian Muslims: two British men arrested by the Turkish police in March 2015 protested that they were going to Syria to help – not to fight.[5]

On 7 January 2015, however, the world's attention was deflected from IS to Paris, where Said and Chérif Kouachi shot twelve journalists in the offices of the satirical magazine *Charlie Hebdo* to avenge its provocative cartoons of the Prophet Muhammad. Two days later, Amedy Coulibaly hijacked a kosher supermarket in the Porte de Vincennes: four Jewish customers were killed during the siege. Of Algerian descent, living in a notoriously deprived suburb of Paris, the terrorists were not traditionally devout: all had criminal records and until he was radicalised by the Abu Ghraib photographs, Chérif could not distinguish Islam from Catholicism.

Focusing almost entirely on the *Charlie Hebdo* massacre, the Western media seemed to assume that it was motivated solely by fanatical devotion to the Prophet and a consequent hatred of Western freedom of expression. Even though al-Qaeda, which always has a strong political agenda, claimed responsibility for the attack, there was no sustained discussion of any political motivation. Furthermore, this concentration on *Charlie Hebdo* meant that the political implications of the supermarket siege, where Coulibaly had explicitly declared that he was acting on behalf of the Palestinians, were also overlooked. This was another example of the scapegoating of 'religion' at the expense of the political – one which the West in this dangerously escalating conflict with Islamic extremism can ill afford.

Al-Qaeda's aim is always to incite a clash of civilisations between Islam and the West but this time, instead of attacking iconic buildings, they orchestrated a clash of sacred values. Free speech is sacred in the West, not because it is supernatural but because it is so central to our identity that is absolute and non-negotiable. When something they hold sacred is assaulted, people can feel that their deepest selves are violated. The speed with which the slogan '*Je suis Charlie*' was adopted showed that many instinctively made that profound identification.

On 11 January, forty-one political leaders linked arms and led 3.7 million people through the streets of Paris, marching in defence of freedom and *liberté*. This was probably exactly what al-Qaeda wanted; they will be able to use the imagery of the West marching against Islam to radicalise disaffected Muslim youth. But it is a mistake to assume that all Muslims are hostile to Western freedom. The Gallup Poll (2001–07) that we cited earlier found that democracy and freedom of expression were among the top three things that most Muslim respondents – even those politically radicalised – admired in Western society. Far from 'hating our freedom', they would like more of it for themselves.[6]

In the West, it is often said that because the Muslim world has not experienced an Enlightenment like our own, it will remain chronically unable to appreciate modernity. But, as we have seen, Enlightenment freedom was strictly for Europeans. There was no *liberté* for the Native Americans or the African slaves who toiled on American plantations. John Locke, pioneer of the liberal state, supported slavery and insisted that the native peoples of the New World had no property rights to their land. During the colonial period, the subject peoples were deprived of self-determination at a crucial stage of their modernisation. This attitude continues: many of the political leaders who marched in Paris headed countries that have for over a century supported regimes in Muslim-majority countries that have deprived their people of any freedom of expression. Immediately after the march, several hastened to pay their respects at the funeral of the Saudi king.

At the end of this book, I concluded that we are now living in such an interrelated world that we are all implicated in one another's tragedies. The terrorism we rightly deplore is, in part, a result of Western behaviour and Western people are not the only targets of Muslim extremism. Just two weeks before the Paris attacks, 145 Pakistanis, most of them children, were killed by the Taliban to avenge an action of the Pakistani military. Four days before the Paris shootings, some 2,000 villagers, mostly women, children and the elderly, were slaughtered by Boko Haram, a militant Sunni sect, in Baga on the Nigerian border with Chad. But in the West, compared with the *Charlie Hebdo* bonanza, media coverage of these atrocities was minimal, even perfunctory. This does not go unnoticed in the Muslim world. Yet again, we should recall the story of Cain and Abel. When Muslims are killed in Syria, Palestine, Nigeria, Pakistan or Iraq – countries whose tragic destinies they have helped to shape – Western people must realise that it is their brothers' blood that cries out to them from the soil.

ACKNOWLEDGEMENTS

This book is dedicated to Jane Garrett, my friend as well as my editor at Knopf for twenty years. From the very beginning, your encouragement and enthusiasm gave me the strength to persevere with the daily jihad of writing; it was a privilege and a joy to work with you.

But I am also blessed with my editors George Andreou and Jörg Hensgen, whose stringent, meticulous work on the manuscript helped me to push the book into another dimension for which I am sincerely grateful. My thanks also to all the people who have worked on the book with such skill and expertise: Stuart Williams (publishing director), Joe Pickering (publicist), Katherine Ailes (assistant editor), James Jones (jacket designer), Beth Humphries (copy-editor) and Mary Chamberlain (proofreader) at the Bodley Head; Romeo Enriques (production manager), Ellen Feldman (production editor), Kim Thornton (publicist), Oliver Munday (jacket design), Cassandra Pappas (text designer), Janet Biehl (copy-editor) and Terezia Cicelova at Knopf; and Louise Dennys (publisher) and Sheila Kaye (publicist) at Knopf Canada. Many of you I have never met but be assured I appreciate all you do for me.

As always, I must thank my agents Felicity Bryan, Peter Ginsberg and Andrew Nurnberg for their tireless support, loyalty and, above all, for their continued faith in me; this time, I really could not have managed without you. Thanks too to Michele Topham, Jackie Head and Carole Robinson in Felicity Bryan's office for helping me so cheerfully through the day-to-day crises of a writer's life, from book-keeping to computer melt-downs. And my sincere gratitude to Nancy Roberts, my assistant, for dealing so patiently with my correspondence and for her adamantine firmness in ensuring that I have time and space to write.

A big thank you to Sally Cockburn, whose paintings helped me to understand what my book was, in part, about. And, finally, thanks to Eve, Gary, Stacey and Amy Mott and Michelle Stevenson at My Ideal Dog, for looking after Poppy so devotedly during her last years and enabling me to do my work. This book is also in loving memory of Gary, who always saw to the heart of things and would, I think, have approved its contents.

NOTES

Introduction

1 Leviticus 16: 21–22. Unless otherwise stated, all biblical quotations – in both the Hebrew Bible and the New Testament – are from *The Jerusalem Bible* (London, 1966)

2 René Girard, *Violence and the Sacred,* trans. Patrick Gregory (Baltimore, 1977), p. 251

3 Stanislav Andreski, *Military Organization in Society* (London, 1968); Robert L. O'Connell, *Ride of the Second Horseman: The Birth and Death of War* (New York and Oxford, 1995), pp. 6–13, 106–10,128–29; O'Connell, *Of Arms and Men: A History of War, Weapons and Aggression* (New York and Oxford, 1989), pp. 22–25; John Keegan, *A History of Warfare* (London, 1993), pp. 223–29; Bruce Lincoln, 'War and Warriors: An Overview', in *Death, War and Sacrifice: Studies in Ideology and Practice* (Chicago and London, 1991), pp. 138–40; Johan Huizinga, *Homo Ludens: A Study of the Play Element in Culture* (Boston, 1955 ed.), pp. 89–104; Mark Juergensmeyer, *Terror in the Mind of God: The Global Rise of Religious Violence* (Berkeley, Los Angeles and London, 2001), p. 90; Malise Ruthven, *A Fury for God: The Islamist Attack on America* (London, 2002), p. 101; James A. Aho, *Religious Mythology and the Art of War: Comparative Religious Symbolisms of Military Violence* (Westport, Conn., 1981), pp. xi–xiii, 4–35; Richard English, *Terrorism: How to Respond* (Oxford and New York, 2009), pp. 27–55

4 Thomas A. Indinopulos and Bryan C. Wilson, eds, *What is Religion? Origins, Definitions and Explanations* (Leiden, 1998); Wilfred Cantwell Smith, *The Meaning and End of Religion: A New Approach to the Religious Traditions of Mankind* (New York, 1962); Talal Asad, 'The Construction of Religion as an Anthropological Category', in *Genealogies of Religion: Discipline and Reasons of Power in Christianity and Islam* (Baltimore, 1993); Derek Peterson and Darren Walhof, eds, *The Invention of Religion:*

Rethinking Belief in Politics and History (New Brunswick, NJ, and London, 2002); Timothy Fitzgerald, ed., *Religion and the Secular: Historical and Colonial Formations* (London and Oakville, 2007); Arthur L. Greil and David G. Bromley, eds, *Defining Religion: Investigating the Boundaries between the Sacred and Secular* (Oxford, 2003); Daniel Dubuisson, *The Western Construction of Religion: Myths, Knowledge and Ideology*, trans. William Sayers (Baltimore, 1998); William T. Cavanaugh, *The Myth of Religious Violence* (Oxford, 2009)

5   Dubuisson, *Western Construction of Religion*, p. 168

6   H. J. Rose, 'Religion, terms relating to', in M. Carey, ed., *The Oxford Classical Dictionary* (Oxford, 1949)

7   Smith, *Meaning and End of Religion*, pp. 50–68

8   Louis Jacobs, ed., *The Jewish Religion: A Companion* (Oxford, 1995), p. 418

9   Smith, *Meaning and End of Religion*, pp. 23–25

10   Ibid., pp. 29–31

11   Ibid., p. 33

12   Cavanaugh, *Myth of Religious Violence*, pp. 72–85

13   Mircea Eliade, *The Myth of Eternal Return, Or, Cosmos and History*, trans. Willard R. Trask (Princeton, NJ, 1991 ed.), pp. 1–34

14   Ibid., pp. 32–34; Karl Jaspers, *The Origin and Goal of History*, trans. Michael Bullock (London, 1953), p. 40

15   Paul Gilbert, *The Compassionate Mind: A New Approach to Life's Challenges* (London, 2009)

16   P. Broca, 'Anatomie compare des circonvolutions cérébrales: le grand lobe limbique', *Revue anthropologie*, 1, 1868

17   Gilbert, *Compassionate Mind*, pp. 170–71

18   Mencius, *The Book of Mencius*, 2A.6

19   Walter Burkert, *Homo Necans: The Anthropology of Greek Sacrificial Ritual*, trans. Peter Bing (Berkeley, Los Angeles and London, 1983), pp. 16–22

20   Mircea Eliade, *A History of Religious Ideas*, 3 vols, trans. Willard R. Trask (Chicago and London, 1978, 1982, 1985), 1, pp. 7–8, 24; Joseph Campbell, *Historical Atlas of World Mythologies*, 2 vols (New York, 1988), 1, pp. 48–49; Campbell, with Bill Moyers, *The Power of Myth* (New York, 1988), pp. 70–72, 85–87

21   André Leroi-Gourhan, *Treasures of Prehistoric Art* (New York, n.d.), p. 112

22   Jill Cook, *The Swimming Reindeer* (London, 2010)

23 Neil MacGregor, *A History of the World in 100 Objects* (London, 2001), p. 22

24 Ibid., p. 24

25 J. Ortega y Gasset, *Meditations on Hunting* (New York, 1985), p. 3

26 Walter Burkert, *Structure and History in Greek Mythology and Ritual* (Berkeley, Los Angeles and London, 1980), pp. 54–56; Burkert, *Homo Necans*, pp. 42–45

27 O'Connell, *Ride of Second Horseman*, p. 33

28 Chris Hedges, *War is a Force That Gives Us Meaning* (New York, 2003 ed.), p. 10

29 Theodore Nadelson, *Trained to Kill: Soldiers at War* (Baltimore, 2005), p. 64

30 Ibid., pp. 68–69

31 Hedges, *War is a Force*, p. 3

32 I. Eibl-Eibesfeldt, *Human Ethology* (New York, 1989), p. 405

33 Lt. Col. Dave Grossman, *On Killing: The Psychological Cost of Learning to Kill in War and Society*, rev. ed. (New York, 2009), pp. 3–4

34 Joanna Bourke, *An Intimate History of Killing: Face to Face Killing in Twentieth-Century Warfare* (New York, 1999), p. 67

35 Peter Jay, *Road to Riches or The Wealth of Man* (London, 2000), pp. 35–36

36 K. J. Wenke, *Patterns of Prehistory: Humankind's First Three Million Years* (New York, 1961), p. 130; John Keegan, *A History of Warfare* (London, 1993), pp. 120–21; O'Connell, *Ride of Second Horseman*, p. 35

37 M. H. Fried, *The Evolution of Political Society: An Essay in Political Anthropology* (New York, 1967), pp. 101–02; C. McCalley, 'Conference Archives', in J. Harris, ed., *The Anthropology of War* (Cambridge, UK, 1990), p. 11

38 Lenski, *Power and Privilege: A Theory of Social Stratification* (Chapel Hill and London, 1966), pp. 189–90

39 O'Connell, *Ride of Second Horseman*, pp. 57–58

40 J. L. Angel, 'Paleoecology, Pleodeography and Health', in S. Polgar, ed., *Population, Ecology and Social Evolution* (The Hague, 1975); David Rindos, *The Origins of Agriculture: An Evolutionary Perspective* (Orlando, Fla., 1984), pp. 186–87

41 E. O. James, *The Ancient Gods: The History and Diffusion of Religion in the Ancient Near East and the Eastern Mediterranean* (London, 1960), p. 89; S. H. Hooke, *Middle Eastern Mythology: From the Assyrians to the Hebrews* (Harmondsworth, UK, 1963), p. 83

42   K. W. Kenyon, *Digging up Jericho: The Results of the Jericho Excavations, 1953–1956* (New York, 1957).

43   Jacob Bronowski, *The Ascent of Man* (Boston, 1973), pp. 86–88; J. Mellaert, 'Early Urban Communities in the Near East, 9000 to 3400 BCE', in P. Mooney, ed., *The Origins of Civilization* (Oxford, 1979), pp. 22–25; P. Dorell, 'The Uniqueness of Jericho', in R. Morrey and P. Parr, eds, *Archaeology in the Levant: Essays for Kathleen Kenyon* (Warminster, UK, 1978)

44   Robert Eisen, *The Peace and Violence of Judaism: From the Bible to Modern Zionism* (Oxford, 2011), p. 12

45   World Council of Churches, *Violence, Nonviolence, and the Struggle for Social Justice* (Geneva, 1972), p. 6

46   Gerhard E. Lenski, *Power and Privilege*, pp. 105–14; O'Connell, *Ride of Second Horseman*, p. 28; E. O. Wilson, *On Human Nature* (Cambridge, Mass., 1978), p. 140; M. Ehrenburg, *Women in Prehistory* (London, 1989), p. 38

47   A. R. Radcliffe, *The Andaman Islanders* (New York, 1948), p. 43

48   Ibid., p. 177

49   John H. Kautsky, *The Politics of the Aristocratic Empire*, 2nd ed. (New Brunswick and London, 1997), p. 374

50   Ibid., p. 177

51   Keegan, *History of Warfare*, pp. 384–86; John Haldon, *Warfare, State and Society in the Byzantine World* (London and New York, 2005), pp. 10–11

52   Bruce Lincoln, 'The Role of Religion in Achmenean Imperialism', in Nicole Brisch, ed., *Religion and Power: Divine Kingship in the Ancient World and Beyond* (Chicago, 2008)

53   Cavanaugh, *Myth of Religious Violence*.

PART ONE: BEGINNINGS

1. Farmers and Herdsmen

1   *The Epic of Gilgamesh*, Standard Version, Tablet I, 38. Unless otherwise stated, all quotations are from Stephen Mitchell, trans., *The Epic of Gilgamesh: A New English Version* (New York, London, Toronto, Sydney, 2004)

2   Ibid., I, 18–20

3   Ibid., I, 29–34; Mitchell's emphasis

4   The earliest extant texts date from the late third millennium; the Old
     Babylonian Epic combined these in a single work (*c.* 1700 BCE); Sin-Leqi's
     poem (*c.* 1200 BCE) is the standard version on which most modern
     translations are based.

5   *Gilgamesh*, Standard Version, I. 67–69; trans. Mitchell, amended by
     Andrew George, trans., *The Epic of Gilgamesh: The Babylonian Epic Poem
     in Akkadian and Sumerian* (London, 1999)

6   George, *Epic of Gilgamesh*, p. xlvi

7   John Keegan, *A History of Warfare* (London, 1993), pp. 126–30; Robert
     L. O'Connell, *Ride of the Second Horseman: The Birth and Death of War*
     (New York and Oxford, 1995), pp. 88–89

8   R. M. Adams, *Heartlands of Cities: Surveys of Ancient Settlements and Land
     Use on the Central Floodplains of the Euphrates* (Chicago, 1981), pp. 60,
     244; William H. McNeill, *Plagues and People* (London, 1994), p. 47

9   McNeill, *Plagues and People*, pp. 54–55

10   Gerhard E. Lenski, *Power and Privilege: A Theory of Social Stratification*
     (Chapel Hill and London, 1966), p. 228

11   A. L. Oppenheim, *Ancient Mesopotamia: Portrait of a Dead Civilization*
     (Chicago, 1977), pp. 82–83; O'Connell, *Ride of Second Horseman*,
     pp. 93–95

12   Samuel N. Kramer, *Sumerian Mythology: A Study of the Spiritual and Literary
     Achievement of the Third Millennium BC* (Philadelphia, 1944), p. 118

13   Ibid., p. 119

14   Gottwald, *The Politics of Ancient Israel* (Louisville, 2001), pp. 118–19

15   O'Connell, *Ride of Second Horseman*, pp. 91–92

16   Georges Dumézil, *The Destiny of the Warrior*, trans. Alf Hiltebeitel
     (Chicago and London, 1969), p. 3

17   Thorkild Jacobsen, 'The Cosmos as State', in H. and H. A. Frankfort,
     eds, *The Intellectual Adventure of Ancient Man: An Essay on Speculative
     Thought in the Ancient Near East* (Chicago, 1946), pp. 148–51

18   *Gilgamesh*, Standard Version, Tablet I, 48

19   I have discussed this more fully in *A Short History of Myth* (London,
     2005)

20   Jacobsen, 'Cosmos as State', pp. 145–48; 186–97; George, *Epic of
     Gilgamesh*, pp. xxxvii–xxxviii

21   Jacobsen, 'Cosmos as State', pp. 186–91; Tammi J. Schneider, *An
     Introduction to Ancient Mesopotamian Religion* (Grand Rapids, Micha. and
     Cambridge, UK, 2011), pp. 66–79; George, *Epic of Gilgamesh*,
     pp. xxxviii–xxxix

22   Schneider, *Introduction*, p. 5; Jacobsen, 'Cosmos as State' p. 203

23   John Kautsky, *The Politics of Aristocratic Empire*, 2nd. ed., pp. 15–16; 107

24   Thomas Merton, *Faith and Violence* (Notre Dame, Ind., 1968), pp. 7–8

25   Walter Benjamin, 'Theses on the Philosophy of History', in *Illuminations* (London, 1999), p. 248

26   Max Weber, *The Theory of Social and Economic Organization*, trans. A. M. Henderson and Talcott Parsons (New York, 1947), pp. 341–48

27   *Gilgamesh,* Standard Version, Tablet I, 80, 82–90

28   Atrahasis I.i; trans. Stephanie Dalley, *Myths from Mesopotamia: Creation, the Flood, Gilgamesh, and Others* (Oxford and New York, 1989), p. 10

29   Ibid.

30   Ibid., I.iii, p. 12.

31   Ibid., p. 14.

32   Ibid.

33   Ibid. II.iii, p. 23

34   Ibid., III.vii, p. 28

35   W. G. Lambert and A. R. Millard, *Atra-Hasis: The Babylonian Story of the Flood* (Oxford, 1969), pp. 31–39

36   Schneider, *Ancient Mesopotamian Religion,* p. 45

37   Keegan, *History of Warfare,* p. 128

38   *Gilgamesh,* Standard Version, Tablet II, 109–10; George translation

39   Ibid., Tablet I, 220–23; George translation

40   Ibid., Yale Tablet, 18; George translation

41   O'Connell, *Ride of Second Horseman,* pp. 96–97

42   A. L. Oppenheimer, 'Trade in the Ancient Near East', *International Congress of Economic History,* 5, 1976

43   Kautsky, *Politics of Aristocratic Empires,* p. 178

44   Thorstein Veblen, *The Theory of the Leisure Class: An Economic Study of Institutions* (Boston, 1973), pp. 41, 45; my emphasis

45   Ibid., p. 30

46   *Gilgamesh,* Yale Tablet, 97; Standard Version, Tablet III, 54; Mitchell translation

47   Kautsky, *Politics of Aristocratic Empires,* pp. 170–72, 346

48   *Gilgamesh,* Standard Version, Tablet II, 233, Yale Tablet, 149–50

49   Ibid., 185–87; Mitchell's emphasis

50   *Gilgamesh,* Standard Version, Tablet III, 44

51   Chris Hedges, *War is a Force That Gives Us Meaning* (New York, 2003), p. 21

52   *Gilgamesh,* Yale Tablet, 269

53   *Gilgamesh,* Standard Version, XI, 322–26

54 R. Cribb, *Nomads and Archaeology* (Cambridge, UK, 1999), pp. 18, 136, 215

55 O'Connell, *Ride of Second Horseman*, pp. 67–68

56 K. C. Chang, *The Archaeology of Ancient China* (New Haven, 1968), pp. 152–54

57 O'Connell, *Ride of Second Horseman*, pp. 77–78

58 Ibid.

59 Tacitus, *Germania*, 14 in Kautsky, *Politics of Aristocratic Empires*, p. 178

60 Veblen, *Theory of the Leisure Class*, p. 45

61 Bruce Lincoln, 'Indo-European Religions: An Introduction', in *Death, War and Sacrifice: Studies in Ideology and Practice* (Chicago and London, 1991), pp. 1–10

62 Mary Boyce, 'Priests, Cattle and Men', *Bulletin of the School of Oriental and African Studies*, 1988, pp. 508–26

63 For example, the Zoroastrian liturgical text Yasna 30:7c; 32; 49: 4b; 50: 7a; 30: 106; 44: 4d; 51: 96; Bruce Lincoln, 'Warriors and Non-Herdsmen: A Response to Mary Boyce', in *Death, War and Sacrifice*, pp. 147–60

64 Lincoln, 'Indo-European Religions', pp. 10–13

65 Ibid., p. 12

66 Bruce Lincoln, 'War and Warriors: An Overview', in *Death, War and Sacrifice*, pp. 138–40

67 Homer, *Iliad*, 12: 310–15, trans. Richard Lattimore, *The Iliad of Homer* (Chicago and London, 1951)

68 Lincoln, 'War and Warriors', p. 143

69 Georges Dumézil, *The Destiny of the Warrior*, trans. Alf Hiltebeitel (Chicago and London, 1969), pp. 64–74

70 *Iliad*, 20: 490–94; Lattimore translation

71 *Iliad*, 20: 495–503; Lattimore translation; Seth L. Schein, *The Mortal Hero: An Introduction to Homer's* Iliad (Berkeley, Los Angeles and London), pp. 145–46

72 Lincoln, 'Indo-European Religions', p. 4

73 Dumézil, *Destiny of the Warrior*, pp. 106–07

74 *Iliad*, 4: 492–88; Lattimore translation

75 Homer, *Odyssey*, 11.500, in Walter Shewring, trans., *Homer: The Odyssey* (Oxford and New York, 1980)

76 James Mellaart, *The Neolithic of the Near East* (London, 1975), pp. 119, 167, 206–07; O'Connell, *Ride of Second Horseman*, pp. 74–81

77 J. N. Postgate, *Early Mesopotamia: Society and Economy at the Dawn of History* (London, 1992), p. 251

78 O'Connell, *Ride of Second Horseman*, pp. 132–42

79 Keegan, *History of Warfare*, pp. 130–31

80 John Romer, *People of the Nile: Everyday Life in Ancient Egypt* (New York, 1982), p. 115

81 Keegan, *History of Warfare*, pp. 133–35

82 Yigal Yadin, *The Art of Warfare in Biblical Lands*, 2 vols (New York, 1963), I, pp. 134–35; Robert Adams, *The Evolution of Urban Society: Early Mesopotamia and Prehispanic Mexico* (Chicago, 1966), p. 149

83 Kramer, *Sumerian Mythology*, p. 123

84 Ibid., p. 120

85 Kautsky, *Politics of Aristocratic Empires*, p. 108; cf. Carlo M. Cipolla, *Before the Industrial Revolution: European Society and Economy, 1000–1700* (New York, 1976), pp. 129–30, 151

86 Robert L. O'Connell, *Of Arms and Men: A History of War: Weapons and Aggression* (New York, p. 38); *Ride of Second Horseman*, pp. 100–01; William H. McNeill, *The Pursuit of Power: Technology, Armed Force and Society since AD ⬜⬜⬜⬜* (Chicago, 1982), pp. 2–3; Schneider, *Ancient Mesopotamian Religion*, pp. 22–23; A. L. Oppenheim, *Ancient Mesopotamia*, pp. 153–54; Gwendolyn Leick, *Mesopotamia: The Invention of the City* (London, 2001), pp. 85–108

87 Joseph A. Schumpeter, *Imperialism and Social Classes: Two Essays* (New York, 1955), p. 25: Perry Anderson, *Lineages of the Absolutist State* (London, 1974), p. 32

88 Anderson, *Lineages*, p. 31; Anderson's emphasis

89 Kautsky, *Politics of Aristocratic Empires*, pp. 148–52

90 Marc Bloch, *Feudal Society* (Chicago, 1961), p. 298

91 Leick, *Mesopotamia*, p. 95. The 'Lower Seas' and 'Upper Seas' were, respectively, the Persian Gulf and the Mediterranean

92 Ibid., p. 100

93 J. B. Pritchard, ed., *Ancient Near Eastern Texts Relating to the Old Testament* (Princeton, 1969), p. 164

94 Code of Hammurabi, 24: 1–8, cited in F. C. Frensham, *Social Justice in Ancient Israel and in the Ancient Near East* (Minneapolis, 1995), p. 193

95 Pritchard, *Ancient Near Eastern Texts*, p. 178; my emphasis

96 Marshall G. S. Hodgson, *The Venture of Islam: Conscience and History in a World Civilization* (Chicago and London, 1974), 3 vols, I, pp. 108–10

97 Schneider, *Ancient Mesopotamian Religion*, pp. 105–06. The meaning and derivation of *akitu* is unknown; Jacobsen, 'Cosmos as State', p. 169

98 N. K. Sanders, ed. and trans., 'The Babylonian Creation Hymn', in

Poems of Heaven and Hell from Ancient Mesopotamia (London, 1971), pp. 44–60

99 Jonathan Z. Smith, 'A Pearl of Great Price and a Cargo of Yams: A Study in Situational Incongruity', in Jonathan Z. Smith, *Imagining Religion: From Babylon to Jonestown* (Chicago and London, 1982), pp. 90–96; Mircea Eliade, *A History of Religious Ideas*, trans. Willard R. Trask, 3 vols, (Chicago, 1978), 1, pp. 72–76; Sanders, 'Babylonian Creation Hymn', pp. 47–51

100 Smith, 'Pearl of Great Price', p. 91

101 Sanders, 'Babylonian Creation', p. 73

102 Ibid.

103 Ibid., p. 79

104 O'Connell, *Ride of Second Horseman*, pp. 141–42

105 Leick, *Mesopotamia*, pp. 198–216

106 A. K. Grayson, *Assyrian Royal Inscriptions*, 2 vols (Wiesbaden, 1972, 1976), 1, pp. 80–81

107 H. W. F. Saggs, *The Might That Was Assyria* (London, 1984), pp. 48–49; I. M. Diakonoff, *Ancient Mesopotamia: Socio-Economic History* (Moscow, 1969), pp. 221–22

108 Grayson, *Assyrian Royal Inscriptions*, pp. 123–24

109 Saggs, *Might That Was Assyria*, p. 62

110 Ibid., p. 61

111 *Ludlul Bel Nemeqi* in Jacobsen, 'Cosmos as State', pp. 212–14

112 Yasna 46. Norman Cohn, *Cosmos, Chaos and the World to Come: The Ancient Roots of Apocalyptic Faith* (New Haven and London, 1993), p. 77; Mary Boyce, *Zoroastrians: Their Religious Beliefs and Practices*, 2nd ed. (London and New York), p. xliii; Peter Clark, *Zoroastrians: An Introduction to an Ancient Faith* (Brighton and Portland, Oreg., 1998, p. 19)

113 Yasna 30

114 Boyce, *Zoroastrians*, pp. 23–24

115 Lincoln, 'Warriors and Non-Herdsmen', p. 153

116 Yasna 44

117 Lincoln, 'Warriors and Non-Herdsmen', p. 158

2. India: The Noble Path

1 Jarrod L. Whitaker, *Strong Arms and Drinking Strength: Masculinity, Violence and the Body in Ancient India* (Oxford, 2011), pp. 152–53

2   Rig Veda, III.32: 1–4, 9–11, trans. Ralph T. Griffith, *The Rig Veda* (London, 1992)

3   Edwin Bryant, *The Quest for the Origins of Vedic Culture: The Indo-Aryan Debate* (Oxford and New York, 2001); Colin Renfrew, *The Puzzle of Indo-European Origins* (London, 1987); Romila Thapar, *Early India: From the Origins to AD* ▧▧▧▧ (Berkeley and Los Angeles, 2002), pp. 105–07

4   Whitaker, *Strong Arms*, pp. 3–5; Wendy Doniger, *The Hindus: An Alternative History* (Oxford, 2009), pp. 111–13

5   Louis Renou, *Religions of Ancient India* (London, 1953), p. 20; Michael Witzel, 'Vedas and Upanishads', in Gavin Flood, ed., *Blackwell Companion to Hinduism* (Oxford, 2003), pp. 70–71; J. C. Heesterman, 'Ritual, Revelation and the Axial Age', in S. N. Eisenstadt, ed., *The Origins and Diversity of Axial Age Civilizations* (Albany, NY, 1986), p. 398

6   J. C. Heesterman, 'Ritual, Revelation and the Axial Age', pp. 396–98; Heesterman, *The Inner Conflict of Tradition: Essays on Indian Ritual, Kingship and Society* (Chicago and London, 1985), p. 206; John Keay, *India: A History* (London, 2000), pp. 31–33; Thapar, *Early India*, pp. 126–30

7   Rig Veda 1.32.5

8   Shatapatha Brahmana (SB), 6.8.1.1, trans. J. C. Heesterman, *The Broken World of Sacrifice: An Essay in Ancient Indian Religion* (Chicago and London, 1993), p. 123

9   Rig Veda 8.16.1; 8.95.6; 10.38.4

10   Whitaker, *Strong Arms*, pp. 3–5; 16–23; Catherine Bell, *Ritual Theory, Ritual Practice* (New York, 1992), pp. 180–81, 221

11   Renou, *Religions of Ancient India*, p. 6; Witzel, 'Vedas and Upanishads', p. 73

12   Whitaker, *Strong Arms*, pp. 115–17

13   Rig Veda 2.22.4

14   Rig Veda 3.31; 10.62.2

15   Witzel, 'Vedas and Upanishads', p. 72

16   Doniger, *Hindus*, p. 114

17   Heesterman, 'Ritual and Revelation,' p. 403

18   SB 7.1.1.1–4, in Mircea Eliade, *The Myth of the Eternal Return or Cosmos and History*, trans. Willard R. Trask (Princeton, 1974), pp. 10–11

19   Maitrayani Samhita 4.2.1.23.2, in Heesterman, *Broken World*, pp. 23–24; 134–37

20   SB 2.2.2.8–10; Heesterman, *Broken World*, p. 24

21   Georges Dumézil, *The Destiny of the Warrior*, trans. Alf Hiltebeitel (Chicago and London, 1970), pp. 76–78

22   John H. Kautsky, *The Political Consequences of Modernization* (New Brunswick and London, 1997), pp. 25–26

23   Whitaker, *Strong Arms*, p. 158

24   Louis Renou, 'Sur la Notion de "brahman"', *Journal Asiatique*, 237 (1949); Jan Gonda, *Change and Continuity in Indian Religion* (The Hague, 1965), p. 200

25   Rig Veda I.164. 46. Garatman was the Sun

26   Rig Veda, 10.129. 6–7

27   Jan Gonda, *The Vision of the Vedic Poets* (The Hague, 1963), p. 18

28   Renou, *Religions of Ancient India*, pp. 220–25; R. C. Zaehner, *Hinduism* (London, New York and Toronto, 1962), pp. 219–25

29   Rig Veda, X.90

30   Ibid., X. 90. 11–14; Griffiths translation, modified

31   Bruce Lincoln, 'Indo-European Religions: An Introduction', in *Death, War and Sacrifice: Studies in Ideology and Practice* (Chicago and London, 1991), p. 8

32   Bruce Lincoln, 'Sacrificial Ideology and Indo-European Society', in *Death, War and Sacrifice*, p. 173

33   Thapar, *Early India*, p. 123

34   Lincoln, 'Sacrificial Ideology', pp. 174–75

35   Ibid., pp. 143–47

36   Reinhard Bendix, *Kings or People: Power and the Mandate to Rule* (Berkeley, 1977), p. 228

37   Max Weber, *The Religion of India: The Sociology of Hinduism and Buddhism*, trans. and ed. Hans H. Gerth and Don Martindale (Glencoe, Ill., 1951), p. 65

38   Alfred Vogts, *A History of Militarism: Civilian and Military*, rev. ed. (New York, 1959), p. 42

39   Pancavimsha Brahmana (PB) 7.7: 9–10, in Heesterman, *Broken World*, p. 62

40   SB 6.8.14; Heesterman, 'Ritual, Revelation and the Axial Age', p. 402

41   J. C. Heesterman, *The Inner Conflict of Tradition: Essays on Indian Ritual, Kingship and Society* (Chicago and London, 1993) pp. 68, 84–85

42   Rig Veda I.132: 20–21; Griffiths translation

43   Taittiriya Samhita (TS) 6.4.8.1., in Heesterman, *Inner Conflict*, p. 209

44   Taittiriya Brahmana (TB) 3.7.7.14, in Heesterman, *Broken World*, p. 34

45   Witzel, 'Vedas and Upanisads', p. 82

46   Shatapatha Brahmana 10.6.5.8, in Heesterman, *Broken World*, p. 57

47   Zaehner, *Hinduism*, pp. 59–60; Renou, *Religions of Ancient India*, p. 18;

Witzel, 'Vedas and Upanisads', p. 81; Brian K. Smith, *Reflections on Resemblance, Ritual and Religion* (Oxford and New York, 1989), pp. 30–34, 72–81

48   Jonathan Z. Smith, 'The Bare Facts of Ritual', in *Imagining Religion: From Babylon to Jonestown* (Chicago and London, 1982), p. 63

49   Doniger, *Hindus*, pp. 137–42; Gavin Flood, *An Introduction to Hinduism* (Oxford, 2003), pp. 80–81

50   Thapar, *Early India*, pp. 150–52

51   *The Laws of Manu*, 7.16–22, trans. G. Buhler (Delhi, 1962)

52   Thapar, *Early India*, pp. 147–49; Doniger, *Hindus*, pp. 165–66

53   Thapar, *Early India*, p. 138

54   Hermann Kulke, 'The Historical Background of India's Axial Age', in S. N. Eisenstadt, ed., *The Origins and Diversity of Axial Age Civilizations* (Albany, NY, 1986), p. 385

55   Thapar, *Early India*, p. 154

56   Richard Gombrich, *Theravada Buddhism: A Social History from Ancient Benares to Modern Colombo* (London and New York, 1988), pp. 55–56

57   Ibid., pp. 58–59; William H. McNeill, *Plagues and Peoples* (Garden City, NY, 1976), p. 60; Patrick Olivelle, ed. and trans., *Samnayasa Upanisads: Hindu Scriptures on Asceticism and Renunciation* (New York and Oxford, 1992), p. 34; Doniger, *Hindus*, p. 171

58   Thomas J. Hopkins, *The Hindu Religious Tradition* (Belmont, Calif., 1971), pp. 50–51; Doniger, *Hindus*, p. 165

59   Chandogya Upanishad (CU) 5.10.7. Quotations from the Upanishads are from Patrick Olivelle, ed., *Upanisads* (Oxford and New York); Brhadaranyaka Upanishad (BU) 4.4.23–35; Thapar, *Early India*, p. 130

60   Olivelle, *Samnayasa Upanisads*, pp. 37–38

61   Olivelle, *Upanisads*, p. xxix; Witzel, 'Vedas and Upanisads', pp. 85–86

62   BU 1.4.6

63   BU 1.4.10

64   BU 4.4.5–7

65   BU 4.4.23–35

66   CU 8: 7–12

67   CU 6: 11

68   CU 6: 12

69   CU 6: 13

70   CU 6: 10

71   Thapar, *Early India*, p. 132

72   Flood, *Introduction to Hinduism*, p. 91; Patrick Olivelle, 'The Renouncer

Tradition', in Gavin Flood, ed., *The Blackwell Companion to Hinduism* (Oxford, 2003) p. 271

73   Steven Collins, *Selfless Persons: Imagery and Thought in Theravada Buddhism* (Cambridge, UK, 1982), p. 64; Paul Dundas, *The Jains*, 2nd ed. (London and New York, 2002), p. 64

74   Manara Gryha Sutra 1.1.6, in Heesterman, *Broken World*, pp. 164–74; Gonda, *Change and Continuity*, pp. 228–35; 285–94

75   Gonda, *Change and Continuity*, pp. 380–84; Patrick Olivelle, 'The Renouncer Tradition', pp. 281–82

76   Digha Nikaya (DN), in Olivelle, *Samnyasa Upanisads*, p. 43

77   Naradaparivrajaka Upanisad (NpU), 143, in Olivelle, *Samnyasa Upanisads*, p. 108

78   Ibid., p. 185

79   A. Ghosh, *The City in Early Historical India* (Simla, 1973), p. 55; Olivelle, *Samnyasa Upanisads*, pp. 45–46

80   Mircea Eliade, *Yoga, Immortality and Freedom*, trans. Willard Trask (London, 1958) pp. 59–62

81   Patanjali, Yoga Sutras 2.42, in Eliade, *Yoga*, p. 52

82   Dundas, *Jains*, pp. 28–30

83   Ibid., pp. 106–07

84   Acaranga Sutra (AS) 1.4.1.1–2, in Dundas, *Jains*, pp. 41–42

85   AS 1.2.3, ibid.

86   Avashyaksutra 32, in ibid., p. 171

87   Western scholars once thought that the Buddha was born *c.*563 BCE, but recent scholarship indicates that he lived about a century later. Heinz Berchant, 'The Date of the Buddha Reconsidered', *Indologia Taurinensin*, 10, n.d.

88   Majjhima Nikaya (MN) 38. Unless otherwise stated, all quotations from the Buddhist scriptures are my own versions of the texts cited

89   I have described the Buddha's spiritual method more fully in *Buddha: A Penguin Life* (New York, 2001). See also Richard F. Gombrich, *How Buddhism Began: The Conditioned Genesis of the Early Teachings* (London and Atlantic Highlands, NJ, 1966); Michael Carrithers, *The Buddha* (Oxford and New York, 1993); Karl Jaspers, *The Great Philosophers: The Foundations*, ed. Hannah Arendt, trans. Ralph Manheim (London, 1962), pp. 99–105; Trevor Ling, *The Buddha: Buddhist Civilization in India and Ceylon* (London, 1973)

90   Edward Conze, *Buddhism: Its Essence and Development* (Oxford, 1951),

p. 102; Hermann Oldenberg, *Buddha: His Life, His Doctrine, His Order*, trans. William Hoeg (London, 1882), pp. 299–302

91   Sutta Nipata (SN) 118

92   Vinaya, *Mahavagga* I:ii; Ling, *The Buddha*, p. 134

93   Anguttara Nikaya (AN) 1.211

94   Ibid. 1.27; SN 700; Bikkhu Nanamoli, ed., *The Life of the Buddha, according to the Pali Canon* (Kandy, Sri Lanka, 1992), p. 134

95   MN 89

96   Thapar, *Early India*, pp. 174–98

97   Patrick Olivelle, ed., *Asoka, in History and Historical Memory* (Delhi, 2009), p. 1

98   Major Rock Edict XIII, trans. Romila Thapar, *Asoka and the Decline of the Mauryas* (Oxford, 1961), pp. 255–56

99   Ibid.

100 Olivelle, *Asoka*, p. 1

101 Pillar Edict VII, in Thapar, *Asoka*, p. 255

102 Major Rock Edict XII, ibid.

103 Major Rock Edict XI, ibid., p. 254.

104 Ananda K. Coomaraswamy and Sister Nivedita, *Myths of the Hindus and Buddhists* (New York, 1967), p. 118

105 Shruti Kapila and Faisal Devji, eds, *Political Thought in Action: The Bhagavad Gita and Modern India* (Cambridge, 2013)

106 Doniger, *Hindus*, pp. 262–64

107 Thapar, *Early India*, p. 207

108 *Mahabharata*, 7.70.44, in J. A. B. van Buitenen, trans. and ed., *The Mahabharata:, Volume 3: Book 4: The Book of Virata; Book 5: The Book of the Effort* (Chicago and London, 1978)

109 Mahabharata 5.70.46–66, van Buitenen translation

110 Ibid., 7.165.63

111 Ibid., 9.60. 59–63, in John D. Smith, trans. and ed., *The Mahabharata: An Abridged Translation* (London, 2009)

112 Ibid. 10.8.3

113 Ibid. 10.10.14

114 Mahabharata 12.15; trans. Doniger, *Hindus*, p. 270

115 Ibid., 17.3

116 *Bhagavad Gita* 1: 33–34, 36–37. All quotations are from *The Bhagavad-Gita: Krishna's Cousel in Time of War*, trans. Barbara Stoler Miller (New York, Toronto and London, 1986)

117 Ibid., 2.9

118 Ibid. 4.20.

119 Ibid. 9.9.

120 Ibid., 11. 32–33

121 Ibid., 11.55.

3. China: Warriors and Gentlemen

1   *Liezi jishi*, 2, in Mark Edward Lewis, *Sanctioned Violence in Early China* (Albany, NY, 1990), p. 200

2   Ibid., pp. 167–72

3   Ibid., pp. 176–79

4   Marcel Granet, *Chinese Civilization*, trans. Kathleen Innes and Mabel Brailsford (London and New York, 1951), pp. 11–12; Granet, *The Religion of the Chinese People*, trans. and ed. Maurice Freedman (Oxford, 1975), pp. 66–68

5   *Taijong yulan*, 79, in Lewis, *Sanctioned Violence*, p. 203

6   Ibid.

7   Ibid., p. 201

8   Granet, *Chinese Civilization*, pp. 11–16; Henri Maspero, *China in Antiquity*, 2nd ed., trans. Frank A. Kiermannn, Jr. (Folkestone, 1978), pp. 115–19

9   John King Fairbank and Merle Goldman, *China: A New History*, 2nd ed. (Cambridge, Mass., and London, 2006), p. 34

10   Jacques Gernet, *A History of Chinese Civilization*, 2nd ed., trans. J. R. Foster and Charles Hartman (Cambridge, UK and New York, 1996), pp. 39–40

11   Ibid., pp. 41–50; Jacques Gernet, *Ancient China: From the Beginnings to the Empire*, trans. Raymond Rudorff (London, 1968), pp. 37–65; Wm. Theodore De Bary and Irene Bloom, eds, *Sources of Chinese Tradition: From Earliest Times to 1600*, 2nd ed. (New York, 1999), pp. 3–25; D. Howard Smith, *Chinese Religions* (London, 1968), pp. 1–11

12   Gernet, *History of Chinese Civilisation*, pp. 45–46; Gernet, *Ancient China*, pp. 50–53; Granet, *Religion of the Chinese People*, pp. 37–54

13   *The Book of Songs*, trans. and ed. Arthur Waley (London, 1937), 35, 167, 185

14   Sima Qian, *Records of a Master Historian*, 1. 56, 79; Granet, *Chinese Civilization*, p. 12

15   Gernet, *Chinese Civilization*, p. 49

16   Marshall G. S. Hodgson, *The Venture of Islam: Conscience and History in a World Civilization*, 3 vols (Chicago and London, 1974), 1, pp. 281–82

17   Lewis, *Sanctioned Violence*, pp. 15–27; Fairbank and Goldman, *China*, pp. 49–50

18   Fairbank and Goldman, *China*, p. 45

19   K. C. Chang, *Art, Myth and Ritual: The Path to Political Authority in Ancient China* (Cambridge, Mass., 1985), pp. 95–100; Fairbank and Goldman, *China*, pp. 42–44

20   Walter Burkert, *Homo Necans: The Anthropology of Ancient Greek Sacrificial Ritual and Myth*, trans. Walter Bing (Berkeley, 1983), p. 47

21   David. N. Keightley, 'The Late Shang State: When, Where, What?', in Keightley, ed., *The Origins of Chinese Civilization* (Berkeley, 1983), pp. 256–59

22   Michael J. Puett, *To Become a God: Cosmology, Sacrifice and Self-Divinization in Early China* (Cambridge, Mass., and London, 2002), pp. 32–76

23   Oracle 23 in De Bary and Bloom, *Sources*, p. 12

24   Lewis, *Sanctioned Violence*, pp. 26–27

25   *The Book of Mozi*, 3.25, in Gernet, *Ancient China*, p. 65

26   'The Shao Announcement (Shaogao)' included in the Confucian classical text *Shujing* ('The Classic of Documents'), cited in De Bary and Bloom, *Sources*, pp. 35–37

27   H. G. Creel, *Confucius: The Man and the Myth* (London, 1951), pp. 19–25; Benjamin I. Schwarz, *The World of Thought in Ancient China* (Cambridge, Mass., and London, 1985), pp. 57–59; remarks by Jacques Gernet in Jean-Pierre Vernant, *Myth and Society in Ancient Greece*, 3rd ed., trans. Janet Lloyd (New York, 1996), pp. 80–90

28   Gernet, *Ancient China*, pp. 71–75

29   Granet, *Chinese Civilization*, pp. 97–100

30   Fung Yu-lan, *A Short History of Chinese Philosophy*, trans. Derk Bodde (New York, 1978), pp. 32–37

31   *Classic of Documents*, 'The Canon of Yao and the Canon of Shun', in De Bary and Bloom, *Sources*, p. 29

32   *Record of Rites* 2.263, in James Legge, trans., *The Li Ki* (Oxford, 1885)

33   Ibid., 2.359; Legge translation

34   Granet, *Chinese Civilization*, pp. 297–308

35   *Record of Rites* 1.215; Legge translation

36   Granet, *Chinese Civilization*, pp. 310–43

37   Gernet, *Ancient China*, p. 75

38   Granet, *Chinese Civilization*, pp. 261–84; Gernet, *History of Chinese*

Civilization, pp. 261–79; Gernet, *Ancient China*, p. 75; Holmes Welch, *The Parting of the Way: Lao Tzu and the Taoist Movement* (London, 1958), p. 18

39   *Zuozhuan* ('The Commentary of Mr Zuo') 1.320, in James Legge, trans., *The Ch'un Ts'ew and the Tso Chuen*, 2nd ed. (Hong Kong, 1960)

40   Ibid., 1.635; Legge translation

41   Ibid., 2.234; Legge translation

42   Ibid., 1.627; Legge translation

43   James A. Aho, *Religious Mythology and the Art of War: Comparative Religious Symbolism of Military Violence* (Westport, Conn., 1981), pp. 110–11

44   Recorded in *Chunqin* ('The Spring and Autumn Annals'), a history of the state of Lu (722–481 BCE) and the fifth Confucian classic, X. 17. 4; trans. J. Legge, *The Ch'un Ts'ew and Tso Chuen*, 2nd ed. (Hong Kong, 1960)

45   Ibid., I. 9. 6

46   Herbert Fingarette, *Confucius: The Secular as Sacred* (New York, 1972)

47   Benjamin L. Schwartz, *The World of Thought in Ancient China* (Cambridge, Mass., 1985), p. 62; Fung, *Short History*, p. 12

48   Wm. Theodore De Bary, *The Trouble with Confucianism* (Cambridge, Mass., and London, 1996), pp. 24–33

49   Analects 12.3, in Edward Slingerland, trans. and ed., *Confucius: Analects* (New York, 2003)

50   Analects 15.24; Slingerland translation

51   Analects 4.15; 15.23, in Arthur Waley, trans. and ed., *The Analects of Confucius* (New York, 1992)

52   Analects 6.30; Slingerland translation

53   Ibid.; Waley translation

54   De Bary, *Trouble with Confucianism*, p. 30

55   Schwartz, *World of Thought*, pp. 155, 157–58

56   Analects 12.1; trans. ibid., p. 77

57   Ibid.; Slingerland translation

58   Analects 5.4

59   Fingarette, *Confucius*, pp. 1–17; 46–79

60   Analects 12.3

61   Analects 7.30

62   Tu Wei-ming, *Confucian Thought: Selfhood as Creative Transformation* (Albany, NY, 1985), pp. 115–16

63   Ibid., pp. 57–58; Huston Smith, *The World's Religions: Our Great Wisdom Traditions* (San Francisco, 1991), pp. 180–81

64   Analects 13.30

65   Don J. Wyatt, 'Confucian Ethical Action and the Boundaries of Peace and War', in Andrew R. Murphy, ed., *The Blackwell Companion to Religion and Violence* (Chichester, 2011)

66   Analects 12.7; Slingerland translation

67   Ibid.

68   Analects 16.2

69   Analects 2.3

70   *The Book of Mencius* III.A.4, in D. C. Lau, trans., *Mencius* (London, 1975)

71   Xinzhong Yao, *An Introduction to Confucianism* (Cambridge, UK, 2000), p. 28

72   Mencius, VII.B.4; Lau translation. My emphases

73   Ibid.

74   Mencius VII.B.2; Lau translation; Wyatt, 'Confucian Ethical Action', pp. 240–44

75   Mencius II. A.1; Lau translation

76   A. C. Graham, *Later Mohist Logic, Ethics, and Science* (Hong Kong, 1978), p. 4; Gernet, *Ancient China*, pp. 116–17

77   *The Book of Mozi*, 3.16, trans. Fung Yu-lan, *Short History*, p. 55

78   Mozi 15: 11–15, in B. Watson, trans. and ed., *Mo-Tzu: Basic Writings* (New York, 1963)

79   A. C. Graham, *Disputers of the Tao: Philosophical Argument in Ancient China* (La Salle, Ill., 1989), p. 41

80   Mozi, 15.

81   Graham, *Later Mohist Logic*, p. 250

82   Lewis, *Sanctioned Violence*, pp. 56–61

83   Zhuozhuan 2.30; Legge translation

84   R. D. Sawyer, *The Seven Military Classics of Ancient China* (Boulder, Co., 1993), p. 254

85   Ibid., p. 243

86   Ibid., pp. 97–118; John Keegan, *A History of Warfare* (London, 1993), pp. 202–08; Robert L. O'Connell, *Ride of the Second Horseman: The Birth and Death of War* (New York and Oxford, 1989), pp. 171–73; R. D. Sawyer, *The Military Classics of Ancient China* (Boulder, Colo., 1993)

87   'The Book of Master Sun (Sunzi)', trans. Thomas Cleary, *Sun Tzu: The Art of War* (Boston and London, 1988), p. 56

88   Ibid., Chapter 3

89   Ibid.

90 'The Book of Master Sun', Chapter 1, trans. De Bary and Bloom, *Sources of Chinese Tradition*, p. 217

91 Ibid.; Cleary translation, pp. 81–83

92 Ibid., p, 86

93 Ibid., p. 5; Bary and Bloom translation

94 Fairbank and Goldman, *China*, pp. 53–54

95 Graham, *Disputers of the Tao*, pp. 172; Schwartz, *World of Thought*, pp. 215–36; Fung Yu-lan, *Short History*, pp. 104–17

96 Graham, *Disputers of the Tao*, pp. 170–213; Schwartz, *World of Thought*, pp. 186–215; Max Kaltenmark, *Lao Tzu and Taoism*, trans. Roger Greaves (Stanford, 1969), pp. 93–103

97 Daodejing 37, in D. C. Lau, trans., *Lao Tzu: Tao Te Ching* (London, 1963)

98 Ibid. 16; Lau translation

99 Ibid. 76; Lau translation

100 Ibid. 6; Lau translation

101 Ibid. 31; Kaltenmark translation

102 Ibid. 68; Kaltenmark translation

103 Ibid. 22; trans. De Bary and Bloom, *Sources of Chinese Tradition*

104 *Shang Jun Shu*, trans. Lewis, *Sanctioned Violence*, p. 64

105 Schwartz, *World of Thought*, pp. 321–23

106 Lewis, *Sanctioned Violence*, pp. 61–65

107 Graham, *Disputers of the Tao*, pp. 207–76; Schwartz, *World of Thought*, pp. 321–43; Fung Yu-lan, *Short History*, pp. 155–65; Julia Ching, *Mysticism and Kingship in China: The Heart of Chinese Wisdom* (Cambridge, UK, 1997), pp. 236–41

108 *Shang Jun Shu*, trans. Mark Elvin, 'Was There a Transcendental Breakthrough in China?' in S. N. Eisenstadt, ed., *The Origins and Diversity of the Axial Civilizations* (Albany, NY, 1980), p. 352

109 *Shang Jun Shu*, trans. Graham, *Disputers of the Tao*, p. 290

110 *Shang Jun Shu*, 15.72, in B. Watson, ed. and trans., *Hsun-Tzu: Basic Writings* (New York, 1963)

111 Ibid.

112 *The Book of Xunzi*, 10, in Graham, *Disputers of the Tao*, p. 238

113 *Han Feizi*, 5; Watson translation

114 Ibid.

115 Ching, *Mysticism and Kingship*, p. 171

116 *Xunzi* 21: 34–38, in Xunzi, *Basic Writings*, trans. Barton Watson (New York, 2003)

117 Fairbank and Goldman, *China*, p. 56; Derk Bodde, 'Feudalism in China', in Rushton Coulbourn, ed., *Feudalism in History* (Hamden, Conn., 1965), p. 69

118 Sima Qian, *Records of the Grand Historian*, 6.239

119 Ibid., 6.87

120 Lewis, *Sanctioned Violence*, pp. 99–101

121 Sima Qian, *Records of the Grand Historian*; 'Introduction', cited and trans. Lewis, *Sanctioned Violence*, p. 141

122 Schwartz, *World of Thought*, pp. 237–53

123 Lewis, *Sanctioned Violence*, pp. 145–57; Derk Bodde, *Festivals in Classical China: New Year and Other Annual Observances during the Han Dynasty, 206 BC to AD 220* (Princeton, 1975)

124 Lewis, *Sanctioned Violence*, p. 147

125 Sima Qian, *Records of the Grand Historian*, 8.1, in Fung Yu-lan, *Short History*, p. 215

126 Fung Yu-lan, *Short History*, pp. 205–16; Graham, *Disputers of the Tao*, pp. 313–77; Schwartz, *World of Thought*, pp. 383–406

127 Fairbank and Goldman, *China*, pp. 67–71

128 Joseph R. Levenson and Franz Schurman, *China: An Interpretive History – from the Beginnings to the Fall of Han* (Berkeley, Los Angeles and London, 1969), p. 94

129 De Bary, *Trouble with Confucianism*, pp. 48–49

130 *Yan tie lun*, 19, trans. De Bary and Bloom, *Sources of Chinese Tradition*, p. 223

131 Hu Shih, 'Confucianism', in *Encyclopaedia of Social Science* (1930–35) IV, pp. 198–201; Ching, *Mysticism and Kingship*, p. 85

132 De Bary, *Trouble with Confucianism*, p. 49; Fairbank and Goldman, *China*, p. 63

4. The Hebrew Dilemma

1 Genesis 2: 7–3: 24. Unless otherwise stated, all biblical quotations are taken from *The Jerusalem Bible* (London, 1996)

2 Genesis 3: 17–19

3 Genesis 4: 10–11; trans. Everett Fox, *The Five Books of Moses* (New York, 1990)

4 Genesis 4: 17–22

5 Genesis 4: 9

6 Genesis 12: 1–3

7   Israel Finkelstein and Neil Asher, *The Bible Unearthed: Archaeology's New Vision of Ancient Israel and the Origins of its Sacred Texts* (New York and London, 2001), pp. 103–07; William G. Dever, *What Did the Biblical Writers Know and When Did They Know It? What Archaeology Can Tell Us About the Reality of Ancient Israel* (Grand Rapids, Mich., and Cambridge, UK, 2001), pp. 110–18

8   George W. Mendenhall, *The Tenth Generation: The Origins of Biblical Tradition* (Baltimore and London, 1973); P. M. Lemche, *Early Israel: Anthropological and Historical Studies on the Israelite Society before the Monarchy* (Leiden, 1985); D. C. Hopkins, *The Highlands of Canaan* (Sheffield, 1985); James D. Martin, 'Israel as a Tribal Society', in R. E. Clements, ed., *The World of Ancient Israel: Sociological, Anthropological and Political Perspectives* (Cambridge, UK, 1989); H. G. M. Williamson, 'The Concept of Israel in Transition', in Clements, *World of Ancient Israel*, pp. 94–114

9   Finkelstein and Asher, *Bible Unearthed*, pp. 89–92

10 John H. Kautsky, *The Politics of Aristocratic Empires*, 2nd ed. (New Brunswick and London, 1997), p. 275; Karl A. Wittfogel, *Oriental Despotism: A Comparative Study of Total Power* (New Haven, Conn., 1957), pp. 331–32

11 Joshua 9: 15; Exodus 6: 15; Judges 1: 16; 4: 11; I Samuel 27: 10; Frank Moore Cross, *Canaanite Myth and Hebrew Epic: Essays in the History of the Religion of Israel* (Cambridge, Mass., and London, 1973), pp. 49–50

12 Cross, *Canaanite Myth*, p. 69; Peter Machinist, 'Distinctiveness in Ancient Israel', in Mordechai Cogan and Israel Ephal, eds, *Studies in Assyrian History and Ancient Near Eastern Historiography* (Jerusalem, 1991)

13 This theme has been explored in more detail by Yoram Hazony, *The Philosophy of Hebrew Scripture* (Cambridge, 2012), pp. 103–60

14 Norman Gottwald, *The Hebrew Bible in Its Social World and in Ours* (Atlanta, 1993), pp. 115, 163

15 Leviticus 25: 23–28, 35–55; Deuteronomy 24: 19–22; Gottwald, *Hebrew Bible*, p. 162

16 I have described this process in *A History of God: The 4,000-Year Quest of Judaism, Christianity and Islam* (London and New York, 1993)

17 Psalms 73: 3, 8; 82: 8; 95: 3; 96: 4ff.; 97: 7; Isaiah 51: 9ff.; Job 26: 12; 40: 25–31

18 Genesis 11: 1–9

19 Genesis 11: 9

20 Genesis 12: 1–3. Strictly speaking, Yahweh called Abraham from Haran

in modern Iraq; but his father Terah had left Ur but only got as far as Haran. Yahweh himself backdates the call to Abraham, taking responsibility for the entire migration, telling Abraham: 'I . . . brought you out of Ur of the Chaldeans' (Genesis 15: 7)

21   Hazony, *Philosophy of Hebrew Scripture*, p. 121

22   Ibid., pp. 122–26

23   Genesis 12: 10

24   Genesis 26: 16–22; cf. 36: 6–8

25   Genesis 41: 57–42: 3

26   Genesis 37: 5–7

27   Genesis 37: 8; Fox translation

28   Genesis 37: 10; Fox translation

29   Genesis 41: 51; Fox translation

30   Genesis 41: 48–49

31   Genesis 47: 13–14, 20–21

32   Genesis 50: 4–9. After Jacob's death, the brothers were permitted to take his body back to Canaan, accompanied by 'a very large retinue' of chariots and cavalry, while their children and possessions were held hostage in Egypt

33   Genesis 12: 15; 20: 2; 26: 17–18; 14: 11–12; 34: 1–2; Hazony, *Philosophy of Hebrew Scripture*, pp. 111–13, 143

34   Genesis 14: 21–25

35   Genesis 18: 1–8; 19: 1–9

36   Genesis 18: 22–32

37   Genesis 49: 7

38   Genesis 49: 8–12; 44: 18–34

39   Exodus 1: 11, 14

40   Exodus 2: 11

41   Hazony, *Philosophy of Hebrew Scripture*, pp. 143–44

42   Exodus 24: 9–11

43   Exodus 31: 18

44   Cf. Exodus 24: 9–31: 18; William M. Schniedewind, *How the Bible Became a Book: The Textualization of Ancient Israel* (Cambridge, UK, 2004), pp. 121–34

45   E.g. Judges 1; 3: 1–6; Ezra 9: 1–2

46   Regina Schwartz, *The Curse of Cain: The Violent Legacy of Monotheism* (Chicago, 1997); Hector Avalos, *Fighting Words: The Origins of Religious Violence* (Amherst, NY, 2005)

47   Mark S. Smith, *The Early History of God: Yahweh and the Other Deities in*

48   Joshua 24; S. David Sperling 'Joshua 24 Re-examined', *Hebrew Union College Annual* 58 (1987); Sperling, *The Original Torah: The Political Intent of the Bible's Writers* (New York and London, 1998), pp. 68–72; John Bowker, *The Religious Imagination and the Sense of God* (Oxford, 1978), pp. 58–68

49   Exodus 20: 3; Fox translation

50   Susan Niditch, *War in the Hebrew Bible: A Study of the Ethics of Violence* (New York and Oxford, 1993), pp. 28–36; 41–62; 152

51   Compare a similar deal in Numbers 21: 2

52   Joshua 6: 20

53   Joshua 8: 25

54   Joshua 8: 28

55   Lauren A. Monroe, *Josiah's Reform and the Dynamics of Defilement: Israelite Rites of Violence and the Making of a Biblical Text* (Oxford, 2011), pp. 45–76

56   Mesha Stele 15–17, in Kent P. Jackson, 'The Language of the Mesha Inscription', in Andrew Dearman, ed., *Studies in the Mesha Inscription and Moab* (Atlanta, 1989), p. 98; Norman K. Gottwald, *The Politics of Ancient Israel* (Louisville, 2001), p. 194; cf. 2 Kings 3: 4–27

57   Mesha Stele 17; Jackson translation

58   H. Hoffner, 'History and the Historians of the Ancient Near East: The Hittites', *Orientalia*, 49 (1980); Nidditch, *War in the Hebrew Bible*, p. 51

59   Judges 21: 25

60   Judges 11: 29–40

61   Judges 18

62   Judges 19

63   Judges 20–21

64   1 Samuel 8: 5

65   1 Samuel 11: 18

66   Gottwald, *Politics of Ancient Israel*, pp. 177–79

67   Nidditch, *War in the Hebrew Bible*, pp. 90–105

68   Samuel 17: 1–13; Quincy Wright, *A Study of Warfare*, 2 vols (Chicago, 1942), 1, pp. 401–15

69   2 Samuel 2: 23

70   2 Samuel 5: 6

71   1 Chronicles 22: 8–9

72   Gosta W. Ahlstrom, *The History of Ancient Palestine* (Minneapolis, 1993), pp. 504–05

73   1 Kings 7: 15–26

74   Richard J. Clifford, *The Cosmic Mountain in Canaan and the Old Testament* (Cambridge, Mass., 1972), *passim*; Ben C. Ollenburger, *Zion, City of the Great King: A Theological Symbol of the Jerusalem Cult* (Sheffield, 1987), pp. 14–16; Margaret Barker, *The Gate of Heaven: The History and Symbolism of the Temple in Jerusalem* (London, 1991), p. 64; Hans-Joachim Kraus, *Worship in Israel: A Cultic History of the Old Testament* (Oxford, 1966), pp. 201–04

75   1 Kings 9: 3; David Ussishkin, 'King Solomon's Palaces', *Biblical Archaeologist*, 36 (1973)

76   1 Kings 10: 26–29

77   1 Kings 9: 3; 5: 4–6

78   1 Kings 4: 1–5: 1

79   1 Kings 5: 27–32 which contradicts 1 Kings 9: 20–21. The Deuteronomist authors were anxious to blame Solomon's idolatry for the catastrophe, because of their reform

80   1 Kings 11: 1–13

81   1 Kings 12: 4

82   1 Kings 12: 17–19

83   Psalms 2: 7–8; 110: 12–14

84   Psalm 110: 5–6

85   Andrew Mein, *Ezekiel and the Ethics of Exile* (Oxford and New York, 2001), pp. 20–38

86   Amos 2: 6

87   Amos 3: 10

88   Amos 7: 17; 9: 7–8

89   Amos 3: 11–15

90   Amos 1: 2–2: 5

91   Isaiah 1: 16–18

92   Gottwald, *Politics of Ancient Israel,* pp. 210–12

93   Finkelstein and Asher, *Bible Unearthed,* pp. 263–64

94   Ibid., pp. 264–73

95   2 Kings 21: 2–7; 23: 10–11

96   Psalms 68: 17; Ahlstrom, *History of Ancient Palestine*, p. 734

97   Schniedewind, *How the Bible Became a Book,* pp. 91–117; Calum M. Carmichael, *The Laws of Deuteronomy* (Eugene, Oreg., 1974); Bernard

M. Levinson, *Deuteronomy and the Hermeneutics of Legal Innovation* (Oxford, 1998); Moshe Weinfeld, *Deuteronomy and the Deuteronomic School* (Oxford, 1972); Joshua Berman, *Biblical Revolutions: The Transformation of Social and Political Thought in the Ancient Near East* (New York and Oxford, 2008)

98   2 Kings 22: 8

99   Exodus 24: 3, 7; Schniedewind, *How the Bible Became a Book,* pp. 121–26

100 Exodus 24: 4–8. This passage was inserted into the older traditions by the reformers; it is the only other place in the Bible where the phrase *sefer torah* is found

101 Deuteronomy 6: 4

102 Deuteronomy 7: 1–4

103 Deuteronomy 28: 64, 68

104 2 Kings 22: 11–13

105 2 Kings 23: 5

106 Jeremiah 44: 15–19; Ezekiel 8

107 2 Kings 23: 4–20

108 Levinson, *Deuteronomy and the Hermeneutics of Legal Innovation*, pp. 148–49

109 Deuteronomy 7: 22–26

110 Deuteronomy 13: 8–9, 12

111 Niditch, *War in the Hebrew Bible*, pp. 65, 77

112 1 Kings 13: 1–2; 2 Kings 23: 15–18; 2 Kings 23: 25

113 2 Kings 24: 16. These numbers are disputed

114 Ezekiel, 3: 15; Schiedewind, *How the Bible Became a Book*, p. 152

115 Mein, *Ezekiel*, pp. 66–74

116 Anshan is called Elam in the Hebrew sources

117 Garth Fowden, *Empire to Commonwealth: Consequences of Monotheism in Later Antiquity* (Princeton, 1993), p. 19

118 The Cyrus Cylinder, 18. Quotations from the Cyrus Cylinder are taken from the translation of Irving L. Finkel in John Curtis, *The Cyrus Cylinder and Ancient Persia: A New Beginning for the Middle East* (London, 2013), p. 42

119 Bruce Lincoln, *Religion, Empire and Torture: The Case of Achaemenian Persia, with a Postscript on Abu Ghraib* (Chicago and London, 2007), pp. 36–40

120 Cyrus Cylinder, 12, 15, 17; Curtis, *Cyrus Cylinder*, p. 42

121 Isaiah, 45: 1

122 Isaiah 45: 1, 2, 4

123 Isaiah 40: 4–5

124 Flavius Josephus, *The Antiquities of the Jews*, trans. William Whiston (Marston Gate, UK, n.d.), 11.8

125 Cyrus Cylinder, 16; Curtis, *Cyrus Cylinder*, p. 42

126 Cyrus Cylinder, 28–30; Curtis, *Cyrus Cylinder*, p. 43

127 Lincoln, *Religion, Empire and Torture*, p. ix

128 Ibid, pp. 16, 95

129 Bruce Lincoln, 'The Role of Religion in Achaemenian Imperialism', in Nicole Brisch, ed., *Religion and Power: Divine Kingship in the Ancient World and Beyond* (Chicago, 2008), p. 223

130 Clarisse Herrenschmidt, 'Désignations de l'empire et concepts politiques de Darius Ier d'après inscriptions en Vieux Perse', *Studia Iranica*, 5 (1976); Marijan Mole, *Culte, mythe, et cosmologie dans l'Iran ancien* (Paris, 1963)

131 Darius, First Inscription at Naqsh-I Rustum (DNa1), in Lincoln, *Religion, Empire and Torture*, p. 52

132 Ibid., pp. 55–56

133 DNa 4, ibid., p. 71

134 Darius, Fourth Inscription at Persepolis, ibid., p. 10

135 Ibid., pp. 26–28

136 Ibid., pp. 73–81; Darius, Inscription 19 at Susa, ibid., p. 73

137 Cross, *Canaanite Myth*, pp. 293–323; Mary Douglas, *Leviticus as Literature* (Oxford and New York, 1999); Douglas, *In the Wilderness: The Doctrine of Defilement in the Book of Numbers* (Oxford and New York, 2001), pp. 58–100; Niditch, *War in the Hebrew Bible*, pp. 78–89; 97–99; 132–53

138 Leviticus 25

139 Leviticus 19: 34

140 Douglas, *Leviticus as Literature*, pp. 42–44

141 Genesis 32: 33

142 Numbers 20: 14

143 Genesis 1: 31

144 Nehemiah 4: 11–12

145 Numbers 31

146 Numbers 31: 19–20

147 2 Chronicles 28: 10–11

148 2 Chronicles 28: 15

149 Isaiah 46: 1

150 Zechariah 14: 12

151 Zechariah 14: 16. See also Micah 4: 1–5, 5; Haggai 1: 6–9

152 Isaiah 60: 1–10
153 Isaiah 60: 11–14

PART TWO: KEEPING THE PEACE

5. Jesus: Not of this World?

1   Luke 2: 1
2   Robert L. O'Connell, *Of Arms and Men: A History of War, Weapons and Aggression* (New York and Oxford, 1989), p. 81
3   E. N. Luttwak, *The Grand Strategy of the Roman Empire* (Baltimore, 1976), pp. 25–26; 41–42; 46–47; Susan P. Mattern, *Rome and the Enemy: Imperial Strategy in the Principate* (Berkeley, 1999), pp. xii; 222
4   O'Connell, *Arms and Men*, pp. 69–81; John Keegan, *A History of Warfare* (London, 1993), pp. 263–71
5   W. Harris, *War and Imperialism in Republican Rome* (Oxford, 1979), p. 56
6   Ibid., p. 51
7   Tacitus, *Agricola*, 30; Loeb Classical Library translation
8   Harris, *War and Imperialism*, p. 51
9   Martin Hengel, *Judaism and Hellenism: Studies in their Encounter in Palestine during the Early Hellenistic Period*, 2 vols, trans. John Bowden (London, 1974), pp. 294–300; Elias J. Bickerman, *From Ezra to the Last of the Maccabees* (New York, 1962), pp. 286–89; *The Jews in the Greek Age* (Cambridge, Mass., and London, 1990), pp. 294–96; Reuven Firestone, *Holy War in Judaism: The Rise and Fall of a Controversial Idea* (Oxford and New York, 2012), pp. 26–40
10   Daniel 10–12
11   Daniel 7: 13–14
12   Richard A. Horsley, 'The Historical Context of Q', in Richard A. Horsley and Jonathan A. Draper, eds, *Whoever Hears You Hears Me: Prophets, Performance and Tradition in Q* (Harrisburg, Penn., 1999), pp. 51–54
13   Gerhard E. Lenski, *Power and Privilege: A Theory of Social Stratification* (Chapel Hill and London, 1966), pp. 243–48
14   John H. Kautsky, *The Politics of Aristocratic Empires*, 2nd ed. (New Brunswick and London, 1997), p. 81
15   Horsley, 'Historical Context of Q', p. 154
16   Flavius Josephus, *The Life*, trans. H. St. J. Thackeray (Cambridge, Mass.,

1926), 10–12; Alan Mason, 'Was Josephus a Pharisee?: A Re-Examination of the *Life*, 10–12', *Journal of Jewish Studies*, 40 (1989); Alan F. Segal, *Paul the Convert: The Apostolate and Apostasy of Saul the Pharisee* (New Haven, Conn., and London, 1990), pp. 81–82

17 Josephus, *The Jewish War* (JW), 6: 51, trans. G. A. Williamson, *Josephus: The Jewish War* (Harmondsworth, 1959)

18 Josephus, *The Antiquities of the Jews* (Ant.), 17: 157; trans. in Richard A. Horsley, *Jesus and the Spiral of Violence: Popular Jewish Resistance in Roman Palestine* (Minneapolis, 1993 ed.), p. 76

19 JW 1: 655

20 Ibid., 2: 3

21 Ibid., 2: 11–13

22 Ibid., 2: 57

23 JW 2: 66–75

24 John Dominic Crossan, *God and Empire: Jesus against Rome, Then and Now* (San Francisco, 2007), pp. 91–94

25 Ant. 18: 4–9; trans. Horsley, *Spiral of Violence*, p. 81; JW 2: 117

26 JW 2: 169–74

27 Philo, *On the Embassy to Gaius*, trans. F. H. Colson (Cambridge, Mass., 1962), 223–24

28 Ant. 18: 292; Whiston translation

29 Ibid., 18: 284; Whiston translation

30 JW 2: 260; Williamson translation

31 Ibid., 2: 261–62

32 Ant. 18: 36.8; Horsley, 'Historical Context of Q', p. 58

33 John Dominic Crossan, *Jesus: A Revolutionary Biography* (New York, 1994), pp. 26–28

34 A. N. Sherwin-White, *Roman Law and Roman Society in the New Testament* (Oxford, 1963), p. 139. Matthew 18: 22–33; 20: 1–15; Luke 16: 1–13; Mark 12: 1–9

35 Matthew 2: 16

36 Matthew 14: 3–12

37 Matthew 10: 17–18

38 Marcus Borg, *Jesus: Uncovering the Life, Teachings, and Relevance of a Religious Revolutionary* (San Francisco, 2006), pp. 67–68

39 Matthew 4: 1–11; Mark 12–13; Luke 4: 1–13

40 Luke 10: 17–18

41 M. Lewis, *Ecstatic Religion: An Anthropological Study of Spirit Possession and Shamanism* (Baltimore, 1971), pp. 31, 32, 35, 127

42 Mark 5: 1–17; Crossan, *Jesus*, pp. 99–106

43 Luke 13: 31–33

44 Matthew 21: 1–11; Mark, 11: 1–11; Luke 19: 28–38

45 Matthew 21: 12–13

46 Horsley, *Spiral of Violence*, pp. 286–89; Sean Frayne, *Galilee: From Alexander the Great to Hadrian, 323 BCE to 135 CE. A Study of Second Temple Judaism* (Notre Dame, Ind., 1980), pp. 283–86

47 Matthew 5: 39, 44

48 Matthew 26: 63

49 Luke 6: 20–24

50 Matthew 12: 1–12; 23

51 Luke 13: 13

52 Luke 9: 23–24

53 Luke 1: 51–54

54 Mark 12: 13–17; Horsley, *Spiral of Violence*, pp. 306–16

55 F. F. Bruce, 'Render to Caesar', in F. Bammel and C. F. D. Moule, eds, *Jesus and the Politics of His Day* (Cambridge, 1981), p. 258

56 Mark 12: 38–40

57 Horsley, *Spiral of Violence*, pp. 167–68

58 A. E. Harvey, *Strenuous Commands: The Ethic of Jesus* (London and Philadelphia, 1990), pp. 162, 209

59 Luke 14: 14, 23–24; Crossan, *Jesus*, pp. 74–82

60 Luke 6: 20–21; Translation amended in Crossan, *Jesus*, p. 68; the Gospel does not use the Greek *penes* ('poor'), describing people making a bare living, but *ptochos*, 'destitute, beggars'

61 Crossan, *Jesus*, pp. 68–70

62 Luke 6: 24–25

63 Matthew 20: 16

64 Matthew 6: 11–13

65 Gerd Theissen, *The First Followers of Jesus: A Sociological Analysis of the Earliest Christians*, trans. John Bowden (London, 1978), pp. 8–14

66 Mark 1: 14–15; my translation

67 Matthew 9: 36

68 Warren Carter, 'Construction of Violence and Identities in Matthew's Gospel', in Shelly Matthews and E. Leigh Gibson, eds, *Violence in the New Testament* (New York and London, 2005), pp. 93–94

69 John Pairman Brown, 'Techniques of Imperial Control: The Background of the Gospel Event', in Norman Gottwald, ed., *The Bible of Liberation: Political and Social Hermeneutics* (Maryknoll, NY, 1983), pp. 357–77;

Gerd Theissen, *The Miracle Stories: Early Christian Tradition* (Philadelphia, 1982), pp. 231–44; Warren Carter, *Matthew and the Margins: A Socio-Political and Religious Reading* (Sheffield, 2000), pp. 17–29, 36–43, 123–27; 196–98

70   Matthew 6: 10

71   Luke 6: 28–30

72   Luke 6: 31–38

73   Acts 2: 23, 32–35; Philippians 2: 9

74   Matthew 10: 5–6

75   James B. Rives, *Religion in the Roman Empire* (Oxford, 2007), pp. 13–20

76   Ibid., pp. 104–14

77   Jonathan Z. Smith, 'Fences and Neighbours: Some Contours of Early Judaism', in *Imagining Religion: From Babylon to Jonestown* (Chicago and London, 1982), pp. 1–18; John W. Marshall, 'Collateral Damage: Jesus and Jezebel in the Jewish War', in Matthews and Gibson, eds, *Violence in the New Testament*, pp. 38–39; Julia Galambush, *The Reluctant Parting: How the New Testament's Jewish Writers Created a Christian Book* (San Francisco, 2005), pp. 291–92

78   Acts of the Apostles 5: 34–42

79   Acts of the Apostles 13: 44; 14: 19; 17: 10–15

80   1 Corinthians 11: 2–15

81   1 Corinthians 14: 21–25

82   Romans 13: 1–2, 4

83   Romans 13: 6

84   1 Corinthians 7: 31

85   Acts of the Apostles, 4: 32, 34

86   1 Corinthians 12: 12–27

87   Luke 24: 13–32

88   Philippians 2: 3–5

89   Philippians 2: 6–11, trans. *The English Revised Bible* (Oxford and Cambridge, UK, 1989)

90   Philippians 2: 2–4

91   John 1

92   1 John 7: 42–47

93   1 John 2: 18–19

94   Tacitus, *History*, 1.11; Marshall, 'Collateral Damage', pp. 37–38

95   Firestone, *Holy War*, pp. 46–47

96   Michael S. Berger, 'Taming the Beast: Rabbinic Pacification of Second-Century Jewish Nationalism', in James K. Wellman, Jr., ed., *Belief*

and Bloodshed: Religion and Violence across Time and Tradition (Lanham, Md., 2007), pp. 54–55

97   Jerusalem Talmud (J), Taanit 4.5; Lamentations Rabbah 2.4 in C. G. Montefiore and H. Loewe, eds, *A Rabbinic Anthology* (New York, 1974)

98   Dio Cassius, *History* 69.12; Mireille Hadas-Lebel, *Jerusalem against Rome*, trans. Robyn Freshat (Leuven, 2006), pp. 398–409

99   Berger, 'Taming the Beast', pp. 50–52

100   B. Berakhot 58a; Shabbat 34a; Baba Batra 75a; Sanhedrin 100a in Montefiore and Loewe, *Rabbinic Anthology*; Firestone, *Holy War*, p. 73

101   Firestone, *Holy War*, pp. 52–61

102   Berger, 'Taming the Beast', p. 48

103   Avot de Rabbi Nathan, B.31, in Robert Eisen, *The Peace and Violence of Judaism: From the Bible to Modern Zionism* (Oxford, 2011), p. 86

104   B. Pesahim 118a in ibid.

105   Eisen, *Peace and Violence*, p. 86; Hadas-Lebel, *Jerusalem against Rome*, pp. 265–95

106   Mekhilta de Rabbi Yishmael 13; B. Avodah Zarah 18a in Montefiore and Loewe, *Rabbinic Anthology*

107   B. Shabbat 336b; B. Berakhot 58a in Montefiore and Loewe, *Rabbinic Anthology*

108   Wilfred Cantwell Smith, *What is Scripture? A Comparative Approach* (London, 1993), p. 290; Gerald L. Bruns, 'Midrash and Allegory: The Beginnings of Scriptural Interpretation', in Robert Alter and Frank Kermode, eds, *A Literary Guide to the Bible* (London, 1987), pp. 629–30; Nahum S. Glatzer, 'The Concept of Peace in Classical Judaism', *Essays on Jewish Thought* (University, Ala., 1978), pp. 37–38; Eisen, *Peace and Violence*, p. 90

109   Michael Fishbane, *Garments of Torah: Essays in Biblical Hermeneutics* (Bloomington and Indianapolis, 1989), pp. 22–32

110   B. Shabbat 63a; B. Sanhedrin 82a; B. Shabbat 133b; Tanhuman 10; Eisen, *Peace and Violence*, pp. 88–89; Reuven Kimelman, 'Non-violence in the Talmud', *Judaism*, 17 (1968)

111   Avot de Rabbi Nathan, A. 23 in Eisen, *Peace and Violence*, p. 88

112   Mishnah (M), Avot, 4:1 in Montefiore and Loewe, *Rabbinic Anthology*

113   Eisen, *Peace and Violence*, p. 89

114   B. Berakhot 4a; Megillah 3a; Tamua 16a in Montefiore and Loewe, *Rabbinic Anthology*

115   Exodus 14; B. Megillah 10b in Montefiore and Loewe, *Rabbinic Anthology*

116   M. Sotah 8: 7; M. Yadayin 4: 4; Tosefta Kiddushim 5: 4; Firestone, *Holy War*, p. 74

117   J. Sotah 8.1 in Montefiore and Loewe, *Rabbinic Anthology*

118   Song of Songs 2: 7; 3: 5; 8: 4; B. Ketubot 110b–111a; Song of Songs Rabbah 2: 7 in ibid.

119   Firestone, *Holy War*, pp. 74–75

120   Aviezer Ravitsky, *Messianism, Zionism and Jewish Religious Radicalism*, trans. Michael Swirsky and Jonathan Chapman (Chicago, 1997), pp. 211–34

121   Peter Brown, *The World of Late Antiquity, AD 150–750* (London, 1989), pp. 20–24; Brown, *The Rise of Western Christendom: Triumph and Diversity, AD 200–1000* (Oxford and Malden, Mass., 1996), pp. 18–19

122   Brown, *World of Late Antiquity*, pp. 24–27

123   Peter Brown, *The Making of Late Antiquity* (Cambridge, Mass., and London, 1978), p. 48; *Rise of Western Christendom*, pp. 19–20

124   Revelation 3: 21; Tacitus, *Annals* 15: 44; Tacitus was, however, writing decades after the event and it seems unlikely that at this early date Christians were recognised as a distinct body. Candida R. Moss, *The Myth of Persecution: How Early Christians Invented a Story of Martyrdom* (New York, 2013), pp. 138–39

125   Tertullian, *Apology* 20 in Moss, *Myth of Persecution*, p. 128

126   W. H. C. Frend, *Martyrdom and Persecution in the Early Church: A Study of the Conflict from the Maccabees to Donatus* (Oxford, 1965), p. 331

127   Jonathan Z. Smith, 'The Temple and the Magician', in *Map is Not Territory: Studies in the History of Religions* (Chicago and London, 1978), p. 187; Peter Brown, 'The Rise of the Holy Man in Late Antiquity', *Journal of Roman Studies* LXI (1971)

128   Rives, *Religion in the Roman Empire*, pp. 207–08

129   Ibid., pp. 68, 82

130   Moss, *Myth of Persecution*, pp. 127–62; G. E. M. De Ste Croix, 'Why Were the Early Christians Persecuted?', in Michael Whitby and Joseph Street, eds, *Martyrdom and Orthodoxy* (Oxford, 2006)

131   James B. Rives, 'The Decree of Decius and the Religion of Empire', *Journal of Roman Studies*, 89 (1999); Robin Lane Fox, *Pagans and Christians* (New York, 1987), pp. 455–56

132   B. Baba Metziah 59b in Montefiore and Loewe, *Rabbinic Anthology*

133   *Collatio Legum Romanarum et Mosaicarum* 15.3 in Brown, *Rise of Western Christendom*, p. 22

134   Ramsey MacMullen, *The Second Church: Popular Christianity AD ▨▨▨–▨▨▨*.

Christians had traditionally worshipped in private houses. Churches like the offending basilica were a recent innovation

135 Moss, *Myth of Persecution*, pp. 154–58

136 Candida R. Moss, *The Other Christs: Imitating Jesus in Ancient Christian Ideologies of Martyrdom* (Oxford, 2010)

137 Victricius, *De Laude Sanctorum* 10.452 B in Peter Brown, *The Cult of the Saints: Its Rise and Function in Latin Christianity* (Chicago, 1981), p. 79

138 *Decretum Gelasianum* in ibid.

139 'The Martyrs of Lyons' 1.4, in H. Musurillo, trans., *The Acts of the Christian Martyrs* (Oxford, 1972)

140 Ibid., 9, in Peter Dronke, *Women Writers of the Middle Ages: A Critical Study of Texts from Perpetua (†203) to Marguerite Poretz (†1310)* (Cambridge, UK, 1984), p. 4

141 Perpetua, *Passio*, 10 in Dronke, *Women Writers*, p. 4

142 Frend, *Martyrdom and Persecution in the Early Church*, p. 15

143 Brown, *World of Late Antiquity*, pp. 82–84

144 Origen, *Contra Celsum* 2: 30, trans. Henry Chadwick (Cambridge, 1980)

145 Cyprian, *Letters* 40: 1; 48: 4

146 Ibid., 30.2; Brown, *Making of Late Antiquity*, pp. 79–80

147 Lactantius, *Divine Institutions*, in William Fletcher, trans., *Lactantius: Works* (Edinburgh, 1971), p. 366

148 Ibid., p. 427

149 Ibid., p. 328

6. Byzantium: The Tragedy of Empire

1   Garth Fowden, *Empire to Commonwealth: Consequences of Monotheism in Late Antiquity* (Princeton, NJ, 1993), pp. 13–16, 34

2   Eusebius, trans. H. A. Drake, *In Praise of Constantine: A Historical Study and New Translation of Eusebius' Tricennial Orations* (Berkeley and Los Angeles, 1976), p. 89

3   Aziz Al-Azmeh, *Muslim Kingship: Power and the Sacred in Muslim, Christian and Pagan Polities* (London and New York, 1997), pp. 27–33

4   Michael Gaddis, *There is No Crime for Those Who Have Christ: Religious Violence in the Christian Roman Empire* (Berkeley, Los Angeles and London, 2005), p. 88

5   Eusebius, *Life of Constantine* (VC) 1.5, 24; 2:19, trans. and ed. Averil and Stuart G. Hall (Oxford, 1999)

6   Ibid., 4: 8–13; Fowden, *Empire to Commonwealth*, pp. 93–94

7   Al-Azmeh, *Muslim Kingship*, pp. 43–46

8   Matthew 28: 19

9   John Haldon, *Warfare, State and Society in the Byzantine World, 565–1204* (London and New York, 2005), pp. 16–19

10   Fowden, *Empire to Commonwealth*, pp. 93–94; Gaddis, *There is No Crime*, pp. 62–63

11   Eusebius, VC 4.61

12   Ibid., 4.6.2; Gaddis, *There is No Crime*, pp. 63–64

13   Gaddis, *There is No Crime*, pp. 51–59

14   Eusebius, VC 4.24

15   Constantine, *Letter to Aelafius, Vicor of Africa*, trans. Mark Edwards, *Optatus: Against the Donatists* (Liverpool, 1997), Appendix 3

16   The Donatists argued that Caecilian had been ordained by Felix of Apthungi, who had apostatised during the persecution of Diocletian. Their protest was an act of piety to the memory of the martyrs

17   Gaddis, *There is No Crime*, p. 51

18   Ibid., pp. 51–58

19   Constantine; trans. Edwards, *Optatus*, Appendix 9; Gaddis, *There is No Crime*, p. 57

20   Richard Lim, *Public Disputation, Power and Social Order in Late Antiquity* (Berkeley, 1995)

21   Peter Brown, *The World of Late Antiquity, AD 150–750* (London, 1989 ed.), pp. 86–87

22   Ibid., pp. 87–89

23   James B. Rives, *Religion in the Roman Empire* (Oxford, 2007), pp. 13–20

24   Genesis 18: 1–17; Exodus 33: 18–23, 34: 6–9; Joshua 5: 13–15

25   Jaroslav Pelikan, *The Christian Tradition: A History of the Development of Doctrine. Vol. 1: The Emergence of the Catholic Tradition* (Chicago and London, 1971), p. 145

26   Eusebius, *The Proof of the Gospel*, trans. William John Ferrer (Charlottesville, 1981) 5–6, Preface 1–2

27   Peter Brown, *The Body and Society: Men, Women and Sexual Renunciation in Early Christianity* (London and Boston, 1988), p. 236

28   Athanasius, *On the Incarnation*, trans. Andrew Louth, *Origins of the Christian Mystical Traditions: From Plato to Denys* (Oxford, 1981), p. 78

29   John Meyndorff, *Byzantine Theology: Historical Trends and Doctrinal Themes* (New York and London, 1975), p. 78

30   Brown, *World of Late Antiquity*, p. 90

31   Evelyne Patlagean, *Pauvreté économique et pauvreté sociale à Byzance, 4e–7e Siècles* (Paris, 1977), pp. 78–84

32   Matthew 6: 25

33   Matthew 4: 20; Acts 4: 35

34   Matthew 19: 21

35   Athanasius, *Vita Antonii*, 3,2. All quotations from the *Vita* are from R. C. Gregg, trans., *The Life of Antony and the Letter to Marcellinus* (New York, 1980)

36   David Caner, *Wandering, Begging Monks, Spiritual Authority and the Promotion of Monasticism in Late Antiquity* (Berkeley, Los Angeles and London, 2002), p. 25

37   2 Thessalonians 3: 6–12

38   Athanasius, *Vita*, 50: 4–6

39   H. I. Bell, V. Martin, E. G. Turner and D. van Berchem, *The Abinnaeus Archive* (Oxford, 1962), pp. 77, 108

40   A. E. Boak and H. C. Harvey, *The Archive of Aurelius Isidore* (Ann Arbor, 1960) pp. 295–96

41   Peter Brown, *The Making of Late Antiquity* (Cambridge, Mass., and London, 1978), pp. 82–86

42   Matthew 6: 34

43   Brown, *Body and Society*, pp. 218–21

44   Evagrius Ponticus, *Praktikos*, 9, in *Evagrius Ponticus: The Praktikos and Chapters on Prayer*, trans. J. E. Bamberger (Kalamazoo, Mich., 1978)

45   *Apophthegmata Patrum* ('Sayings of the Desert Fathers'), Olympios. 2 in J. P. Migne, ed., *Patrologia Graeca* (PG), 161 vols (Paris, 1857–1866), 65, 313d–316a

46   Brown, *Making of Late Antiquity*, pp. 88–90

47   *Apophthegmata Patrum*, Poemon, 78; PG 65.352cd.

48   Ibid., 60; PG 65:332a

49   Douglas Burton-Christie, *The Word in the Desert: Scripture and the Quest for Holiness in Early Christian Monasticism* (New York and Oxford, 1993), pp. 261–83

50   Brown, *Body and Society*, p. 215; Brown, *World of Late Antiquity*, p. 98

51   Athanasius, *Vita*, pp. 92–93

52   *Sayings of the Fathers*, Macarius 32; PG 65:273d

53   Brown, *World of Late Antiquity*, pp. 93–94

54 Gaddis, *There is No Crime*, p. 278

55 Hilary of Poitiers, *Against Valerius and Ursacius*, 1.2.6, trans. Lionel R. Wickham, *Hilary of Poitiers: Conflicts of Conscience and Law in the Fourth-Century Church* (Liverpool, 1997)

56 Athanasius, *History of the Arians*, 81, trans. in Alexander Roberts and James Donaldson, trans. and ed., *Nicene and Post Nicene Fathers* (NPNF), 14 vols (Edinburgh, 1885)

57 Athanasius, *Apology Before Constantius* B3, in NPNF

58 Genesis 14: 18–20

59 Gaddis, *There is No Crime*, pp. 89–97

60 Ibid., p. 93

61 Socrates, *History of the Church*, 3.15; NPNF translation

62 Gaddis, *There is No Crime*, pp. 93–94; cf. Mark Juergensmeyer, *Terror in the Mind of God: The Global Rise of Religious Violence* (Berkeley, 2000), pp. 190–218

63 Harold A. Drake, *Constantine and the Bishops: The Politics of Intolerance* (Baltimore, 2000), pp. 431–36

64 Peter Brown, *Power and Persuasion in Late Antiquity: Towards a Christian Empire* (Madison, Wis., and London, 1992), pp. 34–70

65 G. W. Bowerstock, *Hellenism in Late Antiquity* (Ann Arbor, Mich., 1990), pp. 2–5; 35–40; 72–81; Brown, *Power and Persuasion*, pp. 134–45

66 Gregory of Nazianzus, Oration, 6.6; PG 35. 728 in Brown, *Power and Persuasion*, p. 50

67 Brown, *Power and Persuasion*, pp. 123–26

68 Raimundo Panikkar, *The Trinity and the Religious Experience of Man* (Mary Knoll, NY, 1973), pp. 46–67

69 Gaddis, *There is No Crime*, pp. 251–82

70 Eusebius, *The History of the Church*, trans. G. A. Williamson (London, 1965), 6.43, 5–10

71 Palladius, *Dialogue on the Life of John Chrysostom*, trans. Robert T. Meyer (New York, 1985), 20.561–71,

72 Gaddis, *There is No Crime*, p. 16

73 Hilary of Poitiers, *Against Valerius and Ursacius*, 1.2.6

74 Patlagean, *Pauvreté économique*, pp. 178–81; 301–40

75 Peter Garnsey, *Famine and Food Shortage in the Graeco-Roman World* (Cambridge, UK, 1988), pp. 257–68

76 E. W. Brooks, *The Sixth Book of the Select Letter of Severus, Patriarch of Antioch* (London, 1903), 1.9; Brown, *Power and Persuasion*, p. 148; Brown, *World of Late Antiquity*, p. 110

77   Sozomen, *History of the Church*, 6.33.2, NPNF, 2nd series, vol. 2

78   Gaddis, *There is No Crime*, pp. 242–50

79   Caner, *Wandering, Begging Monks*, pp. 125–49. Cf. 1 Thessalonians 5:17

80   Gaddis, *There is No Crime*, pp. 94–97

81   Libanius, Oration 30: 8–9 in A. F. Norman, ed. and trans., *Libanius: Select Orations*, 2 vols (Cambridge, Mass., 1969, 1977)

82   Gaddis, *There is No Crime*, p. 249

83   Ambrose, Epistle 41; Goddis, *There is No Crime*, pp. 191–96

84   Ramsey MacMullen, *Christianising the Roman Empire, AD ☒☒☒–400* (New Haven and London, 1984), p. 99

85   Rufinus, *History of the Church*, 11.22 in Philip R. Amidon, trans., *The Church History of Rufinus of Aquileia* (Oxford, 1997)

86   Gaddis, *There is No Crime*, p. 250

87   Ibid., pp. 99–100

88   MacMullen, *Christianising the Roman Empire*, p. 119

89   Augustine, Letters, 93.5.17; NPNF translation

90   Augustine, *The City of God*, 18. 54, MacMullen, *Christianising the Roman Empire*, p. 100

91   Peter Brown, 'Religious Dissent in the Later Roman Empire: The Case of North Africa', *History*, 46 (1961); Brown, 'Religious Coercion in the Later Roman Empire: The Case of North Africa,' *History*, 48 (1963); Gaddis, *There is No Crime*, p. 133

92   Augustine, Letter 47:5; NPNF translation

93   Augustine, *Against Festus*, 22.74; NPNF translation

94   Augustine, Letter 93.6

95   Augustine, *On the Free Choice of the Will*, 9.1.5., trans. Thomas Williams (Indianapolis, 1993)

96   Brown, *Rise of Western Christendom*, pp. 7–8

97   Gaddis, *There is No Crime*, pp. 283–89

98   Nestorius, *Bazaar of Heracleides*, trans. G. R. Driver and Leonard Hodgson (Oxford, 1925), pp. 199–200

99   Socrates, *Historia Ecclesiastica* 7.32; NPNF translation

100   Palladius, *Dialogue on the Life of John Chrysostom*, 20. 579

101   Gaddis, *There is No Crime*, pp. 292–310

102   *Letter of Theodosius to Barsauma*, 14 May, 449 in ibid., p. 298

103   Acts of the Council of Chalcedon in ibid., p. 156, n

104   Nestorius, *Bazaar of Heracleides*, pp. 482–83

105   Gaddis, *There is No Crime*, pp. 310–27

106   John Meyendorff, 'The Role of Christ I: Christ as Saviour in the East',

in Bernard McGinn, Jill Raitt and John Meyendorff, eds, *Christian Spirituality: High Middle Ages to Reformation* (London, 1987), pp. 236–37

107 Meyndorff, *Byzantine Theology*, pp. 213–15

108 Brown, *World of Late Antiquity*, pp. 166–8

109 Ibid., p. 166

110 Khusrow I, ibid.

111 Brown, *World of Late Antiquity*, pp. 160–65; Brown *The Rise of Western Christendom: Triumph and Diversity, AD 200–1000* (Oxford and Malden, Mass., 1996), pp. 173–74

112 Maximus, *Ambigua* 42, trans. Andrew Louth, *Maximus the Confessor* (London and New York, 1996) in Louth, *Maximas the Confessor*

113 Maximus, *Letter 2: On Love*, 401D in Louth, *Maximus the Confessor*

114 Matthew 5: 44; 1 Timothy 2: 4; Maximus, *Centuries on Love*, I, 61; Louth translation

115 Meyendorff, *Byzantine Theology*, pp. 212–22

7. The Muslim Dilemma

1   I have discussed the career of Muhammad and the history of Arabia in more detail in *Muhammad: A Prophet for Our Time* (London and New York, 2006)

2   Muhammad A. Bamyeh, *The Social Origins of Islam: Mind, Economy, Discourse* (Minneapolis, 1999), pp. 11–12

3   Toshihiko Izutsu, *Ethico-Religious Concepts in the Qur'an* (Montreal and Kingston, Ont., 2002), pp. 29, 46

4   R. A. Nicholson, *A Literary History of the Arabs* (Cambridge, 1953), p. 83

5   Ibid., pp. 28–45

6   Bamyeh, *Social Origins of Islam*, p. 38

7   Genesis 16; 17: 25; 21: 8–21

8   Quran 5: 69; 88: 17–20

9   Quran 3: 84–85

10 W. Montgomery Watt, *Muhammad at Mecca* (Oxford, 1953), p. 68

11 Quran 90: 13–17

12 Izutsu, *Ethico-Religious Concepts*, p. 28

13 Ibid., pp. 68–69; Quran 14: 47; 39: 37; 15: 79; 30: 47; 44: 16

14 Quran 25: 63, trans., Muhammad Asad, *The Message of the Quran* (Gibraltar, 1980)

15 W. Montgomery Watt, *Muhammad's Mecca: History of the Quran* (Edinburgh, 1988), p. 25

16   W. Montgomery Watt, *Muhammad at Medina* (Oxford, 1956), pp. 173–231

17   Ibn Ishaq, *Sirat Rasul Allah* in A. Guillaume, trans. and ed., *The Life of Muhammad* (London, 1955), p. 232

18   Watt, *Muhammad at Medina*, pp. 6–8; Bamyeh, *Social Origins of Islam*, pp. 198–99; Marshall G. S. Hodgson, *The Venture of Islam: Conscience and History in a World Civilization*, 3 vols (Chicago and London, 1974), I, pp. 75–76

19   Quran 29: 46

20   Michael Bonner, *Jihad in Islamic History* (Princeton and Oxford, 2006), p. 193

21   Martin Lings, *Muhammad: His Life Based on the Earliest Sources* (London, 1983), pp. 247–55; Tor Andrae, *Muhammad: The Man and His Faith*, trans. Theophil Menzil (London, 1936), pp. 213–15; Watt, *Muhammad at Medina*, pp. 46–59; Bamyeh, *Social Origins of Islam,* pp. 222–27

22   Quran 48: 26; trans. Izutsu, *Ethico-Religious Concepts*, p. 31

23   Ibn Ishaq, *Sirat Rasul Allah*, 751, in Guillaume, *Life of Muhammad*. Cf. Quran 110

24   Paul L. Heck, '*Jihad* Revisited', *Journal of Religious Ethics*, 32, 1 (2004); Bonner, *Jihad in Islamic History,* pp. 21–22

25   Bonner, *Jihad in Islamic History*, p. 25; Reuven Firestone, *Jihad: The Origin of Holy War in Islam* (Oxford and New York, 1999), pp. 42–45

26   Quran 16: 125–28

27   Quran 22: 39–41; 2: 194; 2: 197

28   Quran 9: 5

29   Quran 8: 61

30   Quran 9: 29

31   Firestone, *Jihad*, pp. 49–50

32   Quran 15: 94–95; 16: 135

33   Quran 2: 190; 22: 39–45

34   Quran 2: 191, 217

35   Quran 2: 191; 9.5, 29

36   Firestone, *Jihad*, pp. 50–65

37   Quran 2: 216; Asad translation

38   Quran 9: 38–39, in M. A. S. Abdel Haleem, trans., *The Qur'an: A New Translation* (Oxford, 2004)

39   Quran 9: 43; Abdel Haleem translation

40   Quran 9: 73–74; 63: 1–3

41   Quran 2: 109; cf. 50: 59; Abdel Haleem translation

42   Quran 5: 16; Abdel Haleem translation

43   Firestone, *Jihad*, pp. 73, 157

44   Quran 9: 5. Abdul Haleem translation

45   Quran 2: 193; trans. Firestone, *Jihad*, p. 85

46   Ibid.

47   Garth Fowden, *Empire to Commonwealth: Consequences of Monotheism in Late Antiquity* (Princeton, 1993), pp. 140–42

48   John Keegan, *The History of Warfare* (London, 1993), pp. 195–96

49   Peter Brown, *The World of Late Antiquity, AD 150–750* (London, 1989), p. 193

50   Hadith reported by Muthir al Ghiram, Shams ad-Din Suyuti and al Walid ibn Muslim cited by Guy Le Strange, *Palestine under the Moslems: A Description of Syria and the Holy Land from AD 650 TO 1500* (London, 1890), pp. 139–43; Tabari, *Tarikh ar-Rasul wa'l Muluk*, 1: 2405 in Moshe Gil, *A History of Palestine, 634–1099*, trans. Ethel Broido (Cambridge, 1992), pp. 70–72, 143–48, 636–38

51   'Book of Commandments' quoted in Gil, *History*, p. 1

52   Michael the Syrian, *History* 3.226, quoted in Joshua Prawer, *The Latin Kingdom in Jerusalem: European Colonialism in the Middle Ages* (London, 1972), p. 216

53   Peter Brown, *The Rise of Western Christendom: Triumph and Diversity, AD 200–1000* (Oxford and Malden, Mass., 1996), p. 185; Bonner, *Jihad in Islamic History*, p. 56

54   Bonner, *Jihad in Islamic History*, pp. 64–89; 168–69

55   David Cook, *Understanding Jihad* (Berkeley, Los Angeles and London, 2005), pp. 22–24

56   Ibid., pp. 13–19; Bonner, *Jihad in Islamic History*, pp. 46–54; Firestone, *Jihad*, pp. 93–99

57   Jan Wensinck, *Concordance et indices de la tradition musulmane*, 5 vols (Leiden, 1992), 1, 994

58   Ibid., 5, 298

59   Al-Hindi, *Kanz* (Beirut, 1989), 4, p. 282, no. 10,500; Cook, *Understanding Jihad*, p. 18

60   Ibn Abi Asim, *Jihad* (Medina, 1986), 1, pp. 140–41, no. 11

61   Wensinck, *Concordance*, 2.212; S. Bashear, 'Apocalyptic and Other Materials on Early Muslim–Byzantine Wars', *Journal of the Royal Asiatic Society*, Series 3, 1 (1991)

62   Wensinck, *Concordance*, 4.344; Bonner, *Jihad in Islamic History*, p. 51

63   Wensinck, *Concordance*, 2.312

64   Cook, *Understanding Jihad*, pp. 23–25

65   Ibn al-Mubarak, *Kitab al-Jihad* (Beirut, 1971), pp. 89–90; no. 105;
     Cook, *Understanding Jihad*, p. 23

66   Abu Daud, *Sunan* III, p. 4; no. 2484

67   Quran 3: 157, 167

68   Abd al-Wahhab Abd al-Latif, ed., *Al-jami al-sahih*, 5 vols (Beirut, n.d.),
     106, no. 1712 in David Cook, 'Jihad and Martyrdom in Islamic
     History', in Andrew R. Murphy, ed., *The Blackwell Companion to Religion
     and Violence* (Chichester, 2011), pp. 283–84

69   Ibn al-Mubarak, *Kitab al-Jihad*, pp. 63–64, no. 64 in Cook, *Understanding
     Jihad*, p. 26

70   Bonner, *Jihad in Islamic History*, pp. 119–20

71   Ibid., pp. 125–26; Marshall G. S. Hodgson, *The Venture of Islam: Conscience
     and History in a World Civilisation*, 3 vols (Chicago and London, 1974),
     1, p. 216; John L. Esposito, *Unholy War: Terror in the Name of Islam* (Oxford,
     2002), pp. 41–42

72   Al-Azmeh, *Muslim Kingship*, pp. 68–69; the Umayyads learned this
     lore from the Lakhmid Arab dynasty, who had been clients of Persia;
     Timothy H. Parsons, *The Rule of Empires: Those Who Built Them, Those
     Who Endured Them, and Why They Always Fail* (Oxford, 2010),
     pp. 79–80

73   Peter Brown, *The World of Late Antiquity, AD 150–750* (London, 1971,
     1989), pp. 201–02

74   Michael Bonner, *Aristocratic Violence and Holy War: Studies in the Jihad
     and the Arab–Byzantine Frontier* (New Haven, 1996), pp. 99–106

75   Abu Nuwas, *Diwan*, 452, 641 in Bonner, *Jihad in Islamic History*,
     p. 129

76   Bonner, *Jihad in Islamic History*, pp. 127–31

77   Ibid., pp. 99–110

78   Peter Partner, *God of Battles: Holy Wars of Christianity and Islam* (London,
     1997), p. 51

79   Cf. Ibn al-Mubarak, *Kitab al-Jihad*, p. 143, no. 141; Al Bayhagi, *Zuhd*
     (Beirut, n.d.), p. 165, no. 273 in Cook, *Understanding Jihad*, p. 35

80   Parsons, *Rule of Empires*, p. 77; Bonner, *Jihad in Islamic History*, p. 89;
     Hodgson, *Venture of Islam*, 1. p. 305

81   Aziz Al-Azmeh, *Muslim Kingship: Power and the Sacred in Muslim Christian
     and Pagan Politics* (London and New York, 1997), p. 239; Hodgson,
     Venture of Islam, 1, pp. 444–45

82   Hodgson, *Venture of Islam*, 1, pp. 315–54

83   Ibid., p. 317; Bonner, *Jihad in Islamic History*, pp. 92–93; Cook, *Understanding Jihad*, p. 21

84   Hodgson, *Venture of Islam*, 1, p. 323

85   Sunni Muslims form the majority, basing their lives on the *sunnah* or 'customary practice' of the Prophet

86   It was called the Fatimid empire because, like all Shiis, Ismails revere Fatima, the Prophet's daughter, the wife of Ali, and the mother of Husayn

87   Bernard Lewis, *The Assassins* (London, 1967); Edwin Burman, *The Assassins: Holy Killers of Islam* (London, 1987)

8. Crusade and Jihad

1   H. E. J. Cowdrey, 'Pope Gregory VII's "Crusading" Plans of 1074', in B. Z. Kedar, H. E. Mayer and R. C. Smail, eds, *Outremer* (Jerusalem, 1982)

2   Jonathan Riley-Smith, *The First Crusade and the Idea of Crusading* (London, 1986), pp. 17–22

3   Joseph R. Strager, 'Feudalism in Western Europe', in Rushton Coulborn, ed., *Feudalism in History* (Hamden, Conn., 1965), p. 21; Michael Gaddis, *There is No Crime for Those Who Have Christ: Religious Violence in the Christian Roman Empire* (Berkeley, Los Angeles and London, 2005), pp. 334–35; John Keegan, *A History of Warfare* (London, 1993), pp. 283, 289

4   Peter Brown, *The World of Late Antiquity*, AD ☒☒☒–☒☒☒ (London, 1989), p. 134

5   J. M. Wallace-Hadrill, *The Frankish Church* (Oxford, 1983), pp. 187, 245

6   Peter Brown, *The Rise of Western Christendom: Triumph and Diversity*, AD ☒☒☒–☒☒☒☒ (Oxford and Malden, Mass., 1996), pp. 254–57

7   Ibid., pp. 276–302

8   Einard, 'Life of Charlemagne', in Lewis Thorpe, trans., *Two Lives of Charlemagne* (Harmondsworth, UK, 1969), p. 67

9   Karl F. Morrison, *Tradition and Authority in the Western Church*, ☒☒☒–☒☒☒☒ (Princeton, 1969), p. 378

10   Rosamund McKitterick, *The Frankish Kingdoms under the Carolingians*, ☒☒☒–☒☒☒ (London and New York, 1983), p. 62

11   Brown, *World of Late Antiquity*, pp. 134–35

12   Alcuin, Letter 174 in R. W. Southern, *Western Society and the Church in the Middle Ages* (Harmondsworth, UK, 1970), p. 32

13   This letter was actually written for him by Alcuin, Epistle 93 in Wallace-Hadrill, *Frankish Church*, p. 186

14   Brown, *Rise of Western Christendom*, p. 281

15   Talal Asad, 'On Discipline and Humility in Medieval Christian Monasticism', in *Genealogies of Religion: Discipline and Reasons of Power in Christianity and Islam* (Baltimore and London, 1993), p. 148

16   Ibid., pp. 130–34

17   Southern, *Western Society and the Church*, pp. 217–24

18   Georges Duby, 'The Origins of a System of Social Classification', in *The Chivalrous Society*, trans. Cynthia Postan (London, 1977), p. 91

19   Georges Duby, 'The Origins of Knighthood', in ibid., p. 165

20   Foundation Charter of King Edgar for New Minster, Winchester, in Southern, *Western Society and the Church*, pp. 224–25

21   Ordericus Vitalis *Historia Ecclesiastica*, in ibid., p. 225

22   Brown, *Rise of Western Christendom*, p. 301

23   Georges Duby, *The Three Orders: Feudal Society Imagined*, trans. Arthur Goldhammer (London, 1980), p. 151; Riley-Smith, *First Crusade*, p. 3

24   Marc Bloch, *Feudal Society*, trans. L. A. Manyon (London, 1961), pp. 296, 298

25   Georges Duby, *The Early Growth of the European Economy: Warriors and Peasants from the Seventh to the Twelfth Century*, trans. Howard B. Clarke (Ithaca, NY, 1974), p. 49

26   Duby, 'Origins of a System of Social Classification,' pp. 91–92

27   The first extant formulations of this system have been found in a poem by Adalbéron of Laon (*c.* 1028–30) and *Gesta epeiscoporum camera-censiam* by Bishop Gerald of Cambrai, *c.* 1025, but there may have been earlier versions. Duby, 'Origins of Knighthood', p. 165

28   Bishop Merbad of Rennes in J. P. Migne, ed., *Patrologia Latina* (PL) (Paris 1844–64), 1971, 1483–34; Baldric of Bol in PL, 162, 1058–59; R. I. Moore, *The Formation of a Persecuting Society: Power and Deviance in Western Europe, 950–1250* (Oxford, 1987), p. 102

29   Maurice Keen, *Chivalry* (New Haven and London, 1984), pp. 46–47

30   Thomas Head and Richard Landes, eds, *The Peace of God: Social Justice and Religious Response in France around the Year* ⬚⬚⬚⬚ (Ithaca, NY, 1992); Tomaz Mastnak, *Crusading Peace: Christendom, the Muslim World and Western Political Order* (Berkeley, Los Angeles and London, 2002), pp. 1–18; Duby, *Chivalrous Society*, pp. 126–31; H. E. J. Cowdrey, 'The Peace

and the Truce of God in the Eleventh Century', *Past and Present*, 46 (1970)

31   James Westfall Thompson, *Economic and Social History of the Middle Ages* (New York, 1928), p. 668

32   The Council of Narbonne, 1054 in Duby, *Chivalrous Society*, p. 132

33   Glaber, *Historiarum* V. i. 25 in Mastnak, *Crusading Peace*, p. 11

34   Duby, 'Origins of Knighthood', p. 169

35   P. A. Sigal, 'Et les marcheurs de Dieu prirent leurs armes,' *L'Histoire*, 47 (1982); Riley-Smith, *First Crusade* (London, 1986), p. 10

36   Riley Smith, *First Crusade*, pp. 7–8

37   Ibid., pp. 17–27

38   Urban, Letter to the counts of Catalonia, ibid., p. 20

39   Matthew 19: 29

40   Mastnak, *Crusading Peace*, pp. 130–36

41   Sigal, 'Et les marcheurs de Dieu', p. 23; Riley-Smith, *First Crusade*, p. 23

42   Riley-Smith, *First Crusade*, pp. 48–49

43   'Chronicle of Rabbi Eliezer bar Nathan', in Schlomo Eidelberg, trans. and ed., *The Jews and the Crusaders: The Hebrew Chronicles of the First and Second Crusades* (London, 1977), p. 80

44   Guibert of Nogent, *De Vita Sua*, II.1, in Joseph McAlhany and Jay Rubinstein, trans. and ed., *Monodies and On the Relics of the Saints: The Autobiography and a Manifesto of a French Monk from the Time of the Crusades* (London, 2011), p. 97

45   Henri Pirenne, *Economic and Social History of Europe* (New York, 1956), pp. 7, 10–12

46   John H. Kautsky, *The Political Consequences of Modernization* (New York, London, Sydney, Toronto, 1972), p. 48

47   Georges Duby, 'The Transformation of the Aristocracy', in *Chivalrous Society*, p. 82

48   Norman Cohn, *Pursuit of the Millennium: Revolutionary Millenarians and Mystical Anarchists of the Middle Ages* (London, 1984), pp. 68–70

49   Duby, 'The Juventus,' in *Chivalrous Society*, pp. 112–21

50   Ibid., p. 120

51   Cohn, *Pursuit of the Millennium*, p. 63

52   Riley-Smith, *First Crusade*, p. 46

53   Ralph of Caen, *Gesta Tancredi, Recueil des Historiens des Croisade* (RHC), ed. Académie des Inscriptions et Belles-Lettres (1841–1906), 3 in ibid., p. 36

54 E. O. Blake, 'The Formation of the "Crusade Idea"', *Journal of Ecclesiastical History*, 21, 1 (1970); Mastnak, *Crusading Peace*, pp. 56–57

55 *The Deeds of the Franks and the Other Pilgrims to Jerusalem*, trans. Rosalind Hill (London, 1962), p. 27

56 Fulcher of Chartres, *A History of the Expedition to Jerusalem, 1098–1127*, trans. and ed. Frances Rita Ryan (Knoxville, 1969), p. 96

57 Riley-Smith, *First Crusade*, p. 91

58 Ibid., pp. 84–85

59 Ibid., p. 117

60 John Fowles, *The Magus*, revised edition (London, 1997), p. 413

61 Mastnak, *Crusading Peace*, p. 66

62 *Deeds of the Franks*, p. 91

63 Raymond in August C. Krey, ed. and trans., *The First Crusade: The Accounts of Eyewitnesses and Participants* (Princeton, NJ, and London, 1921), p. 266

64 Fulcher, *History of the Expedition*, p. 102

65 Raymond in Krey, ed., *First Crusade*, p. 266

66 Robert the Monk, *Historia Iherosolimitana* (Paris, 1846), RHC, 3, p. 741

67 Fulcher, *History of the Expedition*, pp. 66–67; Robert the Monk, *Historia*, p. 725; Riley-Smith, *First Crusade*, p. 143

68 Keegan, *History of Warfare*, p. 295

69 Bernard, *In Praise of the New Knighthood*, 2.3; 2, 1; quotations from M. Conrad Greenia, RHC, trans., *In Praise of the New Knighthood: A Treatise on the Knights Templar and the Holy Places of Jerusalem* (Collegeville, Minn., 2008)

70 Ibid., 3, 5

71 Amin Maalouf, *The Crusades through Arab Eyes*, trans. Jon Rothschild (London, 1984), pp. 38–39; the figures quoted by Ibn al-Athir are clearly exaggerated, since the city's population at this time was no more than 10,000

72 Michael Bonner, *Jihad in Islamic History* (Princeton and Oxford, 2006), pp. 137–38

73 Izz ad-Din ibn al-Athir, *The Perfect History*, X. 92, in Francesco Gabrieli, ed., *Arab Historians of the Crusades*, trans. E. J. Costello (London, Melbourne and Henley, 1978)

74 Carole Hillenbrand, *The Crusades: Islamic Perspectives* (Edinburgh, 1999), pp. 75–81

75 Maalouf, *Crusades through Arab Eyes*, pp. 2–3

76   Bonner, *Jihad in Islamic History*, pp. 139–40; Emanuel Sivan, 'Genèse de contre-croisade: une traité damasquine de début du XIIe siècle', *Journal Asiatique*, 254 (1966)

77   R. A. Nicholson, *The Mystics of Islam* (London, 1963 ed.), p. 105

78   Ibn al-Qalanisi, *History of Damascus*, 173 in Gabrieli, ed., *Arab Historians of the Crusades*

79   Kamal ad-Din, *The Cream of the Milk in the History of Aleppo*, II, 187–90 in Gabrieli, ed., *Arab Historians of the Crusades*

80   Maalouf, *Crusades through Arab Eyes*, p. 147

81   Imad ad-Din al-Isfahani, *Zubat al-nuores* in Hillenbrand, *Crusades*, p. 113

82   All quotations are from Ibn al-Athir, *Perfect History*, XI, 264–67 in Gabrieli, *Arab Historians of the Crusades*

83   Baha ad-Din, *Sultanly Anecdotes* in ibid., p. 100

84   Ibn al-Athir, *Perfect History* in ibid., pp. 141–42

85   Ibn al-Athir, *Perfect History* in Maalouf, *Crusades through Arab Eyes*, pp. 205–06

86   Christopher J. Tyerman, 'Sed nihil fecit? The Last Capetians and the Recovery of the Holy Land', in J. Gillingham and J. C. Holt, eds, *War and Government in the Middle Ages: Essays in Honour of J. O. Prestwich* (Totowa, NJ, 1984); Norman Housley, *The Later Crusades, 1274–1580: From Lyons to Alcazar* (Oxford, 1992), pp. 12–30; Mastnak, *Crusading Peace*, pp. 139–40

87   Two contrasting views are given in R.W. Southern, *The Making of the Middle Ages* (London, Melbourne, Sydney, Aukland, Johannesburg, 1967), pp. 56–62, and Steven Runciman, *A History of the Crusades*, 3 vols (Cambridge, 1954), pp. 474–77

88   Hillenbrand, *Crusades*, pp. 249–50

89   David Abulafia, *Frederick II: A Medieval Emperor* (New York and Oxford, 1992), pp. 197–98

90   From John Esposito, *Unholy War: Terror in the Name of Islam* (Oxford, 2002), pp. 43–46; David Cook, *Understanding Jihad* (Berkeley, Los Angeles and London, 2005), pp. 63–66; Bonner, *Jihad in Islamic History*, pp. 143–44; Marshall G. S. Hodgson, *The Venture of Islam: Conscience and History in a World Civilisation* (Chicago and London, 1974), pp. 468–71; Natana J. Delong-Bas, *Wahhabi Islam: From Revival and Reform to Global Jihad* (Cairo, 2005), pp. 247–55; Hillenbrand, *Crusades*, pp. 241–43

91   R. I. Moore, *The Formation of a Persecuting Society: Power and Deviance in Western Europe 950–1250* (Oxford, 1987)

92   Ibid., pp. 26–43

93   H. G. Richardson, *The English Jewry under the Angevin Kings* (London, 1960), p. 8; John H. Mundy, *Liberty and Political Power in Toulouse* (New York, 1954), p. 325

94   Moshe Gil, *A History of Palestine, 634–1099*, trans. Ethel Broido (Cambridge, UK, 1992), pp. 370–80; F. E. Peters, *The Distant Shrine: The Islamic Centuries in Jerusalem* (New York, 1993), pp. 73–74; 92–96. The Greeks called the Anastasis that enshrined Christ's Tomb the Church of the Resurrection; the Crusaders would rename it the Church of the Holy Sepulchre

95   Cohn, *Pursuit of the Millennium*, pp. 76–78, 80, 86–87

96   Ibid., pp. 87–88

97   Moore, *Formation of Persecuting Society*, pp. 105–06

98   Ibid., pp. 84–85; Richardson, *English Jewry*, pp. 50–63

99   Peter Abelard, *Dialogus*, 51 in P. J. Payer, trans., *A Dialogue of a Philosopher with a Jew and a Christian* (Toronto, 1979), p. 33

100 M. Montgomery Watt, *The Influence of Islam on Medieval Europe* (Edinburgh, 1972), pp. 74–86

101 Duby, 'Introduction', in *Chivalrous Society*, pp. 9–11

102 Jonathan and Louise Riley-Smith, *The Crusades: Idea and Reality, 1095–1274* (London, 1981), pp. 78–79

103 Ibid., pp. 83, 85

104 Zoe Oldenbourg, *Le Bucher de Montségur* (Paris, 1959), pp. 115–16

105 Ibid., p. 89

106 J. D. Mansi, *Sacrorum Consiliorum nova et amplissima collectio* (Paris and Leipzig, 1903), Vol. 21, 843 in Moore, *Formation of Persecuting Society*, p. 111

107 Norman Cohn, *Warrant for Genocide* (London, 1967), p. 12

108 Peter the Venerable, *Summary of the Whole Heresy of the Diabolic Sect of the Saracens* in Norman Daniel, *Islam and the West: The Making of an Image* (Edinburgh, 1960), p. 124

109 Benjamin Kedar, *Crusade and Mission: European Approaches to the Muslims* (Princeton, NJ, 1984), p. 101

110 Moore, *Formation of Persecuting Society*, pp. 60–67

111 Ibid., pp. 102, 110–11

112 Larry Benson, ed. and trans., *King Arthur's Death: The Middle English Stanzaic Morte d'Arthur and the Alliterative Morte d'Arthur* (Kalamazoo, Mich., 1994), line 247

113 *The Song of Roland*, line 2196; all quotations are taken from the translation of Dorothy L. Sayers (Harmondsworth, 1957)

114   Ibid., lines 2240, 2361

115   Ibid., lines 1881–82

116   Keen, *Chivalry*, pp. 60–63

117   P. M. Matarasso, trans. and ed., *The Quest of the Holy Grail* (Harmonds-worth, 1969), pp. 119–20

118   Franco Cardini, 'The Warrior and the Knight', in James Le Goff, ed., *The Medieval World*, trans. Lydia C. Cochrane (London, 1990), p. 95

119   Keith Busby, trans., *Raoul de Hodence, Le roman des eles: The Anonymous Ordene de Cevalerie* (Philadelphia, 1983), p. 175

120   Richard W. Kaeuper, *Holy Warrior: The Religious Ideology of Chivalry* (Philadelphia, 2009), pp. 53–57

121   A. T. Holden, S. Gregory and David Crouch, trans. and eds, *History of William Marshal*, 2 vols (London, 2002–06), lines 16,853–63

122   Kaeuper, *Holy Warrior*, pp. 38–49

123   Henry of Lancaster, 'Book of Holy Remedies' in A. J. Arnold, ed., *Le Livre de Seyntz Medicines: The Unpublished Devotional Treatises of Henry of Lancaster* (Oxford, 1940), p. 4

124   Geoffroi de Charny, *The Book of Chivalry of Geoffroi de Charny: Text, Context and Translation*, trans. Richard W. Kaeuper and Elspeth Huxley (Philadelphia, 1996), p. 194

125   Ibid., pp. 174, 176–77

126   Ibid.

127   Mastnak, *Crusading Peace*, pp. 233–39

128   Malcolm Barber, *The New Knighthood: A History of the Order of the Templars* (Cambridge, 1995), pp. 280–313; Norman Cohn, *Europe's Inner Demons: The Demonization of Christians in Medieval Christendom* (London, 1975), pp. 79–101

129   Brian Tierney, *The Crisis of Church and State, 1050–1300* (Toronto, 1988), p. 172; J. H. Shennon, *The Origins of the Modern European State 1450–1725* (London, 1974); Quentin Skinner, *The Foundations of Modern Political Thought*, 2 vols (Cambridge, UK, 1978), 1, p. xxiii; A. Fall, *Medieval and Renaissance Origins: Historiographical Debates and Demonstrations* (London, 1991), p. 120

130   Mastnak, *Crusading Peace*, pp. 244–46

131   J. N. Hillgarth, *Ramon Lull and Lullism in Fourteenth-Century France* (Oxford, 1971), pp. 107–11, 120

132   Christopher J. Tyerman, *England and the Crusades, 1095–1588* (Chicago, 1988), pp. 324–43; William T. Cavanaugh, *Migrations of the Holy: God, State and the Political Meanings of the Church* (Grand Rapids, Mich., 2011)

133 John Barnie, *War in Medieval English Society: Social Values in the Hundred Years War* (Ithaca, NY, 1974), pp. 102–03

134 Mastnak, *Crusading Peace*, pp. 248–51; Thomas J. Renna, 'Kingship in the *Disputatio inter clericum et militem*', *Speculum*, 48 (1973)

135 Ernst K. Kantorowicz, '*Pro Patria Mori* in Medieval Political Thought', *American Historical Review*, 56, 3 (1951), pp. 244, 256

PART THREE: MODERNITY

9. The Arrival of 'Religion'

1   Felipe Fernández-Armesto, *1492: The Year Our World Began* (New York, 2009), pp. 9–11, 52

2   Marshall G. S. Hodgson, *The Venture of Islam: Conscience and History in a World Civilization*, 3 vols (Chicago and London, 1974), 3, pp. 14–15

3   Ibid., 2, pp. 334–60

4   John H. Kautsky, *The Politics of the Aristocratic Empire*, 2nd ed. (New Brunswick and London, 1997), p. 146

5   Perry Anderson, *Lineages of the Absolutist State* (London, 1974), p. 505

6   Fernandez-Armesto, *1492*, pp. 2–4

7   Timothy H. Parsons, *The Rule of Empires: Those Who Built Them, Those Who Endured Them, and Why They Always Fail* (Oxford, 2010), p. 117; Peter Jay, *Road to Riches or The Wealth of Man* (London, 2000), p. 147

8   Jay, *Road to Riches*, p. 151

9   Ibid., pp. 152–53

10   Henry Kamen, *Empire: How Spain Became a World Power, 1492–1763* (New York, 2003), p. 83

11   Howard Zinn, *A People's History of the United States: From 1492 to the Present*, 2nd ed. (New York, 1996), p. 11

12   Massimo Livi-Bacci, *A Concise History of World Population* (Oxford, 1997), pp. 56–59

13   Parsons, *Rule of Empires*, p. 121

14   Ibid., p. 117

15   Jay, *Road to Riches*, p. 150

16   Mark Levene, *Genocide in the Age of the Nation-State: The Rise of the West and the Coming of Genocide* (London and New York, 2005), pp. 15–29

17   Cajetín, *On Aquinas' Secunda Secundae*, q. 66; art. 8 in Richard Tuck,

The Rights of War and Peace: Political Thought and the International Order from Grotius to Kant (Oxford, 1999), p. 70

18   Francisco de Vitoria, *Political Writings*, ed. Anthony Pagden and Jeremy Lawrence (Cambridge, 1991), pp. 225–26

19   Thomas More, *Utopia*, ed. George M. Logan and Robert M. Adams (Cambridge, 1989), pp. 89–90

20   Ibid., p. 58

21   Ibid.

22   Tuck, *Rights of War and Peace*, p. 15; Max Weber made the same point in 1906, cf. H. H. Gerth and C. Wright Mills, trans. and ed., *From Max Weber* (London, 1948), pp. 71–72

23   The Tacitus passage is quoted in Gentili's *The Rights of War and Peace, in Three Books* (London, 1738), 2.2.17; Tuck, *Rights of War and Peace*, pp. 47–48

24   Aristotle, *Politics*, 1256.b.22, in Richard McKeon, ed., *The Basic Works of Aristotle* (New York, 1941)

25   Henry Kamen, *The Spanish Inquisition: An Historical Revision* (London, 1997), pp. 45, 68, 137

26   Paul Johnson, *A History of the Jews* (London, 1987), pp. 225–29

27   Haim Beinart, *Conversos on Trial: The Inquisition in Ciudad Real* (Jerusalem, 1981), pp. 3–6

28   Norman Roth, *Conversos, Inquisition and the Expulsion of Jews from Spain* (Madison, 1995), pp. 283–84

29   Ibid., p. 19

30   Fernández-Armesto, *1492*, pp. 94–96

31   Johnson, *History of the Jews*, p. 229; Yirmiyahu Yovel, *Spinoza and Other Heretics: I. The Marrano of Reason* (Princeton, NJ, 1989), pp. 17–18

32   Johnson, *History of the Jews*, pp. 225–29

33   Kamen, *Spanish Inquisition*, pp. 57–59; William Monter, *Frontiers of Heresy: The Spanish Inquisition from the Basque Lands to Sicily* (Cambridge, UK, 1990), p. 53

34   Kamen, *Spanish Inquisition*, p. 69

35   Robin Briggs, 'Embattled Faiths: Religion and Natural Philosophy', in Euan Cameron, ed., *Early Modern Europe: An Oxford History* (Oxford, 1999), pp. 197–205

36   Jay, *Road to Riches*, pp. 160–63

37   Henri Pirenne, *Medieval Cities: Their Origins and the Revival of Trade* (Princeton, 1946), pp. 168–212; Bert F. Hoselitz, *Sociological Aspects of Economic Growth* (New York, 1960), pp. 163–72

38   Norman Cohn, *Pursuit of the Millennium: Revolutionary Millenarians and Mystical Anarchists of the Middle Ages* (London, 1984 ed.) pp. 107–16

39   Euan Cameron, 'The Power of the Word: Renaissance and Reformation', in Cameron, *Early Modern Europe*, pp. 87–90

40   Richard Marius, *Martin Luther: The Christian between God and Death* (Cambridge, Mass., and London, 1999), pp. 73–74, 214–15, 486–87

41   Joshua Mitchell, *Not By Reason Alone: History and Identity in Early Modern Political Thought* (Chicago, 1993), pp. 23–30

42   Martin Luther, 'Temporal Authority: To What Extent It Should Be Obeyed', trans. J. J. Schindel, revised by Walther I. Brandt in J. M. Porter, ed., *Luther: Selected Political Writings* (SPW) (Eugene, Oreg., 2003), p. 54

43   Ibid., p. 55

44   Ibid.

45   Ibid., p. 56

46   Martin Luther, 'Whether Soldiers, Too, Can Be Saved', trans. Charles M. Jacobs, revised by Robert C. Schultz in SPW, p. 108

47   J. W. Allen, *A History of Political Thought in the Sixteenth Century* (London, 1928), p. 16; Sheldon S. Wolin, *Politics and Vision: Continuity and Innovation in Western Political Thought* (Boston, 1960), p. 164

48   Cohn, *Pursuit of the Millennium*, pp. 245–50

49   Martin Luther, 'Admonition to Peace: A Reply to the Twelve Articles of the Peasants in Swabia' (1525), trans. J. J. Schindel, revised by Walther I. Brandt, in SPW, p. 72

50   Ibid., p. 78

51   Ibid., p. 82

52   Martin Luther, 'Against the Robbing and Murdering Hordes of Peasants' (1525), trans. Charles M. Jacobs, revised by Robert C. Schultz in SPW, p. 86

53   Steven Ozment, *The Reformation of the Cities: The Appeal of Protestantism to Sixteenth Century Germany and Switzerland* (New Haven, 1975), pp. 10–11, 123–25, 148–50

54   Charles A. McDaniel, Jr., 'Violent Yearnings for the Kingdom of God: Münster's Militant Anabaptism', in James K. Wellman, ed., *Belief and Bloodshed: Religion and Violence across Time and Tradition* (Lanham, Md., 2007), p. 74. The social danger persisted, even though in the last days of Anabaptist Münster its leader Jan of Leyden set himself up as king, then introduced a pseudo-imperial court and a reign of terror

55   Cohn, *Pursuit of the Millennium*, pp. 255–79

56   I have discussed this at length in *The Case for God* (London and New York, 2009). See also Wilfred Cantwell Smith, *The Meaning and End of Religion: A New Approach to the Religious Traditions of Mankind* (New York, 1962); *Belief in History* (Charlottesville, Va., 1985) and *Faith and Belief* (Princeton, NJ, 1987)

57   William T. Cavanaugh, *The Myth of Religious Violence* (Oxford, 2009), pp. 72–74

58   Thomas More, *A Dialogue Concerning Heresies*, ed. Thomas M. C. Lawlor (New Haven, 1981), p. 416

59   François-André Isambert, ed., *Recueil général des anciennes lois françaises depuis l'an 420 jusqu'à la Révolution de 1789* (Paris, 1821–33), 12, p. 819

60   Brad S. Gregory, *Salvation at Stake: Christian Martyrdom in Early Modern Europe* (Cambridge, Mass., and London, 1999), p. 201

61   Raymund F. Mentzer, *Heresy Proceedings in Languedoc, 1500–1560* (Philadelphia, 1984), p. 172

62   Philip Spierenberg, *The Spectacle of Suffering: Executions and the Evolution of Repression: From a Pre-Industrial Metropolis to the European Experience* (Cambridge, UK, 1984); Lionello Puppi, *Torment in Art: Pain, Violence and Martyrdom* (New York, 1991), pp. 11–69

63   Gregory, *Salvation at Stake*, pp. 77–79

64   David Nicholls, 'The Theatre of Martyrdom in the French Reformation', *Past and Present*, 121 (1998); Susan Brigdon, *London and the Reformation* (Oxford, 1989), p. 607; Mentzer, *Heresy Proceedings*, p. 71

65   Gregory, *Salvation at Stake*, pp. 80–81

66   Deuteronomy, 13: 1–3, 5, 6–11, quoted by Johannes Eck, *Handbook of Commonplaces* (1525) and Calvin to justify his execution of Michael Servetus who denied the doctrine of the Trinity

67   Gregory, *Salvation at Stake*, pp. 84–87

68   Ibid., pp. 111, 154

69   Ibid., pp. 261–69

70   Allen, *Apologie of the English College* (Douai, 1581); Gregory, *Salvation at Stake*, p. 283

71   Gregory, *Salvation at Stake*, pp. 285–86

72   Kamen, *Spanish Inquisition*, pp. 204–13

73   Ibid., p. 203

74   Ibid., p. 98

75   Ibid., pp. 223–45

76   Ibid.

77 Cavanaugh, *Myth of Religious Violence*, p. 122

78 J. V. Poliskensky, *War and Society in Europe, 1618–1848* (Cambridge, 1978), pp. 77, 154, 217

79 Cavanaugh, *Myth of Religious Violence*, pp. 142–55

80 Richard S. Dunn, *The Age of Religious Wars, 1559–1689* (New York, 1970), p. 6; James D. Tracy, *Charles V, Impresario of War: Campaign Strategy, International Finance, and Domestic Politics* (Cambridge, 2002), pp. 45–47, 306

81 William Blockmans, *Emperor Charles V, 1500–1558* (London and New York, 2002), pp. 95, 110; William Maltby, *The Reign of Charles V* (New York, 2002), pp. 112–13

82 Tracy, *Charles V*, p. 307; Blockmans, *Emperor Charles V*, p. 47

83 Klaus Jaitner, 'The Pope and the Struggle for Power during the Sixteenth and Seventeenth Centuries', in Klaus Bussman and Heinz Schilling, eds, *War and Peace in Europe*, 3 vols (Münster, 1998), 1, p. 62

84 Maltby, *Reign of Charles V*, p. 62; Tracy, *Charles V*, pp. 209–15

85 Tracy, *Charles V*, pp. 32–34; 46

86 Maltby, *Reign of Charles V*, pp. 60–62

87 Cavanaugh, *Myth of Religious Violence*, p. 164

88 Dunn, *Age of Religious Wars*, p. 49

89 Ibid., pp. 50–51

90 Steven Gunn, 'War, Religion and the State', in Cameron, *Early Modern Europe*, p. 244

91 Cavanaugh, *Myth of Religious Violence*, pp. 145–47, 153–58

92 James Westfall Thompson, *The Wars of Religion in France, 1559–1576: The Huguenots, Catherine de Medici, Philip II*, 2nd ed. (New York, 1957); Lucien Romier, 'A Dissident Nobility under the Cloak of Religion', in J. H. M. Salmon, ed., *The French Wars of Religion: How Important Were Religious Factors?* (Lexington, Mass., 1967); Henri Hauser, 'Political Anarchy and Social Discontent', in ibid.

93 Natalie Zemon Davis, 'The Rites of Violence: Religious Riot in Sixteenth-Century France', *Past and Present*, 59 (1973)

94 Mack P. Holt, 'Putting Religion Back into the Wars of Religion', *French Historical Studies*, 18, 2 (Autumn 1993); John Bossy, 'Unrethinking the Sixteenth-Century Wars of Religion', in Thomas Kselman, ed., *Belief in History: Innovative Approaches in European and American Religion* (Notre Dame, Ind., 1991); Denis Crouzet, *Les guerriers de Dieu: La violence en temps des troubles de religion* (Seyssel, 1990); Barbara Diefendorf, *Beneath the Cross: Catholics and Huguenots in Sixteenth-Century Paris* (New York,

1991). Some scholars have argued that Davis was herself incorrect to describe the conflict as 'essentially' religious, because religion still permeated all human activities; see Cavanaugh, *Myth of Religious Violence*, pp. 159–60

95 M. P. Holt, *The French Wars of Religion, 1562–1629* (Cambridge, UK, 1995), pp. 17–18

96 Bossy, 'Unrethinking the Sixteenth-Century Wars of Religion', pp. 278–80

97 Virginia Reinberg, 'Liturgy and Laity in Late Medieval and Reformation France,' *Sixteenth-Century Journal*, 23 (Autumn 1992)

98 Holt, *French Wars of Religion*, pp. 18–21

99 Ibid., pp. 50–51

100 J. H. M. Salmon, *Society in Crisis: France in the Sixteenth Century* (New York, 1975), p. 198; Henry Heller, *Iron and Blood: Civil Wars in Sixteenth-Century France* (Montreal, 1991), p. 63

101 Holt, *French Wars of Religion*, p. 99; Salmon, *Society in Crisis*, pp. 176; 197

102 Salmon, *Society in Crisis,* pp. 204–05

103 Holt, *French Wars of Religion*, pp. 50–51

104 Heller, *Iron and Blood*, pp. 209–11

105 Ibid., p. 126

106 Holt, *French Wars of Religion*, pp. 156–57; Salmon, *Society in Crisis*, pp. 282–91

107 Salmon, *Society in Crisis,* pp. 3–4, 126, 168–69; Cavanaugh, *Myth of Religious Violence*, pp. 173–74

108 Cavanaugh, *Myth of Religious Violence,* pp. 147–50

109 Geoffrey Parker, *The Thirty Years War* (London, 1984), pp. 29–33, 59–64

110 Ibid., p. 195

111 Dunn, *Age of Religious Wars*, pp. 71–72

112 William H. McNeill, *Pursuit of Power: Technology, Armed Force and Society since AD 1000* (Chicago, 1982), pp. 120–23; Robert L. O'Connell, *Of Arms and Men: A History of War, Weapons and Aggression* (New York and Oxford, 1999), pp. 143–44

113 McNeill, *Pursuit of Power,* pp. 121–23

114 Parker, *Thirty Years War*, pp. 127–28

115 Jeremy Black, 'Warfare, Crisis and Absolutism', in Cameron, *Early Modern Europe*, p. 211

116 Parker, *Thirty Years War*, p. 142

117 Ibid., pp. 216–17

118 Cavanaugh, *Myth of Religious Violence*, p. 159; John Bossy, *Christianity in the West, 1400–1700* (Oxford, 1985), pp. 170–1

119 Andrew R. Murphy, 'Cromwell, Mather and the Rhetoric of Puritan Violence', in Andrew R. Murphy, ed., *The Blackwell Companion to Religion and Violence* (Chichester, 2011), pp. 528–34

120 Thomas Carlyle, ed., *Oliver Cromwell's Letters and Speeches*, 3 vols (New York, 1871), 1, p. 154

121 Ibid., 2, pp. 153–54

122 Cavanaugh, *Myth of Religious Violence*, p. 172

123 Ann Hughes, *The Causes of the English Civil War* (London, 1998), p. 25

124 Ibid., pp. 10–25, 58–59, 90–97

125 Ibid., p. 89

126 Ibid., p. 85

127 Cavanaugh, *Myth of Religious Violence*, pp. 160–72

128 Parker, *Thirty Years War*, p. 172

129 Jan N. Brenner, 'Secularization: Notes toward the Genealogy', in Henk de Vries, ed., *Religion: Beyond a Concept* (New York, 2008), p. 433

130 Heinz Schilling, 'War and Peace at the Emergence of Modernity: Europe between State Belligerence, Religious Wars and the Desire for Peace in 1648', in Bussman and Schilling, *War and Peace in Europe*, p. 14

131 Thomas Ertman, *Birth of the Leviathan: Building States and Regimes in Early Modern Europe* (Cambridge, 1997), p. 4

132 Salmon, *Society in Crisis*, p. 13

133 Cavanaugh, *Myth of Religious Violence*, pp. 72–85; Russell T. McCutcheon, 'The Category "Religion" and the Politics of Tolerance', in Arthur L. Greil and David G. Bromley, eds, *Defining Religion: Investigating the Boundaries between the Sacred and the Secular* (Oxford, 2003), pp. 146–52; Derek Peterson and Darren Walhof, 'Rethinking Religion', in Peterson and Walhof, eds, *The Invention of Religion*, pp. 3–9; David E. Gunn, 'Religion, Law and Violence', in Murphy, *Blackwell Companion*, pp. 105–07

134 Edward, Lord Herbert, *De Veritate*, trans. Meyrick H. Carre (Bristol, UK, 1937), p. 303

135 Ibid., p. 298

136 Edward, Lord Herbert, *De Religio Laici*, trans. and ed. Harold L. Hutcheson (New Haven, Conn., 1944), p. 127

137 Thomas Hobbes, *Behemoth; or, The Long Parliament*, ed. Frederick Tönnies (Chicago, 1990), p. 55

138 Ibid., p. 95

139 Thomas Hobbes, *On the Citizen*, ed. Richard Tuck and Michael Silverthorne (Cambridge, 1998), 3.26; Thomas Hobbes, *Leviathan*, ed. Richard Tuck (Cambridge, 1991), p. 223

140 Hobbes, *Leviathan*, pp. 315, 431–34

141 Ibid., p. 31

142 Ibid., p. 27

143 Ibid., p. 17

144 John Locke, *A Letter Concerning Toleration* (Indianapolis, 1955), p. 15

145 John Locke, *Two Treatises of Government*, ed. Peter Laslett (Cambridge, 1988), 'Second Treatise', 5. 24

146 Ibid., 5.120–21

147 Ibid., 5.3

148 Hugo Grotius, *Rights of War and Peace, in Three Books* (London, 1738), 2.2.17, 2.20.40; Tuck, *Rights of War and Peace*, pp. 103–04

149 Hobbes, *On the Citizen*, ed. Tuck, 30

150 Donne, *Sermons of John Donne*, ed. George R. Potter and Evelyn M. Simpson (Berkeley, 1959), 4, p. 274

10. The Triumph of the Secular

1 John Cotton and Thomas Morton, 'New English Canaan' (1634–35) and John Cotton, 'God's Promise to His Plantations' (1630), in Alan Heimart and Andrew Delbanco, eds, *The Puritans in America: A Narrative Anthology* (Cambridge, Mass., 1985), pp. 49–50

2 Kevin Phillips, *The Cousins' Wars: Religious Politics and the Triumph of Anglo-America* (New York, 1999), pp. 3–32; Carla Garden Pesteria, *Protestant Empire: Religion and the Making of the British Atlantic World* (Philadelphia, 2004), pp. 503–15; Clement Fatoric, 'The Anti-Catholic Roots of Liberal and Republican Conception of Freedom in English Political Thought', *Journal of the History of Ideas*, 66 (January 2005)

3 John Winthrop, 'A Model of Christian Charity', in Heimart and Delbanco, *Puritans in America*, p. 91

4 John Winthrop, 'Reasons to Be Considered for . . . the Intended Plantation in New England' (1629), in ibid., p. 71

5 Winthrop, 'Model of Christian Charity', in ibid., p. 82

6 John Cotton, 'God's Promise', in ibid. p. 77

7 Cushman, 'Reasons and Considerations Touching the Lawfulness

of Removing out of England into the Parts of America', in ibid., pp. 43–44

8   Perry Miller, 'The Puritan State and Puritan Society', in *Errand into the Wilderness* (Cambridge, Mass., and London, 1956), pp. 148–49

9   John Smith, 'A True Relation', in Edwin Arber and A. C. Bradley, eds, *John Smith: Works* (Edinburgh, 1910), p. 957

10   Perry Miller, 'Religion and Society in the Early Literature of Virginia', in *Errand*, pp. 104–05

11   William Crashaw, *A Sermon Preached in London before the right honourable Lord werre, Lord Gouernour and Captaine Generall of Virginea* (London, 1610), in ibid., pp. 111, 138

12   Ibid., p. 101

13   David S. Lovejoy, *Religious Enthusiasm in the New World: Heresy to Revolution* (Cambridge, Mass., and London, 1985), pp. 11–13; Louis B. Wright, *Religion and Empire: The Alliance between Piety and Commerce in English Expansion, 1558–1625* (Chapel Hill, 1943); Miller, 'Religion and Society', pp. 105–08

14   Samuel Purchas, *Hakluytus Posthumous, or Purchas His Pilgrim,* 3 vols (Glasgow, 1905–06), I, pp. 1–45

15   'A True Declaration of the Estate of the Colonie in Virginia' (1610), in Peter Force, ed., *Tracts* (New York, 1844), 3, pp. 5–6

16   Miller, 'Religion and Society', pp. 116–17

17   Howard Zinn, *A People's History of the United States: From 1492 to the Present,* 2nd ed. (London and New York, 1996), p. 12

18   Ibid., p. 13

19   Andrew Preston, *Sword of the Spirit, Shield of Faith: Religion in American War and Diplomacy* (New York and Toronto, 2012), pp. 15–17

20   Purchas, *Hakluytus Posthumous,* I, pp. xix, 41–45, 220–22, 224, 229

21   Ibid., pp. 138–39

22   Preston, *Sword of the Spirit*, pp. 31–38

23   Ibid., p. 33

24   Ibid., p. 35

25   Bradford, *History of the Plymouth Plantation*, in Zinn, *People's History*, p. 15

26   Ronald Dale Kerr, 'Why Should You Be So Furious? The Violence of the Pequot War', *Journal of American History,* 85 (December 1998)

27   Preston, *Sword of the Spirit*, pp. 41–45; Andrew R. Murphy, 'Cromwell, Mather and the Rhetoric of Puritan Violence', in Murphy, ed., *The Blackwell Companion to Religion and Violence* (Chichester, 2011), pp. 525–35

28   Miller, 'Puritan State', pp. 150–51

29   Sherwood Eliot Wirt, ed., *Spiritual Awakening: Classic Writings of the Eighteenth-Century Devotios to Inspire and Help the Twentieth-Century Reader* (Tring, 1988), p. 110

30   Alan Heimert, *Religion and the American Mind: From the Great Awakening to Revolution* (Cambridge, Mass., 1968), p. 43

31   Miller, 'Puritan State', p. 150

32   Stoddard, 'An Examination of the Power of the Fraternity' (1715), in Heimart and Delbanco, *Puritans in America*, p. 388

33   Perry Miller, 'Jonathan Edwards and the Great Awakening', in *Errand*, pp. 162–66

34   Ibid., p. 165

35   Ruth H. Bloch, *Visionary Republic: Millennial Themes in American Thought, 1756–1800* (Cambridge, UK, 1985), pp. 14–15

36   The original draft of the Declaration listed the self-evident rights as 'life, liberty and property'; only later was that amended to 'the pursuit of happiness'

37   Jon Butler, *Awash in a Sea of Faith: Christianizing the American People* (Cambridge, Mass., and London, 1990), p. 198

38   Bloch, *Visionary Republic*, pp. 81–88

39   Timothy Dwight, *A Valedictory Address to the Young Gentlemen Who Commenced Bachelors of Arts, July 27 1776* (New Haven, Conn., 1776), p. 14

40   Lovejoy, *Religious Enthusiasm in the New World*, p. 226

41   Ibid.

42   Thomas Paine, *Common Sense and the Crisis* (New York, 1975), p. 59

43   Bloch, *Visionary Republic*, p. 55

44   Ibid., pp. 60–63

45   Ibid., pp. 29, 31

46   Edwin S. Gaustad, *Faith of Our Fathers: Religion and the New Nation* (San Francisco, 1987), p. 38

47   Madison to William Bradford, 1 April 1774, in William T. Hutchinson and William M. E. Rachal, eds, *The Papers of James Madison* (Chicago, 1962), 1, pp. 212–13

48   Madison, 'Memorial and Remonstrance' (1785), 7, in Gaustad, *Faith of Our Fathers*, p. 145

49   Jefferson, *Statute for Establishing Religious Freedom* (1786), in ibid., p. 150

50   Henry S. Stout, 'Rhetoric and Reality in the Early Republic: The Case of the Federalist Clergy', in Mark A. Noll, ed., *Religion and American*

Politics: From the Colonial Period to the 1980s (Oxford and New York, 1990), pp. 65–66, 75

51 Nathan O. Hatch, *The Democratization of American Christianity* (New Haven, Conn., and London, 1989), p. 22

52 Ibid., pp. 25–29

53 John F. Wilson, 'Religion, Government and Power in the New American Nation', in Noll, *Religion and American Politics*

54 Gaustad, *Faith of Our Fathers*, p. 44

55 Perry Miller, *Roger Williams: His Contribution to the American Tradition*, 2nd ed. (New York, 1962), p. 192

56 Miller, 'Puritan State', p. 146

57 Jefferson to William Baldwin, 19 January 1810, in Dickenson W. Adams, ed., *Jefferson's Extracts from the Gospels* (Princeton, 1983), p. 345; Jefferson to Charles Clay, 29 January 1816, ibid., p. 364

58 Hatch, *Democratization of American Christianity*, pp. 68–157

59 Daniel Walker Howe, 'Religion and Politics in the Antebellum North', in Noll, *Religion and American Politics*, pp. 132–33; George Marsden, 'Afterword', ibid., pp. 382–83

60 Mark A. Noll, 'The Rise and Long Life of the Protestant Enlightenment in America', in William M. Shea and Peter A. Huff, eds, *Knowledge and Belief in America: Enlightenment Traditions and Modern Religious Thought* (New York, 1995); cf. D. W. Bebbington, *Evangelicalism in Modern Britain: A History from the 1730s to the 1980s* (London, 1989), p. 74; Michael Gauvreau, 'Between Awakening and Enlightenment', in *The Evangelical Century: College and Creed in English Canada from the Great Revival to the Great Depression* (Kingston and Montreal, 1991), pp. 13–56

61 Alexis de Tocqueville, *Democracy in America,* ed. and trans. Harvey Claflin Mansfield and Delba Winthrop (Chicago, 2000), p. 43; De Tocqueville's emphasis

62 Henry F. May, *The Enlightenment in America* (New York, 1976); Mark A. Noll, *America's God: From Jonathan Edwards to Abraham Lincoln* (Oxford and New York, 2002), pp. 93–95

63 Mark A. Noll, *The Civil War as a Theological Crisis* (Chapel Hill, 2006), pp. 24–25

64 John M. Murrin, 'A Roof without Walls: The Dilemma of American National Identity', in Richard Beeman, Stephen Botein and Edward E. Carter II, eds, *Beyond Confederation: Origins of the Constitution and American Identity* (Chapel Hill, 1987), pp. 344–47

65 Noll, *Civil War*, pp. 25–28

66   Claude E. Welch, Jr., *Political Modernization* (Belmont, Calif. 1967), pp. 2–6

67   John H. Kautsky, *The Political Consequences of Modernization* (New York, London, Sydney, Toronto, 1972), pp. 45–47

68   T. C. W. Blanning, 'Epilogue: The Old Order Transformed', in Euan Cameron, ed., *Early Modern Europe: An Oxford History* (Oxford, 1999), pp. 345–60; Michael Burleigh, *Earthly Powers: The Clash of Religion and Politics from the French Revolution to the Great War* (New York, 1995), pp. 48–66

69   M. G. Hutt, 'The Role of the Curés in the Estates General of 1789', *Journal of Ecclesiastical History*, 6 (1955)

70   George Lefebvre, *The Great Fear of 1789*, trans. R. R. Farmer and Joan White (Princeton, NJ, 1973)

71   Philip G. Dwyer, *Talleyrand* (London, 2002), p. 24

72   Ibid., pp. 61–62

73   Mark Noll, *The Old Religion in a New World: The History of North American Christianity* (Grand Rapids, Mich., 2002), pp. 82–83; Gertrude Himmelfarb, *The Roads to Modernity* (New York, 2004), pp. 18–19

74   Burleigh, *Earthly Powers*, pp. 96–101; Claude Petitfrere, 'The Origins of the Civil War in the Vendée', *French History*, 2 (1998), pp. 99–100

75   Instructions from the Committee of Public Safety (1794), cited in Burleigh, *Earthly Powers*, p. 100

76   Reynald Secher, *Le Génocide franco-français: La Vendée-vengé* (Paris, 1986), pp. 158–59

77   Jonathan North, 'General Hocte and Counterinsurgency', *Journal of Military History*, 67 (2003)

78   Mircea Eliade, *Patterns in Comparative Religion*, trans. Rosemary Sheed (London, 1958), p. 11

79   Burleigh, *Earthly Powers*, pp. 79–80

80   Ibid., p. 76

81   Jules Michelet, *Historical View of the French Revolution from its Earliest Indications to the Flight of the King in 1791*, trans. C. Cooks (London, 1888), p. 393

82   Burleigh, *Earthly Powers*, p. 81

83   Boyd C. Schafer, *Nationalism: Myth and Reality* (New York, 1952), p. 142

84   Ibid.

85   Alexis de Tocqueville, *The Old Regime and the French Revolution*, ed. François Furet and Françoise Melonio (Chicago, 1998), 1, p. 101

86   Jean-Jacques Rousseau, *Politics and the Arts, Letter to M. D'Alembert on the Theatre*, trans. Alan Bloom (Ithaca, NY, 1960), p. 126

87   Jean-Jacques Rousseau, *The Social Contract and Other Later Political Writings*, ed. Victor Gourevitch (Cambridge, 1997), pp. 150–51

88   Donald Greer, *The Incidence of Terror in the French Revolution* (Gloucester, Mass., 1935)

89   John Keegan, *A History of Warfare* (London and New York, 1993), pp. 348–59; Robert L. O'Connell, *Of Arms and Men: A History of Weapons and Aggression* (New York and Oxford, 1989), pp. 174–88; William H. McNeill, *The Pursuit of Power: Technology, Armed Force and Society Since AD 1000* (Chicago, 1982), pp. 185–215

90   Russell Weighley, *The Age of Battles* (Bloomington, Ind., 1991); O'Connell, *Arms and Men*, pp. 148–50

91   John U. Neff, *War and Human Progress: An Essay in the Rise of Industrial Civilisation* (New York, 1950), pp. 204–05; Theodore Ropp, *War in the Modern World* (Durham, NC, 1959), pp. 25–26

92   Keegan, *History of Warfare*, p. 344; O'Connell, *Arms and Men*, pp. 157–66; McNeill, *Pursuit of Power*, p. 172

93   Trans. Crane Brinton in McNeill, *Pursuit of Power*, p. 192

94   Keegan, *History of Warfare*, p. 350

95   Ibid., pp. 351–52

96   O'Connell, *Arms and Men*, p. 185

97   George Annesley, *The Rise of Modern Egypt: A Century and a Half of Egyptian History* (Durham, UK, 1997), p. 7

98   Gaston Wait, ed. and trans., *Nicholas Turc, Chronique D'Egypte: 1798–1804* (Cairo, 1950), p. 78

99   Peter Jay, *Road to Riches or The Wealth of Man* (London, 2000), pp. 205–36; Gerhard E. Lenski, *Power and Privilege: A Theory of Social Stratification* (Chapel Hill and London, 1966), pp. 297–392; Marshall G. S. Hodgson, *The Venture of Islam: Conscience and History in a World Civilization*, 3 vols (Chicago and London, 1974), 3, pp. 195–201

100 Hodgson, *Venture of Islam*, 3, p. 194

101 John H. Kautsky, *The Politics of Aristocratic Empires*, 2nd ed. (New Brunswick and London, 1997), p. 349; even Fascist governments were coalitions

102 Hodgson, *Venture of Islam*, 3, pp. 199–201; G. W. F. Hegel, *The Philosophy of Right*, paragraphs 246, 248

103 Kautsky, *Political Consequences of Modernization*, pp. 60–61

104 Hodgson, *Venture of Islam*, 3, p. 208; Bassam Tibi, *The Crisis of Political*

Islam: A Pre-Industrial Culture in the Scientific-Technological Age (Salt Lake City, Utah, 1988), pp. 1–25

105 Hodgson, *Venture of Islam*, 33, pp. 210–12

106 O'Connell, *Arms and Men*, p. 235; Percival Spear, *India* (Ann Arbour, Mich., 1961), p. 270

107 Daniel Gold, 'Organized Hinduisms: From Vedic Truth to Hindu Nation', in Martin E. Marty and R. Scott Appleby, eds, *Fundamentalisms Observed* (Chicago and London, 1991), pp. 534–37

108 Wilfred Cantwell Smith, *The Meaning and End of Religion: A New Approach to the Religious Traditions of Mankind* (New York, 1964), pp. 61–62

109 Patwant Singh, *The Sikhs* (New York, 1999), p. 28

110 Guru Garth Sahib, 1136, in ibid., p.18

111 John Clark Archer, *The Sikhs in Relation to Hindus, Christians and Ahmadiyas* (Princeton, NJ, 1946), p. 170

112 T. N. Madan, 'Fundamentalism and the Sikh Religious Tradition', in Marty and Appleby, eds, *Fundamentalisms Observed*, 602

113 Kenneth W. Jones, 'The Arya Samaj in British India, 1875–1947', in Robert D. Baird, ed., *Religion in Modern India* (Delhi, 1981), pp. 50–52

114 Madan, 'Fundamentalism', p. 605

115 Ibid., pp. 603–6

116 Harjot S. Oberoi, 'From Ritual to Counter Ritual: Rethinking the Hindu–Sikh Question, 1884–1915', in Joseph T. O'Connell, ed., *Sikh History and Religion in the Twentieth Century* (Toronto, 1988), pp. 136–40

117 N. Gould Barrier, 'Sikhs and Punjab Politics', in O'Connell, *Sikh History*

118 Madan, 'Fundamentalism', p. 617

119 Mumtaz Ahmad, 'Islamic Fundamentalism in South Asia: The Jama'at-i-Islami and the Tablighi Jamaat', in Marty and Appleby, eds, *Fundamentalisms Observed*, p. 460

120 O'Connell, *Arms and Men*, pp. 231–35

121 Ibid., p. 191

122 Ibid., p. 233

123 G. W. Steevans, *With Kitchener to Khartoum* (London, 1898), p. 300

124 Speech of Sir John Ardagh, 22 June 1899, in *The Proceedings of the Hague Peace Conference* (London, 1920), pp. 286–87

125 Elbridge Colby, 'How to Fight Savage Tribes', *American Journal of International Law*, 21, 2 (1927); author's emphasis

126 Ernest Gellner, *Nations and Nationalism (New Perspectives on the Past)* (Oxford, 1983)

127 Anthony Giddens, *The Nation-State and Violence* (Berkeley, 1987), p. 89

128 Ibid., pp. 85–89; William T. Cavanaugh, *Migrations of the Holy: God, State, and the Political Meaning of the Church* (Grand Rapids, Mich., 2011), pp. 18–19

129 Benedict Anderson, *Imagined Communities: Reflections on the Origin and Spread of Nationalism* (London and New York, 2003)

130 Mark Levene, *Genocide in the Age of the Nation-State. Vol. III: The Rise of the West and the Coming of Genocide* (London and New York, 2005), pp. 26–27, 112–20; David Stannard, *American Holocaust: The Conquest of the New World* (New York and Oxford, 1992), p. 120; Ward Churchill, *A Little Matter of Genocide: Holocaust and Denial in the Americas, 1492 to the Present* (San Francisco, 1997), p. 150; Anthony F. C. Wallace, *Jefferson and the Indians: The Tragic Fate of the First Americans* (Cambridge, Mass., 1999)

131 Norman Cantor, *The Sacred Chain: A History of the Jews* (London, 1995), pp. 236–37

132 John Stuart Mill, *Utilitarianism, Liberty, and Representational Government* (London, 1910), pp. 363–64

133 Quoted in Antony Smith, *Myths and Memories of the Nation* (Oxford, 1999), p. 33.

134 Cited in Levene, *Genocide*, pp. 150–51; cf. C. A. Macartney, *National States and National Minorities* (London, 1934), p. 17

135 Bruce Lincoln, *Holy Terrors: Thinking about Religion after September 11*, 2nd ed. (Chicago and London, 2006), pp. 62–63

136 Johann Gottlieb Fichte, 'What a People Is, and What Is Love of Fatherland', in Fichte, *Addresses to the German Nation*, ed. and trans. Gregory Moore (Cambridge, 2008), p. 105

137 Zinn, *People's History*, pp. 23–58; Basil Davidson, *The African Slave Trade* (Boston, 1961); Stanley Elkins, *Slavery: A Problem of American Institutional and Intellectual Life* (Chicago, 1959); Edmund S. Morgan, *American Slavery, American Freedom: The Ordeal of Colonial Virginia* (New York, 1975)

138 Leviticus 25: 45–46; Genesis 9: 25–27, 17: 12; Deuteronomy 20: 10–11; 1 Corinthians 7: 21; Romans 13: 1, 7; Colossians 3: 22, 4: 1; 1 Timothy 6: 1–2; Philemon, *passim*

139 Thornhill, 'Our National Sins', in *Fast Day Sermons or The Pulpit on the State of the Country*, ed. anonymous (Charleston, SC, 2009 ed.), p. 48

140 Beecher, 'Peace Be Still', in ibid., p. 276

141 Van Dyke, 'The Character and Influence of Abolitionism', in ibid., p. 137

142 Lewis, 'Patriarchal and Jewish Servitude: No Argument for American Slavery', in ibid., p. 180

143 Noll, *Civil War*, pp. 1–8

144 Ibid., pp. 19–22; 'The Rise and Long Life of the Protestant Enlightenment in America', in William M. Shea and Peter A. Huff, *Knowledge and Belief in America: Enlightenment Trends and Modern Thought* (New York, 1995), pp. 84–124; May, *Enlightenment in America*, passim

145 James M. McPherson, *For Cause and Comrades: Why Men Fought in the Civil War* (New York, 1997), p. 63; 'Afterword', in Randall M. Miller, Harry S. Stout and Charles Reagan Wilson, eds, *Religion and the American Civil War* (New York, 1998), p. 412

146 Noll, *Civil War*, pp. 52–79

147 Beecher, 'Abraham Lincoln', in *Patriotic Addresses* (New York, 1887), p. 711

148 Bushnell, 'Our Obligations to the Dead', in *Building Eras in Religion* (New York, 1881), pp. 328–29

149 O'Connell, *Arms and Men*, pp. 189–96

150 Grady McWhiney and Perry D. Jamieson, *Attack and Die: The Civil War, Military Tactics, and Southern Heritage* (Montgomery, Ala., 1982), pp. 4–7

151 Bruce Cotton, *Grant Takes Command* (Boston, 1968), p. 262

152 O'Connell, *Arms and Men*, pp. 198–99

153 Noll, *Civil War*, pp. 90–92

154 Alastair McGrath, *The Twilight of Atheism: The Rise and Fall of Disbelief in the Modern World* (London and New York), pp. 52–55, 60–66

155 James R. Moore, 'Geologists and Interpreters of Genesis in the Nineteenth Century', in David C. Lindberg and Ronald L. Numbers, eds, *God and Nature: Historical Essays on the Encounter between Christianity and Science* (New York, 1986), pp. 341–43

156 Noll, *Civil War*, pp. 159–62

157 Richard Maxwell Brown, *Strain of Violence: Historical Studies of American Violence and Vigilantism* (New York, 1975), pp. 217–18

158 O'Connell, *Arms and Men*, 202–10; McNeill, *Pursuit of Power*, pp. 242–55

159 I. F. Clarke, *Voices Prophesying War: Future Wars 1763–3749*, rev. ed. (Oxford and New York, 1992), pp. 37–88

160 Paul Johnson, *A History of the Jews* (London, 1987), p. 365

161 Zygmunt Bauman, *Modernity and the Holocaust* (Ithaca, NY, 1989), pp. 40–77

162 Amos Elon, *The Israelis: Founders and Sons*, 2nd ed. (London, 1981), p. 112

163   Ibid. p. 338

164   Eric J. Leed, *No Man's Land: Combat and Identity in World War I*
        (Cambridge, UK, 1979), pp. 39–72

165   Stefan Zweig, *The World of Yesterday: An Autobiography* (New York, 1945),
        p. 224

166   Leed, *No Man's Land*, p. 55

167   Zweig, *World of Yesterday*, p. 24; Leed, *No Man's Land*, p. 47

168   Quoted in H. Hafkesbrink, *Unknown Germany: An Inner Chronicle of the
        First World War Based on Letters and Diaries* (New Haven, Conn., 1948),
        p. 37

169   Rudolf Binding, *Erlebtes Leben* (Frankfurt, 1928), p. 237; Leed transla-
        tion

170   Carl Zuckmayer, *Pro Domo* (Stockholm, 1938), pp. 34–35

171   Franz Schauwecker, *The Fiery Way* (London and Toronto, 1921), p. 29

172   Quoted in Carl Schorske, *German Social Democracy, 1905–1917*
        (Cambridge, Mass., 1955), p. 390

173   Leed, *No Man's Land*, p. 29

174   P. Witkop, ed. *Kriegsbriefe gefallener Studenten* (Munich, 1936), p. 100;
        Leed translation

175   Lawrence, *The Mint* (New York, 1963), p. 32

176   De Beauvoir, *Memoirs of a Dutiful Daughter* (New York, 1974), p. 180

177   Emilio Lussu, *Sardinian Brigade* (New York, 1939), p. 167

11. Religion Fights Back

1   I have explained this at length in *The Battle for God: A History of
        Fundamentalism* (London and New York, 2000)

2   Calvin, Commentary on Genesis 1:6 in *The Commentaries of John Calvin
        on the Old Testament*, 30 vols, Calvin Translation Society, 1643–48, 1,
        p. 86; for a fuller account of the traditional non-literal interpretation
        of scripture in both Judaism and Christianity, see my *The Bible: The
        Biography* (London and New York, 2007)

3   Hodge, *What Is Darwinism?* (Princeton, NJ, 1874), p. 142

4   2 Thessalonians 2: 3–12; Revelation 16: 15; Paul Boyer, *When Time
        Shall Be No More: Prophecy Belief in Modern American Culture* (Cambridge,
        Mass., 1992), p. 192; George Marsden, *Fundamentalism and American
        Culture: The Shaping of Twentieth-Century Evangelicalism, ▨▨▨▨–▨▨▨▨*
        (New York and Oxford, 1980), pp. 154–55

5   Marsden, *Fundamentalism and American Culture*, pp. 90–92; Robert C.
      Fuller, *Naming the Antichrist: The History of an American Obsession* (Oxford
      and New York, 1995), p. 119

6   Marsden, *Fundamentalism*, pp. 184–89; R. Lawrence Moore, *Religious
      Outsiders and the Making of Americans* (Oxford and New York, 1986),
      pp. 160–63; Ronald L. Numbers, *The Creationists: The Evolution
      of Scientific Creationism* (Berkeley, Los Angeles and London, 1992),
      pp. 41–44, 48–50; Ferenc Morton Szasz, *The Divided Mind of Protestant
      America, 1880–1930* (University, Ala., 1982), pp. 117–35

7   Marsden, *Fundamentalism in America*, pp. 187–88

8   Aurobindo Ghose, *Essays on the Gita* (Pondicherry, 1972), p. 39

9   Louis Fischer, ed., *The Essential Gandhi* (New York, 1962), p. 193

10   Mahatma Gandhi, 'My Mission', *Young India*, 3 April 1924, in Judith
      M. Brown, ed., *Mahatma Gandhi: Essential Writings* (Oxford and New
      York, 2008), p. 5

11   Mahatma Gandhi, 'Farewell', *An Autobiography*, in ibid., p. 65

12   Kenneth W. Jones, 'The Arya Samaj in British India, 1875–1947', in
      Robert D. Baird, ed., *Religion in Modern India* (Delhi, 1981), pp. 44–45

13   Radhey Shyam Pareek, *Contribution of Arya Samaj in the Making of Modern
      India, 1875–1947* (New Delhi, 1973), pp. 325–26

14   Daniel Gold, 'Organized Hinduisms: From Vedic Truth to Hindu
      Nation', in Martin E. Marty and R. Scott Appleby, eds, *Fundamentalisms
      Observed* (Chicago and London, 1991), pp. 533–42

15   Vinayak Damdar Savakar, *Hindutva* (Bombay, 1969), p. 1

16   Gold, 'Organized Hinduisms,' pp. 575–80

17   M. S. Golwalkar, *We or Our Nationhood Defined* (Nagpur, 1939),
      pp. 47–48

18   Ibid., p. 35

19   Sudhir Kakar, *The Colours of Violence: Cultural Identities, Religion, and
      Conflict* (Chicago and London, 1996), p. 31

20   Ibid., p. 38

21   Gold, 'Organized Hinduisms', pp. 531–32; Sushil Srivastava, 'The
      Ayodhya Controversy: A Third Dimension', *Probe India*, January 1988

22   Abul Ala Mawdudi, *The Islamic Way of Life* (Lahore, 1979), p. 37

23   Charles T. Adams, 'Mawdudi and the Islamic State', in John Esposito,
      Voices of Resurgent Islam (New York and Oxford, 1983); Youssef M.
      Choueiri, *Islamic Fundamentalism* (London, 1970), pp. 94–139

24   Mumtaz Ahmad, 'Islamic Fundamentalisms in South Asia,' in Marty
      and Appleby, *Fundamentalisms Observed*, pp. 487–500

25   Abul Ala Mawdudi, *Tafhim-al-Qur'an*, in Mustansire Mir, 'Some Features
     of Mawdudi's Tafhim al-Quran', *American Journal of Islamic Social Sciences*,
     2, 2 (1985), p. 242

26   *Introducing the Jamaat-e Islami Hind*, in Ahmad 'Islamic Fundamentalism
     in South Asia,' pp. 505–06

27   Ibid., pp. 500–01

28   Khurshid Ahmad and Zafar Ushaq Ansari, *Islamic Perspectives* (Leicester,
     1979), pp. 378–81

29   Abul Ala Maududi, 'Islamic Government', reprinted in *Asia* 20
     (September 1981), p. 9

30   Rafiuddin Ahmed, 'Redefining Muslim Identity in South Asia: The
     Transformation of the Jama'at-i-Islami', in Martin E. Marty and R.
     Scott Appleby, eds, *Accounting for Fundamentalisms: The Dynamic Character
     of Movements* (Chicago and London, 1994), p. 683

31   The Ahmadis were said to be heretical, because their founder, M. G.
     Ahmad (d. 1908) had claimed to be a prophet

32   Ahmad, 'Islamic Fundamentalism in South Asia,' pp. 587–89

33   Abul Ala Maududi, 'How to Establish Islamic Order in the Country?',
     The Universal Message, May 1983, pp. 9–10

34   Marshall G. S. Hodgson, *The Venture of Islam: Conscience and History in
     a World Civilization*, 3 vols (Chicago and London, 1974), 3, 218–19

35   George Annesley, *The Rise of Modern Egypt: A Century and a Half of
     Egyptian History*, p. 62

36   Ibid., pp. 51–56

37   Hodgson, *Venture of Islam*, 3, p. 71

38   Nikkie R. Keddie, *Roots of Revolution: An Interpretive History of Modern
     Iran* (New Haven, Conn., and London, 1981), pp. 72–73, 82

39   John Kautsky, *The Political Consequences of Modernisation* (New York,
     London, Sydney and Toronto, 1972), pp. 146–47

40   Bruce Lincoln, *Holy Terrors: Thinking about Religion after September 11*,
     2nd ed. (Chicago and London, 2006), pp. 63–65

41   Daniel Crecelius, 'Non-Ideological Responses of the Ulema to
     Modernization', in Nikki R. Keddie, ed, *Scholars, Saints and Sufis: Muslim
     Religious Institutions in the Middle East since 1500* (Berkeley, Los Angeles
     and London, 1972), pp. 181–82

42   Gilles Kepel, *Jihad: The Trail of Political Islam*, trans. Anthony F. Roberts,
     4th ed. (London, 2009), p. 53

43   Alastair Crooke, *Resistance: The Essence of the Islamist Revolution* (London,
     2009), pp. 54–58

44   Bobby Sayyid, *A Fundamental Fear: Eurocentrism and the Emergence of Islamism* (London, 1997), p. 57

45   Hodgson, *Venture of Islam*, 3, p. 262

46   Donald Bloxham, *The Great Game of Genocide: Imperialism, Nationalism and the Destruction of the Ottoman Armenians* (Oxford, 2007), p. 59

47   Quoted in Joanna Bourke, 'Barbarisation vs. Civilisation in Time of War', in George Kassimeris, ed., *The Barbarisation of Warfare* (London, 2006), p. 29

48   Moojan Momen, *An Introduction to Shii Islam: The History and Doctrines of Twelver Shiism* (New Haven, Conn., and London, 1985), p. 251; Keddie, *Roots of Revolution*, pp. 93–94

49   Azar Tabari, 'The Role of Shii Clergy in Modern Iranian Politics', in Nikki R. Keddie, ed., *Religion and Politics in Iran: Shiism from Quietism to Revolution* (New Haven, Conn., and London, 1983), p. 63

50   Shahrough Akhavi, *Religion and Politics in Contemporary Islam: Clergy–State Relations in the Pahlavi Period* (Albany, NY, 1980), pp. 58–59

51   Majid Fakhry, *A History of Islamic Philosophy* (New York and London, 1970), pp. 376–81; Bassam Tibi, *Arab Nationalism: A Critical Inquiry*, trans. Marion Farouk Slugett and Peter Slugett, 2nd ed. (London, 1990), pp. 90–93; Hourani, *Arabic Thought in the Liberal Age*, pp. 130–61; Hodgson, *Venture of Islam*, 3, pp. 274–76

52   Evelyn Baring, Lord Cromer, *Modern Egypt*, 2 vols (New York, 1908), 2, p. 184

53   Hourani, *Arabic Thought in the Liberal Age*, pp. 224, 230, 240–43

54   John Esposito, 'Islam and Muslim Politics', in Esposito, ed., *Voices of Resurgent Islam*, p. 10; Richard P. Mitchell, *The Society of Muslim Brothers* (New York and Oxford, 1969), *passim*

55   Mitchell, *Society of Muslim Brothers*, p. 8; the story and speech may be apocryphal but it expresses the spirit of the early Brotherhood

56   Ibid., 9–13, 328

57   Anwar Sadat, *Revolt on the Nile* (New York, 1957), pp. 142–43

58   Mitchell, *Society of Muslim Brothers*, pp. 205–06

59   Ibid., p. 302

60   John O. Voll, 'Fundamentalisms in the Sunni Arab World: Egypt and the Sudan', in Martin E. Marty and R. Scott Appleby, eds, *Fundamentalisms Observed* (Chicago and London, 1991), pp. 369–74; Yvonne Haddad, 'Sayyid Qutb', in Esposito, ed., *Voices of Resurgent Islam*; Choueiri, *Islamic Fundamentalism*, pp. 96–151

61   Qutb, *Fi Zilal al-Quran*, 2, 924–25

62   Harold Fisch, *The Zionist Revolution: A New Perspective* (Tel Aviv and London, 1968), pp. 77, 87

63   Theodor Herzl, *The Complete Diaries of Theodor Herzl*, ed. R. Patai, 2 vols (London and New York, 1960), 2, pp. 793–94

64   Mircea Eliade, *The Sacred and the Profane*, trans. Willard J. Trask (New York, 1959), p. 21

65   Meir Ben Dov, *The Western Wall* (Jerusalem, 1983), p. 146

66   Ibid., p. 148

67   Ibid., p. 146

68   Meron Benvenisti, *Jerusalem: The Torn City* (Jerusalem, 1975), p. 84

69   Ibid., p. 119

70   Psalm 72: 4

71   Michael Rosenak, 'Jewish Fundamentalism in Israeli Education', in Martin E. Marty and R. Scott Appleby, eds, *Fundamentalisms and Society: Reclaiming the Sciences, the Family, and Education* (Chicago and London, 1993), p. 392

72   Gideon Aran, 'The Father, the Son and the Holy Land', in R. Scott Appleby, ed., *Spokesmen for the Despised: Fundamentalist Leaders in the Middle East* (Chicago, 1997), p. 310

73   Ibid.

74   Ibid., p. 311

75   Ibid., p. 310

76   Interview with *Maariv* (14 Nisan 5723, 1963), in Aviezer Ravitsky, *Messianism, Zionism, and Jewish Religious Radicalism*, trans. Michael Swirsky and Jonathan Chipman (Chicago and London, 1993), p. 85

77   Ian S. Lustick, *For the Land and the Lord: Jewish Fundamentalism in Israel* (New York, 1988), p. 85; Aran, 'Father, Son and the Holy Land,' p. 310

78   Samuel C. Heilman, 'Guides of the Faithful: Contemporary Religious Zionist Rabbis', in Appleby, ed., *Spokesmen for the Despised*, p. 357

79   Ehud Sprinzak, 'Three Models of Religious Violence: The Case of Jewish Fundamentalism in Israel', in Martin E. Marty and R. Scott Appleby, eds. *Fundamentalism and the State: Remaking Politics, Economics and Militance* (Chicago and London, 1993), p. 472

80   Gideon Aran, 'Jewish Zionist Fundamentalism', in Marty and Appleby, eds., *Fundamentalisms Observed*, p. 290

81   Gideon Aran, 'Jewish Religious Zionist Fundamentalism', in ibid., p. 280

82   Ibid., p. 308

83   Keddie, *Roots of Revolution*, pp. 160–80

84   Mehrzad Borujerdi, *Iranian Intellectuals and the West: The Tormented Triumph of Nativism* (Syracuse, NY, 1996), p. 26; Choueiri, *Islamic Fundamentalism*, p. 156

85   Michael J. Fischer, 'Imam Khomeini: Four Levels of Understanding', in Esposito, ed., *Voices of Resurgent Islam*, p. 157

86   Keddie, *Roots of Revolution*, pp. 154–56

87   Ibid., pp. 158–59; Momen, *Introduction to Shii Islam*, p. 254; Hamid Algar, 'The Oppositional Role of the Ulema in Twentieth-Century Iran', in Nikki R. Keddie, ed., *Scholars, Saints and Sufis: Muslim Religious Institutions in the Middle East since 1500* (Berkeley, Los Angeles and London, 1972), p. 248

88   Willem M. Floor, 'The Revolutionary Character of the Ulama: Wishful Thinking or Reality', in Keddie, ed. *Religion and Politics in Iran*, Appendix, p. 97

89   Hamid Algar, 'The Fusion of the Mystical and the Political in the Personality and Life of Imam Khomeini', lecture delivered at the School of Oriental and African Studies, London, 9 June 1998

90   John XXIII, *Mater et Magistra*, 'Christianity and Social Progress', in Claudia Carlen, ed., *The Papal Encyclicals, 1740–1981*, 5 vols (Falls Church, Va., 1981), 5, pp. 63–64

91   Camilo Torres, 'Latin America: Lands of Violence', in J. Gerassi, ed., *Revolutionary Priest: The Complete Writings and Messages of Camilo Torres* (New York, 1971), pp. 422–23

92   Thia Cooper, 'Liberation Theology and the Spiral of Violence', in Andrew R. Murphy, ed., *The Blackwell Companion to Religion and Violence* (Chichester, UK, 2011), pp. 543–55

93   Andrew Preston, *Sword of the Spirit, Shield of Faith: Religion in American War and Diplomacy* (New York, 2012), pp. 502–25

94   Ibid., p. 510

95   Martin Luther King, Jr., *Strength to Love* (Philadelphia, 1963), p. 50

96   Keddie, *Roots of Revolution,* pp. 282–83; Borujerdi, *Iranian Intellectuals,* pp. 29–42

97   Akhavi, *Religion and Politics in Contemporary Iran,* pp. 129–31

98   Algar, 'Oppositional Role of the Ulema', p. 251

99   Keddie, *Roots of Revolution,* pp. 215–59; Sharough Akhavi, 'Shariati's Social Thought', in Keddie, *Religion and Politics in Iran*; Abdulaziz Sachedina, 'Ali Shariati: Ideologue of the Islamic Revolution,' in

Esposito, ed., *Voices of Resurgent Islam*; Michael J. Fischer, *Iran: From Religious Dispute to Revolution* (Cambridge, Mass., and London, 1980), pp. 154–67; Borujerdi, *Iranian Intellectuals*, pp. 106–15

100 Sayeed Ruhollah Khomeini, *Islam and Revolution*, trans. and ed. Hamid Algar (Berkeley, 1981), p. 28

101 Keddie, *Roots of Revolution*, p. 242; Fischer, *Iran*, p. 193

102 Gary Sick, *All Fall Down: America's Fateful Encounter with Iran* (London, 1985), p. 30

103 Keddie, *Roots of Revolution*, p. 243

104 Fischer, *Iran*, p. 195

105 Momen, *Introduction to Shii Islam*, p. 288

106 Fischer, *Iran*, p. 184

107 Momen, *Introduction to Shii Islam*, p. 288

108 Fischer, *Iran*, pp. 198–99

109 Ibid., p. 199; Sick, *All Fall Down*, p. 51; Keddie, *Roots of Revolution*, p. 250. The government claimed that only 120 demonstrators died, and 2,000 were injured; others claimed between 500 and 1,000 dead

110 Fischer, *Iran*, p. 204

111 Ibid., p. 205; Keddie (*Roots of Revolution*, pp. 252–53) believes that only one million took part

112 Amir Taheri, *The Spirit of Allah: Khomeini and the Islamic Revolution* (London, 1985), p. 227

113 Baqir Moin, *Khomeini: Life of the Ayatollah* (London, 1999), pp. 227–28

114 Daniel Brumberg, 'Khomeini's Legacy: Islamic Rule and Islamic Social Justice', in R. Scott Appleby, ed., *Spokesmen for the Despised: Fundamentalist Leaders of the Middle East* (Chicago, 1997)

115 Joos R. Hiltermann, *A Poisonous Affair: America, Iraq and the Gassing of Halabja* (Cambridge, 2007), pp. 22–36

116 Homa Katouzian, 'Shiism and Islamic Economics: Sadr and Bani Sadr', in Keddie, ed., *Religion and Politics in Iran*, pp. 161–62

117 Michael J. Fischer, 'Imam Khomeini: Four Levels of Understanding', in Esposito, ed., *Voices of Resurgent Islam*, p. 171

118 Sick, *All Fall Down*, p. 165

119 Hannah Arendt, *On Revolution* (New York, 1963), p. 18

120 Kautsky, *Political Consequences of Modernisation*, pp. 60–127

121 William Beeman, 'Images of the Great Satan: Representations of the United States in the Iranian Revolution', in Keddie, ed., *Religion and Politics in Iran*, p. 215

12. Holy Terror

1   Rebecca Moore, 'Narratives of Persecution, Suffering and Martyrdom: Violence in the People's Temple and Jonestown', in James R. Lewis, ed., *Violence and New Religious Movements* (Oxford, 2011); Moore, 'America as Cherry-Pie: The People's Temple and Violence', in Catherine Wessinger, ed., *Millennialism, Persecution and Violence: Historical Circumstances* (Syracuse, NY, 1986); Wessinger, *How the Millennium Comes Violently: Jonestown to Heaven's Gate* (New York, 2000); Mary Maaga, *Hearing the Voices of Jonestown* (Syracuse, NY, 1998).

2   Moore, 'Narratives of Persecution', p. 102

3   Ibid., p. 103

4   Huey Newton, *Revolutionary Suicide* (New York, 1973)

5   Moore, 'Narratives of Persecution', p. 106

6   Ibid., p. 108

7   Ibid., p. 110

8   George Steiner, *In Bluebeard's Castle: Some Notes toward the Re-definition of Culture* (New Haven, Conn., 1971), p. 32

9   Zygmunt Bauman, *Modernity and the Holocaust* (Ithaca, NY, 1989), pp. 77–92

10 Joanna Bourke, 'Barbarisation vs. Civilisation in Time of War', in George Kassimeris, ed., *The Barbarisation of Warfare* (London, 2006), p. 26

11 Amir Taheri, *The Spirit of Allah: Khomeini and the Islamic Revolution* (London, 1985), p. 85

12 Michael Barkun, *Religion and the Racist Right: The Origins of the Christian Identity Movement* (Chapel Hill, 1994)

13 Ibid., pp. 107, 109; there may be as few as 50,000 members

14 Ibid., p. 213

15 William T. Cavanaugh, *The Myth of Religious Violence* (Oxford, 2009), pp. 34–35

16 C. Gearty, 'Introduction', in Gearty, ed., *Terrorism* (Aldershot, 1996), p. xi

17 C. Gearty, 'What is Terror?' in Gearty, *Terrorism*, p. 495; A. Guelke, *The Age of Terrorism and the International Political System* (London, 2008), p. 7

18 Richard English, *Terrorism: How to Respond* (Oxford, 2009), pp. 19–20

19 A. H. Kydd and B. F. Walter, 'The Stratagems of Terrorism', *International Security*, 31, 1 (Summer, 2006)

20   P. Wilkinson, *Terrorism versus Democracy: The Liberal State Response* (London, 2001), pp. 19, 41; Mark Juergensmeyer, *Terror in the Mind of God: The Global Rise of Religious Violence* (Berkeley, 2001), p. 5; J. Horgan, *The Psychology of Terrorism* (London, 2005), p. 12; English, *Terrorism*, p. 6

21   Hugo Slim, 'Why Protect Civilians? Innocence, Immunity and Enmity in War', *International Affairs*, 79, 3 (2003)

22   Bruce Hoffman, *Inside Terrorism* (London, 1998), p. 14; C. C. Harmon, *Terrorism Today* (London, 2008), p. 7; D. J. Whittaker, ed., *The Terrorist Reader* (London, 2001), p. 9

23   Harmon, *Terrorism Today*, p. 160

24   Martha Crenshaw, 'Reflections on the Effects of Terrorism', in M. Crenshaw, ed., *Terrorism, Legitimacy, and Power: The Consequences of Political Violence* (Middletown, Conn., 1983), p. 25

25   Richard Dawkins, *The God Delusion* (London, 2007), p. 132

26   Cavanaugh, *Myth of Religious Violence*, pp. 24–54

27   Muhammad Heikal, *Autumn of Fury: The Assassination of Sadat* (London, 1984), pp. 94–96

28   Gilles Kepel, *The Prophet and Pharaoh: Muslim Extremism in Egypt*, trans. Jon Rothschild (London, 1985), p. 85

29   Fedwa El Guindy, 'The Killing of Sadat and After: A Current Assessment of Egypt's Islamic Movement', *Middle East Insight* 2 (January–February 1982)

30   Kepel, *Prophet and Pharaoh*, pp. 70–102

31   Ibid., pp. 152–59

32   Ibid., pp. 158–59

33   Heikal, *Autumn of Fury*, pp. 118–19

34   Patrick D. Gaffney, *The Prophet's Pulpit: Islamic Preaching in Contemporary Egypt* (Berkeley, Los Angeles and London, 1994), pp. 97–101

35   Ibid., pp. 141–42

36   Johannes J. G. Jansen, *The Neglected Duty: The Creed of Sadat's Assassins and Islamic Resurgence in the Middle East* (New York and London, 1988), pp. 49–88

37   Ibid., p. 169

38   Ibid., p. 166

39   Wilfred Cantwell Smith, *Islam in Modern History* (Princeton and London, 1957), p. 241

40   Ibid., pp. 90, 198

41   Ibid., pp. 90, 198, 201–02

42   English, *Terrorism*, p. 51

43   Abdulaziz A. Sachedina, 'Activist Shi'ism in Iran, Iraq and Lebanon', in Martin E. Marty and R. Scott Appleby, eds, *Fundamentalisms Observed* (Chicago and London, 1991), p. 456

44   Alastair Crooke, *Resistance: The Essence of the Islamist Revolution* (London, 2009), p. 173

45   Martin Kramer, 'Hizbollah: The Calculus of Jihad', in Martin E. Marty and R. Scott Appleby, eds, *Fundamentalisms and the State* (Chicago and London, 1993), pp. 540–41

46   Sheikh Muhammad Fadl Allah, *Al-Islam wa Muntiq al Quwwa* (Beirut, 1976); trans. Crooke, *Resistance*, p. 173

47   Kramer, 'Hizbollah', p. 542

48   Sachedina, 'Activist Shi'ism', p. 448

49   Interview with Fadl Allah, *Kayhan*, 14 November 1985; Kramer, 'Hizbollah', p. 551

50   Speech by Fadl Allah, *Al-Nahar*, 14 May 1985; Kramer, 'Hizbollah', p. 550

51   Kramer, 'Hizbollah', pp. 548–49; Ariel Meroni, 'The Readiness to Kill or Die: Suicide Terrorism in the Middle East', in Walter Reich, ed., *The Origins of Terrorism* (Cambridge, UK, 1990), pp. 204–05

52   Crooke, *Resistance*, pp. 175–76

53   Interview with Fadl Allah, *Al-Shira*, 18 March 1985; Kramer, 'Hizbollah', pp. 552–53

54   Interview with Fadl Allah, *La Repubblica*, Rome, 28 August 1989; Kramer, 'Hizbollah', p. 552

55   Crooke, *Resistance*, pp. 175–82

56   Ibid., p. 182

57   Ibid., pp. 183–87

58   Robert Pape, *Dying to Win: The Strategic Logic of Suicide Terrorism* (New York, 2005), pp. xiii, 22

59   Ehud Sprinzak, *The Ascendance of Israel's Far Right* (Oxford and New York, 1991), p. 97; in the event, only two of the targeted mayors were wounded

60   Ibid., pp. 94–95

61   Ibid., p. 96; Aviezar Ravitsky, *Messianism, Zionism and Jewish Religious Radicalism*, trans. Michael Swirsky and Jonathan Chipman (Chicago and London, 1993), pp. 133–34

62   Ibid., pp. 97–98

63   Gideon Aran, 'Jewish Zionist Fundamentalism', in Marty and Appleby,
      Fundamentalisms Observed, pp. 267–68

64   Mekhilta on Exodus 20: 13; M. Pirke Aboth 6: 6; B. Horayot 13a; B.
      Sanhedrin 4: 5 in C. G. Montefiore and H. Loewe, eds, *A Rabbinic
      Anthology* (New York, 1974)

65   Sprinzak, *Ascendance of Israel's Far Right*, p. 121

66   Ibid., p. 220

67   Amartya Sen, *Identity and Violence: The Illusion of Destiny* (London and
      New York, 2006)

68   Raphael Mergui and Philippe Simonnot, *Israel's Ayatollahs: Meir Kahane
      and the Far Right in Israel* (London, 1987), p. 45

69   Ibid.

70   Tom Segev, *The Seventh Million: The Israelis and the Holocaust*, trans.
      Haim Watzman (New York, 1991), pp. 515–17

71   Sprinzak, *Ascendance of Israel's Far Right*, p. 221

72   Ehud Sprinzak, 'Three Models of Religious Violence: The Case of
      Jewish Fundamentalism in Israel', in Marty and Appleby, *Fundamentalisms
      and the State*, p. 479

73   Ibid., p. 480

74   Ellen Posman, 'History, Humiliation, and Religious Violence', in
      Andrew R. Murphy, ed., *The Blackwell Companion to Religion and Violence*
      (Chichester, UK, 2011), pp. 336–37, 339

75   Sudhir Kakar, *The Colours of Violence: Cultural Identities, Religion and
      Conflict* (Chicago and London, 1996), p. 15

76   Daniel Gold, 'Organized Hinduisms: From Vedic Truth to Hindu
      Nation', in Marty and Appleby, eds, *Fundamentalisms Observed*, pp. 532,
      572–73

77   Kakar, *Colours of Violence*, pp. 48–51

78   Paul R. Brass, *Communal Riots in Post-Independence India* (Seattle, 2003),
      pp. 66–67

79   Kakar, *Colours of Violence*, pp. 154–57

80   Ibid., p. 157

81   Ibid., p. 158

82   David Cook, *Understanding Jihad* (Berkeley, Los Angeles and London,
      2005), p. 114

83   Beverley Milton-Edwards, *Islamic Politics in Palestine* (London and New
      York, 1996), pp. 73–116

84   Ibid., p. 118

85   Cook, *Understanding Jihad*, p. 114

86   Heilman, 'Guides of the Faithful: Contemporary Religious Zionist Rabbis', in R. Scott Appleby, ed., *Spokesmen for the Despised: Fundamentalist Leaders in the Middle East* (Chicago, 1997), pp. 352–53

87   Ibid., p. 354

88   G. Robinson, *Building a Palestinian State: The Incomplete Revolution* (Bloomington, Ind., 1997); Jeroen Gunning, 'Rethinking Religion and Violence in the Middle East', in Murphy, ed., *Blackwell Companion to Religion and Violence*, p. 519

89   Gunning, 'Rethinking Religion and Violence', pp. 518–19

90   Milton-Edwards, *Islamic Politics*, p. 148

91   Anne Marie Oliver and Paul F. Steinberg, *The Road to Martyrs' Square: A Journey to the World of the Suicide Bomber* (Oxford, 2005), p. 71

92   Cook, *Understanding Jihad*, p. 116

93   *The Covenant of the Islamic Resistance Movement*, Article 1 (Jerusalem, 1988); John L. Esposito, *Unholy War: Terror in the Name of Islam* (Oxford, 2002), p. 96

94   Cook, *Understanding Jihad*, p. 116

95   *Covenant*, Article 1; Esposito, *Unholy War*, p. 96

96   Talal Asad, *On Suicide Bombing: The Wellek Lectures* (New York, 2007), pp. 46–47

97   Dr Abdul Aziz Reutizi in Anthony Shehad, *Legacy of the Prophet: Despots, Democrats and the New Politics of Islam* (Boulder, Colo., 2001), p. 124

98   Esposito, *Unholy War*, pp. 97–98

99   Bernard Lewis, *The Crisis of Islam: Holy War and Unholy Terror* (New York, 2003); Bruce Hoffman, *Inside Terrorism* (New York, 2006)

100 Gunning, 'Rethinking Religion and Violence', p. 516

101 Asad, *Suicide Bombing*, p. 50

102 Pape, *Dying to Win*, p. 130; these figures differ slightly from those quoted earlier from another survey but both arrive at the same general conclusion

103 Robert Pape, 'Dying to Kill Us', *New York Times*, 22 September 2003

104 May Jayyusi, 'Subjectivity and Public Witness: An Analysis of Islamic Militance in Palestine', unpublished paper (2004), quoted in Asad, *Suicide Bombing*

105 Gunning, 'Rethinking Religion and Violence', pp. 518–19

106 Oliver and Steinberg, *Road to Martyrs' Square*, p. 120

107 Ibid., pp. 101–02; Gunning, 'Rethinking Religion and Violence', pp. 518–19

108 Oliver and Steinberg, *Road to Martyrs' Square*, p. 31

109 Roxanne Euben, 'Killing (for) Politics: Jihad, Martyrdom, Political Action', *Political Theory*, 30, 1 (2002)

110 Ibid., p. 49

111 Judges 16: 23–31

112 John Milton, *Samson Agonistes* (1671), lines 1710–11

113 Ibid., lines 1721–24

114 Ibid., lines 1754–55

115 Asad, *Suicide Bombing*, pp. 74–75

116 Ibid., p. 63

117 Bourke, 'Barbarisation vs. Civilisation', p. 21

118 Jacqueline Rose, 'Deadly Embrace', *London Review of Books*, 26, 21 (4 November 2004)

13. Global Jihad

1   Jason Burke, *Al-Qaeda* (London, 2003), pp. 72–75; Thomas Hegghammer, *Jihad in Saudi Arabia: Violence and Pan-Islamism since 1979* (Cambridge, UK, 2010), pp. 7–8, 40–42; Gilles Kepel, *Jihad: The Trail of Political Islam*, trans. Anthony F. Roberts, 4th ed. (London, 2009), pp. 144–47; Lawrence Wright, *The Looming Tower: Al-Qaeda's Road to 9/11* (New York, 2006), pp. 95–101; David Cook, *Understanding Jihad* (Berkeley, Los Angeles and London, 2005), pp. 128–31

2   Abdullah Azzam, 'The Last Will of Abdullah Yusuf Azzam, Who Is Poor unto His Lord', dictated 20 April 1986; trans. Cook, *Understanding Jihad*, p. 130

3   Burke, *Al-Qaeda*, p. 75

4   Andrew Preston, *Sword of the Spirit, Shield of Faith: Religion in American War and Diplomacy* (New York and Toronto, 2012), p. 585

5   Kepel, *Jihad*, pp. 137–40, 147–49; Burke, *Al-Qaeda*, pp. 58–62; Hegghammer, *Jihad in Saudi Arabia*, pp. 58–60

6   Abdullah Azzam, 'Martyrs: The Building Blocks of Nations'; trans. Cook, *Understanding Jihad*, p. 129

7   Ibid.

8   Ibid.

9   Azzam, 'The Last Will of Abdullah Yusuf Azzam'; trans. Cook, *Understanding Jihad*, p. 130

10   Abdullah Yusuf Azzam, *Join the Caravan* (Birmingham, UK, n.d.)

11   Wright, *Looming Tower*, p. 96

12   Ibid., p. 130

13   Hegghammer, *Jihad in Saudi Arabia*, pp. 8–37, 229–33

14   Natana J. DeLong-Bas, *Wahhabi Islam: From Revival and Reform to Global Jihad* (Cairo, 2005), pp. 35, 194–96, 203–11, 221–24

15   Hamid Algar, *Wahhabism: A Critical Essay* (Oneonta, NY, 2002)

16   DeLong-Bas, *Wahhabi Islam*, pp. 247–56; Cook, *Understanding Jihad*, p. 74

17   Kepel, *Jihad*, pp. 57–59, 69–86; Burke, *Al-Qaeda*, pp. 56–60; John Esposito, *Unholy War: Terror in the Name of Islam* (Oxford, 2002), pp. 106–10

18   Kepel, *Jihad*, p. 71

19   Ibid., p. 70

20   Hegghammer, *Jihad in Saudi Arabia*, pp. 19–24

21   Ibid., pp. 60–64

22   *Al-Quds al-Arabi*, 202 (March 2005); Hegghammer *Jihad in Saudi Arabia*, p. 61

23   *Al-Quds al-Arabi*

24   Hegghammer, interview, *Jihad in Saudi Arabia*, p. 61

25   Ibid., pp. 61–62

26   Ibid. p. 64

27   Nasir al-Basri, *Al-Quds al-Arabi*, in ibid.

28   Michael A. Sells, *The Bridge Betrayed: Religion and Genocide in Bosnia* (Berkeley, Los Angeles and London, 1996), p. 154

29   Ibid., p. 9

30   Ibid., pp. 29–52

31   Ibid., pp. 1–3

32   Ibid., p. 72–79, 117

33   Chris Hedges, *War is a Force That Gives Us Meaning* (New York, 2003), p. 9

34   *New York Times*, 18 October 1995; Sells, *Bridge Betrayed*, p. 10

35   S. Burg, 'The International Community and the Yugoslav Crisis', in Milton Eshman and Shibley Telham, eds., *International Organizations and Ethnic Conflict* (Ithaca, NY, 1994); David Rieff, *Slaughterhouse: Bosnia and the Failure of the West* (New York, 1993)

36   Thomas L. Friedman, 'Allies', *New York Times*, 7 June 1995

37   Cook, *Understanding Jihad*, pp. 119–21

38   Mahmoun Fandy, *Saudi Arabia and the Politics of Dissent* (New York, 1999), p. 183

39   Kepel, *Jihad*, pp. 223–26

40 Cook, *Understanding Jihad*, pp. 135–36; Marc Sageman, *Leaderless Jihad: Terror Networks in the Twenty-First Century* (Philadelphia, 2008), pp. 44–46; Burke, *Al-Qaeda*, pp. 118–35

41 Hegghammer, *Jihad in Saudi Arabia*, pp. 229–30

42 Burke, *Al-Qaeda*, pp. 7–8

43 Esposito, *Unholy War*, p. 14

44 Ibid., pp. 6, 8

45 Kepel, *Jihad*, pp. 13–14

46 Burke, *Al-Qaeda*, pp. 161–64; DeLong-Bas, *Wahhabi Islam*, pp. 276–77

47 Esposito, *Unholy War*, pp. 21–22; Burke, *Al-Qaeda*, pp. 175–76

48 Hegghammer, *Jihad in Saudi Arabia*, pp. 102–03

49 Osama bin Laden, 'Hunting the Enemy'; Esposito, *Unholy War*, p. 24

50 Burke, *Al-Qaeda*, p. 163

51 Hegghammer, *Jihad in Saudi Arabia*, pp. 133–41

52 Ibid., p. 133

53 Ibid., p. 134

54 Matthew Purdy and Lowell Bergman, 'Where the Trail Led: Between Evidence and Suspicion; Unclear Danger: Inside the Lackawanna Terror Case', *New York Times*, 12 October 2003

55 Cook, *Understanding Jihad*, p. 150; Sageman, *Leaderless Jihad*, p. 81

56 Cook, *Understanding Jihad*, pp. 136–41

57 Abu Daud, *Sunan* (Beirut, 1988), 3, p. 108, no. 4297; trans. Cook, *Understanding Jihad*, p. 137

58 Quran 2: 249; Burke, *Al-Qaeda*, pp. 24–25

59 Quran 2: 194; Communiqué from Qaidat al-Jihad, 24 April 2002; Cook, *Understanding Jihad*, p. 178

60 Sageman, *Leaderless Jihad*, pp. 81–82

61 Marc Sageman, *Understanding Terror Networks* (Philadelphia, 2004), pp. 103–08

62 Sageman, *Leaderless Jihad*, pp. 59–60

63 Ibid., p. 28

64 Ibid., p. 57

65 Timothy McDermott, *Perfect Soldiers. The 9/11 Hijackers: Who They Were, Why They Did It* (New York, 2005), p. 65

66 Fraser Egerton, *Jihad in the West: The Rise of Militant Salafism* (Cambridge, UK, 2011), pp. 155–56

67 Sageman, *Understanding Terror Networks*, p. 105

68 Antony Giddens, *The Consequences of Modernity* (Cambridge, UK, 1991), p. 53

69   Osama bin Laden, 'Hunting the Enemy', in Esposito, *Unholy War*, p. 23

70   Andrew Sullivan, 'This *Is* a Religious War', *New York Times Magazine*, 7 October 2001

71   William T. Cavanaugh, *The Myth of Religious Violence* (Oxford, 2009), p. 204

72   Emanuel Sivan, *Arab Historiography of the Crusades* (Tel Aviv, 1973)

73   Hegghammer, *Jihad in Saudi Arabia*, pp. 104–05

74   The translated text is found in Bruce Lincoln, *Holy Terrors: Thinking about Religion after September 11*, 2nd ed. (Chicago, 2006), Appendix A, 'Final Instructions to the Hijackers of September, 11, Found in the Luggage of Muhammad Atta and Two Other Copies'. Two other copies were found: one in the car used by one of the hijackers before he boarded American Airlines Flight 77 in Washington; the other at the crash site of United Airlines Flight 93 in Pennsylvania

75   For example, 'Final Instructions', para. 10, in Lincoln, *Holy Terrors*, p. 98; para. 24, p. 100; para. 30, p. 101

76   Ibid., para 1; Lincoln, *Holy Terrors*, p. 97

77   Trans. Cook, *Understanding Jihad*, Appendix 6, p. 196; Lincoln, p. 97

78   Cook, *Understanding Jihad*, para. 14; Lincoln, *Holy Terrors*, p. 98

79   Cook, *Understanding Jihad*, para. 16

80   Ibid., Lincoln, *Holy Terrors*, p. 200

81   Ibid.

82   Ibid., p. 201

83   Cook, *Understanding Jihad*, p. 234, note 37

84   Quran 3: 173–74; trans. M. A. S. Abdel Haleem (Oxford, 2004)

85   Cook, *Understanding Jihad*, Appendix 6, p. 198

86   Ibid., p. 201

87   Louis Atiyat Allah, 'Moments Before the Crash, By the Lord of the 19' (22 January 2003), ibid., Appendix 7, p. 203

88   Ibid., p. 207

89   Ibid.

90   Ibid.

91   Osama bin Laden, videotaped address, 7 October 2001, Appendix C in Lincoln, *Holy Terrors*, p. 106, para. 1

92   Hamid Mir, 'Osama claims he has nukes. If US uses N. Arms it will get the same response', *Dawn: The Internet Edition*, 10 November 2001

93   Ibid., paras 3, 6, 8, 9, 11, in Lincoln, *Holy Terrors*, pp. 106–07

94   'George W. Bush, Address to the Nation, October 7th, 2001', Appendix B, in ibid.

95   Remarks by the President at the Islamic Centre of Washington DC,
      17 September 2001, http://usinfo.state.gov/islam/50917016.htm

96   'George W. Bush, Address to the Nation', p. 104

97   Paul Rogers, 'The Global War on Terror and its Impact on the Conduct
      of War', in George Kassimeris, *The Barbarisation of Warfare* (London,
      2006), p. 188

98   Cook, *Understanding Jihad*, p. 157; Cook comments: 'Sadly, in the light
      of the revelations at the Abu Ghraib prison in the spring of 2004, this
      description is not as implausible as it should have been.'

99   Anthony Dworkin, 'The Laws of War in the Age of Asymmetric
      Conflict', in Kassimeris, *Barbarisation of Warfare*, pp. 220, 233

100   Joanna Bourke, 'Barbarisation vs. Civilisation in Time of War', in ibid.,
      p. 37

101   Dworkin, 'Laws of War', p. 220

102   Rogers, 'Global War on Terror', p. 192

103   The *Guardian*, Datablog, 12 April 2013; the United Nations began to
      report statistics of civilian deaths in 2007

104   Sageman, *Leaderless Jihad*, pp. 136–37

105   White House press release, 'President Discusses the Future of Iraq',
      26 February 2003

106   White House press release, 'President Bush Saluting Veterans at White
      House Ceremony', 11 November 2002

107   Timothy H. Parsons, *The Rule of Empires: Those Who Built Them, Those
      Who Endured Them, and Why They Always Fail* (Oxford, 2010), pp. 423–50

108   Bruce Lincoln, *Religion, Empire, and Torture: The Case of Achaemenian Persia,
      with a Postscript on Abu Ghraib* (Chicago and London, 2007), pp. 97–99

109   Ibid., pp. 97–98

110   Luke 4: 18–19

111   Lincoln, *Religion, Empire and Torture*, pp. 101–07

112   Ibid., pp. 102–03

113   Susan Sontag, 'What Have We Done?' *Guardian*, 24 May 2005

114   Lincoln, *Religion, Empire and Torture*, pp. 101–02

115   Parsons, *The Rule of Empires*, pp. 423–34

116   Bashir, Friday Prayers, Umm al-Oura, Baghdad, 11 June 2004 in
      Edward Coy, 'Iraqis Put Contempt for Troops on Display', *Washington
      Post*, 12 June 2004; Kassimeris, 'Barbarisation of Warfare', p. 16

117   Rogers, 'Global War on Terror', pp. 193–94

118   Dworkin, 'Laws of War', p. 253

119   Sageman, *Leaderless Jihad*, pp. 139–42

120 Ibid., pp. 31–32

121 Michael Bonner, *Jihad in Islamic History* (Princeton and Oxford, 2006), p. 164

122 Sageman, *Leaderless Jihad*, pp. 156–57

123 Ibid., p. 159

124 John L. Esposito and Dahlia Mogahed, *Who Speaks for Islam? What a Billion Muslims Really Think; Based on Gallup's World Poll – the largest study of its kind* (New York, 2007), pp. 69–70

125 Cited in Joos R. Hiltermann, *A Poisonous Affair: America, Iraq and the Gassing of Halabja* (Cambridge, UK, 2007), p. 243

126 Naureen Shah, 'Time for the Truth about "targeted killings"', *Guardian*, 22 October 2013

127 Rafiq ur Rehman, 'Please tell me, Mr President, why a US drone assassinated my mother'; theguardian.com, 25 October 2013

Afterword

1 Quran 29: 46, to cite just one example

2 Quran 22: 40; trans. M. A. S. Abdel Haleem (Oxford, 2004)

3 It is also due to the prevalence of Wahhabi ideas that have been promoted throughout the Muslim world with the tacit agreement of the United States

4 John Fowles, *The Magus*, revised edition (London, 1987), p. 413

Postscript

1 Recent studies of IS include: John Gray, 'ISIS: An Apocalyptic Cult Carving a Place in the Modern World', *Guardian, Commentisfree.com*, 26 August 2014; Caner K. Dagli, 'The Phony Islam of IS', *Atlantic*, 27 February 2015; Mehdi Hasan, 'How Islamic is Islamic State?' *New Statesman*, 10 March 2015.

2 Mehdi Hasan, 'What the Jihadists Who Bought "Islam for Dummies" on Amazon Tell Us About Radicalisation', *The Huffington Post*, 20 October 2014.

3 Hasan, 'How Islamic is Islamic State?'

4 Hannah Furness, 'BBC Radio 1 Breached Ofcom Rules After ISIS

Jihadist Compared "Quite Fun" murder with Playing "Call of Duty"',
Daily Telegraph, 10 November 2014.

5   Channel 4 News, 17 March, 2015.
6   John L. Esposito and Dalia Mogahed, *Who Speaks for Islam? What A
Billion Muslims Really Think* (New York, 2007), p. 80

BIBLIOGRAPHY

ABDEL HALEEM, M. A. S., trans., *The Qur'an: A New Translation* (Oxford and New York, 2004)

ABELARD, Peter, *A Dialogue of a Philosopher with a Jew and a Christian,* trans. P. J. Payer (Toronto, 1979)

ABULAFIA, David, *Frederick II: A Medieval Emperor* (New York and Oxford, 1992)

ADAMS, Charles, 'Mawdudi and the Islamic State', in John L. Esposito, ed., *Voices of Resurgent Islam* (New York and Oxford, 1983)

ADAMS, Dickenson W., ed., *Jefferson's Extracts from the Gospels* (Princeton, NJ, 1983

ADAMS, R. M., *Heartlands of Cities: Surveys on Ancient Settlements and Land Use on the Central Floodplains of the Euphrates* (Chicago, 1981)

AGEMBEN, Giorgio, *State of Exception,* trans. Kevin Attell (Chicago and London, 2005)

  The Kingdom and the Glory: For a Theological Genealogy of Economy and Government, trans. Lorenzo Chiesa (with Matteo Mandarini) (Stanford, 2011)

AHLSTROM, Gosta W., *The History of Ancient Palestine* (Minneapolis, 1993)

AHMAD, Kharshid and Zafar USHAQ, *Islamic Perspectives* (Leicester, 1979)

AHMAD, MUMTAZ, 'Islamic Fundamentalism in South Asia: The Jamaat-i-Islami and the Tablighi Jamaat', in Martin E. Marty and R. Scott Appleby, eds, *Fundamentalisms Observed* (Chicago and London, 1991)

AHMED, Rafiuddin, 'Redefining Muslim Identity in South Asia: The Transformation of the Jamaat-i-Islami', in Martin E. Marty and R. Scott Appleby, *Accounting for Fundamentalisms: The Dynamic Character of Movements* (Chicago and London, 1994)

AHO, James A., *Religious Mythology and the Art of War: Comparative Religious Symbolisms of Military Violence* (Westport, Conn., 1981)

AKHAVI, Shahrough, *Religion and Politics in Contemporary Iran: Clergy–State Relations in the Pahlavi Period* (Albany, NY, 1980)

'Shariati's Social Thought', in Nikki R. Keddie, ed., *Religion and Politics in Iran: Shiism from Quietism to Revolution* (New Haven, Conn., and London, 1983)

AL-AZMEH, Aziz, *Muslim Kingship: Power and the Sacred in Muslim, Christian and Pagan Politics* (London and New York, 1997)

Islams and Modernities, 3rd ed. (London and New York, 2009)

ALGAR, Hamid, *Religion and State in Iran, 1785–1906* (Berkeley, 1984)

Wahhabism: A Critical Essay (Oneonta, NY, 2002)

'The Oppositional Role of the Ulema in Twentieth-Century Iran', in Nikki R. Keddie, ed., *Scholars, Saints and Sufis: Muslim Religious Institutions in the Middle East since 1500* (Berkeley, Los Angeles and London, 1972)

ALLAH, Louis Atiyat, 'Moments Before the Crash, By the Lord of the 19', in David Cook, *Understanding Jihad* (Berkeley, Los Angeles and London, 2005)

ALLEN, J. W., *A History of Political Thought in the Sixteenth Century* (London, 1928)

ALLEN, William, *Apologie of the English College* (Douai, 1581)

ALTER, Robert and Frank KERMODE, eds, *A Literary Guide to the Bible* (London, 1987)

ANDERSON, Benedict, *Imagined Communities: Reflections on the Origin and Spread of Nationalism* (London and New York, 2003)

ANDERSON, Perry, *Lineages of the Absolutist State* (London, 1974)

Passages from Antiquity to Feudalism (London, 1974)

ANDRAE, Tor, *Muhammad: The Man and His Faith,* trans. Theophil Menzel (London, 1936)

ANDRESKI, Stanislav, *Military Organization and Society* (Berkeley, 1968)

ANGEL, J. L., 'Paleoecology, Paleogeography and Health', in S. Polgar, ed., *Population, Ecology and Social Evolution* (The Hague, 1975)

ANNESLEY, George, *The Rise of Modern Egypt: A Century and a Half of Egyptian History* (Durham, UK, 1997)

ANONYMOUS, 'Final Instructions to the Hijackers of September 11', in Bruce Lincoln, *Holy Terrors: Thinking about Religion after September 11,* 2nd ed. (Chicago and London, 2003, 2006)

ANONYMOUS, ed., *Fast Day Sermons or The Pulpit on the State of the Country* (Charleston, SC, 2009 ed.)

APPLEBY, R. Scott, ed., *Spokesmen of the Despised: Fundamentalist Leaders of the Middle East* (Chicago, 1997)

The Ambivalence of the Sacred: Religion, Violence and Reconciliation (Lenham, Md., 2000)

ARAN, Gideon, 'The Roots of Gush Emunim,' *Studies in Contemporary Jewry*, 2 (1986)

'Jewish Zionist Fundamentalism', in Martin E. Marty and R. Scott Appleby, eds, *Fundamentalisms Observed* (Chicago and London, 1991)

'The Father, the Son and the Holy Land: The Spiritual Authorities of Jewish-Zionist Fundamentalism in Israel', in R. Scott Appleby, ed., *Spokesmen of the Despised: Fundamentalist Leaders of the Middle East* (Chicago, 1997)

ARDAGH, Sir John, Speech in *The Proceedings of the Hague Peace Conference* (London, 1920)

ARENDT, Hannah, *On Revolution* (London, 1963)

On Violence (San Diego, 1970)

The Origins of Totalitarianism (San Diego, 1979)

ARISTOTLE, *The Basic Works of Aristotle,* ed. Richard McKeon (New York, 1941)

ASAD, Muhammad, trans., *The Message of the Qur'an* (Gibraltar, 1980)

ASAD, Talal, *Genealogies of Religion, Discipline and Reasons of Power in Christianity and Islam* (Baltimore and London, 1993)

Formations of the Secular: Christianity, Islam, Modernity (Stanford, 2003)

On Suicide Bombing: The Wellek Lectures (New York, 2007)

ATHANASIUS, 'Life of Antony', in R. C. Gregg, trans., *The Life of Antony and the Letter to Marcellinus* (New York, 1980)

AUGUSTINE, Aurelius, *On the Free Choice of the Will,* trans. Thomas Williams (Indianapolis, 1993)

AVALOS, Hector, *Fighting Words: The Origins of Religious Violence* (Amhurst, NY, 2005)

AZZAM, Abdullah Yusuf, 'The Last Will of Abdullah Yusuf Azzam, Who Is Poor Unto His Lord' (Birmingham, UK, n.d.)

Join the Caravan (Birmingham, UK, n.d.)

The Defence of Muslim Lands (Birmingham, UK, n.d.)

BACHRACH, David S., *Religion and the Conduct of War, c.300–1215* (Woodbridge, UK, 2003)

BAER, Yitzhak, *A History of the Jews in Christian Spain,* 2 vols (Philadelphia, 1966)

BAINTON, Ronald H., *Christian Attitudes toward War and Peace* (Nashville and New York, 1960)

BAIRD, Robert D., ed., *Religion in Modern India* (Delhi, 1981)

BAMMEL, F., and C. F. D. MOULE, eds, *Jesus and the Politics of His Day* (Cambridge, UK, 1981)

BAMYEH, Mohammed A., *The Social Origins of Islam: Mind, Economy, Discourse* (Minneapolis, 1999)

BARBER, Malcolm, *The New Knighthood: A History of the Order of the Templars* (Cambridge, 1995)

BARBER, Richard, *The Knight and Chivalry* (New York, 1970)

BARING, Evelyn, Lord Cromer, *Modern Egypt*, 2 vols (New York, 1908)

BARKER, Margaret, *The Gate of Heaven: The History and Symbolism of the Temple in Jerusalem* (London, 1991)

BARKUN, Michael, *Religion and the Racist Right: The Origins of the Christian Identity Movement* (Chapel Hill, 1996)

BARNIE, John, *War in Medieval English Society: Social Values and the Hundred Years War* (Ithaca, NY, 1974)

BASHEAR, S., 'Apocalyptic and Other Materials on Early Muslim-Byzantine Wars', *Journal of the Royal Asiatic Society*, Series 3, 1 (1991)

BAUMAN, Zygmunt, *Modernity and the Holocaust* (Cambridge, 1992)

BEBBINGTON, D. W., *Evangelicalism in Modern Britain: A History from the 1730s to the 1980s* (London, 1989)

BEECHER, Henry W., *Patriotic Addresses* (New York, 1887)

BEEMAN, Richard, Stephen BOTEIN and Edward E. CARTER III, eds, *Beyond Confederation: Origins of the Constitution in American Identity* (Chapel Hill, 1987)

BEEMAN, William, 'Images of the Great Satan: Representations of the United States in the Iranian Revolution', in Nikki R. Keddie, ed., *Religion and Politics in Iran: Shiism from Quietism to Revolution* (New Haven, Conn., and London, 1983)

BEHR, John, *Irenaeus of Lyons: Identifying Christianity* (Oxford, 2013)

BEINART, Haim, *Conversos on Trial: The Inquisition in Ciudad Real* (Jerusalem, 1981)

BELL, Catherine, *Ritual Theory, Ritual Practice* (New York, 1992)

BELL, H., I. V. MARTIN, E. G. TURNER and D. VAN BURCHEM, *The Abinnaeus Archive* (Oxford, 1962)

BEN DOV, Meir, *The Western Wall* (Jerusalem, 1983)

BENDIX, Reinhard, *Kings or People: Power and the Mandate to Rule* (Berkeley, 1977)

BENSON, Larry, ed. and trans., *King Arthur's Death: The Middle English Stanzaic Morte d'Arthur and the Alliterative Morte d'Arthur* (Kalamazoo, Mich., 1994)

BENVENISTI, Meron, *Jerusalem: The Torn City* (Jerusalem, 1975)

BERCHANT, Heinz, 'The Date of the Buddha Reconsidered', *Indologia Taurinensen,* 10, n.d.

BERGER, Michael S., 'Taming the Beast: Rabbinic Pacification of Second-Century Jewish Nationalism', in James K. Wellman, *Belief and Bloodshed: Religion and Violence across Time and Tradition* (Lanham, Md., 2007)

BERGER, Peter, *The Sacred Canopy: Elements of Sociological Theory* (New York, 1967)

BERMAN, Joshua, *Biblical Revolutions: The Transformation of Social and Political Thought in the Ancient Near East* (New York and Oxford, 2008)

BERMAN, Paul, *Terror and Liberalism* (New York, 2003)

BERNARD of Clairvaux, *In Praise of the New Knighthood: A Treatise on the Knights Templar and the Holy Places of Jerusalem,* trans. M. Conrad Greenia; introduction by Malcolm Barber (Collegeville, Minn., 2008)

BICKERMAN, Elias J., *From Ezra to the Last of the Maccabees* (New York, 1962)

BLACK, Jeremy, 'Warfare, Crisis and Absolutism', in Euan Cameron, ed., *Early Modern Europe: An Oxford History* (Oxford, 1999)

BLAKE, E. O., 'The Formation of the Crusade Idea', *Journal of Ecclesiastical History,* 21, 1 (1970)

BLANNING, T. C., 'Epilogue: The Old Order Transformed', in Euan Cameron, ed., *Early Modern Europe: An Oxford History* (Oxford, 1999)

BLOCH, Marc, *Feudal Society,* trans. L. A. Manyon (London, 1961)

BLOCH, Ruth H., *Visionary Republic: Millennial Themes in American Thought, 1756–1800* (Cambridge, UK, 1985)

BLOCKMANS, Wim, *Emperor Charles V, 1500–1558* (London and New York, 2002)

BLOXHAM, David, *The Great Game of Genocide: Imperialism, Nationalism and the Destruction of the Ottoman Armenians* (Oxford, 2007)

BOAK, A. E. and H. C. HARVEY, *The Archive of Aurelius Isidore* (Ann Arbor, Mich., 1960)

BODDE, Derk, *Festivals in Classical China and Other Annual Observances during the Han Dynasty, 206 BCE to AD 220* (Princeton, NJ, 1975)

    'Feudalism in China', in Rushton Coulborn, ed., *Feudalism in History* (Hamden, Conn., 1965)

BONNER, Michael, *Aristocratic Violence and the Holy War: Studies in Jihad and the Arab-Byzantine Frontier* (New Haven, Conn., 1996)

    Jihad in Islamic History (Princeton and Oxford, 2006)

BONNEY, Richard, *Jihad: From Qur'an to Bin Laden* (New York, 2004)

BORG, Marcus, *Jesus: Uncovering the Life, Teachings, and Relevance of a Religious Revolutionary* (New York, 2006)

BOROWITZ, Albert, *Terrorism for Self-Glorification: The Herostratos Syndrome* (Kent, Ohio, 2005)

BORUJERDI, Mehrzad, *Iranian Intellectuals and the West: The Tormented Triumph of Nativism* (Syracuse, NY, 1996)

BOSSY, John, *Christianity in the West, 1400–1700* (Oxford, 1985)

   'Unrethinking the Wars of Religion', in Thomas Kselman, ed., *Belief in History: Innovative Approaches to European and American Religion* (Notre Dame, Ind., 1991)

BOURKE, Joanna, *An Intimate History of Killing: Face to Face Killing in Twentieth-Century Warfare* (New York, 1999)

   'Barbarization vs Civilization in Time of War', in George Kassimeris, ed., *The Barbarization of Warfare* (London, 2006)

BOUSTAN, Ra'anau S., Alex P. JASSEN and Calvin J. ROETZAL, eds, *Violence, Scripture and Textual Practice in Early Judaism and Christianity* (Leiden, 2010)

BOWERSTOCK, G. W., *Hellenism in Late Antiquity* (Ann Arbor, Mich., 1990)

BOWKER, John, *The Religious Imagination and the Sense of God* (Oxford, 1978)

BOYCE, Mary, *Zoroastrians: Their Religious Beliefs and Practices,* 2nd ed. (London and New York, 2001)

   'Priests, Cattle and Men', *Bulletin of the School of Oriental and African Studies,* 1998

BOYER, Paul, *When Time Shall Be No More: Prophecy Belief in Modern American Culture* (Cambridge, Mass., 1992)

BRACE, F. F. 'Render to Caesar', in F. Bammel and C. F. D. Moule, eds, *Jesus and the Politics of His Day* (Cambridge, UK, 1981)

BRASS, Paul R., *Communal Riots in Post-Independence India* (Seattle, 2003)

BRENNER, Jan N., 'Secularization: Notes toward the Genealogy', in Henk De Vries, ed., *Religion beyond a Concept* (New York, 2008)

BRIGDON, Susan, *London and the Reformation* (Oxford, 1989)

BRIGGS, Robin, 'Embattled Faiths: Religion and Natural Philosophy', in Euan Cameron, ed., *Early Modern Europe: An Oxford History* (Oxford, 1999)

BRISCH, Nicole, ed., *Religion and Power: Divine Kingship in the Ancient World and Beyond* (Chicago, 2008)

BRODIE, Bernard and Fawn BRODIE, *From Crossbow to H-Bomb* (Bloomington, Ind., 1972)

BRONOWSKI, Jacob, *The Ascent of Man* (Boston, 1975)

BROOKS, E. W., trans., *The Sixth Book of the Select Letter of Severus, Patriarch of Antioch* (London, 1903)

BROWN, John Pairman, 'Techniques of Imperial Control: Background of the Gospel Event', in Normal Gottwald, ed., *The Bible of Liberation: Political and Social Hermeneutics* (Maryknoll, NY, 1985)

BROWN, Judith M., ed., *Mahatma Gandhi: Essential Writings* (London and New York, 2008)

BROWN, Peter, *The World of Late Antiquity, AD 150–750* (London, 1971, 1989)

The Making of Late Antiquity (Cambridge, Mass., and London, 1973)

The Cult of the Saints: Its Rise and Function in Latin Christianity (Chicago and London, 1981)

Society and the Holy in Late Antiquity (Berkeley, Los Angeles and London, 1982)

The Body and Society: Men, Women and Sexual Renunciation in Early Christianity (London and Boston, 1988)

Power and Persuasion in Late Antiquity: Towards a Christian Empire (Madison, Wis., and London, 1992)

Authority and the Sacred: Aspects of the Christianization of the Roman World (Cambridge, 1995)

The Rise of Western Christendom: Triumph and Diversity, AD 200–1000 (Oxford and Malden, Mass., 1996)

Poverty and Leadership in the Later Roman Empire (Hanover and London, 2002)

'Religious Dissent in the Later Roman Empire: The Case of North Africa', *History,* 46 (1961)

'Religious Coercion in the Later Roman Empire: The Case of North Africa', *History,* 48 (1961)

'The Rise of the Holy Man in Late Antiquity', *Journal of Roman Studies,* LXI (1971)

BROWN, Richard Maxwell, *Strains of Violence: Historical Studies of American Violence and Vigilantism* (New York, 1975)

BRUMBERG, Daniel, 'Khomeini's Legacy: Islamic Rule and Islamic Social Justice', in R. Scott Appleby, ed., *Spokesmen for the Despised: Fundamentalist Leaders of the Middle East* (Chicago, 1997)

BRUNS, Gerald L., 'Midrash and Allegory: The Beginnings of Scriptural Interpretation', in Robert Alter and Frank Kermode, eds, *A Literary Guide to the Bible* (London, 1987)

BRYANT, Edwin, *The Quest for the Origins of Vedic Culture: The Indo-Aryan Debate* (Oxford and New York, 2001)

BRYCE, T., *The Kingdom of the Hittites* (Oxford, 1998)

BURG, S., 'The International Community and the Yugoslav Crisis', in Milton

Eshman and Shibley Telham, eds., *International Organizations and Ethnic Conflict* (Ithaca, NY, 1995)

BURKE, Jason, *Al-Qaeda* (London, 2003)

BURKE, Victor Lee, *The Clash of Civilizations: War-Making and State Formation in Europe* (Cambridge, UK, 1997)

BURKERT, Walter, *Structure and History in Greek Mythology and Ritual* (Berkeley, Los Angeles and London, 1980)

> *Homo Necans: The Anthropology of Ancient Greek Sacrificial Ritual and Myth*, trans. Walter Bing (Berkeley, 1983)

BURLEIGH, Michael, *Earthly Powers: Religion and Politics in Europe from the Enlightenment to the Great War* (London, New York, Toronto and Sydney, 2005)

BURMAN, Edward, *The Assassins: Holy Killers of Islam* (London, 1987)

BURTON-CHRISTIE, Douglas, *The Word in the Desert: Scripture and the Quest for Holiness in Early Christian Monasticism* (New York and Oxford, 1993)

BUSBY, Keith, trans., *Raoul de Hodence, Le Roman des Eles: The Anonymous Ordre de Cevalerie* (Philadelphia, 1983)

BUSHNELL, Howard, *Building Eras in Religion* (New York, 1981)

BUSSMANN, Klaus and Heinz SCHILLING, eds, *War and Peace in Europe*, 3 vols (Munster, 1998)

BUTLER, Jon, *Awash in a Sea of Faith: Christianizing the American People* (Cambridge, Mass., and London, 1990)

BUTZER, Karl W., *Environment and Archaeology: An Ecological Approach to Prehistory* (Chicago, 1971)

> *Early Hydraulic Civilization in Egypt: A Study in Cultural Ecology* (Chicago, 1976)

CALVIN, John, *The Commentaries of John Calvin on the Old Testament*, 30 vols (1643–48)

CAMERON, Euan, ed., *Early Modern Europe: An Oxford History* (Oxford, 1999)

> 'The Power of the Word: Renaissance and Reformation' in ibid.

CAMPBELL, Joseph, *Historical Atlas of World Mythologies*, 2 vols (New York, 1988)

> (with Bill Moyers) *The Power of Myth* (London and New York, 1988)

CANER, Daniel, *Wandering Begging Monks: Spiritual Authority and the Promotion of Monasticism in Late Antiquity* (Berkeley, Los Angeles and London, 2002)

CANTOR, Norman, *The Sacred Chain: A History of the Jews* (New York, 1994; London, 1995)

CARDINI, Franco, 'The Warrior and the Knight', in James Le Goff, ed., *The Medieval World*, trans. Lydia C. Cochrane (London, 1990)

CARLEN, Claudia, ed., *The Papal Encyclicals, 1740–1981,* 5 vols. (Falls Church, Va., 1981)

CARLYLE, Thomas, ed., *Oliver Cromwell's Letters and Speeches,* 3 vols (New York, 1871)

CARMICHAEL, Calum M., *The Laws of Deuteronomy* (Eugene, Ore., 1974)
The Spirit of Biblical Law (Athens, Ga., 1996)

CARRASCO, David, *City of Sacrifice: The Aztec Empire and the Role of Violence in Civilization* (Boston, 1999)

CARRITHERS, Michael, *The Buddha* (Oxford and New York, 1983)

CARTER, Warren, *Matthew and the Margins: A Socio-Political and Religious Reading* (Sheffield, 2000)
'Construction of Violence and Identities in Matthew's Gospel', in Shelly Matthews and E. Leigh Gibson, eds, *Violence in the New Testament* (New York and London, 2005).

CAVANAUGH, William T., *The Myth of Religious Violence* (Oxford, 2009)
Migrations of the Holy: God, State and the Political Meaning of the Church (Grand Rapids, Mich., 2011)

CHANG, Kwang-chih, *Archaeology of Ancient China* (New Haven, Conn., 1968)
Shang Civilization (New Haven, Conn., 1980)
Art, Myth and Ritual: The Path to Political Authority in Ancient China (Cambridge, Mass., 1985)

CHILDS, John, *Armies and Warfare in Europe, 1648–1789* (Manchester, UK, 1985)

CHING, Julia, *Mysticism and Kingship in China: The Heart of Chinese Wisdom* (Cambridge, UK, 1997)

CHOUEIRI, Youssef M., *Islamic Fundamentalism* (London, 1970)

CHURCHILL, Ward, *A Little Matter of Genocide: Holocaust and Denial in the Americas, 1492 to the Present* (San Francisco, 1997)

CIPOLLA, Carlo M., *Before the Industrial Revolution: European Society and Economy, 1000–1700* (New York, 1976)

CLARK, Peter, *Zoroastrianism: An Introduction to an Ancient Faith* (Brighton, UK, and Portland, Ore., 1998)

CLARKE, I. F., *Voices Prophesying War: Future Wars 1763–3749,* 2nd ed. (Oxford and New York, 1992)

CLEMENTS, R. E., ed., *The World of Ancient Israel: Sociological, Anthropological and Political Perspectives* (Cambridge, UK, 1989)

CLIFFORD, Richard J., *The Cosmic Mountain in Canaan and the Old Testament* (Cambridge, Mass., 1972)

COGAN, Mordechai and Israel EPHAL, eds, *Studies in Assyrian History and Ancient Near Eastern Historiography* (Jerusalem, 1991)

COHEN, Mark Nathan, *The Food Crisis in Prehistory* (New Haven, Conn., 1978)

COHN, Norman, *Warrant for Genocide* (London, 1967)

> *Europe's Inner Demons: The Demonization of Christians in the Middle Ages* (London, 1975)

> *Pursuit of the Millennium: Revolutionary Millenarians and Mystical Anarchists in the Middle Ages* (London, 1984 ed.)

> *Cosmos, Chaos and the World to Come: The Ancient Roots of Apocalyptic Faith* (New Haven, Conn., and London, 1993)

COLBY, Elbridge, 'How to Fight Savage Tribes', *American Journal of International Law,* 21, 2, 1927

COLLINS, Steven, *Selfless Persons: Imagery and Thought in Theravada Buddhism* (Cambridge, UK, 1982)

CONTAMINE, Philippe, *War in the Middle Ages,* trans. Michael Jones (Oxford, 1984)

CONZE, Edward, *Buddhism: Its Essence and Development* (Oxford, 1981)

> *Buddhist Meditation* (London, 1956)

COOK, David, *Understanding Jihad* (Berkeley, Los Angeles and London, 2005)

> 'Jihad and Martyrdom in Islamic History', in Andrew R. Murphy, ed., *The Blackwell Companion to Religion and Violence* (Chichester, UK, 2011)

COOK, Jill, *The Swimming Reindeer* (London, 2010)

COOMARASWAMY, Ananda and Sister NIVEDITA, *Myths of the Hindus and Buddhists* (London, 1967)

COOPER, Thia, 'Liberation Theology and the Spiral of Violence', in Andrew R. Murphy, ed., *The Blackwell Companion to Religion and Violence* (Chichester, UK, 2011)

COOTE, Robert and Keith E. WHITELAM, *The Emergence of Early Israel in Historical Perspective* (Sheffield, 1987)

COTTON, Bruce, *Grant Takes Command* (Boston, 1968)

COULBORN, Rushton, ed., *Feudalism in History* (Hamden, Conn., 1965)

COWDREY, H. E. J., 'The Peace and Truce of God in the Eleventh Century', *Past and Present,* 46 (1970)

> 'Pope Gregory VII's "Crusading" Plans of 1074', in B. Z. Kedar, H. E. Mayer and R. C. Smail, eds, *Outremer* (Jerusalem, 1982)

CRECELIUS, Daniel, 'Nonideological Responses of the Egyptian Ulema to Modernization', in Nikki R. Keddie, ed., *Scholars, Saints and Sufis: Muslim*

Religious Institutions in the Middle East since 1500 (Berkeley, Los Angeles and London, 1972)

CREEL, H. G., *Confucius: The Man and the Myth* (London, 1951)

CRENSHAW, Martha, ed., *Terrorism, Legitimacy and Power: The Consequences of Political Violence* (Middletown, Conn., 1983)

'Reflections on the Effects of Terrorism', in ibid.

CRIBB, Roger, *Nomads and Archaeology* (Cambridge, UK, 1999)

CROOKE, Alastair, *Resistance: The Essence of the Islamist Revolution* (London, 2009)

CROSS, Frank Moore, *Canaanite Myth and Hebrew Epic: Essays in the History of the Religion of Israel* (Cambridge, Mass., and London, 1973)

CROSSAN, John Dominic, *Jesus: A Revolutionary Biography* (New York, 1994)
God and Empire: Jesus against Rome, Then and Now (New York, 2007)

CROUZET, Denis, *Les guerriers de Dieu: La violence en temps des troubles de religion* (Seyssel, 1990)

CRUSEMANN, Frank, *The Torah: Theology and Social History of Old Testament Law,* trans. Allen W. Mahnke (Minneapolis, Minn., 1996)

CURTIS, John, *The Cyrus Cylinder and Ancient Persia: A New Beginning for the Middle East* (London, 2013)

DALLEY, Stephanie, trans. and ed., *Myths from Mesopotamia: Creation, the Flood, Gilgamesh, and Others* (Oxford and New York, 1989)

DANIEL, Norman, *The Arabs and Medieval Europe* (London and Beirut, 1975)
Islam and the West: The Making of an Image, 2nd ed. (Oxford, 1993)

DAVIDSON, Basil, *The African Slave Trade* (Boston, 1961)

DAVIS, Natalie Zemon, 'The Rites of Violence: Religious Riot in Sixteenth-Century France', *Past and Present,* 59 (1973)

DAWKINS, Richard, *The God Delusion* (London, 2007)

DE BARY, Wm. Theodore, *The Trouble with Confucianism* (Cambridge, Mass., and London, 1996)

(with Irene Bloom) eds, *Sources of Chinese Tradition, from Earliest Times to 1600,* 2nd ed. (New York, 1999)

DE BEAUVOIR, Simone, *Memoirs of a Dutiful Daughter* (New York, 1974)

DE STE CROIX, G. E., 'Why Were the Early Christians Persecuted?', in Michael Whitby and Joseph Street, eds, *Martyrdom and Orthodoxy* (New York, 1987)

DE TOCQUVILLE, Alexis, *The Old Regime and the French Revolution,* 2 vols, ed. and trans. François Furet and Françoise Melonio (Chicago, 1988)
Democracy in America, ed. and trans. Harvey Claflin Mansfield and Delba Winthrop (Chicago, 2000)

DE VRIES, Henk, ed., *Religion beyond a Concept* (New York, 2008)

DEARMAN, Andrew, ed., *Studies in the Mesha Inscription and Moab* (Atlanta, NY, 1989)

DELONG-BAS, Natana J., *Wahhabi Islam: From Revival and Reform to Global Jihad* (Cairo, 2005)

DEVER, William G., *What Did the Biblical Writers Know and When Did They Know It? What Archaeology Can Tell Us about the Reality of Ancient Israel* (Grand Rapids, Mich., and Cambridge, UK, 2001)

DIAKONOFF, *Ancient Mesopotamia: Socio-Economic History* (Moscow, 1969)

DIEFENDORT, Barbara, *Beneath the Cross: Catholics and Huguenots in Sixteenth-Century Paris* (New York, 1991)

DONIGER, Wendy, *The Hindus: An Alternative History* (Oxford, 2009)

DONNE, John, *Sermons of John Donne,* ed. George R. Potter and Evelyn M. Simpson (Berkeley, 1959)

DONNER, F., *The Early Islamic Conquests* (Princeton, 1980)
    'The Origins of the Islamic State', *Journal of the American Oriental Society,* 106 (1986)

DORRELL, P., 'The Uniqueness of Jericho', in R. Morrey and P. Parr, eds, *Archaeology in the Levant: Essays for Kathleen Kenyon* (Warminster, UK, 1978)

DOUGLAS, Mary, *Leviticus as Literature* (Oxford and New York, 1999)
    In the Wilderness: The Doctrine of Defilement in the Book of Numbers (Oxford and New York, 2001)

DRAKE, Harold A., *In Praise of Constantine: A Historical Study and New Translation of Eusebius' Tricennial Orations* (London and New York, 1997)
    Constantine and the Bishops: The Politics of Intolerance (Baltimore, 2000)

DRONKE, Peter, *Women Writers of the Middle Ages: A Critical Study of Texts from Perpetua (d. 203) to Marguerite de Parete (d. 1310)* (Cambridge, Mass., 1984)

DUBUISSON, Daniel, *The Western Construction of Religion: Myths, Knowledge, and Ideology,* trans. William Sayers (Baltimore, 2003)

DUBY, Georges, *The Early Growth of the European Economy: Warriors and Peasants from the Seventh to the Twelfth Century,* trans. H. B. Clarke (Ithaca, NY, 1974)
    The Chivalrous Society (London, 1977)
    The Three Orders: Feudal Society Imagined (London, 1980)
    The Knight, the Lady and the Priest (Harmondsworth, UK, 1983)

DUMEZIL, Georges, *The Destiny of the Warrior,* trans. Alf Hiltebeitel (Chicago and London, 1969)

DUMONT, Louis, 'World Renunciation in Indian Religions', *Contributions to Indian Sociology,* 4 (1960)

DUNDAS, Paul, *The Jains,* 2nd ed. (London and New York, 2002)

DUNN, Richard, *The Age of Religious Wars, 1559–1689* (New York, 1970)

DURKHEIM, Emile, *The Elementary Forms of the Religious Life,* trans. Joseph Swain (Glencoe, Ill., 1915)

DUTTON, P. E., *Carolingian Civilization* (Peterborough, Ont., 1993)

DWIGHT, Timothy, *A Valedictory Address to the Young Gentlemen Who Commenced Bachelor of Arts, July 27, 1776* (New Haven, Conn., 1776)

DWORKIN, Anthony, 'The Laws of War in the Age of Asymmetric Conflict', in George Kassimeris, ed., *The Barbarization of Warfare* (London, 2006)

DWYER, Philip G., *Talleyrand* (London, 2002)

EBERHARD, W., *A History of China* (London, 1977)

EDBURY, Peter W., ed., *Crusade and Settlement* (Cardiff, 1985)

EDWARDS, Mark, trans., *Optatus: Against the Donatists* (Liverpool, 1997)

EGERTON, Frazer, *Jihad in the West: The Rise of Militant Salafism* (Cambridge, 2011)

EHRENBERG, M., *Women in Prehistory* (London, 1981)

EHRENREICH, Barbara, *Blood Rites: Origins and History of the Passions of War* (New York, 1997)

EIBL-EIBESFELDT, I., *The Biology of Peace and War: Man, Animals and Aggression* (New York, 1979)

 Human Ethology (New York, 1989)

EIDELBERG, Scholomo, trans. and ed., *The Jews and the Crusaders: The Hebrew Chronicles of the First and Second Crusades* (London, 1977)

EISEN, Robert, *The Peace and Violence of Judaism: From the Bible to Modern Zionism* (Oxford, 2011)

EISENSTADT, S. N., ed., *The Origins and Diversity of Axial Age Civilizations* (Albany, NY, 1986)

EL-GUINDY, Fedwa, 'The Killing of Sadat and After: A Current Assessment of Egypt's Islamist Movement', *Middle East Insight,* 2 (January/February 1982)

ELIADE, Mircea, *The Sacred and the Profane: The Nature of Religion,* trans. Willard R. Trask (San Diego, New York and London, 1957)

 Patterns in Comparative Religion, trans. Rosemary Sheed (London, 1958)

 Yoga, Immortality and Freedom, trans. Willard R. Trask (London, 1958)

 A History of Religious Ideas, 3 vols, trans. Willard R. Trask (Chicago and London, 1978, 1982, 1985)

 The Myth of the Eternal Return, Or, Cosmos and History, trans. Willard R. Trask (Princeton, 1991)

ELISSEEFF, N., *Nur al-Din: un grand prince musulman de Syrie au temps des Croisades,* 3 vols (Damascus, 1967)

ELKINS, Stanley, *Slavery: A Problem of American Institutional and Intellectual Life* (Chicago, 1976)

ELON, Amos, *The Israelis: Founders and Sons,* 2nd ed. (London, 1981)

ELVIN, Mark, 'Was There a Transcendental Breakthrough in China?', in S. N. Eisenstadt, ed., *The Origins and Diversity of Axial Age Civilizations* (Albany, 1986)

ENGLISH, Richard, *Terrorism: How to Respond* (Oxford and New York, 2009)

EPSZTEIN, Leon, *Social Justice in the Ancient Near East and the People of the Bible,* trans. John Bowden (London, 1986)

ERDMANN, C., *The Origin of the Idea of Crusade,* trans. M. W. Baldwin and W. Goffart (Princeton, 1977)

ERTMAN, Thomas, *Birth of the Leviathan: Building States and Regimes in Early Modern Europe* (Cambridge, UK, 1997)

ESHMAN, Milton and Shibley TELHAM, eds, *International Organizations and Ethnic Conflict* (Ithaca, NY, 1994)

ESPOSITO, John L., *Unholy War: Terror in the Name of Islam* (New York and Oxford, 2002)

ed., *Voices of Resurgent Islam* (New York and Oxford, 1983)

'Islam and Muslim Politics', in ibid.

(with John J. Donohue) eds, *Islam in Transition: Muslim Perspectives* (New York, 1982)

(with Dalia Mogahed), *Who Speaks for Islam? What a Billion Muslims Really Think; Based on Gallup's World Poll – the Largest Study of its Kind* (New York, 2007)

EUBES, Roxanne, 'Killing (for) Politics: Jihad, Martyrdom, Political Action', *Political Theory,* 30 (2002)

EUSEBIUS, *Life of Constantine,* trans. Averil Cameron and Stuart G. Hall (Oxford, 1999)

FAIRBANK, John King and Merle GOLDMAN, *China: A New History,* 2nd ed. (Cambridge, Mass., and London, 2006)

FAKHRY, Majid, *A History of Islamic Philosophy* (New York and London, 1970)

FALL, A., *Medieval and Renaissance Origins: Historiographical Debates and Demonstrations* (London, 1991)

FANDY, Mahmoun, *Saudi Arabia and the Politics of Dissent* (New York, 1999)

FATORIC, Clement, 'The Anti-Catholic Roots of Liberal and Republican

Conception of Freedom in English Political Thought', *Journal of the History of Ideas,* 66 (January 2005)

FENSHAM, F. C., 'Widows, Orphans and the Poor in Ancient Eastern Legal and Wisdom Literature', *Journal of Near Eastern Studies,* 21 (1962)

FERGUSON, Niall, *Empire: How Britain Made the Modern World* (London, 2003)

    Colossus: The Price of America's Empire (New York, 2004)

    'An Empire in Denial: The Limits of U.S. Imperialism', *Harvard International Review,* Fall 2003

FERNÁNDEZ-ARMESTO, Felipe, *1492: The Year Our World Began* (New York, 2009)

FICHTE, Johann Gottlieb, *Addresses to the German Nation,* trans. and ed. Gregory Moore (Cambridge, 2008)

FINGARETTE, Herbert, *Confucius – the Secular as Sacred* (New York, 1972)

FINKELSTEIN, Israel, and Neil Asher SILBERMAN, *The Bible Unearthed: Archaeology's New Vision of Ancient Israel and the Origin of Its Sacred Text* (New York, 2001)

FINLEY, M. I., ed., *Studies in Ancient Society* (London and Boston, 1974)

FINN, Melissa, *Al-Qaeda and Sacrifice: Martyrdom, War and Politics* (London, 2012)

FIRESTONE, Reuven, *Jihad: The Origin of the Holy War in Islam* (Oxford and New York, 1999)

    Holy War in Judaism: The Fall and Rise of a Controversial Idea (Oxford and New York, 2012)

FISCH, Harold, *The Zionist Revolution: A New Perspective* (Tel Aviv and London, 1978)

FISCHER, Louis, ed., *The Essential Gandhi* (New York, 1962)

FISCHER, Michael J., *Iran: From Religious Dispute to Revolution* (Cambridge, Mass., and London, 1980)

    'Imam Khomeini: Four Levels of Understanding', in John L. Esposito, ed., *Voices of Resurgent Islam* (New York and Oxford, 1980)

FISHBANE, Michael, *The Garments of Torah: Essays in Biblical Hermeneutics* (Bloomington and Indianapolis, 1989)

FITZGERALD, Timothy, *The Ideology of Religious Studies* (Oxford, 2000)

    ed., *Religion and the Secular: Historical and Colonial Formations* (Oakville, Conn., 2007)

FLOOD, Gavin, *An Introduction to Hinduism* (Cambridge, UK, and New York, 1996)

    ed., *The Blackwell Companion to Hinduism* (Oxford, 2003)

FLOOR, Willem M., 'The Revolutionary Character of the Ulema: Wishful Thinking or Reality?', in Nikki R. Keddie, ed., *Religion and Politics in Islam: Shiism from Quietism to Revolution* (New Haven, Conn., and London, 1983)

FORCE, Peter, *Tracts* (New York, 1844)

FOSSIER, Robert, ed., *The Middle Ages*, 2 vols, trans. Janet Sondheimer (Cambridge, 1989)

FOWDEN, Garth, *Empire to Commonwealth: Consequences of Monotheism in Late Antiquity* (Princeton, 1993)

FOWLES, John, *The Magus. Revised Edition* (London, 1997)

FOX, Everett, trans., *The Five Books of Moses* (New York, 1990)

FRANKFORT, H. and H. A. FRANKFORT, eds, *The Intellectual Adventure of Ancient Man: An Essay on Speculative Thought in the Ancient Near East* (Chicago, 1946)

FRAYNE, Sean, *Galilee from Alexander the Great to Hadrian, 323 BCE–135 CE: A Study in Second Temple Judaism* (Notre Dame, Ind., 1980)

FREND, W. H. C., *Martyrdom and Persecution in the Early Church: A Study of a Conflict from the Maccabees to Donatus* (Oxford, 1965)

FRIED, M. H., *The Evolution of Political Society: An Essay in Political Anthropology* (New York, 1967)

FULCHER of Chartres, *A History of the Expedition to Jerusalem, 1098–1127*, trans. and ed. Frances Rita Ryan (Knoxville, 1969)

FULLER, Robert C., *Naming the Antichrist: The History of an American Obsession* (Oxford and New York, 1995)

FUNG, Yu Lan, *A Short History of Chinese Philosophy*, ed. and trans. Derk Bodde (New York, 1976)

GABRIELI, Francesco, ed., *Arab Historians of the Crusades*, trans. E. J. Costello (London, 1969)

GADDIS, Michael, *There is No Crime for Those Who Have Christ: Religious Violence in the Christian Roman Empire* (Berkeley, Los Angeles and London, 2005)

GAFFNEY, Patrick D., *The Prophet's Pulpit: Islamic Preaching in Contemporary Egypt* (Berkeley, Los Angeles and London, 1994)

GALAMBUSH, Julia, *The Reluctant Parting: How the New Testament Jewish Writers Created a Christian Book* (San Francisco, 2005)

GARLAN, Yvon, *War in the Ancient World: A Social History* (London, 1975)

GARNSEY, Peter, *Famine and Food Shortage in the Graeco-Roman World* (Cambridge, UK, 1988)

GAUSTAD, Edwin S., *Faith of Our Fathers: Religion and the New Nation* (San Francisco, 1987)

GAUVREAU, Michael, 'Between Awakening and Enlightenment', in *The Evangelical Century: College and Creed in English Canada from the Great Revival to the Great Depression* (Kingston and Montreal, 1991)

GEARTY, C., *Terrorism* (Aldershot, 1996)

GELLNER, Ernst, *Nations and Nationalism (New Perspectives on the Past)*, 2nd ed., with an Introduction by John Breuilly (Oxford, 2006)

GENTILI, Alberico, *The Rights of War and Peace, in Three Books* (London, 1738)

GEOFFROI de Charny, *The Book of Chivalry of Geoffroi de Charny: Text, Context and Translation*, trans. Richard W. Kaeuper and Elspeth Huxley (Philadelphia, 1996)

GEORGE, Andrew, *The Epic of Gilgamesh: The Babylonian Epic Poem and Other Texts in Akkadian and Sumerian* (London and New York, 1999)

GERASSI, J., ed., *Revolutionary Priest: The Complete Writings and Messages of Camilo Torres* (New York, 1971)

GERNET, Jacques, *Ancient China: From the Beginnings to the Empire*, trans. Raymond Rudorff (London, 1968)

    A History of Chinese Civilization, ed. and trans. J. R. Foster and Charles Hartman, 2nd ed. (Cambridge, UK, and New York, 1996)

GERTH, H. H. and C. WRIGHT MILLS, eds, *From Max Weber* (London, 1948)

GHOSE, Aurobindo, *Essays on the Gita* (Pondichery, 1972)

GHOSH, A., *The City in Early Historical India* (Simla, 1973)

GIDDENS, Anthony, *The Nation-State and Violence* (Berkeley, 1987)

    The Consequences of Modernity (Cambridge, UK, 1991)

GIL, Moshe, *A History of Palestine, 634–1099*, trans. Ethel Broido (Cambridge, 1992)

GILBERT, Paul, *The Compassionate Mind: A New Approach to Life's Challenges* (London, 2009)

GILLINGHAM, J., and J. C. Holt, eds, *War and Government in the Middle Ages: Essays in Honour of J. O. Prestwich* (Woodbridge, UK and Totowa, NY, 1984)

GIRARD, René, *Violence and the Sacred*, trans. Patrick Gregory (Baltimore, 1977)

GLATZER, Nahum, 'The Concept of Peace in Classical Judaism', in *Essays on Jewish Thought* (University, Ala., 1978)

GOLD, Daniel, 'Organized Hinduisms: From Vedic Truth to Hindu Nation', in Martin E. Marty and R. Scott Appleby, eds, *Fundamentalisms Observed* (Chicago and London, 1991)

GOLWALKER, M. S., *We or Our Nationhood* (Nagpur, 1939)

GOMBRICH, Richard F., *Theravada Buddhism: A Social History from Ancient Benares to Modern Colombo* (London and New York, 1988)

  How Buddhism Began: The Conditioned Genesis of the Early Teachings (London and Atlantic Highlands, NJ, 1996)

GONDA, Jan, *The Vision of the Vedic Poets* (The Hague, 1963)

  Change and Continuity in Indian Tradition (The Hague, 1965)

GOTTWALD, *The Tribes of Yahweh* (Maryknoll, NY, 1979)

  The Hebrew Bible in Its Social World and in Ours (Atlanta, 1993)

  The Politics of Ancient Israel (Louisville, 2001)

  The Hebrew Bible: A Brief Socio-Literary Introduction (Minneapolis, 2009)

  ed., *The Bible of Liberation: Political and Social Hermeneutics* (Maryknoll, NY, 1983)

GRAHAM, A. C., *Disputers of the Tao: Philosophical Argument in Ancient China* (La Salle, Ill., 1989)

  Early Mohist Logic, Ethics and Science (Hong Kong, 1978)

GRANET, Marcel, *Festivals and Songs of Ancient China*, trans. E. D. Edwards (London, 1932)

  Chinese Civilization, trans. Kathleen Innes and Mabel Brailsford (London and New York, 1951)

  The Religion of the Chinese People, trans. and ed. Maurice Freedman (Oxford, 1975)

GRAYSON, A. K., *Assyrian Royal Inscriptions*, 2 vols (Wiesbaden, 1972)

GREER, Donald, *The Incidence of Terror in the French Revolution* (Gloucester, Mass., 1935)

GREGORY, Brad S., *Salvation at Stake: Christian Martyrdom in Early Modern Europe* (Cambridge, Mass., and London, 1999)

GREIL, Arthur L. and David G. BROMLEY, eds, *Defining Religion: Investigating the Boundaries between the Sacred and the Secular* (Oxford, 2003)

GRIFFITH, Ralph T. H., trans., *The Rig Veda* (reprinted New York, 1992)

GROSSMAN, Lt. Col. David, *On Killing: The Psychological Cost of Learning to Kill in War and Society*, rev. ed. (New York, 2009)

GROTIUS, Hugo, *Rights of War and Peace, in Ten Books* (London, 1738)

GUELKE, A., *The Age of Terrorism and the International Political System* (London, 2008)

GUIBERT of Nogent, *Monodies and On the Relics of Saints: The Autobiography and a Manifesto of a French Monk from the Time of the Crusades*, ed. and trans. Joseph McAlhany and Jay Rubenstein (London and New York, 2011)

GUILLAUME, A., trans. and ed., *The Life of Muhammad: A Translation of Ishaq's Sirat Rasul Allah* (London, 1955)

GUNN, David E., 'Religion, Law and Violence', in Andrew R. Murphy, ed., *The Blackwell Companion to Religion and Violence* (Chichester, UK, 2011)

GUNN, Steven, 'War, Religion and the State', in Euan Cameron, ed., *Early Modern Europe: An Oxford History* (Oxford, 1999)

GUNNING, Jeroen, 'Rethinking Religion and Violence in the Middle East', in Andrew R. Murphy, ed., *The Blackwell Companion to Religion and Violence* (Chichester, UK, 2011)

HADAS-LEBEL, Mireille, *Jerusalem against Rome,* trans. Robyn Freshunt (Leuven, 2006)

HADDAD, Yvonne K., 'Sayyid Qutb: Ideologue of Islamic Revival', in John L. Esposito, ed., *Voices of Resurgent Islam* (New York and Oxford, 1980)

HAFKESBRINK, H., *Unknown Germany: An Inner Chronicle of the First World War Based on Letters and Diaries* (New Haven, Conn., 1948)

HALDON, John, *Warfare, State and Society in the Byzantine World, 565–1204* (London and New York, 2005)

HARMON, C. C. *Terrorism Today* (London, 1998)

HARRIS, J., ed., *The Anthropology of War* (Cambridge, UK, 1990)

HARRIS, Marvin, *Cannibals and Kings: The Origins of Cultures* (New York, 1977)

   Our Kind: Who We Are, Where We Come From, and Where We Are Going (New York, 1989)

HARRIS, William, *War and Imperialism in Republican Rome* (Oxford, 1979)

HARVEY, A. E., *Strenuous Commands: The Ethic of Jesus* (London and Philadelphia, 1990)

HASSIG, Ross, *War and Society in Ancient Mesopotamia* (Berkeley, 1992)

HATCH, Nathan O., *The Sacred Cause of Liberty: Republican Thought and the Millennium in Revolutionary New England* (New Haven, Conn., 1977)

   The Democratization of American Christianity (New Haven, Conn., 1989)

HAUSER, Henri, 'Political Anarchy and Social Discontent', in J. H. M. Salmon, ed., *The French Wars of Religion: How Important Were Religious Factors?* (Lexington, Mass., 1967)

HAYES, Carlton J. H., *Essays on Nationalism* (New York, 1926)

   Nationalism: A Religion (New York, 1960)

HAZONY, Yoram, *The Philosophy of Hebrew Scripture* (Cambridge, UK, 2012)

HEAD, Thomas and Richard LANDES, eds, *The Peace of God: Social Violence and Religious Response in France around the Year 1000* (Ithaca, NY, 1992)

HECK, Paul, L., '*Jihad* Revisited', *Journal of Religious Ethics,* 32, 1, 2004

HEDGES, Chris, *War is a Force That Gives Us Meaning* (New York, 2003)

HEESTERMAN, J. C., *The Inner Conflict of Tradition: Essays on Indian Ritual, Kingship and Society* (Chicago and London, 1985)

   The Broken World of Sacrifice: An Essay in Ancient Indian Religion (Chicago and London, 1993)

   'Ritual, Revelation and the Axial Age', in S. N. Eisenstadt, ed., *The Origins and Diversity of Axial Age Civilizations* (Albany, 1986)

HEGEL, G. W. F., *Elements of the Philosophy of Right,* ed. Allen W. Wood (Cambridge, UK, 1991)

HEGGHAMMER, Thomas, *Jihad in Saudi Arabia: Violence and Pan-Islamism since 1979* (Cambridge, UK, 2010)

HEIKAL, Mohamed, *Autumn of Fury: The Assassination of Sadat* (London, 1984)

HEILMAN, Samuel, 'Guides of the Faithful: Contemporary Religious Zionist Rabbis', in R. Scott Appleby, ed., *Spokesmen for the Despised: Fundamentalist Leaders of the Middle East* (Chicago, 1997)

HEIMART, ALAN, *Religion and the American Mind: From the Great Awakening to the Revolution* (Cambridge, Mass., 1968)

   (with Andrew Delbanco) eds, *The Puritans in America: A Narrative Anthology* (Cambridge, Mass. and London, 1985)

HELLER, Henry, *Iron and Blood: Civil Wars in Sixteenth-Century France* (Montreal, 1991)

HENGEL, Martin, *Judaism and Hellenism: Studies in Their Encounter in Palestine during the Early Hellenistic Period,* 2 vols, trans. John Bowden (London, 1974)

HENRY of Lancaster, *Le Livre de Seyntz Medicines: The Unpublished Treatises of Henry of Lancaster,* trans. A. J. Arnold (Oxford, 1940)

HERBERT, Edward, Lord, *De Veritate,* trans. Mayrick H. Carre (Bristol, UK, 1937)

   De Religio Laici, trans. and ed. Harold L. Hutcheson (New Haven, Conn., 1944)

HERRENSCHMIDT, Clarisse, 'Designations de l'empire et concepts politiques de Darius Ier d'après inscriptions en Vieux Perse', *Studia Iranica,* 5 (1976)

HERZL, Theodor, *The Complete Diaries of Theodor Herzl,* 2 vols, ed. R. Patai (London and New York, 1960)

HILL, Rosalind, trans., *The Deeds of the Franks and Other Pilgrims to Jerusalem* (London, 1962)

HILLENBRAND, Carole, *The Crusades: Islamic Perspectives* (Edinburgh, 1999)

HILLGARTH, J. N., *Ramon Lull and Lullism in Fourteenth Century France* (Oxford, 1971)

HILTEBEITEL, Alf, *The Ritual of Battle: Krishna in the Mahabharata* (Ithaca and London, 1976)

HILTERMANN, Joos R., *A Poisonous Affair: America, Iraq and the Gassing of Halabja* (Cambridge, UK, 2007)

HIMMELFARB, Gertrude, *The Roads to Modernity* (New York, 2001)

HOBBES, Thomas, *Leviathan,* ed. Richard Tuck (Cambridge, UK, 1991)

   On the Citizen, ed. Richard Tuck and Michael Silverthorne (Cambridge, UK, 1998)

   Behemoth; or, The Long Parliament, ed. Frederick Tönnies (Chicago, 1990)

HOBSBAWM, Eric J., *Primitive Rebels* (New York, 1965)

   Bandits, rev. ed. (New York, 1985)

HODGE, Charles, *What is Darwinism?* (Princeton, NJ, 1874)

HODGSON, Marshall G. S., *The Venture of Islam: Conscience and History in a World Civilization,* 3 vols (Chicago and London, 1974)

HOFFMAN, Bruce, *Inside Terrorism* (London, 1998)

HOFFNER, H., 'History and the Historians of the Ancient Near East: The Hittites', *Orientalia,* 49 (1980)

HOLT, Mack P., *The French Wars of Religion, 1562–1629* (Cambridge, UK, 1995)

   'Putting Religion Back into the Wars of Religion', *French Historical Studies,* 18, 2 (Autumn 1973)

HOLT, P. M., *The Age of the Crusades* (London, 1986)

HOMER, *The Iliad of Homer,* trans. Richard Lattimore (Chicago and London, 1951)

   The Odyssey, trans. Walter Shewring, with an Introduction by G. S. Kirk (Oxford, 1980)

HOOKE, S. H., *Middle Eastern Mythology: From the Assyrians to the Hebrews* (Harmondsworth, UK, 1963)

HOPKINS, D. C., *The Highlands of Canaan* (Sheffield, 1985)

HOPKINS, Thomas J., *The Hindu Religious Traditions* (Belmont, Calif., 1971)

HORGAN, J., *The Psychology of Terrorism* (London, 2005)

HORSLEY, Richard A., *Jesus and the Spiral of Violence: Popular Jewish Resistance in Roman Palestine* (Minneapolis, 1993 ed.)

   (with Jonathan A. Draper) *Whoever Hears You Hears Me: Prophets, Performance and Tradition in Q* (Harrisburg, Pa., 1999)

   'The Historical Context of Q', in ibid.

HOSELITZ, Bert F., *Sociological Aspects of Economic Growth* (New York, 1960)

HOURANI, Albert, *Arabic Thought in the Liberal Age, 1798–1939* (Oxford, 1962)

HOUSELY, Norman, *The Later Crusades, 1274–1558: From Lyons to Alcazar* (Oxford, 1992)

  'Crusades against Christians: Their Origin and Early Development', in Peter W. Edbury, ed., *Crusade and Settlement* (Cardiff, 1985)

HOWARD, Michael, *The Invention of Peace: Reflections on War and International Order* (New Haven, Conn., 2000)

HOWE, Daniel Walker, 'Religion and Politics in the Antebellum North', in Mark A. Noll, ed., *Religion and American Politics: From the Colonial Period to the 1980s* (Oxford and New York, 1990)

HSU, C. Y., and K. M. LINDOFF, *Western Chou Civilization* (New Haven, Conn., 1988)

HUBERT, Henry and Marcel MAUSS, *Sacrifice: Its Nature and Functions,* trans. D. Halls (Chicago, 1964)

HUGHES, Anne, *The Causes of the English Civil War* (London, 1998)

HUIZINGA, Johan, *Homo Ludens: A Study of the Play Element in Culture* (Boston, 1955 ed.)

HUMBLE, Richard, *Warfare in the Ancient World* (London, 1980)

HUTCHINSON, William T. and William M. E. RAPHAEL, eds, *The Papers of James Madison* (Chicago, 1962)

HUTT, M. G., 'The Role of the Curés in the Estates General of 1789', *Journal of Ecclesiastical History,* 6 (1955)

IBRAHIM, Raymond, ed. and trans., *The Al-Qaeda Reader* (New York, 2007)

IDINOPULOS, Thomas A. and Bryan C. WILSON, eds, *What is Religion? Origins, Definitions and Explanations* (Leiden, 1998)

ISAMBERT, François-André, ed., *Recueil général des anciens lois françaises depuis l'an 420 jusqu'à la Révolution de 1789,* 17 vols (Paris, 1820–30)

IZUTSU, Toshihiko, *Ethico-Religious Concepts in the Qur'an* (Montreal and Kingston, 2002)

JACKSON, Kent P., 'The Language of the Mesha Inscription', in Andrew Dearman, ed., *Studies in the Mesha Inscription and Moab* (Atlanta, NY, 1989)

JACOBI, Hermann, trans., *Jaina Sutras* (New York, 1968)

JACOBS, Louis, ed., *The Jewish Religion: A Companion* (Oxford, 1995)

JACOBSEN, Thorkold, 'The Cosmic State', in H. and H. A. Frankfort, eds, *The Intellectual Adventure of Ancient Man: An Essay on Speculative Thought in the Near East* (Chicago, 1946)

JAITNER, J., 'The Pope and the Struggle for Power during the Sixteenth and Seventeenth Centuries', in Klaus Bussman and Heinz Schilling, eds, *War and Peace in Europe,* 3 vols (Münster, 1998)

JAMES, E. O., *The Ancient Gods: The History and Diffusion of Religion in the Ancient Near East and the Eastern Mediterranean* (London, 1960)

JANSEN, Johannes J. G., trans. and ed., *The Neglected Duty* (New York, 1986)

JASPERS, Karl, *The Great Philosophers: The Foundations,* ed. Hannah Arendt, trans. Ralph Manheim (London, 1962)

   The Origin and Goal of History, trans. Michael Bullock (London, 1953)

JAY, Peter, *Road to Riches or The Wealth of Man* (London, 2000)

JAYUSSI, May, 'Subjectivity and Public Witness: An Analysis of Islamic Militance in Palestine', unpublished paper, 2004

JEREMIAS, J., *Jerusalem in the Time of Jesus* (London and Philadelphia, 1969)

   The Lord's Prayer (Philadelphia, 1973)

JOHN XXIII, Pope (Angelo Giuseppe Roncalli), *Mater et Magistra* and *Pacem in Terris* in Claudia Carlen, ed., *The Papal Encyclicals, 1740–1981,* 5 vols (Falls Church, Va., 1981)

JOHNSON, Paul, *A History of the Jews* (London, 1987)

JONES, A. H. M., *The Later Roman Empire,* 2 vols (Oxford, 1964)

JONES, Kenneth W., 'The Arya Samaj in British India', in Robert D. Baird, *Religion in Modern India* (Delhi, 1981)

JOSEPHUS, *The Jewish War,* trans. G. A. Williamson (Harmondsworth, 1967)

JUERGENSMEYER, Mark, *Terror in the Mind of God: The Global Rise of Religious Violence* (Berkeley, Los Angeles and London, 2001)

   Global Rebellion: Religious Challenges to the Secular State from Christian Militias to Al-Qaeda (Berkeley, 2008)

   The New Cold War? Religious Nationalism Confronts the Secular State (Berkeley, 1993)

   ed., *Violence and the Sacred in the Modern World* (London, 1992)

KAEUPER, Richard W., *Holy Warrior: The Religious Ideology of Chivalry* (Philadelphia, 2009)

KAHANE, Meir, *Listen World, Listen Jew* (Tucson, 1978)

KAKAR, Sudhir, *The Colors of Violence: Cultural Identities, Religion and Conflict* (Chicago and London, 1996)

KALTENMARK, Max, *Lao-Tzu and Taoism,* trans. Roger Greaves (Stanford, 1969)

KAMEN, Henry, *The Spanish Inquisition: An Historical Revision* (London, 1997)

   Empire: How Spain Became a World Power, 1492–1763 (New York, 2003)

KANT, Immanuel, *Lectures on Ethics,* trans. Lewis Infield, ed. Lewis White Beck (New York, 1963)

   Critique of Pure Reason, trans. Norman Kemp Smith (London, 1993)

KANTOROWICZ, K., '*Pro Patria Mori* in Medieval Political Thought', *American History Review*, 3 (1951)

KAPILA, Shruti and Faisal DEVJI, eds, *Political Thought in Action: The Bhagavad Gita and Modern India* (Cambridge, UK, 2013)

KASSIMERIS, George, ed., *The Barbarization of Warfare* (London, 2006)

KAUTSKY, John H., *The Political Consequences of Modernization* (New York, London, Sydney, Toronto, 1972)

    The Politics of Aristocratic Empires, 2nd ed. (New Brunswick and London, 1997)

KEAY, John, *India: A History* (London, 2000)

KEDAR, Benjamin Z., *Crusade and Mission: European Approaches toward Muslims* (Princeton, 1984)

    (with H. E. Mayer and R. C. Smail) eds, *Outremer* (Jerusalem, 1982)

KEDDIE, Nikki R., *Roots of Revolution: An Interpretive History of Modern Iran* (New Haven, Conn., and London, 1981)

    (ed.) *Scholars, Saints and Sufis: Muslim Religious Institutions in the Middle East since 1500* (Berkeley, Los Angeles and London, 1972)

    (ed.) *Religion and Politics in Iran: Shiism from Quietism to Revolution* (New Haven, Conn., and London, 1983)

KEEGAN, John, *The Face of Battle* (London, 1976)

    A History of Warfare (London and New York, 1993)

KEEN, Maurice, *Chivalry* (New Haven, Conn., and London, 1984)

KEIGHTLEY, David N., ed., *The Origins of Chinese Civilization* (Berkeley, 1983)

KENYON, Kathleen, *Digging Up Jericho: The Results of the Jericho Excavations, 1953–56* (New York, 1957)

KEPEL, Gilles, *The Prophet and Pharaoh: Muslim Extremism in Egypt,* trans. Jon Rothschild (London, 1985)

    Beyond Terror and Martyrdom: The Future of the Middle East, trans. Paschale Ghazaleh (Cambridge, Mass., and London, 2008)

    Jihad: The Trail of Political Islam, trans. Anthony F. Roberts, 4th ed. (London, 2009)

    (with Jean-Pierre Milleli) eds, *Al-Qaeda in its Own Words,* trans. Paschale Ghazaleh (Cambridge, Mass., 2008)

KERR, Ronald Dale, 'Why Should You Be So Furious? The Violence of the Pequot War', *Journal of American History,* 85 (December 1998)

KERTZER, David I., *Ritual, Politics and Power* (New Haven, Conn., and London, 1988)

KHOMEINI, Sayeed Ruhollah, *Islam and Revolution,* trans. and ed. Hamid Algar (Berkeley, 1981)

KHROSROKHAVAR, Farhad, *Suicide Bombers: Allah's New Martyrs,* trans. David Macey (London, 2005)

KIERMAN, Frank A., Jr., and John K. FAIRBANK, eds, *Chinese Ways in Warfare* (Cambridge, Mass., 1974)

KIMBALL, Charles, *When Religion Becomes Evil* (San Francisco, 2002)

KIMELMAN, K., 'Non-violence in the Talmud,' *Judaism,* 17 (1968)

KING, Martin Luther, Jr., *Strength to Love* (Philadelphia, 1963)

KRAMER, Martin, 'Hizbullah: The Calculus of Jihad', in Martin E. Marty and R. Scott Appleby, eds, *Fundamentalisms and the State: Rethinking Politics, Economies and Militance* (Chicago and London, 1993)

KRAMER, Samuel N., *Sumerian Mythology: A Study of the Spiritual and Literary Achievement of the Third Millennium BC* (Philadelphia, 1944)

History Begins at Sumer (Philadelphia, 1981)

KRAUSS, Hans-Joachim, *Worship in Israel: A Cultic History of the Old Testament* (Oxford, 1966)

KREISTER, Fritz, *Four Weeks in the Trenches: The War Story of a Violinist* (Boston and New York, 1915)

KREY, August C., ed. and trans., *The First Crusade: The Accounts of Eye-Witnesses and Participants* (Princeton, NJ and London), 1921

KRITZECK, James, *Peter the Venerable and Islam* (Princeton, NJ, 1964)

KSELMAN, Thomas, ed., *Belief in History: Innovative Approaches to European and American Religion* (Notre Dame, Ind., 1991)

KULKE, Hermann, 'The Historical Background of India's Axial Age', in S. N. Eisenstadt, ed., *The Origins and Diversity of Axial Age Civilizations* (Albany, NY, 1986)

KYDD, A. H. and B. F. WALTER, 'The Stratagems of Terrorism', *International Security,* 31, 1 (Summer 2006)

LACTANTIUS, trans. William Fletcher, *Lactantius: Works* (Edinburgh, 1971)

LAL, Deepak, *In Praise of Empires: Globalization and Order* (New York, 2004)

LAMBERT, W. G. and A. R. MILLARD, trans. and eds, *The Atra-Hasis: The Babylonian Story of the Flood* (Oxford, 1969)

LANE FOX, Robin, *Pagans and Christians* (London, 1986)

LAU, D. C., trans. and ed., *Tao Te Ching* (London, 1963)

(trans. and ed.) *Mencius* (London, 1970)

LAWRENCE, T. E., *The Mint* (New York, 1963)

LE GOFF, Jacques, ed., *The Medieval World,* trans. Lydia C. Cochrane (London, 1990)

LE ROI-GOURHAN, Andre, *Treasures of Prehistoric Art* (New York, n.d.)

LE STRANGE, Guy, *Palestine under the Moslems: A Description of Syria and the Holy Land from AD 650 to 1500* (London, 1890)

LEA, H. C., *A History of the Inquisition of the Middle Ages* (Philadelphia, 1866)

LEED, Eric J., *No Man's Land: Combat and Identity in World War I* (Cambridge, UK, 1979)

LEFEBUREM, Leo D., *Revelation, the Religions and Violence* (Maryknoll, NY, 2000)

LEFEBVRE, Georges, *The Great Fear of 1789,* trans. R. R. Farmer and Joan White (Princeton, NJ, 1973)

LEGGE, J., trans., *The Ch'un Ts'ew and the Tso Chuen,* 2nd ed. (Hong Kong, 1960)

(trans.) *The Li Ki* (Oxford, 1885)

LEICK, Gwendolyn, *Mesopotamia: The Invention of the City* (London, 2001)

LEMCHE, Niels P., *Early Israel: Anthropological and Historical Studies on the Israelite Society before the Monarchy* (Leiden, 1985)

LENSKI, Gerhard E., *Power and Privilege: A Theory of Social Stratification* (Chapel Hill and London, 1966)

LEVENE, Mark, *Genocide in the Age of the Nation-State: The Rise of the West and the Coming of Genocide* (London and New York, 2005)

LEVENSON, Joseph R. and Franz SCHURMANN, *China: An Interpretive History – from the Beginnings to the Fall of Han* (Berkeley, Los Angeles and London, 1969)

LEVINE, Lee I., ed., *The Galilee in Late Antiquity* (New York and Jerusalem, 1992)

LEVINSON, Bernard M., *Deuteronomy and the Hermeneutics of Legal Innovation* (Oxford and New York, 1998)

LEWIS, Bernard, *The Assassins* (London, 1967)

'The Roots of Muslim Rage', *Atlantic Monthly,* 1990

LEWIS, James R., ed., *Violence and New Religious Movements* (Oxford, 2011)

LEWIS, M., *Ecstatic Religion: An Anthropological Study of Spirit Possession and Shamanism* (Baltimore, 1971)

LEWIS, Mark Edward, *Sanctioned Violence in Early China* (Albany, 1990)

LIBANIUS, *Select Orations,* trans. A. F. Norman, 2 vols (Cambridge, Mass., 1969, 1970)

LIM, Richard, *Public Disputation, Power and Social Order in Late Antiquity* (Berkeley, 1995)

LINCOLN, Bruce, *Death, War and Sacrifice: Studies in Ideology and Practice* (Chicago and London, 1991)

Holy Terrors: Thinking about Religion after September 11, 2nd ed. (Chicago and London, 2006)

Religion, Empire and Torture: The Case of Achaemenian Persia, with a Postscript on Abu Graib (Chicago and London, 2007)

'The Role of Religion in Achmenean Inscriptions', in Nicole Brisch, ed., *Religion and Power: Divine Kingship in the Ancient World and Beyond* (Chicago, 2008)

LINDBERG, David and Ronald L. NUMBERS, eds, *God and Nature: Historical Essays on the Encounter between Christianity and Science* (Berkeley, Los Angeles and London, 1986)

LING, Trevor, *The Buddha: Buddhist Civilization in India and Ceylon* (London, 1973)

LINGS, Martin, *Muhammad: His Life Based on the Earliest Sources* (London, 1983)

LIVVI-BACCI, Massimo, *A Concise History of World Population* (Oxford, 1997)

LOCKE, John, *A Letter Concerning Toleration* (Indianapolis, Ind., 1955)

Essays on the Law of Nature, ed. W. van Leyden (Oxford, 1970)

Two Treatises of Government, ed. Peter Laslett (Cambridge, UK, 1988)

Political Writings, ed. David Wootton (London, 1993)

LOVEJOY, David S., *Religious Enthusiasm in the New World: Heresy to Revolution* (Cambridge, Mass., and London, 1985)

LOWTH, Andrew, *The Origins of Christian Mysticism: From Plato to Denys* (London, 1975)

Maximus the Confessor (London, 1996)

LUTHER, Martin, *Selected Political Writings,* ed. J. M. Porter (Philadelphia, 1974)

LUTTWICK, *The Grand Strategy of the Roman Empire* (Baltimore, 1976)

LYONS, M. C. and D. E. P. JACKSON, *Saladin: The Politics of the Holy War* (Cambridge, UK, 1982)

MAAGA, Mary, *Hearing the Voices of Jonestown* (Syracuse, NY, 1958)

MAALOUF, Amin, *The Crusades through Arab Eyes,* trans. Jon Rothschild (London, 1984)

MACARTNEY, C. A., *National States and National Minorities* (London, 1934)

MACGREGOR, Neil, *A History of the World in 100 Objects* (London and New York, 2010)

MACHINIST, Peter, 'Distinctiveness in Ancient Israel', in Mordechai Cogan and Israel Ephal, eds, *Studies in Assyrian History and Ancient Near Eastern Historiography* (Jerusalem, 1991)

MACMULLEN, Ramsey, *Christianizing the Roman Empire, AD 100–400* (New Haven, Conn., 1984)

Christianity and Paganism in the Fourth to Eighth Centuries (New Haven, Conn., 1997)

The Second Church: Popular Christianity AD 200–400 (Leiden, 2009)

MALTBY, William, *The Reign of Charles V* (New York, 2002)

MARIUS, Richard, *Martin Luther: The Christian Between God and Death* (Cambridge, Mass., and London, 1999)

MARSDEN, George, *Fundamentalism and American Culture: The Shaping of Twentieth-Century Evangelicalism, 1870–1925* (New York and Oxford, 1980)

'Afterword', in Mark A. Noll, ed., *Religion and American Politics: From the Colonial Period to the 1980s* (Oxford and New York, 1990)

MARSHALL, John W., 'Collateral Damage: Jesus and Jezebel in the Jewish War', in Shelly Matthews and E. Leigh Gibson, eds, *Violence in the New Testament* (New York and London, 2005)

MARTIN, James D., 'Israel as a Tribal Society', in R. E. Clements, ed., *The World of Ancient Israel: Sociological, Anthropological and Political Perspectives* (Cambridge, UK, 1989)

MARTY, Martin E., and R. Scott APPLEBY, eds, *Fundamentalisms Observed* (Chicago and London, 1991)

eds, *Fundamentalisms and Society: Reclaiming the Sciences, the Family and Education* (Chicago and London, 1993)

eds, *Fundamentalisms and the State: Remaking Politics, Economies, and Militance* (Chicago and London, 1993)

eds, *Accounting for Fundamentalisms: The Dynamic Character of Movements* (Chicago and London, 1994)

eds, *Fundamentalisms Comprehended* (Chicago and London, 1995)

MASON, 'Was Josephus a Pharisee? A Re-examination of the *Life* 10–12', *Journal of Jewish Studies,* 40 (1989)

MASPARO, Henri, *China in Antiquity,* 2nd ed., trans. Frank A. Kiermann Jr (Folkestone, UK, 1978)

MASSELMAN, George, *The Cradle of Colonialism* (New Haven, Conn., 1963)

MASTNAK, Tomaz, *Crusading Peace: Christendom, the Muslim World, and Western Political Order* (Berkeley, Los Angeles and London, 2002)

MATARASSO, P. M., trans., *The Quest of the Holy Grail* (Harmondsworth, UK, 1969)

MATTERN, Susan, *Rome and the Enemy: Imperial Strategy in the Principate* (Berkeley, 1999)

MATTHEWS, Shelly and E. LEIGH GIBSON, eds, *Violence in the New Testament* (New York and London, 2005)

MAWDUDI, Abu Ala, *The Islamic Way of Life* (Lahore, 1979)

'Islamic Government', *Asia,* 20 (September 1981)

'How to Establish Islamic Order in the Country', *The Universal Message* (May 1983)

MAY, Henry F., *The Enlightenment in America* (New York, 1976)

MAYER, Hans Eberhard, *The Crusades,* trans. J. Gillingham, 2nd ed. (Oxford, 1993)

MCCALLEY, 'Conference Archives', in J. Harris, ed., *The Anthropology of War* (Cambridge, UK, 1990)

MCCUTCHEON, Russell, *Manufacturing Religion: The Discourse on Sui Generis Religion and the Politics of Nostalgia* (New York, 1997)

'The Category "Religion" and the Politics of Tolerance', in Arthur L. Greil and David G. Bromley, eds, *Defining Religion: Investigating the Boundaries between the Sacred and the Secular* (Oxford, 2003)

MCDANIEL, Charles A., 'Violent Yearnings for the Kingdom of God: Münster's Militant Anabaptism', in James K. Wellman Jr, ed., *Belief and Bloodshed: Religion and Violence across Time and Tradition* (Lanham, Md, 2007)

MCDERMOTT, Timothy, *Perfect Soldiers: The 9/11 Hijackers — Who They Were, Why They Did It* (New York, 2005)

MCGINN, Bernard and John MEYENDORFF, eds, *Christian Spirituality 1: Origins to the Twelfth Century* (London, 1985)

MCKITTERICK, *The Frankish Kingdoms under the Carolingians, 751–987* (London and New York, 1983)

MCNEILL, William H., *The Pursuit of Power: Technology, Armed Force and Society since AD 1000* (Chicago, 1982)

Plagues and People (London, 1994)

MCPHERSON, James M., *For Cause and Comrades: Why Men Fought in the Civil War* (New York, 1997)

MCWHINEY, Grady and Perry D. JAMIESON, *Attack or Die: The Civil War, Military Tactics and Southern Heritage* (Montgomery, Ala., 1982)

MEIN, Andrew, *Ezekiel and the Ethics of Exile* (Oxford and New York, 2001)

MELLAART, James, *Catal Huyuk: A Neolithic Town in Anatolia* (New York, 1967)

The Neolithic of the Near East (London, 1975)

'Early Urban Communities in the Near East, 9000–3400 BCE', in P. Mooney, ed., *The Origins of Civilization* (Oxford, 1979)

MENDENHALL, George W., *The Tenth Generation: The Origins of Biblical Tradition* (Baltimore, 1973)

MERGUI, Raphael and Philippe SIMONNOT, *Israel's Ayatollahs: Meir Kahane and the Far Right in Israel* (London, 1987)

MERONI, Ariel, 'The Readiness to Kill or Die: Suicide Terrorism in the Middle East', in Walter Reich, ed., *The Origins of Terrorism* (Cambridge, UK, 1990)

MICHELET, Jules, *Historical View of the French Revolution from its Earliest Indications to the Flight of the King in 1791,* trans. C. Cooks (London, 1888)

MIGNE, J. P., ed., *Patrologia Latina* (Paris, 1844–67)

MILL, John Stuart, *Utilitarianism, Liberty, Representational Government* (London, 1990)

MILLER, Perry, *Errand into the Wilderness* (Cambridge, Mass., and London, 1956)

    Roger Williams: His Contribution to the American Tradition, 2nd ed. (New York, 1962)

MILTON, John, *Major Works,* ed. Stephen Orgel and Jonathan Goldberg (Oxford, 2008)

MILTON-EDWARDS, Beverley, *Islamic Politics in Palestine* (London and New York, 1996)

MIR, Mustansire, 'Some Features of Mawdudi's Tafhim al-Quran', *American Journal of Islamic Social Sciences,* 2, 2 (1985)

MITCHELL, Joshua, *Not by Reason Alone: Religion, History and Identity in Early Modern Political Thought* (Chicago, 1993)

MITCHELL, Richard P., *The Society of Muslim Brothers* (London, 1969)

MITCHELL, Stephen, *Gilgamesh: A New English Version* (New York, London, Toronto and Sydney, 2004)

MOHAMEDOU, M. M. Ould, *Understanding al-Qaeda: The Transformation of War* (London, 2007)

MOIN, Baqer, *Khomeini: Life of the Ayatollah* (London, 1999)

MOLE, Marjan, *Culte, mythe et cosmologie dans l'Iran ancien* (Paris, 1963)

MOMEN, Moojan, *An Introduction to Shii Islam: The History and Doctrines of Twelver Shiism* (New Haven, Conn., and London, 1985)

MONROE, Lauren A., *Josiah's Reform and the Dynamics of Defilement: Israelite Rites of Violence and the Making of the Biblical Text* (Oxford, 2011)

MONTAGU, Ashley, ed., *Man and Aggression* (New York, 1973)

MONTEFIORE, C. G. and H. LOEWE, eds, *A Rabbinic Anthology* (New York, 1974)

MONTER, William, *Frontiers of Heresy: The Spanish Inquisition from the Basque Lands to Sicily* (Cambridge, 1990)

MOONEY, P., *The Origins of Civilization* (Oxford, 1979)

MOORE, James R., 'Geologists and the Interpreters of Genesis in the Nineteenth Century', in David Lindberg and Ronald L. Numbers, eds,

God and Nature: Historical Essays on the Encounter between Christianity and Science (Berkeley, Los Angeles and London, 1986)

MOORE, Lawrence, *Religious Outsiders and the Making of America, 1880–1934* (University, Ala., 1982)

MOORE, Rebecca, 'America as Cherry-Pie: The People's Temple and Violence', in Catherine Wessinger, ed., *Millennialism, Persecution and Violence: Historical Circumstances* (Syracuse, NY, 1986)

    'Narratives of Persecution, Suffering and Martyrdom in the People's Temple and Jonestown', in James R. Lewis, ed., *Violence and the New Religious Movements* (Oxford, 2011)

MOORE, R. I., *The Formation of a Persecuting Society: Power and Deviance in Western Europe 950–1250* (Oxford, 1987)

MORE, Thomas, *A Dialogue Concerning Heresies,* ed. Thomas M. C. Lawlor (New Haven, Conn., 1981)

    Utopia, ed. George M. Logan and Robert M. Adams (Cambridge, UK, 1989)

MORGAN, Edmund S., *American Slavery, American Freedom: The Ordeal of Colonial Virginia* (New York, 1975)

MORREY, R. and P. PARR, eds, *Archaeology in the Levant: Essays for Kathleen Kenyon* (Warminster, UK, 1978)

MORRIS, Christopher, *The Papal Monarchy: The Western Church from 1050 to 1250* (Oxford, 1991)

MORRISON, Karl F., *Tradition and Authority in the Western Church, 300–1140* (Princeton, NJ, 1969)

MOSS, Candida R., *The Other Christs: Imitating Jesus in Ancient Christian Ideologies of Martyrdom* (Oxford, 2010)

    The Myth of Persecution: How Early Christians Invented a Story of Martyrdom (New York, 2013)

MURPHY, Andrew R., ed., *The Blackwell Companion to Religion and Violence* (Chichester, UK, 2011)

    'Cromwell, Mather and the Rhetoric of Puritan Violence', in ibid.

MURRIN, John M., 'A Roof without Walls: The Dilemma of National Identity', in Richard Beeman, Stephen Botein and Edward E. Carter III, eds, *Beyond Confederation: Origins of the Constitution in American Identity* (Chapel Hill, 1987)

MUSURILLO, H., trans., *The Acts of the Christian Martyrs* (Oxford, 1972)

NADELSON, Theodore, *Trained to Kill: Soldiers at War* (Baltimore, 2005)

NEFF, John U., *War and Human Progress: An Essay on the Rise of Industrial Civilization* (New York, 1950)

NESTORIUS, *Bazaar of Heracleides,* trans. G. R. Driver and Leonard Hodgson (Oxford, 1925)

NETANYAHU, Benzion, *The Origins of the Inquisition in Fifteenth-Century Spain* (New York, 1995)

NEUSNER, Jacob, *From Politics to Piety* (Englewood Cliffs, NJ, 1973)

NEWTON, Huey, *Revolutionary Suicide* (New York, 1973)

NICHOLLS, David, 'The Theatre of Martyrdom in the French Reformation', *Past and Present,* 121 (1998)

NICHOLSON, R. A., *A Literary History of the Arabs* (Cambridge, UK, 1953)
    The Mystics of Islam (London, 1963)

NIDITCH, Susan, *War in the Hebrew Bible: A Study in the Ethics of Violence* (New York and Oxford, 1993)

NOLL, Mark A., *Religion and American Politics: From the Colonial Period to the 1980s* (Oxford and New York, 1990)
    America's God: From Jonathan Edwards to Abraham Lincoln (Oxford and New York, 2002)
    The Old Religion in a New World: The History of American Christianity (Grand Rapids, Mich., 2002)
    The Civil War as a Theological Crisis (Chapel Hill, 2006)
    'The Rise and Long Life of the Protestant Enlightenment in America', in William M. Shea and Peter A. Huff, eds, *Knowledge and Belief in America: Enlightenment Traditions and Modern Religious Thought* (New York, 1995)

NORTH, Jonathan, 'General Hochte and Counterinsurgency', *Journal of Military History,* 62 (2003)

NUMBERS, Ronald L., *The Creationists: The Evolution of Scientific Creationism* (Berkeley, Los Angeles and London, 1992)

O'CONNELL, Robert L., *Of Arms and Men: A History of War, Weapons and Aggression* (New York and Oxford, 1989)
    Ride of the Second Horseman: The Birth and Death of War (New York and Oxford, 1995)

OLDENBURG, Hermann, *Buddha: His Life, His Doctrine, His Order,* trans. William Hoey (London, 1982)

OLDENBURG, Zoe, *Le Bucher de Montsegur* (Paris, 1959)

OLIVELLE, Patrick, ed. and trans., *Samnyasa Upanisads: Hindu Scriptures on Asceticism and Renunciation* (New York and Oxford, 1992)
    'The Renouncer Tradition', in Gavin Flood, ed., *The Blackwell Companion to Hinduism* (Oxford, 2003)
    ed. and trans., *Upanisads* (New York and Oxford, 1996)

OLIVER, Anne Marie and Paul F. STEINBERG, *The Road to Martyrs' Square: A Journey to the World of the Suicide Bomber* (Oxford, 2005)

OLLENBURGER, Ben C., *Zion, the City of the Great King: A Theological Symbol of the Jerusalem Cult* (Sheffield, 1987)

OLMSTEAD, A. T., *History of Assyria* (New York, 1923)

OPPENHEIM, A. L., *Ancient Mesopotamia: Portrait of a Dead Civilization* (Chicago, 1977)

    'Trade in the Ancient Near East', *International Congress of Economic History*, 5 (1976)

ORIGEN, *Against Celsus,* trans. Henry Chadwick (Cambridge, UK, 1980)

ORTEGA Y GASSET, J., *Meditations on Hunting* (New York, 1985)

OZMENT, Steven, *The Reformation of the Cities: The Appeal of Protestantism to Sixteenth-Century Germany and Switzerland* (New Haven, Conn., 1975)

PAINE, Tom, *Common Sense and the Crisis* (New York, 1975)

PALLADIUS, *Dialogue on the Life of John Chrysostom*, trans. Robert T. Meyer (New York, 1985)

PANNIKKAR, Raimundo, *The Trinity and the Religious Experience of Man* (London and New York, 1973)

PAPE, Robert, *Dying to Win: The Strategic Logic of Suicide Terrorism* (New York, 2005)

    'Dying to Kill Us', *New York Times,* 22 September 2003

    'The Logic of Suicide Terrorism', interview by Scott McConnell, *The American Conservative,* 18 July 2007

PAREEK, Radhey Shyam, *Contribution of Arya Samaj in the Making of Modern India, 1975–1947* (New Delhi, 1973)

PARKER, Geoffrey, ed., *The Thirty Years War* (London, 1984)

PARSONS, Timothy H., *The Rule of Empires: Those Who Built Them, Those Who Endured Them, and Why They Always Fail* (Oxford, 2010)

PARTNER, Peter, *God of Battles: Holy Wars of Christianity and Islam* (London, 1997)

PATLAGEAN, Evelyne, *Pauvreté économique et pauvreté sociale à Byzance, 4e–7e* (Paris, 1977)

PELIKAN, Jaroslav, *The Christian Tradition – A History of the Development of Doctrine 1: The Emergence of the Catholic Tradition* (Chicago and London, 1971)

PERRIN, Norman, *Rediscovering the Teachings of Jesus* (New York, 1967)

    Jesus and the Language of the Kingdom (Philadelphia, 1976)

PESTERIA, Carla Garden, *Protestant Empire, Religion and the Making of the British Atlantic World* (Philadelphia, 2004)

PETERS, F. E., *The Distant Shore: The Islamic Centuries in Jerusalem* (New York, 1993)

PETERSON, Derek and Darren WALHOF, eds, *The Invention of Religion: Rethinking Belief in Politics and History* (New Brunswick, NJ, and London, 2002)

PETITFRERE, Claude, 'The Origins of the Civil War in the Vendée', *French History*, 2 (1998)

PHILLIPS, Keith, *The Cousins' Wars: Religious Politics and the Triumph of Anglo-America* (New York, 1999)

PIRENNE, Henri, *Medieval Cities: Their Origins and the Revival of Trade* (Princeton, NJ, 1946)

   Ecclesiastical and Social History of Europe (New York, 1956)

POLGAR, S., ed., *Population, Ecology and Social Evolution* (The Hague, 1975)

POLISKENSKY, J. V., *War and Society in Europe, 1618–1848* (Cambridge, UK, 1978)

POSMAN, Ellen, 'History, Humiliation and Religious Violence', in Andrew R. Murphy, ed., *The Blackwell Companion to Religion and Violence* (Chichester, UK, 2011)

POSTGATE, J. N., *Mesopotamian Society and Economics at the Dawn of History* (London, 1992)

POTTER, David, *A History of France, 1460–1560: The emergence of a Nation State* (London, 1995)

PRAWER, Joshua, *The Latin Kingdom of Jerusalem: European Colonialism in the Middle Ages* (London, 1972)

PRESCOTT, William H., *History of the Conquest of Mexico and Peru* (New York, 1936)

PRESTON, Andrew, *Sword of the Spirit, Shield of Faith; Religion in American War and Diplomacy* (New York and Toronto, 2012)

PRITCHARD, J. B., ed,. *Ancient Near Eastern Texts Relating to the Old Testament* (Princeton, NJ, 1950)

PUETT, Michael J., *To Become a God: Cosmology, Sacrifice and Self-Divination* (Cambridge, Mass., and London, 2002)

PURCHAS, Samuel, *Hakluytus Posthumous or Purchas His Pilgrim* (Glasgow, 1905–06)

PUPPI, Lionello, *Torment in Art: Pain, Violence and Martyrdom* (New York, 1991)

QUTB, Sayed, *Milestones (Ma'alim fi'l-tareeq)*, ed. and trans. A. B. al-Mehri (Birmingham, UK, 2006)

RADCLIFFE, A. R., *The Andaman Islanders* (New York, 1948)

RAVITSKY, Aviezer, *The Roots of Kahanism: Consciousness and Political Reality*, trans. Moshe Auman (Jerusalem, 1986)

　Messianism, Zionism and Jewish Religious Radicalism, trans. Michael Swirsky and Jonathan Chapman (Chicago, 1996)

REDFIELD, Robert, *Peasant Society and Culture: An Anthropological Approach to Civilization* (Chicago, 1956)

REICH, Walter, ed., *The Origins of Terrorism* (Cambridge, UK, 1990)

REINBERG, Virginia, 'Liturgy and Laity in Late Medieval and Reformation France', *Sixteenth-Century Journal*, 23 (Autumn 1992)

RENFREW, Colin, *The Puzzle of Indo-European Origins* (London, 1987)

RENNA, Thomas J., 'Kingship in the *Disputatio inter clericum et militem*', *Speculum*, 48 (1973)

RENOU, Louis, *Religions of Ancient India* (London, 1953)

　'Sur la notion de *brahman*', *Journal Asiatique*, 23 (1949)

RICHARDSON, H. G., *The English Jewry under the Angevin Kings* (London, 1960)

RICHARDSON, Louise, *What Terrorists Want: Understanding the Terrorist Threat* (London, 2006)

RIEFF, David, *Slaughterhouse: Bosnia and the Failure of the West* (New York, 1995)

RILEY-SMITH, Jonathan, *The First Crusade and the Idea of Crusading* (London, 1986)

　The First Crusaders, 1095–1131 (Cambridge, UK, 1997)

　(with Louise Riley-Smith) *The Crusades: Idea and Reality, 1095–1274* (London, 1981)

　'Crusading as an Act of Love', *History*, 65 (1980)

RINDOS, David, *The Origins of Agriculture: An Evolutionary Perspective* (Orlando, Fla., 1984)

RIVES, James B., *Religion in the Roman Empire* (Oxford, 2007)

　'The Decree of Decius and the Religion of Empire', *Journal of Roman Studies* (1989)

ROBERT the Monk, *Historia Iherosolimitana* (Paris, 1846)

ROBERTS, Alexander and James DONALDSON, trans., *The Nicene and Post-Nicene Fathers*, 14 vols (Edinburgh, 1885)

ROBINSON, G., *Building a Palestinian State: The Incomplete Revolution* (Bloomington, Ind., 1997)

ROBINSON, I. S., 'Gregory VII and the Soldiers of Christ', *Historia*, 58 (1978)

ROGERS, Paul, 'The Global War on Terror and Its Impact on the Conduct of War', in George Kassimeris, ed., *The Barbarization of Warfare* (London, 2008)

ROMIER, Lucien, 'A Dissident Nobility under the Cloak of Religion', in J. H. H. Salmon, ed., *The French Wars of Religion: How Important Were Religious Factors?* (Lexington, Mass., 1967)

ROPP, Theodore, *War in the Modern World* (Durham, NC, 1959)

ROSE, Jacqueline, 'Deadly Embrace', *London Review of Books*, 26, 21 (4 November 2004)

ROSENAK, Michael, 'Jewish Fundamentalism in Israeli Education', in Martin E. Marty and R. Scott Appleby, eds, *Fundamentalisms and Society: Reclaiming the Sciences, the Family and Education* (Chicago and London, 1993)

ROTH, Norman, *Conversos, Inquisition and the Expulsion of Jews from Spain* (Madison, 1995)

ROUSSEAU, Jean-Jacques, *Political Writings,* ed. C. E. Vaughan (Cambridge, UK, 1915)

   The Social Contract, trans. Willmoore Kendall (South Bend, Ill., 1954)
   Politics and the Arts, Letter to M. D'Alembert on the Theatre, trans. Alan Bloom (Ithaca, NY, 1960)

   The Social Contract and Discourses, trans. and ed. G. D. H. Cole, rev. J. H. Brumfitt and John C. Hall (London, 1973)

   The Social Contract and Other Later Political Writings, ed. Victor Gourevitch (Cambridge, UK, 1997)

ROUTLEDGE, Bruce, 'The Politics of Mesha: Segmented Identities and State Formation in Iron Age Moab', *Journal of the Economic and Social History of the Orient,* 43 (2000)

   Moab in the Iron Age: Hegemony, Polity, Archaeology (Philadelphia, 2004)

RUFINUS, *The Church History of Rufinus of Aquileia,* trans. Philip R. Amidon (Oxford, 1997)

RUNCIMAN, Steven, *A History of the Crusades,* 3 vols (London, 1965)

RUTHVEN, Malise, *A Fury for God: The Islamist Attack on America* (London, 2003)

SACHEDINA, Abdulaziz Abdulhussein, 'Ali Shariati: Ideologue of the Iranian Revolution', in John L. Esposito, ed., *Voices of Resurgent Islam* (New York and Oxford, 1980)

   'Activist Shi'ism in Iran, Iraq and Lebanon', in Martin E. Marty and R. Scott Appleby, eds, *Fundamentalisms Observed* (Chicago and London, 1991)

SADAT, Anwar, *Revolt on the Nile* (New York, 1957)

SAGEMAN, Marc, *Understanding Terror Networks* (Philadelphia, 2004)
   Leaderless Jihad: Terror Networks in the Twenty-First Century (Philadelphia, 2008)

SAGGS, H. W. F., *The Might That Was Assyria* (London, 1984)

'Assyrian Warfare in the Sargonid Period', *Iraq,* 25 (1963)

SAGI, Avi, 'The Punishment of Amalek in Jewish Tradition: Coping with the Moral Problem', *Harvard Theological Review,* 87, 3 (1994)

SALMON, J. H. M., *Society in Crisis: France in the Sixteenth Century* (New York, 1975)

 ed., *The French Wars of Religion: How Important Were Religious Factors?* (Lexington, Mass., 1967)

SANDERS, N. K., trans. and ed., *Poems of Heaven and Hell from Ancient Mesopotamia* (London, 1971)

SAVAKAR, Vinayat Damdas, *Hindutva* (Bombay, 1969)

SAWYER, R. D., ed., *The Seven Military Classics of Ancient China* (Boulder, Co., 1993)

SAYERS, Dorothy L., trans., *The Song of Roland* (Harmondsworth, 1957)

SAYYID, Bobby, *A Fundamental Fear: Eurocentrism and the Emergence of Islamism* (London, 1997)

SCHAFER, Boyd C., *Nationalism: Myth and Reality* (New York, 1952)

SCHAUWECKER, Franz, *The Fiery Way* (London and Toronto, 1921)

SCHEIN, Seth, L., *The Mortal Hero: An Introduction to Homer's Iliad* (Berkeley, Los Angeles and London, 1984)

SCHILLING, Heinz, 'War and Peace at the Emergence of Modernity: Europe between State Belligerence, Religious Wars and the Desire for Peace in 1648', in Klaus Bussman and Heinz Schilling, eds, *War and Peace in Europe,* 3 vols. (Münster, 1998)

SCHNEIDER, Tammi J., *An Introduction to Ancient Mesopotamian Religion* (Grand Rapids, Mich., and Cambridge, UK, 2011)

SCHNIEDEWIND, William M., *How the Bible Became a Book: The Textualization of Ancient Israel* (Cambridge, UK, 2004)

SCHORSKE, Carl, *German Social Democracy, 1905–17* (Cambridge, Mass., 1955)

SCHUMPETER, Joseph A., *Imperialism and Social Classes: Two Essays* (New York, 1955)

SCHWARTZ, Benjamin I., *The World of Thought in Ancient China* (Cambridge, Mass., 1985)

SCHWARTZ, Regina, *The Curse of Cain: The Violent Legacy of Monotheism* (Chicago, 1997)

SECHER, Reynald, *Le Génocide franco-français: La Vendée-vengé* (Paris, 1986)

SEGAL, Alan F., *Paul the Convert: The Apostolate and Apostasy of Saul the Pharisee* (New Haven, Conn., and London, 1990)

SEGEV, Tom, *The Seventh Million: The Israelis and the Holocaust,* trans. Haim Watzman (New York, 1991)

SELENGUT, Charles, *Sacred Fury: Understanding Religious Violence* (Walnut Creek, Calif., 2003)

SELLS, Michael A., *The Bridge Betrayed: Religion and Genocide in Bosnia* (Berkeley, Los Angeles and London, 1996)

SEN, Amartya, *Identity and Violence: The Illusion of Destiny* (London, 2007)

SHEA, William M. and Peter A. Huff, eds, *Knowledge and Belief in America: Enlightenment Traditions and Modern Religious Thought* (New York, 1995)

SHEHAD, Anthony, *Legacy of the Prophet: Despots, Democrats and the New Politics of Islam* (Boulder, Co., 2011)

SHERWIN-WHITE, A. N., *Roman Law and Roman Society in the New Testament* (Oxford, 1963)

SICK, Gary, *All Fall Down: America's Fateful Encounter with Iran* (London, 1985)

SIGAL, P. A., 'Et les marcheurs de Dieu prirent leurs armes', *L'Histoire,* 47 (1982)

SIVAN, Emmanuel, *L'Islam et la Croisade* (Paris, 1968)

 'The Crusades Described by Modern Arab Historiography', *Asian and African Studies,* 8 (1972)

 'Genese de contre-croisade: une traité damasquine de debut du XIIe siècle', *Journal Asiatique,* 254 (1966)

SKINNER, Quentin, *The Foundations of Modern Political Thought,* 2 vols (Cambridge, 1978)

SLIM, Hugo, 'Why Protect Civilians? Innocence, Immunity and Enmity in War', *International Affairs,* 79, 3 (2003)

SLINGERLAND, Edward, trans., *Confucius: Analects, with Selections from Traditional Commentaries* (Indianapolis, Ind., and Cambridge, UK, 2003)

SMITH, Brian K., *Reflections on Resemblance, Ritual and Religion* (Oxford and New York, 1989)

SMITH, Howard D., *Chinese Religions* (London, 1968)

SMITH, Huston, *The World's Religions: Our Great Wisdom Traditions* (San Francisco, 1991)

SMITH, John, *John Smith: Works,* ed. Edwin Arber and A. C. Bradley (Edinburgh, 1910)

SMITH, John D., ed. and trans., *The Mahabharata: An Abridged Translation* (London, 2009)

SMITH, Jonathan Z., *Map is Not Territory: Studies in the History of Religions* (Chicago and London, 1978)

 Imagining Religion: From Babylon to Jonestown (Chicago and London, 1982)

SMITH, Mark S., *The Early History of God: Yahweh and the Other Deities in Ancient Israel* (New York and London, 1990)

    The Origins of Biblical Monotheism: Israel's Polytheistic Background and the Ugaritic Texts (New York and London, 2001)

SMITH, William Cantwell, *Islam in Modern History* (Princeton, NJ, and London, 1957)

    The Meaning and End of Religion: A New Approach to the Religious Traditions of Mankind (New York, 1962)

    Belief in History (Charlottesville, Va., 1985)

    Faith and Belief (Princeton, NJ, 1987)

    What is Scripture? A Comparative Approach (London, 1993)

SONTAG, Susan, 'What have we done?' *Guardian,* 24 May 2005

SOUTHERN, R. W., *Western Views of Islam in the Middle Ages* (Cambridge, Mass., 1962)

    The Making of the Middle Ages (London, 1967)

    Western Society and the Church in the Middle Ages (Harmondsworth, UK, 1970)

SOZOMEN, *The Ecclesiastical History of Sozomon,* trans. Chester D. Harnaft (Grand Rapids, Mich., 1989)

SPEAR, Percival, *India* (Ann Arbor, Mich., 1961)

SPERLING, S. David, *The Original Torah: The Political Intent of the Bible's Writers* (New York and London, 1998)

    'Joshua 24 Re-examined', *Hebrew Union College Annual, 58* (1987)

SPIERENBERG, Peter, *The Spectacle of Suffering: Executions and the Evolution of Repression — from a Pre-Industrial Metropolis to the European Experience* (Cambridge, UK, 1984)

SPRINZAK, Ehud, *The Ascendance of Israel's Radical Right* (New York, 1991)

    'Three Models of Religious Violence: The Case of Jewish Fundamentalism in Israel', in Martin E. Marty and R. Scott Appleby, eds, *Fundamentalisms and the State: Remaking Politics, Economies and Militance* (Chicago and London, 1993)

SRIVASTA, Sushil, 'The Ayodhya Controversy: A Third Dimension', *Probe India* (January 1998)

STANNARD, David, *American Holocaust: The Conquest of the New World* (New York and Oxford, 1992)

STEINER, George, *In Bluebeard's Castle: Some Notes toward the Re-definition of Culture* (New Haven, Conn.,1971)

STEVANS, G. W., *With Kitchener to Khartoum* (London, 1898)

STOUT, Henry S., 'Rhetoric and Reality in the Early Republic: The Case of the Federalist Clergy', in Mark A. Noll, ed., *Religion and American Politics, From the Colonial Period to the 1980s* (Oxford and New York, 1980)

STRAYER, Joseph R., *On the Medieval Origin of the Modern State* (Princeton, 1970)

    Medieval Statecraft and the Perspectives of History (Princeton, 1971)

    'Feudalism in Western Europe', in Rushton Coulborn, ed., *Feudalism in History* (Hamden, Conn., 1965)

STROZIER, Charles B., David M. TERMAN and James W. JONES, eds, *The Fundamentalist Mindset* (Oxford, 2010)

STUART, Henry S. and Charles Reagan WOLFSON, eds, *Religion and the American Civil War* (New York, 1998)

SULLIVAN, Andrew, 'This *Is* a Religious War', *New York Times Magazine*, 7 October 2001

SUN TZU, *The Art of War: Complete Texts and Commentaries*, trans. Thomas Cleary (Boston and London, 1988)

SZASZ, Ferenc, *The Divided Mind of Protestant America, 1880–1930* (University, Ala., 1982)

TABARI, Azar, 'The Role of the Shii Clergy in Modern Iranian Politics', in Nikki R. Keddie, ed., *Religion and Politics in Iran: Shiism from Quietism to Revolution* (New Haven, Conn., and London, 1983)

TACITUS, Cornelius, *Agricola, Gemania, Dialogus,* trans. M. Hutton and W. Peterson (Loeb Classical Library, 1989)

TAHERI, Amir, *The Spirit of Allah: Khomeini and the Islamic Revolution* (London, 1985)

THAPAR, Romila, *Asoka and the Decline of the Mauryas* (Oxford, 1961)

    Early India: From the Origins to AD 1300 (Berkeley and Los Angeles, 2002)

THEISSEN, Gerd, *The First Followers of Jesus: A Sociological Analysis of the Earliest Christianity,* trans. John Bowden (London, 1978)

    The Miracle Stories: Early Christian Tradition (Philadelphia, 1982)

    The Social Setting of Pauline Christianity: Essays on Corinth, ed. and trans. John H. Schutz (Eugene, Ore., 2004)

THOMPSON, James Westfall, *Economic and Social History of the Middle Ages* (New York, 1928)

    The Wars of Religion in France, 1559–1576: Huguenots, Catherine de Medici, Philip II, 2nd ed. (New York, 1957)

TIBI, Bassam, *The Crisis of Political Islam: A Pre-Industrial Culture in the Scientific-Technological Age* (Salt Lake City, Utah, 1988)

TIERNY, Brian, *The Crisis of Church and State, 1050–1300* (Toronto, 1988)

TILLY, Charles, ed., *The Formation of Nation States in Western Europe* (Princeton, NJ, 1975)

TRACY, James D., *Emperor Charles V, Impresario of War: Campaign Strategy, International Finance and Domestic Politics* (Cambridge, UK, 2002)

ed., *Luther and the Modern State in Germany* (Kirbyville, Mo., 1986)

TU, Wei-ming, *Confucian Thought: Selfhood as Creative Transformation* (Albany, 1985)

TUCK, Richard, *The Rights of War and Peace: Political Thought and the International Order from Grotius to Kant* (Oxford, 1999)

TYERMAN, Christopher J., *England and the Crusades, 1095–1588* (Chicago, 1988)

'Sed nihil fecit? The Last Captians and the Recovery of the Holy Land', in J. Gillingham and J. C. Holt, eds, *War and Government in the Middle Ages: Essays in Honour of J. D. Prestwich* (Woodbridge, UK, and Totowa, NJ 1980)

UR-REHMAN, Rafiq, 'Please tell me, Mr President, why a US drone assassinated my mother', theguardian.com, 25 October 2013

USSISHKIN, David, 'King Solomon's Palaces', *Biblical Archaeologist*, 36 (1973)

VAN BUITENEN, J. A. B., ed. and trans., *The Mahabharata*, 3 vols (Chicago and London, 1973, 1975, 1978)

VEBLEN, Thorstein, *The Theory of the Leisure Class: An Economic Study of Institutions* (Boston, 1973)

VERNANT, Jean-Pierre, *Myth and Society in Ancient Greece,* trans. Janet Lloyd, 3rd ed. (New York, 1996)

VITORIA, Francisco de, *Political Writings,* ed. Anthony Pagden and Jeremy Lawrence (Cambridge, 1991)

VOGTS, Alfred, *A History of Militarism, Civilian and Military,* rev. ed. (New York, 1959)

VOLL, John O., 'Fundamentalism in the Sunni Arab World: Egypt and the Sudan', in Martin E. Marty and R. Scott Appleby, eds, *Fundamentalisms Observed* (Chicago and London, 1991)

WAIT, Gaston, ed. and trans., *Nicholas Turc: Chronique d'Egypte, 1798–1804* (Cairo, 1950)

WALEY, Arthur, trans. and ed., *The Analects of Confucius* (New York, 1992)

WALLACE, Anthony F. C., *Jefferson and the Indians: The Tragic Fate of the First Americans* (Cambridge, Mass., 1999)

WALLACE-HADRILL, J. M., *The Barbarian West: The Early Middle Ages, AD 400–1000* (New York, 1962)

Early Medieval History (Oxford, 1975)

The Frankish Church (Oxford, 1983)

WATSON, B., ed. and trans., *Records of the Grand Historian of China* (New York, 1961)

    ed. and trans., *Mo-Tzu; Basic Writings* (New York, 1963)

    ed. and trans. *Han Fei Tzu: Basic Writings* (New York, 1964)

    ed. and trans., *Xunzi: Basic Writings* (New York, 2003)

WATT, W. Montgomery, *Muhammad at Mecca* (Oxford, 1953)

    Muhammad at Medina (Oxford, 1956)

    The Influence of Islam in Medieval Europe (Edinburgh, 1972)

    Muhammad's Mecca: History in the Qur'an (Edinburgh, 1988)

WEBER, Max, *The Theory of Social and Economic Organization,* trans. A. M. Henderson and Talcott Parsons (New York, 1947)

    The Protestant Ethic and the Spirit of Capitalism, trans. Talcott Parsons (New York, 1958)

    The Religion of China: Confucianism and Taoism, trans. Hans H. Gerth (Glencoe, Ill., 1949)

    The Religion of India: The Sociology of Hinduism and Buddhism, trans. Hans H. Gerth and Don Martindale (Glencoe, Ill., 1958)

WEDGWOOD, C. W., *The Thirty Years War* (New Haven, Conn., 1939)

WEIGHLEY, Russell F. *The Age of Battles* (Bloomington, Ind., 1991)

WEINFELD, Moshe, *Deuteronomy and the Deuteronomic School* (Oxford, 1972)

WELCH, Claude E., Jr., *Political Modernization* (Belmont, Calif., 1967)

WELCH, Holmes, *The Parting of the Way: Lao Tzu and the Taoist Movement* (London, 1958)

WELLMAN, James K., Jr, ed., *Belief and Bloodshed: Religion and Violence across Time and Tradition* (Lanham, Md., 2007)

WENKE, K. J., *Patterns of Prehistory: Humankind's First Three Million Years* (New York, 1961)

    The Origins of Civilizations (Oxford, 1979)

WENSINCK, Jan, *Concordance et indices de la tradition musulmane,* 5 vols (Leiden, 1992)

WESSINGER, Catherine, *How the Millennium Comes Violently: Jonestown to Heaven's Gate* (New York, 2000)

    ed., *Millennialism, Persecution and Violence: Historical Circumstances* (Syracuse, NY, 1986)

WHITAKER, Jarrod L., *Strong Arms and Drinking Strength: Masculinity, Violence and the Body in Ancient India* (Oxford, 2011)

WHITBY, Michael and Joseph STREET, eds, *Martyrdom and Orthodoxy* (New York, 1987)

WHITTAKER, D. H., ed., *The Terrorist Reader* (London, 2001)

WICKHAM, Lionel R., *Hilary of Poitiers: Conflicts of Conscience and Law in the Fourth Century* (Liverpool, 1997)

WILLIAMSON, H. G. M., 'The Concept of Israel in Transition', in E. E. Clements, ed., *The World of Ancient Israel: Sociological, Anthropological and Political Perspectives* (Cambridge, UK, 1989)

WILSON, E. O., *On Human Nature* (Cambridge, Mass., 1978)

WILSON, John F., 'Religion, Government and Power in the New American Nation', in Mark A. Noll, ed., *Religion and American Politics: From the Colonial Period to the 1980s* (Oxford and New York, 1990)

WIRT, Sherwood Eliot, ed., *Spiritual Awakening: Classic Writings of the Eighteenth-Century Devotions to Inspire and Help the Twentieth-Century Reader* (Tring, UK, 1988)

WITTFOGEL, Karl A., *Oriental Despotism: A Comparative Study of Total Power* (New Haven, Conn., 1957)

WITZEL, Michael, 'Vedas and Upanisads', in Gavin Flood, ed., *The Blackwell Companion to Hinduism* (Oxford, 2003)

WORLD COUNCIL OF CHURCHES, *Violence, Nonviolence and the Struggle for Social Justice* (Geneva, 1972)

WRIGHT, Lawrence, *The Looming Tower: Al-Qaeda's Road to 9/11* (New York, 2006)

WRIGHT, Louis B., *Religion and Empire: The Alliance between Piety and Commerce in the English Expansion, 1558–1625* (Chapel Hill, 1943)

WRIGHT, Quincy, *A Study of War,* 2nd ed. (Chicago, 1965)

WYATT, Don J., 'Confucian Ethical Action and the Boundaries of Peace and War', in Andre R. Murphy, ed., *The Blackwell Companion to Religion and Violence* (Chichester, UK, 2011)

YADIN, Yigal, *The Art of Warfare in Biblical Lands: In Light of Archaeological Study,* 2 vols (New York, 1963)

YAO, Xinzhong, *An Introduction to Confucianism* (Cambridge, UK, 2000)

YOVEL, Yirmanyahu, *Spinoza and Other Heretics. Vol. 1: The Marrano of Reason; Vol. 2: Adventures of Immanence* (Princeton, NJ, 1989)

ZAEHNER, R. C., *Hinduism* (London, New York and Toronto, 1962)

ZINN, Howard, *A People's History of the United States: From 1492 to the Present,* 2nd ed. (London and New York, 1996)

ZWEIG, Stefan, *The World of Yesterday: An Autobiography* (New York, 1945)

INDEX